I0349196

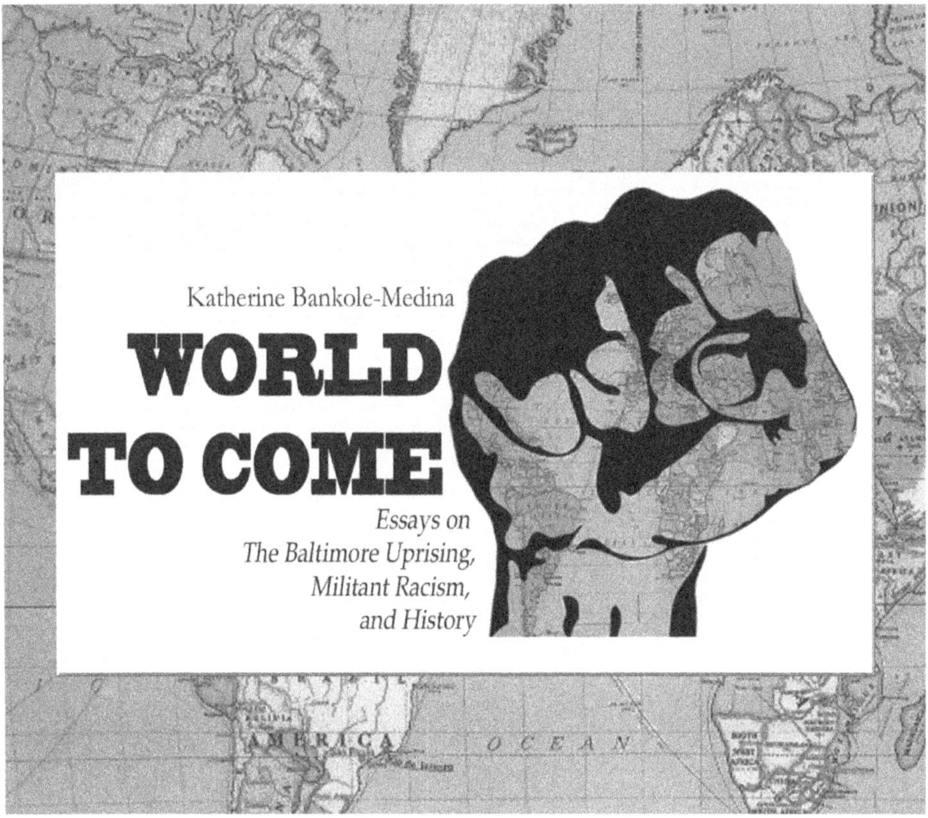
Katherine Bankole-Medina
WORLD
TO COME
Essays on
The Baltimore Uprising,
Militant Racism,
and History
AMERICA
OCEAN

WORLD TO COME
ESSAYS ON THE BALTIMORE UPRISING, MILITANT RACISM, AND HISTORY

KATHERINE BANKOLE-MEDINA, PH.D.

COPPIN STATE UNIVERSITY

WITH A FORWARD BY
REILAND RABAKA, PH.D.

LIBERATED SCHOLARS ASSOCIATION PRESS
IN PARTNERSHIP WITH THE A P FOUNDATION PRESS
WASHINGTON, D.C.
2016

Copyright © 2016 Katherine Bankole-Medina. All rights reserved. No part of this book may be reproduced or transmitted in any form or by any means, electronic or mechanical, including photocopying, recording or by any information storage and retrieval system, without permission in writing from the publisher. Published by the Liberated Scholars Association Press, in partnership with the A P Foundation Press, P. O. Box 56283, Washington, D.C. 20011.

ISBN-13: 978-0692681510
ISBN-10: 0692681515

Library of Congress Cataloging-in-Publication Data

Bankole-Medina, Katherine

World to Come: Essays on the Baltimore Uprising, Militant Racism, and History

Includes Index

1. African American History 2. United States History 3. Race Relations 4. Racism 5. Essays 6. Criticism 7. African American Studies 8. Africana Studies 9. Africology 10. Media Studies

Manufactured in the United States of America

2016

FIRST EDITION

Cover Design/Concept by Zamaniya Baderinwa Bankole
Editorial Consultant, Malaika Khan

✝✝✝

Dedication

For my brothers:

Todd Jr. And Winston,

The Black Men Who Cared for and Protected Us:

Robert J. "Daddy" G.
Stephen G.
Isadore S.
Todd Sr.,

Carlos and Zee,

And our Remarkable Students

History tells a people where they have been and what they have been, where they are and what they are. Most important, an understanding of history tells a people where they still must go and what they still must be.
—John Henrik Clarke

If there is no struggle, there is no progress. Those who profess to favor freedom, and yet depreciate agitation, are men who want crops without plowing up the ground. They want rain without thunder and lightning. They want the ocean without the awful roar of its many waters. This struggle may be a moral one; or it may be a physical one; or it may be both moral and physical; but it must be a struggle.
—Frederick Douglass

Nobody's as powerful as we make them out to be.
—Alice Walker

Not everything that is faced can be changed; but nothing can be changed until it is faced.
—James Baldwin

I for one believe that if you give people a thorough understanding of what confronts them and the basic causes that produce it, they'll create their own program, and when the people create a program, you get action.
—Malcolm X

History, we should realize, separates the 'first fundamental' reality of a people's existence, namely, the past, from the second fundamental reality of their existence, namely, the present. There is a third element which completes the triad, namely, the future. But the future exists, by definition, only in a people's vision and in their plans which only become actualized in the present.
—C. Tsehloane Keto

If you have been questioning whether black lives really and truly matter in the twenty-first century, *World to Come* cogently demonstrates that you are not alone.—Reiland Rabaka

WORLD TO COME: ESSAYS ON THE BALTIMORE UPRISING, MILITANT RACISM, AND HISTORY

CONTENTS

DEDICATION

ACKNOWLEDGEMENTS—17

FORWARD BY DR. REILAND RABAKA—19

PREFACE—THIS IS MADNESS—25
- On Police and Grandparents—a Sixteen-Year-Old Black Girl's Disquisition
- Studying The Immediate Past in the Miasma of the Present and a Note on Sources
- The Shape of the World to Come—Chapter Summaries
- Racial Justice In Search of a Proactive Audience

1. INTRODUCTION—BLACK LIVES IN THE NEW MILLENNIUM—45
   - The Assassination of Martin Luther King, Jr. and the 1968 Baltimore Riot
   - The Freddie Grays of the World, Police-Encounter Deaths, and the Universal Community-Of-Care
   - From Police-Encounter Death to Patterns and Practices of Unlawful Conduct: The Cases of Michael Brown and Freddie Gray
   - Racial Insult and the 'While Black' Phenomenon

2. BETWEEN ENSLAVEMENT AND FREEDOM—THE APEX OF RACIAL POWER—65
   - The Link between Historic Slavery and the Police Killings of Blacks
   - Henry Watson's Story of Jo, the Enslaved African Put to Death
   - Frederick Douglass Fought for his Life at Fells Point
   - An Historical Overview of Post-Civil War Racism

3. HISTORY, SOCIAL NETWORK CONSERVATION, AND INTOLERABLE BLACKNESS—81
   - Nat Turner, Negative Racial Stereotypes, and Social Network Conservation
   - Intolerable Blackness and the Refinement of Racism
   - Involuntary Segregation and Intolerable Blackness
   - The New Racism in Post-Racial America and the Price of Prejudice

4. POPULAR MEDIA GHETTOIZATION AND AN INTRODUCTION TO THE POLICE-ENCOUNTER NARRATIVE—95
   - The Media And The Ghettoization Of Black Life And Culture
   - Truth is: We are all 1 Bullet Away From Being a #Hashtag
   - Leaking And Sharing Information Advantageous to the Police Narrative
   - The Media Framing The Message and The Murder of Emmett Till

World To Come: Essays On The Baltimore Uprising, Militant Racism, And History

5. THE AGE OF NEW MEDIA AND THE YETTE HYPOTHESIS—109
   - The Age of New Media, The Citizen Journalist, and Independent Reporting
   - The Africanization of American Media: Other Paradigms Influencing Black Public Media
   - Citizen Journalism, the Testimony of Kevin Moore, and Original Local Media
   - The Yette Hypothesis and the Nefarious Option

6. BALTIMORE'S WILDERNESS + "RIOT" = "UPRISING"—123
   - Freddie Gray and the Wilderness
   - The Baltimore Wished for and The State of Black Baltimore
   - The Riot—A Synopsis of Domestic Civil Unrest and Race in American History
   - In the Moment of Our Birth: Baltimore's Historic Uprising

7. THE MILLENNIALS AND IGENS IN THE WILDERNESS STATE AND AT THE MALL—149
   - The Millennials Will be Heard
   - The IGens, the "Purge" or Teens at the Mondawmin Mall
   - The BGF-Crips-Bloods Gang Fatwa
   - The New Governor, the Molded Mayor, and Curfew As Prophecy

8. INTO THE REBELLION: SELECTED FACETS OF THE BALTIMORE UPRISING—159
   - The Protest Moment, CVS and Police Presence
   - Police Misinformation, and the Gang Response
   - Rawlings-Blake, The Uprising, and the Interruption of City Culture
   - In Solidarity with the Baltimore Uprising and Black Protest versus White Revelry

9. RACISM, KILLOLOGY AND DISBELIEF IN HISTORY—167
   - Racism as a Violent Social Force in Human History
   - Killology—The Study and the Ideology Of War
   - Racism, Disbelief, Denial, And Fashionable Forgetting
   - Racism, Signage, And Maximum Discomfort In The Community

10. BALTIMORE AND THE NEW URBAN POLICE STATE—181
    - COINTELPRO Surveillance, the ISD in Baltimore, and the Elimination of "Primitive Man"
    - The High Cost Of Fatal Police-Community Conflict
    - BMore Police Technology—Tools for Mass Surveillance
    - Post-Uprising—A Window Into the ATF and the Quest for Punishment

WORLD TO COME: ESSAYS ON THE BALTIMORE UPRISING, MILITANT RACISM, AND HISTORY

11. VARIETIES OF COPS, POLITICAL LEADERS, AND THE RACIAL PARADOX THAT WASN'T—197
    - Racial Premises Regarding Black Cops And The Baltimore 6
    - African American Police Officers, Good Cops Gone Rogue, And The "Line That Protects The Innocent"
    - The "Z-Man" And The Dark Side Of Para-Policing
    - Black Political Leaders and the Black President at the Nexus of the Baltimore Uprising?

12. THE BALTIMORE UPRISING AND THE GREAT BLACK LEGACY OF SOCIAL JUSTICE—219
    - This Was No "African American Spring"
    - Marilyn J. Mosby, The Quest For Justice, And Strategic Challenges
    - The Police As Sacred Symbols, Money Bail, The Baltimore 6, And Alan Bullocks
    - The Militarization Of Baltimore And The Live Disappearance Of Joseph Kent

13. AFRICAN AMERICANS, THE PSYCHOPOMP OF MEDIA, AND *THE WIRE*—235
    - The New Attorney General Visits Baltimore
    - Polling the Baltimore Uprising, Charitable Expressions, and the Rally 4 Peace
    - The Gendered Nuisances of Afrofemiphobia
    - The Socio-Political Theater Of Baltimore And *The Wire*

14. THE MILITARIZATION OF URBAN AMERICA—255
    - Notes On The Domestic Military Build-Up
    - The Zero-Sum Game To Crime Deterrence And Broken Windows
    - The Human Terrain For Military Operations And Police Overcompensation
    - On Biker Gangs And The Blurred Dimensions Of Contested Territory

15. CONCLUSION—THE WORLD TO COME AND THE POST-MILLENNIAL REVOLUTION—277
    - The Pedagogy of Protest, Critical Public Discourse and Disruptive Activism
    - What Does It Mean To Be Human And Humane In The World?
    - Social Justice Beyond Policing—Deconstructing Violent Racist Paradigms
    - Dismantling Police-Encounter Killings and African Americans as a World Historical People

EPILOGUE—THE PAST CATCHES ALL OF US—307
- Maroons in the Mountains
- A Colleague's Hidden Fear and the Forces of History in an Ahistorical World
- On Research and the Upwelling of Souls
- A Movement Reborn, or The Past Catches All Of Us

WORLD TO COME: ESSAYS ON THE BALTIMORE UPRISING, MILITANT RACISM, AND HISTORY

APPENDICES

A—TIMELINE OF THE 2015 BALTIMORE UPRISING—327

B—BALTIMORE UPRISING PROTEST SIGNS—343

C—A COMPENDIUM OF AFRICAN AMERICANS WHO DIED IN POLICE-ENCOUNTERS, 1994-2015—349

D—GRAND JURY CHARGES AGAINST THE BALTIMORE 6, MAY 21, 2015—391

E—DOMESTIC RIOT/CIVIL DISOBEDIENCE AND PROTEST EVENTS RELATED TO RACE IN THE UNITED STATES, 1863-2015—393

BIBLIOGRAPHY—399

ABOUT THE AUTHOR—439

GENERAL INDEX—441

ABBREVIATIONS

ATC—Air Traffic Control
ATF— Bureau of Alcohol, Tobacco, Firearms and Explosives
BB—BB Gun, Ball Bearing, Bullet Ball
BCPD—Baltimore City Police Department
BGF—Black Guerilla Family
BIM—Building Information Modeling
BPP—Black Panther Party
BWC—Body Worn Camera
CBC—Congressional Black Caucus
CCTV—Closed Circuit Television Systems
COC—Community-of-Care
COINTELPRO—Counter Intelligence Program
CPR— Cardiopulmonary Resuscitation
C.S.A.—Confederate States of America
CVS—CVS Pharmacies
DA—District Attorney
DEA—Drug Enforcement Administration
DOA—Dead on Arrival
DOJ—Department of Justice
DPW—Department of Public Works

FBI—Federal Bureau of Investigation
FEMA—Federal Emergency Management Agency
FOP—Fraternal Order of Police
GBI—Georgia Bureau of Investigation
GPS—Global Positioning System
HBCU—Historically Black Colleges and Universities
IDS—Inspectional Services Division
LAPD—Los Angeles Police Department
LBS—Leaders of a Beautiful Struggle
LEOBOR—Law Enforcement Officers Bill of Rights
LEMC—Law Enforcement Motorcycle Club
NAACP—National Association for the Advancement of Colored People
NYPD—New York Police Department
PERF—Police Executive Research Forum
STEM—Science, Technology, Engineering, Medicine
SWAT—Special Weapons and Tactics
TPP—Trans-Pacific Partnership
Y2K—The year 2000

World To Come: Essays On The Baltimore Uprising, Militant Racism, And History

Acknowledgements

We may differ slightly in our ideas, but we are all one in the great cause of humanity. A grateful heartfelt acknowledgement is made to the following individuals:

Abena Lewis Mhoon
Reiland Rabaka
Roger Davidson
Ibrahim Kargbo
Claudia Nelson
Kokahvah Zauditu-Selassie
Elizabeth Clark-Lewis
Elizabeth Kilungya
Debra Vines
Elaine Sykes
Larry Martin
Linda Brown-Davenport
Gary Hyatt
Doug Reardon
Michelle Haskins
Rashida Forman-Bey
Kenneth Jackson
Lopez Matthews
Charles Minor
Joanne Jackson
Michael Thomas
Shawn Brooks
Errol Bolden
Emmanuel Anorou
Rolande Murray
Ron Collins
Alcott Arthur
Trulestine Jefferson
José Díaz-Garayúa
Sumanth Reddy
Shaquille Carbon
Kofi Ogungbende

Forward

After reading this book, it will be difficult to come to the conclusion that *the world to come* will be – indeed, *needs to be* – anything other than a world free from anti-black racism. After centuries of struggle a new collective cry has risen from the ashes and anger, the heartache and moral outrage of the aftermath of the Civil Rights Movement. It is important to emphasize here at the outset that the Black Lives Matter Movement is not about *hating* white people, but about *loving* black people, and defending them against anti-black racist assaults (both physical and psychological).

When the history of anti-black racist violence in the U.S. is taken into serious consideration then, and perhaps only then, does the Black Lives Matter Movement make any sense. Even though the media has more or less focused on the "shouting" and "ranting" of a few members of the movement, more often than not, in practice the major expressions of the movement have followed more carefully defined and, for the most part, more familiar African American socio-political movement methods (e.g., direct-action protests, street rallies, marches, demonstrations, conferences, concerts, etc.). In fact, although the Black Lives Matter Movement is mainly social and political, the cultural and artistic impact of the movement should not be overlooked: Kendrick Lamar's *To Pimp A Butterfly* and Beyoncé's "Formation," for instance, did not emerge out of the ether. The movement is simultaneously social and political, as well as cultural and artistic. Consequently, the ideals and ethos of the movement manifest themselves in a variety of ways and in a variety of works: some social and political, some cultural, and some intellectual.

Katherine Bankole-Medina's *World to Come: Essays on the Baltimore Uprising, Militant Racism, and History* is one of the most illuminating scholarly works to emerge from the Black Lives Matter Movement thus far. Part deep history, and part black political theory, *World to Come* is a book about bearing witness. Echoes of Ida B. Wells and W.E.B. Du Bois, Georgia Douglas Johnson and Marcus Garvey, Zora Neal Hurston and Langston Hughes resound from the tear-soaked and blood-stained pages of this book, eerily recalling the anti-lynching activism during the first decades of the twentieth century. As is often said: *plus ça change, plus c'est la même chose*—the more things change, the more they stay the same. In other words, for those of us who have a serious sense of African American history, culture, and struggle, it would seem that we are sadly passing through an epoch in the twenty-first century that is essentially the "Red Summer of 1919" *redux*.

As African Americans fanned out across the country in the early years of the twentieth century most thought very little of the Red Scare of 1919, but anti-communism quickly translated into xenophobia, and xenophobia almost immediately mutated into fickle forms of anti-black racist violence that in many ways rivaled the horrors African Americans endured during the 1880s and 1890s—an era that noted historian Rayford Logan, in *The Negro in American Life and Thought: The Nadir, 1877-1901* (1954), famously characterized as "the nadir of American race relations." African Americans had many reasons for migrating to the North, including escaping lynching, Jim Crow laws, anti-black racist restrictions on their voting and civil rights, and the collapsing economy of the rural South, where the boll weevil was devastating cotton crops. By most accounts the Red Summer of 1919 began in May in Charleston, North Carolina, where a white sailor shot an African American civilian to death. The "race riot" that ensued left seven African Americans dead and more than thirty-five wounded, as well as three white sailors and one policeman injured.

Ellisville, Mississippi exploded in late June. There a fanatical gang of white men fatally wounded an alleged black rapist by the name of John Hartfield as he sought to escape from capture by way of a cane field. Reports indicate that a local white physician fiendishly kept Hartfield alive so that he could be "properly" lynched the next day. The local newspapers gleefully announced the time and place of Hartfield's lynching, while the then Governor of Mississippi, Theodore Bilbo, callously remarked that "[n]obody can keep the inevitable from happening." On the day after Hartfield's lynching the local newspapers shamelessly reported that more than three thousand townspeople and "upstanding" citizens gathered at the appointed tree and, after fervently debating the "best" way to torture him before they killed him, Hartfield's executioners hanged, burned, and then, for good measure, repeatedly shot his lifeless and brutally charred and bludgeoned body.

By summer's end this sickening scene was repeated in more than three-dozen U.S. cities, including the nation's capital. In response to the carnage one of the leading lights of the Harlem Renaissance, Claude McKay, drummed out his most defiant and most famous poem, the immortal "If We Must Die." It became both the battle oath and battle anthem of the New Negro Movement: "If we must die, let it not be like hogs/ Hunted and penned in an inglorious spot/ While round us bark the mad and hungry dogs/ Making their mock at our accursed

WORLD TO COME: ESSAYS ON THE BALTIMORE UPRISING, MILITANT RACISM, AND HISTORY

lot." Indeed, this was not Paul Laurence Dunbar's much-heralded "dialect poetry." It represented something altogether different, something clearly distinguished from even those race-conscious writings offered up by notable nineteenth century black radicals, such as Frederick Douglass, Frances Ellen Watkins Harper, Martin Delany, Alexander Crummell, Pauline Hopkins, and Bishop Henry McNeal Turner. Similar to McKay's passionate plea almost a hundred years ago, Bankole-Medina's essays in this volume symbolize a salvo, a chronicle and a critique.

Where others have made facile references to the origins and evolution of the Black Lives Matter Movement, Bankole-Medina develops a deep history that takes us back to historical figures and events that prefigured and provided a foundation for one of the most provocative black social and political movements of the dawning decades of the twenty-first century. From Nat Turner and Frederick Douglass, Emmett Till and the media coverage of the murders of Michael Brown and Freddie Gray, Bankole-Medina provides an awe-inspiring interpretation of the Baltimore Uprising. Her attention to historical detail, her ability to ask critical historical and cultural questions from an unapologetically African American perspective are the hallmarks of the essays to follow. In characteristic fashion, Bankole-Medina guides her readers through a much-misunderstood episode in African American history, culture, and struggle and, ultimately, offers us a much-needed micro-history of the Black Lives Matter Movement. Shifting the frame and focus from the mainstream media to the activists and organic intellectuals of the movement, she demonstrates that the recent unrest in Baltimore is a response to the continuation and, perhaps, a kind of culmination of decades of black social and political neglect. However, Bankole-Medina's work here is not merely aimed at the community. It is also intended as a distinct kind of critique of the staid, bourgeois, and unambiguously Eurocentric historiography of the American academy in the twenty-first century.

Surviving in the jungles of Europe's ivory towers and quarantined to racially colonized and ghettoized spaces in the European and American academies, often quietly combating the constantly "on safari" attitudes of well-meaning whites' unrepentant refusal to acknowledge their power and privilege in a white supremacist world, and amid the current intellectual trepidation and word-wizardry of many of the long-lauded "conventional" or "mainstream" critics, the distinct discourse(s) of *Africology*/Africana Studies exists furtively in the insurgent intellectual-activist imagination, seemingly stripped of its

WORLD TO COME: ESSAYS ON THE BALTIMORE UPRISING, MILITANT RACISM, AND HISTORY

critical potency, and even mocked by postmodernists, postcolonialists, and post-Marxists (among many others) who argue that black radicalism is out-dated or old fashioned. It seems as though black radicalism in the twenty-first century continues to represent a riddle, or series of riddles, which remain the hallowed hallmark(s) of the "wretched of the earth," and this even though "conventional" critics consistently downplay and attempt to diminish the salience of race, racism, racial violence and, of course, white supremacy. Black radicalism has been all but banished in contemporary critical theory, as it was with classical critical theory, blithely relegated to the status of a ruse put forward by the unruly blacks of bygone eras—that is to say, those "Pan-African insurgents," "Negritude nuisances," "Civil Rights radicals" and, of course, "Black Power pests" of the past.

However, for those of us with unquenchable commitments to continuing the fight for freedom, for those of us deeply disturbed by what is going on in our global warming and war-torn world, and for those of us who desperately search for solutions to our most pressing social and political problems, black radicals' anti-imperialist ideas and actions, black radicals' increasing commitments to racial *and* gender justice, black radicals' revolutionary humanist political vision and theories of social change are far from antiquated and have historically and continue currently to offer a much needed *Africological* alternative to, and through the mazes of ever-increasing Eurocentrism, postmodernism, postcolonialism, postfeminism, and post-Marxism, among other contemporary conceptual distractions and disruptions. Along with other black radical figures, like W.E.B. Du Bois, Marcus Garvey, Claudia Jones, C.L.R. James, Frantz Fanon, Ella Baker, Malcolm X, Fannie Lou Hamer, Amílcar Cabral, and Angela Davis, Bankole-Medina provides us with the means through which we can begin to critically rethink the possibilities of resistance to, and the transgressive transformation of the new global imperialism(s) of our age. Her thought clearly cuts across several disciplines and, therefore, closes the chasm between *Africology* and historiography, constantly demanding that intellectuals not simply think deep thoughts, develop new theories, and theoretically support radical politics, but *be* and constantly *become* political activists, social organizers and cultural workers— that is to say, folk the Italian critical theorist Antonio Gramsci referred to as "organic intellectuals." In this sense, then, the series of studies gathered in *World to Come* contribute not only to Africana Studies, Popular Movement Studies, and Cultural Studies, but also to contemporary critical discourse across an amazingly wide-range

WORLD TO COME: ESSAYS ON THE BALTIMORE UPRISING,
MILITANT RACISM, AND HISTORY

of "traditional" disciplines, and radical political activism outside of (and, in many instances, absolutely *against*) Europe's insidious ivory towers and the apartheid-like absurdities of the American academy. If you have been questioning whether black lives really and truly matter in the twenty-first century, *World to Come* cogently demonstrates that you are not alone. Even if no one else believes that black lives matter, Bankole-Medina audaciously asserts that when all the smoke clears and all the dust settles there will be those of us who hold firm and find solace in the subaltern, grassroots social organizing and political activism of black America in the Age of Obama and its aftermath.

REILAND RABAKA
Professor of African, African American & Caribbean Studies
Department of Ethnic Studies
University of Colorado at Boulder
February 23, 2016 (*W.E.B. Du Bois's birthday*)

Preface—This Is Madness

> *This Is Madness…*
> *This Is Madness…*
> *All This Madness Is Madness…*
> *This Madness Must Stop…*
> *Madness This Is…Please Stop All This Madness!*
> *Please Stop All This Madness!*
> *Please Stop All This Madness…Stop!*—The Last Poets[1]

On Police and Grandparents—A Sixteen-Year-Old Black Girl's Disquisition

In the 1970s, there was a curious traffic stop involving a young African American woman. She had just turned sixteen years old, and was driving to the home of her grandparents. She had on a knee-length denim pinafore with the newly popular pantyhose because her grandmother liked dresses, and thought that "young ladies" should wear hose—even in the summer. Like all the girls, she wore them with high-top sneakers. The visit to her grandparents was no different from any of the others she had made since she received her learner's permit and driver's license. This day she was pulled over by a police car and asked for her license, registration and proof of insurance. As she complied, two other police cruisers joined the scene. Suddenly there were six white male police officers. They took turns looking at her and then past her. One of the police cars blocked traffic. There were light bars mounted on each car that rapidly flashed red, white and blue.

She knew immediately that this was trouble, and she was afraid. Mostly she was angry. The lead officer asked her if she had any weapons (in the car, glove compartment or her purse). She said no and began asking him repeatedly *why* she had been pulled over. There was no response. He glared at her and told her to get out of the car. As she stepped lightly from the car, she noticed that the lead officer placed his right hand on his service revolver. She kept asking why she had been pulled over. What had she done wrong? This seemed to annoy the officer. He asked her if she had any drugs. She said no, and continued with her questions. He told her to calm down, to be quiet. *Be quiet?* At

---

[1] The Last Poets, "This is Madness," *This is Madness*, Douglass, 1971.

that point, she was informed that she would be searched. He ordered her to place her hands on the hood of her car. *It was burning hot. She was hot.* As she acquiesced, he pushed her down over the car. That was when the other officers who had been in a huddled clandestine discussion, closed in around her. *She started to resist.* Her hands were burning and she could still feel the palm of his hand on her back. Then the lead officer kicked her legs apart. This was madness. She almost fell. He began "patting" her down…pulling, tugging…one side…the other…up top…and back again down below…tearing at her pantyhose. All the while he kept asking if she had any weapons or drugs in her possession—or on her person. *She is beyond angry—she is livid.* The young woman demanded to know why they were doing this. She had a right to know. *This was madness.* Her questions and protests went unanswered, and she was visibly shaking. She had been pushed, poked, prodded and groped—slammed against the hood of her hot car, and now they were all leering.

At that moment, another police car came on the scene and a lone black officer emerged. He approached, almost reluctantly, looking awkwardly at his fellow officers and upon breaking their circle, eyed the sixteen-year-old black girl. She peered at him, still bent over the hood of the car, with her legs spread apart. In the broad daylight, various and sundry motorists and bystanders were starting to look. Mostly the cars carefully moved around the awkwardly parked police cars, and the people on foot looked, but said nothing. The black officer stood with the cluster of men. It was a surreal scene. Two were deep in conversation. Two others smirked and poked one another. One of them looked somber and severe. Then there was the lead offer with a specious wry smile on his face. The black officer moved toward the girl and asked the lead officer, "Can you tell me what this is about?" He was ignored. The lead officer shook his head, satisfied that she possessed no weapons on her body, stood her upright, and with a wicked smile told her again to relax. The officers, including the lead, went back into a sequestered conversation.

The transition from white to black officer looked seamless. However, it was mostly a function of the white officers crudely ignoring him. Now he began to question her. He looked down at his feet for a moment and then straightened himself. First, he wanted to know about *her people*—who were they? Where did they live? *They lived just outside of the city.* They were one of the first black families to buy a house there. Where did they go to church? *It was a prestigious black church* whose venerable minister had just retired, and a young, vibrant, highly

World To Come: Essays On The Baltimore Uprising, Militant Racism, And History

trained pastor took over the congregation. Where did she go to school? The girl prattled to keep from crying. She did not have to be bussed because it was a racially mixed high school (one of the first) downtown with a collegiate course of study and a vocational program. She was a junior steered into typesetting and printmaking to avoid cosmetology. But she hoped to go to college one day. The black policeman shook his head, and then went over to the cluster of white officers.

No matter how reserved he seemed, the black officer was pleading. He then hurried back to her. *Why did they stop me? Why did they do that?* As he answered, his eyes looked as if he could not believe the response he would give. He told the girl that she had been pulled over, not for a traffic violation, but because she (and her car) had "fit the description" of a suspect they were looking for. The more he talked, the more it sounded like they were looking for a black man. *He did not know.* So, maybe it was the car—they were looking for an old green Ford Pinto like the one she drove? No, he said—they were looking for a suspect who had fled on foot into the nearby housing projects. It didn't make sense. At this point, exasperated, beyond anger, and with all of the disgust and attitude a privileged sixteen-year-old can muster she yelled, "Can I go now?" The black officer scurried back to the group to retrieve her license, registration and insurance card. He handed them back with kindness and a shameful "they had to do this" apology. Then he humbly gave her his name and repeated it, as if he wanted her to remember it…

…As they listened intently, my grandparents never raised an eyebrow or their voices. They had a deeper understanding that I would one day only hope to know. My grandmother "Bunny" took me to the back of the house to inspect my person—and my mind. I did not tell her about the public "cavity search." When she was satisfied that the two were "right" (in tack) she brought me out again, talking incessantly, trying to keep me busy with her epic stories of the Deep South—some real "Mississippi Goddamn" mess. However, my grandfather, always quiet, authoritative and reserved, was deep down, filled with outrage. He was not willing to accept the *up north* madness. We could see that "Daddy" was incensed, mainly because he never got upset. Even still, there was always a sense of wry coolness about him. He talked over my grandmother's musings and told me to go roller-skate or play records (he drolly suggested Parliament-Funkadelic attempting to wrench a smile from my face) because he was "going to handle this." As if he had command of a thousand troops, Daddy announced that he had a few calls to make. Within a couple of hours, he had called one to the pastors of the church, some of the deacons he served with, some people downtown, a few distant cousins, some "good white folks," and the NAACP. I remember people coming by that evening, some from the church of my youth. Many knew the black officer's people. It was all matter of fact. They spoke quietly and calmly. *They had been here before. They knew what this was.* They were used to it, and in every generation they had taught their black sons how to deal with it. That I was a black girl in this day and age—in this new, and at times promising, post-Civil Rights world, did give them pause—but not much. The girls had learned to navigate in other arenas ... but, like wise and weary time travelers to the future, the point was *they had been here before.*

I have had years to think about this encounter with police; and have only shared it with a few people up to this point. Nevertheless, it was important to do so here. Especially since the contemporary police-encounter deaths of black men and women in the United States has come under intense public scrutiny—particularly the recent claims of police-custody suicides and other mysterious deaths of black and transgender women.[2] I was fortunate. I can still hear the love, calm rage, indignation and courage in my grandfather's voice, as he said, "...dey put dey hands on *my* Chile."

Studying the Immediate Past in the Miasma of the Present, or This is My Protest Sign

This essay collection is concerned with the historical moment surrounding the spring 2015 Baltimore Uprising (excluding the subsequent legal trials of the Baltimore 6). The book has five linked objectives. *First,* the work chronicles the Baltimore Uprising and explores how the death of Freddie Gray continued to galvanize black protest over police misconduct in the United States. This manuscript considers the Baltimore Uprising as critical to our understanding of the militarization (the use of military philosophy and technology) of urban

---

[2]In July, 2015 five black women were found dead and deemed suicides in police-custody within days of being jailed—Sandra Bland* (Texas), Kindra Chapman* (Alabama), Joyce Curnell (South Carolina), Ralkina Jones* (Ohio), and Raynetta Turner* (New York). Though no less important, this number should also include the Lakota woman, 24-year-old Sarah Lee Circle Bear, who was found unconscious in a Brown County Jail holding cell in Aberdeen, South Dakota on July 6, 2015. *These women are listed in Appendix C: A Compendium of African Americans Who Died in Police-Encounters, 1994—2015.

WORLD TO COME: ESSAYS ON THE BALTIMORE UPRISING, MILITANT RACISM, AND HISTORY

communities, which can be viewed as an initial step toward concretizing the police state in America. Facets of The Baltimore Uprising, as a focal point (though we could have easily used the Ferguson Movement), have been interspersed throughout the essays. Therefore, the essays are not intended to present a formal chronology of the Baltimore Uprising, but are meant to provide a particular perspective for beginning to comprehend the event. The *second* objective highlights the meaning of inordinate police-encounter deaths among largely unarmed African Americans in the United States. The work examined 150 past and recent cases of fatal police-encounters that have caused black communities to protest against perceptions of violent policing. The *third* objective surveys the general role of the media and the African American experience. Specifically, this objective explores how the media has, and continues to shape, our construction of blackness. The *fourth* objective discusses racism, and specifically militant racism in the United States. In this manuscript, *militant racism* is defined as the rhetoric or activity that incorporates operationalized racial bigotry (racism) with the intention or actual use of marshal force. In every generation, African Americans are compelled to remind the nation of grievances gone unaddressed, and of injustices still in force. The colonization of the world's people, including the large forced migration of African people introduced into the New World, helped to establish the form of human oppression that we now call racism. It is an ideology that has oppressed, exploited, and contained various groups of people for centuries through a carefully crafted social, legal and military apparatus. Given the normalization of stringent government social controls and surveillance, this manuscript is particularly concerned with the persistent significance of racism for people of African descent in America, and for world society as a whole.

    The *fifth* objective supports our appreciation and understanding of history as crucial to the intellectual decisions we make about the real world experiences of African Americans. The important idea of grasping history is also connected to the Black Lives Matter movement in the United States, an expression of black protest that has important antecedents, as well as a uniquely modern strategic thrust. Black Lives Matter is a social justice/civil/human rights crusade that focuses on empowering African American people. It is youth driven, even though in its broadest sense, members of every generation are involved and directly attached to those activists who came before them. Like the Civil Rights movement of the 1960s, we have seen that Black Lives Matter is the kind of struggle that galvanizes the world. This

World To Come: Essays On The Baltimore Uprising, Militant Racism, And History

manuscript finds distinction and value in recent historical events, based on our understanding of a much deeper sense of the past. Far from an insider, home-grown, or behind-the scenes assessment, *World to Come* is an historical introduction, a beginning—one reflexive documentary account and opinion in support of the histories that will one day be written about the Baltimore Uprising.

Historical events take considerable time to process. It would be very difficult, if not foolhardy to attempt to write a definitive history, or even an historical report of the 2015 Baltimore Uprising. The researcher would not have the wealth of necessary records. It would take years for certain documents and administrative reports to become available; and even more time to collect, verify, and analyze this material. For historians and social scientists who conduct oral interviews, there is the task of organizing and interviewing the many people who were key participants and observers in the Baltimore Uprising, including those whose stories were never featured in the national mainstream media or even the local news. Scholars undertaking such a task would not have the fullest sense of perspective afforded by time in order to see how the issues have been shaped, evolved or how they resolved themselves. Since most historians, over the course of research, immerse themselves in documents, the work of critical analysis, and the processes necessary to effectively ruminate over and find meaning in the past would be missing. Finally, it is important to have a multiplicity of disciplines representing scholarly voices in order to examine the subject. This makes recent history more difficult, nearly impossible to write—and this is why historians are cautioned never to consider such an undertaking.

However, we must begin to ask critical questions about how to study black lives within the context of the 2015 Baltimore Uprising. Initially, these questions are private, subjective, and varied in scope. There are also questions that come from our collective self. How do we live in the midst of history? How do we search for accuracy and meaning within the context of the past? How do we deny what is right before our eyes? *How do we tell a story that is unfinished?* We all have a multitude of unasked and unanswered questions about race, racism, and the Baltimore Uprising, including police-encounter deaths, mass incarceration, systemic poverty, the school-to-prison pipeline, modern apartheid schools—and how mass media chooses to interpret these issues. We can initiate our questions with the knowledge that every historical moment—every event, perspective, idea, and action has a history.

World To Come: Essays On The Baltimore Uprising, Militant Racism, And History

This manuscript was written mainly from the perspective of the people most affected by the fatal police-encounters in the United States; the nation of blacks who question and dispute this extreme police action. These people are the descendants of those who knew the face of national terrorism, those who experienced "The mass lynchings, public executions, and burnings at the stake of thousands of African Americans in the early twentieth century...."[3] In terms of methodology, this manuscript intentionally used important sources (and theories) that are too often overlooked in the corporate media, scholars whose cutting-edge ideas are ignored, co-opted, or marginalized. The essays in this manuscript rely on primary and secondary sources, including scholarly articles and books, news articles, judicial materials, websites, videos and social media. There were some barriers to accessing information including restricted material, largely due to pending legal concerns. Among the materials utilized, the document formats acquired included electronic reproductions, transcriptions, photocopies, original documents; and internet accessed resources. The use of disparate sources, historically driven but interdisciplinary in nature, was necessary because of the less than rigorous, (though prolific) production and reproduction, of news stories. At this time, most of the records on the Baltimore Uprising and the Freddie Gray case are confined to publically available news reports and pretrial sources. And since this is an effort to inspect recent historical incidents, there is a multitude of newspaper (print and online) sources, and many of the online materials are updated and when they expire, are archived and sometimes purged. Even news stories that provide little substantive analysis or thoughtful organizational perspective (i.e. blogs) are important for study. We learn, if nothing else, what is of great importance to individuals, groups, and communities.

Finally, however, the lack of historical distance, and the ever-changing news cycle, has not limited the efforts of several scholars. Many academic researchers, from the very beginning, have shared their insights about the 2015 Baltimore Uprising, the case of Freddie Gray, and the general landscape of police-encounter deaths among black citizens. Within six months of the Baltimore Uprising (from late April through the end of September 2015), over two hundred scholarly articles, commentaries, assessments and critical blogs were pre-

---

[3]Manning Marable, *The Great Wells of Democracy*, New York: BasicCivitas Books, 2002, 296.

published or published; and at least two masters level thesis were successfully defended. These works were either wholly concerned with the event or referenced the Freddie Gray case (and often the Michael Brown episode) in a meaningful way.

Cassandra Chaney and Ray V. Robertson presented an analysis of the police-encounter deaths of unarmed African Americans in the U.S. and the frequency with which police officers are charged. Their work covered a fifteen year period (1999 to 2015) documenting that the Freddie Gray case produced a rare indictment of police officers who cause or contribute to the death of citizens.[4] Concerned about the role of medical ethics, the silence of ethicists and medical professionals in light of the death of Freddie Gray, Derek Ayeh presented "Bioethical Silence & Black Lives."[5] Similar to Ayeh, Karen Kelly-Blake, in the field of medical anthropology, analyzed the national issue of police-encounter deaths as a black public health dilemma.[6] Leana S. Wen, Katherine E. Warren and Shirli Tay et al addressed the issue of public health and planned emergency intervention after the Baltimore Uprising.[7] In the study of democracy and civil disobedience, Edward L. Glaeser and Cass R. Sunstein produced a working paper, which noted the significance of the Brown and Gray cases to their analysis.[8] In addition to the subject of democracy, the issues of social justice, caste and racism was addressed in the article "Value, Visibility and the Demand for Justice" by Anupama Rao.[9] Darryl Scriven comparatively analyzed the anti-Black activities of police and the resistance of the

---

[4]Cassandra Chaney and Ray V. Robertson, Armed and Dangerous? An Examination of Fatal Shootings of Unarmed Black People by Police, *The Journal of Pan-African Studies*, Vol. 8, No. 4, September 2015, 45-78.
[5]Derek Ayeh, "Bioethical Silence & Black Lives," Voices in Bioethics, An Online Journal, Columbia University School of Continuing Education, August 3, 2015. http://voicesinbioethics.org/2015/08/03/bioethical-silence-black-lives/, accessed September 27, 2015.
[6]Karen Kelly-Blake, "Racism and the Public's Health: Whose Lives Matter?" Center for Ethic and Humanities in the Life Sciences at Michigan State University, July 23, 2015, http://msubioethics.com/2015/07/23/whose-lives-matter/, Accessed July 27, 2015.
[7]Leana S. Wen, Katherine E. Warren, Shirli Tay, Joneigh S. Khaldun, Dawn L. O'Neill, and Olivia D. Farrow, "Public Health In The Unrest: Baltimore's Preparedness And Response After Freddie Gray's Death," *American Journal of Public Health*, October 2015, Vol. 105, Issue 10, p. 1957, 3pp.
[8]Glaeser, Edward L., and Cass R. Sunstein. *A Theory of Civil Disobedience*. No. w21338. National Bureau of Economic Research, 2015.
[9]Anupama Rao, "Value, Visibility and the Demand for Justice," *Economic & Political Weekly*, September 5, 2015, Vol. 1, No. 36, 37-42.

WORLD TO COME: ESSAYS ON THE BALTIMORE UPRISING, MILITANT RACISM, AND HISTORY

courts in South Africa and Baltimore, Maryland.[10] Johari R. Shuck and Robert Helfenbein examined how knowledge acquisition and civic identity converge in community protest movements.[11] Frank R. Baumgartner, Derek A. Epp, Kelsey Shoub, and Bayard Love statistically analyzed disparities in racial profiling in North Carolina. The authors contextualized the "driving while black" phenomena by presenting results from over 18 million traffic stops, finding an increase in racial bias.[12] Michael Pinard considered the police-encounter deaths of blacks within the contexts of Ferguson, Missouri and Baltimore, Maryland, noting the structural methods used to target poor communities of color within the criminal justice system.[13]

In addition to the scholarship (and innumerable workshops, conferences and meetings), Baltimore universities developed and offered academic courses and professional support around many of the key issues surrounding the death of Freddie Gray and the Baltimore Uprising. University of Baltimore President (and former mayor of Baltimore) Kurt L. Schmoke announced the fall 2015 course: "Divided Baltimore: How did we get here, where do we go?" The course was offered to both graduate and undergraduate students.[14] The dean of the University of Maryland's Carey School of Law also saw the immediate need for an academic course which would examine the Baltimore Uprising. The one credit hour course, "Freddie Gray's Baltimore: Past, Present, and Moving Forward," was designed as an eight-week offering.[15] The course was led by law Professor Michael Greenberger (and facilitated by several members of the law faculty). Greenberger outlined the rationale: "The idea for this course emanates from the

---

[10] Darryl Scriven, "Blue on Black Violence: Freddie Gray, Baltimore, South Africa, and the Quietism of Africana Christian Theology," *The Journal of Pan African Studies*, August 2015, Vol. 8, Issue 3, 119-126.
[11] Johari R. Shuck, and Robert J. Helfenbein. "Civic Identity, Public Education, and the African-American Community in Indianapolis: Mending the Fracture." *Journal of Civic Literacy* 2, No. 1 (2015): 24-42.
[12] Frank R. Baumgartner, Derek A. Epp, Kelsey Shoub, and Bayard Love. "Driving While Black: It's Getting Worse." *Politics, Groups, and Identities*, June 22, 2015.
[13] Michael Pinard, "Poor, Black and 'Wanted': Criminal Justice in Ferguson and Baltimore." Digital Commons, The University of Maryland School of Law, (2015), http://digitalcommons.law.umaryland.edu/cgi/viewcontent.cgi?article=2536&context=fac_pubs, accessed September 27, 2015.
[14] Daniel Leaderman, *The Daily Record*, "New UB Course Will Focus On Fixing Divided Baltimore," August 3, 2015.
[15] Delece Smith-Barrow, "Freddie Gray Course Teaches Social Justice to Law Students," *U.S. News and World Report*, September 21, 2015.

WORLD TO COME: ESSAYS ON THE BALTIMORE UPRISING, MILITANT RACISM, AND HISTORY

recent disturbances in Baltimore arising from Freddie Gray's arrest and his resulting death. These events have highlighted and/or uncovered serious on-going social and financial dislocations within the City. The course will examine the recent unrest itself and then examine the causes of, and possible solutions..."[16] The work of many universities, particularly some of the schools within the University of Maryland, presented the idea of community concern and self-help in the wake of the Baltimore Uprising. In addition to the Carey School of Law, the dean of the University of Maryland School of Social Work, Richard Barth, reached out to Police Commissioner Anthony Batts after Gray's death and *before* the uprising, and offered to work with the police department to "prevent such future tragedies."[17] The University of Maryland School of Social Work also held a forum on race ("A Discussion about Race in Baltimore"), invited people to share their stories and images, and reminded the community of their counseling support.

    The early research and academic offerings, along with the institutional services of higher education which encompassed the Baltimore Uprising and the case of Freddie Gray have much in common. These formal queries can also be seen as important demonstrations of civil protest that allow scholars professional forums in which to critically discuss the larger issues of the criminal justice system, racial profiling, and public health. Obviously, scholars from a multiplicity of disciplines were compelled to respond to the historicity of the moment. Pinard explained that his work "…offers a couple of ways to move forward and contributes to the efforts currently undertaken by communities, individuals, and families who have been impacted by police violence and the criminal justice system …."[18] These scholars and institutions took an immediate intellectual stand to research and dialogue about the issues of police brutality and suspicious

---

[16]University of Maryland Francis King Carey School of Law, Course Catalog, "Special Topic: Freddie Gray's Baltimore: Past, Present and Moving Forward," http://www.law.umaryland.edu/academics/program/curriculum/catalog/course_details.html?coursenum=552M, Accessed August 12, 2015.

[17]Letter to Baltimore Police Department Police Commissioner Anthony W. Batts from Richard P. Barth, Dean and Professor of the University of Maryland School of Social Work, April 22, 2015.

[18]Michael Pinard, "Poor, Black and 'Wanted': Criminal Justice in Ferguson and Baltimore." Digital Commons, The University of Maryland School of Law, (2015), http://digitalcommons.law.umaryland.edu/cgi/viewcontent.cgi?article=2536&context=fac_pubs, accessed September 27, 2015.

World To Come: Essays On The Baltimore Uprising, Militant Racism, And History

police-encounter deaths. In keeping with their sense of urgency, this manuscript is my protest sign.

The Shape of the World to Come—Chapter Summaries

Chapter 1, the introduction to this essay collection, "Black Lives in the New Millennium," begins with a reminder of the 1968 Baltimore riots, which were a direct result of the assassination of the Reverend Dr. Martin Luther King, Jr., signaling an end to the modern Civil Rights movement, and fueling the advancement of Black power. The chapter introduces the current discussion about the idea of black men as the embodiment of "Freddie Gray" within the context of the police-encounter deaths of African Americans. This introduction also takes a look at two of the important police-encounter death cases (out of many) since the death of Trayvon Martin (Sanford, Florida) in 2012—Michael Brown (Ferguson Missouri) in 2014 and Freddie Gray (Baltimore Maryland) in 2015. In addition, this chapter presents the idea of the Community-of-Care (COC)—how groups tend to operate in order to preserve a great social cause. The introduction ends with a summary of how the police-encounter scenario relates to the 1990s "while black" rhetoric and phenomena in which African Americans likened their racialized experience to living under constant formal and informal constructs of police surveillance. Succinctly, "driving while black," "shopping while black," etc. was to live in a world highly reactive to blackness while at the same time ignoring the structural processes of racism's impact on black humanity.

Chapter 2, "Between Enslavement and Freedom—the Apex of Racial Power" suggests that the American institution of slavery is connected to the long history of police killing in the black community. This connection is explored through a general discussion of the master narrative, the legal nuisances, and operational apparatus (the slave patrollers) of controlling the enslaved African population. This chapter presents the story of one slave as paradigmatic of the brutality inherent in the slave system; and considers how the scope of the institution of slavery was rooted in obedience and an embedded sense of white racial supremacy. The chapter then notes how Frederick Douglass, probably one of the first critical race theorists, actualized freedom by exercising his own edict, "If there is no struggle, there is no progress." Even though blacks worked as laborers in Baltimore's Fells Point (both enslaved and free) they represented much smaller numbers. Douglass found that in antebellum Baltimore Maryland black lives were

World To Come: Essays On The Baltimore Uprising, Militant Racism, And History

disposable; and that whites who may have sympathized with him did not raise their voices to stop the brutality he and other blacks suffered. Douglass realized two truths about racism in this experience. First, his blackness was the target for whites who sought to act out capricious racial aggression and cruelties. Second, only the enslaved African could secure his freedom. The chapter ends with a concise history of the rise and maintenance of post-Civil War racism.

Social networking is the theory behind the Community-of-Care concept, and it is an ancient idea, which is at the heart of our contemporary technological world and the issues involving race. Social networking is the idea that groups of people establish and maintain highly influential discursive communities around any purpose—but particularly around a shared understanding of their own humanity. Chapter 3, "History, Social Network Conservation and Intolerable Blackness" explores the fundamental concept of social network preservation in modern society and the issue of anti-black racism. The chapter discusses the importance of the 1831 Nat Turner revolt and the maintenance of racial stereotypes within this context. The Nat Turner event is important for many reasons—one is the paradoxical nature of racialized thinking. On the one hand, Turner and other blacks rebelled against the institution of slavery in the South were thought incapable of planning and executing armed liberation movements. Yet, blacks were demonized for assertively pursuing their freedom. The two ideas revealed denial, because racist thinking understood the liberatory thrust, but chose not to recognize it in African people. The chapter introduces the idea of social network conservation—in essence the need for people to coalesce racial (and ethnic) group voices in order to present the most positive mass media image. In addition, the concept of intolerable blackness is addressed—how anti-Black sentiment has honed through systemic racism. The chapter also addresses ideas surrounding "new" and "post" racial discussions, which uncover how modern racism is slightly different from the past; especially how it seeks to shut down discussions which attempt to eliminate racism.

Mass media is one of the most important tools in molding racist thinking in modern society. Chapter 4, "Popular Media, Ghettoization, and an Introduction to the Police-Encounter Narrative," examines how popular media preserved the contemporary black "Ghetto" in 2007, at the same time President Barack Obama announced his candidacy. The material in this chapter came from news and other sources, which demonstrated that negative racial stereotypes, overall, had changed very little since the beginning of the turn of the

World To Come: Essays On The Baltimore Uprising, Militant Racism, And History

century 2001. This chapter discusses how police-encounters are controlled and presented in the media. Largely based on the selected cases of police-encounter deaths in this manuscript, law enforcement agencies have enhanced the careful management of their public image. They use the latest media tools and technologies to establish their infallibility to the public, especially regarding the issue of police-encounter deaths of African Americans. This includes leaking and sharing information to reporters within mass media outlets. Most significantly, this research has determined that law enforcement agencies actually control most of the news articles that involve police-custody deaths—with few exceptions, regardless of the journalist or the reporting periodical. This is largely because of the way news is instantly created and swiftly distributed today. The end of this chapter briefly explores the two medias—traditional mainstream and independent.

Given the force of mass media in the Black Lives Matter movement, Chapter 5, "The Age of New Media and the Yette Hypothesis," addresses how media culture, the quality of black life, and notions of racial cleansing (physical, cultural and psychic) converge. Without the imposition of new media, via the cellphone video camera, the critical documentation about contemporary police-encounter deaths would not have emerged. This chapter looks at new age media—largely the impact of social media, news, and the citizen journalist. The chapter also considers how African Americans have taken control of media as a result of the emerging technologies. Using this command of media, we see the example of Kevin Moore in the Freddie Gray case as representative of media-activism. This chapter also reviews Samuel Yette's classic work *The Choice* and proffers, the Yette hypothesis. The Yette hypothesis is the theory, gleaned from Yette's important work, which suggested that the contemporary landscape of black America is found in the past. This landscape emerged from the post-Civil Rights/Black Power/Vietnam War era. It was during this timeframe that American society recognized that African Americans (and African descended people in general, no matter their country of origin) were no longer crucial to western economy. Blacks had become anachronistic to the labor market because they were no longer enslaved (or enslavable) or they were considered economically burdensome as low-wage workers, or dismissible as impoverished people, and therefore, and especially within a racist prism, were wholly expendable.

Chapter 6 "Baltimore's Wilderness + 'Riot' = 'Uprising'" is an attempt to show that the events that took place at the end of April and the beginning of May 2015 were broader than the frameworks of riot and protest. In the city of Baltimore the media frequently saw protest as riot and vice versa. However, while there was a clear distinction, the inability to separate the two expressions often caused clashes in public perceptions. Chapter 6 then is concerned with some of the immense challenges faced by the city of Baltimore, challenges that predate the current political landscape. This chapter shows that while Baltimore can cite many growth sectors (and countless funded development programs), the fact remains that for a significant portion of the black residents life is restricted to, or teetering on, poverty. While we want to speak about all that is good in the city of Baltimore—and we should—this life of poverty is directly tied to the past *and* to the present through countless reports of over policing and police brutality. Chapter 6 also briefly relates the history of civil disobedience in the United States, as these events concern issues of race.

Chapter 7 takes an interesting look at some of the city-induced, media-fueled features of the Baltimore Uprising. This chapter, "The Millennials and IGens in the Wilderness State and at the Mall," assesses the youth culture of the "Millennial generation" and the concept of youth dissent. More often however, the youth involved in this aspect of Baltimore's civil disobedience were rarely considered within the larger context of youth culture. The chapter also takes a look at their younger counterparts, the IGens and the controversy surrounding rumors of a "purge" that permeated the media and painted Baltimore youth as violent and less than human. Related to this were additional reports that groups of Baltimore criminal gangs were positioning themselves to attack (and even kill) local law enforcement officers. These examples demonstrate that the "early and often" rumor mill fed the mass media, and some assert helped to create a sense of looming violence in the city. Chapter 7 also briefly introduces us to two of the frontline leaders in the Baltimore Uprising. These leaders faced some inordinate challenges, and while they were praised for proactive efforts, they were also heavily criticized for heightening the militaristic climate of the city, particularly the curfew.

There was significant discussion about how the riot aspect of the Baltimore Uprising affected businesses. While mostly local small businesses were impacted (i.e. black and Korean businesses), the media's attention was on the national CVS chain store located in West Baltimore. In part, this was because of the televised images of black smoke rising from the building. Chapter 8, "Into the Rebellion: Selected Facets of the Baltimore Uprising," continues the discussion of the Baltimore Uprising, at the moment of its creation. The chapter goes

World To Come: Essays On The Baltimore Uprising, Militant Racism, And History

further into the rebellion, noting the focus on the CVS, the military formation of police officers, and rioting; as well as the impact of police misinformation and the response of local gangs. Chapter 8 explores the criticisms of the mayor; and further, the notion that the uprising disturbed the city's art and culture scene. In these kinds of situations, it has been said that blacks riot, while whites protest. Therefore, chapter 8 also notates the spread of civil disobedience actions across the nation in support of Baltimore, and how these protest events, when compared to the disruptions fueled largely by white counterparts—and sometimes for different reasons—are perceived very differently in the mass media.

As a historical force, the concept of racism has done more to change the human landscape of the world than we are willing to concede. Yet rarely is racism credited, as a major historical concept or a seminal factor of causation for social strife and militarization. In connecting the basic principles of racism and killing, Chapter 9, "Racism, Killology and Disbelief in History," surveys this idea and the concept of killology. Killology is the study of killing as a chief ideology of military philosophy and of modern western warfare. In addition, the human capacity to see or not see systemic racism is explored. Systemic racism is founded on and completely indebted to the ideas of disbelief and denial—profound ahistorical psychological conditions (akin to cognitive dissonance), which the chapter also explores. Furthermore, chapter 9 discusses the many protest signs featured during the Baltimore Uprising; and, finally, draws our attention to how racism, in a militaristic context, dismembers black communities by intentionally inflicting maximum discomfort upon the residents.

For Black Lives Matter protesters across the nation, African American communities resembled the epitome of the dystopic police state (crime, police killing, and eco-racism). Yet there is a history leading to and surrounding this sense of public disorder. Chapter 10, "Baltimore and the New Urban Police State," considers the important legacy of the FBI's Counter Intelligence Program (COINTELPRO), and the military imperative of surveillance. Here we see theories, training programs and equipment acquisitions specifically developed to respond to national fears of black uprising. The chapter summarizes the history of conflict between traditional law enforcement and African American people. Observing the primacy of the Baltimore Uprising, the chapter examines some of the technologies used. Historically, the use of technology was very important in law enforcement's relationship to black communities. The use of technology then was exceedingly important in the Baltimore Uprising. The chapter also notes the

World To Come: Essays On The Baltimore Uprising, Militant Racism, And History

presence of the Bureau of Alcohol, Tobacco and Firearms (ATF) and their investigative role post-uprising. Finally, the chapter discusses the efforts to locate and punish rioters in the Baltimore Uprising.

Chapter 11, "Varieties of Cops, Political Leaders, and the Racial Paradox that Wasn't" addresses an important popular idea about how racism functions in American society. The chapter looks at the mainstream notion of whether blacks, who operate within a racist system, can be racist when they are bound to the system. The chapter reviews what it means to be part of a blue police culture, where one's loyalties are to fellow officers and not to the people-at-large. The chapter gives a few examples of the experiences of African American members of law enforcement, and the struggles in discussing the aims and intents of white officers who participate in racially bias speech and actions, while denying that this effort fulfills a racist mandate. In addition, the chapter details the experiences of white officers who do not subscribe to the pervasive unofficial police code. Further, the chapter gives some attention to para-police, individuals who operate in police-like capacities and become involved in police-encounter style shootings of African Americans. The chapter ends with a discussion on the meaning of black leadership and the Baltimore Uprising.

In Chapter 12, "The Baltimore Uprising and the Great Black Legacy of Social Justice," the essay addresses the media's attempt to devalue the historic role of black protest movements in the United States. This chapter also outlines the role of the State's Attorney for the city of Baltimore Marilyn Mosby; and how the decision to charge the six officers involved in the death of Freddie Gray was received as a national watershed event. The discussion also includes some attention to the politically inspired criticisms of the State's Attorney's speech and actions. The chapter looks at how police are revered and protected even as the public perceives that they might be guilty of wrongdoing. As a consequence of how policing is viewed, the chapter recounts the issue of bail, the reception to the Baltimore 6, and the case of Alan Bullocks. Finally, this chapter relates the "live disappearance" of Joseph Kent during the Baltimore Uprising as an indication of state militarization and social media spectacle.

The Baltimore Uprising featured an incredible sensational aspect fueled by mass and social media. So much of the imagery introduced by mass media presented a distinctive frame that felt like live theater or interactive television. Chapter 13, "African Americans, the Psychopomp of Media, and *The Wire*," briefly reviews post-uprising media events such as the new United States Attorney General's visit to

World To Come: Essays On The Baltimore Uprising, Militant Racism, And History

Baltimore, an initial survey (a Pew poll) using data to characterize the uprising, and the notion of blacks as refugees in their own city. This chapter examines a few of the cultural, social and gender issues surrounding the Baltimore Uprising. These include Prince's *Rally for Peace*; and in light of *Afrofemiphobia*—the perverse fear of black women—the issue of how African American women in the Black Lives Matter movement are presented, perceived and omitted in the serious discussion of police-encounter deaths. The chapter concludes with an analysis of the HBO serial, *The Wire*; specifically how the show depicted the African American community in the city of Baltimore in a constricted pop culture scope.

Chapter 14, "The Militarization of Urban America," discusses the military frameworks appearing in major cities. This chapter adds to this discussion the important concepts of crime prevention, and explores the zero-sum game and broken windows approaches. These concepts contributed to the advancement of racism in Black communities; and these ideas have been viewed as part of the aggressive program of policing in the United States. Chapter 14 also considers that in the Baltimore Uprising, particularly after the introduction of the National Guard, the streets appeared to be military training grounds; and the actual terrain for combat operations. This chapter also examines the concept of police overcompensation within the context of police-encounter deaths of African Americans. The chapter ends with how biker gangs were portrayed in the media; specifically their role in the 2015 Waco Texas massacre which resulted in the deaths of 9 people, and how these homicides were interpreted. This discussion is surrounded by a brief treatment of the *black-on-black* crime concept, the notion of contested territory, and how the violent activity of biker gangs was depicted in the media with less ferocity than the actions of those that chose to riot during the Baltimore Uprising.

The concluding Chapter 15, "The World to Come and the Post-Millennial Revolution," covers the idea of the Baltimore Uprising as a learning tool for addressing the issues of civil disobedience, and police-encounter deaths of African Americans. The summation suggests that the new methods of civil disobedience incorporated tactical legacies of the civil rights movement, including a heightened sense of disruptive activism. This chapter then asks the question, "What does it mean to be human and humane in the world?" The question is addressed by looking at the selected thoughts of public personas, mostly characterized as public intellectuals, whose work embodies the theme of "human/humane" in world society. There is also a section on "social justice beyond policing," which incorporates critical events post-Baltimore Uprising that intersect with the overall discussion of Black Lives Matters activists. These events include the 2015 tragedy of the "Emanuel 9", the killing of Senator Clementa Pinckney and black parishioners in Charleston South Carolina by Dylann Roof, and the national fervor over the Confederate battle flag; which culminated in the civil disobedience act of Bree Newsome who removed the Confederate flag from the state grounds.

Racial Justice In Search of a Proactive Audience

    This manuscript was written expressly for people who are pro-humanity, and in favor of humane relations. It is for those who truly want to study and remember the past, are anti-racist, and champion black life. This book is especially for the heroes of the twenty-first century human rights movement, the youth who told the world Black Lives Matter. While this manuscript is not intended to be a definitive history of the Baltimore Uprising, or even a history of Baltimore, it is a collection of disparate essays that attempts to chronicle and situate the Baltimore Uprising within the broad themes of: *Racism, Media, Human Rights, and Militarization.* These essays are concerned with the questionable police-killings of African Americans as an historic and contemporary human rights issue. The manuscript also endeavors a critique of the media's traditional presentation of race issues, while at the same time, acknowledging the immense influence of social media and calls for a deeper racial discourse. As the essays imply, we are at an alarming place in world history, and each person is compelled to ask *unthinkable questions*, once again, about the value of black life. Questions people should not have to ask—inquires predicated on a bitter past.

    As far as police-community relations are concerned, there are varying perspectives. According to Kurt L. Schmoke, "Some people believe very strongly, or are supportive of the police in all they do. Other people are very skeptical of the police, so it depends on your encounter and the history of your encounter with police."[19] The reverend Al Sharpton maintained that, "...while the vast majority of

---

[19]Andrew R. Koch, "UB President Schmoke Discusses Upcoming Police Officer Trials," *The UB Post*, September 29, 2015, https://theubpost.wordpress.com/2015/09/29/ub-president-schmoke-discusses-upcoming-police-officer-trials/, accessed September 30, 2015.

police officers are serving our communities bravely there is a real and urgent problem with policing in America."[20] The extralegal killing of blacks by police *and history* has demanded a multitude of questions—and more importantly, has insisted upon humane answers that ensure justice. The present moment makes our questions, not just embellished inquiries or part of a rhetorical posture, but part of a necessary public dialogue and activist discourse about race, racism, justice, power, authority and agency in the twenty-first century. Most of the time, the specific questions we must ask of ourselves and others about police conduct begins with a first, formative encounter with law enforcement—as noted above—sometimes it begins with a traffic stop.

KATHERINE OLUKEMI BANKOLE-MEDINA, PH.D.
Professor of History
Department of Humanities
Coppin State University
Baltimore, Maryland

---

[20] Al Sharpton, "Statement by Reverend Al Sharpton on Criminal Charges of Six Baltimore Police Officers in Death of Freddie Gray," May 1, 2015, the National Action Network (NAN), http://nationalactionnetwork.net/press/statement-by-reverend-al-sharpton-on-criminal-charges-of-six-baltimore-police-officers-in-death-of-freddie-gray/, accessed May 31, 2015.

CHAPTER 1

INTRODUCTION—BLACK LIVES IN THE NEW MILLENNIUM

> I am convinced that if we are to get on the right side of the world revolution, we as a nation must undergo a radical revolution of values. We must rapidly begin the shift from a "thing-oriented" society to a "person-oriented" society. When machines and computers, profit motives and property rights are considered more important than people, the giant triplets of racism, materialism, and militarism are incapable of being conquered... The choice is ours, and though we might prefer it otherwise we must choose in this crucial moment of human history.—Martin Luther King, Jr.[1]

The 1968 King Assassination Riots in Baltimore

Baltimore is a grand historic city. Like many major cities today, Baltimore houses two distinct worlds—one white and the other black. While these worlds are filled with all races of people, which routinely come together; it is only when they collide that we truly see the estrangement. One such collision occurred almost 47 years ago, from April 7-9 in 1968. The city of Baltimore experienced one of the most challenging civil uprisings in its history. The unrest and massive protests in the city were sparked by the assassination of the reverend Dr. Martin Luther King, Jr. in Memphis Tennessee. Over one hundred cities experienced turmoil when King was killed. King, along with Malcolm X, was arguably the first black man whose words and deeds placed African Americans on the world stage of history. However, King's assassination was the tragic capstone to the long and protracted struggle of African Americans. African Americans were fighting for real quality of life issues such as education, housing and employment. Dr. King, who had been arrested by police sixteen times in the movement, became the de facto spokesperson for these rights. He did this in part,

---

[1] Martin Luther King Jr, "Beyond Vietnam: A Time to Break Silence." Speech, Riverside Church, New York, NY, April 4, 1967.

World To Come: Essays On The Baltimore Uprising, Militant Racism, And History

through his fundamental advocacy and practice of civil disobedience—the idea that people have a right and responsibility to challenge unjust treatment and laws. King's philosophy was to be actively nonviolent, attempt to convert the enemy into a friend, eschew hate, and understand and accept that struggle was a core part of the process. His moral strategy to ensure black equality as a "humanicentric philosopher"[2] was embraced by many, and dismissed by some. However, his criticism of the Vietnam War and the military build-up of the United States armed forces caused a wave of established order condemnation, and some asserted might have even cost him his life.

Yet King acted with conviction, and by 1968, he was one of the most revered men in the United States. When he was assassinated on April 4, 1968, the brutal act cast dispersions on the aims and tactics of the Civil Rights movement. Many suggested that only King stood between the peaceful protests and Black power, the notion that advocates of social agency and self-defense was the violent alternative. His death also symbolically crushed the dreams of a "nation within a nation."[3] Blacks had expected that Jim Crow would pass a way, not necessarily without racist animosity, but that it would do so leaving a more politically progressive and equal society in its wake. However, the history of persistent deprivation, false hopes, continued calls for gradual change, day-to-day racial bigotry, and the denial of real opportunity was the spark that ignited the flames. The violent public death of Martin Luther King, Jr. in 1968 was a blow to the nation. Collectively, the cities in revolt experienced intense forms of despair, anger, depression, disillusionment, rioting and other forms of violence associated with the destruction of property.

Maryland Governor Spiro Agnew authorized the National Guard on April 6, 1968. The Army set up command centers, marched in formation, and searched citizens. The city was under siege. In addition to the Army National Guard, local police led the mission to quell the uprising. A curfew was imposed and travel in and out of the city of Baltimore was restricted. In cities like Baltimore several people were killed, property damaged soared into the millions, and thousands of people were arrested. Armed guards, using armored vehicles,

---

[2]Greg Moses, *Revolution of Conscience: Martin Luther King, Jr., and the Philosophy of Nonviolence.* New York: The Guilford Press, 1997, 42.
[3]A "nation within a nation," was articulated by W.E.B. DuBois in 1934, who saw economic leverage as a tool for blacks to advance in the United States.

World To Come: Essays On The Baltimore Uprising, Militant Racism, And History

patrolled the streets with rifles at the ready. West Baltimore was most affected by the riots. The 1968 Baltimore riot ranks among the major urban American cities to experience widespread discontent and extensive military occupation. The Baltimore riot of 1968 caused about $14 million dollars in damage. Many of the urban cities that experienced rage over King's murder can profess today that the areas directly affected, especially those that had already lost their industrial base, have virtually remained the same—essentially left undeveloped for a half century. After the 2015 Baltimore Uprising, former director of the ACLU Washington Legislative Office, Laura W. Murphy remarked "…it's clear today that many of the problems that plagued Baltimore 50 years ago are still plaguing us now."[4] However, as the city of Baltimore once again exploded, it proved to be more than the recollection that a familiar racial history was upon us. It was the feeling, as Baltimore radio talk show host Marc Steiner suggested, that, "…something's been happening all the time, now we all see it."[5]

The Freddie Grays of the World, Police-Custody Deaths, and the Universal Community-of-Care

Charm City has captured national and international attention over the 2015 police-custody death of Freddie Carlos Gray, Jr. and the Baltimore Uprising. Freddie Gray was a 25-year-old African American man who has become an important symbol in America. Too many African Americans live a quasi-existence in the United States—in a world that promises so much opportunity and delivers very little to the masses of the black, working class, and the poor. There has been a lot of talk about "the Freddie Grays of the world," meaningful conversations that speak to the exploitation and the deep humanity of black men. The Freddie Grays of this world seem to look at life through a closed window—watching and witnessing—but unable to access or fully participate in this world. Sometimes they are the embodiment of the black male characters in classic literary works like

---

[4]Laura W. Murphy, "Preventing the Next Death in Police Custody," Op-Ed, *The Baltimore Sun*, April 24, 2015, http://www.baltimoresun.com/news/opinion/oped/bs-ed-police-custody-deaths-20150425-story.html, accessed May 15, 2015.
[5]Marc Steiner, *The Marc Steiner Show*, Center for Emerging Media, Baltimore, Maryland, July 29, 2015.

World To Come: Essays On The Baltimore Uprising, Militant Racism, And History

Native Son, Invisible Man, and *Manchild in the Promised Land.*[6] They are always struggling, sometimes succeeding, and at other times falling—but constantly trying to envision a better life. Black men, regardless of their socio-economic status, have a long history of being targeted by law enforcement and framed in the popular culture and the media as being angry and embittered, under educated, prone to criminality, brutish, violent and hypersexual. The American myths and stereotypes applied to black men that serve society also have a black female counterpart.

Recently, however, and because of the preponderance of "endangered black male" literature from the 1980s; in addition to their higher numbers in the criminal justice system, black men have been the focus of contemporary queries into extralegal, in-custody, or police-encounter deaths.[7] Moreover, we know that as the standard police-custody death narrative unfolds in each individual case, uninhibited racial stereotypes and demonstrative displays of force emerge when profiling black males.[8] According to one parent, "My sons both black have been pulled over by police (,) hand cuffed, and harassed, not because they are criminals but because they are black. One was (stopped) for speeding 10 miles over the speed limit when he was 16. Three cop cars arrived to help the cop who pulled him over for speeding. He was cuffed (,) his car searched and he was arrested. He was sitting on the street with cops surrounding him…the other son (was stopped) for an expired registration rag. He was almost shot by the cop not because he was doing anything illegal but because he was so scared he was shaking (—) he was 18.…"[9] The long history of this particular policing milieu has been so pervasive that legislators like

---

[6]Richard Wright, *Native Son,* New York: Harper & Row, 1969. Ralph Ellison, *Invisible Man,* New York: Random House, 1952; Claude Brown, *Manchild in the Promised Land,* New York: Collier Macmillan, 1965.
[7]This manuscript also uses the term police-encounter deaths.
[8]Kelly Welch, "Black Criminal Stereotypes And Racial Profiling," *Journal of Contemporary Criminal Justice* 23, No. 3 (2007): 276-288.
[9]Public comments made regarding the report by Ryan Gabrielson, Ryann Grochowski Jones and Eric Sagara, "Deadly Force, in Black and White: A ProPublica analysis of killings by police shows outsize risk for young black males," *ProPublica,* October 10, 2014, http://www.propublica.org/article/deadly-force-in-black-and-white, accessed August 8, 2015.

World To Come: Essays On The Baltimore Uprising, Militant Racism, And History

Representative John Conyers, Jr. (D-MI) introduced the "End Racial Profiling Act of 2015."[10]

Research and findings on the deaths of blacks in police-custody are consistent with what independent investigative journalists, blactivists,[11] and community leaders have known all along—that black men die at the hands of law enforcement—or legal intervention[12]—in much greater numbers than white males.[13] Nancy Krieger and others have identified the racial issues that led to the police-custody deaths of Michael Brown and Eric Garner (and now certainly would include Freddie Gray), as symptomatic of one of society's major public health issues—racism.[14] The editorial board of the *Harvard Public Health Review* stated in 2015,

> …racism has driven health inequities among historically underserved and marginalized populations nationwide, evidenced not only in the extraordinarily disparate rate at which Blacks are killed at the hands of the police compared to Whites, but also through inequities in environmental exposures, limitations in access to health care, and other factors that affect optimal health and well-being.[15]

However, all of the new interest in racism and police-custody deaths began to reveal that many states were not reporting this information;

---

[10] H.R. 1933, the "End Racial Profiling Act of 2015" was introduced and referred to the House Committee on the Judiciary on April 22, 2015.
[11] Black activists who work exclusively on black, Africana issues.
[12] Legal intervention is defined as "deaths due to law enforcement actions," see Nancy Krieger, Mathew V. Kiang, Jarvis T. Chen, and Pamela D. Waterman, "Trends in US deaths due to legal intervention among black and white men, age 15-34 years, by county income level: 1960-2010," *Harvard Public Health Review*, Vol. 3, January 2015, 1-5, 1, http://harvardpublichealthreview.org/wp-content/uploads/2015/01/HPHRv3-Krieger-Trends-in-Deaths.pdf, accessed May 15, 2015.
[13] Ryan Gabrielson, Ryann Grochowski Jones and Eric Sagara, "Deadly Force, in Black and White: A ProPublica analysis of killings by police shows outsize risk for young black males," *ProPublica*, October 10, 2014, http://www.propublica.org/article/deadly-force-in-black-and-white, accessed August 8, 2015.
[14] Nancy Krieger, "Police Killings, Political Impunity, Racism and the People's Health: Issues for our Times," *Harvard Public Health Review*, Vol. 3, January 2015, 1-3, http://harvardpublichealthreview.org/wp-content/uploads/2015/01/HPHRv3-Krieger-Police-Killings.pdf, accessed May 15, 2015.
[15] Harvard Public Health Review Editorial Board, "HPHR Editorial: Racism Is a Public Health Problem," *Harvard Public Health Review*, Vol. 3, January 2015, http://harvardpublichealthreview.org/hphr-editorial-racism-is-a-public-health-problem/, accessed May 15, 2015.

and if they were, the data provided by law enforcement agencies excluded race, or was not in-depth. In addition, it has been suggested that we probably only have knowledge of half of the police-custody deaths in the United States. To address this, in December 2014 H.R. 1447, known as the "Death in Custody Reporting Act of 2013" became law. This bill was sponsored by Representative Robert C. "Bobby" Scott (D-VA) and co-sponsored by Representative John Conyers, Jr. (D-MI); and a number of congressional representatives and senators supported or assisted with the bill. Representative Scott stated,

> It is clear that the federal government needs to exercise greater oversight of federal, state and local law enforcement personnel to ensure that they are protecting and serving all of our citizens and that the protections embodied in our Constitution apply equally to all citizens. To aid in that measure, we need data on deaths that occur within our criminal justice system. Without accurate data, it is nearly impossible to identify variables that lead to an unnecessary and unacceptable risk of individuals dying in custody or during an arrest.[16]

The black community has known for quite some time that mass media reported heavily on race and crime issues because it was sensational and supported national racist beliefs of black pathology—the odious idea that blackness itself was a disease. However, the excessive numbers of police-custody deaths of black men, especially at the hands of white officers, called into question the actions of police. The recent high profile deaths of blacks in police-encounters confirmed that blacks were more likely to be killed by police than any other people. As this problem became a fixture in news media, it also raised more questions about the data. There were doubts about the accuracy of state and county data (the numbers killed) as reported to the federal government. Critiques of the federal reporting criteria and mandates have declared that data has been stalled, exists in an unorganized (and rendered inaccessible) state, and that some law enforcement agencies have

---

[16]"Scott Statement on the Signing of Death In Custody Reporting Act of 2013 into Law by President Obama," Press Release, December 18, 2014, Congressman Bobby Scott Representing the 3rd District of Virginia, http://bobbyscott.house.gov/media-center/press-releases/scott-statement-on-the-signing-of-death-in-custody-reporting-act-of-2013, accessed May 15, 2015.

World To Come: Essays On The Baltimore Uprising, Militant Racism, And History

deemed it unnecessary to keep race data when it involved the killing of black citizens.■

When people perceive a profound injustice they rise-up to form a community-of-care (COC). This is true for any issue, and is usually present after a disputed police-encounter that results in death. The community-of-care is often a diverse group of people (physically and virtually) who feel a commitment to a person (or a group of people), or to a greater cause (a common symbol). For example, a community-of-care led by journalist and anti-lynching activist Ida B. Wells-Barnett rose up in outrage over the 1892 lynching of Will Stewart, Calvin McDowell, and Tom Moss. The group of black men opened their own business—a grocery store that was a success and caused a white mob to attack them. They were arrested, jailed and shot to death with the support of law enforcement.[17] The community-of-care operated for decades to address the issue of justice over the convictions of the Scottsboro Boys in 1931.[18] Through sometimes competing COCs, the International Labor Defense (ILD) and the NAACP worked to free the young black males who were falsely accused. Two decades later in 1950 the Scottsboro Boys were exonerated. COCs can change the course of history. When Rosa Parks was arrested in 1955 for refusing to give up her bus seat to a white rider, the planned act of civil disobedience started the Montgomery bus boycott, drew attention to the emerging leadership of the reverend Dr. Martin Luther King Jr., and for many formally ushered in the modern Civil Rights Movement.

Today, the COC operates, as strong as ever, around the issues of police misconduct and excessive-use-of-force. A half century after Rosa Park's defiance, a global community-of-care developed to support the case of Mumia Abu-Jamal. In 1981 Abu-Jamal, a journalist and activist who worked part-time as a taxi driver, found himself shot, semi-conscious and lying next to a police officer on the streets of Philadelphia. The officer, Daniel Faulkner, who was also gunned down later died. Abu-Jamal was "…arrested, savagely beaten, thrown into a

---

[17] Ida B. Wells-Barnett, *A Red Record: Tabulated Statistics and Alleged Causes of Lynchings in the United States, 1892-1893-1894*. Chicago: Donohue and Henneberry, 1895, 84.
[18] Nine African American boys—Clarence Norris, Charlie Weems, Haywood Patterson, Olen Montgomery, Ozie Powell, Willie Roberson, Eugene Williams, Andy Wright, and Roy Wright—faced the death penalty for the alleged rape of a white woman.

paddy wagon and driven to a hospital a few blocks away…"[19] Abu-Jamal's case is replete with overwhelming evidence and allegations of Philadelphia judicial misconduct, false and coerced testimony, police harassment, botched ballistics and forensics, missing and suppressed evidence, and the rejection of a 1999 confession of another individual. Even so, Abu-Jamal was found guilty of killing officer Faulkner and sentenced to the death penalty. As *the* symbol for black political prisoners in the United States Abu-Jamal's supporters, the world over, have maintained that his race, beliefs and activist affiliations along with a police vendetta were aggressively used against him. For 35 years Abu-Jamal's community-of-care fought to have him removed from death row[20], demanded that he be granted a new trial, advocated for medical treatment, and always called for his immediate release from prison.

The community-of-care possesses a shared sense of responsibility to the person and/or the cause—and they act out expressions of support. Their goal is to eliminate injustice, combat error, correct omission, refute negativity, and call attention to insensitivity. They endeavor to interpret the story, question the issues and events, find truth, and ultimately to secure justice. The COC is the collective voice and concerted action of people that seek to represent the interests of citizens *and* the police. Members of the community-of-care are dynamically inspired in their endeavors because they speak to the media, create media, and as crusaders they encourage others to act. They hold meetings, post public comments, advance legislation, raise money, circulate petitions, inform the community, and organize protests. The community-of-care can be family, friends, co-workers, or complete strangers. The COC may espouse any ideology, but they all have one sentiment in common, they deeply believe in the person or the cause. As a result, the community-of-care is hypervigilant. They defend their message to ensure that it remains *on point*. The COC challenges any disarticulation or misunderstanding of their main idea. Individuals without a visible and vocal community-of-care are often lost to a system, believing no one is interested in them. People without a committed community-of-care involved in questionable police-encounters, are as doomed as those trapped inside of a Greek tragedy.

---

[19] *The Case of Mumia Abu-Jamal Information Booklet*, Philadelphia, PA: International Concerned Family and Friends of Mumia Abu-Jamal, November, 2005, 26pp, 2.
[20] Abu-Jamal was removed from Death Row in 2012; and his supporters had to fight for his transfer to the General Population.

World To Come: Essays On The Baltimore Uprising, Militant Racism, And History

The community-of-care is often, but not always, an informal, ad hoc group of people—a micro-movement. It can be a collection of open source activists—an accessible group that is not predicated on acceptance or even interpersonal relationships. The COC is rarely closed to genuine supporters. They don't need permission to join the struggle. Members do not have to look or sound alike—but they must share similar thought processes about the issues. Unless the community-of-care is a highly organized and structured, they don't vote, or formulate consensus. They don't even have to communicate personally with one another in order to be part of the support system. When the COC is exclusively online (and many are), they can be an entirely different entity in terms of how vigorously they mobilize and engage supporters, establish the basis for their cause, and *how well* they look after the subject over time. No matter the structure, COCs have come forward to advance a singular idea—and by doing so to challenge power—and most importantly, to wield power.

Sometimes the COC is based on personal proximity to the issue. Because people know what they care about, they are able to identify themselves in relation to the individual or the cause—as a concerned citizen, a neighbor, a colleague or a family member. The community-of-care shares an emotional experience and a moral bond. Members within the COC truly believe their voice will make a difference. They form these clusters with a common purpose. They almost always identify and expose an enemy or an injustice; and uphold and bring to light a friend or a circumstance of righteousness. Finally, the community-of-care can be ubiquitous. They can disappear as quickly as they form, for many reasons. If their call for justice has been met, they might disband as organically as they began. They can lose faith in the meaning of their struggle; or they are defeated in the battle for public message proliferation. But it is rare that a virtuous just cause loses its community-of-care. The people have bound themselves to a potent idea—historic, mythic, and epochal; they have assembled themselves intellectually to a cause greater than themselves.

From Police-Encounter Death to Patterns and Practices of Unlawful Conduct: The Cases of Michael Brown and Freddie Gray

There were many early comparisons made between the Freddie Gray and Michael Brown cases regarding the arrest-related deaths of young black men in America. While both cases continue to present a number of unanswered questions, there are some important differences. The Michael Brown case brought the issue of shooting unarmed black men and the over-policing (zero-tolerance) of the black community in the United States to the forefront. Michael Brown symbolized the long history of blacks dying in police-encounters—and his tale catalyzed a movement. In many ways he was later immortalized in the lyrics for the 2014 film *Selma*,

> Justice for all just ain't specific enough
> One son died, his spirit is revisitin' us
> Truant livin' livin' in us, resistance is us
> That's why Rosa sat on the bus
> That's why we walk through Ferguson with our hands up.[21]

On August 9, 2014, Michael Brown was killed in a conflict with police officer Darren Wilson in Ferguson Missouri, a town often considered a suburb of St. Louis. The unarmed 18-year-old was "walking in the middle of the street" with a friend, purportedly headed to the home of his grandmother. Brown had recently earned his high school diploma (on August 1) and he was slated to start classes at Vatterott College in a few weeks. Despite the effort to turn Brown into a delinquent, he had no criminal background that anyone knew of; nor was he ever convicted of a serious felony. One version of the story suggested that Brown struggled with Officer Wilson for control his gun in and outside of the police car. Another version said that Brown resisted arrest while being placed into the police car and then ran. Witnesses have maintained that Brown held both of his hands up in the air. Others say he didn't have time to raise his hands. In the encounter, Brown was killed by Officer Wilson who was immediately placed on administrative leave and was not subject to arrest. However, the story, as common as it was, took on a surreal edge. Brown had been shot at least six times—twice in the head; and then his body lay in the street for "several hours." The community was outraged and major demonstrations followed. Protests, marches, candlelight and silent vigils, rioting, injuries, and arrests occurred. The situation was militaristic and so volatile and suspicious that the F.B.I. stated they would conduct a parallel investigation into the shooting of Brown. The U.S. Attorney General Eric Holder authorized a second, separate federal autopsy of

---

[21]Lyrics from the song "Glory," featured in the motion picture soundtrack for *Selma* (directed by Ava DuVernay and produced by Christian Colson, Oprah Winfrey, Dede Gardner, and Jeremy Kleiner), Common and John Legend, ARTium/Def Jam Recordings a division of UMG Recordings & Getting Out Our Dreams/Columbia Records/Sony Music Entertainment, December 11, 2014.

his Brown's body. Attorney General Holder also held meetings regarding possible civil rights violations; and later he launched a broad civil rights investigation into the Ferguson, Missouri Police Department.

    The situation in Ferguson Missouri escalated and it looked like a war zone. The St. Louis County Police initially stated they would not release the name of the officer involved in the shooting (due to threats made on social media). He was shielded for a time. Darren Wilson's name was not made public until six days later. As the community continued their protests, the militarization of the city intensified. When the armed operation in Ferguson got underway, protesters were clearly defined as "enemy forces." Moreover, they were thought to be adversaries who were assumed to possess dangerous intelligence resources such as social media. Ordinary citizens were viewed as domestic enemy combatants. The FAA announced air restrictions over Ferguson, in order to facilitate the use of law enforcement helicopters. President Obama released a statement and later addressed the nation about the situation. Protests and vigils were to be held in the daytime. In addition to the activists, journalists (and photographers) were detained (*Huffington Post*, *Getty Images*, and the *Washington Post*) by police. The police used tear gas and a full complement of tactical assault equipment (i.e. high-powered rifles, stun/flash grenades, smoke bombs, rubber bullets, armored vehicles) in response to the peaceful protests.

    The Governor issued a state of emergency for the city of Ferguson (including curfews) and called in the National Guard. Amnesty International sent monitors to document any human rights violations. In addition to local law enforcement, the State Highway Patrol (to support the National Guard) was dispatched to maintain order. Schools were initially cancelled in the Ferguson-Florissant School District. 10 days after the Michael Brown shooting, a 23-year-old man by the name of Kajieme Powell was shot by north St. Louis Police (a few miles from Ferguson) for stealing pastries and then *wielding* a knife at police—and with that the situation was amplified and protests increased. A veteran Missouri officer deployed to Ferguson after the slaying of Brown resigned after pointing an assault rifle directly at protesters and threatening to kill them. In the aftermath of Michael Brown's tragic death, Ferguson police officers began using body cameras. The attorney representing the Brown case was also the legal counsel for the Trayvon Martin family in Florida.[22] There were also online fundraisers for Michael Brown and police officer Darren Wilson. Brown's funeral was held August 25, 2014 (the day he was to begin college) and more than 5,000 mourners attended. Brown's death symbolized the apparent escalation of police use of deadly force against African Americans and sparked the chant and gesture of surrender, "Hands up—Don't Shoot" used in protest campaigns and the development of the Hands up Don't Shoot United movement. Michael Brown's death also revealed a system of for-profit policing in the city[23], one that contributed to the deleterious quality of life for many blacks in Ferguson Missouri. A year and a half after the death of Michael Brown, the Department of Justice filed a lawsuit against the city, citing patterns and practices of unlawful conduct.

Less than a year later in the city of Baltimore, on April 12, 2015, the local media reported that Freddie Carlos Gray, Jr. observed police officers in his West Baltimore neighborhood. Apparently he looked them in the eye and then decided to run. The police chased him for at least two blocks. Gray was apprehended quickly, searched and then arrested (for purportedly possessing a switchblade that later was determined to be a legal pocketknife). The police-charging document stated that Gray "fled unprovoked upon noticing police presence. The Defendant was apprehended in the 1700 block of Presbury St (.) after a brief foot chase. This officer noticed a knife clipped to the inside of his front right pants pocket. The defendant was arrested without force or incident. The knife was recovered."[24] Gray was then taken, literally dragged to the police transport vehicle for a weapons possession charge. Despite the various police policies on transporting detainees,[25] and while paramedic assistance was needed, his calls for help were ignored. Somewhere in the arrest and transport of Gray by police, his

---

[22]Trayvon Martin was the 17-year-old high school student shot and killed on February 26, 2012 in Sanford Florida by George Zimmerman, a self-appointed neighborhood watch volunteer/advocate. Zimmerman was acquitted of any wrong-doing in the death of Martin in July 2013.
[23]Ryan J. Reilly and Mariah Stewart, "Fleece Force: How Police and Courts Around Ferguson Bully Residents and Collection Millions," *The Huffington Post*, www.huffingtonpost.com, March 28, 2015, accessed October 8, 2015.
[24]District Court of Maryland for Baltimore City, *State of Maryland vs. Grey, Freddie Carlos Jr.*, Case No. 6B02294074, April 12, 2015, 2.
[25]The Baltimore Police Department had several policies in place regarding the treatment of citizens in custody. This included the revised Policy 1114, "Persons in Police Custody," issued April 3, 2015, as well as several other associated policies.

larynx and eighty percent of his spinal cord were severely crushed. Gray was eventually taken to the Maryland Shock Trauma Center. After falling into a coma, he died a week later on April 19, 2015.

News of Gray's death initiated protests in the city of Baltimore. Some media outlets had already reported on Gray's "lengthy arrest record"; and it was widely stated that when he was apprehended, another prisoner being transported by police witnessed him attempting to injure himself. The next day, April 20, 2015, the six officers involved in Gray's arrest (the Baltimore 6) were suspended from duty. As in the case of Michael Brown, the Justice Department opened a federal investigation to determine whether Gray's civil rights had been violated. The peaceful protests in Baltimore continued, and some community groups stated that they would launch their own investigation into Gray's death.[26] The situation looked more and more like the Ferguson Missouri militarized zone after the shooting death of Michael Brown. The city of Baltimore was imploding. The president of the Baltimore City Fraternal Order of Police (FOP) Lodge #3—the police union—compared protestors to a lynch mob.[27] This angered the community even further because of the brutal and tragic legacy of blacks being lynched by whites in the United States. There were angry calls for Baltimore's Police Commissioner Anthony Batts to resign,[28] but he respectfully declined to leave office. The peaceful demonstrations grew considerably. However, the night of April 25 also saw stores damaged, cars vandalized, debris thrown at police officers, and dozens of people arrested. The next day, Commissioner Batts told the officers that he was proud of their conduct, impressed with their professionalism, and he urged them to remain calm.[29]

As people filed into New Shiloh Baptist Church for Gray's funeral, the digital marquee scrolled, "Black Lives Matter & All Lives Matter." Freddie Gray's funeral services were held on April 27 at one of Baltimore's historic churches. New Shiloh Baptist church was founded in 1902. The current pastor's late father, the Reverend Harold A. Carter, Sr. was a civil rights/community activist and a well-regarded Christian spiritual leader in the city of Baltimore. The Reverend Harold

---

[26]This notably included The People's Power Assembly and the Baltimore chapter of the Southern Christian Leadership Conference (SCLC).
[27]Gene Ryan, President of the Baltimore FOP (Fraternal Order of Police), April 22, 2015.
[28]Interdenominational Ministerial Alliance, April 24, 2015.
[29]Anthony Batts, "Police Commissioner's Message" Email to BCPD, April 26, 2015.

WORLD TO COME: ESSAYS ON THE BALTIMORE UPRISING, MILITANT RACISM, AND HISTORY

A. Carter Jr. presided over Gray's funeral. Thousands of people attended the services for Gray including numerous local leaders like attorney William "Billy" Murphy (legal counsel for the Gray family), the Reverend Dr. Jamal Bryant (pastor of Empowerment Temple A.M.E. Church, and Gray's eulogist), Rep. Elijah Cummings (D-MD), Mayor Stephanie Rawlings-Blake, and former mayor of Baltimore Sheila Dixon. There was also an entourage of national leaders and personalities. The White House sent a small delegation which included Broderick Johnson, an assistant to President Obama; and also in attendance were veteran activists like the Reverend Jesse Jackson, Jr., Dick Gregory, Michael Eric Dyson, and Kweisi Mfume. Several family members from previous police-encounter deaths from other cities, some under the auspices of Families United for Justice, also attended Gray's funeral. There were photographers and reporters from around the world.

The events surrounding his high profile funeral were characterized by organized peaceful protests, plaintive calls for activist restraint, requests for community assistance, condemnations of random violence, sporadic lawlessness that included looting businesses, and damage to property. On that day, Governor Larry Hogan issued a state of emergency for the city of Baltimore. The police also issued a statement saying they had been threatened by local gangs. Then a citywide curfew was enacted. A number of people defied the curfew. The city was filled with military presence. Several people identified Black Hawk Helicopters in the sky, the specter of armored vehicles, and police donning riot gear had assault weapons and pepper spray at the ready. For many, the city felt like it is under military siege. The atmosphere also supported post-conflict relief efforts. Churches and community organizers were conducting forums and teach-ins. Members of the Baltimore Ravens football league met with young people and assisted with food distribution. Various protests and town hall meetings continued, and the Reverend Al Sharpton, president of the National Action Network (NAN), held a community meeting in Baltimore, labeled the "Use Your Voice" summit.[30] Three days after Gray's funeral, the police department gave the office of the State's Attorney their internal investigation into the death of Freddie Gray.

---

[30] Sharpton was invited to Baltimore by local area leaders to assist the protest effort and to dialogue about peace; he was also publically welcomed by Mayor Stephanie Rawlings-Blake.

World To Come: Essays On The Baltimore Uprising, Militant Racism, And History

The capstone to all of this was that on May 1, the city's State's Attorney Marilyn J. Mosby held a much anticipated press conference announcing that the six police officers involved in Gray's arrest would be charged for his death.

The cases of Michael Brown and Freddie Gray were often compared, even though the manner of their deaths was very different. Brown was shot by one police officer; while Gray's death appeared to be caused by six officers. Brown died at the scene. Gray was hospitalized, lingered in a coma, and died later. The officer in Brown's case was not indicted by a Grand Jury; and as the story unfolded, a number of irregularities involving militant racism and the entire prosecutorial process in Ferguson would be revealed. While there was some resolution in the death of Brown, both cases continued to unfold. Yet the violent deaths of Brown and Gray (and there were many others around the nation) would see major protests and demonstrations against the use of deadly force by law enforcement. Together the cases highlight the tragic death of young black men in the presence of police. Both cities would expose the stark realities of the lives of many African Americans in towns and cities like Ferguson and Baltimore. Moreover, because of the brave voices raised about these tragic events, their stories are no longer invisible and unheard. The members of the community talked about the consequences of extreme and aggressive policing. The multitude of accounts lay bare the overwhelming sense that predominately African American and impoverished communities everywhere in the nation, but especially in working-class and poor neighborhoods, were being "over policed" for minor non-violent offenses and under-policed in terms of major crimes involving general public safety.

In addition to the tragic loss of human life and potential, the most important issue emanating from the publicity over the law-enforcement deaths of these two black men, is that they are only representative of the many deaths of blacks, Latinos, Native Americans, and poor whites across the nation. However, for the masses of blacks in America's major cities, a new millennial era has come into view; one where the presence of fear, the stark reality of community abandonment, and at times the loss of hope for a better life has become the norm. In spite of the best efforts of some community leaders, these spaces feel under siege, inadequately served, and neglected. Unfortunately, these communities also supply the school-to-prison pipeline; are heavily taxed, provide jobs and revenue for cities largely in the criminal justice employment sector. Every facet of daily life can make or break struggling individuals, families, and communities. These are the neighborhoods with apartheid (segregated) schools, missing community centers, absolute food wastelands, distant or nonexistent medical health facilities, predacious neighborhood stores—and plenty of criminal activity, which either overwhelms or utterly prevents, law enforcement's ability to remove illicit drugs and people who are determined to prey on the community. In these black communities, it seems that there is no differentiation of crime when it comes to arrest and sentencing—petty and violent crimes can often exact nearly the same penalty. More to the point, completely linked to this is an endemic terror of the capability and intent of law-enforcement powers to take a black life at a moment's notice for any reason—and with impunity.

Racial Insult and the 'While Black' Phenomenon

The threat to black life is cemented inside of extraordinarily hostile perceptions of black humanity. It takes time and effort to create and maintain a social climate that tolerates public racial insult. Racial antipathy is often first expressed through, and sustained by, language. Racial insult almost always revives stereotypes and frames blacks as less than human. However, in a land that values free speech, why are racial insults in the public domain problematic? In one way, organized (historic) racial slurs have the power to incite people to act out their insensitivity, personal rage, and societal fears towards others. Though some do not rise to the level of death threat, racial insults may appear harmless, but there is a difference between freedom of expression and the intent of racial hate speech. When people of the governing group possess the power to actualize discriminatory speech, seemingly innocuous utterances take on a completely new meaning. Publically charged racial slurs do need to be scrutinized because they are not created in a vacuum—they are targeted at a specific group of people. The key however is how media manages discriminatory rhetoric in a context of an immense racial power imbalance. Before the internet and social media, American media tended to dismiss hate speech made publically against African Americans; and whites who called blacks "niggers" in the public domain were defended by asserting that since some blacks may use the term (publically or privately) then whites should be able to do so.

Despite the opportunities afforded to black media hosts, commentators, experts and others featured in the mainstream news,

World To Come: Essays On The Baltimore Uprising, Militant Racism, And History

none of the professional advancements for African Americans individually has translated into full media justice and equality for blacks as a people. There is a climate of comfort that engenders anti-black and racially disparaging rhetoric. An example from recent history would include the 2007 NCAA playoffs, when talk show host "shock jock" Don Imus caused a national media storm when he (and others) insulted the black women players on the Rutgers University women's basketball team on his show, *Imus in the Morning*:

> IMUS: So, I watched the basketball game last night between –a little bit of Rutgers and Tennessee, the women's final.
> ROSENBERG: Yeah, Tennessee won last night – seventh championship for [Tennessee coach] Pat Summitt, I-Man. They beat Rutgers by 13 points.
> IMUS: That's some rough girls from Rutgers. Man, they got tattoos and –
> McGUIRK: Some hard-core hos.
> IMUS: That's some nappy-headed hos there. I'm gonna tell you that now, man, that's some – woo. And the girls from Tennessee, they all look cute, you know, so, like –kinda like – I don't know.
> McGUIRK: A Spike Lee thing.
> IMUS: Yeah.
> McGUIRK: The Jigaboos vs. the Wannabes – that movie that he had.
> IMUS: Yeah, it was a tough –
> McCORD: Do The Right Thing.
> McGUIRK: Yeah, yeah, yeah.
> IMUS: I don't know if I'd have wanted to beat Rutgers or not, but they did, right?
> ROSENBERG: It was a tough watch. The more I look at Rutgers, they look exactly like the Toronto Raptors.
> IMUS: Well, I guess, yeah.
> RUFFINO: Only tougher.

WORLD TO COME: ESSAYS ON THE BALTIMORE UPRISING, MILITANT RACISM, AND HISTORY

McGUIRK: The [Memphis] Grizzlies would be more appropriate.[31]

Imus and the commentators, found a way to humiliate black women, calling them whores and comparing them to animals—even using the not so subtle double entendre, "raptors." Pointed at black women, this was also about black men—, which suggested that the women looked (and acted) like men. The comment also slighted filmmaker Spike Lee and his movies, which were perceived as an extension of the black cultural experience. Even the job terminations of media hosts such as Don Imus and others for mass communicated racial slurs was countered with powerful defenses of both the individual and the comments made, usually culminating in blacks being blamed for the racial offenses levied against them. Viewers have witnessed, through the media's negative presentation of African Americans, critical aspects of the vocalized backlash against the social justice efforts afforded by the Civil Rights movement.

By the late 1990s the curious phrase "while black" (which was often derisively dismissed as the complaint of underachieving African Americans) gained popular attention for its social significance. For more than a decade, the Internet was replete with stories and anecdotes of people discussing "living while black." Blacks may have first seen this in the "driving while black" trend—the preponderance of blacks to be pulled over as a consequence of racial profiling by law enforcement agencies.[32] From there the phrase, which not only captured the attention of intensely affected communities, was also being used by scholars to discuss such issues as "learning while black," "testing while black," and "working while black," etc. The first two ideas were linked to the failing public education system. This was the belief that black children in the public schools were intentionally being uneducated. Regarding the latter work concept, Barbara Marshall defined the term in relation to the criminal component as a form of "...racial profiling in the American labor market. It takes place in workplace contexts in which perceptions of black workers are distorted and where black employees and applicants are targets of a regimen of stereotypes and

---

[31]Media Matters for America, "Imus called women's basketball team 'nappy-headed hos'" April 4, 2007, http://www.mediamatters.org/research/2007/04/04/imus-called-womens-basketball-team-nappy-headed/138497, accessed April 13, 2007 and October 6, 2015.

[32]John Lamberth, "Driving While Black; A Statistician Proves That Prejudice Still Rules the Road," *Washington Post*, August 16, 1998; C01.

biases that function to exclude, disadvantage and otherwise disqualify them in the competitive labor market of the United States."[33] Black workers from entry to exit endure the potential for a variety of challenges, based on race, in the labor market. This includes the fact that African Americans generally have much higher rates of unemployment, especially black youth between the ages of 16 and 24 years old.

Furthermore, regarding the health of African Americans, Professor Emerita of Law Vernellia R. Randall, in *Dying While Black*, linked the health crisis of blacks to the legacy of enslavement and contemporary racial domination.[34] Years ago, the notion of dying while black was mostly linked to medical health issues including biogenetic and social disorders that impact well-being; as well as access to medical care. Overall, however, "while black" has been termed a contemporary manifestation of the persistence of extreme racial bias as well as a call for a new national dialogue about issues of race in American society and around the world. As a reassertion of neo-Jim Crow power, the black person is singled out (and usually verbally maligned) for imagined questionable or malevolent behaviors because he or she is black. The racial presumption of accepted difference challenges identifiable issues beyond the prevalence of skin color. In this racial schema, blacks must prove that their very existence is not a threat to or a crime against the established state order. Just as the stranger faces a different world, he/she is also introduced to another, but not necessarily a better way of life. This is reminiscent of James Baldwin's encounters in Switzerland in the 1950s, which followed a familiar U.S. southern racist script whereby he (as a black man) was compelled to be "pleasant." Baldwin explained, "…it being a great part of the American Negro's education (long before he goes to school) that he must make people like him."[35] Baldwin confirmed that this was a universal construct that automatically controlled and alienated blackness. Thus, there was historical precedent to the "while black" phraseology and racial phenomena of the 1990s through the early 2000s, which anticipated the coming of the new American century in which people of African descent would be expected to act as though they were alien, work against their own

---

[33]Barbara Marshall, "Working While Black: Contours of an Unequal Playing Field," *Phylon*, Vol. 49, No. 3/4 (Autumn-Winter, 2001), 137-150, 138.
[34]Vernellia R. Randall, *Dying While Black: An In-Depth Look at a Crisis in the American Healthcare System*. Dayton, OH: Seven Principles Press, October, 2006.
[35]James Baldwin, *Notes of a Native Son*. New York: Beacon Press, 1955.

interests, deny and disparage their heritage and culture, and to accept racism. To do any or all of this meant that there was indeed the shade of death on the horizon, and it did whispered "dying while black." This time the phrase had nothing to do with standard measures of health. "Dying while black" came to be most associated with fatal police-encounters. The greatest challenge ahead would be to circumvent the destructive forces that were anti-life—and to learn to live *and* thrive "while black."

Chapter 2

Between Enslavement And Freedom—The Apex Of Racial Power

> I speak advisedly when I say this, that killing a slave, or any colored person, in Talbot county, Maryland, is not treated as a crime, either by the courts or the community.—Frederick Douglass[1]

The Link between Historic Slavery and the Police Killings of Blacks

African Americans have endured generations of unrelenting intellectual, social, cultural, psychological and physical assault since the introduction of chattel slavery in the United States. Stripped of their ancestral homeland, names, language, and kinships ties, the legacy of American slavery gives us deep insight into the persistent militant racist impetus. The apex of racial power is not to subjugate—the ultimate goal is the ability to destroy life. For some the contemporary police (extralegal) killings of African Americans are reminiscent of the racial violence found in the American institution of slavery. We cannot understand the indiscriminate killing of Blacks until we recognize the deeply embedded militant racist philosophy. Contrary to popular belief, this is not racial bigotry and petty acts of discrimination. Racism deals specifically with systems, institutions, networks, communities, and relationships involving "co-conspirators for its perpetration."[2] In the American antebellum period, where most people of African descent were enslaved, varieties of racial violence were the norm. Yet even the term *racial violence* implies to some that Blacks acted offensively against whites with the same force and frequency, because they were white. This was never true in the history of American slavery. Before the Civil War, Blacks were subjected to a wide range of brutal racial punishments for two apparent reasons: they were an African people who had been subjected to bondage. However, the main reason enslaved Africans

---

[1] Frederick Douglass, *Narrative of the Life of Frederick Douglass, an American Slave: Written by Himself.* Edited by Benjamin Quarles. Cambridge, MA: Harvard, 1960.
[2] Joseph J.E. Williams, *The Principles of American Slavery: An Interesting and Authentic Pamphlet Giving a Full and Satisfactory Description of the Principles of the Slave Code of the South, with the Morals and Improvements of the Colored People of Canada, of the Elgin Association.* Hamilton, Ontario: Christian Advocate Office, 1858, 5.

were dehumanized was that the power inherent in racism was conceived of as absolute.

In the American system of slavery African people were first and foremost property and the scheme of bondage was racial, hereditary and meant to be one of perpetual captivity. Our popular and national culture tends to ignore, distort, minimize, or apologize for the system of slavery; mostly because it is difficult for our modern-day minds to grasp. Deep down we understand that slavery was anathema to freedom and democracy, yet we avoid critical examinations of just how disturbing it was; or how the foundations of slavery have reverberated throughout the history of the nation. The study of slavery in world history is important. Slavery teaches us what it means to be human and humane. To be sure, Europeans didn't invent chattel slavery, but arguably they perfected it in the modern world. There is no doubt that a distinctly racialized slavery changed the course of world history.

The many laws, acts, statues, rules, and unwritten practices regarding what it meant to be a slave in antebellum America—the slave codes—tell an important story of human bondage. Viewed as a whole, the various (and only slightly differing) slave codes in the United States defined the country's perception of humanness and the use of absolute power. The composite slave code was clearly delineated, and offers an organized understanding of human ownership. It was fundamental that there was a master and a slave, and that the master considered himself superior (in every way) to the person held in bondage. This bond person was human chattel who could be bought and sold, and moved around, or made part of any financial arrangement which involved valuable property. Some of these financial arrangements included using enslaved Africans to satisfy a debt; or in the settlement of estates and wills which allowed them to be inherited by surviving family members. The slave was, in theory and practice, the absolute property of the slave-holder. When we think of some of the basic needs for human survival, we think of food, water, clothing, housing, and medical care. These items were issued at the discretion of the slave owner. Further, the slave-holding class defined slaves as beings that could not own anything or attempt to own anything. They could not marry because essentially marriage was a binding legal contract. Slave marriages were never recognized in the courts, "…not a single slave in the United States is legally married. The nominal marriages they contract are not marriages in the proper sense of the word, and may be, and are broken at any time, to suit the will or interest of the master."[3] One of the most important aspects of any society, marriage and the formation of families was also denied to enslaved Africans. For white males, the cultivation of families generally meant power over wives and children, so the slave master assumed this unlimited power. This particular power protected the financial investment made in slave property. Since the main purpose of the slave was to supply labor, the African could be used in any number of ways—agricultural labor, domestic service, skilled crafts, etc. Even when an enslaved person was "hired-out" and allowed to keep some of his wages, it was done with the legal and common understanding that he was not a free wage earner.

The slave master was in complete possession of the slave body and issues which involved punishment and brutality (irrespective of the law or the number of slaves owned) was his decision. The laws did not super cede the investment in white racial identity either—the power to do what one willed to the person legally considered subordinate and inferior. Often the legal concerns over an injured slave were about the destruction or maiming of chattel property, and not about the rights of enslaved Africans or the responsibility to treat them humanely. Cases like Dolly Chapple were frequent, as the courts attempted to derive meaning from the law about what it meant to be a slave. In 1811 Chapple was charged with and indicted for the "malicious stabbing" of a slave. One of the main issues of the case was whether a slave, who was property and therefore not legally entitled to own property, could receive remuneration for the crime. If the fine levied against the defendant could not be legally received by the slave, does that render the judgement voided? The other issue was whether the "malicious stabbing" was nothing more than the effort to "correct" or punish the enslaved person.[4] The slave could be punished for any number of legally identified and unnamed offenses, including refusing to obey the demands of the slaveholder and in some locales slaves were jailed for general disobedience offenses. The slave-owner not only had the law

---

[3]Joseph J.E. Williams, *The Principles of American Slavery: An Interesting and Authentic Pamphlet Giving a Full and Satisfactory Description of the Principles of the Slave Code of the South, with the Morals and Improvements of the Colored People of Canada, of the Elgin Association*. Hamilton, Ontario: Christian Advocate Office, 1858, 13.
[4]*A Collection of Cases Decided By the General Court of Virginia, Chiefly Relating To the Penal Laws of the Commonwealth. Commencing In the Year 1789, And Ending in 1814*, Philadelphia: James Webster, 1815, 184-185.

WORLD TO COME: ESSAYS ON THE BALTIMORE UPRISING, MILITANT RACISM, AND HISTORY

on his side, he was the law. Though rare, in the case against Chapple it mattered little that she was convicted of the crime or that the fine was upheld. What was important was the various legal questions that delineated and consolidated the slave status, i.e. "...that there is nothing in the law which shews clearly that an injury to was not intended to be made punishable: that there were no words of exclusion, or exception, and that a slave in this country has been frequently decided to be legally and technically a person, on whom a wrong can be inflicted..." [5] Slave statutes were legally malleable; but personhood, for the purposes of maintaining the law, remained under the purview of the slave owner.

The court wanted to know if indeed it was conceivable to legally inflict harm on an enslaved person who had been brutalized or injured. In addition, it was also argued that a slave could not be viewed as a "competent witness" against whites—because slaves were not persons, and thus could not be witnesses in courts of law. Other aspects of the slave codes determined that it was against the law for slaves to trade goods of any kind. Slaves could not interfere with white people attending church. Enslaved persons could not resist being loaned or "hired out" to anyone the slave-owner chose. And in some places it was an act of treason for a slave to "excite" a revolt[6] against his condition; and when blacks did this, it was often considered "justifiable homicide" when he or she was killed.[7] Further, during the antebellum period while some states were making radical provisions for the education of poor white children, most state codes punished people for teaching slaves how to read and write and stipulated other penalties for slaves caught demonstrating such knowledge. Then there were the provisions that forbade the sale of weapons to slaves, and expressly banned slaves from possessing firearms. The 1845 code of Georgia stated that any slave using a firearm must be accompanied by a white person 16 years old or older; and that a slave "...using or carrying firearms or other offensive weapon contrary to the true intention of this act, such person may lawfully seize and take away such offensive

---

[5] *A Collection Of Cases Decided By The General Court Of Virginia, Chiefly Relating To The Penal Laws Of The Commonwealth. Commencing In The Year 1789, And Ending In 1814*, Philadelphia: James Webster, 1815, 185.
[6] *A Codification Of The Statute Law Of Georgia: Including The English Statutes Of Force, In Four Parts: To Which Is Prefixed, A Collection Of State Papers, Of English, American, And State Origin*, Savannah: John Cooper, 1845, 704.
[7] *A Codification of the Statute Law of Georgia*, 1845, 707.

weapon or firearms."[8] Other standard proscriptions outlawed groups of black men from traveling together, prevented slaves from holding meetings and pretending to meet for religious purposes, or did not allow slaves to leave the slaveholders property without written permission.[9]

The martial apparatus for policing enslaved people in the United States was both formal an informal. The patrollers were well-known to the enslaved African population of the south. Their purpose was "…to seize and whip any slave they may find wandering from the plantation. They ride on horseback, headed by a captain, armed, and accompanied by dogs. They have the right, either by law, or by general consent, to inflict discretionary chastisement upon a black man caught beyond the boundaries of his master's estate without a pass, and even to shoot him, if he attempts to escape."[10] There were places in the south where slave patrols were expertly managed and highly structured. In Georgia slave patrols were developed in each district and judges (justices of the peace) appointed the patrols. The laws held that white males between sixteen to sixty years old could be compelled to serve in the patrols, and fined for failing to work or for dereliction of duty. Slave masters were also required to provide white male servants for patrol duty, along with any necessary equipment (i.e. a horse, weapon, ammunition). Patrollers were paid for their mileage, beginning at the point where they took the slave into custody. Like the slave-owner and the overseer, the duty of the slave patrol was to prevent "…their (Africans from) using and carrying mischievous and dangerous weapons, or using and keeping drums, horns, or other loud instruments, which may call together or give sign or notice to one another of their wicked designs and intentions…."[11] Specifically patrolmen were to "…examine the several plantations in their divisions…take up all slaves which they shall see without the fences or cleared ground of their owners' plantations, who have not a ticket or letter, or other token, to show the reasonableness of their absence, or

---

[8] *A Codification Of The Statute Law Of Georgia: Including The English Statutes Of Force, In Four Parts: To Which Is Prefixed, A Collection Of State Papers, Of English, American, And State Origin*, Savannah: John Cooper, 1845, 813.
[9] Ibid., 814-815.
[10] Solomon Northup, Twelve Years A Slave. *Narrative of Solomon Northup, a citizen of New York, kidnapped in Washington City in 1841, and rescued in 1853, from a cotton plantation near the Red River, in Louisiana*, London: Sampson Low, Son & co., 1853. 237.
[11] *A Codification of the Statute Law of Georgia*, 1845, 813.

World To Come: Essays On The Baltimore Uprising, Militant Racism, And History

who have not some white person in company to give an account of his, her, or their business...."[12] To further this mission the patrollers were authorized to search slaves for weapons and to whip them. They could also look through the homes of slaves and free people of color for runaways. Slaves attempting to hide from patrollers, particularly runaway slaves, were subjected to immediate arrest. But these fugitive slaves were not only the responsibility of the plantation patrolman; any white person could "...take, apprehend and secure, any runaway or fugitive slave..."[13] While this was usually handled by those with some aptitude or experience, the apprehension of a fugitive slave involved several aspects—the arrest, delivery to the constable, advertising and publishing, jail housing and feeding the apprehended slave, managing the distribution of capture rewards, and ultimately authorizing the sale of runaways who were not claimed within a specified period of time. These fees for "catching and keeping"[14] slaves had to be paid by the slave-owner. Some patrolmen could expect compensation if a fugitive slave attacked or wounded them; and their families were the beneficiaries of a death payment if the patrolman was killed by the slave while on duty.

No matter the legal issue, the antebellum slave codes were unmistakable that African people in bondage were property, and everything else understood about the system of slavery flowed from this conceptual foundation. The idea was singular, potent and articulated by Chief Justice Roger B. Taney in the 1857 *Dred Scott v. Sandford* case, "The Black man has no rights which the White man is bound to respect.... He may justly and lawfully be reduced to slavery... and treated as an ordinary article of traffic and merchandise."[15] It did not matter if they were bound in servitude, or quasi-free, the United States Supreme Court ruled that blacks only lived as a result of the moral largesse of whites. The Civil War and the thirteenth amendment to the constitution ceded the freedom of people of African descent. However, another Supreme Court ruling maintained, essentially, that black people would never be truly "free" unless whites deemed it so.

---

[12]*A Codification Of The Statute Law Of Georgia: Including The English Statutes Of Force, In Four Parts: To Which Is Prefixed, A Collection Of State Papers, Of English, American, And State Origin*, Savannah: John Cooper, 1845, 818.
[13]*A Codification Of The Statute Law Of Georgia*, 1845, 819.
[14]William Wells Brown, *Narrative of William W. Brown a Fugitive Slave Written By Himself*, Boston: The Anti-Slavery Office, 1847, 45.
[15]Chief Justice Roger Brooke Taney, *Dred Scott v. Sandford*, 1856.

World To Come: Essays On The Baltimore Uprising, Militant Racism, And History

This sentiment was expressed in the 1896 *Plessy v. Ferguson* Supreme Court ruling, which upheld racial segregation. It was, ultimately, the privilege of white society to choose who would be free, whom they would live and work among, and how all of this would be accomplished. There is a solid link between the history of slavery and police killings. Both are bound to an ideology that wields godlike power—the power of life and death. It is a total power, the ability to take a life with the highest sacred and secular authority, and more often than not, with immunity. However, it is not always easy for people to kill. One of the ways to facilitate this power is for people to accept, and participate in, the processes of subjugating and dehumanizing others. Slavery, by definition, is oppression and it always demands extreme and explicit forms of prejudice.

Henry Watson's Story Of Jo, The Enslaved African Put to Death

Slavery represented the height of the militant racist impulse in antebellum America, and this racism was a life-threatening form of power. Slavery made race synonymous with the lowest social class. African people learned this very early in America's history. Blacks also learned, no matter their sense of comfort or insecurity, that their lives were always precarious. From the Deep South to northern slave states like Maryland, the lives of African Americans were predicated on the force of racial bondage. Henry Watson, who was enslaved in Baltimore, Maryland, possessed a deep understanding of this violence. In 1848, Watson related in detail the common story of an enslaved African man called Jo in the area of Vicksburg, Virginia. In the Deep South, Jo's existence was defined by unqualified social control, as well as the embedded knowledge that one's life could be taken in an instant.

> There was a slave on the farm by the name of Jo. The overseer had threatened to put him in the stocks, for some trivial offence. Jo, dreading the severity of the punishment, ran away, which fact was soon brought to my master's knowledge, who ordered the overseer to shoot him the first time he saw him. The overseer, being a bloodthirsty fiend, like my master, kept strict watch for Jo; and the second night, he saw him but a short distance from his cabin, where he was probably going for the purpose of seeing his wife, and getting something to eat; but he never saw those eyes light up with pleasure,—never heard the sweet music of their

> voices, or felt their warm embrace,—for the incarnate fiend's aim was too sure; he was stretched dead in an instant. Yes; this man was hurried into the presence of his Maker, without the power of speaking one word of prayer. On the master being informed that his brutal order had been obeyed, he gave orders that his body should not be removed from the spot where he fell, as he wished it to serve as an example to the rest of us; and there it remained, the vultures rioting and feasting on the remains of a man, whose only fault was a black skin.[16]

Through Watson's narrative, we understand that enslaved Africans ran away for any number of reasons, especially arbitrary brutality, but mostly because they wanted freedom. It was important to shoot disobedient slaves like Jo on sight when they attempted to escape punishment. Watson's narrative, in an effort to personify Jo's image, demonstrated the inhumanity of slave system. Jo's body in essence was put on display and served as a warning to the black population. The plantation overseer was often perceived as the emblem of antebellum wickedness, however, he was not an out-of-control tyrant; he and the slave holder shared the same master-mind regarding the killing of Jo. The master-mind accepted and advanced systematic punishment. This supremacist way of thinking supported Jo's body left as carrion for prey and decomposing in the ground, in order to strike fear in the black population.

    Henry Watson and his wife eventually freed themselves from slavery, and he lived to tell the cruel story of Jo. To tell a story like this was to put one's life at risk and Watson, like so many others, was determined to be a witness to history. The social ideology of slavery established and maintained complete control of African people; and subjugated blacks to perpetual servitude and blind obedience. To argue or verbally abuse whites could result in certain death as much as refusing to work, or especially the act of running away. A form of police power was vested in the slaveholder, the patrollers, and especially in the overseer of enslaved Africans. Regarding the latter, these poor white males were able to elevate their self-esteem (though not necessarily their economic status) through terrorizing blacks for their labor. While his main function was to extract human labor, the overseer

---

[16]*Narrative Henry Watson, A Fugitive Slave*. Boston: Bela Marsh. 1848. 15-16.

accomplished this though brute disciplinary force and his own sense of the absolute power of life over death.

Frederick Douglass Fought for his Life at Fells Point

One of Maryland's most outspoken personalities, Frederick Douglass, was born in Talbot County Maryland on the Eastern shore on (circa) February 14, 1818. Among the nation's greatest orators and statesmen, his leadership included a dedication to the radical abolitionist cause and a vigorous advocacy for the rights of African Americans. Douglass often spoke of contrasting racial worlds that obstructed the lives of black men and women. In this regard all whites (including non-slave holders) functioned in the slave system as de facto self-appointed overseers. When Frederick Douglass was hired out as an apprentice to the white carpenter shipbuilders at Fell's Point (1836-1838), he found that once again, black life was precarious. Douglass was placed "…at the beck and call of about seventy-five men." According to Douglass, his apprenticeship meant, "I was to regard all these as masters. Their word was to be my law."[17] In a brief period of time, the white carpenters decided that they did not want to work with free blacks. The small number of free blacks threatened the jobs they held; and if allowed to continue in the occupation, they would take over the profession and eliminate white workers. The white workers demanded that the free blacks be dismissed. The carpenters however were not satisfied. They found it demeaning to work with Douglass who was enslaved. They had determined that blacks were taking over, and some expressed that their ultimate goal was to kill all of the blacks in the community. Douglass had no fear of the white carpenters, and when they attacked him, he fought back; yet they operated against him in numbers, "…armed with sticks, stones, and heavy handspikes. One came in front with a half brick."[18] Douglass was disappointed that the whites who did not take part in the attack on him, offered no assistance, and some encouraged the attack. The precarious nature of black lives in the antebellum period both enslaved and free, was even more poignant in his latter point—that whites allowed it to happen; and

---

[17]*Narrative of the Life Of Frederick Douglass An American Slave Written By Himself.* Edited with an Introduction by David W. Blight. New York: Bedford/St. Martin's, 1993, 91.
[18]*Narrative of the Life of Frederick Douglass an American Slave Written By Himself.* Edited with an Introduction by David W. Blight. New York: Bedford/St. Martin's, 1993, 92.

that he had nowhere to turn for justice. Douglass surmised long after his escape to freedom from Fell's Point:

> If I had been killed in the presence of a thousand colored people, their testimony combined would have been insufficient to have arrested one of the murderers. Master Hugh, for once, was compelled to say this state of things was too bad. Of course, it was impossible to get any white man to volunteer his testimony in my behalf, and against the young white men. Even those who may have sympathized with me were not prepared to do this. It required a degree of courage unknown to them to do so; for just at that time, the slightest manifestation of humanity toward a colored person was denounced as abolitionism…Such was, and such remains, the state of things in the Christian city of Baltimore.[19]

Like Watson's account, Douglass' testimony about the value of black life in the antebellum period is damming. With one's humanity completely disregarded, slavery was a violent system of social control, including intergenerational terror that saw the plundering of families to the slave market. Slave offenses, trivial or great, were counted the same because they were the sum of disobedience. In addition, vast numbers of slaves were as threatening as small numbers. This meant that, the fear was not the great numbers of blacks—it was blackness itself. Finally, slave-owners and overseers often agreed that there was one act that a slave could engage in that was inviolate—self-emancipation. For the slave to free him or herself from bondage was the worst kind of defiance because it directly challenged the slave system. One could be severely punished—maimed and whipped for seeking freedom. One could also be put to death.

An Historical Overview of Post-Civil War Racism

Most Africans in America began their life legally bound to white society. Slavery in the United States was predicated on the control and containment of blacks and maintained through the brutal use of force as well as the threat of violence. For enslaved blacks

---

[19]*Narrative of the Life of Frederick Douglass an American Slave Written By Himself*. Edited with an Introduction by David W. Blight. New York: Bedford/St. Martin's, 1993, 93.

World To Come: Essays On The Baltimore Uprising, Militant Racism, And History

housed on larger farms and plantations, the overseer served as *the police*. However, locally organized slave patrollers functioned as *the police force*; and at times militia, volunteers, and vigilantes served as an *occupying force*. In the aftermath of the Civil War, blacks emerged as a free people, through the 13th Amendment to the Constitution, but in the period of reconstruction they were immediately under military occupation in the south. Military troops were sent to the southern states to supervise the former Confederate state governments. The south was divided into five military districts. One of the duties of federal troops was to oversee the rights of African Americans. When African Americans were granted the vote through the Reconstruction Acts of 1867, southerners were outraged. When the 15th Amendment to the Constitution was passed in 1868, it gave all males the right to vote, and this included black males. For a brief time after the end of slavery, a small number of African American males were able to vote and assume political office, which included elections to state legislatures and Congress. Seven African Americans were elected to congress. After the 1870s what appeared to be the beginning of promising civil rights gains receded. When the northerners withdrew their passionate support for blacks, the Compromise of 1877 saw an agreement between the democrats and the republicans, one which essentially abandoned African American people. The Compromise was a political agreement in which the south saw the removal of military troops. The U.S. Supreme Court rendered the Civil Rights Act of 1875 unconstitutional in 1883. The ability of blacks to vote was of paramount importance to the states, particularly in the south. The popular methods for restricting the black vote from the 1890s through the 1960s were intimidation, violence, moving poll stations, adding poll taxes, administering literacy tests, and sanctioning the infamous and offensive Grandfather clauses.

 The post-Civil War South used the authority and efficiency of state laws, the force of social coercion, and long accepted practices to implement and maintain racial segregation. This had its foundation in the Black Codes and in organized militant racial violence. While the Black Codes varied, their intent was to re-enslave African American people. The Black Codes restricted or eliminated voting, forced people into exploitative work contracts, limited travel and the acquisition of personal property, and in states like South Carolina, the Black Codes denied blacks the opportunity to become skilled workers or to own their own businesses unless they were granted a fee-based, judge approved license. The states Black Codes were nearly universal in denying blacks the ability to possess weapons. White clandestine groups in the south like the Ku Klux Klan augmented the discrimination against blacks. They worked to instill terror in the African American community, especially in the area of voting rights. This was done through cross burnings, mob attacks, and lynchings. State and local governments, along with auxiliary racist organizations moved to ensure that whites kept complete control of local governments.

When the Freedmen's Bureau (the Bureau of Refugees, Freedmen, and Abandoned Lands) was established in 1865, it was designed to assist white post-war southerners, and the newly freed men and women. Blacks were, as the official name of the agency stated, in effect, refugees of war. They were provided food, clothing, medical care, education and assistance with employment. Economic independence (specifically through land ownership) was not a fully realized aspect of the assistance provided to blacks. It has been effectively argued and documented that after the Civil War, blacks expected to become landowners en masse, but that racism coupled with the desire to punish the rebel south conspired against any real, and enforceable, land acquisition for the freed people.[20] The dilemma of a sustainable labor pool for southern lands caused challenging decisions to be made in the face of prevailing social forces. White landowners needed black labor. Some blacks left the plantations and moved to the North and the west; and some remained on the familiar farms and slave manors. Southern white landowners exploited the refugee status of African Americans, some with the mindset that they were contraband of war, by instituting abusive sharecropping arrangements. These measures meant that blacks rented the land they worked and lived on and gave part of the harvest to the owner. The sharecropping system was necessary for whites to continue their agricultural production and despite the assistance of the Freedmen's Bureau—served to keep many blacks economically and social dependent.

African Americans sought employment opportunities in the North, especially in factories and other kinds of industrial work. However, blacks were usually given more inferior jobs than their white counterparts. Northern discrimination was widespread. States readily passed Jim Crow laws that racially segregated schools, public facilities, hospitals, parks and transportation. Jim Crow laws were meant to control and demean blacks, send a message that not only were they

---

[20] *The Forty Acres Documents*, with an Introduction by Amílcar Shabazz. Baton Rouge, LA: The House of Songhay, 1994.

World To Come: Essays On The Baltimore Uprising, Militant Racism, And History

deemed inferior, but also that they were somehow a public health threat. This was expressed in the racial practices that forbade blacks access to the same toilets, pools, water fountains and theaters as whites. However, separate never meant equal for blacks. Scholars have written extensively about the racial discrimination in the south and the north—as de jure and de facto segregation. Through the *Plessy v. Ferguson* Supreme Court ruling Jim Crow laws advanced the idea of a "separate but equal" society, and these laws were further strengthened locally. "Separate but equal" gave the illusion of racial equality, but the segregated institutions and facilities were never equal to that of whites. Social structures like Jim Crow racial segregation served to "police" blacks. African Americans were expected to live within strict boundaries and to accept second-class citizenship.

By the turn of the century 1900, the accommodationist philosophy and methods of Booker T. Washington, was widely accepted by white society. Washington's accommodationist plan, which emphasized black self-help and a strong industrial education base, was also meant to save black lives from the racist killing impulse. At the time it was considered a progressive race-relations plan. However, in 1905, through the Niagara Movement, W.E.B. DuBois, Monroe Trotter, Lafayette M. Hershaw, John Hope and many others, countered Washington's accommodationist theories and the practices of racial segregation, by emphasizing higher education and confronting racism in society. These radical organizers believed that whites should be held accountable for the crimes against blacks. The Niagara Movement addressed political, civil and economic discrimination. The movement severely denounced Jim Crow practices in the United States, which especially included the violent crime of lynching. The lynch mobs could include men, women and children either participating in or observing blacks being kidnapped and taken to locations where they were tortured and killed. Because of their stance against lynching, as well as racial discrimination, the Niagara conference conveners were labeled as black militants because they refused to advance the social accommodationist tone of Washington. The organizational successor to the Niagara Movement, the NAACP which was founded in 1909, included the participation and patronage of white liberals, and also challenged Jim Crow racism. The NAACP used their resources to condemn the murders of blacks, and leveraged the courts to challenge voting restrictions. Yet without the uncompromising spirit of Niagara men and women, there would have been no NAACP.

WORLD TO COME: ESSAYS ON THE BALTIMORE UPRISING, MILITANT RACISM, AND HISTORY

The steady demographic shift of African Americans from the south to the north (and from southern rural areas to rising southern cities) was known as The Great Migration of African Americans (1890—1920). It was evidence of black people fleeing from racial discrimination, arbitrary racial violence and exploitation, and in search of a better life. Blacks moved for these main reasons and the available opportunities brought about by World War I and the challenges to southern agriculture. More than one million blacks took part in this mass migration. There were places in the south where blacks were criminalized for migration efforts (this included imprisonment and monetary fines). Northern reaction became visceral as well. The notion that African Americans were taking over contributed to racial violence, notably the Red Summer of 1919 race riots. In 1890, African Americans represented less than twenty percent of the urban population. By 1930, blacks were nearly 45 percent of the urban population. Large numbers of blacks migrating to the north began to produce intense fears of labor competition, miscegenation, and crime. White society controlled where black migrants could live, and codified their actions through racially restrictive covenants. Baltimore, Maryland swiftly established racially segregated housing districts in 1910.[21] In the north, as well as in the south, racial discrimination meant that blacks would be largely contained in specific housing areas, and provided the least available services to those neighborhoods.

It was the numbers, and the vitality of African Americans that gave rise to our contemporary idea of urban America. Blacks relocated to areas that were allowed to them; and they congregated among family, friends, churches. As blacks were permitted more space, whites began to move in great numbers from the inner cities to the developing suburbs. When they did so municipal infrastructures were improved and services were better. When they moved, community wealth and genuine access to wealth went with them. Again, for blacks, separate was never equal; and the inner cities became the locale for the impoverished. There were different states of poverty in post-World War II. Some people experienced transitory or short-term poverty; while others endured a persistent poverty. The efforts to address poverty would ultimately make the situation worse. Federal and state programs, along with the housing industry ultimately created "ghettos"

---

[21]See Antero Pietila, *Not in My Neighborhood: How Bigotry Shaped a Great American City*, Chicago: Ivan R. Dee, 2010 (chapter 2, "Good Government,"), 22-31.

and the "slums"—areas that provided a basic form of housing for poor people, and often retained the popular construction label, "the projects." What appeared to be the partnerships and investments of city governments, private business, and real estate developers, quickly turned into containment centers for the massively poor—people who would later be defined as sociologically diseased by Senator Daniel Patrick Moynihan (1927-2003).

By the late 1950s, housing was a definitive crisis for African Americans. It was a common practice for "...sellers, renters, real estate agents, builders, and lenders" to discriminate against blacks in housing.[22] Original public housing was generally all white, and when blacks sought access, race riots broke out. As whites eventually fled the cities, these urban areas became very quickly, for large numbers of blacks, the place where you struggled to live—paid more for services and were subjected to rising crime. In 1965, a Grand Jury report for the city of Baltimore, Maryland stated "...the environment, overcrowding and other deplorable conditions..." in black areas was a problem for law enforcement and "...the welfare of the entire City..."[23] Society set the parameters of existence for blacks, which when compared to whites was devolved, absent, or marginalized. However, blacks were usually blamed for the structural outcomes of racism. Cities were generally thought of as the locus of industry, the hub of municipal services, and the seat of political power. However, overtime, as blacks attempted to remove themselves from an intergenerational cycle of poverty, the dire social conditions impacting the community were being consistently described by mainstream scholars, politicians, and the mass media as a *plight* (a social problem), a *pathology* (an innate disease), and also as a *culture* (a way of life).

---

[22]William J. Collins, "The Housing Market Impact of State-Level Anti-Discrimination Laws, 1960–1970." *Journal of Urban Economics* 55, No. 3 (2004): 534-564, 534.
[23]Grand Jury Report, September Term 1965, Baltimore City, The Special Collections Department, Langsdale Library, University of Baltimore. Used with permission of the University of Baltimore, 5.

CHAPTER 3

HISTORY, SOCIAL NETWORK CONSERVATION, AND INTOLERABLE BLACKNESS[1]

> The rise of a nation, the pressing forward of a social class, means a bitter struggle, a hard and soul-sickening battle with the world such as few of the more favored classes know or appreciate.—W.E.B. DUBOIS[2]

Nat Turner, Negative Stereotypes, and Social Network Conservation

At the end of his spiritual-cosmic visioning, Nathaniel (Nat) Turner launched one of the most notable slave revolts in United States history. On August 20, 1831, in the midnight hour, Turner, along with nearly fifty others, covered several square miles of Virginia. Their goal was to kill the representation of slave tyranny—the owner-masters, which included fifty-five white men, women and children. It must be observed, from the beginning, that Africans came to the Americas with an embedded ethos of actualizing freedom. This liberatory consciousness was pervasive and necessary. It was different from European ethnics groups who came as an early transnational colonial experiment, or those who entered later through Ellis Island. It is important to make the distinction that though enslaved Africans made their way from a relative sense of freedom to an expectation of a greater realization of liberty. The people who came in bondage came with the presumption of liberty as a thrust of collective identity. Groups in the process of finding freedom were also in the process of building power and conserving their sense of self as a people. The protection of language and customs are just two examples suggesting that to guard the group meant defending the individual. There are many examples of blacks asserting this liberatory consciousness; and one of the most discussed is the Nat Turner Revolt. By the end of August,

---

[1]Previously published version of this essay appears in *Africalogical Perspectives*—Katherine Bankole-Medina, "History, Racial Stereotypes, and Social Network Conservation: The Legacy of Intolerable Blackness," *Africalogical Perspectives*, Vol. 6, No. 1, November/December 2009, 14-26.
[2]William Edward Burghardt DuBois, edited by Nathan Irvin Huggins, *W.E.B. DuBois Writings*. Vol. 34. New York, NY: Library of America, 1986. See *The Souls of Black Folk*, Chapter VIII, "Of the Quest of the Golden Fleece," 474.

World To Come: Essays On The Baltimore Uprising, Militant Racism, And History

1831 Virginia clearly did not understand the meaning of this African ethos. The prevailing white notion that blacks were intellectually incapable of organized rebellion was popular—even though the threat of such an uprising was a looming specter, but one more evident of the generic baseness of slaves. The direct and brutal confrontation of two worlds that emerged from the Nat Tuner revolt in Southampton County Virginia revealed that black and white death was emphatically differently. What lay underneath was the difficult and racially convoluted reasoning that black people had no conception of wanting to be free. In the aftermath of the Turner revolt, with all of its mysticism tied to an atmospheric phenomenon (a solar eclipse), was the memory of Turner's legacy of prophesizing, and the death of whites and blacks. In Turner's attack on slavery, blacks not involved with the revolt were murdered and punished; and harsher penalties were developed to control and contain blacks. For Virginia this included banning black men from preaching, and reinforcing the laws that expressly forbade black literacy, principally through schools.[3] There was a heightened sense of vigilance among whites looking for the reality and the image of the savage, or the bad black man.[4] The revolt, Turner's trial, and the new laws that followed demonstrated how people who lived in two separate, but interdependent worlds, used their community-of-care to passionately actualize and interpret their lives.

Negative stereotypic references are keyed to historical messages about blacks, translated by the mass media, and are either enlarged or diminished by the concept of social network conservation. Social network conservation emanates from a racial group dynamic, but it is broader than racial politics or the public manipulation of racial ideas. The concept is concerned with how racial identity (based on both our historical and contemporary understanding) influences how people view and protect themselves within society. As a basis for inspecting the terms of the meaning of collective group personality, one of the principal elements for this research was the work of Davis and Gandy who, like other scholars, have asserted that racial identity is important

---

[3]"Anti-Slavery in Virginia: Extracts from Thos. Jefferson, Gen. Washington and others Relative to the 'Blighting Curse of Slavery.' Debates on the 'Nat Turner Insurrection,' Queries by William Crane, &c." Baltimore: J. F. Weishampel, Bookseller and Stationer, 1865, 7.
[4]"Insurrection of the Blacks," *Niles' Register*, September 10, 1831.

World To Come: Essays On The Baltimore Uprising, Militant Racism, And History

to all people—particularly African Americans.[5] However to suggest this is not meant to convey the idea that racial identity is not also important to whites. Racial identity has different meanings for whites and blacks. American history has demonstrated that whiteness has been expressed in various forms—directly and indirectly—in the formation of the American nation. The overarching difference is the language used to convey racial identity in the media. Social network conservation suggests that there are understood standards related to how groups within a society cooperate to define and safeguard their pubic interests and image. In addition to race—class, gender, wealth, power and media access impact actions associated with this form of cultural and community care. Social network conservation is dependent upon the values of the group regarding particular issues before mass media. As a theory, social network conservation is also in every respect subject to the extent people perceive themselves as a part of a group—whether or not they articulate this membership. Social network conservation can be either internally creative or competitive. Creatively, the principle holds that there is a collection of activities, which support the interests of a specific group, but are not designed or intended to diminish other groups. In terms of competition, each group perceives another group's exercise of social network conservation as suspicious, politically motivated, and intrinsically oppositional. Contemporarily, social network conservation operates without using terms to indicate racism, and racial dominance is asserted as a silent construct to ensure survival of even "little domains."[6]

Social network conservation is not limited to the media because its nature is to secure favorable images in every area of human life (education, housing, labor, consumerism, neighborhoods), and any aspect involving social interactions in general. For social network conservation to reach the widest audience, the media (or a media forum) is its most powerful expression. Wherever the media is involved, social network conservation is a basic defense of the group's affinity and interests. Minimally social network conservation is sympathetic to the public group image. In its most vigorous and

---

[5] Jessica L. Davis and Oscar H. Gandy, Jr., "Racial Identity and Media Orientation: Exploring the Nature of Constraint," *Journal of Black Studies*, Vol. 29, No. 3 (January 1999), 367-397.
[6] Amy Goodman, Cleveland Riser, Jr., "Voices from Jena: African American Educator from Jena Accuses DA of Conflict of Interest in Handling of Jena Six Case," Interview, September 19, 2007, Retrieved from Democracynow.org September 20, 2007.

WORLD TO COME: ESSAYS ON THE BALTIMORE UPRISING, MILITANT RACISM, AND HISTORY

competitive articulation it is the deliberate condemnation of another groups' public image. In this research, it was clear that racial groups define themselves differently publicly with respect to the concept of race.[7] There appears to be two main categories of social network conservation thought with respect to racial identity dynamics. This includes groups that define themselves fundamentally by: (1) power, control, and authority; and those that are attentive to (2) culture, customs and a sense of community. This does not mean that both groups do not at times convey the same essential thrust of the other. This also assumes that they recognize skin color and many other features of group affinity as well as a common history and culture. Based on the history in this study, people classified as white are identified by the first primary category; African Americans are characterized by the latter. They are in direct competition with one another because both groups see their very different basic definitions of the group self-reflected in the other group. The presumption here is that in places where racial dialogues are polemical there is the heightened threat of groups being labeled adversely. Institutions direct such discussions and groups scramble to either support the management function or expand the discussion. In addition, social network conservation can be facilitated by external group alliances. This does incorporates both inter- and intra-racial cooperation and partnerships. Mission-oriented representatives from diverse groups seek the most optimal image and interests for each other, as well as for their own group. In this case, the overarching messages of care, compassion, justice, equality, etc. are just as important as group advancement. However, social network conservation alliances do not deny or attempt to mitigate the struggles of other partners. Despite these efforts, people are inculcated to act, first and foremost, in defense of their communities and their group's specific interests. Concerning the mass media, social network conservation is an unwritten form of cultural and community care. In late 1831, there were newspaper accounts from all over the country detailing the exploits of Nat Turner. Determined that he would not be remembered as Christ-like, or

---

[7]The concept of race impacts everyone and is a larger concern than black-white issues. It involves most people classified as nonwhite, even those who perceive of themselves in an *honorary white* category. In this research, as in much of the discussion in America, race was viewed from the black-white because of some of the themes of these essays—African Americans in the news media, and the historic relationship between blacks and whites in the pursuit of social justice.

martyred in anyway, most news stories referred to him as a "demon."[8] Turner and his allies operated at the behest of God and on behalf of enslaved Africans. They were obligated to take an active, leadership role in aggressively securing freedom. Even among the sympathizers of blacks, there was the failure to conceive of black agency, but there was the recognition of black community. Whites saw the violent pursuit of liberty among blacks, as a threatening conservation effort, and the loss of white life at the hands of blacks was utterly reprehensible, or beyond the pale.

Intolerable Blackness and the Refinement of Racism

Within three decades after the Civil War, many were concerned about how history would be written, specifically how the war and slavery would be remembered. Jubal Anderson Early, a Confederate lieutenant general in the war, wrote in his narrative that in effect slavery had been used to stir up mob action and to foment antagonism between the north and the south. However, of Africans he wrote "High dignitaries in both church and state in Old England, and puritans in New England, had participated in the profits of a trade by which the ignorant and barbarous natives of Africa were brought from that country and sold into slavery in the American Colonies. The generation in the Southern States which defended their country in the late war, found amongst them, in a civilized and Christianized condition, 4,000,000 of the descendants of those degraded Africans … The Creator of the Universe had stamped them, indelibly with a different color and an inferior physical and mental organization. He had not done this from mere caprice or whim, but for wise purposes. An amalgamation of the races was in contravention of His designs or He would not have made them so different."[9] Early freely expressed some of the widely accepted ideas about Africans on both sides of the conflict. The inferiority, divine mandate, and civilization themes were very popular beliefs throughout the late 1800s. Lieutenant Early ventured that millions of African descendants could not be returned to their homeland. He believed that the only real solution was that "…the

---

[8]"Insurrection of the Blacks," *Niles' Register*, September 3, 1831.
[9]Lieutenant General Jubal Anderson Early, C.S.A. *Autobiographical Sketch and Narrative of the War Between the States*. Philadelphia: J.B. Lippincott, 1912, vii.

inferior race should be kept in a state of subordination."[10] The press during the period of Reconstruction was predisposed to support these views by mocking blacks in print in an effort to maintain African people in a perpetual state of enslavement.[11] After more than a half a century, much of race relations' sentiment was described, not as an embedded form of absolute racism, but the failure of people of color (blacks, Asians, Native Americans and Latinos) to perceive three factors of racial power. First that they (nonwhite people) have failed to remain unconscious about the oppression they experienced. Second, if people of color would not accept the ascribed subordinate status within American society they would be responsible for conflict. Finally, this conglomerate of emerging people of color, subjugated through war, colonization, and slavery, did not appear to comprehend or appreciate the limits of toleration among the dominant group. Thus, these marginalized people were subjected to involuntary segregation where "…racial minorities (specifically people of African descent) tend to be the most enduring minorities of all."[12] Their existence rested on whether or not the dominant group felt secure with their presence within society. Moreover, a social context emerged that would influence other people of color to distance themselves from African people, and even gauge their own progress and acceptance by the way blacks were viewed and treated.

By the late 1960s, race relations' perspectives had not shifted much from the assigned responsibilities of people of color to provide a sense of comfort to whites during their assertion of human rights. There was an overwhelming sense among whites that the government had done enough to help blacks. Scholarly perspectives on assimilation, acculturation and the status of nonwhite groups classified as minorities, began a vigorous response to the demands of the Civil Rights movement. African Americans were encapsulated within a specific racial history:

> …Slavery and the Reconstruction period of history created a large aggregate of persons identifiable as Negroes. They were effectively segregated and excluded from the larger society via an ideology of

---

[10]Lieutenant General Jubal Anderson Early, 1912, vii.
[11]Cal M. Logue, "Racist Reporting During Reconstruction," *Journal of Black Studies*, Vol. 9, No. 3 (March, 1979), 335-349.
[12]See Louis Wirth's essay in Ralph Linton (ed.) *The Science of Man in the World Crisis*. New York: Columbia University Press, 1945, 347-372, 347.

> racial inferiority, yet devoid of any centripetally
> [internally] unifying sense of collective fate or
> peoplehood ... Booker T. Washington's acceptance of
> the status quo represented an attempt at a segregated
> pluralist accommodation despite the grossly
> disadvantaged status of Negroes ... the twentieth
> century saw the beginning of a change in settlement an
> status of Negroes ... [which included] Urban
> concentration and socio-economic improvement ....[13]

Blacks were still perceived, despite the contributions and the gains they made, as largely outside of American society. There were critical discussions about how blacks, Asians, Latinos and Native Americans have made efforts to be accepted by white cultures, particularly about their ability to achieve racial conversion.[14] The idea of institutional racism was noted, but not fully explored on the part of white society. Blacks and other people of color were always perceived as accountable for optimal race relations. American racial studies began to shift over the next two decades to address such ideas as multiculturalism, cultural pluralism, the Afrocentric analysis of race, and critical race theory.[15] These discussions congealed in the 1990s in the form of whiteness studies. The call for whiteness studies was initiated not only to understand white racism, but expanded to include further inquiry into the ethnic and cultural components in our understanding of modern whiteness. This also includes the commonly nebulous and convoluted ways whites perceive their involvement in matters of race and racism.[16] These studies also incorporated how whiteness as a concept and human reality has evolved and expanded in American society.[17] Even with the

---

[13]Irwin D. Rinder, "Minority Orientations: An Approach to Intergroup Relations Theory Through Social Psychology," *Phylon*, XXVI (Spring, 1965), 5-17; 15-17.
[14]Walter P. Zenner, "Ethnic Assimilation and Corporate Group," *The Sociological Quarterly*, VIII (Summer 1967), 340-348.
[15]Molefi Kete Asante, *The Afrocentric Idea*. Philadelphia: Temple University Press, 1987; and also his *Kemet, Afrocentricity, and Knowledge*. Trenton: Africa World Press, 1990. Jean Stefancic, Richard Delgado, *Critical Race Theory: An Introduction*. New York: New York University Press, 2001.
[16]Karl Dach-Gruschow, Ying-yi Hong, "The Racial Divide in Response to the Aftermath of Katrina: A Boundary Condition for Common Ingroup Identity Model," *Analyses of Social Issues and Public Policy* 6 (1), 125–141, 2006.
[17]Jonathan W. Warren; France Winddance Twine, "White Americans, the New Minority?: Non-Blacks and the Ever-Expanding Boundaries of Whiteness," *Journal of Black Studies*, Vol. 28, No. 2. (November, 1997), 200-218.

variety of literature emerging from this area, the one constant about black life in the United States continued to be the thought that "Neither gradual nor radical assimilation are possible solutions [for blacks], even for the elite ..."[18] The exception here was "secret 'conversion'"—or passing for white for those blacks with little discernable physical African or biracial heritage.[19] However, for most African Americans the issue was not assimilation, but the agency they asserted, their autonomous voice (in all areas of life), which was deemed a threat and an affront to established racial subordination, not a contribution to society's quest for democracy.

Involuntary Segregation and Intolerable Blackness

Society moved blacks from the "strict involuntary segregation" of American slavery, to the "involuntary segregation" (but equally rigid) of Jim Crow.[20] By the late twentieth century African Americans were subjected to a form of physical, social and intellectual racial separation identified here as "intolerable blackness." As a major concept of racism, it reflects society's maintenance of the idea of black inferiority, which also defines black agency as a form of militancy. It is theorized that this expression of militancy produced an overall backlash, or resistance to the greater goals of the Civil Rights and Black Power movements. It is similar to the discussion of pervasive and persistent racism in much of Derrick Bell's arguments.[21] The idea of intolerable blackness is analogous to, but not the same as how the expression "unforgivable blackness" was used to capture the life and persona of heavyweight boxing champion Jack Johnson.[22] Considered an audacious and flamboyant black man, Johnson won the championship

---

[18]Walter P. Zenner, "Ethnic Assimilation and Corporate Group," *The Sociological Quarterly*, VIII (Summer 1967), 340-348, 348.
[19]Ibid., 340-348, 348.
[20]D. Y. Yuan, "Voluntary Segregation: A Study of New York Chinatown," *Phylon* (Fall 1963), 255-265, 256.
[21]Derrick A. Bell, *And We Are Not Saved the Elusive Quest for Racial Justice; Faces At The Bottom Of The Well: The Permanence Of Racism*. I would also include Bell's, *Silent Covenants: Brown V. Board of Education and the Unfulfilled Hopes for Racial Reform*. New York: Oxford University Press, 2005.
[22]Geoffrey C. War, *Unforgivable Blackness: The Rise and Fall of Jack Johnson*, New York: A.A. Knopf, 2004. See also Randy Roberts, *Papa Jack: Jack Johnson and the Era of White Hopes*, London: Collier Macmillan, 1983, and Al-Tony Gilmore, *Bad Nigger!: The National Impact of Jack Johnson*, New York: Kennikat Press, 1975.

WORLD TO COME: ESSAYS ON THE BALTIMORE UPRISING, MILITANT RACISM, AND HISTORY

in 1908. The concepts share some of the same components but differ in some areas. Johnson possessed a fundamental disregard for racism and racial prejudice and engaged in direct confrontation and defiance of racial bigotry as an individual choice. In this sense, Johnson was the embodiment of the "bad nigger." He consorted with white women in spite of the social proscriptions, ignoring the punishment of lynching as a result of this boldness (in the year he won the heavyweight championship a minimum of 89 blacks were lynched in America).[23] The most frequently cited rationale for the lynching of black men was sexual aggression against white females. The idea of unforgivable blackness is the highly symbolic personal offense to interracial relationships predicated upon the prohibition of black male/white female sexual contact around the turn of the century 1900. The legacy of intolerable blackness is reflected in many racial phenomena, one of the most significant examples is how the terms used to describe blacks as a group (negro, colored), were once considered libelous and slanderous when mistakenly applied to whites (particularly white women).[24] In the twenty-first century intolerable blackness is assigned to African Americans in what Stephen Bright called a "tolerance of racial discrimination in the criminal courts"[25] (as in death penalty cases) where racial bias is accepted and racial profiling is an institutional norm. Intolerable blackness is a refined aspect of racism which privileges—or signals highly expressive sentiments against blacks and the idea of blackness. Intolerable blackness is another aspect of racial subjugation in which broad intellectual and public discussions about race are carefully selected and scripted and where racial debates are fundamentally mediated by the mass media within the popular culture.

In a retreat to pre-1950s racial discourse, as Jerry Mander proclaimed, "the seventies became an advanced version of the fifties,"[26] as a result, intolerable blackness was forcefully articulated as a seminal

---

[23]*1952 Negro Year Book*, Tuskegee Institute, Department of Records and Research, William H. Wise and Co., 278. This is from the year book's lynching data beginning in 1882 to 1956.
[24]See *Express Pub. Co. v. Osborn* (Texas 1912) 151 S. W. 574; *Flood v. News and Courier Co.*, 71 S.C. 112, 50 S. E. 637; *Upton v. Publishing Co.*, 104 La. 141, 28 So. 970.
[25]Stephen B. Bright, "Discrimination, Death, and Denial: The Tolerance of Racial Discrimination in Infliction of the death Penalty," in Charles J. Ogletree, Jr. and Austin Sarat's *From Lynch Mobs to the Killing State: Race and the Death Penalty in America*. New York: New York University Press, 2006, 211-259.
[26]Jerry Mander, *Four Arguments for the Elimination of Television*, New York: Quill, 1978, 31-33.

theme in the news media. It was a frustration emanating from the national psyche. Not only had blacks forced their way into American society from the bottom rungs of slavery, but they also introduced inferior cultural elements, and within this process did not fully acknowledge the civil rights gains that society afforded them. Moreover, the statistical data that supported institutional racism in health care, the penal system, education, and employment, etc. confirmed embedded notions of an imperfect transplanted African culture, not the legacy of organized institutionalized and systemic racism. Thus intolerable blackness is an explicit category of dominant culture racial and social justice exhaustion and discomfort, and is concurrently a vigorous philosophical reassertion of white supremacy without using these terms to indicate racial authority. Blacks were relegated to the racial frontier, a "wilderness" decidedly outside of the American dream experience and into the mythic condition of intolerable blackness.[27] According to Molefi Asante this represented blacks living "...under a siege of disrespect, whether you are a person of high visibility or of no visibility." For African Americans there are some necessary risks in addressing the elimination of racism, including "The attempt on the part of the prisoner is to escape the wilderness by rearranging the field of struggle—that is, to find one's own ground."[28] This means that the antebellum disposition for advancing the in perpetuity nature of American slavery was a potent desire whose meaning transcended the dominant discourse on democracy and equality, and became a fixed theme in how black acquiescence or agency would be recognized and acted upon within society. One of the scholars who best understood the nature of intolerable blackness was Franz Fanon, reflected in his work *Black Skins, White Masks*.[29] Fanon's famous quote captures the synonymy of derision for blacks with the familiar observation of blackness: "'Dirty nigger!' or, 'Look, a Negro!'"[30] Homi K. Bhabha analyzed Fanon's argument and further illustrated this phenomenon of the African American as being, "...a member of the marginalized, the displaced, the diasporic. To be amongst those whose very presence is both 'overlooked'—in the double sense of social surveillance and psychic disavowal—and, at the

---

[27]Molefi K. Asante, *Erasing Racism*, Amherst, NY: Prometheus Books, 2003, 33-68.
[28]Molefi K. Asante, 2003, 200.
[29]Franz Fanon. *Black Skin, White Masks*. London: Pluto, 1986. See the important forward by H. Bhabha.
[30]Franz Fanon, 1986; see "The Fact of Blackness."

same time, overdetermined—psychically projected made stereotypical and symptomatic."[31] The 1980s saw a consolidation of these binary views of blacks, where blackness itself came to represent a depreciating social condition for all Americans.[32]

The New Racism in Post-Racial America and the Price of Prejudice

The early anti-African sentiment of intolerable blackness moved from idealizing inferiority and affirming justificatory bondage, towards a conclusion that assimilation was not possible. Furthering our fundamental definition, intolerable blackness is the modern idiom for the attempt to recreate America as a slave republic. Joe Feagin posed the question in a critical discussion of the ideological position of white America on the issues of race. He called this "semislavery," where the issue is whether or not nonblacks are willing to give up the power to dominate and the privilege associated with this power.[33] Today, the penal system coupled with the institutionalized ghetto has produced a new version of the "peculiar institution."[34] Added to this the commercialization and marketing of the ghetto which idealizes and entrenches blackness within a poverty consciousness. This is one example of how the passionate social justice discourse of rap and hip-hop music was recast as an anti-black dialogue in what Maulana Karenga called a milieu of "self-disrespect, and self-mutilation." [35] In this context the privileging of negative rap, and the assertion that it has a cultural place, is the negation of affirming and politically inspired forms of new music and cultural expression.[36] In the media, this has

---

[31]Homi K. Bhabha. *The Location of Culture*. London: Routledge, 1994, 236.
[32]Herman Gray, *Watching Race: Television and the Struggle for Blackness*. Minneapolis, MN: University of Minnesota Press, 1995, See Chapter 3, "African American Discourses and the sign of Blackness," 35-56. See also Maurice A. St. Pierre, Reaganomics and Its Implications for African-American Family Life, *Journal of Black Studies*, Vol. 21, No. 3. (March, 1991), 325-340.
[33]Joe Feagin, "Slavery Unwilling to Die: The Background of Black Oppression in the 1980s," *Journal of Black Studies*, Vol. 17, No. 2, The Economic State of Black America. (December, 1986), 173-200.
[34]Loïc Wacquant, "Race as Civic Felony," *International Social Science Journal* 57 (183), 127–142, 2005.
[35]Maulana Karenga, *Introduction to Black Studies*. Los Angeles: University of Sankore Press, 2002, 482-483.
[36]M.K. Asante Jr., "Enough Disrespect: Return Rap To Its Artistic Roots," *USA Today*, Pg. 13a, October 26, 2004.

World To Come: Essays On The Baltimore Uprising, Militant Racism, And History

become propagandistic and highly argumentative. This is but one manifestation of the "new racism." It is linked to what Teun A. van Dijk referred to as a 'discursive" discourse, "expressed, enacted and confirmed by text and talk, such as everyday conversations, board meetings, job interviews, policies, laws, parliamentary debates, political propaganda, textbooks, scholarly articles, movies, TV programmes and news reports in the press, among hundreds of other genres." Like the force indispensable to the enslavement of African people, this discourse on racism is "just as effective to marginalize and exclude minorities."[37] Significantly, it further encapsulates the inability to recognize black humanity, offering only a sense of finality of societal loss within a context of an unforgivable existence complete with demonstrative assertions of bigotry (i.e. the "the living while black" phenomena).

The costs of racism to people of African descent—all people—have been high. *First*, buttressed by racial stereotypes, black crimes have become the standard by which crimes committed by all others are measured. Scientific information is often used to support biological perspectives on race and to argue against the position that race is a social construction.[38] Ignoring the social construction of race negates the power dynamic and continues to blame blacks for a long history of oppression. This unfairly reinforces erroneous perceptions and attitudes about people of African descent adding to the basis for intolerable blackness. *Second*, it gives nonblacks a false sense of racial security and superiority. For some it is an unspeakable legacy, for others a troublesome social privilege with dire consequences for inspired race relationships. This does not exclude the risks that nonblacks take in speaking out and in support of serious antiracism discourses and activities specifically in support of blacks. Intolerable blackness has given license to others to mount vicious attacks against blacks as a whole, and to justify these attacks with racial literature from the past. One example was Kenneth Eng's column during Black History Month, 2007 in which he justified his hatred for blacks this way: "Contrary to media depictions, I would argue that blacks are weak-willed. They are the only race that has been enslaved for 300

---

[37]Teun A. van Dijk, "New(s) Racism. A Discourse Analytical Approach," In Simon Cottle (Ed.), *Ethnic Minorities and the Media*. Milton Keynes, UK: Open University Press, 2000, 33-49, 34.
[38]J. Philippe Rushton, *Race, Evolution, and Behavior: A Life History Perspective*, 2nd Special Abridged Edition, Port Huron, MI: Charles Darwin Research Institute, 2000.

years."[39] Leith Mullings has theorized: "...one of the ranking crimes of racism is the tremendous squander of human potential: the intellectual time and energy spent theorizing this construct that must, in the course of human history, be seen as one of the more bizarre approaches to human organization."[40] Perennially locked out of global time and space, and unable to disengage the *in perpetuity* emblem of slavery, the African in America as well as those in the diaspora were ascribed the status of intolerable blackness—a condition fueled by obstructive stereotypes and by negating source racism. The post-Civil Rights Movement message was clear and straightforward—society would no longer tolerate the assertion of, or the responsibility for blacks, as racial victims in America. Nancy Snow defined this kind of propaganda as, "…. Any organized or concerted group effort or movement to spread a particular doctrine or a system of doctrines or principles."[41] Most widely expressed in the mass media, particularly in the news, intolerable blackness exists among the most potent expressions of the science of racism within society and the mass media. As Snow has described, like the propaganda associated with the war in Iraq (2003 through 2011), the primitive doctrine of racism is also deliberate and singularly beneficial.

---

[39] Kenneth Eng, "Why I Hate Blacks," *AsianWeek*, February 23, 2007.
[40] Leith Mullings, *On Our Own Terms: Race, Class, and Gender in the Lives of African American Women*. New York: Routledge, 1997, xii. In addition to the monetary liability associated with civil rights violations, there are many costs to racism including the experiences of black women and the gender specific mechanisms of racism. Hazel V. Carby, "White Woman Listen! Black Feminism and the Boundaries of Sisterhood," in Heidi Safia Mirza, (ed.), *Black British Feminism: A reader*, London: Routledge, 1997.
[41] Nancy Snow, *Information War American Propaganda, Free Speech and Opinion Control since 9-11*, New York: Seven Stories Press, 2003, 61.

CHAPTER 4

Popular Media Ghettoization And An Introduction To
The Police-Encounter Narrative

> The ghetto, in short, operates as an ethnoracial prison:
> it encages a dishonored category and severely curtails
> the life chances of its members in support of the
> 'monopolization of ideal and material goods or
> opportunities' by the dominant status group dwelling
> on its outskirts.—Loïc Wacquant[1]

The Media and the Ghettoization of Black Life and Culture

2007 was an important year in the United States (and around the world). Among other events, the year marked the global financial crisis, and assisted our effort to understand the connection between the media and the ghettoization of African American culture. Before the "Great Recession" began to have an enormous impact on the American economy, Barack Obama announced his candidacy for President of the United States on February 10, 2007. He entered the 2008 presidential election at a time when black popular culture and the mass media was firmly entrenched in the notion that the black urban (and rural) ghetto—defined by poverty, unemployment, crime, etc.—was a cultural phenomenon, instead of a social construction. During the summer of 2007, the mass media, fixated on its own conceptualization of the ghetto, created fallacious visions of an African American subculture.[2] To counter and eliminate these negative images, it has been hypothesized that if blacks consistently and vigorously protested racist images in the media that these images would be reduced.[3] In addition, black control of media images has been called for along with the

---

[1] Loïc Wacquant, "The New 'Peculiar Institution': On the Prison as Surrogate Ghetto," *Theoretical Criminology*, Vol. 4 (3), 377-389, 383, 2000.
[2] For one of the most recent treatments on this see Cora Daniels, *Ghettonation A Journey into the Land of Bling and the Home of the Shameless*. New York: Doubleday, 2007.
[3] Ellen Holly, "The Role of Media in the Programming of an Underclass." *Black Scholar*, Vol. 10, No. 5, January-February 1979, 31-37.

acquisition of television stations and other media outlets.[4] These are certainly important strategic methods. However, one of the most significant obstacles to mass media ownership has been capital formation and sustained investment for a larger vision—multiple networks. Blackness in the news, as in other forms of media, demonstrated that a key issue regarding images and ideas is how black voices are limited in terms of perspective and worldview. It has also been argued that when blacks assume greater creative and executive control of established media outlets that the images and range of information would significantly improve. The one prominent example often given is Black Entertainment Television (B.E.T.), which revealed that this was not the case either.

From the very beginning, cultural and quality expectations were too high for the network; and still today, selected members of the 18 to 34 year old market felt compelled to defend its existence as then, the nation's only black owned and operated television network irrespective of programming. As the name confirmed, Black Entertainment Television's scheduling in 2007 focused primary on entertainment geared toward a narrowly defined black youth audience. This programming included mostly situation comedies, comedy specials, music and rap videos, variety shows, and movies. Regarding the latter, during the week of September 17-23, 2007 the prime time movies scheduled by B.E.T. consistently included irreverent features or updated renderings of the Blackploitation film genre. The movies provided during this week were listed as "Soul Plane" (comedy, 2004), "Truth Be Told" (2003, crime drama), "Lockdown" (2003, prison drama), "State Property 2" (2005, gangster drama), "Civil Brand" (2003, women's prison drama), and "Gang of Roses" (2003, Hip Hop western).[5] Beyond this the network selected "The Wire: Season 3" (the drug war in Baltimore Maryland), incorporated a moderate dose of religious and gospel music programming, and a small number of news briefs. The criticism of B.E.T. in 2007, which admittedly was primarily interested in the 18-34 market, was that it was narrowly focused. The network was also viewed as defensive instead of expansive, one that consistently pandered to racial stereotypes, virtually ignored (with rare exception) essential news and social justice commentary and had clung

---

[4] James Haskins, "New Black Images in the Mass Media—How Educational is Educational TV?," *Freedomways*, 14, 3, 200-208, 1974.
[5] See B.E.T.'s website at http://www.bet.com/OnTV/Schedule/default.htm.

to the decision that older (the post 34 year old group) and more varied markets of African Americans were deemed less important.[6] B.E.T. had been fiscally responsive to the paradoxical nature of blackness and negative images in the American media by positioning itself, from the very beginning, to exploit the salability of highly constructed notions of the black underclass, and defending this position as representative of black popular culture. Even as B.E.T. sought to adjust the programming, it remained committed to profit over quality and controversy over social justice empowerment.

    The problem is not entirely reflected in the past or current criticisms levied at B.E.T. The crisis is much larger than network programming, the news, or the media in general. Using Ronald W. Walters' analysis of the media, public policy and the African American experience, the difficulty is the "…consistent, comprehensive and substantive coverage of Blacks and their agenda."[7] One aspect is an issue that the news appears to readily accept and advance its singular coverage of artificial ideas about the low socio-economic background of many African Americans. That issue has been called the "Ghettoization" of black culture, or is sometimes referred to as black street culture. From the rural to the urban landscape, blacks and the dominant society have described street culture in many different ways. While society used its negative aspects to affirm racial beliefs about blacks, African Americans often interpreted the experience differently, and more broadly. Beyond media images, the ghetto is a multi-layered discourse, which denotes, among other things, a reluctant and transient refuge from domination and a sense of where the people are. Its expressions, both antagonistic and creatively constructive, are viewed as defiant to the power structure. In addition, the discussion has been avoided because it demands serious attention to the class conflicts among African Americans. In his chapter, "The Culture of Hip Hop," Michael Eric Dyson described rap music as "emblematic of the glacial shift in aesthetic sensibilities between blacks of different generations, and it draws attention to the severe economic barriers that increasingly divide ghetto poor blacks from middle- and upper-middle-class blacks. Rap reflects the intra-racial class division that has plagued African-

---

[6]Felicia R. Lee, "Network for Blacks Broadens Its Schedule," *The New York Times*, July 9, 2007. See also, Beretta Smith-Shomade, *Pimpin' Ain't Easy: Selling Black Entertainment Television*, Taylor and Francis, Inc., 2007.
[7]Ronald W. Walters, *White Nationalism, Black Interests: Conservative Public Policy and the Black Community*. Detroit: Wayne State University Press, 2003, 267.

American communities for the last thirty years."[8] The serious dialogue has been evaded because of the reading of hip-hop as a form of public journalism, the conflicts over the varying interpretations of black street culture, and whether the consistently adverse public expressions of black culture as a whole are viable components of African American ways of life or merely a reflection of American society's commercial drive. Yet the variety of black speech and idiom in popular culture are constantly surveilled (notably by consumer interests). Often if interpreted as pedestrian, black expression is used as comic fodder by both blacks and whites. In addition, and more importantly, the creation of and reliance on a black low-culture is regularly seized upon for political purposes. The historical, intellectual, and social force of black expression is routinely ignored, while whites chide or dismiss an already circumspect black "culture." Conversely, if viewed as modern and stylish, black expression is imitated in order to exhibit the historically coveted black "soul," "cool" or "hip" pose in American society.

Maulana Karenga addressed "The Problem of Ghettoization" as a multifaceted racist mechanism for controlling African Americans, which included, among other things, how "social reality is defined."[9] Afrocentric culturalists have long argued that there are many ways of being black in the world. While tenuous challenges and passionate discourse related to the idea have been mounted, we know that news media readily engaged the idea of its own conception of blackness—usually sensation and associated with notions of street culture—notably such phenomena promoting misaligned stories involving baggy pants, black women street fighting, etc. However, society does not seek to know black street culture, or any aspect of African culture, as much as it attempts to interpret it. As an element of this, that American popular culture embraced modern day forms of minstrelsy is no secret. Nor were black viewers unaware that much of black life and culture was misrepresented in the global public sphere. In one example from 2007, a German Defense department training video encouraged the mock shooting of blacks, complete with racial epithets (the soldiers were told to pretend that they were in the Bronx New York). One German

---

[8]Michael Eric Dyson, *Reflecting Black: African-American Cultural Criticism*, Minneapolis, MN: The University of Minneapolis Press, 1993, 7. See chapter one, "The Culture of Hip Hop," 3-15.
[9]Maulana Karenga, *Introduction to Black Studies*, Los Angeles: University of Sankore Press, 2003. See section 6.2, "The Problem of Ghettoization," and the 6 basic dimensions of the ghetto, 300-306.

WORLD TO COME: ESSAYS ON THE BALTIMORE UPRISING, MILITANT RACISM, AND HISTORY

reporter stated: "There are quite of a lot of B movies or hip-hop songs, about black people, African Americans are portrayed as gangsters, are portrayed as criminals, and then some people here in Germany, they take it for real."[10] However, this was consistent with the history of the attack on black struggles with economic, social and political equality; along with messages which emphasize undeserved welfare and crime. Poor people in general are regarded as a drain on American society; but the black poor are regarded with particular repugnance. The media establishment's concerted attention to this phenomenon tends to reinforce negative stereotypes and diminishes the national exposition of a multi-faceted black culture. It was an effort to redefine black culture in meagre terms. The issue was not the validity of black street culture; but the commercialization, distortion, and marketing of a stylized ghetto concept—the attempt to create and delineate a "Ghettonation."[11] Mass media fed on the commercial aspect of this through privileging coarse rap music and granting star power to those entertainers who created and defended careers delivering scatological messages. The mass media was powerful in this regard, but fortunately not exclusive to our understanding of cultural delivery systems.

Truth is: We are all 1 Bullet Away From Being a #Hashtag[12]

Not since the mob violence associated with the post-Reconstruction lynching of African Americans and the history of indiscriminate Ku Klux Klan-style murders of black people — through the 1960s Civil Rights Movement—have we seen such pervasive racialized killing of African American men, women, and children. In addressing this, the Black Lives Matter Movement supported and embraced the preservation of all black people. The three brave young black women who stepped forward as co-founders of Black Lives Matter were Alicia Garza, Patrisse Cullors, and Opal Tometi. Each woman also provided separate leadership to her own grassroots movement, encompassing labor, the criminal justice system, and immigration. According to Garza, "Black Lives Matter was born out of

---

[10]"Racist German Army Clip Targets NY Blacks: German Military Instructor Tells Soldier to Envision Black Bronx Residents, Yell Obscenity and Fire Gun," ABC News Now, Show: Inside the Newsroom #1 6:08 AM EST, April 16, 2007.
[11]Cora Daniels. *Ghettonation A Journey into the Land of Bling and the Home of the Shameless.* New York: Doubleday, 2007.
[12]See Appendix B: Baltimore Uprising Protest Signs.

the incredible pain and rage that each of us feels and that black people across the world feel when any of our lives are taken unnecessarily, particularly in relationship to state-sanctioned violence."[13] The Black Lives Matter movement emphasized the statistic that "Every 28 hours a black man, woman, or child is murdered by police or vigilante law enforcement."[14] Their goal is the cessation of police shootings of blacks. Black Lives Matter organizations in communities have exhibited a comprehensive investment in the wellbeing of black society. Like other suspicious deaths of African American males at the hands of law enforcement, the death of Freddie Gray made headlines around the world—far "beyond Baltimore" to West Africa, Latin America, the United Kingdom, Canada, and South Africa. The casual observer cannot help but to note the frequency with which young black men (females, and older blacks as well) have been killed by law enforcement officers under suspicious circumstances. It was never an issue of the responsibility of law enforcement to protect and serve the community by "apprehending the bad guy." However, citizens should have the right to question the deaths of blacks in police-encounters. This noticeable upsurge in questioning police actions suggested that the pattern of high profile killings was eerily similar. More than this, just as corporations now routinely mine vast amounts of data for information and profit leverage, citizens want to unearth credible knowledge and they want justice. They have a different appreciation and expectation of how information is constructed and shared. In addition, they also want to know how data is critically analyzed for accuracy. Citizens are no longer willing to accept the traditional police narrative, especially in some of the cases disputing the deaths of citizens. This approach to information has demanded transparency and independent external scrutiny. Citizens also want the same information from corporate, education, and government spheres. They are no less interested in a formal examination of evidence than the historian and scholars from the multiplicity of disciplines. This mindset is very different from what society as a whole has been accustomed.

---

[13] Alicia Garza, Patrisse Cullors, and Opal Tometi, interviewed by Amy Goodman and Nermeen Shaikh, *Democracy Now*, July 24, 2015, http://www.democracynow.org/blog/2015/7/24/part_2_blacklivesmatter_founders_on_immigration, accessed August 9, 2015.
[14] Black Lives Matter website, http://blacklivesmatter.com/about/, accessed May 14, 2015.

World To Come: Essays On The Baltimore Uprising, Militant Racism, And History

The construct of law enforcement shootings of African Americans across the nation has a specific scenario—one, which consistently presents a narrative that the deceased black person was responsible for his or her own death in the presence of police. Finally, public knowledge of police actions, especially fatal encounters, are accompanied by a highly scripted media production. In the emerging police-encounter death narrative, a black person usually has a conflict with law-enforcement, which leads to being killed by the police. [15] In the cases that raise questions, often the person is unarmed or the only visible weapon they possess is their blackness—their very existence. The police, in conjunction with media, hasten to mitigate the death, by reporting that the person "might" have been armed, or that police "thought" they were armed. In addition, we are told that the person in question attempted to take the officers weapon, or the officer "thought" he or she was "going for" his weapon; and, so they shot them. These kinds of statements alone are enough to justify the killing. We are often led to believe that most law-enforcement officers, who are purportedly highly trained, experienced, operating in sufficient numbers, and armed with state-of-the-art weapons, were in extraordinary fear for their own lives. Or, that the citizen-suspect posed an immediate deadly threat to the police. In the case of 12-year-old Tamir Rice, a 911 call was made, indicating that a generic black male, who might be a juvenile, was pointing a pistol at people "gangster style" on the grounds of the Cudell Recreation Center in Cleveland, Ohio. The caller could not ascertain that he was a child playing with a toy/pellet gun; he thought Rice looked about 20-years-old. Two officers tactically charged and in a matter of seconds, one of them killed the child instantly. The officer who fired his weapon was "…4.5 feet and 7 feet from RICE."[16] Black men, women and children become the living embodiment of mythological "monsters" to be vanquished. This idea is similar to "The Big Black Man Syndrome" in traditional judicial advocacy where (using Rodney King as the prototype) the person is "…portrayed as larger than life, with superhuman strength."[17]

---

[15] In addition to shooting, other police-encounter deaths have resulted from physical restraint, beating, trauma from taser, etc., or other mysterious causes.
[16] Cuyahoga County Sheriff's Department, File #: 15-00004, "Synopsis of CCSD Case #15-004 Use of Deadly Force Incident," June 2, 2015, 4.
[17] Lawrence Vogelman, "The Big Black Man Syndrome: The Rodney King Trial and the Use of Racial Stereotypes in the Courtroom," *Fordham Urban Law Journal*, Vol. 20, No. 3, 1992, 571-578, 574.

World To Come: Essays On The Baltimore Uprising, Militant Racism, And History

Mythologized blacks present an imminent danger to society. There must always be a justification for the shooting. This must be something, anything, which will legally and credibly explain, absolve, or mitigate the extra-legal police shooting to the public.

Furthermore, in this construction we are reminded with each incident that police do not kill decent law-abiding citizens. They kill murderers, drug abusers, batterers, thieves, weapons dealers, gang-bangers, and the mentally psychotic. There is a "slam-dunk" kind of attitude where anyone, with any kind of prior arrest record (including a parking ticket), who dies in a police-encounter, somehow deserved that death. This is very important to the overall public discussion because it means that everyone is at risk. The various classifications of misdemeanors (including traffic violations) will be used to taint the victim; while prior felonies simply stop the conversation altogether. It should be noted that people thought to be deserving of lethal police action, but who present no criminal history, can be successfully publically framed to appear guilty of personal problems, mental instability, or low character. Then there is the problem of the "clean" person. For example, Everette Howard, Jr. was an 18-year-old Upward Bound student at the University of Cincinnati in 2011. His encounter with campus police led to him being tased and he died thereafter. Howard's parents, who won their wrongful death suit, were interested in making sure that no other police-taser deaths occurred. Many articles failed to mention constructive details like Howard was a college student or anything else that would make him appear human and worthy of life. The real problem for police is the "clean" person. This is the person who does not fit the criminal mold, and who has a vocal community-of-care. However, as we have seen, there have been consistent attempts to "dirty" the victim in the media.

The officers involved in questionable police-encounter death cases, especially if their actions cannot be adequately explained away before an internal investigation takes place, are usually placed on leave, per department protocols. They typically receive paid leave during the internal review. For some, the initial formal inquiry moves very slowly, and factual information surrounding most cases is limited and takes an interminable amount of time to uncover—leading to even more speculation about what is unknown. Public information is carefully released, and some of this material is not allowed because of any potential or pending litigation. And that is the whole point. The narrative that police cite publically, what they give to the media is the story they have already prepared in the event of any future legal proceedings. Families of the victims often cite that they are usually not provided adequate information about the case, or even an acknowledgement of their loss, if they are engaged at all. Time is the genuine factor here. The longer it takes to provide the public with credible information, the more distrustful people become of police motives. Police-encounter deaths may involve the collection and examination of video, the gathering of witness statements, an inspection of the scene, etc. However, time is the critical factor when a narrative must be carefully fashioned to support the law enforcement agency's public brand and its policies. One need only examine hundreds of questionable police-encounter death cases reported in the newspapers, radio, television, and the internet to understand that even the death of an ordinary citizen is often *a corporate media production*.

There are areas of last resort in the construction of questionable police-encounter deaths. It is very rare that officers and police organizations admit to the public that an accident or a serious mistake was made. Such cases often appear egregious and indefensible. To be fair this is not necessarily done for the preservation of the individual officer in question, this is done for the integrity of the law enforcement agency and the national union of police. Police have often made mistakes that cost people their lives. This has included invading homes for possessing drugs or illegal weapons, only to find out that it was the wrong home, or the wrong warrant.[18] There are also cases of mistaken identity. In one scenario, where a person has been robbed or assaulted by a black person, police have been known to round-up and arrest the nearest black individual who "fit the description"—only to find that these people were innocent.[19] This does not include the unctuous "a black guy did it" accusation, where whites falsely blamed a crime on a fictitious black person because they understood that the prevailing racial climate would easily support such an allegation, irrespective of the evidence (i.e. the cases of Susan Smith and Charles Stuart).[20] In addition, death-by-cop (also known as suicide-by-cop[21]) at

---

[18] As in the cases of Alberta Spruill and Prince Jones, see Appendix C: A Compendium of African Americans who Died in Police-Encounters, 1994-2015.
[19] See Kendrec McDade, Appendix C: A Compendium of African Americans who Died in Police-Encounters, 1994-2015.
[20] See Erika L. Johnson, "Menace to Society: The Use of Criminal Profiles and Its Effects on Black Males, A." *Howard LJ* 38 (1994): 629; Barak, Gregg. "Between the waves: Mass-mediated themes of crime and justice." *Social Justice* (1994): 133-147.

one time referred to a person who intentionally forced a police officer to shoot him, for example, by pointing a gun the person knew was empty of bullets. As implausible as it sounds, death-by-cop now has an expanded meaning in terms of how the in-custody suicide/death transpires —including beating, kicking, slamming, and even asphyxiation deaths. Then there are the truly bizarre "it could happen" claims. Many of these involve mysterious or supernatural suicides. This includes cases like Chavis Carter in Jonesboro Arkansas who in 2012 was said to have killed himself while handcuffed in the back of a police car. In 2014, Victor White, III of Iberia Parish Louisiana was also thought to have committed suicide in the same manner. However, in the case of White this idea is still disputed, even after the U.S. Justice Department declined to charge Louisiana law enforcement officers in his death. Since the high visibility of the Black Lives Matter movement, the typical police-shooting media production has involved stories that invariably state or reiterate information telling the public that the police followed appropriate protocol. This is introduced whether we know it to be true or not. In addition to the reliance upon racial stereotypes, we have the essential presentation of *criminal history-like* information as well as the liberal use of actual criminal histories even when they are not violent felonies. The people affected in these police-encounter deaths are commonly stripped of any humanity and this is evident in mainstream news stories. This is also clear from the September 2015 police shooting of a wheelchair bound black man[22]— indicating that not even physical disability, especially when the threat of a weapon is asserted, can prevent the use of lethal force. Since news agencies rely on the police for their information, police adeptly use the mass media to absolve themselves of culpability.

Leaking and Sharing Information Advantageous to the Police Narrative

It seems that there is little need these days for law enforcement agencies to leak information to the media. Law enforcement representatives (media liaisons) work hand-in-hand with news outlets to

---

[21]"...refers to an individual who wishes to die and uses the police to effect that goal." See V. Geberth, "Suicide by cop." *Law and Order* 41, No. 7 (1993): 105-109.
[22]Cory Alexander Haywood, "NAACP Wants Special Prosecutor in Police Shooting Death of Man in Wheelchair," *Eurweb, Electronic urban Report*, September 28, 2015, http://www.eurweb.com/2015/09/naacp-wants-special-prosecutor-in-police-shooting-death-of-man-in-wheelchair/, accessed September 28, 2015.

transmit stories about police-encounter shootings. Too often, news agencies simply reprint the police narrative without any effort at investigation, or basic fact checking. However, leaking material does exist and one of the most pernicious examples is the creation, reprinting, or disclosing of information that condemns citizens and absolves police officers of responsibility before an investigation takes place. This is a kind of public myth making, where police agencies recognize the importance of the phenomenon of adjudicating cases in the 24-hour media. As noted above, this includes, establishing (or merely suggesting) a prior criminal history (or any assertion of unlawful behavior) of the victim. We saw this in the cases of Michael Brown and Freddie Gray. The other crucial strategy was to construct the presence of a deadly weapon. Blacks must be perceived as deviant and threatening, therefore a weapon enhances this conception. History has shown us that any object can be construed as a weapon when there is an encounter with law enforcement: wallets, keys, cell phones, cars[23], etc. These objects assist in *dirtying* a deceased person suspected of a crime or who was confronted by police. In the never-ending news cycle, the person lives long after his or her death to be vilified by police.

Not only were Freddie Gray's struggles with the criminal justice system asserted immediately (including arrests for illicit drugs) after his death, but the media spread the word that he was in possession of a switchblade knife at the time of his arrest. His childhood was also placed under intense scrutiny, not the environment that affected all (predominately) black residents of the area, but specifically the extent that lead paint poisoning, deposited early in his system, might have contributed to the situation. When it became apparent that his arrest and subsequent death would be very difficult to explain away, the media ran stories suggesting that Gray might have attempted to kill himself in the back of the police transport vehicle. This purportedly came from another arrestee-suspect riding in the police transport van; but the eyewitness later vigorously denied the whole notion. However, the strength of this kind of carefully shaped narrative is considered indefensible. As the story of one black man's mysterious death at the hands of law enforcement receded into yet another, we were littered

---

[23]Scottsdale, Arizona police claimed that Dewayne Carr (along with three others) used the Mercedes car he was driving as a weapon against police. Carr, who had an arrest record, was being surveilled by police for credit card fraud and was shot by police on January 19, 2015.

WORLD TO COME: ESSAYS ON THE BALTIMORE UPRISING, MILITANT RACISM, AND HISTORY

with mainstream media examples of "blacks behaving badly" across the country, complete with video clips and mug shots (police booking photographs) filling the screens of our smartphones, tablets and personal computers. This occurred because individuals rely on highly controlled and easily accessed media to understand the world and ultimately the media can "…enhance discrimination in the justice system…."[24] It represented the exploitation of racial fears–using coded headlines and photographs—without necessarily employing traditional coarse racial language.

The Media Framing the Message and the Murder of Emmett Till

If the brutal death of one black man anywhere in America warrants national attention, the two Medias—mainstream and powerful versus small, independent and formidable —tend to do battle. One of the earliest examples includes the murder of Emmett Till. Sixty years ago, the fourteen-year-old Chicago boy was sent to visit relatives near the town of Money, Mississippi. Unaware of the visceral nature of racism and white supremacy in the south in 1955, Till allegedly violated the edict that black males did not endeavor to look at, much less speak to (or gesture) a white woman. The boy on a dare, after buying candy at a store, whistled or made a comment to the storeowner's wife. The storeowner and his brother-in-law (J.W. Milam and Roy Bryant) came to Till's uncle's home in the middle of the night and took him. They tortured him, brutalized his body and eventually shot him. They then weighted down and dumped his body in the Tallahatchie River. When Tills body was found three days later, it was virtually unrecognizable. His mother, Mamie Bradley, in an act of citizen journalism, demanded that the public be allowed to view his damaged and disfigured body— she authorized an open casket. *Jet magazine* published the photograph of Emmett Till's bloated and mutilated corpse. African Americans across the nation became witness to the racial violence of the south through his tragic death, and this helped to galvanize people in the Civil Rights movement. It was Mamie Bradley who said, "The murder of my son has shown me that what happens to any of us, anywhere in the world, had better be the business of us all." The black media was instrumental

---

[24]Alicia Summers, "Racial Disparity Begins In Childhood: How Disproportionality In Child Abuse Cases Impacts Adult Justice System Inequities," *Critical Issues in Justice and Politics*, Vol. 1, No. 1, March 20008, 47-62, 54.

in bringing Milam and Bryant to trial, even though they were found not guilty of kidnapping and murder. Shortly thereafter, the two men who were known to boast about killing Till, sold their story to *Look* magazine confessing to the crime. Their message was a reminder about the rule of white supremacy in the South. Mamie Bradley's message was a call to action against the lawlessness, brutality, and brazen attitude of the system which permitted her son's death. In addition to the media frames, the story of Emmett Till has several important themes, but one of the most important was the "Black man at risk,"[25] theme because his murder was intended to destroy the black male body. Further, the Emmett Till case demonstrated the lengths people in the south would go to preserve Jim Crow codes of social conduct; and to inspire fear, terror, and obedience in African American people. The Emmett Till case also illustrated the immense resolve of black people to unify and risk their lives in pursuit of justice.

The circumstances surrounding the deaths of Emmett Till and Freddie Gray are very different. They are separated by time, space, and specific social conditions. However, they do share some important aspects. *First*, both events, though sixty years apart, revealed that black males in the United States are still at risk. *Second*, Gray's death was perceived as a function of law-enforcement brutality and/or malfeasance. Till's vicious death came at the hands of local white residents who enjoyed a historic de facto role in policing members of the black race. *Third*, neither Till or Gray could have anticipated that their deaths would impact a massive human rights movement that included legislative response. Though it took more than a half century, Till's case gave rise to the Emmett Till Unsolved Civil Rights Crimes Act of 2007. Introduced by Representative John Lewis (D-GA) the bill was signed into law in 2008 by President George Bush.[26] After Gray's death, Maryland Senators Ben Cardin (D) and Barbara Mikulski (D) introduced (or cosponsored along with others) legislative initiatives which addressed criminal justice reform in the U.S.[27] *Fourth*, these cases

---

[25]Clenora Hudson-Weems, *Emmett Till: The Sacrificial Lamb of the Civil Rights Movement*. Bloomington, IN: Authorhouse, 2006, 80.
[26]The Emmett Till Unsolved Civil Rights Crime Act of 2007, Public Law 110-344, 110th Congress, October 7, 2008. The act will expire in 2017 if not re-approved.
[27]These proposals included: S.2168-Law Enforcement Trust and Integrity Act of 2015; S.1610-BALTIMORE Act ("...to eliminate racial profiling by law enforcement officers...; S.1056-End Racial Profiling Act of 2015; and S. 1476-PRIDE Act

are encircled by the concept of lynching. While Emmett Till was intentionally lynched in the classical American sense, Freddie Gray was also lynched, at the very least, through aggressive policing, indifference, and insensitivity.

Finally, both cases were also important in the media battles, particularly in the case of Freddie Gray. Together the cases saw a concerted use of independent black media, which was very effective in galvanizing the citizenry. In Gray's circumstance, independent and social media networks immediately reported the story of his arrest, hospitalization, and subsequent death. The mainstream media barely perceived that the story would grow beyond their sway—and that in time some of the material case content (i.e. cellphone video) on the internet would become viral. Further, the case of Freddie Gray gained notoriety because of the death of Michael Brown and countless other black males before him. Within days, there was scarcely a single mass media subject that did not find a way to incorporate the incident involving Freddie Gray and the Baltimore Uprising. With consistency, corporate media followed the established narrative—that blacks were lawless in the urban city of Baltimore. To counter positive narratives challenging this perception, digital and print sources ran far-flung articles and news items about the heroic deeds of American troops abroad and local police, alongside of carefully framed police-encounter shootings of blacks—as examples of the public good. The neo-conservatives decried the Baltimore Uprising as just another example of blacks "pretending to be victims" of American society. And, the officers who found themselves embroiled in Gray's police-custody death, the Baltimore 6, were described as trained officials whose actions were upstanding, and duly empowered within the law. Yet, the cases of Emmett Till and Freddie Gray demonstrated how blacks, at different times in American history, found the will and way to pierce through the veil of messages and demand justice.

("…requires states to report to the Attorney General certain information regarding shooting incidents involving law enforcement officers…"

CHAPTER 5

THE AGE OF NEW MEDIA AND THE YETTE HYPOTHESIS

> It is axiomatic in the history of power seized by totalitarians that they must first bind to their will the media of expression between themselves and the people to be controlled. No tactic is more essential to despots than this.—Samuel Yette[1]

The Age of New Media, The Citizen Journalist and Independent Reporting

The *new media* is no longer new; however, what is novel is how we navigate the overlapping news platforms across society and employ the competencies required for ever-changing technologies. The new media encompasses mass communication and emerging technologies on a global scale. New media is a vast area, and not easily defined as merely coalescing the internet, it involves the way we communicate using technology; how social mores and laws are developed to address our communication, and how the technologies involving websites, social media, blogging, texting, gaming, videos, digital news, podcasts, and the primacy of tweeting, offers society useful and critical tools. New media allows for mobile cross-cultural information exchange and communication that can influence vast numbers of people. New media is able to influence and shape public opinion, educate, guide and inspire our relationships. New media has become a central part of contemporary social change and social justice initiatives involving digital education centers and in constructing cyber protests. In the process we are not only creating and operating within virtual communication realms, we are privileging voices that have been unheard, maligned or marginalized. In addition to local, state, and federal agencies—citizens are now an integral part of emergency response, event-analysis, and public service announcements (i.e. voter registration). For some the new media is God-like—all seeing, powerful—and incredibly time consuming. The new media is the most recent modern challenge to how citizens define, actualize and otherwise engage democracy in society. Moreover, the concern over privacy is

---

[1]Samuel F. Yette, *The Choice: The Issue of Black Survival in America*, Silver Spring, MD: Cottage Books, 1996.

WORLD TO COME: ESSAYS ON THE BALTIMORE UPRISING, MILITANT RACISM, AND HISTORY

exceedingly important at this time, because the new media transcends our conception of what is possible in communication as a relational tool while we embrace it as a social movement.

Like *new media*, the term *citizen journalist*, has commanded our attention within the Black Lives Matter movement. The term is actually meant to refer to the *online citizen journalist* since the fundamental activity of citizen journalism—is the work of ordinary people reporting news and information—has been around a long time. An elegant definition of the online citizen journalist is "…an individual who intends to publish information online meant to benefit a community."[2] However, for our purposes, the citizen journalist involves in-depth public participation in the development of news and documentary stories (and sometimes where people work with established journalists); and includes the amateur aspects of news sites, blogging, video, images, and twittering by individuals and groups of ordinary citizens. Armed with new media tools the citizen journalist has been a powerful instrument in shaping our contemporary world. We know that the citizen journalist had a tremendous impact on the 2008 election in Zimbabwe.[3] The "Arab Spring" in the Middle East was influenced by the work of citizen journalists. Scholars like Khamis and Vaughn cite the power of cyberactivism in changing the political climate in Egypt.[4] The citizen journalist has claimed the privilege of participating in and leading the quest for a more democratic society. Technological ease and the atmosphere of online sharing, support citizens as participants, observers, and makers of news. According to Indian journalist and historian Amaresh Misra, "For us everyone is a journalist. And everything is news!"[5] In the Baltimore Uprising a number of grassroots activists, citizen journalists, and organizations (like Kwame Rose, LBS, and Baltimore Bloc) used social media to report events as they happened, and they spoke directly to police and city leaders through Twitter. Thus, the citizen journalist is by definition an activist. As a

---

[2]Serena Carpenter, "A Study of Content Diversity in Online Citizen Journalism and Online Newspaper Articles," *New Media and Society*, 12(7), November 2010, 1064-1084, 1064.
[3]Dumisani Moyo. "Citizen Journalism and the Parallel Market of Information in Zimbabwe's 2008 Election." *Journalism Studies* 10, No. 4 (2009): 551-567.
[4]Sahar Khamis and Katherine Vaughn, "Cyberactivism In The Egyptian Revolution: How Civic Engagement And Citizen Journalism Tilted The Balance." *Arab Media and Society* 14, No. 3 (2011): 1-25.
[5]Amaresh Misra, editor-in-chief, News796, "Aims and Objectives," http://www.news786.in/aboutus.php, accessed September 10, 2015.

result of the global citizen journalist movement, people have become empowered to challenge police-encounter deaths, inform others through distributing information, establishing meaningful discussions, providing real time event timelines, and by coming forward with testimony. The qualifications and ability of the citizen journalist has been decried by professional journalists. These lay correspondents have been praised, criticized and mocked in American popular culture, but that the presence and products of the citizen journalist can have a formidable role in shaping public dialogue and policy cannot be denied.

The new independent media encapsulates the power of self-governing print news outlets, internet blogs, radio, and social media, such as Twitter and Facebook. Far less professional, but arguably more palpable is the aspect of the new independent media which is the ever-vigilant citizen-journalist armed with a camera phone. This also includes the new forms of online-activism that does not including hacking, but developing sophisticated forms of using current social media forums to distribute the message of protestors and to galvanize activists on the streets. However, one of the hallmarks of the best independent media is that it tends to see the situation in much broader and historically relevant terms. The independent media, including the citizen-journalists, made an attempt to capture this, to tell his story. Regarding the latter, many asserted that if not for the citizen on the street with cell-phone cameras—brave enough to record the police-event, countless acts of brutality and even deaths, would not have received any real measure of justice or public scrutiny. Just as the advent of television revolutionized the Civil Rights movement by showing the world the violence against activists, the internet, particularly social media, has galvanized social justice initiatives because of the speed in which information and images can be transmitted. In addition, this media information—, which has attached itself to *YouTube*—is subject to perceptions and interpretations of recorded events that exceed that of traditional media. However, people can still choose, more than ever before, to ignore the serious engagement of media content and perspectives that are contrary to their own organized worldview. This is no less true than the citizens' perception that police use their authority to shape the media to support their worldview and interpretation of citizen encounters.

WORLD TO COME: ESSAYS ON THE BALTIMORE UPRISING, MILITANT RACISM, AND HISTORY

The Africanization of American Media: Other Paradigms Influencing Black Public Media

African Americans have challenged the idea of what constitutes mass media in America. For blacks, any large and concerted media communication outlet (pulpit, e-mail, music, World Wide Web, theater, art, and lecture) can qualify as media—as long as the community receives the information. Alternative media for blacks has been a mainstay in African American history. One of the most talked about alternative sources for empowerment is computers and specifically the Internet. More than ten years ago, Colin Beckles called the Internet "the latest source of social power."[6] In his analysis of web sites, Beckles found that, "...people of African descent have established informal structures known as movement centers, free spaces, or Pan-African sites of resistance."[7] He also referred to these sites as BIGs (Black Information Gateways). These are sites that "...archive, organize, and disseminate information online that is specifically relevant to the political, cultural, and socioeconomic needs of the African diaspora community."[8] His main criticism was that internet sites reflect the diversity and social and political interests, as well as entertainment, of the masses of African Americans; and that they tend to rent cyberspace rather than own it. This also supports the author's analyses of the challenges associated with the digital divide, specifically how poor and working class individuals do not have the same access to technology. This does not include black college students who use computers with the same frequency as their peers.[9] The massive use of the internet has spawned a cyber-élite—those with entrée to the new technologies that create and profit from internet dependencies. This is important to diversity in the advancement of images of blacks on the Internet and the need to hear from non-mainstream voices. As a kind of model for the black radical and communitarian journalist, Samori Marksman, the late program director

---

[6]Colin A. Beckles, "Black Liberation and the Internet: A Strategic Analysis," *Journal of Black Studies*, Vol. 31, No. 3, Special Issue: Africa: New Realities and Hopes (January 2001), 311-324, 311.
[7]Ibid., 312.
[8]Ibid., 314.
[9]Kelly S. Ervin and Geoff Gilmore, "Traveling the Superinformation Highway: African Americans' Perceptions and Use of Cyberspace Technology," *Journal of Black Studies*, Vol. 29, No. 3. (January 1999), 398-407.

WORLD TO COME: ESSAYS ON THE BALTIMORE UPRISING, MILITANT RACISM, AND HISTORY

for WBAI (99.5 FM Pacifica) in New York City used the vehicle to establish a "University of the Air," where the audience experienced alternative news from the African diaspora. In addition to its Pan-African focus, Marksman's media was viewed as advocacy for progressive anti-racist whites and oppressed people, around the world. Yet the issue of highly constructed black images in the news is an important component of intolerable blackness. For African Americans it is a matter of theorizing and practicing liberation strategies for social justice equality. It is also a matter of expanding social network conservation among Africana people, including the efforts to consolidate and manage media representation.

Addressing the massive scale of news within the media entails reviewing and developing community-based strategies and cultural constructs that confront the persistence of intolerable blackness. This is done by articulating the meaning of black culture and unity, and delineating paradigms of African agency and language. In the 1940s, Paul Robeson connected the struggles of African Americans to Africans and other people of color. He advocated the concept of coordinated action, bringing together many organizations with a common cause. He believed that African Americans must learn to speak with one voice on central issues where the leadership's role is to respond to the needs of a unified people.[10] By the 1960s Maulana Karenga had developed the African cultural paradigm, which contained the Kawaida theory (the philosophy of the organization Us), the creation of Kwanzaa as a national holiday commemoration for African Americans, and the widespread study and use of the concepts within the Nguzo Saba. Karenga maintained that the issue of culture was, without question, at the heart of the African American experience.[11] In addition to the importance of the African cultural paradigm advanced by Karenga and others, Sutherland identified several expressions of liberation, "...four non-ideal orientations-the non-struggler, the reactive struggler, the opportunistic individual, and the partially committed struggler, -and an ideal orientation, the authentic struggler." This categorization is important because it helps individuals and groups to identify obstacles and benefits of responses to seeking liberation or

---

[10]Paul Robeson, *Here I Stand. Boston:* Beacon, 1971.
[11]Karenga, *Introduction to Black Studies*, 193-197.

being in "the struggle."[12] Furthermore, Reiland Rabaka articulated a critical reading of Malcolm X's theory of social change in the advancement of African liberation. In 1963 while still with the Nation of Islam (NOI), Malcolm X espoused a plan for African Americans that broadly advocated "complete freedom, justice and equality" while discrediting the view that the NOI taught hate. In accomplishing these goals, he stressed the importance of unity, individual upliftment, and collective problem solving.[13] Rabaka demonstrated that in moving towards these goals, Malcolm X was grounded in the theoretical positions of African forebears, that he used this philosophical canon in his rhetoric and the practice of his life and work.[14]

Also in the scholarly tradition of Molefi Kete Asante, Mark Christian and Zizwe Poe advanced African agency as a critically viable tool for divesting western society of white supremacy. Evaluating the U.S. and the U.K. together, Christian suggested a broad and thorough understanding of the history and current unfolding of white supremacy. He also discussed the relevancy of the reparations debate as an essential part of the liberation discourse.[15] Zizwe Poe argued the importance of the agency framework in the philosophy of Kwame Nkrumah. Specifically within his construct of Pan-Africanism, Poe discussed the concepts of individual and organizational agency, precisely the primacy of African values as an important community-based strategy.[16]

Scholars have also asserted that language and the process of naming are essential to this overall process. This includes the origins of rap (and spoken word music) initially as a tool for social justice, and how the music industry privileged negative and violent rap music in the

---

[12]Marcia E. Sutherland, "Individual Differences in Response to the Struggle for the Liberation of People of African Descent," *Journal of Black Studies*, Vol. 20, No. 1. (September 1989), 40-59, 43.
[13]This was espoused in a 1963 television interview produced and moderated by Jim Hurlbut in Chicago, Illinois. The three NBC reporters who participated in the interview (which was framed as a discussion about the Nation of Islam's hatred of whites) were Charles McCuen, Floyd Kalber and Len O'Connor. See "City Desk: Malcolm X," WMAQ-TV (Chicago, IL), March 1, 1963.
[14]Reiland Rabaka, "Malcolm X and/as Critical Theory: Philosophy, Radical Politics, and the African American Search for Social Justice," *Journal of Black Studies*, Vol. 33, No. 2, (November 2002), 145-165.
[15]Mark Christian, "An African-Centered Perspective on White Supremacy," *Journal of Black Studies*, Vol. 33, No. 2, (November 2002), 179-198.
[16]Zizwe Poe, "The Construction of an Africalogical Method to Examine Nkrumahism's Contribution to Pan-African Agency," *Journal of Black Studies*, Vol. 31, No. 6 (July 2001), 729-745, 738.

public domain has eclipsed this thrust.[17] This speaks to the force of mass media's representation (particularly in the news) of people of African descent. Understanding the use of language reflects one of the highest forms of African agency because "naming, definition, interpretation, and conceptualization have been integral components of the African American struggle for liberation, freedom, and progress in the United States. Nevertheless, these components do not necessarily mirror reality. There are times when they impose meaning on a particular reality. The cultural and political status of African Americans has often been subject to the whims of definition, interpretation, and conceptualization."[18] For blacks it is the recognition that negatively labeling the black youth called the Jena 6, for example, as the model for juvenile criminality in Louisiana or the United States, is a selectively deleterious marker on the black community.[19] Naming representation is also the essential theme in the concept of social network conservation where the public's attention to community care ensures that perceptions are managed favorably or at least accurately.

Citizen Journalism, the Testimony of Kevin Moore, and Original Local Media

However, in terms of citizen journalism and ad hoc vigilante reporting, it can be argued that the man directly responsible for the 2015 Baltimore Uprising was Kevin Moore. Moore captured just one of

---

[17] Among the many early articles tracing the socially conscious origins of rap music see Errol A. Henderson, "Black Nationalism and Rap Music," *Journal of Black Studies*, Vol. 26, No. 3 (January 1996), 308-339; T. Rose, "'Fear Of A Black Planet': Rap Music And Black Cultural Politics In The 1990s." *Journal of Negro Education*, 60, 276-290, 1991; T. Rose, *Black Noise: Rap Music and Black Culture in Contemporary America*. Hanover, NH: Wesleyan University Press, 1994.
[18] Anthony Neal, "The Naming: A Conceptualization of an African American Connotative Struggle," *Journal of Black Studies*, Vol. 32, No. 1 (September 2001), 50-65, 51.
[19] Six African American teenagers (student athletes) in Jena, Louisiana (Robert Bailey, Mychal Bell, Carwin Jones, Bryant Purvis, Jesse Ray Beard, and Theo Shaw, all between 14-17 years old). In late 2006 they were convicted of beating (attempted murder) a white teenager. When racial hate "pranks" (the hanging of nooses, etc.) went unaddressed at the school, the students protested, and the school and local authorities ignored and threatened them. Racial animus among school students escalated, resulting in widespread interracial altercations. The case demonstrated how black students were singularly and excessively charged in such cases.

the video images of Freddie Gray's April 12 arrest.[20] Cautious video activists like Moore know the power of the camera. Moore's remarks to the media about his video suggested that he, a member of Baltimore Copwatch, not only understood the value of the tape in the current moment, but as an important asset to the history of the case. Copwatch, an organization committed to documenting (via videotape) the policing of citizens, has helped to make the practice an officially recognized public activity. California based Copwatch are "a group of community residents and students who have become outraged by the escalation of police misconduct, harassment and brutality in recent years."[21] The group seeks to decrease law enforcement violence against citizens through documenting the public practices of police and educating the community. According to Moore's public statements, he was on the street at the time Gray was arrested. Moore has maintained that Gray was tased and yelling in fear. Moore stated that the police held Gray in impossible holds, bending him "…like he was a crab or a piece of origami." Moore cooperated with the police at all levels, including volunteering his statement and giving them his video of the Freddie Gray arrest. Nevertheless, he languished in the police department for several hours. The police did not seem to recall this, or coordinate their efforts in this aspect of data gathering.

  Not long after he gave his statement to police, Moore stated that he was "wanted" by the BCPD for questioning, as if he were a person of interest. Moore was very concerned about his role in the whole matter. He had never recorded police activity before; and when he posted the video to the internet, it went viral. In terms of charges of police misconduct, most police departments had already discerned that video uploaded to the internet *was the most important determining factor* in how the public would react, in what way police agencies would be viewed, and whether officers would be held accountable. The Baltimore Police department's policy on video recording was not new, the 2011 document stated, "It is the policy of the Baltimore Police Department to ensure the protection and preservation of every person's

---

[20]There were a number of videos of Gray's arrest, including individuals like Moore. There was also the Michelle Gross cell phone video, and city's street surveillance cameras.
[21]*Copwatch Handbook an Introduction to Citizen Monitoring of the Police*, n.p., n.d., Berkeley, California, 2, 4-5.

Constitutional Rights."[22] The policy reiterated the rights of citizens to record, but defined the circumstances under which police can arrest the recorder, or confiscate the video (which usually meant a search and seizure order). According to the 2011 policy, people who record the police in public are "uninvolved bystanders" who can be jailed if they hinder the police.[23] Despite this policy Kianga Mwamba sued the Baltimore City Police Department in early spring of 2014 when she was "...brutally attacked in her vehicle" by police as she attempted to record a man in handcuffs she observed being beaten by police. In addition to one officer referring to her as a "dumb bitch," Mwamba was arrested and held on a $75,000 bond.[24] More than a year later, the city of Baltimore settled Mwamba's case for $60,000.

Even so, Moore knew that throughout the nation police were targeting ordinary citizens who used their cell phones to videotape their public activities. One of the most notable cases was that of Ramsey Orta in New York City. Orta captured police activity in the chokehold death of Eric Garner in New York on July 17, 2015. The medical examiner found that Garner died from a chokehold and the force police applied to his chest. This was another high profile police-custody death, caught on video, which initiated citywide protests and national outrage. Orta was arrested on possession of weapons charges. He maintained that this arrest was police-revenge; and that since the video was made public the police followed and harassed him and his family. Orta was held on $75,000 bail. Kevin Moore went on his Facebook page and asked people not to post his photograph because "...it's very uncomfortable knowing that the law is looking for me!!" Like Orta, Moore believed that a campaign of police intimidation for voluntarily coming forth with information that might indict the law enforcement officers was taking place. Moore was arrested within days of giving these kinds of statements to the mass media. He was arrested for a minor traffic stop violation, along with Chad Jackson and Tony White (aka Talal Ahmad). The men had been involved in the earlier protests

---

[22]Baltimore Police Department, General Order J-16, "Video Recording of Police Activity," November 8, 2011, 7pp. https://ia801005.us.archive.org/3/items/291576-j-16-video-recording-of-police-activity/291576-j-16-video-recording-of-police-activity.pdf, accessed May 15, 2015.
[23]Baltimore Police Department, General Order J-16, "Video Recording of Police Activity," accessed May 15, 2015.
[24]*Kianga Mwamba v. Baltimore City Police and Mayor and City Council of Baltimore et al,* Circuit Court for Baltimore City, 2014.

World To Come: Essays On The Baltimore Uprising, Militant Racism, And History

during the day (with Moore sporting a Guy Fawkes mask), and they were in a car with Missouri tags. Jackson and Ahmad, along with Moore, were also meeting to establish a Baltimore chapter of *WeCopwatch*. While Moore was released from custody within in a few hours, his associates were not. He believed this was further evidence of police harassment and intimidation. From Moore's perspective, his arrest had nothing to do with a routine traffic stop. This was about citizen journalism—filming Gray's arrest, participating in the Ferguson, Missouri protests; and his willingness to speak freely to print and digital media outlets about his perceptions of police harassment.

In the days surrounding the Baltimore Uprising, television, print and digital outlets all over the world feverishly recycled stories about the riot. Investigative reporters from Baltimore television stations provided constant coverage of the Baltimore Uprising, often emphasizing the riot aspect. The local television stations included major corporate networks *ABC, NBC, CBS*, and *Fox*. It should also be noted that *Al Jazeera America* produced on-the-ground documentaries and numerous news features on Ferguson and Baltimore in 2015. For the most part, original news stories were supplied by local agencies such as the *Baltimore Sun, The City Paper*, and the *Afro-American*. When the news cycle waned, there were only a few media sources that continued to discuss the meaning of the uprising to the city and the community of Sandtown/Winchester. *The Baltimore Sun* added "Freddie Gray case updates" to its email subscription newsletter gallery. This historic local newspaper led the original reporting beyond the riot event. *The Baltimore Sun's* constant attention to the many facets of the Baltimore Uprising, especially the police officers under indictment, threatened their defense attorneys who feared their coverage would bias the cases. Local AM radio stations like WBAL News Radio 1090 contributed coverage to the Baltimore Uprising. This was also true of local public radio, which was attentive to the uprising in the midst of the event, and long after. WYPR 88.1 and WEAA 88.9 collaborated to produce significant content. WYPR ("Your Public Radio") covered the uprising in its mission to "…enrich the minds and spirits of our listeners and ultimately strengthen the communities we serve."[25] These stations and notably WEAA provided continuous coverage, from a variety of perspectives, and with attention to problem solving. However, WEAA ("We Educate African Americans") 88.9, a Baltimore public radio

---

[25]About WYPR, 88.1, Wypr.org., http://wypr.org/about-wypr, accessed May 29, 2015.

World To Come: Essays On The Baltimore Uprising, Militant Racism, And History

channel that presents jazz and talk programming that "strives to educate and enlighten,"[26] ultimately commanded the on-air news coverage of the Baltimore Uprising. The station, which began in 1977, is an NPR affiliate and serviced by Morgan State University, one of Baltimore's premier Historical Black Colleges. From the beginning, WEAA created a strong presence in connecting with the black community over the riots. On air talk-show personalities like Farajii Muhammad, Sean Yoes, Charles D. Ellison, Marilyn Harris-Davis, Anthony McCarthy, and Beverly Burke contributed significantly to the talk programming, which allowed for intensive community-based dialogue after the riot. Two prominent shows on WEAA, Baltimore's *The Marc Steiner Show*, hosted by Marc Steiner; and the nationally syndicated news program *Democracy Now!* created and hosted by Amy Goodman, continued to feature original news and commentary about the Baltimore Uprising, and events central to the city of Baltimore in the aftermath of the event, and long after other talk media moved to other subjects. However, the most up-to-date information came from independent social media—including feeds from professional and lay journalists—but mostly from ordinary citizens and activists.

The Yette Hypothesis and the Nefarious Option

The Black Lives Matter movement is deeply connected to the issues of racial justice, solidarity among African American people, and the preservation of the black nation. On this later point, one of the most important books ever written addressing the African American experience, which was received with high distinction (as well as an inordinate amount of distress)—and then forgotten—is Samuel F. Yette's work, *The Choice, the Issue of Black Survival in America*. Born in 1929, Samuel Yette was an active professional journalist, with years of extensive experience in researching and analyzing the American media, especially the issue of racism. In 1968, Yette became the first black correspondent for *Newsweek*, covering the Washington desk. He also wrote significant columns and opinions for numerous newspapers across the country. His career included a term in higher education and a government appointment as special assistant for Civil Rights at the U.S. Office of Economic Opportunity in 1964. Yette's insight exposed the media's stagnation over and reticence to fairly covering African

---

[26]About WEAA 88.9, WEAA.Org., http://weaa.org/node/1, accessed May 29, 2015.

WORLD TO COME: ESSAYS ON THE BALTIMORE UPRISING, MILITANT RACISM, AND HISTORY

Americans in the news—and the concerted efforts to frame Blacks negatively. The media was just an apparatus of a society that seemingly had abandoned ideals of racial equality. In 1971, Yette published *The Choice*, which outlined the basic premises regarding the future of black people in American society. First, Yette stated that African Americans were perceived, as an obsolete people in the United States.[27] Blacks were considered obsolete because their labor as slaves was no longer needed. Second, the United States government had declared war on Blacks at the same time it was engaged in the Vietnam War.[28] This declaration of war was a direct result of black obsolescence, and their demands for racial equality and justice. Yette's analysis of the state of Black America formed an interesting hypothesis. Blacks had shown historically that they would challenge persistent racism, and assertively protest the assassinations of respected leaders like Martin Luther King, Jr. and Malcolm X. The established order, concerned over rogue (independent) media and the national implications of the protests, revolts, riots—and even the rhetoric of Black Power, set out to resolve the problem. Yette surmised that there were three options before the American nation regarding African American people—liberation, pacification and liquidation. However, there were only two real courses of action that appealed to the system—pacification and liquidation. The Yette Hypothesis exposed the American media's continued complicity in the sixties and seventies pacification and liquidation intentions and schemes directed toward people of African descent.

The Yette Hypothesis states that society's motives concerning African Americans teeters between various expressions of these two plans. Pacification would be used to quell radical and even moderate demands for equal opportunity and justice. As Yette noted, one strategy was to appoint Blacks to high-level posts, but for the most part, they simply displayed their own "powerless visibility."[29] This would be effective in persuading the black masses that *some* action towards expanding human diversity and equality had taken place. Pacification programs would be developed to demonstrate the government's interest in the dilemma of the black poor, but these entities would possess other important functions, which included monitoring black

---

[27]Samuel F. Yette, *The Choice: The Issue of Black Survival in America*, Silver Spring, MD: Cottage Books, 1996, 17-18.
[28]Ibid., 15.
[29]Ibid., 20.

radicals and moderates, surveillance and a physical survey of ghettos, and aiding the capital expansion aspirations of the urban business sector. If society decided that pacification would be the primary course, certainly there was a shift in the actual strategy and movement toward the latter. Yette detailed the concerns and the interests many had; both white and black, that genocide and concentration camps were the future for the masses of African Americans. The movement that took place was the moral and ethical problem of wholesale genocide in the shadow of the Jewish Holocaust in Europe. The question was how to control and contain the black masses without direct physical liquidation—and with the tacit diminishment and dismissal of pacification programs. The media would be used to sustain the image of the historic black threat. Continuing with the black public spectacle theme would accomplish this. The media could continue to perpetuate the framed negative beliefs about black people—and as the 1990s bore out—African Americans, other people of color, and all poor people would essentially be left to their own devices regarding how to shape their own public image.

Yette confirmed that the actual act of liberation, including full and free access to society, would never be allowed to African American people. Therefore, the only options left were pacification and liquidation. According to Yette, President Lyndon Johnson's Great Society pacification programs for African Americans ended in failure in 1965.[30] Thereafter, a course of liquidation was embarked upon. Any gains made by Blacks to date are vestiges of the sixties and seventies— remnants that have not yet been dismantled. To be sure, liquidation can take many forms (physical, psychological, cultural)—and the most potent weapon for Blacks striving for the American Dream, while forging a Wilderness existence, is the mass media. This too can be linked to Yette's analysis concerning the "The Psychic Preparation" of Blacks to accept pacification.[31] In addition, Black Colleges and Universities would be subjected to various policy controls, forms of surveillance, and perennial public attacks, usually culminating in racially burdensome questions about their viability and ultimate value to American society. In 1971, Samuel Yette revealed that key national decisions had to be made in order to deal with the urban revolt of Backs weary of the outcomes of systemic racism—poverty, under and

---

[30]Ibid., 20, 21, 72.
[31]Ibid., 80-89.

unemployment, poor education, and a legacy of political disfranchisement. It was important to deal with the implications of the Civil Rights movement, and especially Black Power expression in the sixties. Yette's findings were truly apocalyptic for African Americans. He saw what the established order of the sixties and seventies already knew—that if left unchecked—the agency inherent in Black Power, black activism, and even Black Colleges could lead to the freedom that Blacks envisioned in American society. Black empowerment would not allow them to remain in a subordinated and pacified place. Yette also illustrated that authentic demonstrations of African American racial, cultural, social, economic or political unity would be recast as a threat to society and cause the implementation of extreme methods of social control. The two choices relegated to the Black nation—pacification or liquidation—were based on the racial belief that Blacks, whose original purpose was to provide a large free labor force as enslaved persons, had outlived this role in American society. Thus, as Yette surmised, the Black nation seemingly had the choices of liberation, pacification or liquidation. Unfortunately, the liberation that African Americans so passionately sought—one free from racism—was not in reality ever among the options.

CHAPTER 6

BALTIMORE'S WILDERNESS + "RIOT"= "UPRISING"

> History does not take place in a vacuum. Historical events, be they great or small, do not exist in isolation, but are a product of the age during which they occurred. Often times, the reasons why a particular historical incident turned out the way it did can be readily located, while for others, the causes may be more difficult to locate. In both cases, one rule still holds true: that the events of the past cannot be separated from the era when they occurred.—Scott Ellsworth[1]

Freddie Gray and the Wilderness

Freddie Gray was martyred as his family, friends, community leaders, Civil Rights dignitaries and hundreds of others attended his funeral. He was sacrificed for many reasons, but one reason was because he lived in the Wilderness, and the people found a powerful narrative in his life and death. According to Molefi Kete Asante, the Wilderness is filled with racial discontent. It is the reflection of a society in conflict over the American Dream. The Wilderness is the opposite of the American Dream; and contains the struggles of gender. It is a geographical distortion produced by racism.[2] A defining feature of the Wilderness is the failure of society to comprehend the outcomes of long-term disorientation and oppression experienced by blacks. It is the act of seeing people, but not knowing who they are. It is the art of creating mystery, enabling disbelief, and embracing denial—by accepting the long history of police aggression against blacks.[3] However, to be a Wilderness dweller is not to be a thug, gangster, ne'er-do-well, or a disposable person. People are compelled to live on the fringes of society, in a world historically and narrowly defined by systemic racist external forces that have existed for generations; and

---

[1]Scott Ellsworth, *The Tulsa Race Riot. Tulsa Race Riot: A Report*, 2001.
[2]Molefi Kete Asante, *Erasing Racism: The Survival of the American Nation*. Amherst, NY: Prometheus Books, 2003. See Chapter 2.
[3]Ibid., See Chapter 4.

World To Come: Essays On The Baltimore Uprising, Militant Racism, And History

one that has sustained "concentrated poverty." Unaddressed historic inequities are very often misunderstood and sacrificed in the contemporary discussion. Long-term deprivation is political fodder, especially when it comes to the Wilderness experience. To eliminate the Wilderness requires local, regional and national commitment to an ideal that all humans have a right to an equal quality of life; to just resolutions for past inequities and atrocities.

The Wilderness is a highly complex police state that shapes a way of being. In the Wilderness, people do have a tipping point. This is not about demographics or population density. This is the place where the anger and frustration of people spill over. We do not know exactly when the shift in collective consciousness took place in the Baltimore Uprising. However, we can find early warning signs in the diminishing quality of life indicators. The least of the disaffected have their reasons, especially when it comes to police-encounters. The Wilderness generates immense psychic chaos as citizens try to make sense of their existence. Residents learn that the police can stop them for no reason, because they *look* suspicious or evasive. Based on the vast number of people stopped and released; those who are frisked, searched, and/or detained, are oblivious—beyond race—as to why they were targeted. Wilderness dwellers are meant to understand that police beat, harass, and arrest them because *they* are afraid of them. They learn that anyone can be arrested for petty crimes, or that low-level drug dealers can be arrested, but major traffickers and purveyors of drug violence are elusive. It is not unusual for citizens to be subjected to physical force in the process of being stopped by the police. What shape does the world take when police-encounters devolve into incredible forms of brutality and disrespect? What happens when a woman is slapped by a police detective for "bumping into him…?" Why would an officer engage in "Punting a handcuffed, face down, suspect in the face, after a foot chase (?)." What do people learn from police-encounters that involve "Pissing and shitting inside suspects' homes during raids, on their beds and clothes?"[4] People will perceive several appalling messages—but most of all they learn from police that their lives do not matter.

---

[4] Michael A. Wood, Jr., Twitter feeds (@MichaelAWoodJr), June 24, 2015. Wood was a sergeant in the Baltimore Police department for ten years; see also *Over Policed, Yet Underserved: The People's Findings Regarding Police Misconduct in West Baltimore*, Baltimore, MD: No Boundaries Coalition and the West Baltimore Commission on Police Misconduct, March 8, 2016, the appendix, "Highlights of Interviews by the Commission," 25-29.

World To Come: Essays On The Baltimore Uprising, Militant Racism, And History

The Baltimore Wished For and the State of Black Baltimore

Everyone was aware that the actions of the Baltimore City Police Department (BCPD) "...represented Baltimore on a worldwide stage..."[5] Freddie Gray died in the late spring of 2015 and it took less than two months for the city of Baltimore to react to the massive national and international coverage over his death and the Baltimore Uprising. Summer was coming and city officials and residents were claiming that there was too much negative focus on a city with so much to offer its residents and tourists. Baltimore needed to be known publically, as the popular urban destination it had always been, as Charm city, a Monument town, home of the Inner Harbor seaport, the Baltimore Ravens and the Orioles. Besides Baltimore was the state's flagship city poised to recapture its demographics and increase commercial growth. Baltimore had numerous legacies in support of this aim as demonstrated by many universities, and a dedicated medicine, science and technology corridor. Anyone can cite the innumerable problems in a major American inner city, and Baltimore was no exception. The city, through print and online media sources attempted to reeducate the world about the city of Baltimore.

The Baltimore Sun reminded its readers "...of the many things that make Baltimore wonderful on any given day or night."[6] The refocused message, from a variety of sources, included mention of scenic destinations, as well as familiar sites like the National Aquarium, the Baltimore Symphony, the Maryland Zoo, and Pimlico—in addition to the many museums, neighborhood pubs and eateries—and eclectic attractions such as the house of Edgar Allan Poe and his grave. This effort to rebrand the city also included the many prominent landmarks in the history of black Baltimore, and educational destinations such as the Great Blacks in Wax Museum, the Reginald F. Lewis Museum of African American History and Culture, and the historic *Afro-American Newspaper*. Then there are the subaltern cultures of Baltimore that speak to great artistic and intellectual spaces (cooperatives, environmentalists), undoubtedly including havens such as Red Emma's. The overall message was about pride, history, cultural diversity, healing, unity, and—consumer opportunity. The threads of this message could be seen emanating from institutions, offices, agencies and individuals—

---

[5] Anthony Batts, "Police Commissioner's Message" Email to BCPD, April 26, 2015.
[6] "101 Days & Nights in Baltimore," *The Baltimore Sun*, June 14, 2015, 4.

WORLD TO COME: ESSAYS ON THE BALTIMORE UPRISING,
MILITANT RACISM, AND HISTORY

that Baltimore was more than Freddie Gray's death, the critical questions about police-custody encounters, and the Baltimore Uprising.

Meanwhile, Baltimore has more than a half million residents and the city is predominately black. At least a third of the city's eastern population is below the established poverty indicators. The children of Baltimore share the same poverty statistics for health as those found in major world urban cities such as Johannesburg, New Delhi, and Shanghai.[7] This includes forgotten neighborhoods—some of them affected by the predatory lending schemes that caused foreclosures during the recession. These Baltimore neighborhoods are filled with cramped and abandoned buildings (specters of once beautiful old row houses), liquor stores, funeral parlors, but are generally bereft of parks, recreational centers, full-service grocery stores, and medical (including mental) health centers. Moreover, with ample trash, Baltimore has been ranked among the top 10 dirtiest cities in the United States. Poor residents are charged more for goods and services and are at risk of losing basic needs such as water due to high bills and a purportedly disorganized bureaucracy. Moreover, because of historic racial housing covenants in the city black neighborhoods were always racially restricted and contained. Over time black neighborhoods were not allowed to expand and develop (ultimately forced into commercial development or gentrification) in the way urban ethnic neighborhood communities tend to when they are part of a larger city plan. Baltimore native, author, and university lecturer D. Watkins called this latter development "Gentri-fuckin-cation," the routine displacement of black communities. Watkins saw the city of Baltimore "…becoming a place for the rich and I don't speak their language."[8]

In terms of public education (K-12), Baltimore city schools were never truly integrated, they experienced persistent inadequate funding,[9] and this challenge, in part, helped to produce some of its systemic issues. The education system in Baltimore has received its share of severe criticism over the years. Baltimore city schools have had

---

[7]Kristin Mmari, et al., "A Global Study on the Influence of Neighborhood Contextual Factors on Adolescent Health," *Journal of Adolescent Health*, Vol. 55, No. 6, Supplement, December 2014, S13-S20. http://www.jahonline.org/article/S1054-139X%2814%2900355-3/fulltext, Accessed May 2, 2015.
[8]D. Watkins, "Black History Bulldozed For Another Starbucks: Against the New Baltimore," *Salon*, March 23, 2015.
[9]Diane W. Cipollone, "Gambling on a Settlement: The Baltimore City Schools Adequacy Litigations." *Journal of Education Finance* (1998): 87-107.

among the lowest high school graduation rates in the state, and where, at best, 60-69 percent of the students graduate.[10] Baltimore has also been cited as an example of an urban school district, which punitively suspends black students. In the state of Maryland, black students are more likely to attend segregated public schools, which are referred to across the nation as "apartheid schools" because of the concentration of low-income and impoverished students. In apartheid schools students are not only segregated by race and class; they are then provided an inferior education. The final component of this is advancing students to higher grades and allowing them to graduate when they are not academically prepared. In the poorest communities, another problem is that half the high school students experience chronic absenteeism. This was true for Baltimore city schools in 2008.[11] Further, this includes the fiscal challenges and institutional failures of Baltimore public schools. Public schools with ideal academic track records (like Langston Hughes Elementary) were closed, ostensively to make room for charter schools. In addition, some schoolchildren are subjected to the same typical racial micro-aggressions as their parents. Apparently when schools resumed after the riot aspect of the Baltimore Uprising, some children, if they appeared to be wearing new clothing, were queried—suggesting that any new items were part of the material procured by looters. Within a few weeks of the uprising, on June 3, 2015 150 layoff notices were given to Baltimore City School employees.

Baltimore is similar to other major cities with large black and poor populations forced to live in overcrowded, neglected housing "projects" and left to white-collar predators peddling nearly every scheme known to man; as well as other opportunists (internal and external) fomenting petty economic chaos in the community. The challenges are many. Local living wage jobs are nearly nonexistent for the average Baltimore high school graduate. In addition, add any kind of arrest record, and the odds of finding even a low-wage job are scarce. One estimate suggests "…if you grow up in Baltimore from birth, you're earning 17 percent less than if you were to grow up in an

---

[10]"High School Graduation Rates in Maryland," *Maryland Equity Project*, Data Brief, January 2014; see also Rachel E. Durham, Marc L. Stein, and Faith Connolly, "College Opportunities and Success: Baltimore City Graduates through the Class of 2014," Baltimore: BERC, November, 2015, 41pp, 7.
[11]Martha Abele Mac Iver, and D. J. Mac Iver. "Gradual Disengagement: A Portrait of the 2008-09 Dropouts in the Baltimore City Schools." *Baltimore Education Research Consortium* (2010), 7-8.

average place."[12] These neighborhoods are typically described as food deserts with residents who are food insecure. This is because, as defined by the U.S. Department of Agriculture, a food desert is a "…area in the United States with limited access to affordable and nutritious food, particularly such an area composed of predominantly lower income neighborhoods and communities."[13] For many areas including West Baltimore this means the "…literal absence of retail food"[14] outlets. These communities in the city are also defined by inordinate environmental risks. For example, lead paint poisoning, which for decades was widely denied as posing any public health risk in American urban areas, is a potential health factor for many children. These areas are places that give birth to the many Freddie Grays of the world. Residents repeatedly complain about being "occupied," brutalized, disrespected, and harassed by the police. Moreover, they know when they have been miseducated by underprepared, overwhelmed, or disinterested teachers. Most of the youth are no stranger to the various forms of random acts of violence perpetrated by desperate people. It has been asserted that Gray and his sister had been victims of severe lead paint poisoning as a child; that he was severely miseducated in the schools, and at some point had a drug addiction. Yet he lived in an area preyed upon by the purveyors of illicit drugs. The mainstream media quickly pointed this out and emphasized that Gray had been arrested 24 times—nearly one arrest for everyday he was alive; and that he had a recent arrest for drug possession, which he denied, and even suggested that the police had framed him. Whether or not this is true, Gray understood that when he made eye contact with the police the only path that lay before him in the Wilderness was incarceration. His community, that of Pennsylvania and West North Avenues and in West Baltimore (Sandtown-Winchester) specifically, as

---

[12] Emily Badger, Jonathan Rothwell, and Margery Turner. "Panel," "Place And Opportunity: What Now For Policy? A Conversation with Harvard's Raj Chetty," Proceedings, The Brookings Institution, *POLICY,* Washington, D.C., June 1, 2015, 68pp.
[13] The U.S. Department of Agriculture used the definition of food desert from the Farm Bill of 2008. See Report to Congress, "Access to Affordable and Nutritious Food, Measuring and Understanding Food Deserts and Their Consequences," United States Department of Agriculture, June 2009, 1.
[14] Julie Beaulac, Elizabeth Kristjansson, Steven Cummins, "A Systematic Review of Food Deserts, 1966-2007." *Preventing Chronic Disease* 2009; 6 (3): A105. http://www.cdc.gov/pcd/issues/2009/jul/08_0163.htm, Accessed November 21, 2015.

World To Come: Essays On The Baltimore Uprising, Militant Racism, And History

courageous and socially active as many of its members are, was not truly meant to thrive and neither was he. Gray, West Baltimore, and a host of other impoverished areas inhabited by blacks in the city, and around the country, are immersed in the Wilderness experience—one that has systemically denied them the promise of the American Dream.

One of the most pervasive problems in the city of Baltimore has to do with the murder rate—those fatalities that do not directly involve police officers. Long before the Baltimore Uprising, the city had earned a reputation for leading the nation in violent crimes, especially murder, vying with New York and Chicago, Charm City was dubbed "the murder capital of the United States." By the 1990s Baltimore was considered one of the most violent and drug-ridden cities in the country. The mayor during this timeframe (1987-1999), Kurt L. Schmoke recalled that the city experienced within a decade, over 300 homicides annually.[15] These deaths were largely the result of the illegal crack-cocaine trade and the gang wars. Black males, especially those between the ages of 18 and 24, were more likely to die in major cities like Baltimore (as well as Chicago, Washington, D.C., Los Angeles, and Detroit) than any other place. The city has been battling this critical issue and this image for years. By the early 2000s, the city had determined that the main reason for the high murder rate was the infusion of illicit drugs into the community. The domestic war on drugs was not successful and it passed over the city of Baltimore. The prison population rose, but also the cases of drug addiction seemed to rise with no end in sight. Immediately after the Baltimore Uprising, there was a surge in the number of murders in the city. The city had not seen such numbers for more than forty years. Some people blamed the police for ostensively "standing down" or slowing down their efforts to police communities after the riots. Others said that the high murder rate was something that the city was never able to get a firm grasp on; and certainly, the issue and incidence of record-breaking homicides would receive attention as a result of the riots. Still, other critical comments were meant to indict the community's protests over police brutality.[16] The logic here separated the issue of policing from that of

---

[15] Andrew R. Koch, "UB President Schmoke discusses upcoming police officer trials," *The UB Post*, September 29, 2015, https://theubpost.wordpress.com/2015/09/29/ub-president-schmoke-discusses-upcoming-police-officer-trials/, accessed September 30, 30215.
[16] This was being called the "Ferguson Effect" (a reference to social media, demonstrations, policing behavior, and increased homicides following the Ferguson

World To Come: Essays On The Baltimore Uprising, Militant Racism, And History

violence within the community, suggesting that since concentrations of blacks experienced high mortality rates, *they* should not be concerned over allegations of police brutality. It was a troubling form of racial logic. Yet, it didn't explain the failure of past policing practices—especially the frequency with which illegal weapons are acquired, random gun violence, and the constant infiltration of illicit drugs. Charges of police brutality by Baltimore activists and protesters further underscored the prevalent failures of crime prevention in the city.

In May 2015, Baltimore's murder rate climbed higher than it had ever been, and the greater community was perplexed and outraged. City officials and police were compelled to respond in the wake of the uprising, forced to give the community answers. On June 3, 2015, Police Commissioner Anthony Batts held a press conference and gave an official response to the spike in the murder rate. Essentially, that the new homicide level was directly related to the riots. Batts stated that during the riot, 27 area pharmacies (and 2 methadone clinics) had been looted of drugs, and these medications had made it to the streets. As a result, people were dying because they were fighting over the newfound illicit drug trade. According to Batts, the amount of drugs taken during the riots was so significant that it could keep the city "…intoxicated for a year."[17] The *Baltimore City Paper* took issue with the impact of the amount of drugs that had been taken during the looting. They called the assertion "preposterous," recalculated the results, and did not find the same outcome.[18] Yet the press conference served several aims. It gave a definitive reason for the rise in the city's mortality rate. The Baltimore Uprising was one crisis, now with the high homicide rate the city was immediately plunged into yet another state of emergency. Once again the press conference centered drugs as the main problem. Drugs contributed to increased violence, engendered crime, created health issues, and overall lowered the quality of life for the communities hit the hardest. It appeared to be one of those "too big" social problems that law enforcement could not get a handle on. The 1970s "war on drugs" implemented by President Nixon and carried on in earnest by

---

Missouri police-encounter death of Michael Brown). The term caused a media uproar in the Fall 2015 when FBI Director James Comey made reference to it.
[17] City of Baltimore, Baltimore Police Department, Press Conference, June 3, 2015.
[18] Edward Erickson, Jr. and Evan Serpick, "Enough Narcotics to keep the city Intoxicated for a year? Checking Batts' Fuzzy Drug Math," *Baltimore City Paper*, June 4, 2015, http://www.citypaper.com/blogs/the-news-hole/bcpnews-checking-batts-fuzzy-drug-math-20150604,0,5269132.story, accessed June 4, 2015.

World To Come: Essays On The Baltimore Uprising, Militant Racism, And History

President Reagan, had many facets, but one—the drug addicted person—had been so vilified (largely using Marijuana as the gateway drug example) that American society saw only a criminal offender, not a person in a serious health crisis. The war on drugs created a complex drug enforcement industry—so convoluted, bureaucratic, and propagandized that it was easy to blame illicit drugs—and thus dependent users—for all of society's ills without any further argument. It was a moral issue, and the press conference criminalized the Baltimore Uprising as an opportunity for some to flood the city with illicit drugs. Finally, the press conference appeared to absolve police for any role in the city's increased mortality rate and for criticisms over the immediate post-Freddie Gray policing practices.

When state's attorney Marilyn Mosby announced May 1, 2015 that Freddie Gray should have never been subject to arrest, mass incarceration became another more visible domestic racial issue stemming from the Baltimore Uprising. The United States incarcerates more people than anywhere else in the world;[19] and more members of its demographic minority groups than any other nation. Mass incarceration of African Americans in the United States has been a pervasive social element for so long there has been an attempt to normalize the experience. It was similar to the efforts to standardize poverty, drug addiction, and miseducation in black communities, and then turn these quality of life negations into an aspect of black "culture." Anti-mass incarceration activists have said that the systemic practice of placing blacks in prison is directly connected to poverty, unemployment, increased crime, disfranchisement, gentrification, eugenics, slavery, and promotes domestic social and economic irresponsibility. The general statistics of who is more subject to incarceration vary slightly. We know that approximately 2 million people are incarcerated and that 60 percent of the prison population is made up of African Americans and Latinos. However, black men (especially under the age of 30) have a much higher risk than any group (1/35) of serving time in the criminal justice system.

Of the many important recent perspectives on mass incarceration, two views came from scholar-analysts James Braxton Peterson and Michelle Alexander. Peterson, in his review of President

---

[19]Roy Walmsley, *World Prison Population List* (tenth edition), International Centre for Prison Studies (ICPS), London: The University of Essex, 2003.

World To Come: Essays On The Baltimore Uprising, Militant Racism, And History

Obama's mass incarceration speech to the NAACP[20] and his visit to the El Reno Federal Correction Institution (both in July 2015) linked the education system directly to mass incarceration. Peterson emphasized that black youth are more often subjected to school suspensions that eventually lead to dropping out.[21] Thereafter they either become involved in criminal activity or are subjected to racial profiling and criminalization. The other current thesis that captured academic and public attention on the criminal justice system was explored by Michelle Alexander in her work *The New Jim Crow*. Alexander likened the history of Jim Crow racial segregation to the mass incarceration approach of law and order that specifically targets blacks. Not only is mass incarceration a national problem—it is a crisis, "a national emergency."[22] The processes of the New Jim Crow are directly linked to the trendy (though not new) race relations concept of colorblindness, which in its most benevolent understanding seeks to deny race (as cultural construct, or a biological health category) in an effort to eliminate racism (the use of race to establish primacy over other humans). Alexander astutely contended (that despite declared forms of deracination) that mass incarceration developed into a "…stunningly comprehensive and well-disguised system of racialized social control…"[23]

The Riot—A Synopsis of Domestic Civil Unrest and Race in American History

While it is a disconcerting disruption to the established order, the tendency to riot—a form of domestic civil unrest—is as old as humanity. Riots have changed the course of world history. By a strict definition, a riot is a public disturbance that can include a number of activities deemed hazardous to the general population. These actions encompass wide-ranging disorder, nonviolent resistance, confrontation with law enforcement, assault, arson, looting, bodily injury, loss of life, and destruction of property. A riot is an extreme action against the

---

[20]106th Annual NAACP Convention, Philadelphia, PA, July 14, 2015.
[21]James Braxton Peterson, "America's Mass Incarceration System: Freedom's Next Frontier," *Reuters,* July 24, 2015, http://blogs.reuters.com/great-debate/2015/07/23/americas-mass-incarceration-system-freedoms-next-frontier/, accessed August 3, 2015.
[22]Cornell West is quoted in Michelle Alexander, *The new Jim Crow: Mass Incarceration in the Age of Colorblindness.* The New Press, 2012, x.
[23]Michelle Alexander, 2012, 4.

World To Come: Essays On The Baltimore Uprising, Militant Racism, And History

established order, and is usually fixed in a specific cause or a series of causes. Some analysts believe a riot is a function of the group mind, where people have collectively reached a threshold. As a result, a riot has elements of destruction and violence that meet the strict definition. While the riot is a form of mass behavior, it does not necessarily involve large numbers of people. In some states, it takes at least two people to riot. A generic definition of inciting a riot involves advocating others to participate in public disorderly conduct, the nature of which is considered injurious to the public health and well-being of the citizens. Riots can occur spontaneously—but rarely happen for no underlying reason. Tacticians know that a riot has a cause, a history, and a trajectory. It is maintained here that the issue of racism (specifically anti-African) is primary and static in the ritual of riot in the history of the United States. Added to this, we find distinct causal sub-factors (labor, education, voting, housing, etc.) that are repetitive, and like the issue of racism, these rarely change over time.

In the summer of 1863, the New York Draft Riots, an event whose major causes was anti-black racism and labor competition—was a major civil disturbance that had a number of concerns and consequences. The rioters were living in a time of great change—African freedom was at stake. The Civil War brought about National Conscription, which angered white males who resented being forced into fighting a war to end slavery. The massive mob violence that defined the event was targeted and aggressive: "…every unfortunate negro who appeared was chased and beaten, inflammatory speeches were being made, and threats openly uttered."[24] Within the riot, there was the attempt to annihilate people of African descent. This included the random pursuit and murder of blacks, and the burning down of the Colored Orphan Asylum. Thirty-five years later, in the Wilmington Race Riot of 1898, one of the main impetuses for the disturbance was fear over the black vote. Hundreds of whites invaded the black neighborhood and killed, intimidated, and harassed the residents. Thirty African Americans were killed. In this particular uprising, the rioters developed war-like strategies in advance of the invasion. When the first among the "Promised Land" riots began in 1900, initially in Harlem New York, the main issue was the impact of black migration on labor

---

[24] David M. Barnes, *The Draft Riots in New York July, 1863. The Metropolitan Police Their Services During Riot Week*. New York: Baker & Godwin, Printers and Publishers, 1863, 21-22.

in the north. Whites were anxious about black labor competition. When a fight occurred between a white police officer and a black man, the black man died. The event sparked two days of rioting in which police "stood down." Consequently, blacks were brutally beaten at random, and only blacks were arrested. In the August 1906 Brownsville Riot in Texas, African American soldiers from the 25th infantry were blamed for white lawlessness in the town, and because they had criticized racial discrimination. There was no evidence that the soldiers caused any disturbance in the town. However, black men in uniform posed a threat in white towns whose citizens were intimidated by them. The entire 25th Infantry was discharged, and only 14 were allowed back into military service. In the effort to disfranchise blacks, the "Atlanta Revolution" that shut down the city in 1906 was characterized by the beatings and terror that blacks suffered. Some blacks left the city, others fought back in self-defense. Like the riots that resulted from the early black migrations to the north, the Springfield, Illinois riot of 1908 also included the sub-factor of labor competition. In the Springfield Riot, black miners were used as strikebreakers, and this was also accompanied by calls for equality. In addition, a false accusation of rape was made. The Illinois state militia was called in. Eight blacks were killed in the riot. More than 2000 African Americans were intimidated and harassed—forced to leave their homes. As these blacks left the city as refugees, the white riot leaders went unpunished; and whites who did not cooperate in the attack on blacks were threatened.

 The World War I era riots were as challenging as those in previous years, but some scholars argue that they were more violent and inclusive of law enforcement. In July 1917, The East St. Louis riot, defined by the great migration of blacks during the war, fueled concerns over job and housing competition among whites. But seething underneath this was the fear that armed blacks would not only retaliate against brutality, but would seek to massacre whites. Blacks with political aspirations who demanded equality in the vote and education, etc. were subjected to random racial violence. In the St. Louis riot, blacks were tortured, burned out of their homes, and then shot. Black men were lynched and black women and children were abused and shot. Law enforcement officers allowed the terror to take place; and police and militia participated. White mobs killed 40 blacks, while nine whites lost their lives. The Chester, Pennsylvania riot of 1917 also saw rioting that produced both black and white mortality. In the same year, the Houston Texas riot saw black troupes angry over the racism, racial segregation and police brutality. The black soldiers were not allowed to have weapons; and black women were arrested. When white soldiers resented being questioned by black solider they shot at him. Black soldiers responded, took weapons, went into town and killed 17 whites. Yet some of the worst rioting in the United States occurred in the "Red Summer" of 1919. The post-war migrations contained the same stressors as those in other cities. The cities were becoming more crowded. There were concerns about blacks competing with whites for jobs and housing. African Americans had higher expectations after the war. They expected racial equality, political power, and they rejected the efforts to "keep blacks in their place." Blacks continued to demonstrate that they would engage in self-defense when attacked. Even so, 25 towns were burned, and hundreds of people were wounded.

  Other post-war riots involved the reemergence of the Ku Klux Klan. In the 1920 Florida riots, encompassing several towns, the Klan mounted an organized campaign of parades and activities to prevent African Americans from voting. The Klan threatened the black voting population, especially those blacks who dared to go to the polling stations. In some the Florida towns, blacks were not allowed to vote at all. Klan mobs invaded black neighborhoods and burned homes, schools and churches. The Klan openly threated black leaders who organized voting activities; and several blacks were killed. In addition to the assertion of voting rights, in most city disturbances, the charge that a white female was assaulted by a black male was enough to promulgate a riot. This was a spark for the 1921 Tulsa Race Riot and Massacre. When charges were made that a white girl was raped by a black boy, 75 blacks held a vigil at the jail in order to keep the boy from being lynched. The sheriff stated that the boy would not be removed or lynched. This assurance caused blacks to disperse, and as they left the jail, a white man attempted to disarm one of the black men and a shot was fired. The confusion that followed included thousands of armed whites invading the city in an effort to destroy the thriving Greenwood community, the people of "Little Africa." Black people were forced to flee their homes and property, some were beaten, shot at, killed, arrested and interned; homes and business were burned and personal possessions were looted. The entire community was razed to the ground, and the destruction included airplanes that released parcels of dynamite. In 2001, State Senator Maxine Horner (Oklahoma State Senate, 1987-2005) called the 1921 Tulsa Race Riot, "…potentially an act of ethnic cleansing..."[25] The chaos and carnage that ensued was massive. Untold numbers of blacks were killed and survivors and scholars have asserted that mass graves were uncovered. However, the conservative number of those who lost their lives included 300 blacks and 50 whites.

The period surrounding the Great Depression through the end of World War II (1929-1945) spawned a number of fractious race riots. The underlying factors included the maintenance of white supremacy, unemployment, and economic hardship. Blacks continued to have little political power. The period also included an increase in the lynching of African Americans. In the south fears heightened that blacks engaged in sharecropping and tenant farming were attempting to create unions. In one of the Great Depression riots in Camp Hill, Alabama (July 1931), a white mob invaded a black church were sharecroppers were holding a meeting. Blacks were attacked inside of the church, and thereafter whites began "hunting" blacks down. In the north, African Americans also responded to their imposed second-class citizenship status. In the Harlem Riot of 1935, the unrest that took place was a culmination of northern migration, intentionally crowding blacks seeking housing into slum areas, unemployment, discriminatory hiring, and poverty. Blacks boycotted, organized rent strikes, and attacked white businesses and property owners. The riot began when a rumor spread that a black youth attempted to steal a knife, and was killed by a white shop owner. Angry rioters looted and destroyed property. The Harlem post-riot commission found that people were angry over racial discrimination and the issue of concentrated poverty in the midst of abundance. By 1942, some of these kinds of disturbances were characterized as "Military Riots." They encompassed the post-depression boom in war production employment; the Presidential order calling for blacks to be hired to support wartime labor; and the March on Washington for jobs. African Americans demanded full equality, though the racial climate of the time alleged that blacks were attempting to move *too fast* for equality and civil rights.

There were many in American society, who thought that the reasons the wartime race riots took place was that African Americans

---

[25]Tulsa Race Riot: A Report by the Oklahoma Commission to Study the Tulsa Race Riot of 1921," Final Report of Findings and Recommendations of the 1921 Tulsa Race Riot Commission, February 28, 2001, 177. See also Scott Ellsworth, *Death In A Promised Land: The Tulsa Race Riot Of 1921*. Baton Rouge, LA: LSU Press, 1992.

were demanding too much (jobs, housing, education, social and public services, etc.)—which was interpreted as the quest for supremacy over whites. There were many clashes between black and white soldiers and civilians in the towns and cities that resulted in the deaths and serious injuries in both races. In 1943 the Mobile Alabama race riots was representative of the kinds of events that took place when employment opportunities opened up to African Americans. On May 25, 1943, one of the worst riots took place at the Alabama Dry Dock and Shipbuilding Company Yards. The city of Mobile actively recruited to increase the black and white population in order to support war industry work. Nearly thirty thousand people held jobs at the Alabama Dry Dock and Shipbuilding Company Yards. African Americans secured 6 thousand of these jobs, mostly in the shipyard, comprising only 20 percent of the workforce. Skilled workers were needed (and heavily recruited) among whites and blacks. The company decided to upgrade the jobs of 12 black workers. They would work as skilled welders. This advancement immediately inspired rumors that African Americans were replacing whites at the shipyard. The move was seen as an affront to the skilled white workers. The animosity and rumors intensified and morphed into highly organized work-place membership drives for such groups as the League for White Supremacy. The employers and the union allowed the League to organize, instigate violence, and threaten black workers. Fifty black workers were severely beaten, and this included black women. Whites refused to return to the shipyard by the thousands; and blacks started looking for other employment. The shipyard was forced to shut down war-production operations for a week.[26] Local and national leaders knew (or cared) little about how to prepare whites to share space as equals with blacks in the labor force.

By the 1950s, civil rights activity of any kind led and supported by blacks was increasingly labeled as communist (as in the New York Peekskill/Paul Robeson riots of 1949). There were three capstones to the civil rights activity of the 1950s, the 1954 *Brown v. Board of Education* case, the 1955 Montgomery Bus Boycott, and the 1957 Little Rock crisis. These activities generated increased and intense fears among whites, and helped to continue to fuel racial riots in the United States.

---

[26]"Summary of a Report on the Race Riots in the Alabama Dry Dock and Shipbuilding Company Yards in Mobile, Alabama," New York: National Urban League for Social Service Among Negroes, June, 1943.

WORLD TO COME: ESSAYS ON THE BALTIMORE UPRISING, MILITANT RACISM, AND HISTORY

For generations racist practices within most institutions were unwritten in addition to those codified. There was an entrenched anti-black (anti-African) attitude that permeated society and this included the ranks of law enforcement. The media had created the problem of the "negro protest" (boycotts, sit-ins, freedom rides" etc.), while at the same time dismissing black desires to realize equality. Black protest events, and thereby black people, were in essence the obstacle—not the persistence of white racism. This was especially evident with respect to the issue of housing. Throughout the North, African American migrants had been relegated to racially segregated neighborhoods that were overcrowded, and underserved, thus creating deplorable living conditions. When whites tried to integrate (advocating for black citizens) white neighborhoods, they were overruled or dismissed. Blacks risked their lives when they attempted to improve their housing situation by moving into white communities. For example, when a small group of Blacks tried to integrate Chicago's Trumbull Park beginning in 1953, it generated white rage expressed through riots that openly attacked black residents. White mobs in Trumbull Park damaged black apartments, and assaulted blacks anywhere they were found in the neighborhood, while police more often than not looked the other way. White citizens were empowered to destroy the property of blacks, and even resorted to using bombing devices. For African Americans, the mob attacks were no less than like living in a war zone were strikes took place around the clock. This was done in order to "....remind Blacks of the dangers of continuing to live there."[27] In 1957, approximately one hundred white residents broke into an African American apartment and completely destroyed it and the contents before setting the flat on fire. Many cities like Chicago experienced racial violence against black families who struggled to live in white communities. In the case of Trumbull Park, even the most conservative scholarship has suggested that the attacks on black citizens lasted at least a decade.

In American the 1960s, which included the rebelliousness and freethinking expression of white counter culture, involved numerous civil actions that defined the decade as well as shaped the Civil Rights movement. Thousands of protest actions as well as reactions took place. African Americans began a campaign of organized sit-ins and

---

[27]Leonard S. Rubinowitz and Imani Perry, "Crimes Without Punishment: White Resistance to Black Entry," *Journal of Criminal Law and Criminology*, Vol. 92, No. 2, Fall, 2001, 335-428, 394-395.

World To Come: Essays On The Baltimore Uprising, Militant Racism, And History

activities such as the "Freedom Rides" in order to press for equal treatment. The 1963 March on Washington, a capstone event, also served as a precursor to the intense civil disobedience actions that would come. In addition, the September 15, 1963 bombing of the 16th Street Baptist church in Birmingham Alabama killed four girls,[28] served as a form of violent southern terrorist-protest to the Civil Rights movement. A series of major race riots took place in 1964 known as the first of the "Long Hot Summers," these events were nationwide and included major cities in the north and the south. The Civil Rights movement raised the issue of social justice fatigue among blacks. African Americans were tired of waiting for positive change. Impoverished ghettos had been firmly established and the Jim Crow over-policing of blacks was an enduring feature. "Freedom Summer's" efforts to firmly secure voting rights and eliminate the ongoing lynching of blacks were dominant themes in the south that affected both regions. The year 1965 was characterized by the assassination of Malcolm X, the March on Selma, Alabama, and the Watts Riot in Los Angeles. Civil disobedience continued in 1966 with James Meredith's march (from Memphis to Jackson) for voting rights, and activist demonstrations in Chicago, Dayton and Cleveland.

From July 23 through July 28, 1967, in the midst of the Civil Rights movement, Detroit Michigan experienced one of the worst race riots in the nation's history since the 1943 unrest in Belle Isle. The riot was explained as "...a class confrontation which impoverished Negroes led against the wealthy merchants, landlords and police."[29] Like similar up-and-coming urban cities, there was great post-war growth and prosperity in Detroit followed by a steady decline. In addition, there was also a long history of unaddressed issues in the black community. These issues included a protracted history of police harassment and abuse, a shortage of affordable housing (because blacks were effectively barred from living in the white suburbs), rapid urban renewal, and economic inequality coupled with a decline in manufacturing jobs. There was also a new expression of confidence and intergroup identity that the African American youth called Black Power, and the established order immediately labeled the sentiment as black militancy.

---

[28]Denise McNair, Cynthia Wesley, Carole Robertson and Addie Mae Collins were killed in this attack. There was no indictment on this case until the year 2000. Spike Lee's 1997 documentary film *Four Little Girls* galvanized interest in closing the case.
[29]Editorial, "Massacre at Newark," *Freedomways*, Vol. 7, No. 3, Summer, 1967 (Third Quarter), 198.

World To Come: Essays On The Baltimore Uprising, Militant Racism, And History

This period also featured the consciousness-raising activities among black production and factory workers. This new assertion of black agency largely came from the soldiers who returned from fighting in Vietnam. When police attempted to raid a bar where a black celebration of returning veterans was taking place, they arrested 80 people. Because of the large number of black arrestees, who were forced to wait around for police transport, the crowds that gathered manifested their frustration and resentment. In less than 48 hours, the National Guard was called in, and there after President Johnson ordered the 82nd Airborne to assume riot duty. It seemed that they stopped and arrested nearly every black person they saw in the city. The governor instituted a curfew. Seven thousand people were arrested, two thousand people were injured,[30] and at least 43 people died. Most of the deaths that occurred were from the police and National Guard. The damaged was estimated to have been over five million dollars, though amounts as high as one billion have been cited.[31] There were innumerable violations of people's rights—regardless of whether they had participated in the actual riot. Searches and seizures without warrants, excessively high bails, extended detentions in harsh conditions (up to a month) were also marked features. Many people were forced to accept misdemeanor pleas, in what has been described as a criminal justice processing assembly line. The message was an old one, "The flames of Detroit should serve to light up a great truth: It's that time, America. Grant Negroes freedom and equality or invite catastrophe!"[32] The term *riot* effectively described the destructive aspect of civil disobedience—but it completely dismissed the serious issue of racial oppression that lay beneath.

For seven months in 1968, the last of the major multi-city riots called the "Long Hot Summer" took place. Most of these events were characterized by the persistent push of the Civil Rights movement (as in the Poor People's campaign) and the affirmation of Black Power. The threshold for the riots that took place was the assassination of Martin Luther King, Jr. By that time the nation was weary of black protest. Civil disobedience, which included rioting and peaceful protests, were often perceived to be the same activity. When peaceful

---

[30]Editorial, "Massacre at Newark," *Freedomways*, Vol. 7, No. 3, Summer, 1967 (Third Quarter), 198.
[31]Ibid.
[32]Ibid.

World To Come: Essays On The Baltimore Uprising, Militant Racism, And History

protests were not violent, they were still seen as an impetus for a violent action to occur. President Johnson established a commission to study the civil disorders that took place in 1967. There were a number of commissions created to examine the urban violence that took place in the 1960s. Like most of these endeavors, the President's commission, appointed only two blacks, and wanted to know how and why the riots started, and most importantly, how they could be prevented. In 1968, The Kerner Commission[33] Report (nearly 1500 pages) presented its findings to the public, and stated, "Our nation is moving toward two societies, one black, one white—separate and unequal." It was an honest outcome, but the sentiment was not necessarily new or noteworthy. It did infer that American society had been moving in the same direction, but this was never true. The Kerner Commission did implicate "White Racism" in the 1967 "Long Summer" riots. The report also confirmed that institutions created and maintained by white society, had implemented and sustained racial discrimination that gave rise to poverty and the ghetto. All institutions were culpable, and this included the mainstream media (radio, print and television). The media had difficulty in presenting accurate portraits of blacks and the civil disorders. They shifted responsibility squarely to black society. They ignored the squalor of the ghettos. The media also misled the public (with acts of commission and omission) which often suggested that blacks (viewed as an organized military force) were routinely engaging law enforcement officers. The report found that law enforcement officers did not understand the black community, particularly the sense of rage. Some people felt that the Kerner Commission report was not fair, and were highly critical of its findings. "White racism" was not a topic that made people comfortable in the late 1960s. The belief advanced was that there was no such thing as "white racism." Another criticism of the report was that the many reforms—in jobs, housing, and education— necessary to advance American society for everyone would be impossible to implement. Yet another assessment was that the Kerner Commission Report was too broad in its scope regarding liability—essentially the idea that "'Everybody is guilty, but no one is to blame.'"[34] It was paradoxical and

---

[33] Also known as The National Advisory Commission on Civil Disorders.
[34] Philip Meranto, *The Kerner Report Revisited, Final Report and Background Papers*, Illinois: University of Illinois Institute of Government and Public Affairs, 1970, 155.

surreal upon reflection—the notion that racism was not able to understand the affects and impacts of racism.

Civil unrest and riots continued throughout the remainder of the 1960s and into the 1970s. The Attica prison revolt in 1971 raised awareness about black political prisoners,[35] and particularly the death of George Jackson, who was killed by a prison guard. Attica prisoners seized the institution and began negotiations. The rebellion also sought to address issues regarding the living conditions of inmates. The rebellion ended when nearly forty inmates and a hostage died after law enforcement, in an effort to take back the prison, open fired. The 1970s was also important for the protests over school racial integration. Two of the most notable were the Boston riots over bussing, and the Escambia high school "mascot riot" in Florida. Both events demonstrated the challenges over racism, and the desire to maintain the status quo in dealing with the desegregation of public schools. At the end of the 1970s, the Greensboro Massacre in North Carolina was one of the most tragic outcomes of civil protests during the decade. The multiracial group of activists,[36] represented by the Communist Workers' Party, were protesting racism and the Klan, as well as organizing black laborers. On November 3, 1979, the Ku Klux Klan with the support of the American Nazi party, in a pre-planned action, opened fired (in a kind of convoy "drive by" shooting) on the activists. Five of the activists were killed. The police were present in small numbers, though the contingent did not arrive until after the shooters had fled the scene, and they then proceeded to arrest some of the protesters.

Several events from the 1980s through the 2000s reflected peaceful demonstrations which supported social justice issues, riots over charges of police brutality (i.e. Tompkins Square Park in 1988), or conflicts between members of the community (i.e. between the Jews and African Americans in Crown Heights in 1991). Ultimately, the 1990s are defined by the Los Angeles Riots of 1992 (also known as the

---

[35] In this context, a political prisoner is someone who is legally, but unjustly, confined to a penal institution because they have openly opposed or criticized the government. Political prisoners often cite that they were framed for crimes in order to incarcerate them for their political beliefs and/or protest activities. Political prisoners are captives of the state, but their imprisonment is also meant to send a message of caution to the masses of the people. One of the most famous political prisoners in world history was Nelson Mandela (1918-2013), former South African President and Human Rights Activist.
[36] Those killed in the Greensboro Massacre included: Sandi Smith, Jim Waller, Bill Sampson, Cesar Cauce, and Michael Nathan.

WORLD TO COME: ESSAYS ON THE BALTIMORE UPRISING, MILITANT RACISM, AND HISTORY

Rodney King Riots) when four white police officers viciously beat Rodney King, an African American man. The recording which captured the beating was one of the first major public uses of video that informed the community about police brutality. The video also served as a tool which motivated activists. The riot occurred when the officers implicated in the beating of King were acquitted of any wrongdoing. In the 1990s there were also massive peaceful protests that included the Million Man March Day of Absence in Washington, D.C. (October 16, 1995) and the Million Woman March in Philadelphia (October 25, 1997). These historic protests in particular were more than social justice protest initiatives; they were also affirmations of black culture. By the end of the 1990s, police brutality was of great concern to the black community, but also white racial violence at the hands of vigilante citizens was an issue. This included the beating, kidnapping and cruel vehicle-dragging murder of James Byrd, Jr. on June 7, 1998. Byrd was killed by three self-identified white supremacists in Jasper, Texas.[37] At a time when the words *hate crime* were rarely used to describe white attacks on blacks, the end of the 1990s launched a huge debate over the federal legislation of hate crimes in the United States.

Most of the protest and riot events after the year two thousand turn of the century continued to cite systemic racism, economic inequality, and relentless poverty. However, the years between 2000 and 2015 are notable for the citizens' intense focus on racial profiling, police brutality, and police-encounter killings of black citizens. It seemed as if police authority had consolidated an independent right to arbitrarily abuse and kill blacks at will. Nearly all questionable cases involved the excessive use of force. A notable case during this time was the Fall 2006 murder of 23-year-old Sean Bell. Bell was killed in a hail of bullets outside of a Queens New York club the evening before his wedding. Years later it is still a strange and ever shifting story of a group of plainclothes/undercover police officers who shot at an unarmed Bell and his two friends 50 times as they left a bachelor party. Bell died, his two friends were severely wounded and arrested, and the officers involved in the shooting were acquitted. In addition to the sense of injustice felt by the community, the Bell case revealed the difficulty in obtaining documents and statistical information, especially

---

[37]Byrd was murdered by ex-convicted criminals William King, Lawrence Brewer, and Shawn Berry.

those related to the training and practices of law enforcement officers.[38] The city of New York, for more than a decade, would be the flashpoint that illuminated the questionable police practices (written and unwritten) in other cities around the country. The controversial 2007 RAND Report revealed that New York police increased their stop-and-frisk practices from less than one hundred thousand to over a half million people in 2006. Very few people were ever arrested in these stops; however, blacks and Latinos combined were stopped by the police 90 percent of the time. African Americans were stopped more than 53 percent of the time, and when they were stopped, routinely subjected to searches, endangered by the use of force, and more often arrested. The small numbers of whites stopped in 2006 were the least likely to be arrested.[39] In New York and other major cities, by the mid-2000s through 2015, the key concept/theme in cases where African Americans died in police-encounters, was excessive lethal force.[40]

In the Moment of Our Birth: Baltimore's Historic Uprising

In the city of Baltimore, we will always be mindful of the honorable protests and calamitous rioting that took place in early April 1968 and then again 47 years later, during last week of April 2015. Many citizens were clear that an uprising is a form of resistance and the term *Baltimore Uprising* offered more accurate insight into what took place, and the term caught on very quickly. Media outlets were looking for a name—something to describe what was happening. If you just called the event a protest then you had to explain what they were protesting against, and then you had to include the riots, and the burning of property as a form of dissent— ultimately linking legal activity with illegal activity. A rebellion always has a cause, but a rebellion assumes many things—more widespread protest efforts—but also acknowledges lawlessness and the reasons for it. Mainstream media did not hesitate to call the disruption in Baltimore a riot. However, this

---

[38]New York Civil Liberties Union Letter to Raymond Kelly, Commissioner, NYCPD, Re: Sean Bell Shooting and Stop-and-Frisk Reports, November 30, 2006; *New York Civil Liberties Union v. New York City Police Department et al*, November 12, 2009.
[39]See Greg Ridgeway, "Analysis Of Racial Disparities In The New York Police Departments Stop, Question, And Frisk Practices," Sponsored by the New York City Police Foundation, Santa Monica, CA: RAND Corporation, 2007.
[40]See Appendix C: "A Compendium of African Americans Who Died in Police-Encounters, 1994-2015."

was a more punitive label since it classified the protests and demonstrations as an unlawful activity. The blurring of many interests and frustrations occurred when the police tweeted, "Groups of violent criminals are continuing to throw rocks, bricks, and other items…."[41] In general, the people who throw rocks and bottles, and yell epithets at the police are not organized to riot, "…they are interested not in killing policemen, but in humiliating them."[42] More than likely, they are caught up in the moment, in the experience of long-standing anger over aggressions unaddressed. As a Baltimore Uprising eyewitness noted, this was one possible response to oppression.[43] Journalist Matthew Reece further observed, "The rioters are not anarchists," and "To understand the rioters is not to condone their actions."[44] "Generally, people who taunt the police are not highly structured revolutionaries. Those who spontaneously face-off with police officers who are dressed in riot gear and armed to the hilt, equipped only with a sharp tongue or a steely stare, are usually prepared to die. Rocks and bottles are petty and minuscule weapons of opportunity, not the tools of heavily armed and organized rebels with a well-thought-out tactical plan of action.

Yet, more often, clashes with police are about the people's very right to raise their voices in civil demonstration. One of the leading activists who gained public attention and recognition in the Baltimore Uprising was Kwame Rose. Rose challenged *Fox News* Host Geraldo Riviera about the exploitation of the media in the midst of the unrest on April 28. Rose later reflected on Twitter that "…property was destroyed because city officials and law enforcement tried to block people's right to protest."[45] Like many others Rose's experience and criticisms indicated that what happened in Baltimore the last week of

---

[41]Baltimore Police, (#BaltimorePolice), "Groups of Violent Criminals Are Continuing To Throw Rocks, Bricks, and Other Items at Police Officers." April 27, 2015, 9:28PM.
[42]Louis C. Goldberg, "Ghetto Riots and Others: The Faces of Civil Disorders in 1967," in Gary T. Marx, *Racial Conflict Tension and Change in American Society*, Boston: Little, Brown and Company, 1971, 273-285, 284.
[43] O'Reilly, Bill. "The Baltimore Rioting Now Leading to Madness," *Fox News,* FoxNews.Com, May 1, 2015 (Interview with Kenneth Jackson).
[44]Matthew Reece, "Ten Observations on the Baltimore Riots," www.examiner.com, May 2, 2015, accessed http://www.examiner.com/article/ten-observations-on-the-baltimore-riots, March 1, 2016.
[45]Kwame Rose, [kwamerose]. (2015, Dec 14). In April/May Property was destroyed because City officials and law enforcement, tried to block people's right to protest. [Tweet]. Retrieved from https://twitter.com/kwamerose/status/676431026172899328. Tweeted during the end of the first of the Baltimore 6 Trials, Officer William G. Porter.

World To Come: Essays On The Baltimore Uprising, Militant Racism, And History

April and first week of May in 2015 was an uprising. The Baltimore Uprising involved organized and impromptu protests and demonstrations; community members coming together to articulate long-standing grievances; in addition to expressions of rioting, looting, and damage to property. The uprising also included spaces for healing, places where people could address the trauma of racism; and the effort of citizens—from everywhere—to help clean up the aftermath (as well as attend to current neglected conditions). An uprising recognizes the totality of the community's effort and the historical significance of the civil disturbance event.

The city of Baltimore experienced an historic uprising. Though not as extensive in duration as the uprising in Ferguson, Missouri, the Baltimore Uprising was a major social event encompassing several critical, and related, elements:

First, the Baltimore Uprising had historical roots that were local, national and global. There is a web of historical relationships and actions that led to the uprising. In addition to the 1968 riots over the assassination of Martin Luther King, Jr. and the failure to rebuild the areas hit the hardest; this historical web also includes the demise of industry in Baltimore, the decline of the significance of the city as a major port town—and the substantial loss of manufacturing jobs.

Second, the Baltimore Uprising was caused by persistent, and embedded social issues affecting the black community. The entrenched problems were resistant to the implementation of countless community development programs and stopgap measures; overtime the city's long-term municipal problems remained intact and compounded. Joblessness and racism combined and helped contribute to the persistence of adverse social issues.

Third, many mass uprisings have an immediate and identifiable catalyst. Most people agreed that the immediate catalyst for the Baltimore Uprising was the arrest and death of Freddie Gray. Others argue that the direct catalyst was the numerous police-custody deaths of African Americans that took place in the city of Baltimore (and across the nation) prior to Freddie Gray.

Fourth, uprisings involve an intellectual awakening among the masses of people. This is an awareness of challenges beyond individual problems. The potent idea becomes a collective movement. The people start to consciously examine, analyze and discuss critical information and make connections that are pertinent to the event. Freddie Gray's arrest turned into a grassroots enquiry into issues of police brutality, negligent policing, the criminal justice system, and persistent poverty.

Community issues were elevated to state, national and international levels.

Fifth, uprisings include displays of traditional protest and civil disobedience. In the Baltimore Uprising this involved symbolic protests, such as silent and candlelight vigils to acts of civil disobedience, like defying curfew. Other aspects of this kind of civil disobedience involved the "die-in," laying down and pretending to be dead or immobile in support of people who actually died.

Sixth, like all popular disturbances, the Baltimore Uprising included flashes of violent civil unrest. This involved the random damage to property and clashes with police. Here we found uncoordinated displays of rage among individuals; possibly apolitical opportunists who used the anger of the masses as a cover to commit crimes.

Seventh, the community became engaged in concerted dialogue and problem-solving. This not only involved grassroots organizers, activists and religious leaders, but also educators, police, city government representatives and legislators. There was sustained engagement of social issues through the media, politicians, and community leaders—all of whom asserted a stakeholder role, and articulated a desire to serve the needs of the community.

Eighth, due in part to the use of the mass media (including social), the Baltimore Uprising possessed the ability to sustain its momentum long after the catalyst (the arrest and death of Freddie Gray).

Finally, the Baltimore Uprising is defined by message saturation. A specific message (about definite issues) had permeated society. This saturation point initiated further intellectual discourse and physical activity.

Chapter 7

The Millennials And IGens In The Wilderness State And At The Mall

Our youth can be our fate or our future.—Maulana Karenga[1]

Each generation out of relative obscurity must discover their mission, fulfill it or betray it.— Frantz Fanon[2]

The Millennials Will be Heard

In the shadow of Freddie Gray's tragic death, and the long history of police-encounter killings of black people, The Baltimore Uprising as a whole (especially the aspect that included erratic looting and damage to property), was among many things, an extreme cry for justice, a complicated struggle to be heard. Freddie Gray's peers, especially if black, were aware of two paths in this country's system of public education—one mostly white and of means where they would find their way out of high school to college; the other was predominately black and Latino, and these young people socialized to street life would fill the proverbial K-12 pipeline to prison.[3] The millennials (aka Generation Y, the Net Generation) are people born after 1978 and through 2000, and is usually a reference to the 18 to 24 years old in this group. As a whole, they are often defined by being born and immersed in emerging technology. The millennials are greatly impacted by technology, especially in terms of the portability of their computer devices. Many university professors will tell you how vexing it is to get freshmen students, in a 50-minute (3 times a week) course to stop checking their email, Instagram, Facebook, Twitter and other apps during class time. They want to be connected so badly, to be visible and interactive in a world that seems to have forgotten them. They speak their native language, and they also speak technology. They live for and use technology to live. Perhaps in keeping with the anxieties of people actually occupying a unique 21st century existence, the millennials are

---

[1]Maulana Karenga, Interview, *The Source*, February 1996.
[2]Franz Fanon, *The Wretched of the Earth*, New York: Grove Press, Inc., 1963.
[3]William Oliver, "'The Streets' an Alternative Black Male Socialization Institution," *Journal of Black Studies*, Vol. 36, No. 6, July 2006, 918-937.

comfortable with living in two worlds—often blurring the lines. They believe their brutal honesty and willingness to share everything with the world is one of their defining features. Too often however the millennials are erroneously characterized as ageistly disrespectful of adults (anyone over 35), blissfully ignorant of the significance of history, and that they proudly wallow in and defend their own self-deceptive narrative. They have inherited monumental problems of society, which includes racism, sexism, classism, rampaging capitalism and corporate greed, environmental abuse, and the lingering impact of the 2007-2008 housing bust and the subsequent economic recession.

The millennials are believed to be the generation, which will usher in a powerful future encompassing science, technology, engineering, and medicine (STEM). While this broad expectation of an even brighter technological future seems fine, it does not truly apply to the masses of the black poor within this group. It does not address systemic racism and the persistent audacity of white supremacy. There is a distinct Wilderness Experience, which is diametrically opposed to the illusory concept of the American Dream, and it is filled with Lost, Dislocated, and Abandoned Millennials. They are lost because their communities have been systemically neglected and they know—from birth—that they have been discarded. Beyond the Siren's song of popular culture, they are dislocated from their own historic and global Africana experience. They have been abandoned to a world of racial fascism, a place where color-blind mirages and illusions of choice abound. As an often-touted way out of poverty, higher education is extremely cost prohibitive; and those who can cull the expensive financial aid packages (coupled with a low-wage job or two) may not yet have the necessary skills to matriculate successfully. Those who don't make it for whatever reason are laden with massive student debt and no knowledge—and no degree. As far as mainstream society is concerned, these millennials are more than welcome to participate in popular culture (music, entertainment, and consumerism) and to become assorted service-workers, but they are not perceived as potential intellectual leaders of the future. The continuing trauma of their lives is never taken seriously. The people, the millennials in particular, are desperate to have a real voice in this society. But our idea of youth engulfed in a "millennial haze" does not account for the many Black Lives Matter activists. Like the people who came before them, they want, need—and will be heard.

World To Come: Essays On The Baltimore Uprising, Militant Racism, And History

The IGens, the "Purge" or Teens at Mondawmin Mall

Some of these young people were seen and heard on the night of the Baltimore Uprising, Monday, April 27, 2015. However, the younger counterparts of the millennials, sometimes called the *iGeneration*, were said to have been at the heart of what happened—events which eventually led to a state of emergency and the National Guard being brought in. There are many starting points, but the one that captured the attention of the public was the announcement that local high school students had texted or tweeted that they were going to engage in a "purge." Law enforcement had intercepted this threat through their surveillance of social media. What could be more frightening than raising the specter of the 2013 major motion picture, *The Purge*, which depicted a dystopic American society that sanctioned one night of rampant violence? In this film, American citizens are legally permitted to maim, rape, and kill with impunity.[4] In this chaos and carnage, there are no public policing services—no one to help you. The film also strongly suggested that it was the upper classes of people (predominately white) who engaged in this activity, preying on anyone, but particularly the poor and vulnerable (through the character "Bloody Stranger" who is black). In this fictitious world, what was as chilling as the Hollywood depiction of legalized violence was the accompanying philosophy of purging—that it was morally good for American society. Thus, when the announcement was made that Baltimore's black children would be purging—a seemingly new complexity was layered on top of the tensions surrounding Freddie Gray's death—and a black rebellion came into view. The students, these mostly black IGens, were dismissed early from school[5] with no city-wide public transportation available. They were already under a youth curfew enacted in 2014.[6] The rationale for Baltimore's newest youth curfew law was the belief that children under the age of 14 were mainly responsible for criminal activity in the city and a significant problem for police.

Ostensively, these teens—angry and frustrated over the death of Freddie Gray—joined with local residents to roam the area, designed

---

[4]*The Purge*, 2013, Universal Studies, Released June 7, 2013, http://www.imdb.com/title/tt2184339/?ref_=nv_sr_1, accessed May 19, 2015.
[5]A few months later, city officials would not be immediately able to recall who gave the order to dismiss city schools.
[6]This is a mandatory curfew for young people. Children under the age of 14 must be inside by 9 p.m. For teens 14-16, the curfew is 10 p.m. on school nights.

WORLD TO COME: ESSAYS ON THE BALTIMORE UPRISING, MILITANT RACISM, AND HISTORY

actual, makeshift, and faux protests, while others decided to later storm the Mondawmin Mall. The mall contained the metro subway and bus station. Mondawmin Mall is a transportation hub in West Baltimore and it was normal for school and college students (including Baltimore City Community College and Coppin State University) to converge there to take trains and busses home. However, on the afternoon of April 27, 2015, more than anything else, the pre-looting event at Mondawmin mall appeared to be nothing less than a training exercise for the police. They stood in blue-wall formation with body shields, batons at the ready and of course, they were armed. This initial scene also included the appearance of a Baltimore Police Tactical Unit van. Some of the youth who faced the police at Mondawmin Mall, looked vulnerable and confused. The police marched in formation with guns drawn. In addition to their perplexity, the young people were concerned, amused, and curious to say the least. However, the students did two things to taunt and disrupt the police: 1) they held both hands up (in the "hands up don't shoot" gesture of protest), and 2) using their cell phones, they took countless photographs and videos of the police (along with news and freelance photographers jockeying for positions); and they took pictures of themselves. The barrage of selfies were bad enough, yet when small groups of young people moved anywhere toward the police, they stepped forward. Other students just watched the encounter. It appeared that most of the students had no idea of the danger they were in, and the police were prepared for a military-grade insurgency. At one point, the police blocked the view of a young man who was sequestered, and then taken to the ground.

The BGF-Crips-Bloods Gang Fatwa[7]

There are at least four baseline theories about the rise of black criminal gangs in American society. The *first* suggests that like other organized criminal groups in the United States, black gangs have always been a fixture in American history. In many respects black gangs are not different, though perhaps less structured and networked than Italian mafia families, and other groups (Irish, Poles, etc.) that operated

---

[7] A fatwa is an Islamic religious ruling reflecting a scholarly opinion of Islamic law. (See Hussein A. Agrama, "Ethics, Tradition, Authority: Toward an Anthropology of the Fatwa," *American Ethnologist*, 37, No. 1 (2010) 2-18). Just as the term Jihad means struggle, not war; mainstream U.S. media used fatwa to indicate the issuance of a formal death sentence. The term was used to describe the supposed gang hit on police.

WORLD TO COME: ESSAYS ON THE BALTIMORE UPRISING, MILITANT RACISM, AND HISTORY

and preyed on their own ethnic communities. The *second* theory proposes that black gangs only truly emerged after the waning of the Civil Rights and Black Power movements in the 1960s and early 1970s. Young black men, left out of society and disillusioned, created gangs as a direct response to the race riots, Jim Crow racial segregation, unfulfilled promises of racial equality, and to honor the legacy of martyred heroes. The *third* theory of gang origins is more clearly delineated—the appearance of gangs in the prison system. These are groups who operate in the penal system and at some point (especially after release) set up network operations outside of prison walls. The *fourth* theory of the rise and proliferation of black gangs in the United States maintains that they are a direct result of the ghetto/wilderness experience. Not effectively aligned with an ideology beyond human survival, gangs developed out of the harsh persistent social, political and economic landscape of the black experience in America. These gangs created families as well as criminal enterprises in order to meet the basic needs of outcast people in society (providing for income, employment, a sense of purpose, filial association, and recreation [i.e. sports and social clubs]). All of these theories can be proven true, but only to an extent. Unlike the collective experience of white Anglo-Saxon and other white ethnic groups, black gangs in the United States, regardless of immediate origins, are all tied to the latter, survival theory, and firmly attached to the history of racism and race relations.[8] In all of these scenarios black gangs of any type, rarely achieved the broad economic and political criminal status of their white counterparts because, yet again, racism thwarted any such parallel criminal success. While gangs and gang activity have changed over time, and given their nefarious criminal endeavors, black gangs have often asserted that they operate, somehow, in support of or on behalf of the community.

In the Baltimore Uprising, key narratives and events helped to establish a state of emergency on April 27, 2015. The Baltimore City Police Department announced before Freddie Gray's high profile funeral that area gangs—specifically the Black Guerilla Family (BGF), the Crips (Cribs, or Crypts) and the Bloods (and perhaps other prison gangs)—had created an alliance and issued a fatwa on the Baltimore City Police department. These three gangs were classified as the city's

---

[8]John M. Hagedorn, "Race Not Space: A Revisionist History of Gangs in Chicago." *The Journal of African American History* (2006): 194-208.

top security threats[9], and all have their origins on the west coast in the 1960s. The BGF has a history of being a street and a prison gang founded in California. In the state of Maryland, the BGF engaged in "...narcotics trafficking, robbery, assault and murder."[10] The Crips were described as "...one of the largest and most violent associations of street gains in the United States"[11] in 2002. Among other purported crimes, the Crips were involved in drug dealing, robbery, murder, rape and kidnapping.[12] The Fruit Town Brims sect of the Bloods eventually became the South Side Brims and set up their operation in Maryland.[13] The South Side Brims were cited for "...attempted murders, murder, aggravated assaults, robberies, burglaries, home invasions, drug trafficking, counterfeiting, fraud..."[14] As protests over the death of Freddie Gray mounted, essentially the public was told that a "credible" threat from these gang members had been issued to execute police officers. The media was encouraged to circulate the credible threat information "to the public and law enforcement nationwide." This was despite the fact that some local area leaders and activists had asserted, before the threat was made public, that at least some of these high profile gangs actively attempted to help the community. The show of police force that took place in West Baltimore—complete with riot/tactical gear had to do with the idea that law enforcement fully expected an urban conflict of epic proportions. Beyond the basic methodologies for crowd management, this included several assumptions based on the notion of inherent black violence. First, that a violent outbreak in the black community as a result of the funeral ceremonies for Freddie Gray would take place. Second, that black youth would run uncontrollable through the city streets in a "purge-like" activity. Third, those brutal organized criminal gangs in the city, specifically identified as the Black Guerilla Family, the Crips and the

---

[9]Baltimore City Criminal Justice Coordinating Council, Baltimore City Gang Violence Reduction Plan, Baltimore, Maryland, November 15, 2006, 55pp, 21, from "Table 4: Members of Security Threat Groups Released to Baltimore."
[10]*United States of America v. Tavon White, et al*, United States District Court for the District of Maryland, 2013, 2.
[11]"Crips," Drugs and Crime Gang Profile, National Drug Intelligence Center, U.S. Department of Justice, November, 2002, 1.
[12]*People v. Hall*, California Appellate Court, 2008.
[13]*United States v. Dontell Lamont Guy*, Stipulated Facts, 2012, 9.
[14]Ibid., 12.

World To Come: Essays On The Baltimore Uprising, Militant Racism, And History

Bloods, were prepared for armed street fighting, and had issued, a believable threat to take down the police.

The New Governor, the Molded Mayor, and Curfew as Prophecy

Larry Hogan, Maryland's new republican governor, was consistently described as a professional politician and business executive. He worked closely with his father, Maryland Congressman Larry Hogan, Sr., who was the first Republican Party member to vote for the impeachment of Richard Nixon in the Watergate scandal (1972-1974). From 1866 through 2015, the state of Maryland has had a succession of white male Democratic Party governors (31). When Hogan was inaugurated on January 21, 2015 he became the seventh Republican since the Civil War to lead the state of Maryland. In his inauguration speech, the governor emphasized the need for bipartisan cooperation. He also stated four principals, which would help successfully guide the people of the state of Maryland:

"Fiscal responsibility. Our state government must provide essential services, yet still live within its means. We must run our state government more efficiently and more cost effectively.

Economic growth. Maryland has an educated workforce, world-class universities and colleges, great community colleges, and public schools. We have our beautiful Chesapeake Bay, the Port of Baltimore, and a great location in the heart of the Mid-Atlantic region. We must leverage these amazing assets to transform Maryland into a place where businesses can flourish and create more jobs and opportunities for our citizens. Starting today let me say loudly and clearly: Maryland is open for business.

Reform. We must improve our state government's ability to be more responsive to, and to better serve and represent all of our citizens.

Fairness. We must restore a sense of fairness and balance for Maryland's hardworking and beleaguered taxpayers, in order to rebuild our forgotten middle class. We must get the state government off our backs, and out of our pockets, so

> that we can grow the private sector, put people back
> to work, and turn our economy around."[15]

Within the first one hundred days of his administration, Hogan was faced with a crisis that had national consequence. The Baltimore Uprising would begin to test the application of the principals of governance he had outlined. On April 27, 2015, Governor Hogan issued the "Declaration of Emergency" (Executive Order 01.01.2015.16). It was a day seemingly filled with inner-city chaos. More than anything, it was the day of Freddie Gray's funeral, and the city was poised to experience a breakdown. The executive order was issued to address a grave concern over public safety, because Mayor Rawlings Blake requested it; and the Maryland Emergency Management Agency had "advise(d) and informed" Governor Hogan of the "need to take protective actions to protect lives and property of citizens…" This authorized the use of the Maryland National Guard and paved the way for additional federal support.[16] For the residents of Baltimore, this was martial law, as the order effectively removed internal security authority from the city leaders.

Service to people seemed to be the main theme in Stephanie Rawlings-Blake's life. If her father, Howard "Pete" Rawlings was any example, his daughter learned political service from a man who was a force to be reckoned with. Howard Rawlings, a mathematics professor, turned politician served in the Maryland General Assembly (House of Delegates—40th district) for 23 years beginning in 1987. Her mother Dr. Nina Cole Rawlings was considered a pioneering pediatrician, a woman who spent forty years caring for the well-being of infants and children. Stephanie Rawlings-Blake emerged from that legacy of intellectuality, leadership, self-sacrifice, and service. Rawlings-Blake has had a prominent career as a leader in the city of Baltimore. She was born and raised in the city, is a product of the Baltimore Schools, and earned her law degree from the University Of Maryland School Of Law. Her form of activism was direct political involvement and at the age of 25 she became the youngest person elected to the Baltimore City Council; and then went on to become city council president for three

---

[15]The Office of Governor Larry Hogan, "Inaugural Address—Governor Larry Hogan," January 21, 2015, Maryland.gov,
http://governor.maryland.gov/2015/01/21/inaugural-address-governor-larry-hogan/, accessed May 15, 2015.

[16]The State of Maryland, Executive Department, Executive Order 01.01.2015.16, "Declaration of Emergency," April 27, 2015.

WORLD TO COME: ESSAYS ON THE BALTIMORE UPRISING, MILITANT RACISM, AND HISTORY

years (2007-2010). When Mayor Sheila Dixon resigned over a bitter gift-card scandal that led to embezzlement charges, Rawlings-Blake assumed her remaining time in office, and then in the 2011general election garnered one of the highest vote counts (87%). By the time Rawlings-Blake became Baltimore's 49th mayor (and the second black woman elected to the office), she was considered a rising political star far beyond the city of Baltimore. This was evident when she became secretary of the Democratic National Committee (DNC) after President Obama's reelection. More than five years into her term as Baltimore's mayor, Rawlings-Blake had developed numerous initiatives to address the myriad of systemic issues that troubled the city.

Like Governor Hogan, the Baltimore Uprising was an event intended to test the mettle of new and seasoned political leaders. When Mayor Rawlings-Blake conducted the essential news briefing at 8:00 P.M. on April 27, 2015, she had already been criticized for "waiting too long" to communicate with the residents of the city. This was despite the fact that she held countless meetings days prior, which included discussions with protesters and the clergy. This criticism was in part due to information being circulated by the governor's office that he and Blake were not able to coordinate their communication in order to issue the executive order that would call in the National Guard.[17] Cable television news networks fueled this speculation, with varying degrees of commentary, which ultimately demonized the mayor's efforts. When the mayor's press conference got underway, she called those residents who had burned cars and looted businesses "thugs." She was not the only one to use the term—the President and many others referred to them as thugs. Most people vehemently disagreed with their violent actions. However, the use of the term unleashed yet another—of what would become a series of disappointments from city leaders. People publically talked about the fact that many had also referred to the organized protesters as thugs, gangs, and "ghetto." The problem was not the lack of public disparagement over the reckless behavior of rioters—but that the word *thug*, in particular, was meant to be synonymous with the infamous word *nigger;* and that in some instances *thug* was applied to all factions of demonstrators, including peaceful protesters. This was immediately pointed out by Baltimore City

---

[17]See Paul Schwartzman, Ovetta Wiggins and Cheryl W. Thompson (with contributions from John Wagner), "In the Crucial Hours in Baltimore, a Communication Breakdown," *The Washington Post*, May 11, 2015.

WORLD TO COME: ESSAYS ON THE BALTIMORE UPRISING, MILITANT RACISM, AND HISTORY

Councilman Carl Stokes on CNN.[18] However, the alleged gangland fatwa against the police only served one real purpose—it gave law enforcement an enhanced rationale, and the official opportunity to tactically mobilize for increased civil unrest in the city.

In addition, when the city of Baltimore issued an emergency curfew (in addition to the youth curfew already in place) on the night of August 28, 2015, the measure which was meant to keep the community safe, felt more like a determined effort to keep the people contained; i.e. out of and away from predominately white and well-to-do neighborhoods. The presence of military support was even more evident as the police helicopters used for the routine aerial patrol of the streets, were employed to survey protesters and to announce via public address system, that the 10:00 p.m. curfew was in effect. It was apparent to many however that the citywide curfew was not enforced in some white or middle to upper-middle class Baltimore neighborhoods. They were not subjected to the blaring announcement that the restriction had commenced and that residents were legally required to get off the streets. The curfew had a chilling effect on the community. Some residents with jobs had work hours that exceeded the limits of the curfew, and they were concerned, though technically they were exempt. This did not matter. There were several reports of those who were arrested and detained because their job mandates violated the curfew. There was some discussion, at least publically at the time, as to whether Rawlings-Blake even possessed the authority to issue the curfew, but these questions emerged later. The heightened sense of injustice surrounding curfew-arrests also demanded that these cases be dismissed.[19]

---

[18]Baltimore City Councilman Carl Stokes interviewed by Erin Burnett live on CNN by, April 28, 2015.
[19]It was announced that Mosby would vacate the curfew arrests. May 12, 2015.

CHAPTER 8

INTO THE REBELLION: SELECTED FACETS OF THE BALTIMORE UPRISING

> "Criminal gang" means a group or association of three or more persons whose members...individually or collectively engage in a pattern of criminal gang activity.[1] —Maryland Code Criminal Law

The Protest Moment, CVS, and Police Presence

One of the most popular chants in the Baltimore Uprising was "All night, all day—we will fight for Freddie Gray." While this message was consistent, the civil disobedience protests in the city of Baltimore involved many people, numerous organizations, and multiple issues. Like other major demonstrations for human rights, the Baltimore Uprising was comprised of large numbers of citizens and supporters, organizations, and journalists (including local and national reporters, photographers and writers). For the most part, the people protested to express their deep discontent with the established order. Other people came out to see what was happening. Still, there were people looking for opportunities to exploit the situation. This included those who would prey on the community-at-large even without the context of social upheaval, as well as a host of agent provocateurs and embedded plainclothes law enforcement officers. As with any major protest, there were initiators, organizers, activists, agitators, and extremists. There were also interested spectators, people aimlessly standing around, observing, documenting—just trying to understand the milieu. Inside of the protest we found groups in solidarity with Freddie Gray, and those who would have little real interest in the cause; but his name was big now, and this meant their message might be heard. Then there were the virtual activists, those not physically involved with the many protests, but who supported the effort online, through social media, and at other venues such as places of work and worship. But for the people in the streets, in addition to feelings of anger and frustration, there was also righteousness, commitment, curiosity, anticipation, and

---

[1] MD Code Criminal Law § 9-801 (2013), Definitions.

camaraderie. The people involved knew they were having a transformative experience. Citizens were moved in many ways by the moment they helped to define. They knew that they were no longer individuals who were only interested in themselves, but that they were one, a group dedicated to a higher consciousness of civic duty. The people marched, chanted, and looked on—and when they did so, it was with a profound sense of purpose.

On April 27, 2015, news anchors associated with the long-established cable television shows attempted to inform our understanding of what was taking place in the city of Baltimore. As the videos of random violence were constantly repeated, the mainstream media audience shook its head and lamented that black people were burning and looting their own neighborhoods, and for no apparent or good reason. The conservative media viewers salivated over the images of blacks breaking glass at the CVS (Consumer Value Stores) and the Mondawmin Mall and thereafter. At the mall, they watched in disgust, as people filed in on foot, or drove up to the mall entrance, and exited with armfuls of off-the-rack clothing, while some piled the loot into the back seats or trunks of cars. No piercing security alarms from the stores could be heard on the video, no emergency sirens were evident, and more importantly, no one attempted to stop the looting (save the few brave community members trying to serve as guardians and mediators). The news also featured a police car burning (one of a few law enforcement vehicles vandalized)—an incredibly frightening image for many—but no one offered any explanation of how this happened—and what occurred to the police officers attached to this vehicle. In addition, the clash near the CVS, among the images presented which showed police in full riot gear—demonstrated that the show of force on national media outlets was critical to the emerging narrative. At a time when black men could be shot by law enforcement for running down the street, the tactically clad police officers pointed their weapons directly at irate residents, but did not shoot when they were pelted with rocks and water bottles. Local talk shows incessantly parsed the significance and necessity of the police presence in Baltimore, which included city and county police—and eventually the National Guard.

Police Misinformation and the Gang Response

Some media outlets suggested that the Baltimore Police Department was responsible, at least in part, for events that lead to the escalation of tensions in the city. They had warned the general public

World To Come: Essays On The Baltimore Uprising, Militant Racism, And History

that the Black Guerilla Family (BGF), the Crips *and* the Bloods were out to kill them. However, the idea, from the beginning, was thought to be false—a story leaked by the police to get a head start on the narrative they would shape. There were calls for either the police chief, or at least those who had planted the false gang-threat story, to resign. The rationale was that the fabricated story was not only disingenuous; it put the residents of West Baltimore at further risk of lethal police action. The gangs in question were disturbed because they felt that they were being negatively branded by the police; and they were not acknowledged for their work in the West Baltimore community. Roberto Alejandro interviewed three gang members (Goldie, Bonez and Mugga) who claimed that they had no plans to join forces in order to harm the police.[2] The three men, who purportedly represented only the Crips and Bloods, suggested that they had unified, but they did so over efforts to positively assist the community. In addition, at least one of the group members, Bonez was an aspiring self-published author.[3] Apparently, the police and the community were completely at odds with respect to the role of the gangs. The police had positioned them as would-be assassins of cops; the community had said that during the Baltimore Uprising that there were examples of gang members attempting to work together in order to assist the community and to defuse hostilities. Once again, the media embraced both frames; but particularly the latter since the "black gang" is a stock trope in American popular culture. It was interesting that one news show, "The Young Turks," on *Al-Jazeera America* condemned *Fox News* over the malicious framing of Blacks in Baltimore, particularly regarding the issue of gang involvement.[4] They maintained that the network's goal was to present a coordinated and dangerous black threat to white society.

Even so, criminal gangs in reality are genuine threats to the public wellbeing of our communities. In 2007, Maryland legislators passed House Bill 713, the "Maryland Gang Prosecution Act" which

---

[2]Roberto Alejandro, "Gang Members Discuss Role in Baltimore's Uprising," (Special to the AFRO http://www.afro.com/gang-members-role-in-baltimores-uprising/), *New Pittsburgh Courier*, May 7, 2015, http://newpittsburghcourieronline.com/2015/05/07/gang-members-discuss-role-in-baltimores-uprising/, accessed May 9, 2015.
[3]*Gangster Statistics: The Untold Story.*
[4]"The Young Turks," hosted by John Iadarola, Ana Kasparian, and Jimmy Dore, Al-Jazeera America, April 28, 2015.

was approved by then Governor Martin O'Malley.[5] By accepting that organized urban gangs engaged in criminal activity were capable of doing good works, the media was able to link them (irrespective of their motives) to the interests of the black community. In doing so, the meaning of good deeds by gangs was ignored, and the black community was in effect criminalized. Gangs, by definition, are illegal entities operating within communities.[6] This meant that the community itself would be described as being in league with criminal gangs. Gangs like the Crips and the Bloods have an extensive history in America. As many scholars have noted succinctly, "The presence of gangs in African-American communities poses serious threat to the quality of life for community residents largely because they prey on community residents and engage in criminal activities including violent confrontations with rival gangs."[7] If the police had credible evidence of a gang threat against local law enforcement then why did they not arrest or question known gang members immediately, at least the self-identified followers or leaders? In addition to the Crips and the Bloods, the BGF was consistently described as notorious and infamous. The police had them tied to over a dozen murders in 2005. Two years before this, the group, operating in Baltimore's Greenmount community, were said to terrorize residents—threaten and intimidate people, and that they were responsible for the areas drug trade—in addition to murder. In 2013, the Baltimore City Police issued a massive indictment against 48 members of the BGF. These arrest warrants were executed by police and federal agents. On January 6, 2015, Jason Armstrong, a BGF gang member, walked into the Northeastern District station with a loaded gun. He indicated that he had been ordered to enter a police district (with a gun and drugs—apparently he emitted the odor of Marijuana) in order to test police security. The police immediately alerted officers with a citywide bolo; and the FBI offered their support.[8] Armstrong was charged with drug and weapons offenses and jailed. Countless news outlets ran the story, and all

---

[5]Maryland House Bill 713, Chapter 496, "Maryland Gang Prosecution Act of 2007," May 17, 2007.
[6]MD Criminal Law Code §9-801 (2013).
[7]James F. Anderson, Laronistine Dyson, and Tazinski Lee, "Ridding the African-American Community of Black Gang Proliferation," *The Western Journal of Black Studies*, Vol. 20, No. 2, 1996, 83-88, 85.
[8]Justin George and Justin Fenton, "Man Says Gang Told Him to Take Gun Into Baltimore Police Station, Police Say," *The Washington Post*, January 6, 2015.

World To Come: Essays On The Baltimore Uprising, Militant Racism, And History

emphasized the obvious danger police were in. Yet none of the information available revealed that the police (or the media) expressed any concern for the citizens. The BGF, an original prison gang almost fifty years old, was counted among "Maryland's most active prison gangs....(whose) leaders still control much of the groups' outside criminal activities from behind bars."[9] If the gangs in question were criminal enterprises fueling illicit drugs and violent acts against the citizens of Baltimore, then why would local activists and ministers' support, acknowledge and even praise their role? Moreover, if the gangs were left to the streets in the Baltimore Uprising, would they not want to take advantage of the heightened tensions and national spotlight, by instigating, leading, and/or in some way participating in the looting and riots?

Rawlings-Blake, The Uprising, and the Interruption of City Culture

As with any social upheaval that strains the imagination, the first order of business was to begin looking for someone to blame. The community and the police shared external blame. However, some critics laid everything at the feet of the mayor, Stephanie Rawlings-Blake. Before Mosby had presented her decisive press conference, Rawlings-Blake had been mostly criticized for using the term "thug" to refer to the looters and those who vandalized property. She had been widely condemned for her comment suggesting that the city would give "...them the space to destroy..." and then, bearing the weight of the mayor's office, seemingly allowed it to happen. Dark grey and black smoke billowed out of every orifice of the CVS. Cars, including the infamous police cruiser were burned. Neighborhood businesses were looted and torched in the black community. Despite the strong position she took to ensure the people that the situation was under control—along with Police Commissioner Batts and members of the city council, the Baltimore Uprising had local, national, and international attention. The country wanted to know how the event would unfold, because this would give some indication of what might occur in other major cities if the uprising spread.

One of the first sources of concern was the Inner Harbor, Baltimore's historic seaport. The area is a major commercial and tourist

---

[9] "2012 Gang Threat Assessment," Maryland Coordination and Analysis Center (MCAC), Baltimore, Maryland, 2012, 10.

attraction and it appeared to some as if the National Guard was explicitly protecting this waterfront area. The other issue involved, at least one major clash of protestors and baseball fans outside of Camden Yards that caused the Orioles and White Sox game to be held without spectators. This was a national affront as the media intimated that blacks had shut down America's favorite past time for the evening. When the stadium reopened, some baseball fans responded with "Birds Lives Matter" signs and other derogatory retorts. In addition, the state of emergency and curfew, which affected everyone, included the postponement of such high profile arts events as the performances of the Alvin Ailey American Dance Theatre. In addition, public schools closed the day after the uprising; and many universities either closed or modified their hours of operation. The Baltimore City Police Department also urged the city to encourage parents to keep their children at home on April 29, 2015.[10] Those who criticized the closing of the public schools suggested that the act denied students safe places to discuss and "decompress" the uprising events. Rawlings-Blake would be blamed for much more than this in the weeks and months to come. Yet, notwithstanding the long-term criticisms of Rawlings-Blake's tenure by West Baltimore citizens and other residents, most of the denunciations of her actions appeared politically motivated and came from a variety of sources. When Rawlings-Blake returned to clarify her statements about thugs and the destruction of city property, the message from the media was demeaning. Politicians in general could not take back their rhetorical gaffes or highly insensitive racial remarks (though controversial Republican presidential hopeful Donald Trump would prove to be the exception). However, black women politicians, even in times of crisis, were given no quarter to make mistakes and be human.

In Solidarity with the Baltimore Uprising and Black Protest versus White Revelry

It was not surprising that one of the protest signs from the Baltimore Uprising read "Ferguson Missouri Standing in Solidarity with Baltimore!" Across the country there were coalitions of activists forming inter-state alliances and supporting mutual causes since the shooting of Michael Brown in Ferguson. As in Baltimore, protesters

---

[10]Drew Vetter, BCPD, "Situation Update," email to the city, April 28, 2015.

WORLD TO COME: ESSAYS ON THE BALTIMORE UPRISING, MILITANT RACISM, AND HISTORY

aligned the death of Freddie Gray with other police-encounter deaths of black (and Latino) men:
> Freddie Gray, (Akai) Gurley, Trayvon Martin, Ramarley Graham, Sean Bell and too many others…
> Justice for Freddie Gray, Walter Scott, Eric Garner, Michael Brown, Akai (Gurley) No Justice, No Peace
> No Justice for Gray Brown Garner Grant Nieto Zambrano-Montes No Peace[11]

However, not many could have predicted that Freddie Gray's death would spark thousands to participate (and some would be arrested and injured) in nationwide anti-police brutality protests in numerous major cities. The demonstrations spread mostly in the northeast, the Deep South and southern California. Some of the cities hosting major protests in support of the Baltimore Uprising included Philadelphia, New York, Los Angeles, Chicago, Oakland, Houston, Boston and Washington, D.C. By the time the Baltimore citywide curfew was lifted on May 3, 2015, some of the citizens of Des Moines Iowa had joined the Baltimore Uprising, along with many other cities including Ferguson, Missouri, with a protest in support of Freddie Gray. It was clear that across the nation, Black Lives Matter activists and ordinary citizens recognized the need to speak up against police violence in the community, systemic racial discrimination, and structural deprivation. While groups held specific interests, it is important to note the inter-racial and cross cultural character of demonstrators who saw the contemporary face of institutional discrimination. This was not a signal that traditional racism and racial discrimination was coming to an end, but that people understood the need to unite in order to address these issues. An isolated series of protests over the death of Freddie Gray was considered troubling enough for the establishment, but it was the "in solidarity" demonstrations held throughout the nation that truly concerned private, state and federal law enforcement agencies.

However, in analyzing the Baltimore Uprising, the significance of these massive citywide protests within the context of white privilege to engage in revelry did not go unnoticed. Derrick Clifton presented a series of examples demonstrating that the standard for depicting black and white riots have been very different in our recent history. The

---

[11]See Appendix B: Baltimore Uprising Protest Signs.

author noted that "…when a mob of mostly white people take to the streets, vandalizing cars, storefronts and street signs in the process it usually means someone either won or lost a game."[12] Quite a few universities have a long tradition of mob rioting, "couch burning" and torching cars.[13] These examples involve both collegiate and championship sports games, where groups of whites have been known to destroy public and private property, and to loot. As Clifton pointed out, the media determines that their activities are less of a threat to public safety, then when blacks protest and lose control over the factors that have led to systemic intergenerational deprivation. However, the heavy-handed military response to youth-led liberal social and political movements (i.e. World Trade Organization [WTO] in 1999, and Occupy in 2011) indicated that they knew young people recognized immediate and root causes of societal oppression. The Baltimore Uprising protestors in urban sister-cities emphasized a host of contemporary issues: police brutality, racial profiling, differential justice, hate crimes, homelessness, apartheid schools, de facto segregation, the exploitation of low-wage labor, homophobia, transgender hate crimes, and challenges to environmental justice—and this was just the beginning. The philosophy that bound these fundamentally anti-racist coalitions can be elegantly summed up in a forty-five year old open letter of support James Baldwin wrote to Angela Y. Davis in 1970[14] "…if they take you in the morning, they will be coming for us that night."[15] Decades later, the powerful statement still meant that strong and dedicated alliances of people needed to prepare, and speak with a louder, unified voice—because ultimately in the world to come, they would have no other choice.

---

[12]Derrick Clifton, "11 Stunning Images Highlight the Double Standard of Reactions to Riot Like Baltimore," The Mic.com, http://mic.com/articles/116680/11-stunning-images-highlight-the-double-standard-of-reactions-to-riots-like-baltimore, April 27, 2015, accessed May 13, 2015.
[13]See Krista Baker, Terry Fletcher, Jonathan Nelson, "How WVU's Couch-Burning Tradition Spawned Riots," *Mountaineer News Service*, WVU Reed College of Media, November 8, 2012.
[14]Davis faced criminal charges over, and was acquitted of, the August 7, 1970 Marin County California courtroom takeover.
[15]James Baldwin, "An Open Letter to My Sister, Angela Y. Davis," in Angela Y. Davis, et al, *If They Come in the Morning*, New York: New America Library, 1971, 19-23, 23.

CHAPTER 9

RACISM, KILLOLOGY AND DISBELIEF IN HISTORY

Closely supervised intensive practice is the only path to practical knowledge. There are no easy methods or short cuts. Practice must be intensive enough to render the mechanics of each technique automatic. There is seldom time to stop and think when the pressure of combat is on.—Lieutenant Colonel Rex Applegate USA-Ret.[1]

Racism as a Violent Social Force in Human History

Racism is a specific form of operationalized prejudice. It is pernicious because it acts upon the idea of racial entitlement based on the assumption of human superiority. However, racism has almost always been a means to an end—rather than a construct, which has no functional basis. While, today we might argue the various permutations of racism within a given society (including the domineering white-black scheme), the most effective expression and operation of racism has been a western societal value positioned over the rest of the globe. Native Americans were victims of white racism because they stood in the way of New World lands. Racism revealed its perniciousness when the indigenous people fought back. They were labeled as savages who had hostile intentions against white settlers. Racism always possesses an intricate rationale to accomplish its goals. Therefore, Native American lands were either unoccupied or uncultivated, and therefore, subject to seizure. All forms of critical resistance, including peaceful spiritual actions (i.e. The 1890 Ghost Dance), was met with declarations of war. Nations of peoples, whose cultures and ancestors extended back into the recesses of time, found their existence threatened to annihilation and their lands brutally confiscated.

Racism is dependent upon grandiose perceptions of superior ancestry. The threat of non-whites (and sometimes, white ethnics) always loomed large, but increased during times of war. The United States had always felt threatened by the Orientals, or their idea of the

---

[1]Rex Applegate, *Kill or Get Killed: Riot Control Techniques, Manhandling, and Close Combat, for Police and the Military*. Boulder, CO: Paladin Press, 1976.

"yellow peril," (just one of the terms derisively applied to Japanese, Chinese, and South Asiatic peoples) a convenient foreign immigrant labor force. Again, these were people who possessed ancient cultures and civilizations—and seemingly another category of people who would never be capable of assimilating into white western society. There was a considerable history of legally excluding Asians—Chinese, Japanese and Korean.[2] The fear of Asians raised the old threat that a "Mongol hoard" would be unleashed, intent on enslaving whites and supplanting western civilization. After Japan bombed Pearl Harbor on December 7, 1941, thousands of Japanese Americans (Japanese and mostly American-born) were forcibly relocated and placed in internment camps during World War II. The state of war certainly meant that there was a suspension of tolerance toward immigration—and a question as to whether Japanese Americans possessed the capacity to be loyal to the United States. Japanese Americans were vilified as a people who could not be trusted; and the government emphasized their difference in order to make the point. The Japanese were considered upstart Asians, inferior to the European, a people who dared to have dreams of global imperial power. Their descendants in the United States, principally California, lost their opportunity to create a new life in America, because they were a threat to national security. More often, the so-called Asiatics were thought of as "positively threatening." They were considered a people so industrious that they were a threat to the American system of slavery; or a group perceived as so hard working that they were exploitable. Within the context of World War II, the Japanese Americans lost their homes, livelihoods, and their freedom.

People of African descent have always posed a special problem in the advancement of western civilization. The vastness of the continent of Africa, and the multitude of ethnicities and languages, was a large aspect of this problem. The imperial and colonial challenge of "taking" the African continent took decades; and it was here that the skills needed to advance an absolute racist agenda were honed. This program culminated in the enslavement of African people and the subsequent colonization of the continent. Unlike Native American peoples who possessed an aboriginal birthright to North America, the Africans were forcibly transplanted from their continent. In the

---

[2]For example, The Chinese Exclusion Act (1882), The Immigration Act (1917, 1924), and Executive Order 9066 (1942).

World To Come: Essays On The Baltimore Uprising, Militant Racism, And History

process, blacks would never be depicted as the noble savage—a nostalgic euphemism to concede the loss of great ancient Indian ways of living. Africans would be caste as unmitigated savages. The conquest needed to be perfect. The diverse African ethnic groups shared remarkable cultures, and a collective history that harkened back to the world's first people. The continent of Africa would not only yield humans for trafficking, but also precious and semi-precious resources. African people were, in the western European intellectual canon, stripped of humanity. The emphasis on racial science and categorizations of hierarchies allowed for a creatively biased justification for the removal and subjugation of a people and the exploitation of resources. It also supported the colonization of white Europeans, as in the case of South Africa. It was one thing to take the territory through better military force; and it was another thing to assert, and then maintain, a history that suggested—once again—that the land was either unoccupied or uncultivated—thus, in any case, available for European settlement and resource extraction. At least over time, more than any other exploited group in the history of the United States, it became immensely important to dominate African descended people in a distinct way in order to ensure unchallenged subjugation. Blacks would be forced to immigrate, enslaved, renamed, tainted, and subjected to a host of legal and common brutalities designed to control the body, mind and spirit. For centuries, it was not enough for black people to be enslaved in the United States; Africans were required to affect subservience; and to give deference to white supremacy in western society.

The Baltimore Uprising immediately initiated a strong and contentious public discussion about the nature of racism in the United States. Based on this discussion, particularly from the perspective of activists and other concerned citizens, there were several important elements that characterize the immense concept of racism. To sum up some of the acquired or learned discourse of Black Lives Matter activists, racism is *structural, chaotic, pathogenic,* and *oppressive*. Much less discussed in American society is the *structural* aspect of racism; the idea that it is embedded and infused in U.S. culture and drives institutions and policies. However, activists referenced, from an historical perspective, racism as an old and violent social force. In this discussion, it was clear that many more people were beginning to understand the profound difference between racism and racial bigotry. Yet in structural racism racial bigotry is extremely important to our understanding because, even though it exists without the actual power to effect racist policies—it is a basic sign of the intent to advance militant (armed) racism. Racism is an important foundation in the development of the history of the United States, identified through overt and covert expressions of prejudice as a sign of racist intent, as well as a violent construction (i.e. slavery).

Structural and systemic racism and racial prejudice not only subjugates people in the moment, it incapacitates people through the advance of *chaotic* themes, discourses and actions. Racially oppressed people are kept in a constant state of mistrust and confusion. Racism foments mass anxiety in modern society—where it often attempts to conceal, or obfuscate its motive. For African descended people in particular, racism thwarts the development of black cultural and social consciousness. People generally have difficulty developing culturally and socially because they are not supposed to; and when they fail to understand this, they will often attribute their challenges to other issues and circumstances. In this chaos, racism absolves and protects bigoted speech and actions which culminate in staunch denials of racism. No other feature of modern racism is more effective than absolute denial. As a result, people remain confused and dazed in the face of blatantly racist acts—especially when the state refuses to acknowledge, investigate, and hold accountable, racist individuals, organizations, and institutions. The main reason the concept spreads confusion, is because it cannot exist alongside of counter ideals that mark high-achieving civilizations—such as freedom, democracy, equality, liberty, etc. When racism lives side-by-side with these societal ideals, they are negated.

Some have compared racism to a disease; and it can be argued that racism is not a disease, but that it is the *pathogen*, capable of producing (like a virus or bacteria) any number of social diseases. Racism is an embedded social character disorder. This means that those deemed members of a superior race are empowered and emboldened to support the system; while those considered part of an inferior group are constantly reminded of this imposed status. In our modern configuration, whites who deviate from this imposed social status might be called race traitors or progressives; blacks who reject the inferior assignment are usually labeled radicals, combatives, or at the very least angry persons. For decades, scholars have analyzed the psychopathy of racism. Some fundamental ideas in the psychopathologic racial system include the "…inability to accept blame or learn from previous experience …"; the intention to "…reject constituted authority and discipline…"; and the willingness to "…consistently take advantage of Blacks without any guilt, anxiety, or threat to their self-esteem..."[3] In addition, another aspect of the disease quality of racism mandates that society immunize itself against black humanity; or any target other deemed a direct cultural, social or political threat to white society (i.e. Native Americans, Latinos, Muslims, etc.). This means that they feel the need to take measures to shield and/or remove themselves from people thought to threaten their existence. This immunity includes the acceptance and advancement of racial stereotypes; as well as idealistic confirmations of western values, especially among non-whites. This immunization is particularly potent as a popular culture expression of visual images and public storytelling (films, television series, and photographs)—shared media events that support the racist narrative. Much of today's moderate racism-as-a-disease discourse and scholarship has its roots in the analysis of courageous black scholars (including, but not limited to, Franz Fanon, Bobby E. Wright, Amos N. Wilson, Na'im Akbar, Frances Cress Welsing and many others).[4]

Racism *oppresses* most effectively through an unrelenting opposition to the target other. Racism—as it relates to the African American experience—dictates that fundamentally all blacks are, at least theoretically, if not in actuality, fugitives from justice. This is such a prevalent theme in the African American experience that there are standardized anecdotes, derived from historical precedent, that speak to the circumstance. For example, there were always concerns about groups of enslaved blacks "congregating" because it violated racial convention. Blacks have had to appeal to the federal government for racial social justice, which they believed would be available at the state and local levels. This was an important indication to the extent a racist society will go to protect the system. It showed that racial equality and democracy can be illusive on the state level; and that there is no guarantee that the federal government will address the issues. To be sure, racism is symbolic power; the ever vigilant human effort to

---

[3] Bobby E. Wright, *The Psychopathic Racial Personality And Other Essays*. (Second Edition) Chicago: Third World Press, 1997, 7-9.
[4] See Franz Fanon, *The Wretched of the Earth*. New York: Grove Press, Inc., 1963; Bobby E. Wright, *The Psychopathic Racial Personality And Other Essays*. (Second Edition) Chicago: Third World Press, 1997; Amos N. Wilson, *The Falsification Of Afrikan Consciousness: Eurocentric History, Psychiatry, And The Politics Of White Supremacy*. Afrikan World InfoSystems, 1993; Na'im Akbar, *From Miseducation to Education*, New Mind Productions, 1984; and Frances Cress Welsing, *The Isis Papers The Keys to the Colors*, Chicago: Third World Press, 1991.

establish and maintain supremacy over another human being. Because racism far exceeds our expedient conceptions of race relations, diversity, and even powerless racial bigotry, we must address the somber foundation of structural oppression based on race. The micro-aggressions and the macro-expressions of racism belie a serious "us versus them" mindset. This mindset has always operated as a zero-sum contest. In American society, it is almost impossible—especially in a racial context—for people see a "win-win" outcome. Generally, even a modest gain for Blacks (i.e. a "win" [Civil Rights, Voting Rights, Reparations, etc.]) is viewed as a categorical "loss" for Whites.

Killology—The Study and Ideology of War

The act of actually killing someone begins in the mind. Authentic militarists and scholars know this; and they also know that there are many ways to kill people without removing the physical body. Cultural genocide is demonstrative of the fact that it is not necessary to kill people physically.[5] Yet, it is very difficult to kill spirit and hope in people, at least for a time—because the human will is indomitable. As difficult as it is, we must consider the historic impact of "soul murder" on the lives of people, especially children.[6] Black male children learn at a very early age that they are considered a problem in society— and are saturated with negative labels like "angry" and "intimidating." Black females have reported that the moment they walk into a room, nonblack people are immediately "uncomfortable" with their presence. Racial hostility is a shared public space where even the imagery of blackness can fill a room where no black people exist. This notion is bound to the past and alive in the present. The imagery is stock and trade in American popular fantasy culture—i.e. Hollywood zombies. In the ideology of war, blackness becomes a stimulus for defensive vigilance and offensive reaction. The symbology of killing blackness is as evident as the reality of neighborhoods where no black people live; schools in which few, if any, black students attend, and retail outlets that never see black customers. This absence of blacks in any space is a form of social death. To kill someone—before the act of killing the

---

[5]Anthony T. Browder, *Survival Strategies for Africans in America*. Washington, D.C.: The Institute of Karmic Guidance, 1996, 123-129.
[6]Nell Irvin Painter, *Soul Murder and Slavery: Toward A Fully Loaded Cost Accounting*. na, 1995.

World To Come: Essays On The Baltimore Uprising, Militant Racism, And History

body—is a social undertaking that includes destroying culture, history, creativity—and intellect. This is more than the denigration of the human being, in the historical record this is an annihilation of the totality of the human experience. This is the removal of human self-consciousness. Especially when people no longer recognize that their particular existence is rooted and expansive, they are less of a racial threat. However, what remains is the shell of consciousness in a world filled with the expression of primitive motives. When we are no longer able to have honest self-conscious internal dialogues that seek to examine and elevate the human spirit—we are dead before we die.

There are many places in the civilized world where ordinary citizens realize that they can literally be killed at any moment. American society is so aggressive in this regard, particularly as a result of random gun violence; killing can occur anywhere—the neighborhood store, the movie theater, and in schools. Even in these venues involving gun violence, the act of killing is still associated with the idea of warfare. According to Dave Grossman in times of war, "Execution of innocent civilians … is … a highly personal act of psychotic irrationality that openly refutes the humanity of the victims."[7] To kill someone, especially at close range is personal and is predicated on absolute intentionality. Poor African Americans are deemed common and appealing enemies in society. Blacks on the main are not publically perceived as unique individuals, but an aggregate threat to society. Therefore, a culture of killing (killology) makes multiple black deaths not only possible but also predictable. Killing, over any other form of immobilization and restraint, becomes the favored reality. However, as popular as it is to "trash" law enforcement, police killings of unarmed African Americans are not the primary issue of the police force, but are a measure of racism in society. The deaths of black men affect the entire society by establishing and reinforcing community trauma. The police, equipped with the latest weaponry and riot gear, are depicted as super soldier guardians of non–black communities. The racial relational aspect of killology is legitimized through culture, ethical, psychological, social and technology means. Police are a symptomatic emblem of what actually ails society. Yet they are the new world Watchmen—protecting society and policing blacks as a race of people. The frequency with which they pull the trigger on black males is a learned response that

---

[7]Dave Grossman, *On Killing: The Psychological Cost of Learning To Kill In War And Society*. Boston: Back Bay Books, 1995, 106.

speaks to their sense of proximity to humanity and the need for psychic distance. Armored and trained as military police, equipped with riot gear they set up behind enemy lines. The historic rituals of purification begin. The real fear held by the guardians of society is not the outcomes of black anger or enlightened empowerment; but white intellectual readjustment about racism in American society.

Racism, Disbelief, Denial, and Fashionable Forgetting

Disbelief is generally defined as the inability to accept, or the absolute denial of, something that is true. In the Baltimore Uprising, it appears that some are as baffled by the whole idea of why blacks would want to protest, in the same way that protestors were perplexed regarding how Freddie Gray got his spine and neck crushed in a police-encounter. However, disbelief is the refusal to accept what is real, and this negation justifies fantasy. It is the surrender of reality in order to embrace a sheltered perception of the world. Disbelief is central to the acceptance of militant racist authority. It is far more comfortable for the reality-challenged to believe that great numbers of blacks have not been victims of the American Dream; that they are a "pathological" people; and that they deserve to be incarcerated, or killed for possessing "weaponized" objects such as a key, wallet, cellphone, or a pocketknife. Still, racism is the supreme art of mythmaking, and it is obedient to its own aggrandizing narrative. Racism is also a simple metaphysical idea. The phantasmagorical nature of racism means that black children can be easily depicted as violent and dangerous grown-ups and treated accordingly. This allowed Michael Brown to be transformed into a demon by the officer who shot him, which justified his killing, and further permitted his dehumanization by media and police advocacy groups. The creation of black monsters, the effort to embody black males and the notion, is necessary for society. The diversion shifts attention away from a host of social, political and economic concerns. In the mythology of black monsters, black males are not presented as exceptions to the rule—they are the rule. However, while structural racism has powered social normative behavior; grotesque public expressions of white racial bias-bigotry (without the necessary force to carry out the threat) are generally frowned upon.

Disbelief and denial are often wrapped around the struggle with historical knowledge. Some people, who encounter histories that make them terribly uncomfortable, want to know how to remove that past. They want to negate history, diminish this information, and stop the transmission of historical knowledge from generation to generation. If reformers cannot eliminate the study of history altogether, then denial is one of the most effective ways of reducing the power of history. However, denial is also pernicious in other ways. Denial obliterates memory; maintains that an historical event or action never occurred. Denial helps to keep oppression alive and functioning. Denial also neutralizes the moral authority of people—their ability to persuade others of good will to stand against injustice.

One example is the modern Jewish holocaust denial movement.[8] Through the experience of the Jews in Western Europe, we learn that planned genocide never looks that way at the time. Long before the strategic extermination of the Jews in Nazi Germany during WWII, they were viewed as the ultimate enemy of the state. The German propaganda media demonized Jews, maintained at all times that they were a threat to national security, and a danger to the very existence of Germans as an ancient racial group. In the process of rejecting the history of the Jewish holocaust, there is the absolute denial of the existence of or any responsibility for the "final solution," the concentration camps; or that any harm was caused to the Jewish, local German, and world communities. This is part of the art and practice of definitely stigmatizing people for the purposes of genocide. Another aspect of denial is the minimization of history. It sounds simplistic today, but it explains some of the processes of modern media and men; especially the fundamental idea that the control of peoples' thinking about historical events/issues ultimately determines how that event/issue will be interpreted, and then acted upon. Deniers and minimizers of history do not limit their robust activities to the Jewish Holocaust; they have also been busy with the promulgation of a profound global anti-African sentiment and historiography.

If we consider African Americans in the context of historical denying and minimizing, we find a complex web of negative popular assertions designed to reduce or eliminate the capacity for blacks to unify their efforts. Not long after the Baltimore Uprising, there emerged a handful of unassuming news stories which questioned

---

[8]One of the texts considered foundational to the Holocaust denial movement is Arthur R. Butz. *The Hoax of the Twentieth Century: The Case Against The Presumed Extermination Of European Jewry.* Torrance, CA: Institute for Historical Review, 1985.

whether African Americans were "appropriating" African culture. This is a comfortably persistent racist theme in the African American experience. And this is similar to the annual public discourse suggesting that Kwanzaa, the federal holiday for Martin Luther King, Jr., and Black History Month are racially divisive. The 2015 appropriation stories were often subsumed under the harmless idea of fashion—African clothing, textiles and jewelry. These stories stayed alive for months as various commentators weighed in on both sides. The problem was the underlying assumption that African Americans had no biological, cultural, or historical connection to their Africanity. This meant that no matter what side people chose, the original premise was flawed. It already made the issue of black culture suspect; and it allowed people to feel that they had to debate the foundations of the African American experience. To remove African Americans from their African cultural roots, added to the notions of difference and deviance; disconnected them from other blacks worldwide; and supported indifferent, if not inhuman treatment.

  The articles consistently used the term "appropriating" which was unmistakably meant to bring to mind its synonyms: seizing, stealing, removing, etc.—in other words taking something that did not belong to them. In essence, this was an African American *cultural crime* that fell into the realm of popular public conversations-no-other-race-is-subjected-to. What the casual observer was not privy to was that the innocuous conversations about African Americans wearing African clothing today, had nothing to do with fashion. It was really an extension of an older racial assault on the cultural constructs of Afrocentricity from the late 1990s. It had only one purpose, to disconnect people of African descent from their ancestral African roots. If no one speaks for the cultural unity of African Americans, then blacks the world over also remain vulnerable to physical and temporal attacks. If African Americans were truly appropriating African cultural apparel and accoutrements, then they had no genuine link to Africana heritage, and were thus, a false or crypto people. The timing of this discussion (whether intended or not) was flawless. At a time when large swathes of blacks across the nation were uniting loosely under the umbrella of Black Lives Matter, a subtler conversation questioned their relationship to one another. In the end, the question of appropriation was not a question at all—it was a carefully cultivated denial of African American humanity within the larger context of national and global assertions of Africanity.

World To Come: Essays On The Baltimore Uprising, Militant Racism, And History

Racism, Protest Signage, and Maximum Discomfort in the Community

From a military perspective, racism ensures maximum discomfort in poor black communities; and supports the containment approach to law enforcement often applied to people who are forced to live poverty. As a national public health issue, racism demoralizes and destabilizes the community, advances malicious cycles of exploitation, and consistently fuels internal confusion and widespread mistrust. Neighborhoods are more often managed from the outside, with the limited ability of community members to be directly involved in the decision-making process, which then only too often provides a petite role. However, the people, as a whole are viewed as social threats in need of public control. The war on the poor is actually a high form of social neglect. Specifically, this work refers to the officers who work on the street and in the community. It has been cited that police have taken on more and more of a burden-some social intervention and referral service role. Domestic, mental and emotional disturbances, which require professional services, are often first addressed by the police, which in turn, criminalize health issues. Dispensing with such procedures as probable cause—and embracing views that people are guilty of *something* until proven innocent—undermines communities. Keeping families and communities on the edge of human existence means the difference between a home and a place to live. This idea is reinforced when the public believes that the structural goal is to dislodge and ultimately remove them from the community.

One way to view the perception that maximum discomfort has been inflicted on the black community is to look at the protest signs. In the Baltimore Uprising, there is no question that many residents were angry with the police, and the protest signs clearly indicated this. Overall they charged police brutality and called for an end to it. Some of the uprising signs read, "Black Power! Stop Police Brutality," "End Police Terror!," "No good cops in a racist system," and "Police Brutality is a systematic problem." Baltimore residents and many supporters also expressed concern about the bleak social-economic conditions through signs like, "We can't breathe," "Fund State Schools not a police state," "I'd Love a job, Got one?," "End the Curfew," and "End Police Killings of Black Lives now." To a city pushed to the edge of madness over the death of Freddie Gray, several of the signs did not plead for justice, these announcements demanded it. These signs read, "Arrest, prosecute & Jail Cops Guilty of Police Brutality," "Justice 4 Black Lives," and "We want real justice." The protest banners also featured the words of American personages, such as signage attributed to Thomas Jefferson, Malcolm X, Martin Luther King, Jr., and James Baldwin. The signs also (which were sometimes carried by white protesters) indicated the racial demarcation between blacks and whites and the issues of white racial privilege. Among these were signs that read: "Black Lives Matter More than White Supremacy," "Is Life a White Privilege," "Is my life worth more than theirs?" (Carried by a white protester), "My 2 white nephews have white privilege in USA my 3 black nephews are Freddie Gray!!!," "White Silence is Violence," and "White Silence = White Consent." Overwhelmingly the protest banners addressed the police and policing practices. These posters and placards—some printed, many handwritten—were centrally focused on the death of Freddie Gray (and many others) and the issue of accountability for the police officers involved these deaths.[9]

Black communities experience maximum discomfort when the normative policing policy is to aggressively control and contain the residents. According to Michael Tillotson's work, *Invisible Jim Crow*, this discomfort is an established position of Eurocentric racist philosophy, which ensures that positive change does not take place. Further, his concepts of Agency Reduction Formation and the Post-Racial Project explain the ongoing efforts to destabilize black minds and entire communities through ideological dependency and domination.[10] Therefore, blacks suffer a multiplicity of restrictive quality of life issues that, for others, would signal the government that critical and immediate assistance is needed. These environmentally-compromised neighborhoods often have no employer base; endure exploitative goods and services, as well as high rents for inferior housing. In the past, some residents have been denied water for unpaid bills, do not have regular trash pick-ups, are forced to combat rodents, walk through streets that are not regularly cleaned—in addition to a hostile policing climate. Residents have said that they are subjected to constant arrests for contrived nuisance crimes (such as standing on the corner), but that the police cannot seem to get a handle on major drug and robbery crimes. It is not uncommon for frequent arrests to take place, where citizens are released without being charged with any crime. The quasi police-state maneuver leaves people angry, afraid, and traumatized.

---

[9]See Appendix B: Baltimore Uprising Protest Signs.
[10]Michael Tillotson, *Invisible Jim Crow: Contemporary Ideological Threats to the Internal Security of African Americans*, Trenton, NJ: Africa World Press, 2011, 60-62, 101-116.

World To Come: Essays On The Baltimore Uprising, Militant Racism, And History

There is a basic understanding among the residents about how they live—and this is a hallmark of such neighborhoods—*they know* they exist under conditions of maximum discomfort. The residents often have an intense personal experience with law enforcement, formative meetings with police; or they know someone who has been abused or died in police-encounters. Residents also tolerate routine disrespect, harassment, and humiliation. As a result, there is a plain sense of survival that states: the police are to be avoided. Because there has been long-term community-police mistrust (us versus them), fostered over generations, there is a constant state of suspicion and anxiety.

When we add a domestic policing philosophy that permits *shoot-to-kill*, we have established one of the most efficient ways to create maximum discomfort in communities. However, districts like Sandtown-Winchester (and other areas) in Baltimore do not exist in a vacuum and without an historical context. To reject the history of these neighborhoods—too conveniently forget that once they thrived—dismisses their value and potential. There are also other policy histories that, though well meaning, are relegated to failed development attempts. This results in the dis-investment of communities. Often there is a cycle of community development plans, which are task-forced, assessed, discussed, and reported, but actual long-term investment is limited. In the process, people are offered hope without the intent or ability to create lasting change. Distressed communities are continually denied economic self-sufficiency. As people struggle and live in adversity, the challenges that work against them reflect law enforcement crisis management situations. For example, neighborhoods are structurally contained and movement is restricted. Black Baltimoreans are used to CCTV (Closed Circuit Television) cameras; and police helicopters that routinely patrol communities with the liberal use of floodlights at night. Random police "pick-ups" for no apparent cause also serve as a tool to meet arrest quotas, and to later identify and monitor residents. Individuals are trained to have low expectations of investors, government officials, and the police, as they struggle for everything needed to live. Yet, there are citizens who are not demoralized and they resolve to *get out* so that they can gain the skills needed to come back and help their neighbors. Others believe the battle cannot wait, that skill-building is on the ground, and they remain for the same reason. Either way, too often, citizens operate in a world that promises development, yet delivers maximum discomfort.

CHAPTER 10

BALTIMORE AND THE NEW URBAN POLICE STATE

...in a modern, highly technological society, with its CIA, FBI, electronic surveillance, and cops armed and equipped for overkill, here are black Americans demanding our constitutional rights, and demanding that our basic desires and needs be fulfilled, thus becoming the vanguard of a revolution, despite all attempts to totally wipe us out.—Bobby Seale[1]

COINTELPRO Surveillance, the ISD in Baltimore, and the Elimination of "Primitive Man"

COINTELPRO (code name for the FBI's Counter Intelligence Program), was initially set up in 1956 to monitor and destabilize the US-based Communist Party. Later the program was later extended to address white supremacist hate groups, namely the Ku Klux Klan in 1964. The FBI's COINTELPRO operation became quite infamous as a program concerned with damaging and eliminating those groups deemed radical in the United States. The operation was secret and committed to using proven Cold War methods of military intelligence gathering to weaken these groups. COINTELPRO used an extensive surveillance apparatus to carry out the activities of infiltration, harassment, persecution, deception (including forgery, burglary, and fraud), intimidation, sabotage, and violence. Officially authorized to target blacks on August 25, 1967[2], every major U.S. city with appreciable numbers of African Americans had at least one field office for conducting the program. Some of the black groups subjected to COINTELPRO surveillance and disruption campaigns included:
- The Black Panther Party
- The Congress of African People
- The Congress of Racial Equality (CORE)
- The Dodge Revolutionary Union Movement (DRUM)

---

[1]Bobby Seale, *Seize The Time: The Story Of The Black Panther Party And Huey P. Newton.* New York, NY: Random House, 1970, ix-x.
[2]COINTELPRO also targeted the "New Left" (white student activists and anti-war protest groups) in 1967.

World To Come: Essays On The Baltimore Uprising, Militant Racism, And History

- The League of Black Revolutionary Workers
- The Nation of Islam ("Black Muslims")
- The National Welfare Rights Organization
- The Republic of New Afrika (RNA)
- The Revolutionary Action Movement (RAM)
- The Student Non-Violent Coordinating Committee (SNCC)

From the very beginning—black organizations were defined as national security threats, groups who were "engaged in black extremism." This included black organizational initiatives that involved civil and human rights, political participation and leadership, cultural enhancement, and community self-help. The program also targeted Black Student Unions at colleges and universities (including HBCUs), as well as an anchor of black society—religious institutions. Any black community organization dedicated to advancing the civil and human rights of African Americans fell under the purview of the bureau. From the beginning, COINTELPRO, according to J. Edgar Hoover, honed in on black nationalist groups, including "...their leadership, spokesman, membership, and supporters..."[3] However, under the FBI's definition, and even with their vague acknowledgement of "responsible Negroes,"[4] any black group, organizational entity, or public activity was a target. As with other groups surveilled by COINTELPRO in the 1960s and 1970s, the bureau identified white supremacist, liberal leftist and dissident groups—and other organizations that posed a threat because of their political activism and rhetoric. However, African Americans as a specific race of people (based on the breath of the program's operations) were expressly pinpointed. The history of COINTELPRO has demonstrated that the government operation used media and military strategy (in the broadest sense) to covertly monitor and disrupt the activities of black Americans.

The city of Baltimore has gained a reputation for being one of the most militarized towns in the U.S.; and concomitant to this, an urban center that values the intelligence gained from surveillance. However, the black community has always been under some form of surveillance in the United States. Historically, this has included the enslavement experience, the period throughout post-emancipation Jim

---

[3]Ward Churchill, *Agents of Repression: The FBI's Secret War Against the Black Panther Party and the American Indian Movement.* Boston, MA: South End Press, 1988, 58.
[4]FBI Memorandum to SAC, Albany, Counterintelligence Program, Black Nationalist—Hate Groups, Racial Intelligence, March 4, 1968, 3.

WORLD TO COME: ESSAYS ON THE BALTIMORE UPRISING,
MILITANT RACISM, AND HISTORY

Crow racial segregation, and during the Civil Rights/Black Power movements. Following the assassination of Martin Luther King, Jr., and the 1968 riots in the city of Baltimore, Inspectional Services Divisions (ISD) of police departments emerged, and they were primarily interested in spying on, in the spirit of and in cooperation with COINTELPRO, the activities of civil rights workers and other perceived leftist militants. The IDS was concerned with the widespread probe of African Americans in the city of Baltimore. In the 1970s, the BCPD, through the Inspectional Services Division (ISD), engaged in a comprehensive surveillance program against the black community.[5] This included attempts to infiltrate grassroots Baltimore groups like the Black Panthers, Mother Jones, and John Brown collectives. George Derek Musgrove outlined how black politicians, especially those who had been in the vanguard of the Civil Rights movement, were easily perceived as part of the "...insurgent black population...."[6] Musgrove examined how black congressional representatives were routinely (and heavily) surveilled by state police agencies under IDS or other police intelligence units. Throughout the country black political leaders like John Conyers (D-MI), Barbara Jordan (D-TX), and Charles Rangel (D-NY) were monitored.[7] In addition to being a target of the IDS, Shirley Chisholm (D-NY), while on the presidential campaign trail in 1972, was subjected to a mysterious attempt to discredit her with a fake press release which scurrilously questioned her psychological state.[8]

In Baltimore, Parren Mitchell (D-MD), Maryland's first black congressman, served the 7th congressional district from 1971 through 1987. For six years (and before he was elected to congress), the Baltimore IDS meticulously monitored Mitchell's life including the recording of his home and office activities.[9] According to Musgrove's research and account, the IDS made it no secret that they were surveilling Mitchell.[10] The IDS's activities were so dubious that when

---

[5]Judson L. Jeffries, "Black Radicalism and Political Repression in Baltimore: The case of the Black Panther Party." *Ethnic and Racial Studies* 25, No. 1 (2002): 64-98.
[6]George Derek Musgrove, *Rumor, Repression, and Racial Politics: How the Harassment of Black Elected Officials Shaped Post-civil Rights America*. Athens: University of Georgia Press, 2012, 58.
[7]Ibid., 58.
[8]Barbara Winslow, *Shirley Chisholm*. Boulder, CO: Westview Press, 2014, 124-125.
[9]George Derek Musgrove, *Rumor, Repression, and Racial Politics: How the Harassment of Black Elected Officials Shaped Post-civil Rights America*. Athens: University of Georgia Press, 2012, 58.
[10]Ibid., 58.

they were slated for investigation by the state senate, the police intelligence agency managed to "eliminate" operational files before the inquiry could progress.[11] Just as COINTELPRO morphed into state-led Inspectional Services Divisions, Musgrove documents how the decline of police-intelligence gathering units, who worked to specifically go after black congressional representatives, was transformed into the widespread political harassment of these civic leaders.[12] This harassment included programs like "Operation Fruehmenschen," a campaign against black elected officials.[13] "Operation Fruehmenschen" (which means Operation Primitive/Early Man) was "… the FBI's own designation for the Justice Department/FBI campaign to frame-up, jail, and drive from office, hundreds of African-American elected officials…" It was important to oust black elected officials because the bureau thought they were "'… intellectually and socially incapable of governing major governmental organizations and situations.'"[14] From the 1960s through the 1990s, the rationale was that "black extremists" were the threat. Again however, through various federal and state agencies, there was no difference made between black organizations and political leaders deemed radical or moderate. Black participation in government leadership and community development was perceived as a threat to national security, black leaders were systematically surveilled, their activities monitored, and they were targeted for campaigns to discredit and/or remove them from office.

The High Cost of Fatal Police-Community Conflict

Like Baltimore, many other cities have a history of conflict between the police and its black residents, and sometimes this struggle has been litigious and costly. Millions of dollars are spent defending police officers and on settlements paid to victims and their families. In

---

[11]George Derek Musgrove, *Rumor, Repression, and Racial Politics: How the Harassment of Black Elected Officials Shaped Post-civil Rights America.* Athens: University of Georgia Press, 2012, 70, 81.
[12]Ibid., 70.
[13]Debra Hanania-Freeman, T. Mitchell, L. Young, and C. Mitchell. "Baltimore Coalition Mobilizes Against Hit Squad in the DOJ." *Executive Intelligence Review* 25 (1998): 26-31; see also P. S. Kane, "Why Have You Singled Me Out? The Use of Prosecutorial Discretion for Selective Prosecution." *Tulane Law Review* 67 (1993): 2293-2371.
[14]Testimony of the Schiller Institute Submitted to the Committee on the Judiciary, United States Senate July 13, 1998, http://american_almanac.tripod.com/dojtest.htm, accessed October 5, 2015.

World To Come: Essays On The Baltimore Uprising, Militant Racism, And History

cases not involving the death of citizens, the city of Pittsburgh and the police department, between 2011 and 2012, paid nearly 400,000 dollars for charges of police misconduct. In addition, as a result of the Ferguson riots over the death of Michael Brown, police agencies have settled a legal action that will ban the use of tear gas (and other chemical weapons) on protesters. Not all deadly encounters with police result in monetary or non-monetary settlements for the victim's families. Even some of the most brazen cases indicating abuse of power more often absolve the officers of any liability. However, when police departments, state and city governments pay to settle deadly encounters with police, the price is considered high. Not because they are attempting to place a monetary value on any human life, but because a message of deterrence is being sent. In 2001, the city of Chicago approved a settlement of 18 million for the 1999 police-encounter shooting of LaTanya Haggerty, a computer analyst and college graduate. The police thought that Haggerty had a gun; however, she was holding a cell phone. The University of Cincinnati paid 2 million dollars to settle the taser-death of 18-year-old Everette Howard, Jr., an Upward Board student. In 2011, a University of Cincinnati Police officer fired a taser gun at Howard after "encountering" him on campus "in the early morning hours...."[15] Furthermore, in 2014, the city of New York awarded 5.9 million in the case of Eric Garner. Garner died as a result of a chokehold administered by police. In the Flint Michigan collateral damage lawsuit against the police in the death of Jaqueline Nichols, the family was awarded $7.7 million dollars. In the fall of 2015, the North Charleston city council unanimously voted to award the family of Walter Scott 6.5 million. Scott was stopped for a broken taillight, and then shot in the back by Officer Michael Slager, as he ran away. One might think that frequent multimillion-dollar settlements would curb the tide of questionable police-encounter deaths. They do not. Except in the rarest of cases, officers are defended, shielded, and often retained their positions. City and state governments pay—and taxpayers find, at some point, that they pay for deadly encounters with the police. All the while, as the monetary settlements are awarded, citizens are told that the police agencies and the officers involved "admit no wrong-doing." In rare recent cases, in

---

[15]United States District Court, *Travonna Howard v. Richard Hass*, Settlement Agreement, Full Release and Covenant Not to Sue, Richard Haas and The University of Cincinnati with Travonna Howard and Everette Howard, January 7, 2013.

acts that represented imperfect logic and the callousness of post-encounter shooting deaths, some officers have filed lawsuits (or sought other forms of legal remunerations) against the deceased victims "estates" and their families. In these cases the victims is held financially accountable for expenses related to his or her death; or officers have maintained that they were harmed in the encounter because of the fear and trauma they suffered in killing the person.

The city of Baltimore has an extensive history of tension and hostility between the police and its black residents. Many blacks feel that Baltimore is a police brutality city. It has been reported in many venues that the city has paid out nearly six million dollars to residents to settle lawsuits or judgements stemming from assertions of excessive force and outright police brutality. At one point, they had to cap the settlements to a half a million dollars. There were many cases that never made it to judgement or settlement, but those that did were considered egregious. Court documents reveal that citizens were brutalized in the process of being arrested, while others probably should not have been arrested or jailed at all. Most of the people targeted by police were African American, and most of the time they were unarmed. In the hours, days and weeks after the pinnacle of the Baltimore Uprising, people were trying to "make sense" of why and how it happened. In early May, *The Baltimore Sun*, and other media outlets reported within a three-year period, that thousands of people who were arrested had severe injuries, which prevented them from being admitted to the Baltimore City Detention Center.[16] This means that arrestees might have been subjected to police brutality, were routinely denied medical care; that police are not adequately trained to address injuries and suspect requests for medical care, and police records on the issue are too often nonexistent, incomplete or later are redacted. Baltimore, like other cities, pays settlements to avoid costly lawsuits, the cases that might be tried by juries and awarded more damages. The high profile cases, those that cause cities to erupt, seem to pay settlements to preclude a trial, rather than cases that do not capture mass media attention, or garner communities-of-care around victims. In 2010, Baltimore City Police officers were ordered to settle with the family of

---

[16] Mark Puente and Meredith Cohn, "Freddie Gray Among Many Suspects who do not get Medical care from Baltimore police," *The Baltimore Sun*, May 9, 2015; Scott Falkner, "Baltimore Arrest Report Says Thousands of Suspects Too Injured to Enter Jail," *Inquisitr*, http://www.inquisitr.com/2080983/baltimore-arrest-report-says-thousands-of-suspects-too-injured-to-enter-jail/, May 11, 2015, accessed May 11, 2015.

World To Come: Essays On The Baltimore Uprising, Militant Racism, And History

Dondi Johnson who died in a situation eerily similar to Freddie Gray. In 2005, Johnson was arrested for urinating in public, experienced a "rough rides" and died two weeks later of spinal injuries. The family demanded $100 million; the police were ordered to pay 7.4 million. Baltimore has purportedly paid out approximately $12 million (from 2010 to 2014) to settle police misconduct cases. In keeping with this tradition, by early September 2015, the city of Baltimore (4 months after the Baltimore Uprising) agreed to a $6.4 million settlement in the case of Freddie Gray.

Bmore Police Technology—Tools for Mass Surveillance

Baltimore city is 81 square miles and contains a population of approximately 640,000 people. To address some of the public safety and security the needs of the city, Baltimore purportedly utilizes the highest technology involved in law enforcement surveillance. This includes targeting telecommunication, street cameras, aerial policing, and as a direct result of the riots, surveying the city. One example of techno-policing involving telecommunications, is the city police's use of StingRay (and Hailstorm), a product which can physically locate mobile phones. The Baltimore police department has used this device, for nearly a decade now, to acquire cell phone information including geolocation data; though they are not permitted to disclose any information that would reveal the devices technical specifications. It is believed that these types of devices can also be used to monitor conversations. While other city police departments also use these kinds of military derived devices, at times, Baltimore's use has been considered excessive. Another tool in use meant to aid law enforcement was the installation of public surveillance devices. This includes, for example, microphones (in addition to the video) on city busses. Furthermore, the city, for a time, utilized another form of public surveillance in order to curb speeding. It installed speed cameras, which were found to have high error rates costing drivers to pay fees in the millions—the problems with its errors, more than any other argument, forced the city to table the program. However, the city has for quite some time, utilized an extensive system of street cameras. In high crime neighborhoods, the cameras emitted at one time a rather cautionary flashing blue light. While Baltimore grappled with the high cost of body cameras for police officers, the death of Freddie Gray added another urgent example of why so many felt that police should have this public surveillance gear.

World To Come: Essays On The Baltimore Uprising, Militant Racism, And History

Baltimore has also been at the forefront of aerial policing. The city started its helicopter unit in 1970 and since then has spent millions of dollars on police helicopters. By the mid-nineteen nineties, the Baltimore helicopters had "…VHF transceivers with which the police communicates with Air Traffic Control (ATC). They are also equipped with a siren, public address system, police radios, searchlight, and an infrared heat sensing system."[17] The helicopters and the technology they possess have been substantially upgraded since then, but their tactical advantage to law enforcement has not changed. Their purpose is to track suspects and go unnoticed in the process. They are able to assist officers who are in trouble on the ground, and they can tell police about issues of traffic or other concerns. Most important, they are meant to be a "show of force."[18] These helicopters were used in the Baltimore Uprising to monitor protestors; and to broadcast the citywide curfew, largely to the residents of the western districts. In addition to police helicopters, there were also initial reports that "mysterious" surveillance planes were flying over West Baltimore days after the riots had ended.[19] The city has had GIS technology for many years, with software and visual imaging services purportedly to "…enable city agencies to operate at maximum efficiency."[20] Weeks after the Baltimore Uprising, the city in essence, was declared a crime scene. LiDAR USA[21] donated their high tech scanning technology to assist the city in surveying the damage. The company is considered cutting-edge because they offer "…solutions for GIS, surveying, civil engineering, agriculture, forensics, BIM,[22] heritage mapping—all things 3D and beyond." Apparently, it would be the first time that such forensics would be used to analyze a domestic riot. The police would be able to use this mapping software to determine the extent of the physical damage and to estimate costs.

---

[17]Geoffrey P. Alpert, "Helicopters in Pursuit Operations." *Research in Action*, Washington, DC: National Institute Of Justice, August 1998, 1-6, 4.
[18]Ibid., 1-6, 1.
[19]"Surveillance Planes Spotted in the Sky for Days after West Baltimore Rioting," Craig Timberg, May 5, 2015, *The Washington Post*, http://www.washingtonpost.com/business/technology/surveillance-planes-spotted-in-the-sky-for-days-after-west-baltimore-rioting/2015/05/05/c57c53b6-f352-11e4-84a6-6d7c67c50db0_story.html.
[20]"City of Baltimore Adds Pictometry to Enterprise GIS Program," *Directions Magazine*, September 14, 2004.
[21]LiDAR USA, http://www.lidarusa.com/company.php, accessed May 21, 2015.
[22]BIM refers to "Building Information Modeling," the use of software applications to generate digital images and graphics of physical locations.

World To Come: Essays On The Baltimore Uprising, Militant Racism, And History

On April 27, 2015 in the first major clash of the Baltimore Uprising, the police and other law enforcement agencies had a number of surveillance operations in place. Not only were Baltimore City Police (like police agencies across the country) actively using social media to report their observations and activities, they were also monitoring the content of residents' social media. The Baltimore police department (along with city government) gathered intelligence from Twitter, Facebook, and Instagram. They compiled Twitter hashtags that gave threads of content regarding citizen chatter and potential threats. Some of the hashtags the police department recorded included #JusticeforFreddie and #FuckthePolice.[23] They were also aware of the live feeds of the riot streaming through YouTube. While many believed the police misled the public about the gang death threats, they did have indications of potential dangers from a wide variety of what appeared to be largely juvenile sources. In a May 1 Baltimore City Situation Report "Students from Douglass High School on social media trying to organize a protest" was listed as a "significant incident."[24] In addition to cyber and onsite physical observations of protesters and rioters, the Baltimore police also used the system of CCTV street cameras to monitor Baltimore Uprising events around the city.

There were also media reports that during the Baltimore Uprising, the city used, or were at least solicited to consider the services of private security companies (Zerofox, Exelon, and CISS) that critically assessed cyber and physical threats against the city and officials. Black Lives Matter activist and Baltimore mayoral candidate DeRay McKesson (with over 300 thousand Twitter followers) was identified by at least one security firm as representing a high level threat in the Baltimore Uprising. We do not know the extent to which private, local and/or federal law enforcement officers embedded with protesters (and rioters for that matter) and surveilled events as they unfolded, but failed to prevent crimes in progress. But we do know from the investigative reporting of *The Intercept* that Homeland Security monitored Black Lives Matter protesters, at least beginning with the

---

[23]City of Baltimore, Social Media Tracking Spreadsheet, April 27, 2015 ("Emails from the Baltimore Unrest: Explore Documents and Findings," "Finding: Monitoring Social Media," *The Baltimore Sun*, July 30, 2015, http://www.baltimoresun.com/news/maryland/freddie-gray/bal-emails-from-the-unrest-20150730-htmlstory.html, accessed July 30, 2015.

[24]City of Baltimore, Mayor's Office of Emergency Management, Situation Report #13, "Civil Unrest," May 1, 2015, 3.

WORLD TO COME: ESSAYS ON THE BALTIMORE UPRISING,
MILITANT RACISM, AND HISTORY

uprising in Ferguson Missouri in 2014 up to and including those who participated in the Baltimore Uprising.[25] One of the most interesting if not pernicious aspects of the Baltimore Uprising was the surge of activity from private surveillance companies. Many of these companies sold their products and services by tapping into the fears of police agencies, residents, municipal leaders, and businesses. In the midst of the Baltimore Uprising such companies offered cyber and physical surveillance services and threat assessments; in addition to nonlethal weapons such as pepper and skunk sprays, and DNA markers.

For the Baltimore City Police Department, there was considerable interest in and surveillance of out-of-town activists like attorney Malik Zulu Shabazz. Shabazz, President of the Black Lawyers for Justice, was at one time, chair of the New Black Panther Party. On April 25, 2015, the day before Freddie Gray's wake, Shabazz's organization planned a peaceful protest at the Gilmore Homes and City Hall,[26] which later culminated into chaos. When he told protestors to "Shut it down..."[27] it was interpreted as his instructions to incite a riot. This was not unlike H. Rap Brown who in 1967, was arrested after he gave a speech to Cambridge, Maryland demonstrators to "burn this town down."[28] Moreover, this includes the 1967 congressional enactment of the "Stokely Bill," "...an anti-riot bill for imposing stringent criminal penalties upon anyone crossing state lines for the purpose of inciting 'disturbances'."[29] Shabazz later explained to the *New York Times* that it was the rhetoric of civil disobedience, and not the solicitation of violence. Shabazz was often featured as an outside agitator, among the peaceful protesters, and yet police did not find any

---

[25] George Joseph, "Exclusive: Feds Regular Monitored Black Lives Matter Since Ferguson," *The Intercept*, July 24, 2015, accessed https://theintercept.com/2015/07/24/documents-show-department-homeland-security-monitoring-black-lives-matter-since-ferguson/.
[26] Black Lawyers for Justice, www.bljustice.org, "Massive March & National Rally Against the Brutality of the Baltimore Police Department Freddie Gray," Event Flyer, April 25, 2015.
[27] Sheryl Gay Stolberg and Stephen Babcock, "Scenes of Chaos in Baltimore as Thousands Protest Freddie Gray's Death," *The New York Times*, April 25, 2015, http://www.nytimes.com/2015/04/26/us/baltimore-crowd-swells-in-protest-of-freddie-grays-death.html?_r=0, accessed August 2, 2015.
[28] July 25, 1967.
[29] The bill was named for SNCC's Stokely Carmichael (Kwame Ture), "Massacre at Newark," *Freedomways, A Quarterly Review of the Negro Freedom Movement*, Vol. 7, No. 3, Summer 1967 (Third Quarter), 197-198.

acts, which constituted the crime "inciting to riot." However, later Shabazz, as representative of some of the out-of-town protesters, moved the group to Camden Yards, where they were "...attempting to disrupt game day operations." Shabazz was implicated in broken car and storefronts windows. However, the police observed, he did not stop this activity "in any way."[30] Shabazz had already been branded a categorical "racist" and "black separatist" in the conservative mainstream media and this positioned him against some of the local black leaders. On May 1, the Maryland Coordination and Analysis Center issued its unclassified "Officer Safety Bulletin" to inform law enforcement personnel about a "possible threat." The bulletin stated that Shabazz was planning a protest at city hall, and that "...heightened awareness for intentional acts of violence committed during events associated with Shabazz" should be maintained.[31] It was an interesting warning in that it did not directly tie Shabazz to any acts of violence. However, the bulletin essentially surrounded Shabazz with information about his associations (past and current which were deemed problematic by state and federal agencies), and by implication linked him to the activities of others. The carefully crafted statement suggested that Shabazz was a potential threat—that he would incite citizens to engage in violence. The bulletin iterated to law enforcement officers that, "...protest activity is a constitutionally protected activity; in and of itself it should not be looked upon as problematic or undesirable..." At this point, the important statement was rendered moot. Being associated with groups whose existence and rhetoric was deemed threatening, was enough to place Shabazz' life in jeopardy as an activist. The curious aspect was that activists like Shabazz were treated as threats for using rhetorical declarations in the absence of any violent activity. When there is evidence of violent acts in their presence by others, they are indicted by proximity, but not in actuality.

---

[30] David McMillan to Robert Maloney and Connor D. Scott, "Substantial Update email, April 25, 2015, 6:16 PM.
[31] Maryland Coordination and Analysis Center, "(U) Warning of Possible Incitement in Baltimore, Maryland," *Officer Safety Bulletin*, No.: 2015-0138, May 1, 2015.

World To Come: Essays On The Baltimore Uprising, Militant Racism, And History

Post-Uprising—A Window into the ATF and the Quest for Punishment

The Bureau of Alcohol, Tobacco and Firearms (ATF) claims a long and unique history, and has possessed throughout its lifetime, some very broad law enforcement powers. In its early days the agency has been involved in tax collection and the prosecution of citizens who violated the nation's prohibition laws. They have been engaged in America's effort to control guns from the 1934 National Firearm Act to the Gun Control Act of 1968. The ATF has possessed many titles (under several agencies), but the modern idea of the ATF as Alcohol, Tobacco and Firearms (and Explosives) came into being in the 1970s. The ATF is known for some major controversies and scandals linked to what many believed at the time was the creeping militarization of the country, including a reputation for agents that pursue citizens and groups in an "over the top" fashion. The recent controversial histories of ATF's involvement in Ruby Ridge, Idaho and Waco, Texas in the early 1990s (and Operation Fast and Furious [2009-2011][32]) are still important memories for the general public. These particular events solidified, in the minds of many, the belief that the government had adopted obsessive military ideology, technology, training and tactics (and with a 2014 budget of over a billion dollars[33]) and used these tools against citizens. But the Baltimore Uprising was different. The rioting and looting that took place in the city didn't involve black organizations—just individuals. Blacks are not understood historically as aggressively anti-government, even if some blacks have called for revolutionary changes. The Baltimore Uprising didn't involve white American patriot and militia groups that felt deeply betrayed and threatened by the government. However, this was an important urban terrain involving riot activity, and it was arguably (like Ferguson,

---

[32]Operation Fast And Furious (sometimes known as the "gunwalking scandal") was a failed attempt to track illicit firearms sales from Arizona through Mexico by knowingly allowing criminal suspects to illegally purchase guns so they could be tracked. See United States Department of Justice, Office of the Inspector General, A Review of ATFs Operation Fast and Furious and Related Matters (Redacted), November, 2012, 103-142 ("Operation Fast and Furious"); and John G. Malcolm, "Operation Fast and Furious: How a Botched Justice Department Operation Led to a Standoff Over Executive Privilege," The Heritage Foundation, Washington, D.C. No. 83, July 25, 2012.

[33]"Facts and Figures" Bureau of Alcohol, Tobacco, Firearms and Explosives Factsheet, "Budget," February 1, 2015, https://www.atf.gov/resource-center/pr/facts-and-figures, accessed 1/10/2016.

World To Come: Essays On The Baltimore Uprising, Militant Racism, And History

Missouri) a military training ground, for the nation. Even given the racial animus, disaffected urban blacks and white militiamen at least shared some similar ideas—that American civil liberties were at risk, and that government paramilitary forces have emerged, honed their strategies, and would exhaust their vast resources to forcefully maintain law and order.

On the day that Marilyn Mosby formally charged the Baltimore 6, and Governor Larry Hogan announced the "Maryland Unites" community assistance program, the Bureau of Alcohol, Tobacco, Firearms and Explosives (ATF) stated on Facebook and on their website that they were investigating the burnings of buildings and vehicles in the city. Through two early press releases, the ATF said that they would give as much as $10,000 for information leading to the arrest and conviction of persons responsible for riot related fires.[34] They cited in particular, "...the fires that occurred at the Mary Harkins Senior Center on North Chester Street, the CVS Pharmacies on Pennsylvania Avenue and West Franklin, and the Rite Aid Pharmacy on North Martin Luther King Highway."[35] The ATF special agent in charge, William P. McMullan, expressed in the press release, "The ATF and our local counterparts are committed to identifying, investigating and recommending for prosecution the individuals responsible for the violent acts of arson committed throughout our city." He further emphasized, "Arson is a crime of violence" and that guilty persons would be "held accountable for their dangerous actions."[36] The ATF followed up the reward notice with a call to citizens to help them investigate the fires that took place during the Baltimore Uprising. They promoted the ATF hotline, and set up a website for the uploading of fire videos noting, "The website is secure, anonymous and works with mobile devices." The anonymous website did request a name (for the upload), phone number, email, and had room for a short message. The site, hosted through DriveHQ, allowed for the digital deposit of

---

[34] Bureau of Alcohol, Tobacco, Firearms and Explosives (ATF), Facebook, https://www.facebook.com/HQATF, May 1, 2015, accessed, May 15, 2015.
[35] Bureau of Alcohol, Tobacco, Firearms and Explosives (ATF), Baltimore Field Division, Reward Announcement, May 1, 2015.
[36] Bureau of Alcohol, Tobacco, Firearms and Explosives (ATF), Baltimore Field Division, Press Release, May 1, 2015, https://www.atf.gov/news/pr/atf-offers-10000-reward-baltimore-fire-investigations, accessed, May 15, 2015.

World To Come: Essays On The Baltimore Uprising, Militant Racism, And History

"…photos, videos, documents, audio and other digital media…"[37] There would be a number of services, programs and technologies used to assess the damage, and to identify criminal activity for future prosecution. In this regard, the city's residents would be considered a highly valuable resource for law enforcement.

By the middle of May 2015, an early estimate of damage to the city (in the residential areas) from the rioting aspect of the Baltimore Uprising was $9 million dollars—and this number rose dramatically to $30.5 million when the overall economic impact—tourism and other consumer worker and leisure spending patterns were factored in.[38] While only a few dozen businesses were initially classified as having suffered major damage, a few hundred businesses were listed as having some minor damage, and that number grew to about 400. However, the CVS in West Baltimore was at the heart of the issue of damage. The burning CVS became the symbol for rioting and lawlessness in the city. By the end of June, the ATF had identified at least one person they believed was responsible for the fire at the CVS and posted an announcement for his arrest. The ATF, again, offered $10,000 for assistance leading to the "…identification, arrest, and conviction" of 24-year-old Raymon Carter.[39] The agency received tips to its hotline and this is how they were able to identify Carter. Within weeks, Carter was arrested (on June 1), and charged with crimes related to federal arson totaling $1.3 million dollars in damage. While the ATF considered Carter the primary person responsible for starting the fire, they were also working to find other CVS arsonists besides Carter; and they were also pursing looters.

The ATF believed they apprehended one of these looters when they charged 25-year-old Rashad Robertson in September. Robertson was charged with stealing prescription medication from the CVS. He was found in possession of Alprazolam (the generic formula for Xanax, an anti-anxiety medication used to prevent panic attacks). In addition to the bottle of Alprazolam, Robertson is thought to be the person on the

---

[37]"ATF Baltimore Fire," Dropbox, DriveHQ, http://www.atfbaltimorefire.com/, accessed May 15, 2015.
[38]Request for Presidential Disaster Declaration Governor's Request Cover Letter Major Disaster, State of Maryland, Office of the Governor, May 21, 2015, 5.
[39]Department of Justice, U.S. Attorney's Office, District of Maryland," Press Release, "Baltimore Man Charged with Arson of CVS Pharmacy," July 2, 2015.

store video looking for narcotics on the shelves.[40] Just as surveillance cameras were used to identify and apprehend Carter and Robertson, video implicated another young man in arson and looting. 21-year-old Darius Raymond Stewart was charged with destruction second-degree assault, arson and malicious destruction of property, and arrested for setting fire to a liquor store. The police believe that Stewart set fire to the Fireside North Lounge & Liquor Store causing $350,000 worth of damage. The ATF used a wanted poster, the surveillance video from the store, and received a tip from a confidential source. The ATF maintained that Stewart was identified by witnesses who saw him on the CitiWatch surveillance system of cameras.[41] In fall 2015, 19-year-old Donta Betts also faced federal charges related to arson. In addition to possibly looting the CVS, the ATF had video and still images indicating that Betts tampered with the fuel pipeline of a police cruiser and set it on fire.

In the Baltimore Uprising, The Bureau of Alcohol, Tobacco and Firearms (ATF) displayed their considerable expertise in rounding up young men for petty looting and opportunistic law breaking. They demonstrated their adept ability to act swiftly in the identification and apprehension of criminal suspects. They used the substantial resources at their disposal, particularly the city's video cameras. Their operations, at least in this respect, plainly articulated an agency philosophy of rigorous law and order. With these early arrests and convictions, The Bureau of Alcohol, Tobacco and Firearms, were able to neatly stack their column of wins in the Baltimore Uprising. One wonders what the outcome of Freddie Gray's life and death might have been, and especially for the young men arrested, had local government agencies far beyond the ATF, used their resources to improve the lives of citizens. Federal law enforcement agency models that do not consider wasted human potential and the role and responsibility of city and state government for creating the contexts that engender crime should rethink the meaning of justice. We are a world that prefers to compartmentalize how we live. We firmly believe that these young men (not strangers to the criminal justice system) are either criminally

---

[40]Department of Justice, U.S. Attorney's Office, District of Maryland," Press Release, "Defendant Charged in Federal Court for Possessing Medication Stolen From a CVS Pharmacy During the Baltimore Riots," September 9, 2015.
[41]Department of Justice, U.S. Attorney's Office, District of Maryland," Press Release, "Suspect Charged for Arson of Liquor Store During the Baltimore Riots," October 1, 2015.

predisposed, made a string of unfortunate bad choices, or were simply given to opportunistic crimes. We prefer to ignore how poverty and crime are commercial products—bought and sold—like those items we still manufacture. Given the state of the city, and the catalyst for the Baltimore Uprising, at least some of those who engaged in criminal behavior were treated very much like proverbial laboratory subjects caught and held in an inscrutable maze. They followed the carefully constructed path provided to them and then were experimented upon, studied, and later held fully accountable for a multiplicity of choices and opportunities that never really existed.

CHAPTER 11

VARIETIES OF COPS, POLITICAL LEADERS, AND THE RACIAL PARADOX THAT WASN'T

> Contrary to the view that violence in policing is a matter of a few "bad apples,"... violence is part of the institutional culture of policing. The issue therefore is a function of a "rotten barrel."—Judith A.M. Scully[1]

Racial Premises Regarding Black Cops and the Baltimore 6

The principal discussion about the root causes of the 2015 Baltimore Uprising was the legacy and persistence of structural racism. We have come to view the nature of racism as "...a pathology, a mental and social disorder"[2] that is abnormal to the human condition. However, there has always been the exclusion of people based on the perception of a different physiology, ancestry, and culture. The western focus on the racial binary of black and white in the overarching racial discussion speaks to the greatest impression of human distinction. Notwithstanding this, there is still paucity in discussing racism outside of the ideological and rhetorical context of activism. The Baltimore Uprising made it possible for people who do not usually talk about systemic racism (and specifically as it relates to the African American experience)—as opposed to generic conversations about race relations, or race as a biological category—to speak openly and candidly. The talk about racism ranged from candid assertions about the embedded nature of white supremacy; to anti-racist ideas and movements; to the classic denial of any discriminatory social practice known as racism. Two paradoxical ideas emerged. First that the assertion of racism in the death of Freddie Gray and other blacks in Baltimore (and around the country) at the hands of law enforcement officers could not exist if any of the officers accused were black. Second, the preponderance of black political leadership in such matters meant that there was a failure among the collective of black leaders, and thus not evidence of

---

[1] Judith A.M. Scully, "Rotten Apple or Rotten Barrel?: The Role of Civil Rights Lawyers in Ending the Culture of Police Violence," *National Black Law Journal*, 21, 137-172, 2008.
[2] Molefi Kete Asante, *Erasing Racism the Survival of the American Nation*, New York: Prometheus Books, 2003, 239.

systemic racism. So the logic persists that black people can never be mediators and facilitators of structural racism and white supremacy because they are black. However, blacks can play an unwitting and willing part in advancing racism, largely because some "…have taken on the responsibility of compensating for the white abnormality"[3] of racism. The idea that white racism cannot exist if blacks (or mixed race African Americans[4]) are present or participatory is false. Blacks, like other groups in world history, have been complicit in white racial oppression schemes. It is an insidious argument, which absolves the expansive system of white racism, and allows for token-black environments to preempt charges of racism. While this claim could not be further from the truth, it is an argument that does not challenge or change embedded racism; and which makes for an intellectually expedient, if not superfluous discourse. The complex structural system of racism and white supremacy can render some people instrumental in helping to achieve its goals.

The activists in the Baltimore Uprising did not buy either argument. Among the six officers charged in Freddie Gray's death, half were white, half were black and among the blacks there was a woman. Within hours of their having been charged and arrested, a few stories emerged that seemingly sought to separate them from one another. One of the main stories involving Officer Rice clearly attempted to paint him as an "immoral cop." However, there was an immediate adjustment to "giving up" the officers as individual bad apples. The media frame was modified and advanced a discussion about the officers as a group—and then shifted the emphasis to an attack on the state's attorney for the city of Baltimore, Marilyn Mosby. Though assumed impartial, most state attorney offices are usually perceived as favoring the police in law enforcement shootings. The Fraternal Order of Police refused to accept that the officers had been charged with a crime. The immediate strategy was to vigorously discredit Marilyn Mosby (professionally and personally) and the processes and procedures used by her office to bring the charges against the six officers. In the days that followed, they did everything possible to halt, or "un-charge" the six officers. Public comment seized on the racial diversity of the six, as

---

[3]Molefi Kete Asante, *Erasing Racism The Survival of the American Nation*, New York: Prometheus Books, 2003, 239.
[4]This also includes the tendency to dismiss or deny any racial impulse in cases involving bi-racial victims, such as in the September 2015 James Blake police "take down."

World To Come: Essays On The Baltimore Uprising, Militant Racism, And History

well as a police department with visible numbers of black officers on the city's force, though less than the population percentage-wise. These thoughts would be seed for suggesting that Freddie Gray's civil rights could not have been violated by the six officers because some of them were black.

African American Police Officers, Good Cops Gone Rogue, and the "Line That Protects the Innocent"

African American police officers have experienced historic challenges to serving in predominately-white bureaus; and also when established white authority critically gazes upon the inner workings of black-led agencies. There is a price for being blue. It is maintained here that either scenario matters little when it comes to mainstream policing of black communities. Black officers must negotiate their professional place in the white police power structure. They may still be seen as "token" hires to placate the black community; and this suggests that they are not as qualified regardless of their exam scores, training, experience, education and/or certifications—or especially in administrative decision-making positions. Black police officers must often go out of their way to prove that they are "blue," that they have a deep organizational commitment. The initiation of or participation in the elevation of conflicts among some officers within the black community should come as no surprise. While some black cops are able to act as a go-between between the white officers and the black community, others may lead the way in carrying out abuses that involve racial profiling, including the prodigious inclination to stop, detain, question, search, ticket and arrest African Americans. When excessive force is used against blacks, African American police may direct, participate in, or ignore abuses. This is a form of professional self-preservation, at the expense of the black community, one, which in truth protects the black officer from crude retaliation by white officers and supervisors. This is a fundamental directive of structural racism. However, the cruelest of the black officers in this scenario truly believes in the pseudo-pathology of the black community, and they "act-out" not to impress white officers, but out of guilt and shame because they are disconnected and dislocated from the community. Most importantly, they may abuse blacks in order to distinguish themselves as the "good blacks" in the white mind. Their goodness is not defined by aspirations to uphold the highest moral and ethical standards, but to the extent blacks attempt to comfort, please, and obey the established order. The genealogical, cultural, and historical blackness of a law-enforcement officer does not obfuscate or eliminate the customary operations of institutional racism. What is significant is that law enforcement administration and prosecutors will tend to readily use the involvement of a black officer—or any black person—to deny the racist impulse—and ultimately to dismiss the role of systemic racism in the police-encounter deaths of black citizens.[5]

    White police officers can tell us much about the inner workings of racism and routine acts of racial bias. When former Chicago police detective Timothy McDermott attempted to deny that he was involved in the humiliation, if not abuse, of a black man, he revealed the mindset of some members of law enforcement. When an old photograph surfaced, showing "an unidentified black man lying on a floor and wearing deer antlers,"[6] McDermott, and another officer (Jerome Finnigan, who was serving time for corruption) stood over the man, a suspect, holding rifles. McDermott, who was fired in 2014 and under investigation by the FBI, denied any wrongdoing. Apparently, the picture was more than ten years old. McDermott suggested the black man was complicit in taking the photograph and that he was not mistreated; and ultimately blamed the whole affair on his youth and poor judgment. McDermott said he was an "… impressionable police officer who was trying to fit in."[7] The admission, as well as the iconography is more than chilling. The black man is lying on his stomach, wearing the deer antlers on his head, tongue hanging from his mouth as if the officers had just bagged a 10-point buck. His eyes are rolled back and there is the semblance of blood on the side of his face. The message from the old Polaroid image was clear that the black man was a trophy, a dehumanized person, and symbolically hunted down like an animal. McDermott had argued that the photograph was prejudicial against him. Since so much time had passed, he could not identify the black man, who he was sure would corroborate his story.[8]

---

[5]Two notable cases of this involve the police-encounter deaths of LaTanya Haggerty and Robert "Bobby" Russ. Both were killed in two separate incidents in Chicago in 2009 by black police officers.
[6]"Photo Shows Chicago Cops Posing Over Black Man With Antlers," The Associated Press, May 28, 2015.
[7] Ibid.
[8]In The Matter Of Charges Filed Against Detective Timothy McDermott, No. 14 PB 2855 STAR No. 21084, Department Of Police, City Of Chicago, (CR No. 1061847) Respondent. Findings and Decision, 2014.

WORLD TO COME: ESSAYS ON THE BALTIMORE UPRISING, MILITANT RACISM, AND HISTORY

While McDermott never admitted wrongdoing, and saw no harm in his actions, or any racist meaning—other officers are proud of how police "do it."

Some police officers, and their local supporters, have privately and publically expressed generalized contempt for black life. In doing so, they display an inordinate sense of power over citizens. In the 2003 Orlando Barlow domestic violence case, in Las Vegas, Nevada, officers were not held accountable for the 28-year-old man's execution-style death, while he attempted to surrender to authorities. However, the officers were fired only after they printed t-shirts featuring a rifle and the abbreviation BDRT ("Baby's Daddy Removal Team")[9]. These actions were not only related to killing, they were meant to degrade and humiliate Barlow after the fact. In Alexander City Alabama Troy Middlebrooks bragged about wanting to kill Vincent Bias, a black man he had arrested. Middlebrooks' rant, which was secretly recorded, outlined the police-killing scenario: Bias would be killed during a routine traffic stop and then he would claim self-defense. Middlebrooks, a former Marine, stated that he would "...make it look like he was trying to fucking kill me..."[10] Middlebrooks also lamented that something was wrong with the "system," because Bias, "a nigger," had been able to make bail. The police chief defended Middlebrooks' death threat against Bias, stating, "He was just talking. He didn't really mean that..."[11] However, Bias received $35,000 to settle any potential civil lawsuit, and Middlebrooks retained his position in Alexander City.

In the federal government's investigation into the Ferguson Police department after the death of Michael Brown, one black man reminded a police officer that he had done nothing that warranted an arrest. He was told, "N*****, I can find something to lock you up on." When the man scoffed at the likelihood of this, the officer then physically assaulted him.[12] In August 2015, to coincide with the one

---

[9]Purportedly, this t-shirt acronym theme was adopted by a Florida police department in 2011.
[10]Jon Swaine, "Alabama Officer Kept Job After Proposal to Murder Black Man and Hide Evidence," *The Guardian*, August 4, 2015; John Johnson, "Cop Rants About Killing Black Man, Covering it Up," *Newser*, August 4, 2015, http://www.newser.com/story/210812/cop-rants-about-killing-black-man-covering-it-up.html, accessed August 4, 2015.
[11]Ibid.
[12]United States Department of Justice, Civil Rights Division, *Investigation of the Ferguson Police Department*, March 4, 2015, 73.

year anniversary of Michael Brown's death (August 9, 2014), a police support group circulated an offensive "memorial plaque" on Facebook, which featured the limerick:

> There once was a thug named Brown
> Who Bum-rushed a Cop with a Frown
> Six bullets later
> He met his creator
> Then his Homies burned down the town.[13]

Again, the "memorial" was not only intended to dishonor Brown, but also to demean the protestors in the town of Ferguson, Missouri. The post was eventually removed from Facebook. The unrest in Ferguson was fresh in the public mind, and within days of the Baltimore Uprising, a Detroit Michigan assistant prosecutor, frustrated by the media images of rioting, posted on social media that demonstrators should be *shot*, "end of discussion." Her post (and account) was also removed from Facebook. Thereafter she was defended for her professionalism, and at least one colleague suggested that the post was not reflective of her character.[14]

In addition, by September 2015, one police chief, Mike Halstead was forced to retire after he defamed the Black Lives Matter movement. Using his personal Facebook account, the head of the Surf City North Carolina police department posted a statement, which, in effect, called Black Lives Matter protestors "terrorists," implied that they were black supremacists, and that they encouraged race murder. His "Open Letter from a Police Chief" also urged law enforcement officers to be vigilant and on guard for their own safety, and indicted President Obama for fueling national racial tensions. The local and state NAACP (through Deborah Dicks Maxwell and the Reverend William J. Barber, II) and community leaders moved to meet about the statement; and the town council acted quickly to remove the chief.

---

[13]David Ferguson, "Cops Make Disgusting Online 'Memorial' Mocking Death of Ferguson's Michael Brown," *RawStory*, August 7, 2015,
http://www.rawstory.com/2015/08/cops-make-disgusting-online-memorial-mocking-death-of-fergusons-michael-brown/, accessed August 9, 2015.
[14]"White Supremacist Detroit Prosecutor wants US to kill Baltimore Protesters," *News786*, May 1, 2015, http://www.news786.in/article.php?id=MTU5MzU=, accessed September 10, 2015.

World To Come: Essays On The Baltimore Uprising, Militant Racism, And History

Though obviously compelled, Halstead was allowed to retire, praised for his service, and given two months' severance pay.[15]

It is rare that police officers formally break ranks to divulge non-public expressions of racial prejudice within the organization. However, after consulting the police union and the NAACP, among other agencies, Officer Dustin Stone of the Clatskanie Oregon police department did just that. Dustin Stone, along with Officer Zack Gibson, filed a complaint against police chief Marvin Hoover, who allegedly went on a racist tirade after the arrest of an African American woman. In the process of the arrest, the woman threatened to sue Stone, and another officer for racial discrimination. According to Stone the black woman commented, "When you look at me, my black skin and my nappy hair, all you see is an animal." When Stone related her remarks to the police chief, Hoover stated, "That's what she is." What took place thereafter was an amalgam of racist mockery, which included Hoover elaborately acting out primate behavior, crudely "...comparing African-Americans to monkeys..." Police chief Hoover did not stop there. He launched into a performance of the southern slave-plantation minstrel song, "Dixie,"[16] while pantomiming a violent scene. All of this made Stone uncomfortable, and his complaint against Hoover demanded an official reply. An investigation was initiated and Hoover was placed on paid administrative leave. Weeks later, he was permitted to retire and then given a bonus. When Hoover retired, the mayor publically praised his service to the Clatskanie police department.[17] In addition to the dire implications for and disrespect of the African American community, after the complaint, Stone received death threats. He reported that his wife was twice forced off the road.[18] Stone was frequently harassed and called "nigger" on numerous occasions. On the other hand, Hoover's career was lauded by the mayor: "Without honorable officers, we would live in a world of chaos and lawlessness. I consider Chief Hoover an honorable man and

---

[15]Andrew Blake, "Surf City, N.C., Police Chief, Retires after labeling Black Lives Matters a 'Terrorist Group,'" *The Washington Times*, September 16, 2015; Ashley Norris, "N.C. Police Chief Retires Over Facebook Post," *Star-News*, Wilmington, N.C., September 16, 2015; Iris Duncan, "Police Chief Ousted After Calling Black Lives Matters a 'Terrorist Group,'" *Forex Report Daily*, September 19, 2015.
[16]Incident Report of D. Alex Stone, Oregon Department of Public Safety Standards and Training, Professional Standards Complaint Form," July 20, 2015.
[17]"Letter to the Editor: Mayor Pohl," *The Chief*, September 4, 2015.
[18]Lindsay McCane, "Oregon Police Chief Marvin Hoover, Who Compared African Americans to monkeys, Resigns," *Inquisitr*, September 9, 2015.

officer."[19] It was the ACLU of Oregon that offered any praise for Stone and Gibson. They cited the two officers for their courage in speaking out against Hoover, stating that their actions represented those of "…police who witness hateful behavior from colleagues."[20] However, these are the kinds of attitudes and deeds that intrepid white and African American officers allude to if and when they tell the story of how "life imitates art, more than art imitates life"[21] in law enforcement administrative environments. Most of the time, the underlying message is chilling as well as intimidating, and speaks to a blue—and often larger national community—a subculture steeped in privilege, a code of silence, exceptional behavior, and a gaping disgust for particular segments of the population they serve. Overall, this blue "boys will be boys" point of view represented part of what some officers (especially African American police) have referred to as the *unwritten code of policing*.

Arthur Doyle spent nearly three decades as a New York City police officer, and by the time he retired, he was a Lieutenant. As an African American, Doyle had entered the police force before the modern Civil Rights movement, and while his career can be described as successful, his challenges inside the police force were consistent with those of many veteran black officers. After a tour in the Marine Corps, Doyle attempted to join the ranks of the police in the 1950s. He was immediately rejected for a minor physical condition—one that did not hinder the routine admission of white officers. It was standard procedure to reject black applicants, but with some persistence and a little help, he entered the force and paved the way for other African Americans in New York. Doyle's tale is one of deep love for law enforcement and people. However, he learned that the blue line was more racially convoluted than most people understood. His first education about being in the police force was that the "…department has both a formal and an informal leadership structure."[22] According to

---

[19]"Letter to the Editor: Mayor Pohl," *The Chief*, September 4, 2015.
[20]"Clatskanie Police Chief Engaged in Racist Mockery," ACLU Oregon, Blog, September 2015, http://www.aclu-or.org/blog/clatskanie-police-chief-engaged-racist-mockery, accessed September 10, 2015.
[21]From Oscar Wilde's, "The Decay of Lying—An Observation," (1889) in *Intentions*, New York: Dodd Mead and Co., 1891.
[22]Lieutenant Arthur Doyle (Retired), "From the inside Looking Out: Twenty-nine Years in the New York Police Department," in Jill Nelson's (ed.) *Police Brutality An Anthology*. New York: W.W. Norton & Company, 171-186, 173.

WORLD TO COME: ESSAYS ON THE BALTIMORE UPRISING, MILITANT RACISM, AND HISTORY

Doyle, the informal structure of policing was the norm, one that he rejected because it involved certain unwritten policies. *First*, a suspect was never allowed to walk into a police precinct if he assaulted or abused an officer while in custody. *Second*, the practice of beating suspects who were handcuffed was acceptable behavior, and tolerated by those officers who did not participate in or stop the assault. *Third*, if an officer was forced to "give chase," the suspect was automatically beaten. Doyle suggested that this culture existed because "The system came to their (the officers) defense." New police officers immediately learned that they would be shielded and protected by other officers and supervisors.

Doyle described a culture where other officers were coerced into following unwritten rules; and where they knew that they would always possess the upper hand over citizen-suspects. Doyle maintained that police often retaliated against citizens in police-custody. He also witnessed and experienced the deep racial bias and discrimination of the police force. Doyle made note of the "Black tax"[23]—the price one paid to be a member of the police force if one were black. The Black tax meant that African American officers were deliberately given inferior assignments and equipment and micro managed by supervisors. He lived through decades where overt racial bias and racist attitudes were prevalent among the police. During his time, it was not only common to be personally subjected to racist remarks, but to hear bigoted comments over the police radio. It was an environment where racial epithets were written on walls inside the police station, and off-color jokes were replete. In addition, as a black police officer Doyle endured a litany of challenges because he sought to treat suspects "like people." He was disrespected by fellow officers and often humiliated when white officers openly degraded blacks by asserting they were less than human, when white communities engaged in the same behaviors. According to Doyle, a typical police response to black citizens was "Why don't they police their own community?"[24] The most egregious examples of acceptable informal police practices involved the disparate treatment of black and Latino youth. In New York, Black and Latino juveniles would be routinely arrested while white youth were treated like mischievous wayward family members and taken home.

---

[23]Lieutenant Arthur Doyle, 2000, 171-186, 183.
[24]Lieutenant Arthur Doyle, 2000, 171-186, 179.

WORLD TO COME: ESSAYS ON THE BALTIMORE UPRISING, MILITANT RACISM, AND HISTORY

In recalling his 29 years in law enforcement, Doyle did not indicate a lessening of the informal police practices that have dire consequences for the black community. Doyle discussed the shootings of black plainclothes officers, notably between 1969 through 1971. The situation was so disastrous the police had to devise a way to tell the difference between plainclothes officers and regular citizens who were black. The issue of so-called mistaken-identity did not alleviate the main problem—that police felt empowered to harm black citizens suspected of any crime. Police brutality was a situation admitted by many, but only a brave few citizens would come forward. Doyle noted that those citizens who went to police stations to complain about police brutality were "...often treated discourteously."[25] For some, frustration would prevail, and complaints would never be filed. The absurdities of informal policing were in effect deep tragedies that remained part of his recorded memory. Doyle recounted his perspectives on the 1991 Rodney King beating, the 1997 Abner Louima assault, and the 1999 Amadou Diallo shooting. Doyle felt that public scrutiny was important for each case. He wondered, specifically regarding Louima, if the officer had not admitted his crime what would be the difference between him and the proverbial old southern law enforcer, culpable in the lynching of a black man, yet able to convince the public that it was a suicide. Throughout Doyle's career, we have the sense that he was a "good cop." He did his job, refused to abuse suspects, and stopped other officers from mistreating citizens. And Doyle never looked for a "clean shooting," he focused on peace and justice. Ultimately, Arthur Doyle believed that professional discipline and diversity was the key to good policing.

Many things have changed since Doyle served as a New York City police officer; and yet much appears to remain the same. There is still the issue of what it means to be a "good cop." It is a redundant concept since all law enforcement officers are considered "good" i.e. incapable of intentional wrongdoing and are absolved of inadvertent mistakes that impact the lives of citizens. To be a good cop, means to be "a blue cop"—and whether they agree with the formal and informal ideology and culture of policing—essentially all black cops are blue. There are internal and external perceptions of good cops as well; but

---

[25]Lieutenant Arthur Doyle (Retired), "From the inside Looking Out: Twenty-nine Years in the New York Police Department," in Jill Nelson's (ed.) *Police Brutality An Anthology*. New York: W.W. Norton & Company, 2000, 171-186, 181.

World To Come: Essays On The Baltimore Uprising, Militant Racism, And History

significantly, within the ranks of law enforcement, a good cop is one that functions well as a part of the macrocosm of the police force. Police who inform on the illegal, extralegal, or questionable conduct of other police officers are rarely considered good cops. In fact, they might experience more turmoil and risk to their own lives; their jobs in law enforcement are jeopardized, and family members may even be threatened.

In 2014 when Joe Crystal sued the Baltimore City Police Department, over the mistreatment of a narcotics suspect (Antoine Green) and the subsequent cover-up, he "…began to endure harassment and threats from fellow officers…."[26] Crystal was a city police officer, who rose to the status of detective. Instead of transferring Green to central booking for processing, he was returned to the scene and assaulted by an off duty sergeant and another officer. This event was reported to the Baltimore City State's Attorney Office and to the media. Crystal suffered within a police culture of intimidation, shunning, and innuendo that harm would come to him if he testified. The most telling aspect of this experience was that Crystal was frequently labelled a "rat" complete with a dead rat affixed to the windshield of his car. He was stripped of his detective shield and while working in the streets, denied backup when requested. Based on Crystal's case files, he was the target of "pervasive retaliation." The situation became so intolerable that Crystal was forced to leave the Baltimore police department the first week of September 2014 and he eventually moved to Florida.

It can be argued that by the time the six officers were formally charged in the case of Freddie Gray on May 1, 2015, Police Commissioner Anthony Batts had done all he could to preserve a sense of professional unity within the department. Batts had conceded that over the course of days, members of the force probably had "conflicted emotions." He acknowledged the stress of the officers, noted their professionalism, and emphasized that the members of the Baltimore City Police Department were a family. He also reminded officers once again, that the world was watching. The Baltimore Uprising had global import. His emails to the rank-and-file members of the Baltimore City Police Department, often suggested a search for balance between the duties of the officers and the lives of the citizens. Batts told the officers

---

[26]*Joseph Crystal v. Anthony W. Batts, Robert Amador, and the Baltimore City Police Department*, Case 1:14-cv-03989-JKB, Filed December 22, 2014.

World To Come: Essays On The Baltimore Uprising, Militant Racism, And History

"We are sworn to protect the people of Baltimore. We must be the line that protects the innocent." Even with this sentiment, near the end of July, it was obvious that the Baltimore Police, in many ways, do "take care of their own." If this was indeed true, then it was no surprise when a former Baltimore police officer (forced into retirement) organized a dinner theater fundraiser for the Baltimore 6. The event was intended to assist the families of the six officers charged in the death of Freddie Gray. Robert "Bobby" Berger had not been a member of the Baltimore police force since the 1980s, but his name was well-known.

Berger fought the department to continue his off hours activity which involved locally performing in blackface.[27] Berger's act included renditions of "Mammy" and other songs as popularized by Al Jolson in the 1920s and the 1930s. Berger had been fired three decades ago, and with the legal wrangling involved in suing the Baltimore police department, he eventually settled his case, according to *The Baltimore Sun*, for $200,000 in 1989.[28] His efforts to assist the Baltimore 6 with a fundraiser that had already taken in nearly $30,000, was cancelled by the venue. In fact, nearly everyone created distance from the planned event. In addition to the Baltimore Uprising, the nation had just experienced the horrific deaths of Senator Clementa Pinckney and eight other parishioners inside of the Emanuel A.M.E. Church in South Carolina, and the debate that ensued over the flag of the Confederate States of America. The city of Baltimore did not need additional national media attention that encompassed the word "racist." The Baltimore NAACP condemned the planned blackface affair as they had done thirty years prior in 1985 (which then included a contingent determined to physically prevent Berger's performance). Even the police union found a way to dissociate the organization from the event, while admitting their respect for Berger as an ex-police officer. And before their legal rift with Berger, the police department condoned, encouraged, and as much as possible supported his affable "singing-cop" blackface routine. In Baltimore and many other towns and cities, blackface was not only an amateur pursuit for some, it was a leisure activity for others, "…into the 1960s…friends would occasionally have a bit too much to drink on lazy weekend afternoons and would stage impromptu blackface revues in the backyards of their all-Italian neighborhood. Blacked up with shoe

---

[27] *Berger v. Battaglia*, 779 F. 2d 992 (4th Cir. 1985).
[28] Kevin Rector, "Ex-Cop and Blackface Performer's Fundraiser for Officers in Freddie Gray Case Canceled," *The Baltimore Sun*, July 22, 2015.

World To Come: Essays On The Baltimore Uprising, Militant Racism, And History

polish, the dads would sing X-rated lyrics to popular songs with some Southern feel to them."[29] Consistent with the strange alchemy of racism, neither Berger nor the Maryland appellate court found any racist impulse in his blackface performance, or that this peculiar mockery of, and Jim Crow reminder to, blacks was conceivably insulting to many concerned citizens. This aspect of "Freddie Gray," as the case would come to be causally known, added that tinge of spectacle that either embarrassed, angered or amused those who were bothered enough to be interested. It continued to demonstrate however, that great gulf in what blacks and whites deemed acceptable racialized behavior; and how the police stand by their own—regardless of an embattled history, or the grotesque racial menageries that surface.

The "Z-Man" and the Dark Side of Para-Policing

Community policing, or rather partnerships between police and the community, even from the early days of the colonial militia and the slave patrollers, have been an important part of American law enforcement operations. When para-police (volunteers, reserves, security guards, etc.) are in the field, and armed with law enforcement privilege, citizens can and do suffer. The two recent, most discussed cases involve the killing of Trayvon Martin and Eric Harris. If there was a single case that galvanized the Black Lives Matter movement, Trayvon Martin was it. On February 26, 2012, 17-year-old Trayvon Martin was returning from a convenience store (he was visiting his father), when he was confronted by George Zimmerman. Zimmerman, a neighborhood watch volunteer, was often described in the media as "self-appointed." However, Zimmerman served as the neighborhood watch captain for the rental community, and in their effort to reduce crime, residents were encouraged to contact him after calling the police department.[30] For years, Zimmerman called 911 to report activities he thought might warrant police attention. [31] In addition to reporting strange men he saw while on patrol, he also notified the police about stray dogs and potholes. Zimmerman thought that Martin looked

---

[29]John Strausbaugh, *Black Like You: Blackface, Whiteface, Insult and Imitation in American Popular Culture*, New York: Penguin Group, 2006, 147.
[30]The Retreat at Twin Lakes HOA Newsletter, *Retreat Reflections*, Vol. 5, Issue 1, February 2012.
[31]Sanford Police Department, 911 Event Report, George Zimmerman, August 12, 2004—February 26, 2012.

suspicious and called the police at 7:20 PM. 911 recorded the remarks that Zimmerman had made, indicating that he was observing a black male, "late teens LSW (Last Seen Wearing) Dark Gray Hoodie Jeans or Sweatpants Walking Around Area..."[32] The police advised Zimmerman not to confront Martin. Zimmerman ignored these instructions. At one point Zimmerman noted to 911 that Martin was "...now running towards back entrance of complex."[33] Zimmerman pursued Martin and an altercation took place, one in which Martin was killed. The police found the teen "face down in the grass."[34] Zimmerman claimed that he was defending himself against Martin who was unarmed.

There was considerable outrage when the Sanford Florida police department did not promptly arrest and charge Zimmerman in the case. In addition, there was an immediate effort to tarnish the young life of Martin and portray him as an extremely troubled teen;[35] though his family pointed out the normal behavior of a teen coming of age. The social media and political discussions ranged from Florida's controversial "stand your ground laws" (though it was not used in Zimmerman's defense) to the racial profiling of African Americans and the wearing of "hoodies." The wearing of hoodies became a form of social protest. When Illinois Congressman Bobby Rush (D-IL) did so to protest racial profiling he was reprimanded for wearing the "street apparel" into the congressional chamber and was removed. Like many others, Congressman James Clyburn (D-SC) also wore a hoodie at a Trayvon Martin rally that took place on the steps of the South Carolina State House on July 20, 2013.

Zimmerman was eventually charged with second-degree murder, and acquitted of the crime on July 14, 2013. He has always maintained that he was the victim who was defending himself from an overgrown teenager. Zimmerman, who repeatedly found himself in legal trouble after his acquittal (for issues including domestic violence and a road rage shooting) even blamed President Obama publically for fueling racial tensions in the country, when he spoke out about the incident in a comprehensive statement saying that, "Trayvon Martin

---

[32]Sanford Police Department, 911 Event Report, George Zimmerman, February 26, 2012.
[33]Sanford Police Department, 911 Event Report, George Zimmerman, February 26, 2012.
[34]Sanford Police Department, Partial Report, February 26, 2012, 3.
[35]George E. Curry, "Zimmerman's Team Will Seek to Discredit Trayvon Martin," *The Baltimore Afro-American*, Vol. 121, No. 43, 1, June 1, 2013—June 7, 2013.

could have been me 35 years ago."³⁶ However, Zimmerman's own words and deeds displayed intent and a strong sense of righteousness in the murder of Trayvon Martin. Some believe he had the gun at the ready when he exited his car. Three years after his acquittal, Zimmerman said that he inadvertently re-Tweeted a crime scene photo of the deceased Trayvon Martin. One of his Twitter followers dubbed him the "Z-Man," noting that Zimmerman "is a one man army."³⁷ The callousness and indifference to black lives also included listing Martin as a deceased John Doe, and issues regarding the timely notification of his death to the family. The Trayvon Martin case was not only an extreme form of racial injustice, it represented an utter disregard for human life in para-law enforcement encounters that end in the deaths of blacks.

Ten days before Freddie Gray was arrested in Baltimore, Eric Harris was shot and killed in Tulsa, Oklahoma on April 2, 2015. The case unfolded as one of the most remarkable examples of questionable police-custody deaths and alleged acts of law enforcement corruption and/or negligence. Harris was targeted for a sting operation involving the Violent Crimes Task Force. Members of the Violent Crimes Task Force "…were conducting a controlled buy of guns and ammunition…" at the Dollar General Store parking lot.³⁸ An undercover officer had arranged to purchase a firearm from Harris. Harris gave the firearm to the undercover officer, and at that point, the operation's coordinated arrest team moved in. When Harris realized that a police sting was taking place, he ran. After a foot and vehicle chase, Harris was taken down by police. Four officers subdued an unarmed Harris on the ground when a reserve deputy Officer Robert Bates drew his revolver and fired into Harris' back. Harris can be heard on video yelling about having been shot and he told officers, "I'm losing my breath." One of the officers replied to Harris, "Fuck your breath!"

---

³⁶"Remarks by the President on Trayvon Martin," Press Release, The White House, Office of the Press Secretary, July 19, 2013.
³⁷David K. Li, "Zimmerman allegedly retweeted photo of Trayvon Martin's Body," *The New York Post*, September 28, 2015; Shane Bauer, "George Zimmerman Posted a Photo of Trayvon Martin's Dead Body," *Mother Jones*, September 28, 2015; Khaleda Rahman, "George Zimmerman's sick Twitter rant: Killer shares photos boasting about his freedom with vulgar racist rant at Obama just hours after posting image of Trayvon's dead body," *Daily Mail*, dailymail.com, September 28, 2015, accessed September 29, 2015.
³⁸Tulsa County Sheriff's Office, News Release, "Reserve Deputy Involved Shooting," April 2, 2015, Tulsa Oklahoma.

Other officers commented to Harris, "You shouldn't have run," and "Shut the fuck up." There seemed to be no urgency in getting Harris medical assistance. In fact, he was still being forcefully subdued as he lay wounded and bleeding on the ground.[39] Harris' death was one flagrant issue, yet there was little or no discussion about the personnel and resources expended (through the Violent Crimes Task Force) to buy one weapon.

The volunteer officer, Robert Bates was a millionaire who retired from the insurance business. Bates purportedly was officially assigned to the undercover sting operation when Eric Harris was killed. Bates stated that he meant to use his stun gun on Harris, but made a mistake and fired a service weapon (his personal firearm). Harris' death was ruled a homicide. The 73-year-old was charged with second-degree manslaughter and pled not guilty. Bates came to police-service as a reserve deputy volunteer; however, he had donated thousands of dollars and equipment to the police department. After the incident, he was frequently featured in the media for showing remorse over the killing of Harris. When a judge gave him permission to leave the country for a month, Bates (having received much public criticism) cancelled his vacation to the Bahamas. The killing of Harris raised issues about the extent wealth directly influenced personal inroads into the ranks of the police; and the role of volunteer policing in terms of actual fieldwork experience. Community protesters in Harris' case wondered how much force was necessary to secure an arrestee who was already taken down by several officers—a man who was unarmed and not resisting. They also wanted know why such an elaborate tactical scheme was necessary in order to recover one weapon. This case was different for a number of extremes. It is uncharacteristic in police-custody shootings for law enforcement officers to publically admit guilt or show remorse over the death of a shooting victim. And yet, there was quite a bit of media-generated sympathy for Bates, but not Harris. The effort to shield and distance Bates from "legitimate" police officers was also evident. Bates had received no formal training and the gun he killed Harris with was not approved by the police department. By the time Bates was arrested and photographed, his age was subtly questioned. Yet there were many other problems associated with the case, which continued to mount for the Tulsa Oklahoma police

---

[39]United States District Court for the Northern District of Oklahoma, *Scott W. Birdwell, et al v. Stanley Glanz, Sheriff of Tulsa County, et al.*, Case No.: 15-CV-00304-TCK-TLW.

department—charges of excessive force, the forging of training records, the primacy of personal relationships and professional duty, the power of patronage, an inadequately trained police volunteer, ad infinitum. In the end, instead of depicting a capable and qualified law enforcement field-volunteer, the media (acting as a member of his community-of-care) attempted to convert Robert Bates into the sympathetic figure of a doddering old man.

Black Political Leaders and the Black President at the Nexus of the Baltimore Uprising?

The significance of black political leadership after the Civil Rights Movement is often ignored in American history, unless the goal is to highlight the perceived controversies, contradictions or abject failures (i.e. Marion Barry, Kwame M. Kilpatrick). When black leadership is considered effective and competent, there is a paucity of discussion about the strength of these leaders. Most black political leaders today come directly out of the Civil Rights, Black Power movements, or they have a deep personal history of community activism. The mainstream media seized upon, but never fully developed, this idea of community activism and a black feminine political triad wielding power and influence in the midst of the Baltimore Uprising—the new Attorney General of the United States Loretta Lynch, the States prosecutor for the city of Baltimore, Marilyn Mosby and the Mayor of the city, Stephanie Rawlings-Blake. It is possible to add to that the considerable efforts of Maryland State Senator Catherine Pugh who, like many black leaders were visible and active during the city's unrest, and also served as a co-chair of a working group created to study police issues. However, there was also a black male dynamic which included the nation's first African American President Barack Obama, the Baltimore City Police commissioner Anthony Batts, the former Attorney General, Eric Holder; as well as Maryland Congressman Elijah Cummings. In addition to legislators like Cummings and Pugh, there was several other black Maryland elected officials involved in the efforts to engage in dialogue and to improve the city of Baltimore. The critical issues that emerged were systemic, exhaustive, and there was a tremendous expectation about what these black leaders would be able to accomplish after the Baltimore Uprising. With the city's crisis still searing in the national consciousness, no politician appeared to work harder, or was more maligned than Baltimore's Mayor, Stephanie Rawlings-Blake. Within days of the uprising, the mayor's office announced how new initiatives would be broached; and within months began to discuss reforms that would directly affect the Sandtown/Winchester area. At times, it seemed to matter little what Rawlings-Blake said or did, there were many who were ready to criticize her efforts and others prepared to amplify any reproach. More than citizen disapproval, it was at least in part, a function of the culture of perpetual catharsis and blame. The people had been wounded for so long that apparently no effort—no matter how great—would suffice to alleviate the wrongs. There was a 2016 mayoral primary looming in Baltimore, and while Rawlings-Blake appeared to have run out of political capital as a result of the Baltimore Uprising, she had established her intent to run with her "Stephanie Rawlings-Blake for Baltimore" campaign.[40]

In the history of modern American politics, beginning in the late 1960s with the first black elected officials and through the 1980s, African American citizens fully anticipated that these leaders would be attentive to issues that concerned the community.[41] Yet most of the issues that defined the contours of black life in America were structural, and predated their terms. Whites under black city governance expected the same care; except perhaps, there was the need to *hear* black leaders say that they represented all of the people—and *not just blacks*. The needs of black citizens, no matter how aligned with those of whites, were perceived as separate and particular. However, black leaders were often managing historic crisis (including Obama's assumption of the Presidency during the recession, at the apex of the financial crisis, and the war in the Middle East). Black leaders are constantly embattled in political struggles that directly challenge their positions and hinge on racial perceptions. As a result, they are also perennially embroiled in racialized diminishments of their power. So as the Freddie Gray case unfolded publically and several other high-profile police-shootings across the nation were called into question, along with some extraordinary examples of racial hostility—the nation was fixed on the responses of President Obama. Even before he took office in 2008, President Obama has had to address the vestiges and realities of racism

---

[40]Stephanie Rawlings-Blake for Baltimore campaign website, 2015, http://www.rawlingsblake.com/, accessed September 16, 2015.
[41]Some of the first black elected officials included: Carl Stokes (first black mayor of a large U.S. city in 1967; Shirley Chisholm, the first black woman elected to Congress in 1968; and Barbara Jordan, the first black person from the south since period of Reconstruction to be elected to Congress in 1971.

WORLD TO COME: ESSAYS ON THE BALTIMORE UPRISING, MILITANT RACISM, AND HISTORY

and white supremacy in the United States. Since the beginning of his two terms (2008-2016), President Obama has received more death threats than any president in the history of the United States. Most of the threats were issued online. In the timeframe surrounding his 2008 election, there was a rise in the activity of white radical separatist groups. It has also been suggested that early in Obama's presidency (during his first term) he should be credited for motivating some of the robust political activity of the various Tea Party organizations. There was the sense that whether we were observing the operations of city government in the management and aftermath of the Baltimore Uprising, or the end of the last term of President Obama and his administration's regard for Civil Rights issues, in many ways we were witnessing a new attitude about black social justice advocacy.

Nothing catalyzes politicians more than a high profile social problem. Some politicians (local and national) seized the Baltimore Uprising moment for political gain; others attempted constructive leadership in the effort to understand and address the associated problems. Within days of Freddie Gray's death, Maryland Senators Barbara A. Mikulski, Benjamin L. Cardin, and Congressmen, Elijah Cummings, Dutch Ruppersberger, and John Sarbanes called for a Federal Civil Rights investigation. During the Baltimore Uprising, politicians from the presidential hopefuls to local representatives of Baltimore City made space for their public messages. Former Secretary of State Hillary Clinton was among the first of the Presidential candidates to speak out about the Baltimore Uprising. Like many, she lamented the state of emergency and called for law and order. But to the surprise of some, she contextualized her comments within the plight of African American men. In one of the first public speeches of her campaign, Clinton stated that she supported reform of the penal system, and used the term *mass incarceration* to reference the inordinate numbers of blacks who make up the prison inmate population—and promoted an end to this practice within the criminal justice system.[42] The story ran widely, and ABC News reported that social media paid considerable attention to the issue. It was liked on Facebook 4.2 million times, received over 300 tweets and more than 2000 comments at the

---

[42] Liz Dreutz (via Good Morning America), "Amid Baltimore Violence, Hillary Clinton Calls for End to 'Era of Mass Incarceration,'" *ABC News*, April 29, 2015, http://abcnews.go.com/Politics/amid-baltimore-violence-hillary-clinton-set-unveil-plan/story?id=30664649, accessed July 26, 2015.

story's webpage.[43] Two months later, Bernie Sanders (D-VT) and Martin O'Malley (D-MD) offered similar commentary, though both were thought to have failed to connect with the Black Lives Matter protest at a Democratic presidential forum in Arizona in mid-July. It was at the Netroots Nation convention, an event that was deemed a dynamic conference for liberal activists with about 11,000 people in attendance. Protesters disrupted Sanders and O'Malley at the event over the issue of black police-custody deaths. Both candidates found themselves defending their record on black human rights. At the time it was their largest presidential-election convention. O'Malley, who had been mayor of Baltimore (1999-2007) and Governor of the state of Maryland (2007-2015), had more to defend. Protesters and citizens of Baltimore often cited that O'Malley had supported a zero-tolerance policing policy, which led to the harassment of community members and the arrests of 1/6th of the city's predominately-black population.

The bold challenge to these two presidential candidates was also a clash over the norms, philosophy and the trajectory of modern political engagement. Sensing that the liberal candidates—regardless of independent or democratic affiliation—understood or cared little about the plight of African Americans, the crowd booed them. They had encountered the new age of political disrupters—people who are highly motivated, technologically connected, beyond urgency, if not perhaps at times bereft of civility—a generation with a low tolerance for rhetorical folly and political insensitivity. The black political insurgents not only wanted to know that they were heard and understood, they wanted to feel it. Sanders, who offered to leave the forum after being booed, might have missed the point altogether—not that his independent-democratic-socialist-liberal credentials were in question—but that among other things, the people wanted the 2016 presidential candidates to "stay on point." In another time, at another venue perhaps the parting assertion offered by Martin O'Malley, "Black lives matter. White lives matter. All lives matter," might have made sense to the crowd. But the comment insulted Black Lives Matter activists and supporters. O'Malley did apologize (more than once), however, his remarks appeared indifferent (if not insensitive) because of the inability

---

[43]Liz Dreutz (via Good Morning America), "Amid Baltimore Violence, Hillary Clinton Calls for End to 'Era of Mass Incarceration,'" *ABC News*, April 29, 2015, http://abcnews.go.com/Politics/amid-baltimore-violence-hillary-clinton-set-unveil-plan/story?id=30664649, accessed July 26, 2015.

to stay focused on the subject—*black lives*—thus giving it the weight, time, and attention that the activists believed it deserved. As the summer moved into fall, the Black Lives Matter movement impatiently waited for politicians, particularly the many presidential hopefuls, to say something meaningful about the racial moment. When it occurred, it came from a former law professor and Massachusetts Senator Elizabeth Warren (D) who was not running for President of the United States. *The Washington Post* called her fall 2015 "Civil Rights" address, "…the speech that Black Lives Matter have been waiting for."[44] Senator Warren delivered one of the defining statements on racial inequality as it affected African Americans, centered squarely on the issue. On September 27, 2015, she made these remarks at the Edward M. Kennedy Institute. Senator Warren boldly asserted:

> In the same way that the tools of oppression were woven together, a package of civil rights laws came together to protect black people from violence, to ensure access to the ballot box, and to build economic opportunity. Or to say it another way, these laws made three powerful declarations: Black lives matter. Black citizens matter. Black families matter.[45]

However, since the Netroots Nation conference Sanders and O'Malley had clarified their public message on the phrase and meaning of Black Lives Matter. At the first of the debates of the Democratic National Convention held in Las Vegas Nevada in early October, 2015 all of the presidential candidates, including Sanders and O'Malley, had refined their responses. O'Malley simply defended his crime prevention record during his time as mayor of the city of Baltimore, and as provocative as it was he somehow suggested—using analytics—that the zero-tolerance policy saved lives, rather than wrecked them. Sanders' message was succinct; he stated emphatically that "Black Lives Matter," with a clear "period" at the end of the sentence, and his elucidation of the idea remained on point. Still, what would have happened had there been no great reminder to the nation that "Black Lives Matter," especially with

---

[44]Wesley Lowery, "Elizabeth Warren just gave the speech that Black Lives Matter Activists have been waiting for," *The Washington Post*, September 27, 2015.
[45]Senator Elizabeth Warren, "Remarks at the Edward M. Kennedy Institute for the United States Senate," September 27, 2015, transcript, p. 3, Elizabeth Warren U.S. Senator for Massachusetts website http://www.warren.senate.gov/?p=home, http://www.warren.senate.gov/?p=press_release&id=967, Accessed September 27, 2015.

respect to the focus on the police-encounter deaths of African Americans. Would any of the presidential candidates have addressed these issues on their own? Nevertheless, there were more sophisticated attempts to change the national conversation—by firmly acknowledging that "Black Lives Matter," but failing to offer a clear proposal on how to address the crisis and concerns of black citizens. In this regard, politicians and the 2016 Presidential candidates offered a miniscule hope in the moment, but not an actionable vision.

CHAPTER 12

THE BALTIMORE UPRISING AND THE GREAT BLACK LEGACY OF SOCIAL JUSTICE

> Those were busy days of busy men. They had no time to give the prisoner a bill of exception or stay of execution. The only way a man had to secure a stay of execution was to behave himself.—Ida B. Wells-Barnett[1]

This was no "African American Spring"

Beginning in late 2010, into early 2011 there were a number of protests and uprisings across the modern Middle East (Tunisia, Egypt, Yemen, Syria). These Uprisings were called "Arab Spring" because they represented a massive civil rights crusade of citizens protesting against the repressive actions of their governments. The western media paid close attention to the unrest, opportunely noting the public pleas for democracy and the condemnation of authoritarian rule. Social media played an important role in disseminating independent information about the various protests—including the considerable civil unrest. At the beginning of the Baltimore Uprising in late April 2015 there was an immediate analogy made to the "Arab Spring" events. It was a conventional marginalization and distortion of African American liberatory ambition. Peaceful and dynamic protest and marches are nothing new to black people. Civil dissent and disobedience is a great legacy of the African American community. It is the highest manifestation of the voice of people thought to be voiceless. Like Ferguson, this aspect of the Baltimore Uprising is a testament to our important history—the enduring strength and commitment of a people. Ignoring this black tradition, some commentators struggled to find meaning in the event and called the Baltimore Uprising an "African American Spring." However, the comparison diminished, if not discounted, the long and eloquent history of African American civil disobedience. While black struggles for human rights began centuries before, the civil rights movement (post-World War II) spanned approximately three decades. It represented a series of protest

---

[1] Ida B. Wells-Barnett, "Lynch law in America," *The Arena* 15 (1900).

WORLD TO COME: ESSAYS ON THE BALTIMORE UPRISING, MILITANT RACISM, AND HISTORY

initiatives that redefined the struggle for freedom across the globe. The movements of the 1960s were at times multiracial, interreligious, and interdenominational. In its totality, the movement exposed structural racism as a serious human relations issue. The Civil Rights movement informed and inspired concurrent human rights struggles around the world; and served as a foremost model for civil disobedience discourse and domestic resistance movements influencing the crusades for women, and later LGBTQ (lesbian, gay, bisexual, transgender, and queer) and immigrant rights. There is scarcely a modern social interest group in the United States, which does not owe its rhetorical, methodological and philosophical underpinnings to the African American Civil Rights movement.

Many American cities, including Baltimore, have a great civil rights legacy. This history has included some notable (if not countless unsung) people and events. Regarding the well-known examples, Thurgood Marshall was born on July 2, 1908 in Baltimore, Maryland and grew up in the middle-class, but racially segregated area of Druid Hill. Under the mentorship of Howard University law dean Charles Hamilton Houston, Marshall became Chief Counsel for the NAACP, was later was appointed U.S. Solicitor General in 1965 by President Lyndon Baines Johnson, and in 1967, he became a United States Supreme Court Justice. Marshall is most remembered as chief counsel for the 1954 watershed Supreme Court case, *Brown v. Board of Education*. The span of Marshall's life has been described as one filled with activism and an indefatigable humor. The first U.S. woman supreme court justice Sandra Day O'Connor called Marshall a man of "…wit and charm, and rambunctiousness…."[2] Marshall was a man who possessed one of the sharpest legal minds of his time, and was singularly dedicated to racial justice.

Juanita Jackson Mitchell (1913-1992), a lawyer, educator and activist, was a revered civil rights legend in the city of Baltimore. She was a well-known youth leader and organizer; and the first black woman to attend the University of Maryland School of Law, and to become a practicing attorney in the state of Maryland. Admitted to the bar in 1950, Mitchell initiated and co-counseled (with Thurgood Marshall and others) a series of lawsuits to end racial segregation in Baltimore city schools. She also used her legal training and activism to

---

[2]Sandra Day O'Connor, "Thurgood Marshall: The Influence of a Raconteur," *Journal of Supreme Court History*. 1992 Dec 1; 17(1):9-14, 10.

World To Come: Essays On The Baltimore Uprising, Militant Racism, And History

address customary racial discrimination in employment, voting rights, public facilities, and police misconduct. Thus, she was the first black woman in the state of Maryland to practice civil rights law.[3]

Juanita Jackson Mitchell was part of just one black dynasty dedicated to human rights in the city; Walter P. Carter (1923-1971) is still considered a foremost Civil Rights pioneer in Baltimore. Carter's dedication, power, and influence earned him the label of "too radical" in the city of Baltimore and the State of Maryland. Carter served as chair of the Baltimore chapter of the Congress of Racial Equality (CORE), and was a state coordinator for the 1963 March on Washington. He organized massive protests and campaigns for a variety of issues including the racial desegregation of public accommodations, for equality and fairness in the areas of housing and voting rights, and he was a major activist for the black poor in the city. One of his daughter's Jill P. Carter (D) is an attorney who was elected (2003) to the Maryland House of Delegates, representing the 41st District. For those citizens who supported Jill Carter's run for the mayor's seat in Baltimore (2007)[4], like her father, she was described as a "...capable leader who is not afraid to speak the truth even when it makes the powerful uncomfortable. She walks the walk."[5]

If anything, the 2015 Baltimore Uprising was an extension of the work of countless activists in the modern Civil Rights movement. Moreover, it was, like the call for Black Power, part of the protracted struggle of blacks to define, secure and guard their freedoms in American society. To compare the "Arab Spring" to the Baltimore Uprising, and especially without the full historical scope of African and Arab struggles in the countries of north Africa and those of the Middle East, does a great disservice to the remarkable legacy of the Civil Rights movement and the Pan-African quest for liberation and democracy. The real story of the Baltimore Uprising was not that it was reminiscent of the "Arab Spring," but that, in the context of the dynamic struggle for human rights, how significant events and meaningful discussions were minimized; and how, major crisis-level community issues were now perceived as "real." After the rioting aspect of the Baltimore

---

[3]Taunya Lovell Banks, "Setting the Record Straight: Maryland's First Black Women Law Graduates," *Maryland Law Review* 63, No. 4, 752-772 (2004), 764.
[4]Sheila Dixon (D) won this election.
[5]Jill Carter for Baltimore, "Why Jill Carter?," June 12, 2007, https://jillcarter4baltimore.wordpress.com/, accessed January 7, 2016.

World To Come: Essays On The Baltimore Uprising, Militant Racism, And History

Uprising, residents banded together to clean up the city after the initial night where rioting occurred. In the days that followed countless peaceful protests and demonstrations were initiated. In addition, food, water and other "relief supplies" were collected and distributed to the residents of West Baltimore. The military presence in Charm City, specifically in Black Baltimore, punctuated the stark reality of the city's street cameras and surveillance helicopters. Politicians initiated and responded to discussions about reconstructing the criminal justice system, particularly the mass incarceration of African Americans. In addition to the overwhelming incidence of police brutality, the activists also wanted to talk about the wealth gap, the health outcomes, and life expectancy of Blacks. These were systemic issues the black community had been talking about and working to correct for generations. The Baltimore Uprising proved, once again, that it takes a movement to raise a nation.

Marilyn J. Mosby, the Quest for Justice, and Strategic Challenges

In less than a week after the mayor's press conference, the State's Attorney for the city, Marilyn Mosby, shocked everyone on May 1, 2015 when she presented charges against the six police officers implicated in the death of Freddie Gray. Mosby had made it very clear, from the beginning of her campaign for the office of the city's states attorney, that criminal justice was broader than police powers and in the judicial apparatus—"we are the justice system."[6] She wanted positive change for the city of Baltimore. And she conducted the press conference with the same passion and sense of mission exhibited as when she first announced her run for this office. In the shadow of the death of Freddie Gray, Mosby for nearly twenty minutes, read a detailed statement of the charges against the Baltimore City Police officers involved in the death of Freddie Gray, and then responded to questions. Within days, the *Baltimore Sun*, which held much of the media spotlight as reporters from all over the country converged on the city, ran a series of stories which not only addressed the impact of Mosby's statement—but included stories about the police officers charged with manslaughter and misconduct, assault, and false imprisonment. They also featured a young black photographer, Devin Allen, who had one of

---

[6]Marilyn Mosby, "Marilyn Mosby's Announcement Speech for the Office of Baltimore City State's Attorney," June 24, 2013, accessed May 14, 2015.

World To Come: Essays On The Baltimore Uprising, Militant Racism, And History

his Baltimore Uprising pictures selected for the cover of *Time Magazine*.[7] There was also a story about how a local teacher used coloring books and the rap genre to engage her students; and of course, news items about the potential insurance claims that would be filed after the riots. It was already a complete media frenzy, which seemingly had no end. However, the stories about the six police officers involved in Freddie Gray's arrest, and Marilyn Mosby's quest for justice, held the greatest interest.

Marilyn Mosby had done something that the nation had not seen before—at least not with this magnitude of media attention, and certainly not with the sense of force and determination she conveyed. First, she, without delay, charged the six police officers for the death of a young unarmed black man. Second, the charges included second-degree murder in which one officer could receive up to 30 years; and the charge of manslaughter was also levied, carrying ten-year maximum penalties. This meant that Gray was human and that the officers allegedly intentionally killed him and violated his eighth amendment rights (in terms of "cruel and unusual punishments"). Third, the State's Attorney made it clear that Gray should have never been arrested. She stated that it had been an exhaustive investigation and she emphasized, "no one is above the law."[8] Some people cheered when Mosby made the announcement. There was an overwhelming sense of relief which spread throughout the community. Within a matter of minutes, we also learned that Baltimore's police union would defend all six of the officer's charged, citing that in their opinion the charges were a "rush to judgement." Not only would the union refute assertions of any potential wrongdoing by the officers in question, they made it clear they would stand by their brothers and sister. Others rallying around the police department would question whether there were possible ethical violations emanating from Mosby's office, including questions about conflicts of interests respective to her husband who sat on the Baltimore City council; and regarding her connection to the lawyer for the Gray family (William "Billy" Murphy) and campaign contributions.

By May 5, 2015, Page Croyder, a retired Baltimore deputy state's attorney severely criticized Mosby in a *Baltimore Sun* opinion-editorial piece, stating that Mosby's decisions were "…either (a result

---

[7]*Time Magazine*, May 11, 2015.
[8]The State's Attorney for the City of Baltimore, Press Conference, May 1, 2015, Baltimore, Maryland.

of) incompetence or an unethical recklessness."[9] In addition, just as she asserted in the opinion/editorial in her blog, her condemnation also suggested that inexperience and political ambition prompted Marilyn Mosby's actions.[10] Croyder, who seemed to argue from her past experience and current inside information, said in a CNN interview that Mosby, was "terribly inexperienced" and that she did not use all of the investigative tools available to her office. She even went further to suggest that Mosby might want to leave the city of Baltimore. Within less than twenty-four hours of Croyder's attack, a plethora a stories emerged and latched onto the assault on Mosby. As with most racially charged, or high profile cases, the media trial was underway. The lawyers for the Baltimore 6 filed a motion to have the case dismissed and they also wanted Marilyn Mosby to recuse herself. Carefully parsing Mosby's statement at the May 1, 2015 press conference, the officers' attorneys were essentially arguing that there had been a rush to judgement on Mosby's part, and that the six officers were charged and arrested too quickly. It was not long after Croyder, the police union, and the Baltimore 6 defense attorneys' challenges that assorted media began to call for the resignation of Mosby. The response of the State's Attorney for the city of Baltimore was immediate, dispassionate, and concise; Mosby issued a statement that she would not "...litigate this case through the media." The statement also confirmed what several local activists already assumed, when Mosby stated, "I strongly condemn anyone in law enforcement with access to trial evidence, who has or continues to leak information prior to the resolution of this case."[11] Her resolve to secure justice for Freddie Gray won her praise throughout the city and the nation, particularly among African American citizens.

Part of the problem in assessing the attack on Marilyn Mosby was that obviously African Americans were continuing their tradition of enlarging and deepening their role in the political governance of the

---

[9] Page Croyder, "Police Charges in Freddie Gray case are Incompetent at Best," *The Baltimore Sun*, May 5, 2015, http://www.baltimoresun.com/news/opinion/oped/bs-ed-freddie-gray-mosby-20150505-story.html, accessed May 6, 2015.
[10] "Baltimore's Hasty Prosecutor," Baltimore criminal Justice Blogger Page Croyder, May 4, 2015, http://pagecroyder.blogspot.com/, accessed May 6, 2015.
[11] Office of the State's Attorney for the City of Baltimore, Press Release, "Statement from State's Attorney Mosby on Freddie Gray Case," May 5, 2015.
http://www.stattorney.org/media-center/press-releases/716-statement-from-state-s-attorney-mosby-on-freddie-gray-case, Accessed May 16, 2015.

World To Come: Essays On The Baltimore Uprising, Militant Racism, And History

city. The media spent quite a bit of time focusing on Mosby's age (35); and this was exhibited in part to suggest that she was too young and inexperienced. However, it was her blackness, intelligence, sense of self, and self-assuredness that was the real problem. The racist impulse demanded that the message about the wrongful deaths of black men at the hands of police, morph into criticisms of black women. If Mosby was effectively judged as too young, untested, or zealous, then no one would be held responsible for the death of Freddie Gray. Just on the cusp of the millennial cohort, these black leaders see themselves as an important part of the social and political process. Rather than being content with merely being "in the room with Whites," the post-civil rights generations see themselves as part of, and equal participants in, the discussion. If some of the previous black leaders felt compelled to define their power through a willingness to show an inordinate deference to whites, the post-civil rights generations have normalized Black power. If society declared that structural racial inequity and Jim Crow Racism was dead—then they, having been raised to hold society accountable—would not to go along with a rouse. When they assume power, they are able to set the discourse *and* influence policy because they categorically deny the racist impulse. Assertions about Mosby's supposed naiveté had little to do with political innocence. Her critics were frustrated that she refused to acquiesce to the overarching racist agenda; and unapologetically rejected the idea that she would recuse herself from the case. On May 21, 2015, Mosby announced that a Baltimore Grand jury had indicted the six police officers. Some of the initial individual charges were revised, and all officers were accused of reckless endangerment in the death of Freddie Gray. Marilyn Mosby stated that they would be arraigned on July 2, 2016; and this time she did not take questions from the reporters. Later, the trials for the Baltimore 6 were scheduled to begin in October 2015.

The Police as Sacred Symbols, Money Bail, The Baltimore 6, And Alan Bullocks

Police are regarded as the absolute embodiment of American law and order; or they are perceived as a source of state terror. In the United States, the police are important sacred symbols, and even their pain is privileged. They have difficult jobs and they work hard. They have to make critical decisions in a nano-second. They are subjected to undue occupational stressors and pressures that also have a psychological component. The police who are in the field—on the streets—risk their own lives every day. In addition, like all those who

World To Come: Essays On The Baltimore Uprising, Militant Racism, And History

are public servants and work directly with the community, police-encounters with citizens can be fraught with serious challenges—including life-threatening situations that impact the citizens. Despite the social service support that we might find in any major city, police are ultimately there to "protect and serve" and for many the one task they must carry out —is to uphold the law.

America can be a tremendously ahistorical nation, especially when it comes to the story of African American people. While police as an institution can and do boast of long histories of service and heroism—blacks were not allowed to seriously participate in the forces until after the gains of the Civil Rights movement. Even today, that conveniently forgotten history of concerted racial chauvinism in the police force, speaks to the major racial difficulties that currently exist. In addition to racial exclusion, police have also been part of a long history of oppressing African Americans and other people of color. When history is read from the perspective of the downtrodden, the police would know that historically, their role was always to control and contain the African American community—not to protect and serve. The adversarial relationship has been nurtured for generations; and it impacted the poor, working, middle and upper classes of African Americans.

To demonstrate police privilege in the recent history of American law enforcement, we need only look at the standards for community policing white neighborhoods. While poor blacks complain that police do not come when called, or that they are treated like perpetrators (not as citizens who are possible victims or witnesses) when police arrive, it is not uncommon for a black person to be regarded as a criminal suspect even on his or her own residential property. Many will recall that in 2009 all it took was a 911 call from an affluent white neighborhood that two black men were breaking into a home in Cambridge Massachusetts, to set off a national racial firestorm. The call led to the arrest of well-known black Harvard professor Henry Louis Gates by police Sgt. James Crowley and eventually to a controversial "Beer Summit" at the White House. Gates could not conceal his disgust over the arrest as he told *The Root* in 2009,

> I'm outraged. I can't believe that an individual policeman on the Cambridge police force would treat any African-American male this way, and I am astonished that this happened to me; and more importantly I'm astonished that it could happen to any citizen of the United States, no matter what their race.

WORLD TO COME: ESSAYS ON THE BALTIMORE UPRISING, MILITANT RACISM, AND HISTORY

> And I'm deeply resolved to do and say the right things so that this cannot happen again. Of course, it will happen again, but ... I want to do what I can so that every police officer will think twice before engaging in this kind of behavior.[12]

Gates knew that this would happen again. Yet it was the ancestry of the President that promulgated an unwieldy national discussion about history and the complexities of race, racism and policing. No other modern President, except Barack Obama, would have attempted to bring the parties together for a kind of racial reconciliation, but even the President knew the troubled history that brought them there.[13] For Gates, neither his public profile, income, nor his Ivy League professorial status mattered—just his race.

While Gate's disturbing experience was said to have enhanced his celebrity, the police-encounter he endured paled when compared to Fay Wells' ordeal six years later. Wells, a Duke and Dartmouth graduate who worked as a Vice President in Santa Monica California, accidentally locked herself out of her apartment in September 2015. She called a locksmith and gained entry to her home. Three hours later she was confronted by 19 armed policemen and a police dog. A 911 caller, a neighbor, reported it as a break-in by three Hispanics. Apparently, even after Wells emerged from her apartment as ordered with her hands up, the 5-foot-7, 125-pound woman was still problematic for police. Having been invaded, falsely accused, and traumatized, the woman assumed she would be treated with a modicum of respect. However, she discovered that the police didn't have to identify themselves to her, answer any of her questions, tell her why they were there, lower their guns, examine her identification when she offered it; and certainly did not have to provide their names and badge numbers.

Additionally, the 911 caller didn't appear to have any empathy or concern for her either, nor did he appreciate being questioned by Wells. Based on her account, the neighbor didn't care that she could

---

[12]Dayo Olopade, "Skip Gates Speaks: The Root's Editor-in-Chief Henry Louis Gates Jr. talks about his Arrest and The Outrage of Racial Profiling in America." *The Root*. Posted July 21, 2009,
http://www.theroot.com/articles/culture/2009/07/professor_henry_louis_gates_jr_speaks_out_on_racial_profiling_after_his_arrest_by_cambridge_police.html?auto=true, accessed May 21, 2015.
[13]In the 1990s the Clinton administration's President's Initiative on Race, promoted a national dialogue on race relations.

have been killed. Wells surmised "...What mattered was that I was a woman of color trying to get into her apartment—in an almost entirely white apartment complex in a mostly white city—and a white man who lived in another building called the cops because he'd never seen me before."[14] There was no presidential beer summit for Wells. However, Santa Monica Police Chief Jacqueline A. Seabrooks, who is African American, issued a heartfelt if not racially and legally strategic public statement in response to Wells' *Washington Post* article detailing the encounter. Police Chief Seabrooks essentially acknowledged everyone's pain, noting that individuals involved in these situations tend to see things differently.[15] But the truth is, both Gates and Wells (and many others) were racially profiled and disrespected; and they were fortunate to have survived their experiences. Despite black intra-racial debates and struggles with issues surrounding wealth and class, we should remember that there was nothing about Gates and Wells' obvious socio-economic status that gave them any immunity from hostile police-encounters. ■

    The mainstream media has always treated law enforcement officers as exceptional persons—and everyone else as marginal to their mission and function. In the midst of the Baltimore Uprising, after one week, the media regularly reported that approximately 130 police officers had been injured. However, there was never any real interest in or attempt to report the injuries sustained by demonstrators. One standard news report made an effort to state that, "There were no immediate reports of injuries among the rioters."[16] Nearly 500 people were arrested in the protests; and there were claims of more than 200 instances of destruction of city and personal property including the burned out CVS pharmacy and shops at Mondawmin Mall.[17] These numbers varied, however what is certain is that a massive and wide variety of people were arrested and detained. Apparently, the city police could not handle the number of mass arrests and by mid-week (April

---

[14]Fay Wells, "My White Neighbor Thought I was Breaking into My Own Apartment. Nineteen cops showed up." *The Washington Post*, November 18, 2015.
[15]Jacqueline A. Seabrooks, Chief of Police, Santa Monica Police Department, "The Chief's Perspective," City of Santa Monica, undated,
http://santamonicapd.org/Content.aspx?id=54286, accessed December 19, 2015.
[16]Holly Yan and Dana Ford, "Baltimore Riots: Looting, Fires Engulf City After Freddie Gray's Funeral," CNN, April 28, 2015.
http://www.cnn.com/2015/04/27/us/baltimore-unrest/, accessed May 27, 2015.
[17]The mall closed for a week, and then reopened on a limited basis.

29, 2015), at least a hundred people were released. For protestors the path to arrest was fraught with brutality. Activists, along with numerous photographers, videographers, and journalists were pushed to the ground (faces smashed into concrete), some injured with batons, tear gas and flash bangs. A group of university student activists from Washington, D.C., in solidarity with the Palestinian cause, seemed to feel "…more frightened of police in Baltimore than Israeli forces at protests they had attended in Palestine."[18] The media took little interest in reporting the injuries sustained by protestors and for months after the uprising, it was always important to headline the wounds of law enforcement officers, including psychological trauma and minor physical damage.

On May 1, 2015, six police officers were charged and arrested in the death of Freddie Gray. Within a few days, they were freed on bail, which was levied between 250,000 and 350,000 dollars. However, with the same clamor you would find in a post-war crimes tribunal, there was the case of the 18-year-old Alan Bullock, who was caught on camera vandalizing a police car. The image was posted and reposted everywhere. He turned himself in with his parents (mother and stepfather) by his side. He had no prior convictions and took responsibility for the property damage he had caused. His bail was set at 500,000; he faced eight criminal charges and up to eight years in prison. The black public was outraged that six officers, legally indicted, and shielded by the police, had lower bails for causing and/or contributing to the death of a man who had not committed any crime. This issue, early in the battle to gain justice for Freddie Gray and the criminal justice system, demonstrated the clear disparities in sentencing.[19] Our history has demonstrated that it is difficult for African Americans to gain bail, or they are more often levied bail that is impossible to pay. As a result, people who would otherwise remain outside of the judicial system, risk a permanent criminal record; and for others, even minor past violations threaten a term confinement. There were many questions about the half million-dollar bail levied against the 18-year-old; activists and legal analysts looked into having the bail

---

[18]Rania Khalek, "Israeli-Trained Police Invade Baltimore in Crackdown on Black Lives Matter," *The Electronic Intifada*, http://electronicintifada.net/blogs/rania-khalek/israeli-trained-police-invade-baltimore-crackdown-black-lives-matter, May 7, 2015, accessed May 9, 2015.
[19]Cynthia E. Jones, "'Give us Free': Addressing Racial Disparities in Bail Determinations," *Legislation and Public Policy*, Vol. 16, 919-961, 2013.

lowered. However, Bullocks' attempt to destroy a police car windshield was seen as an act of attacking an actual police officer. Bullocks' was willing to admit his mistake and accept the penalty. Despite the support of family—who encouraged him to do the right thing—his crime was deemed more pernicious than the police officers who ignored Freddie Gray's cries for help. The officers assumed Gray had "jailitis," and among other arrest tactics, they may have intentionally used a "rough ride" which contributed to his death.[20] Bullocks' was released after his family and attorney was able to raise the funds through online crowdfunding. Over three hundred people contributed to Bullocks' legal fund; and had this not taken place, he probably would have remained in jail. The excessive bail levied sent a chilling message to the black community. First, that money—economic power—would be used to limit equitable participation in the criminal justice system. Second, that African American youth have no credibility in the criminal justice system. Bullocks displayed virtuous intent and good will in his effort to take responsibility for his actions. His parents and supporters engendered and reflected that outlook, and stepped forward to in essence, vouch for their child. The courts determined that in the Baltimore Uprising, no amount of personal or community integrity, social networking, or resolve to advance moral and civic good, was enough to mitigate fears of black urban terror. In the Baltimore Uprising excessive bails were levied on the protestors and others who were arrested for nonviolent offenses. Many were held longer than twenty-four hours without having any charges filed against them, and some cited that they were being held in the deplorable conditions of Baltimore's Central Booking.

On Sunday May 3, 2015, the 10:00 p.m. city curfew was lifted by Mayor Rawlings-Blake. Thereafter, major media outlets began preparing to leave. The heightened mainstream media cycle for the Baltimore Uprising faded. The governor ordered the removal of the National Guard. The guard eventually departed their posts around the city hall and other prominent locations. Their Monday May 4, 2015

---

[20]"Jailitis" is defined as a condition where a person becomes suspiciously ill while in police-custody or housed in a jail cell; and purportedly is a rationale for police to not seek medical assistance for arrestees. This was suggested in Freddie Gray's case when he asked for medical help; and a "rough ride" (also known as a "nickel ride") was provided—the informal police practice of leaving a prisoner for transport unbelted along with reckless driving—which can force the body to move violently inside the vehicle, and cause injury.

World To Come: Essays On The Baltimore Uprising, Militant Racism, And History

release from Baltimore city duty coincided with reports, led by *Fox News* that a black man had been shot by the police while running away. While the story proved to be false, and *Fox News* issued an apology, the police appeared on the defensive in their attempt to assure protestors on the scene—and the nation at large—that the black man had not been shot by police—that he, while running from police had discharged a weapon. He had actually thrown the gun down as he ran from police. Several people saw the man, Robert Tucker, being placed into an ambulance. Some thought the police had shot him, and Tucker was accused of inciting people to riot against the police.[21] Without questioning the routine familiarity of the exaggerated media encounter, very few interrogated this particular case. The crucial message was to ensure that this event was not perceived as "another Freddie Gray."[22]

The Militarization of Baltimore and the Live Disappearance of Joseph Kent

The sense of militarization in the city of Baltimore was even more evident surrounding the case of Joseph Kent. Kent majored in music at Morgan State University and worked part-time at Mondawmin Mall. The 21-year-old was known as a prominent local activist who had also assisted in the peaceful organizing efforts of Ferguson Missouri. The night of the curfew, April 28, 2015, he was instantly heralded a hero who was *disappeared* by police on camera. The event was caught on film by *CNN*. About 10:30 P.M. Kent defied curfew, and defiantly marched in front of the tactical line of Baltimore police. He carried no weapons except a water bottle attached to his hip. Pacing and chanting his protest in front of rows of guardsmen and police, an armored car (a Hummer) approached and Kent was immediately whisked into the vehicle by police. During the process, the military vehicle did not slow down or stop. At the time Kent was grabbed no one knew where he was held. Social media advanced the idea that Kent had been *disappeared*. The implications produced a viral response—that Kent was the victim of a state-sponsored kidnapping. Kent was arrested that

---

[21]Bureau of Alcohol, Tobacco, Firearms and Explosives, U.S. Department of Justice, Press Release, "Man Arrested in Penn-North One Week after Baltimore Riots Sentenced to 42 Months in Prison for Federal Gun Charge," December 14, 2015. https://www.atf.gov/news/pr/man-arrested-penn-north-one-week-after-baltimore-riots-sentenced-42-months-prison-federal, accessed December 18, 2015.
[22]Robert Tucker, was convicted of federal weapons possession.

World To Come: Essays On The Baltimore Uprising, Militant Racism, And History

night for violating the curfew, and held until Thursday.[23] Apparently he was recognized and this facilitated his release while, countless other protestors were not so fortunate. Kent's crime was defying curfew, but his real offense was that he publically challenged the police line. A number of people intentionally disobeyed curfew in order to sustain the message that "Black Lives Matter." Independent journalist, Rania Khalek reported that a week after Kent was arrested and released, "…around 80 protesters held their ground in the courtyard in front of City Hall. They were in high spirits and determined to break the 10p.m. curfew…"[24] For civil disobedience adherents, challenging a legal curfew in a state of emergency, is an important tool. It forces the activist to be seen and his or her message to be heard by the public.

There was a price for civil disobedience, even peaceful protests, and this fact was not lost on the protestors; or any of the photographers and journalists who were swept up into the swathe of military-style aggression. However, in some cases the issue was never direct provocation, or even an explicit threat, the issue was aggressive control. Social media either roiled against the swift tactical disappearance of Kent or chided the intimation that a military conspiracy was afoot. But black people do not have the luxury of conspiracy theories—they have reality. The Twitter hashtag #JosephKent was used to gather information and to make public comments about Kent's location. The #hashtag was also a form of protest inquiry and kept his name alive until his whereabouts became known. Kent did confirm that he was "disappeared." The young activist, whose message had consistently been a peaceful one, saw himself as a reliable community-based mediator between the people and the police. Conservatives assailed him as a professional activist (meant derisively that he was "without credibility") who was rightly arrested for breaking the state-of-emergency citywide curfew. Black activists and white liberal progressives were very concerned about his physical well-being. Even using a modest conceptualization, there is truth in the data analysis that "More than one out of every six black men who today should be between 25 and 54 years old have

---

[23]His attorney was Stephen Patrick Beatty.
[24]Rania Khalek, "Israeli-trained police invade Baltimore in Crackdown on Black Lives Matter," The Electronic Intifada, http://electronicintifada.net/blogs/rania-khalek/israeli-trained-police-invade-baltimore-crackdown-black-lives-matter, May 7, 2015, accessed May 9, 2015.

disappeared from daily life" due to incarceration or mortality.[25] What was muted in the conversation was the deepening mythology about the existence of covert urban military operations facilities. The recent allegations and investigations into Chicago's Homan Square police center raised the issue as a valid concern.[26] Homan Square is the police warehouse that critics have compared to a foreign military "black site" (like Guantanamo Bay and Abu Ghraib) where purportedly people have been kidnapped, tortured, and denied legal counsel. Homan Square detained and disappeared thousands of people—mostly blacks. In another more malevolent interpretation of the situation in Baltimore, without photographers and citizens with cellphone cameras—Joseph Kent might have disappeared into one of these black hole sites altogether. Martial Law was in effect, and at the time of the Baltimore Uprising curfew, heavily armed riot-gear clad law enforcement officers outnumbered any lingering protestors seeking justice.

---

[25]Justin Wolfers, David Leonhardt and Kevin Quealy, "1.5 Million Missing Black Men," *The New York Times*, April 20, 2015.
[26]*The Guardian* led the reporting on the citizen charges against Homan Square facility, see their comprehensive coverage at http://www.theguardian.com/us-news/homan-square; Spencer Ackerman, "Homan Square Revealed: How Chicago Police 'Disappeared' 7,000 People," *The Guardian*, October 19, 2015; Spencer Ackerman, "Homan Square Detainee: I Was Sexually Abused By Police At Chicago 'Black Site,'" *The Guardian*, May 14, 2015; Steven W. Hawkins, Amnesty International, USA, "Letter to Chicago Mayor Condemning Police Torture at Homan Square," *Voice of the Revolution*, March 6, 2015, 23.

CHAPTER 13

AFRICAN AMERICANS, THE PSYCHOPOMP OF MEDIA, AND *THE WIRE*

> Every phase of Negro life is highly dramatised. No matter how joyful or how sad the case there is sufficient poise for drama. Everything is acted out. Unconsciously for the most part of course. There is an impromptu ceremony always ready for every hour of life. No little moment passes unadorned...These little plays by strolling players are acted out daily in a dozen streets in a thousand cities, and no one ever mistakes the meaning.—Zora Neale Hurston[1]

The New Attorney General Visits Baltimore

Following the six year (2009-2015) tenure of Eric Holder, the first black Attorney General, Loretta Lynch became the 83rd United States Attorney General, an appointment to the most important law enforcement position on the federal level. Lynch was born in the segregated south in Greensboro, North Carolina and from an early age, showed interest in the legal proceedings held at the Durham courthouse. Her attraction to the law was supported by the stories of her grandfather, who was a pastor and had created his own modern day Underground Railroad in the 1930s in order to assist blacks with Jim Crow racism.[2] Lynch was a dedicated scholar determined to work hard in school and encouraged by her parents who, like many of her generation, emphasized the importance of education. She attended Harvard University where she co-founded a Delta Sigma Theta chapter. Lynch received her A.B., cum laude from Harvard College in 1981, and a J.D. from Harvard Law School in 1984. In 1990, Lynch joined the United States Attorney's Office for the Eastern District of New York (Brooklyn). While in New York, Lynch's career as a prosecutor

---

[1] Zora Neale Hurston, "Characteristics of Negro Expression," in *Signifyin (g), Sanctifyin', and Slam Dunking: A Reader in African American Expressive Culture* (1934): 293-308.
[2] "Attorneys At The Succeeding In Spite Of Top Dismal Diversity Trends." *The Network Journal*. n.d. http://www.tnj.com/archives/2007/december_jan2008/decjan08issue/cs_decjan08_llynch.php (accessed October 5, 2015).

included bringing to trial suits involving narcotics, violent crime, public corruption, and some of the highest profile civil rights cases the nation faced (including the police brutality case involving Abner Louima). In 1999, President Clinton appointed Lynch to lead the office of the United States Attorney—a post she held until 2001.[3] Thereafter she worked as a partner in the New York firm Hogan and Hartson. From 2002 through 2007, Lynch worked pro bono as counsel to the prosecutor at the United Nations International Criminal Tribunal for Rwanda in Arusha, Tanzania.[4] This tribunal helped to indict those responsible for the 1994 genocide committed in Rwanda. After a successful career as one of the highest-profile federal prosecuting attorneys in the nation, President Obama nominated Lynch for the position of attorney general in November 2014, stating that: "Loretta doesn't look to make headlines; she looks to make a difference."[5]

The day the new Attorney General took office was the day that Freddie Gray was buried. Lynch was sworn-in on April 27, 2015 by vice president, Joe Biden.[6] Lynch became the first African American woman to hold the post. By the time civil unrest in Baltimore developed in earnest, several media pundits observed that this event, which unfolded quickly, would be a defining issue for the Lynch administration. Then about a week later, on Tuesday, May 5, 2015 the new head of the justice department led a delegation to Baltimore to meet with city leaders and discuss the Baltimore Uprising. Lynch reached out to the family of Freddie Gray, students at the University of Baltimore, and city law enforcement officers which included a visit to the Central District of the Baltimore police department. Lynch thanked the officers for their service, and yet in some ways her call seemed like an inspection—one that ensured that law enforcement understood that she would oversee a balanced investigative process. This message was reinforced when

---

[3]"Meet the Attorney General." *The United States Department of Justice*. August 28, 2015. http://www.justice.gov/ag/meet-attorney-general (accessed October 5, 2015).
[4]"President Obama Nominates Five to Serve as U.S. Attorneys." *The White House*. January 20, 2010. https://www.whitehouse.gov/the-press-office/president-obama-nominates-five-serve-us-attorneys (accessed October 5, 2015).
[5]The White House, Press Conference, Attorney General Nomination, November 8, 2014 (video archived on C-Span at http://www.c-span.org/video/?322643-1/president-obama-nominates-new-attorney-general).
[6]Raf Sanchez and David Lawler. "Who is Loretta Lynch, the US Attorney General taking on Fifa?" *The Telegraph*. May 27, 2015. http://www.telegraph.co.uk/news/worldnews/us-politics/11375588/Meet-Loretta-Lynch-Barack-Obamas-pick-for-attorney-general.html (accessed 5 October, 2015).

WORLD TO COME: ESSAYS ON THE BALTIMORE UPRISING, MILITANT RACISM, AND HISTORY

Lynch also met with Baltimore mayor Stephanie Rawlings-Blake in City Hall. These meetings were considered among the first official visits of her new tenure as Attorney General. It was during this stop that the city of Baltimore formally requested assistance from the Justice Department. Within twenty-four hours, the Justice Department announced that it would launch a federal investigation into the Baltimore City Police Department. There was only one main question, and it was the question posed to countless police departments across the nation—whether the Baltimore Police Department had an evidence-based "pattern or practice" of using illegal and/or extreme force against the citizens. In one of the most recent federal investigations of city police in Ferguson Missouri, after the police shooting of Michael Brown, the DOJ found (among many troubling particulars) that the police overwhelmingly targeted African Americans for violations that appeared to support an effort to enhance the municipal budget.[7]

Polling the Baltimore Uprising, Charitable Expressions, and the Rally 4 Peace

The Pew Research Center immediately conducted a survey assessing peoples' opinions about the Baltimore Uprising from April 30 through May 3, 2015[8] and other polls followed from news outlets. The Pew's national survey on the Baltimore Uprising reported that most people believed that criminal behavior was at the heart of the unrest—fomented by people who chose to take advantage of the situation. The report also found that most people believed that hostilities did exist between police and the black community. It documented that citizens held "Anger over the death of Freddie Gray," and the survey found significant acknowledgement of poverty conditions in Baltimore. The survey reported that among the causes of the Baltimore Uprising was the "initial response by city officials." In addition, while most whites thought that some people took advantage of the situation in order to participate in criminal activity, fewer whites than blacks thought that poverty and lack of opportunity in the community was a factor. More blacks than whites thought that the charges against the Baltimore 6

---

[7]United States Department of Justice, Civil Rights Division, *Investigation of the Ferguson Police Department*, March 4, 2015, 42-61 (see "Ferguson's Municipal Court Practices").
[8]The Pew Research Center, "Multiple Causes seen for Baltimore Unrest," May 4, 2015, http://www.people-press.org/2015/05/04/multiple-causes-seen-for-baltimore-unrest/, accessed May 11, 2015.

World To Come: Essays On The Baltimore Uprising, Militant Racism, And History

represented the right decision. Blacks were consistent in their views about the recent police-custody deaths involving Freddie Gray, Eric Garner (New York) and Michael Brown (Ferguson, Missouri). While blacks supported charging officers in Freddie's Gray's case, blacks also in significant numbers, thought it was wrong not to charge police officers in the Garner and Brown cases. Most people between the ages of 18 and 29 years old thought that the press "gave too little coverage to non-violent protests."[9]

In the aftermath of the Baltimore Uprising, there was some immediate discussion, and attention paid to the idea that the long neglected neighborhoods in question actually needed help. There was little discussion about what citizens were entitled to, as opposed to, what would be the role of private philanthropy. The conversation turned immediately to the processes of giving and volunteering. However, giving did not necessarily include dollars emanating from city budgets and resources. The initial message was clearly one that suggested the city of Baltimore and the state of Maryland were "rallying" in support of the people. However, the undercurrent of national austerity trends was always a prevailing factor. On May 1, 2015, Governor Larry Hogan announced that charitable donations and volunteers were being coalesced under the "Maryland Unites" program. It was one of the governor's "... effort(s) to provide assistance, food, and donations to those directly affected by the week's events."[10] A week later, the public statement that Mayor Rawlings-Blake would launch the #OneBaltimore program, which sought to galvanize the city's resources to "assist residents in need,"[11] coincided with the legal news that the Justice Department would initiate a "pattern or practice" probe into Baltimore City Police. It appeared that the state, city, as well as the federal government, were moving without delay to address some of the underlying causes of The Baltimore Uprising. Yet everyone was concerned with determining the causes of the unrest.

---

[9]Pew Research Center, May, 2015 "Multiple Causes Seen for Baltimore Unrest," May 4, 2015, 18pp., www.pewresearch.org.
[10]The Office of Governor Larry Hogan, Press Release, "Maryland Unites for Baltimore," May 1, 2015, http://governor.maryland.gov/2015/05/01/maryland-unites-for-baltimore/, accessed May 8, 2015.
[11]City of Baltimore, #OneBaltimore, http://www.baltimorecity.gov/onebaltimore, assessed May 8, 2015. City of Baltimore Press Release, "Mayor Rawlings-Blake Announces One Baltimore Initiative," Thursday, May 7, 2015.

World To Come: Essays On The Baltimore Uprising, Militant Racism, And History

However, the consolidation of state and citywide charitable efforts was notable; many concerned observed that the efforts served a number of purposes and sent multiple messages to the community. It assisted the political interests of officials who would later be able to cite these initiatives as aiding the community post-uprising. Still, in the midst of inspiring support, smaller, independent, and grass-roots community-driven efforts of the people to help themselves was also ceremoniously ignoring. As noted, the rush to charity preempted what some believed to be an ever-increasing fiscal austerity. One that would make the state's belt-tightening in the past, resemble the height of the "Great Society" spending initiatives. The philanthropic announcements were also wanting of long-term endeavors to elevate and rebuild the community structurally. While the efforts were much needed, the idea of charity maintained the established frame of blacks as worthy of "handouts" in times of crisis, but not worthy of genuine long-term city and state investment. Thus, the residents of the Sandtown-Winchester neighborhood of West Baltimore were often framed as refugees or persons in exile—as if they were outsiders in their own country. This brought up parallels to the victims of Hurricane Katrina in 2005, especially the people caught on video cameras looting. The old ideas of "the deserving poor" surfaced with notions that blacks who were economically and socially disadvantaged—were a drain on society—and thus not truly worthy of federal or charitable assistance. However, the philanthropic effort to address the emergency basic needs of the people who lived in West Baltimore would not be denied. During this brief period of time it was actively encouraged.

Then emergency charity turned into creative activist agency. The critically acclaimed musician Prince (Prince Rogers Nelson) has been called "One of the most prolific and multifaceted performers of his generation…,"[12] and he has had a long and storied career. In recent history, he is well known for battling his one time record label, Time Warner. Prince changed his name to a symbol, and for nearly a decade he was known as ⚥ (O or O([13], a contemporary expression reminiscent of Egyptian hieroglyphics, which represented for many in the public, his defiance to commercial exploitation. In embracing iconography for the world of speech, Prince reclaimed his name from

---

[12]Patricia (Patty) Dean, "Punk Funk Rock Pop," *Minnesota History Magazine*, Minnesota Historical Society, MHS Collections, Vol. 58, Issue 1, 29-39, 33, 2002.
[13]He was also referred to as "The Artist Formerly Known as Prince."

enslavement. It was no surprise that he was among the first artists (and there appeared to be many including Rhianna) to lend his name and support to the Baltimore Uprising. Prince had written a protest song, entitled *Baltimore,* and this contributed to the rumor that he was coming to the city to support the demonstrator's and the legacy of Freddie Gray. The rumor was soon confirmed, that his Rally 4 Peace concert— which was free to the public— would be held at Royal Farms Arena. Prince asked that people wear the color gray, in memory of Freddie Gray. Not only would the concert be free to the public, Jay Z's streaming music service, Tidal, committed to broadcasting the event. In addition, Tidal would match donation funds to support the youth of Baltimore. This was the latest, most visible example of high profile protest music, and other creative endeavors, intended to unite people. Other concerts, planned and impromptu, filled the streets of the city days after the riots. Prince, coupled with Jay Z's Tidal, did represent a black intergenerational effort to support the Baltimore Uprising; and these and other artists donated money to assist the citizens in many ways. The Rally 4 Peace concert continued the sense of defiance, as well as offering a determined community progressive ways to address the significance of civil dissent. However, it did surprise some, when Marilyn Mosby and her husband Nick Mosby, attended the concert and was made a place on stage alongside Prince. It was a Mother's Day event for the Mosby's, one that spoke to the social justice impulse of the family. Yet while there was a sense of rebelliousness in the appearance, because of the recent virulent attacks on Marilyn Mosby, there was also the image that Mosby was a woman who stood with the people. Prince delivered his important message to the city, reflected in the lyrics from his song *Baltimore*, that "Peace is so much more than the absence of war."[14]

The Gendered Nuisances of Afrofemiphobia

Within The Baltimore Uprising there was a great carnival atmosphere perpetuated by mainstream and social media. News outlets exhibited considerable sensationalist interest in black women, particularly Toya Graham, who upon recognizing her sixteen-year-old

---

[14]*Baltimore,* lyrics by Prince, from the album *Hitnrun Phase Two*, NPG Records, copyright 2015.

World To Come: Essays On The Baltimore Uprising, Militant Racism, And History

son on television with a stone in his hand, rushed to the scene at Mondawmin Mall and began shouting at and hitting her son. As part of the Baltimore Uprising coverage, *CNN* billed it as breaking news with the headline "Angry Mother Smacks Teen Protester." Police Commissioner Anthony Batts praised her actions. The local and national media dubbed her the *slap mom*, *riot mom*, and in some media outlets she was more derisively referred to as the "Mother of the Year." While one group cheered her, another was appalled that she struck her child, and on national television. Her minister, the well-known Reverend Jamal Bryant said, "…I wish all of the parents of Baltimore would take on her spirit and go pull your children out of the streets."[15] Independent *Pan-African News Wire* editor and journalist Abayomi Azikiwe remarked that the constant attention given to the "Slap Mom" diverted attention away from the major social and economic issues of the residents. Azikiwe also noted that this interest gave further credence to the racialized idea that black youth in general were in special need of discipline. In addition, the sensationalism further reinforced the image of the stereotypic aggressive, loud and violent black mother. It was clear that Graham struggled to remove him from the scene. She explained later and with immense clarity that she was trying to *save her son's life*. She knew how easily he could be killed for acts far less dangerous than rebelling and engaging in the public destruction of property. The importance of that message seemed misplaced as she was paraded through the brief hypermedia cycle as the "Slap Mom." Yet only days later, and with similar social media flourish, 17-year-old Edwardsville Kansas motorist Kali Chatmon found herself in a minor traffic near miss with a white male City Councilman. According to Chatmon, the so-called road rage incident, which was an *almost* collision, caused the councilman to purportedly call her a "black nigger bitch." In addition, in keeping with historically conventional racist calls for blacks to "go back to Africa," the city councilman (who was a retired police officer) supposedly told Chatmon to "go back to Baltimore." A month later, he denied using any such racial slurs against Chatmon.

In United States history, black women have been relentlessly maligned—some scholars and activists have labeled this gendered racial hatred and dismissal of the humanity of the black feminine as,

---

[15] The Reverend Jamal Bryant interviewed by Steven Fabian, *Inside Edition*, CBS Television, April 29, 2015.

WORLD TO COME: ESSAYS ON THE BALTIMORE UPRISING, MILITANT RACISM, AND HISTORY

Afrofemiphobia. In the southern antebellum experience, the labor of black women was exploited; and she was sexually abused, and then blamed and punished for having been a victim of the system.[16] The concept of Afrofemiphobia—how the black female body is constructed within a racist context—is meant to capture the irrational fear of black women that results in assault, marginalization, alienation, defamation, and even death. Black women have suffered from the consequences of this gendered phobia, and this has been especially true of black mothers—and unquestionably real for poor single black mothers who are the most denigrated. In the early days of the Baltimore Uprising, many blamed the problem on the break-down of families, honing in on the black woman. Besides the embedded generalized stereotypes of black women—single mothers (poor, working, middle and upper class) have been blamed for everything from the national crime rates to economic stagnation. To add to this, black women are not just victims of racism—but also routinely wounded by sexism and classism. However, even though the stressors are many, black women have demonstrated tremendous resilience and adaptive capabilities and this includes single mothers. Black mothers provided for the basic needs of children, including socialization, discipline, and nurturing—often as wageworkers. Sometimes the single black mother is the grandmother, aunt, older sister, or some other member of the extended family. In African American historical studies, socio-economic and psychological studies of African American mothers inform and advise women how to survive and thrive.[17] With reference to children however, many scholars

---

[16]Katherine Bankole, *Slavery and Medicine: Enslavement and Medical Practices in Antebellum Louisiana*, New York: Garland Publishing, Inc., 1998.

[17]See Safoura Boukari, "20th Century Black Women's Struggle for Empowerment in a White Supremacist Education System: Tribute to Early Women Educators," (2005) *Information and Materials from the Women's and Gender Studies Program*, Paper 4. http://digitalcommons.unl.edu/wgsprogram/4; Sandra M. Grayson, Black Women in the Antebellum America: Active Agents in the Fight for Freedom, Occasional paper, William Monroe Trotter Institute, University of Massachusetts at Boston, 1996, 32pp. Clenora Hudson-Weems, *Africana Womanist Literary Theory*. Trenton, NJ: Africa World Press, 2004; Christine Renee Robinson, "Black Women: A Tradition of Self-Reliant Strength." *Women & Therapy* 2, No. 2-3 (1983): 135-144; Niara Sudarkasa, "African American Families and Family Values," (1997); Niara Sudarkasa, "Strength of Our Mothers: African and African-American Women and Families: Essays and Speeches" (1996); Niara Sudarkasa, "Female-Headed African American Households: Some Neglected Dimensions." *Family Ethnicity: Strength In Diversity* (1993): 81-89; Freeman A. Hrabowski III, Kenneth I. Maton, and Geoffrey L. Greif, *Beating the Odds: Raising Academically Successful African American Males*. Oxford University Press, 1998; Freeman A.

WORLD TO COME: ESSAYS ON THE BALTIMORE UPRISING, MILITANT RACISM, AND HISTORY

and historians opposed and debunked Daniel Patrick Moynihan's 1967 malicious but influential black family assessment[18], which reinforced the flawed black mother thesis in the United States. These scholars have emphasized brave and noteworthy attributes of black women such as "...the protective instincts...regardless of her, age, economic strata, or educational level."[19] Despite the black woman's dynamic sense of agency in the American Wilderness, *Afrofemiphobia* is often evident as an unnatural racialized hatred that devalues human possibilities, while assigning or assuming both racial and gender inferiority. Ultimately, it is a base, illogical, and inexplicable fear of the black feminine.

There were a myriad of racialized attacks on black women in the mass media (overt and veiled) during and immediately after the Baltimore Uprising. These criticisms included public denunciations specifically targeting Marilyn Mosby and Stephanie Rawlings-Blake; but also included Sgt. Alicia White, who was completely ignored as a black woman named among the Baltimore 6 police officers charged in the death of Freddie Gray. The assaults on the character and intentions of Rawlings-Blake were persistent; while the attacks on Mosby and her motives intensified and seemed pointedly strategic. However, within days of the Baltimore Uprising, both Mosby and Rawlings-Blake were praised by the United States Conference of Mayors. The nonpartisan group said that Mosby's "...strong public statement regarding the charges against the six police officers involved should assure the people of Baltimore and the nation that the pursuit of justice in this case will be diligent, transparent, and prompt."[20] They also supported Rawlings-Blake and recognized "...her immediate and forceful response to the State's Attorney's action." They noted that Rawlings-Blake "...instructed Police Commissioner Batts to suspend and arrest the six

---

Hrabowski, Kenneth I. Maton, Monica L. Greene, and Geoffrey L. Greif, *Overcoming the Odds: Raising Academically Successful African American Young Women*. Oxford University Press, 2002; and Silvia Dominguez and Celeste Watkins, "Creating Networks for Survival and Mobility: Social Capital Among African-American And Latin-American Low-Income Mothers." *Social Problems* 50, No. 1 (2003): 111-135.

[18] Daniel Patrick Moynihan, Lee Rainwater, and William L. Yancey, *The Negro Family: The Case For National Action*. Cambridge, MA: MIT Press, 1967.

[19] Jean Childs Young, "The Black Child," in *Proceedings, Conference on the Black Family*, Cleveland, Ohio, September 25-28, 1985, edited by Janice Hale-Benson, 44-48, 47.

[20] The United States Conference of Mayors, Press Release, "Statement by U.S. Conference of Mayors President Sacramento Mayor Kevin Johnson on the Baltimore State's Attorney's Announcement In The Freddie Gray Case And Baltimore Mayor Stephanie Rawlings-Blake's Response Following It," Washington, D.C., May 1, 2015.

officers. And she reflected the feelings of mayors across America when she stated that the vast majority of police officers serve their communities with pride, courage, honor, and distinction, and that there is no place for brutality, misconduct, racism or corruption in the policing of our cities."[21] Had Mosby and Rawlings-Blake been males in these high profile and powerful positions, within the context of a city-wide emergency, their proactive activities and professional conduct would have been regularly reported on. And regardless of how people perceived them personally or professionally, their competence and desire to preserve human life would have been publically applauded.

Yet it seemed that the exact opposite was more prevalent in assessing their behavior. The Baltimore branch of the NAACP, headed by Tessa Hill-Aston,[22] was forced to send a letter to the President of the FOP on May 18, 2015 regarding "Concerns about rhetoric used towards African American female leadership."[23] The NAACP's letter made it clear that they would not ignore the police union's condemnation of Mosby when her office decided to file charges against the six officers involved in the death of Freddie Gray. Nor did the veteran civil rights organization appreciate that after it was announced that the DOJ would investigate the BCPD, the FOP requested (more or less in retaliation) that the DOJ "…investigate the Mayor of the City of Baltimore…" The NAACP read the not-so-subtle strike as a political attempt to ultimately, "…pollute the possible jury pool…," in order to exonerate the Baltimore 6. According to the NAACP's letter, the statements made by the FOP were an attempt "…to all but subtly threaten these women who are merely doing the job we elected them to do …."[24] Notwithstanding traditional displays of Afrofemiphobia, somewhere in the most virulent of the criticisms levied against these two women lay the truth about the longstanding difficulties in attempting to reform police practices in the city of Baltimore.

---

[21]The United States Conference of Mayors, Press Release, "Statement by U.S. Conference of Mayors President Sacramento Mayor Kevin Johnson on the Baltimore State's Attorney's Announcement In The Freddie Gray Case And Baltimore Mayor Stephanie Rawlings-Blake's Response Following It," Washington, D.C., May 1, 2015.
[22]Hill-Aston is the first woman president of the Baltimore City NAACP.
[23]Letter to Gene S. Ryan, President, Fraternal Order of Police, Lodge #3 from Tessa Hill-Aston, President NAACP and Hassan Giordano, Chairman, NAACP Criminal Justice Committee, Baltimore Branch, May 18, 2015, 3pp.
[24]Letter to Gene S. Ryan, May 18, 2015, 3pp.

World To Come: Essays On The Baltimore Uprising, Militant Racism, And History

However one of the main issues in the national discussion of police-encounter deaths was that mainstream media failed to address that black women were also mortal victims of aggressive policing and were being ushered into the criminal justice system in greater numbers. Historically, black women were perceived to be as guilty as black men were, when confronted by police or in facing criminal charges. One infamous example from the 1970s was the Joan ("Jo Anne") Little case (or "yearlong crisis") in Washington, North Carolina.[25] At the age of twenty-one, Little found herself on trial for the murder of a white jail guard. She faced first-degree murder charges and the death penalty, which would have meant the gas chamber. Little's defense was that she had protected herself against a sexual assault while she was held in the Beaufort County jail on charges of theft. The jailer was found dead inside of the jail cell naked from the waist down. Little, who had escaped after the incident, immediately surrendered to the authorities. She later explained the reason for this, "I knew that if the Beaufort County police or the Washington policemen had seen me on the streets, they would have shot me down...I wouldn't a had a chance to be in this courtroom now to tell what happened ...."[26] Rep. John Conyers (D) characterized the North Carolina justice system in the mid-1970s as "...one of the most oppressive in the entire country..." where the majority of death row inmates were black.[27] Her case received national attention, and she was eventually acquitted in 1975. However, Little's legal defense had to document the racist beliefs of the county (through a behavioral survey) in order to gain a change in venue; and her legal team had to prove that the jailer sexually assaulted other females prior to the purported attack on Little. Everyone seemed to understand that, "Historically... the justice system hasn't protected black women from sexual assault."[28] At that time, in American society it

---

[25] Fred Harwell, *A True Deliverance: The Joan Little Case*, New York: Alfred A. Knopf, 1980; McConahay, J., Mullin, C. & Frederick, J. "The Uses of Social Science in Trials with Political and Racial Overtones: The Trial of Joan Little," 41 *Law and Contemporary Problems*, 1977, 204-229.
[26] James Reston, Jr. *The Innocence of Joan Little a Southern Mystery*, New York: Times Books, 1977, 319.
[27] "The Joanne Little Case," *CBC for the People*, Vol. 1, No. 2, May, 1975, 5.
[28] Rachael Anspach of the African American Policy Forum quoted in Molly Redden and Lauren Gambino, "Attorney Defends Alleged Serial Rapist Cop by Attacking the Credibility of Vulnerable Black Women," *The Guardian*, November 27, 2015. On December 11, 2015 police officer Daniel Holtzclaw was convicted of serially raping African American women.

was thought inconceivable that a black woman could be raped, and especially by a white male. Racial stereotypes in the popular culture held that black women were innately hypersexual and thus, as maintained in the antebellum slave period, were unrapable. For black women, misanthropic police-encounters can involve dimensions of gendered abuses, ranging from plain sexual chauvinism to pure sexual exploitation.

A haunting protest sign featured in the Baltimore Uprising was one that read: "Aiyanna was 7! Black Girls Matter."[29] Her placard was necessary. Aiyanna Jones was shot by a Detroit Michigan SWAT team in her bed during a raid in 2010. The story gained national attention, but not long term interest. The Black Lives Matter movement, through the "Say Her Name" campaign, revealed persistent disparities in the media coverage of black females who died under mysterious or questionable circumstances in police-encounters. One reason for the disparate treatment had to do with blackness conveniently reduced to the male gender, and then intended to encompass black female humanity. It was conceptually dismissive, but in a racialized society that historically abhorred gender as well as race, black women were nonentities. There was a need for the "Say Her Name" campaign because of the long held assumption that black women in America, as a whole, were less threatened by the criminal justice system. This was never true, but as black men were incarcerated in ever increasing numbers, the myth was created and sustained, and undoubtedly related to the popular culture notion of the strong (i.e. superhuman) black woman.[30] This meant that like black men, black women would be defined by their ability to withstand (with requisite dignity) racism, and not understood for the fullest capacities of our being. The African American Policy Forum was just one think tank committed to addressing the deaths of black women as a result of police-encounters and as a data-driven scholarly project with recommendations. They published *Say Her Name: Resisting Police Brutality against Black Women* in 2015.[31] The report drew attention to the multiple deaths of black

---

[29]See Appendix B: Baltimore Uprising Protest Signs.
[30]See Michelle Wallace's, *Black Macho and the Myth of Superwoman*, New York: Verso, 1999.
[31]Kimberle' Williams Crenshaw and Andrea J. Ritchie (with Rachel Anspach, Rachel Gilmer, and Luke Harris), "Say Her Name: Resisting Police Brutality against Black Women," African American Policy Forum, Center for Intersectionality and Social Policy Studies, 48pp.

women at the hands of police long before the high profile police-encounter deaths of African American males. The media had long embraced the "endangered black male" thesis and relegated the copious and mysterious deaths of black women to their back pages. Among a number of issues, the report highlighted the sex offenses perpetrated by police officers against women that included forcible rape. In addition, the *Say Her Name* report documented that black women were: subjected to racial profiling during routine traffic stops; victimized through excessive sentencing in narcotics offenses; abused when they needed mental health assistance; were victims of collateral damage; mistreated in domestic violence calls; discriminated against as mothers with children present; and were targets of police-custody deaths. Especially egregious was the treatment of black transgender women, juveniles, those who led vulnerable lifestyles,[32] and black women who defended family members that had been brutalized or killed by the police.[33]

Then again it was the summer 2015 Sandra Bland case that continued to strain the nation's imagination. Bland was stopped for an alleged traffic violation ("failure to signal a lane change"[34] as she attempted to move out of the officer's way). Bland was threatened verbally and assaulted physically (menaced with a Taser), arrested, and jailed. She was charged with assaulting the officer (Brian Encinia), processed as if she was a thrice convicted felon and recommended for the third highest security level for prisoners, "medium assaultive-escape."[35] Bland was found dead in her holding cell three days later. Authorities maintained that Bland hanged herself with a "…transparent white plastic trash bag tied into a ligature…"[36] As the news cycle initiated the coverage of Bland's arrest and death, there was an immediate media frame of her presumed flaws. Bland was described as an hostile, angry, belligerent, black woman, who was high, depressed,

---

[32] Women addicted to alcohol or narcotics, engaged in prostitution, are parolees, or who simply struggle to live below the poverty line.
[33] Kimberle´ Williams Crenshaw and Andrea J. Ritchie (with Rachel Anspach, Rachel Gilmer, and Luke Harris), "Say Her Name: Resisting Police Brutality against Black Women," African American Policy Forum, Center for Intersectionality and Social Policy Studies, 48pp.
[34] *U.S. District Court Southern District of Texas, Reed-Veal v. Encinia*, 4:15-cv-02232, Filed August 4, 2015, p. 5.
[35] Waller County Sheriff's Department, "Primary Security Level Assessment," (from Booking Sheet, Sandra Annette Bland," Waller County Sheriff's Office, July 10, 2015.)
[36] Autopsy Report, Case No. OC15-030, July 14, 2015, On the Body of Sandra Annette Bland, Harris County Institute of Forensic Sciences, July 22, 2015, p. 2.

given to postpartum suicidal ideation—and an epileptic. Before this message could become successfully conveyed social media and family members allowed for Bland to be seen as a vibrant, young, attractive, and articulate college-educated woman. She was alternatively described as the kind of person who had made the decision to deepen her service to community. She would be able to fulfill this dream because she had recently interviewed and received an offer of employment from her alma mater Prairie View A&M University, an HBCU. Many people refused to believe that Sandra Bland killed herself inside of a jail cell. Bland's disputed suicide touched so many because it was senseless as well as suspicious. People called for justice, and her massive community-of-care was "…profoundly troubled by the circumstances surrounding the sudden and tragic death…"[37] However, her case succeeded in highlighting three important elements. *First*, the Sandra Bland case drew even greater attention to the hidden police-encounter deaths of African American women. *Second*, it confirmed that the police-custody deaths of black females were also a community issue rather than specifically the sole concern of black males. *Third*, the case signaled to people of all races that perhaps there was an unthinkable dystopic future on the horizon. On this latter point, Daniel Lazare concluded, "If you want a picture of the future, to paraphrase Orwell, imagine an endless succession of Sandra Blands hanging in their cell—forever."[38] It was an unimaginable, chilling point. But the activist scholarship aligned with the Black Lives Matter movement, again, confirmed that it was anachronistic to speak of black women as occasional or marginal victims of police-encounter deaths, when black women were also dying in disproportionate numbers.

The Socio-Political Theater of Baltimore and The Wire

From 2002 through 2008, HBO presented the drama series, *The Wire*.[39] It was a cable television show created by David Simon[40]

---

[37]"Alpha Kappa Alpha Sorority Expresses Concern about Death of Sandra Bland," Press Release, Chicago, Illinois, July 20, 2015.
[38]Daniel Lazare, "Why US Police are out of Control," *Consortiumnews.com*, August 20, 2015. https://consortiumnews.com/2015/08/20/why-us-police-are-out-of-control/, accessed September 28, 2015/.
[39]See Home Box Office, *The Wire*: About the Show, http://www.hbo.com/thewire/about/.

WORLD TO COME: ESSAYS ON THE BALTIMORE UPRISING, MILITANT RACISM, AND HISTORY

(also known for *Homicide: Life on the Street* [1993] and *Treme* [2010]) who also served as the show's executive producer. *The Wire*, featured a huge cast including Wendell Pierce, Dominic West, Lance Reddick, Idris Elba, and Sonja Sohn, was set in the city of Baltimore—and the main theme of the show was the city's "inner-city drug scene." When it comes to assessing any serious situation involving Baltimore, more than one conversation begins with, "Baltimore is more than *The Wire*." These words are always presented as a defense against the authenticity of the city and the fictional realism of the television series. Like most major crime dramas, *The Wire* conceivably depicted every problem faced in urban America with large numbers of blacks. This included, but was not limited to drug dealing, drug addiction, crime, violence, police brutality, poverty, prostitution, and gangs. These problems were compounded by an ineffectual, if not incompetent and at times unconcerned, city bureaucracy, dysfunctional families, neglected residents, baffled and beleaguered law enforcement officers, abandoned children, and greedy politicians. *The Wire* was not intended to offer a lofty sense of hopefulness or to depict blacks as a visionary people. The show took every opportunity to display the "gritty" side of shattered black city life—prolific and vicious murders, self-congratulatory ignorance, and filthy streets with blighted houses. Even though the ratings were considered small, *The Wire* won several awards, received widespread media acclaim, and *MSNBC* called it "The best show in the history of television."[41] Fans of *The Wire* are inestimable, most completely convinced that the series represented "the best" of modern television. Defenders of *The Wire* insisted that the genuine appeal of the show was its seemingly meticulous attention to reality; specifically that it told the story of the contemporary drug scene (which still claimed to be in the realm of the protracted, yet failed war on drugs) from many perspectives.

Some people believed that *The Wire* was actually, in part, a serial documentary but no one never claimed such status for the production. Several scholarly and laudatory writings likened the series

---

[40]Simon was once a police reporter for *The Baltimore Sun*, and in 1988, he shadowed three of the city's homicide squads.
[41]Featured on product packaging of "*The Wire*: The Complete Series Blu-ray with Digital HD," available to the public June, 2015. HBO Home Video, http://store.hbo.com/detail.php?p=814002&ecid=PRF-HBO-803451&pa=PRF-HBO-803451#tabs, accessed May 23, 2015.

WORLD TO COME: ESSAYS ON THE BALTIMORE UPRISING, MILITANT RACISM, AND HISTORY

to a televised novel.[42] The show was not only set in Baltimore, Maryland, much of it was filmed in the city. In addition to the intricate politics of criminal and narcotics investigations, *The Wire* attempted to depict the inter-generational aspect of drug-related criminal activity. Similar to the fictional characters in family crime organization shows like *The Sopranos*, *The Wire* showed how parents, adult figures, and other relatives engaged in illegal drug activity and involved children. This supported the show's theme that illicit narcotics were big business, one that fueled petty neighborhood economies and lined the pockets of criminals, corrupt police officers, government officials and other community leaders. Some of the criticisms of *The Wire* were that while it also included every depraved stereotype of blacks that could be imagined; it failed to equally emphasize the genuine struggle for economic social justice. This was also demonstrated in the negative depiction of the Nation of Islam (though not expressly stated), through the character of Mouzone,[43] as a methodical Black Muslim hit man. Further, it dismissed, diminished or simply chided the prevailing cultural nationalism of Baltimore as a reality for black people. While there were always minor storylines and brief scenes of blacks in the upper classes, the show failed at presenting a black working and middle class population that was not pathologically motivated. The show intimated white racism, but with all of its moving complexity never addressed the entrenched history of structural racism and the city of Baltimore. However, shows like *Oz*, *Homicide: Life on the Streets*, and *The Wire*, were consistent with the new Blackploitation series and films of the 2000s, which coincided with the actual steady rise of black prison incarceration, and the decline of quality of life. People who appreciated the show, refused to see *The Wire* as merely television. In the vast realm of popular culture, *The Wire* was the perfect backdrop to the Baltimore Uprising—society had a carefully crafted cinematic narrative of blacks, nearly indistinguishable from a documentary that fans called "realistic," "graphic," "gritty," and "noir."

The Wire was so important to American popular culture, that universities became involved in studying the show's content. University courses were developed to discuss the show within the context of

---

[42]Simon Parker, "From Soft Eyes to Street Lives: *The Wire* and Jargons of Authenticity." *City* 14, No. 5 (2010): 545-557.
[43]Portrayed by actor Michael Potts.

WORLD TO COME: ESSAYS ON THE BALTIMORE UPRISING, MILITANT RACISM, AND HISTORY

serious present-day urban American issues.[44] Through a variety of academic disciplines, *The Wire* was taught to college students. In addition to Johns Hopkins University in Baltimore and the University of Texas (San Antonio), Brown and Harvard[45] universities offered classes based on the content gleaned directly from *The Wire*. A student at Georgetown University submitted a master's thesis on *The Wire* in 2009, "'Can't Knock the Hustle:' The Modernization of the Gangster Image in '"The Wire."'"[46] In addition, there were a number of writers and scholars that contributed critical book literature based entirely on analysis of the series.[47] Furthermore, newspaper and scholarly articles[48] about *The Wire* and contemporary issues of the American drug scene were exhaustive. *The Wire* certainly spawned interest in the issues it presented, and these were evident in the media stories that ran concurrent with the show. With the exception of some of the scholarly attention to *The Wire*, the criticism of the series has been in favor of the fan response and reproach was restrained. With a dedicated but much smaller following than they had hoped for, but which purportedly *has grown* since the show ended in 2008, and with glowing reviews, *The Wire* dismissed severe local and national scrutiny that vigorously challenged the demoralizing depiction and perception of African Americans.

---

[44]Andrew Moore, "Teaching HBO's *The Wire*." *Transformative Dialogues: Teaching & Learning Journal* 5, No. 1 (2011); Lageson, Sarah, Kyle Green, and Sinan Erensu. "The *Wire* Goes To College." *Contexts* 10, No. 3 (2011): 12-15.

[45]Anmol Chaddha, and William Julius Wilson, "Why We're Teaching 'The Wire' at Harvard," *The Washington Post* 12 (2010); Sheehan, Helena, and Sheamus Sweeney, "The *Wire* and the World: Narrative and Metanarrative," *Jump Cut* 51, No. Spring 2009 (2009); Marsha Kinder, "Re-wiring Baltimore: The Emotive Power of Systemics, Seriality, and The City," *Film Quarterly*, Vol. 62, No. 2 (Winter 2008): 50-57; James Trier, "Representations of Education in HBO's *The Wire*, Season 4." *Teacher Education Quarterly* (2010): 179-200.

[46]Scott Andrew Rossow, "Can't Knock the Hustle": The Modernization of the Gangster Image in '*The Wire*,'" MA Thesis, Georgetown University (2009).

[47]See Rafael Alvarez and David Simon, *The Wire: Truth Be Told*, 2010; Tiffany Potter and C.W. Marshall, *The Wire: Urban Decay and American Television* (2009); David Bzdak, Joanna Crosby and Seth Vannatta, *The Wire and Philosophy: This America, Man*, Chicago: Open Court Publishing, 2013; Kathleen Olmstead, *The Wire: The Untold History of Television* (2011); and Arin Keeble and Ivan Stacy, *The Wire and Post-9/11 America Critical Essays* (2015); Liam Kennedy and Stephen Shapiro, *The Wire: Race, Class, and Genre* (2012); and Brett Martin, *Difficult Men: Behind the Scenes of a Creative Revolution: From The Sopranos and The Wire to Mad Men and Breaking Bad* (2014).

[48]Ruth Penfold-Mounce, David Beer, and Roger Burrows, "*The Wire* as Social Science-Fiction?" *Sociology* 45, No. 1 (2011): 152-167.

World To Come: Essays On The Baltimore Uprising, Militant Racism, And History

The Wire was not the only crime show on television that depicted blacks, black politicians, and the city of Baltimore in a challenging negative framework. However, the show was most effective in presenting Baltimore as an inner city war zone.[49] In this view the city was no different than the battlefields in other parts of the world where governments are unstable and rebels are vying for territory. Other shows that offered this view and featured the realism of the city implicating Baltimore included *Homicide: Life and the Streets* (1993-1999) and *The Corner* (2000). Stern critics of *The Wire* were more concerned with the image of the city of Baltimore, than with any demeaning race-specific popular culture representation of African Americans. The *Baltimore City Paper* discussed the various ways in which city officials over the years have attempted to rebrand Baltimore and separate it from the impact of the devastating images presented in shows like *The Wire*.[50] The legacy of *The Wire*, coupled with the mainstream interpretations of the Baltimore Uprising, may have had an impact on securing sustained development projects in the areas of the city that needed it the most. There is no question that developers, and everyone else who saw the show, already held a firm context for the city, its leaders, and residents based on *The Wire*. In terms of image, and the challenge to rebrand the city, one could hardly be separated from the other. For many, *The Wire* was "…an exaggerated, nihilistic, and cynical pox on the city…"[51] but for African Americans, the show continued the media tradition, especially in melodramatic serials, of destructive negative stereotyping and of consistently relegating blacks to hapless futures. It is not that these kinds of serials do not depict some semblance of reality that encompasses the African American urban experience in particular. *The Wire* may have gotten some issues right about the political, social, and economic struggles in Baltimore; but it

---

[49]See Philip Joseph's "Soldiers in Baltimore: *The Wire* and the New Global Wars," *CR: The New Centennial Review*, Vol. 13, No. 1, Spring, 2013, 209-240.
[50]Bret McCabe, "Was '*The Wire*' Just Another Obstacle Standing in the Way of the City?" *Baltimore City Paper*, June 2, 2015.
http://www.citypaper.com/news/features/bcpnews-was-the-wire-just-another-obstacle-standing-in-the-way-of-selling-the-city-20150602,0,1003317.story, accessed June 4, 2015.
[51]Bred McCabe, "Was '*The Wire*' Just Another Obstacle Standing in the Way of the City?" *Baltimore City Paper*, June 2, 2015.
http://www.citypaper.com/news/features/bcpnews-was-the-wire-just-another-obstacle-standing-in-the-way-of-selling-the-city-20150602,0,1003317.story, accessed June 4, 2015.

ultimately failed African American society as a whole because it neglected systemic racism and reinforced the popular culture racial narrative of black pathology. This is an old pernicious narrative entrenched in the racist excesses of mainstream visual media, which maintains that no black/Africana story can (or should) be told without a framework that does not emphasize degraded and/or exaggerated human flaws. However, in the end, this is not really about the television phenomenon known as *The Wire,* which by the time of the Baltimore Uprising was synonymous with black life in the city of Baltimore. This is about truncating the black past, perverting the present; and at the same time, dispensing with worthy visions of the future for black people. Consequently, we are concerned about the stories we choose to tell, with what frequency, who we choose to tell these stories to, and for what purpose. We must consider all of this and remember that ultimately "We are the stories we tell ourselves."[52] For African Americans, and all liberated people, this meant disrupting the traditional narrative of black media distortion and exclusion, to ensure equity, accuracy and vision.

---

[52]Shekur Kapur, "We Are The Stories We Tell Ourselves," *TED India,* November, 2009.

CHAPTER 14

THE MILITARIZATION OF URBAN AMERICA

ARGOULET.— An ancient dragoon. Also an inferior sort of musket made at Liege for trading with the negroes.—*Farrow's Military Encyclopedia*, 1884[1]

Notes on the Domestic Military Build-Up

It has been effectively argued that America, since its inception, has steadily become particularly militaristic, and this movement also extends not only to analysis of war and combat preparedness, but also to the domestic work of local law enforcement agencies.[2] However, many scholars have documented the widespread increased militarization of the United States after the wars in Afghanistan and Iraq, and especially since the September 11, 2001 World Trade Center and Pentagon attacks.[3] When the Twin Towers and the Pentagon was attacked on September 11, 2001, an expanded, full-scale war on terrorism implicating the Middle East was declared. In those horrific and dramatic moments, the world shifted and the weight of a history rarely discussed was upon us. Nearly three thousand people died, and thousands of others suffered in the aftermath. The nation was poised to heighten its fight to protect American freedoms, yet in the process, most Americans did not perceive that they were no longer free. Immediately after September 11, in the early days of the War on Terror, media control and self-censorship meant that any public condemnation or criticism of the country's war was deemed anti-patriotic—in essence, a threat to national security.

With the uncertainty of a new millennium, popular interest in Y2K and the tragedy of 9/11, there was the sense that the world was being massively reordered. Though not a new concept, bulk domestic

---

[1] Edward S. Farrow, Farrow's *Military Encyclopedia A Dictionary of Military Knowledge Illustrated with Maps and About Three Thousand Wood Engravings*, Vol. 1, New York: Published by the Author, 1885, 64.
[2] Radley Balko, *Rise of the Warrior Cop: The Militarization of America's Police Forces* (First edition). New York: Public Affairs, 2013; Catherine Lutz, "Making War At Home in the United States: Militarization and the Current Crisis," *American Anthropologist* (2002): 723-735.
[3] This also includes the Boeing 757 that crashed near Pittsburgh, PA.

World To Come: Essays On The Baltimore Uprising, Militant Racism, And History

surveillance was argued as the main weapon needed to combat the threat of terrorism, and the USA Patriot Act was signed into law in October 2001. Established a year later, the work of the controversial 9/11 Commission (2002-2004),[4] included not only the investigation of the terrorist attack, but launched concerted threat assessment in order to make recommendations about how to improve and defend the nation's infrastructure to prevent future attacks. However, as noted political analyst and public scholar Noam Chomsky has pointed out there is a distinct difference between actual terrorism and the development and uses of terrorist propaganda.[5] The ungainly War on Terror quickly morphed into a War on Islam—and all expressions of Islam (and Islamic people) was deemed fundamentalist and threatening—which meant terrorist. In addition to international deployments, the search for potential domestic Islamic extremists was initiated in earnest. This included the investigation into the recent murders of four Marines at two military reserve centers in Chattanooga, Tennessee on July 16, 2015.[6] There was a real terrorist threat against the United States, however most Americans were privy to massive domestic acts of terrorism and gun violence that did not involve Islamic perpetrators.

While some scholars have argued that the responses to Middle East terrorism were in part a modern substitute for the post-WWII Cold War Russian enemy, domestic wars have always existed. Two of the most important of these domestic war themes is essentially characterized by the idea of an armed, angry and disengaged fringe white rural populous intent on radically resisting or overthrowing the government. The other has been the view that a hostile and violent black urban America exists and threatens the entire white mainstream way of life. Regarding the latter, at least four premises are evident. In the *first* premise war analysts suppose an urban war theatre or the potential for one whether or not organized and armed combatants actually exist. The *second* premise suggests that international and domestic war-games include an urban area component, thus justifying training in the national sphere. The *third* premise is that from a military

---

[4]The official title of the 9/11 working group: the National Commission on Terrorist Attacks upon the United States.
[5]Noam Chomsky, *9-11*, New York: Seven Stories Press, 2002.
[6]The murdered soldiers included Thomas Sullivan, Squire Wells, David Wyatt, and Carson Holmquist. The alleged shooter was Mohammad Youssuf Abdulazeez, an engineer who was a naturalized U.S. citizen, originally born in Kuwait.

perspective, urban warfare is synonymous with street fighting. This includes any expression of open hostility, including brawling and fist-fighting. The *fourth* premise proposes that as urban areas expand, opportunities for negative urban conflict grow. Urban warfare, from a global perspective, has been characterized as "…one of the most destructive forms of warfare."[7] This assumes that any urban-initiated challenge to the established order (including protest)—organized or disorganized, aware or unconscious, is a credible threat.

Urban warfare includes the idea of a "multi-dimensional" physical terrain with "…subterranean and high-rise threats."[8] Related to the image of a volatile urban center is the nearly twenty-year-old prediction that, "The enormous problems of infrastructure and the demand for social services that threaten to swamp governing authorities in the urban center of emerging states will most likely worsen."[9] The psychic preparation for domestic war is rooted in the impression that crumbling city infrastructures cannot sustain population growth; and urban people will assert their rights to the same structural resources available in nonurban areas (i.e. water, utilities); and add to this, popular notions of an apocalyptic American future. Urban citizens are then deemed domestic adversaries or enemy combatants because, "…the proximity of the disfranchised to the ruling elite provides the spark for further unrest and sporadic violence."[10] Urban centers that possess locales of national interest, elite infrastructures, seaports, etc.—and citizen proximity to these areas—are of vital concern. Finally, in these urban areas the leaders of disenfranchised groups are often the first targeted as key threats to national security.

The urban social unrest of the 1960s demanded many reforms in the policing of people. This included the transfer of weapons technologies that had been employed in foreign wars, especially the War in Vietnam (1954-1975). Militaristic crowd control measures were developed to address the fears that social discontent of blacks and whites who embraced the counterculture would harm the larger white population. Organized black groups represented among the greatest threats, principally because of their ability to galvanize a historically

---

[7]Robert H. Scales Jr., *The Indirect Approach: How US Military Forces Can Avoid the Pitfalls of Future Urban Warfare.* Center for Army Lessons Learned Fort Leavenworth KS Virtual Research Library, 1998, 2.
[8]Ibid.
[9]Ibid.
[10]Ibid.

World To Come: Essays On The Baltimore Uprising, Militant Racism, And History

oppressed people. Among the foremost-organized black radical groups of the 1960s was the Black Panther Party. The nation had a rigid frame for the Black Panthers, shaped largely by the government and mainstream media. Together they advanced the idea of an irreconcilable class and intergenerational struggle between the rebellious black youth and the responsibly compliant Negro adults who represented the Civil Rights movement. However, class and intergenerational strife among blacks did not mean an actual or permanent rift. J. Edgar Hoover appeared to have cared little about the internal struggles of blacks, except when their problems could be exploited by the aims of the bureau.

In June of 1969, it was Hoover who determined that the Black Panthers were "...the greatest [single] threat to the internal security of the country."[11] However, Yohuru Williams and Jama Lazerow found that the history of the Panther's was not only rooted in personalities and images, especially that of co-founder Huey Newton, but that a much broader history was found in the local studies of the panthers.[12] In the public construction of the Black Panthers, what was consistently omitted was their organizational attention to self-determination for African American people; and the agency they espoused and created in support of the basic needs of the community. The one idea that defined the Panther's reputation in the mass media as violent, was their defiance to police brutality, their severe critique of social and political inequality, the intellectuality exuded through selected leaders and members in articulating their identity and goals—and most importantly, their stance on legally armed self-defense. The bureau used all of its resources in the effort to discredit, destabilize and destroy black groups that were considered "extremist." And most black groups were viewed as extremist—the Black Panthers (along with Maulana Karenga's US, and the Black Muslims) were at the top of the list. Local law enforcement agencies, emboldened by the legacy and customary practice of racial discrimination, worked with the bureau to shape negative public opinion, and to destroy these groups internally.

In addition to the application of aggressive counterintelligence programs, day-to-day harassment, and plans to kill Panther leaders and

---

[11] Ward Churchill and Jim Vander Wall, *The COINTELPRO Papers Documents from the FBI's Secret Wars Against Domestic Dissent*, Boston: South End Press, 1990, 123.
[12] Yohuru Williams and Jama Lazerow, *Liberated Territory Untold Local Perspectives On The Black Panther Party*, Durham, NC: Duke University Press, 2008, 1-31.

members, state-of-the-art weapons technology was used to eliminate the organization. In the late 1960s, there were a number of lethal (and harmful non-lethal) weapons being used by police on groups like the Black Panthers. Some of these weapons included equipped "Commando Police Vehicles" and "Stoner guns." Police also used mace, pepper gas, gas grenades, protective body armor, sound equipment, and instant barbed wire.[13] David Hilliard, the National Chief of Staff of the Black Panther Party, discovered a detailed police "battle plan," which included a wide range of weaponry to be used in an invasion of the Black Panther's national headquarters.[14] In this planned assault there would be a massive amount of force used that would result in the recovery of "…the wounded and/or dead."[15] When Black Panther leaders Fred Hampton and Mark Clark were killed by police in Chicago on December 4, 1969, there was an open order to shoot Black Panthers and it appeared that such a battle plan was in effect.

A show of police force was always necessary for individual Black Panthers as well—it took 50 officers to arrest David Hilliard as he left a wedding party.[16] It is no surprise that one of the first major uses of SWAT (Special Weapons and Tactics) was against African Americans. In 1969, Daryl Gates unsuccessfully dispatched SWAT on the Black Panthers in Los Angeles.[17] The use of SWAT gained increased public acceptance after this deployment.[18] The Black Panthers represented the first highly organized threat to the American government which prompted a critical military presence in all of the cities where they were organized. Borrowing from the U.S. armed forces, police departments more than fifty years ago began using heavy weaponry, and had increased their use of traditional weapons of war. Local law enforcement agencies had access to state and federal resources and grants to facilitate the domestic application of military equipment and training tactics. Today SWAT teams are employed more

---

[13]Reginald Major, *A Panther is a Black Cat*, New York: William Morrow, Inc. 1971, 27-28.
[14]Ibid., 30-31.
[15]Ibid., 31.
[16]Ibid., 31.
[17]Karan R. Singh, "Treading the Thin Blue Line: Military Special-Operations Trained Police SWAT Teams and the Constitution." *Wm. & Mary Bill Rts. J.* Vol. 9, No. 3 (2000): 673-717, 678-679.
[18]Radley Balko, *Overkill The Rise of Paramilitary Police Raids in America*. Washington, D.C.: The Cato Institute, 2006, 6.

frequently for non-violent offenses and against ordinary people, with extreme force. In some cases, according to Cadman R. Kiker III, "The use of SWAT has become so prolific that it seems at times to border on the absurd."[19] While numerous black organizations of the 1960s were labeled major threats by the government, the real threat was the embedded racialized fears of black people, the black body, and blackness itself. In 2015 it seemed true, that the black individual, seemingly more vulnerable and at times without a powerful community-of-care, was the easiest target.

The Zero-Sum Game to Crime Deterrence and Broken Windows

Based on a review of recent police-custody deaths and the response of the community, there are three broad approaches to crime prevention—conservative, liberal and martial. The *conservative* approach sees crime as an issue of social control. People who violate laws must be punished. The extreme conservative model sees crime as pathology, but does not need to consider the causes of crime—just the idea or existence of crime. The purpose of law enforcement is to reduce crime through a variety of methods. While the participation of the community is important, this model generally perceives the community as marginal to the work of law enforcement. The *liberal* method of deterring crime does not eschew the traditional law and order model, which accepts crime prevention as a fundamental challenge to the whole of society. It regards crime is a function of several factors and opportunity—jobs, education, housing, etc. Given the reaction of Black Lives Matter protestors, crime prevention is also a social justice issue. The liberal method fully recognizes that there is a political struggle where inequality has produced extreme social distance and disaffection. The basic theory is that society can prevent crime by advancing opportunity. Liberal criminalists also see social problems such as drug addiction as a public health challenge rather than a criminally innate human failing. They also see the wealth gap as a result of economic failings and exploitation of the masses, and seek corrective measures. The *military* approach to crime prevention is a strict law and order model. The issue is not equity, root causes or the traditional processes of the criminal

---

[19]Cadman R. Kiker III, "From Mayberry to Ferguson: The Militarization of American Policing Equipment, Culture, and Mission." *Washington and Lee Law Review Online* 71, No. 4 (2015): 282-298.

World To Come: Essays On The Baltimore Uprising, Militant Racism, And History

justice system, but the present moment of control and containment. The military approach does not necessarily exclude the conservative method, but it does reject any ideological basis. The military approach has a tactical objective and this method is supposed to reduce crime through sheer force. The conservative and liberal approaches operate within some notion of an open society; the military approach does not.

Over the past thirty years, many scholars have contended that a broken windows model of policing was first introduced by Wilson and Kelling in 1982.[20] Kelling responded to this idea in 2015, months after the Baltimore Uprising, by denying that the theory was intended for that purpose and among other concerns, stated that law enforcement agencies had misused the concept.[21] However, the model suggested that community disorder, such as broken windows in a neighborhood, is important in engendering dangerous crimes. This disorder creates a sense of increased fear in residential areas and promotes community disengagement. This permits serious crimes to manifest, because of the perceived diminished level of relaxed social control. Police become important responders to broken windows by addressing the idea of disorder, thus stopping serious crimes from occurring. The police, then, focus on disorder and less serious crime, in an effort to reduce fear and prevent significant offenses. Theoretically, this social control empowers residents and prevents crime from happening. The underlying notion of the much-discussed broken windows approach to policing is the belief that people are not able to control their environment or their impulses; and they ultimately do not respect their communities or police authority.

---

[20]James Q. Wilson and George L. Kelling, "Broken Windows." *Atlantic monthly* 249, No. 3 (1982): 29-38; Reed Collins, "Strolling while poor: How Broken-Windows Policing Created a New Crime in Baltimore." *Geo. J. on Poverty L. & Pol'y* 14 (2007): 419; Babe Howell, "Broken Lives from Broken Windows: The Hidden Costs of Aggressive Order-Maintenance Policing." *New York University Review of Law & Social Change* 33 (2009): 271; Gary Stewart, "Black Codes and Broken Windows: The Legacy of Racial Hegemony In Anti-Gang Civil Injunctions." *Yale Law Journal* (1998): 2249-2279; Ralph B. Taylor, *Breaking Away From Broken Windows: Baltimore Neighborhoods and the Nationwide Fight Against Crime, Grime, Fear, And Decline.* Boulder, CO: Westview Press, 2001; Brandon C. Welsh, Anthony A. Braga, and Gerben Bruinsma, "Reimagining Broken Windows from Theory to Policy." *Journal of Research in Crime and Delinquency* 52, No. 4 (2015): 447-463.
[21]George Kelling, "Don't Blame my 'Broken Windows' Theory for Poor Policing," *Politico*, August 11, 2015.

World To Come: Essays On The Baltimore Uprising, Militant Racism, And History

The broken windows concept has become an important criminal theory that establishes a baseline for social behavior in blighted communities. If seemingly small issues such a broken window are not corrected immediately it means that people do not care, and with this lack of concern, in due time, all the windows will soon be broken—and this would signal the opportunity for chaos to occur. The theory was applied broadly to any theoretical neighborhood, but it was specifically directed at poor urban communities. Broken windows were an obvious signal that such neighborhoods were not safe. The theory quickly moved out of the realm of speculation. By the 1990s, federal and local governments had taken a strict stance on crime. The law enforcement agencies in many cities adopted a firm approach to policing. The theory of broken windows had evolved into zero-tolerance. There has been considerable criticism of the concept itself as well as debate about the effectiveness of broken windows policing. Broken windows is similar to the reliance on law enforcement analytics or the science-fiction idea of "pre-crime" in many ways, because they make assumptions about an entire community's motives towards law-breaking, criminalizes them in advance, and then eliminates state ownership of the core problems. In broken windows state authority and public security trumps individual rights. Like the racial profiling of stop and frisk, broken windows policing, assumed a posture of zero-tolerance, and this included the use of lethal force.

The Human Terrain for Military Operations and Police Overcompensation

Fallacious ideology, deceptive rhetoric and unmitigated power can cause war in civilian spaces. The law enforcement-military operation begins and ends with the convergence of these factors and the dismantling of the important conversations about culpability. As Pulitzer Prize winning journalist, Leonard Pitts, Jr. surmised: "In America these days, a bad cop is more likely to win the lottery then to be held accountable for his misbehavior. While we are apportioning blame for that sorry state of affairs, let's not forget the politicians and members of the punditocracy who pretend questioning police is equivalent to hating them or that the person who is critical of law enforcement is the moral equivalent of the psycho who guns a cop

World To Come: Essays On The Baltimore Uprising, Militant Racism, And History

down for fun."[22] The war that absolves bad cops is the domestic battle against the American people. The war began with the rising suspicion and animosity between the people and a government steeped in a bitter national history and in contemporary geopolitical conflicts abroad. The domestic war is also connected to the struggles over innumerable social issues such as the economy, pro-choice/prolife, global warming and environmental exploitation, cyber privacy, labor and wage abuses, gun control, illegal immigration, and the class divisions between the ninety-nine percent and the one percent. Moreover, of course, racism is absolutely essential in this military drama. We have seen the militarization of major cities through the Baltimore Uprising; and prior to this we were witness to the military show of force in Ferguson Missouri. Both recent examples involved black people and the protest over the black lives lost.

American cities are increasingly becoming centers of military demonstration, training, and theaters of operation. While white residential enclaves, including the suburbs are not immune to this development in any way; urban and predominately black and brown areas are much more vulnerable. We could credibly discuss and theorize about the various campaigns, but the ghetto is a major contest in this theater. It is an obvious understatement that the people are not prepared—do not even understand, are not aware, or cannot conceive—that war has been declared. Contemporary populous urban encampments like Occupy Wallstreet have come and gone. We found in this highly publicized social demonstration that the management of intelligence and public relations was absolutely essential. While technology is an important resource, alone it will not win a war. West Baltimore was just one small stage in a terrain that is highly contested—and where the people are sometimes demoralized—but not defeated. They have been in a struggle for five hundred years. While there are rules to engagement, this is a new kind of war. This is a war where, at least in the recently illustrated tragedy of Freddie Gray, people do not perceive that they hold any actual rights. This is a war where the people are barely acknowledged as citizens; the use of excessive police force is

---

[22]Leonard Pitts, Jr., "No Accountability for Take-Down of James Blake," *Sun Journal*, September17, 2015, http://www.sunjournal.com/news/columns-analysis/2015/09/17/leonard-pitts-no-accountability-take-down-james-black/1783276, accessed September 21, 2015.

frequent; and the adversarial soldiers and citizens may even be from the same family and community.

    Within this terrain what does police overcompensation look like? Eric Sanders, the attorney for the family of Miriam Carey, has stated that law enforcement "overcompensation" was one of the causes of her untimely death.[23] The October 3, 2013 case of Miriam Carey was not only tragic, it was bizarre.[24] The 34-year-old dental hygienist from Connecticut was killed by secret service and capital police officers as she attempted to get away from law enforcement. In the most consistent account of the fluctuating story, Carey, who had driven to Washington, D.C. with her 13-month-old daughter, found herself at an outer White House security checkpoint and confronted by an off-duty plainclothes agent. She tried to leave the area after being ordered to stop and a circuitous chase took place, which ended in her death. Law enforcement officers fired 26 rounds at her car; she was struck five times, and died of "multiple gunshot wounds"[25] including a shot to the head. Carey was unarmed and her infant daughter was unharmed in the altercation. The story was initially interpreted by the media as a threat against the Nation's capital. At the outset, legislators praised law enforcement officers' actions in killing Carey thus thwarting a potential terrorist attack. Immediately after her death, there was media speculation that Carey suffered from post-partum depression and a police report surfaced online detailing claims made by an ex-boyfriend. Carey had said earlier that the boyfriend had been stalking and harassing her.[26] Information relevant to this case is incomplete,[27] and there were few answers about why it took such a deadly show of force

---

[23]Eric Sanders was interviewed by Amy Goodman, *Democracy Now*, March 17, 2015.
[24]David Montgomery, "Her Name Was Miriam Carey. She Drove To D.C. From Connecticut with Her Baby Daughter. A U-Turn At A Checkpoint Led To Her Being Killed—And A Slew Of Unanswered Questions," *The Washington Post*, November 26, 2014; David Montgomery, "Official Silence on Capitol Hill Shooting Draws Watchdog Lawsuit," *The Washington Post*, April 15, 2015.
[25]Government of the District of Columbia, Office of the Chief Medical Examiner, Autopsy Report, Case No. 13-02470, October 4, 2013.
[26]Jennifer Gonnerman, "The Wrong Way: Miriam Carey Drove Through A White House Checkpoint And Died In A Hail Of Bullets, Her Infant In The Back Seat. Was A Secret Service Screwup To Blame?" *Mother Jones*, March, 2015, http://www.motherjones.com/politics/2015/03/miriam-carey-whitehouse-rammer-police-death, accessed August 5, 2015.
[27]*Worldnetdaily.com, Inc. v. U.S. Department of Justice*, Civil Action Complaint, April 14, 2015, Case: 1:15-cv-00549.

to stop a young black woman—who, for lack of any other contravening evidence—made a wrong turn.

Police-encounter deaths that are subject to heightened public scrutiny are invariably the cases in which law enforcement officers employed excessive use of force.[28] Citizens have demanded to know why such deadly force—a function of overcompensation— is necessary in hundreds of police-encounters. In another example, Levar Jones at least lived to tell his side of the story. In North Augusta, South Carolina on September 4, 2014, Jones was stopped at a gas station for an alleged seat belt violation. Trooper Sean Groubert asked for his driver's license, and when Jones went to retrieve it from the car, Groubert pulled his weapon, and told him to "get out of the car." Jones backed away and put his hands in the air, yet Groubert shot at him four times. Jones, who was wounded and in pain, explained that he was getting his license, and he wanted to know why he was shot. Still, with a bullet in his hip, he was told to put his hands behind his back—then police backup and an ambulance was called. The encounter only took a few seconds. Jones was struck by only one of the bullets and recovered. Even on that day, the first press release reporting the incident, commented on the safety of the officer and carefully framed Jones: "The trooper was not injured and the violator was injured and transported to a local hospital."[29] What laws had Jones violated? Most of the media presented this case as highly unusual, and emphasized that Jones *did not appear* to provoke the officer in any way. They also positioned the trooper's reaction as an anomaly.

However, in South Carolina as well as other parts of the country, this scenario would not be perceived as uncommon by many in the black community. There was the dash cam video that recorded the event. We can only speculate what the story might have been had Jones died, and had there been no video recording released to the public. One of the counters to community criticisms over questionable police shootings is that the individual in question was *thought* to have been armed, or did not comply with police instructions. Jones clearly was not armed, he immediately complied with the officer's request, and he was still shot. Jones was shot, not in an effort to disable him from

---

[28]Not the micro-aggressive harassment that citizens complain about that does not rise to the point of physical abuse.
[29]South Carolina Department of Public Safety, Press Release, "SCDPS Releases Statement Regarding Trooper-Involved Shooting," September 4, 2014.

causing fatal harm to the trooper—the four shots were meant to kill him. What was unique about the case was that Groubert was charged, arrested, released on bail; and lost his job with the highway patrol. The South Carolina Department of Public Safety (SCDPS) Director admitted "…the force administered in this case was unwarranted…" With the lens firmly fixed on the extralegal deaths of blacks in police-encounters, the SCDPS went on to state that their officers were trained, professional, and with "…750,000 traffic contacts per year…," i.e., experienced.[30] In this case the trooper could not declare inexperience; he had been with the department for ten years.

On the other side of the country, two cases in Aurora Colorado give us a comparative view of how police overcompensation and the issue of race converge. On July 20, 2012 around midnight, 24-year-old James Holmes perpetrated the worse mass shooting in the state of Colorado since the Columbine high school massacre (1999). Holmes, a white male, went into a Century 16 movie theater, which featured *The Dark Knight Rises*. He exploded tear gas in the theater and fired upon unsuspecting moviegoers. He murdered 12 people and wounded 70 others. Except for one, all of his victims were under the age of 31. Police arrested Holmes outside of the theater; he was sitting in his parked car. In this mass shooting, Holmes came to the theater prepared, organized (he kept a notebook of his plans), and determined. He wore a tactical outfit, and in addition to the tear gas, he brought a rifle, a defensive shotgun and a Glock handgun—and he had prior to the shooting—rigged his apartment with explosives. One report said that Holmes might have been mistaken for a law enforcement officer because of his clothing. After his arrest, he was placed on suicide watch. His attorneys pleaded mental incapacity (arguing that he had a psychotic break inside of the theater). It was later revealed that he had a long preoccupation with the idea of killing. He was found guilty of first-degree murder on July 16, 2015.

While Naeschylus Vinzant was no saint, he was not a mass murderer. However, we did not have much verifiable information on him, except that he was "…a parole violator with a violent, lengthy criminal history …"[31] and deemed dangerous. On March 6, 2015

---

[30]South Carolina Department of Public Safety, Press Release, "Second Follow up: Trooper-Involved Shooting in Richland County on September 4, 2014," September 19, 2014.
[31]Carlos Illescas, "Aurora ID's Cop Involved in Fatal Shooting of an Unarmed Black Man," *The Denver Post*, March 12, 2015.

WORLD TO COME: ESSAYS ON THE BALTIMORE UPRISING, MILITANT RACISM, AND HISTORY

Vinzant, a 37-year-old black man, was killed by law enforcement officer Paul Jerothe in Aurora, Colorado. Officer Jerothe was called a hero in the aftermath of the 2012 Aurora Theater shooting because he served as a paramedic. By the time Jerothe encountered Vinzant nearly three years later, he had broken the terms of his parole by removing a correctional ankle monitor a few days earlier. The early news stories were scant and all the same—vague, probably with some truths, but all circumstantially damming. Vinzant had been previously incarcerated but the details were not fully released. He had a criminal history, but specifics were not shared with the public. Vinzant had been suspected of carrying a concealed weapon, and "attempted homicide, first-degree assault, possession of a weapon and felony menacing."[32] In addition, Vinzant was reported as having used multiple aliases, and was arrested for suspicion of assault, in addition to his parole violation.

In this police-encounter, officer Jerothe, who was just one of the members of the fugitive recovery unit/SWAT team, fired the shot during the arrest of Vinzant. If the early accounts are correct, Vinzant's immediate crime was the parole violation, resisting arrest and being confronted by law enforcement, by happenstance, walking near an elementary school. The day SWAT moved in with the fugitive recovery team, from what we know, Vinzant had not killed anyone. However, several months later when a grand jury exonerated officer Jerothe, Vinzant's criminal history, still sketchy, was firmly asserted in the media. Public accounts added newer disturbing elements to Vinzant's case—that he beat his wife, stole her money, kidnapped their infant child, was a drug abuser, threatened police—and most important, that he tried to run away from law enforcement officers with his hand in his pocket. It was this latter move that caused him to be killed. Witnesses said that Vinzant was attempting to surrender.

However, no one denied the preponderance of criminal intent in the hearts of these two men, yet in looking at both cases, activists' wanted to know why did a white mass murderer get to live, while a black man noted for lesser crimes, was sentenced to death. James Holmes possessed enough weaponry to kill hundreds of people in the Aurora movie theater, and after the 911 calls and text messages from terrified theatergoers; and even after he killed 12 people and wounded 70 others—and was known to be heavily armed, a tactical squad was

---

[32]Kieran Nicholson and Jesse Paul, "Aurora Police: Man Killed By Officer Was An Unarmed Parole Absconder," *The Denver Post*, March 9, 2015.

not needed on the scene to arrest him. It was not necessary to shoot and kill him. The stories about Naeschylus Vinzant suggested that the officers feared that he was armed; and yet it turned out that he had no weapon. The media portrayed him as a much deadlier threat than Holmes. If the same level of lethal force (used on unarmed black ordinary citizens, as well as convicted felons) were applied to James Holmes, he would not have been sentenced to multiple life prison terms without parole (in a private cellblock for his personal security) for orchestrating a highly coordinated and executed mass murder.

To a nation of people who felt under siege, this is what police overcompensation looks like. Police overcompensation might serve as an adjustment for perceived deficiencies (material, physical or temporal, or even a combination of the three) or a sense of insurmountable threat. If officers felt unprepared, he/she might overcompensate in the performance of duties. For the black community, overcompensation in police-encounter deaths is more than adjusting for job performance challenges. In a patriarchal society, police overcompensation is a function of institutional, not personal gender—which historically is male, white, and authoritarian. Though not at all unheard of among female police officers, males in law enforcement are more likely to use excessive force, kill citizens, and cost cities millions of dollars in support of their actions.[33] The overreaction to black bodies is the racialized effort to achieve balance, to bring back a contorted sense of equilibrium. To do this, Blacks who question police officers *in any way* pose a credible threat to arrant masculine authority. Those who are unarmed and resist officers, and especially those who run, are subjected to exaggerated demonstrations of police power. Police overcompensation is masculine-aggressive which is further strengthened by the law enforcement code of silence, LEOBORs (Law Enforcement Officers Bill of Rights)[34], and the strength of their community-of-care.

The law enforcement COC supports overcompensation allowing for and defending the most deviant behaviors associated with

---

[33]See Kim Lonsway, Michelle Wood and Megan Fickling et al, "Men, Women, and Police Excessive Force: A Tale of Two Genders: A Content Analysis of Civil Liability Cases, Sustained Allegations and Citizen Complaints," National Center for Women and Policing, Division of the Feminist Majority Foundation, Los Angeles, CA, 2002, 11pp.

[34]In addition to the legal protections of citizens, some states enacted LEOBORs (Law Enforcement Officers Bill of Rights), specialized laws intended to assist and protect police (and other agents of law enforcement) from criminal investigation, interrogation, and prosecution; especially in the procedures that involve officers who kill citizens.

World To Come: Essays On The Baltimore Uprising, Militant Racism, And History

police brutality within the policing of black citizens. This includes the appallingly sensational 1990s cases (as noted previously) involving Amadou Diallo and Abner Louima in New York City. In 1997 Abner Louima, a Haitian immigrant, was speciously arrested and cruelly tortured. Louima's case involved him being sodomized with a broom handle by an officer and the case also included perjured testimony. The officers involved were charged with obstruction of justice, convicted, and later the verdict was overturned. Amadou Diallo, an immigrant from Guinea, was shot 41 times in 1999 inside the entrance of his apartment building by police officers who were later acquitted. The police said that they thought Diallo had a gun—he only possessed a wallet. These cases not only emphasized the anti-black thrust (regardless of African ethnicity and nationality) of policing, they more than demonstrated that overcompensation (and at times abject cruelty) is not the same as proactive community policing. The police-encounter cases that have come under intense scrutiny over the past several years often revealed that any challenge, or perceive defiance to police sovereignty is considered a punishable threat. In its malignant form, police overcompensation is an attempt to create distance between the individual (the person identified not as a threat—but, as *the* threat) and the law enforcement officer (who is *the* annihilator of the threat). The decisive way to cause distance is to eliminate the threat. Death creates this distance—as well as an absolute physical detachment and psychic disassociation from the event, the outcomes—and the people.

On Biker Gangs and the Blurred Dimensions of Contested Territory

Was West Baltimore an occupied space before the arrest and later death of Freddie Gray? How did media shape this idea of territorial contest in the aftermath? For our purposes, a contested territory is a physical area that is in serious dispute. It involves where we live—the physical needs, temporal desires, historical knowledge, and the will of the people; in addition to the aims of the governing authority. The Baltimore Uprising raised a number of issues about territory, opening up the past to be viewed with contemporary lenses. The uprising revealed more of the ways the mainstream media attempted to shape the discourse. Weeks after the uprising, newer—yet related stories—began to dominate the headlines—including the one year anniversary of the shooting of Michael Brown. There was also the rush to "correct" and "address" some of the false and overlooked issues that emerged from the Baltimore Uprising, including the

World To Come: Essays On The Baltimore Uprising, Militant Racism, And History

insertion of angry community and humble resident profiles, and even these stories had begun to wane by the middle of May 2015. Furthermore, there were more immediate critical comparisons between Baltimore, Maryland and Ferguson, Missouri.

However, in the southwest United States, there was, still, the desperate search for meaning in the Baltimore Uprising by looking at the violent meeting in Waco, Texas.[35] Like a script from the original FX television series *Sons of Anarchy*, on May 17, 2015 there was a shootout in the Central Texas Marketplace mall parking lot of the Twin Peaks restaurant by members of feuding biker gangs. Among the groups identified by law enforcement were the Bandidos, Cossacks, and Scimitars. One of the first, most popular and hotly debated images on social media after the deadly shootout was that of bikers (many without disposable handcuff restraints) casually sitting around with a law enforcement officer.[36] This image angered some who were witness to the heated condemnation of the peaceful protests and the riots that had occurred previously in the Baltimore Uprising. The young black people had already been called thugs and hoodlums, now they were labeled animals. Media outlets were still running the same video loop showing the looting at Mondawmin Mall—while at one point, you could literally count the people involved—the mainstream media suggested however that hundreds, perhaps even thousands of people in the city of Baltimore directly participated in the looting and rioting activity.

Apparently, law enforcement officials anticipated the potential for biker gang violence at the Twin Peaks restaurant on that Sunday. Police purportedly had 22 SWAT and state troopers stationed in the parking lot. When the bloody struggle ended, nine people died and twenty people were wounded in the shootout. Nearly 200 gang members were arrested and almost all faced criminal charges. After this melee in Waco Texas, law enforcement officers seized over 400 weapons.[37] The police found a considerable arsenal, including,

---

[35] Twenty-two years ago, the town experienced the *1993 Siege at Waco*, this involved a shootout between ATF agents and the Branch Davidians (a Christian sect that split from the Seventh-Day Adventist church). The standoff with law enforcement lasted six weeks. The FBI moved in with tear gas, and a fire destroyed the Branch Davidian compound, including the group's messianic leader David Koresh and 76 followers. The event remains one of the most debated clashes between citizens and law enforcement.
[36] This was an image of a McLennan County deputy standing guard near a group of bikers after the shootout taken by the *Waco Tribune-Herald* (Rod Aydelotte).
[37] The police originally estimated, based on the initial crime scene, that 1,000 weapons were involved. They revised (lowered) this number.

World To Come: Essays On The Baltimore Uprising, Militant Racism, And History

handguns, knives, chains, brass knuckles—even an AK-47 assault rifle—and bulletproof vests. In this gory fight, the potential causes included a conflict that began in the restroom of the restaurant; or someone had a foot run over; or there was a clash over a parking space. Whatever the actual cause, the issue of paramount importance was one of respect. Gangs of any persuasion do not tolerate disrespect of any kind and members will die defending their dignity rather than be disrespected. In addition to SWAT, police rushed to the scene where bikers where fighting and firing guns. Four officers purportedly fired their weapons. All those arrested were held on a $1 million dollar bond (this amount was eventually reduced for most).

The unfortunate story was sensational, but the country was still reeling from the Baltimore Uprising and the narrative that had been forcefully drawn about the lawlessness of blacks in the city. The media consistently used the term *brawl* to describe the bloody shootings and deaths in Waco, Texas. Yet, in the Waco Massacre, the early media stories did not attempt to apply derisive labels to the bikers or to their actions. However, a comedian was one of the first to chide media and call the bikers "thugs."[38] Of course, the bikers resented any impunity to their character. Several of those arrested in the Waco Massacre made early efforts to file lawsuits against the city. A few others, under public protest, made bail and were released. Other bikers planned letter-writing campaigns and protests on behalf of the rights of motorcycle clubs. Moreover, some of them did not appreciate being stereotyped as biker outlaws (i.e. criminal gangs). Over one hundred of those arrested were allowed to wear GPS ankle monitors and released. By the end of September 2015, most of these tethers were removed—and no one was charged for the shooting deaths and injuries in Waco, Texas.

Mainstream news outlets promptly left the Waco Biker Massacre story as a consistent national news item, and returned to Charm City and the plight of West Baltimoreans. These stories noted that the *regular* violence that took place in the city, including murder—and not just in West Baltimore—had continued since the death of Gray. It was implied that all of the attention given to the city should have abated the area's usual mortality statistics; or, it meant that the public was simply not paying attention to the deaths. Then, rank-and-file police, who had already pointed out that the indictments of the

---

[38] Erik Wemple, "Comedy Central's Larry Wilmore: 'Let Me Be the First to Call [Waco] Bikers 'Thugs'" *The Washington Post*, May 27, 2015, accessed May 30, 2015.

World To Come: Essays On The Baltimore Uprising, Militant Racism, And History

Baltimore 6 had sent a chilling message to law enforcement, especially to police on the streets, strongly suggested that they could not effectively do the job. The message was not hidden. The public was meant to understand that after the Baltimore Uprising, the police were apprehensive, perhaps even afraid, of carrying out their sworn duty.

Kurt L. Schmoke surmised, "…there has been a very brief but telling slowdown in some police enforcement action after the indictment of the six police officers, and I think that has hurt the situation and allowed some things to get out of control in the neighborhoods …."[39] Now, more than ever, the police had to consider the risks. Besides, the black community could not have it "both ways"—expect to be "protected and served" *and* possess the ability to accuse police of brutality—and even deliberate homicide. Local news documented the struggles of unnamed officers, who talked candidly about the aftermath and psychological challenges of the Baltimore Uprising. Meanwhile, the mortality rate for the city, including West Baltimore, began to soar. Purportedly blame was exchanged within the echelons of city hall, and the media talked about the possibility of an orchestrated post-Freddie Gray police work slow-down. It was a terrifying theory—which seemed to have begun as a rumor—that Baltimore police had initiated a work stoppage—a campaign intended to mount a protest themselves. However, partisan commentators took advantage of the opportunity to resume name-calling blacks as a race of people—with epithets, animal imagery, and by evoking fears of criminal vagrancy (for sitting on porches and stoops and standing in their own communities). This view depicted Blacks as a people who were not worth the risk police officers were taking;[40] and therefore, they did not deserve safer communities.

The worst of the post-Baltimore Uprising commentary essentially asserted that "black-on-black" crime was the real problem. In fact, ordinary citizens and seasoned politicians candidly and liberally used the term "black-on-black" crime to describe intra-racial homicides in the city of Baltimore. However, few people, with the exception of

---

[39] Andrew R. Koch, "UB President Schmoke discusses upcoming police officer trials," *The UB Post*, September 29, 2015, https://theubpost.wordpress.com/2015/09/29/ub-president-schmoke-discusses-upcoming-police-officer-trials/, accessed September 30, 30215.
[40] News Hound Ellen, "Mark Fuhrman Endorses Baltimore Police Slowdown, Suggests African American Community is full of 'Animals'" *Crooks and Liars*, May 28, 2015, accessed May 30, 2015.

WORLD TO COME: ESSAYS ON THE BALTIMORE UPRISING, MILITANT RACISM, AND HISTORY

scholars and activists, challenged the historical, academic, or disciplinary basis for the term, which in its least offensive popular rendering was meant to discuss, from a sociological perspective, the numerical incidence and complexities of intra-racial crime.[41] While the actual roots of the term are somewhat obscure, it was used in the 1970s. *Jet Magazine* printed the term "black-on-black crime" on a 1973 cover, complete with a black man aiming a gun directly at the reader.[42] By the 1980s, the expression "black-on-black" homicide, crime or violence was widely used.[43] Sociologists, statisticians and criminologists wrote extensively about "black-on-black" crime. Yet few asked questions about the striking absence of a parallel "white-on-white" label to describe the commission of intra-racial crime among white people. That blacks liberally used the concept in public, along with avowed racists who wanted to make a point, meant that everyone could—and perhaps should—accept the pathological implications of the idea. However, the term was more often used as an indictment of black communities; and an emergent threat to white urban and rural enclaves.

Amos N. Wilson crystallized the concept in the fields of African Studies, psychology and criminology. He defined how the term operated in black communities, and yet situated it squarely within the context racial narcissism. In Wilson's analysis, "black-on-black" crime is a distinct effect—and racism is the specific cause.[44] However, critics have argued that the term was also meant to speak to the idea of black alienation, rootlessness and cultural dislocation. In addition, "black-on-black" has been defined as a kind of "Manchurian candidate"[45] construct where, due to the racist impulse in society, black youth are programmed toward self-destruction and in-group annihilation. The unqualified use of "black-on-black" crime is an underhanded proclamation about black life. Without any credible thought, it presupposes that African Americans are inordinately predisposed to

---

[41]Amos N. Wilson, *Black-On-Black Violence: The Psychodynamics Of Black Self-Annihilation In Service Of White Domination*. Brooklyn, NY: Afrikan World Infosystems, 1990.
[42]*Jet Magazine*, cover, July 12, 1973.
[43]David Wilson, *Inventing Black-On-Black Violence: Discourse, Space, and Representation*, Syracuse University Press, 2005.
[44]Amos N. Wilson, *Black-on-Black Violence: The Psychodynamics of Black Self-Annihilation In Service Of White Domination*. Brooklyn, NY: Afrikan World Infosystems, 1990, xx, 67.
[45]*The Manchurian Candidate* by Richard Condon refers to the 1950s cold war book within the backdrop of the Korean War, which was later turned into a major motion picture, and addresses government-sponsored mind-control and the psychological development of soldier assassins.

killing one another; when in reality, equity, proximity and access tend to determine how and where people kill. In addition, "black-on-black" crime in American society always imagines animalistic and bestial behavior. As a result of this pathological construction, blacks are expected to die in appreciable numbers at the hands of other blacks.[46]

The reckless use of the term supports a pathologically violent relationship construct assigned to blacks, while absolving whites of the same deterministic burden. The term has evolved to serve as an indictment of black society, rather than a lament, or even a complaint about the issue of community violence as a whole. In public spaces, the term requires no further explanation or disciplinary context. "Black-on-black crime" has become rhetorically convenient for well-meaning people; and a damning accusation used by those who categorically devalued black life. For the latter group displaying their racist credentials, "black-on-black" crime not only meant that African Americans possessed a compulsive disposition to kill other blacks, but it included the "where's the rage" argument. This assertion implied that when blacks kill each other, they don't complain or protest about the tragedy of these deaths; but that they vigorously voice disapproval and condemnation when police officers kill blacks. As deplorable as it is, "black on black" crime (namely homicide) is not the same as when police kill blacks. By state authority police are licensed to carry and discharge firearms, and to use force if necessary. They kill under oath and presumably, with public trust and consent so that they might uphold law and order. However, as *Operation Ghetto Storm* suggested there was an inscrutable labyrinth to all of this:

> ...police, sheriffs, security guards and, to a certain extent self-appointed enforcers of law (vigilantes) ARE "authorized" by governments and paid for by taxes. They are hardly accountable for these killings and even less frequently charged in a court of law. In contrast, both the victims who survive and the perpetrators of "Black-on-Black" crime end up as part of the million Black people incarcerated in the U.S. at any given time.[47]

---

[46]David Wilson, "Constructing a 'Black-on-Black' Violence: The Conservative Discourse." *ACME: An International E-Journal for Critical Geographies*, No. 1 (2002): 35-54.
[47]*Operation Ghetto Storm*, 2012 Annual Report on the Extrajudicial Killings of 313 Black People by Police, Security Guards and Vigilantes, with a Preface by Kali Akuno,

WORLD TO COME: ESSAYS ON THE BALTIMORE UPRISING, MILITANT RACISM, AND HISTORY

The popular "where's the rage" argument was racially specious, intended to reduce the complexities of race, policing, and the criminal justice system. The prevalent claim deftly shifted municipal responsibility for state and city law enforcement to individuals and communities. More importantly, the idea rested on the need to transmit standard false notions of black people as criminally pathogenic.

As erroneous and insensitive as some of the post-Baltimore Uprising comments were, including the profuse use of the phrase "black-on-black" crime, the nation began to address issues of embedded racism—and the idea of contested territory. In addition to the physical and temporal component, the principle of contested territory encompasses a number of other areas related to community-police relations. For Baltimore, the fundamental questions about this territory involve where can people live and under what circumstances? Who owns, controls, and inhabits (thus who is responsible for) the land and housing? What goods and services are demanded/available/ allowed? Other questions included whether the urban landscape is poised to grow and develop *with the people*—or is the plan to develop the area without the people—i.e. gentrification, removal, assisted relocation, etc.? More specifically, the immediate question is, where can power-seeking working-class and poor people live? Given these questions, is it even a contest? The reality of a contested territory in West Baltimore, speaks to the national state of African Americans. Further, the contest is historical and filled with inconsistencies. For example, are people truly residents—or are they thought of as a transient population until affluent gentrification emerges; are they owners of proper housing or exploited renters and subsidizers of forgotten spaces because no one else will inhabit the area? After the spring 2015 Baltimore Uprising and the Waco Massacre, the issue of contested territory remains complex. Yet it did not appear that the police or rival bikers gangs were actually fighting over the space they all occupied—the conflict was subjective and personal, but not necessarily territorial and not about social justice.

However, all seemed to take for granted, including the police, that the space belonged to the bikers. Initial reports suggested that the Waco Massacre bikers fought over petty issues, an example of biker-on-biker crime. Yet there was an older theme too, the "Wild Wild

---

Produced by the Every 36 Hours Campaign, Issued by Malcolm X Grassroots Movement, April 2013, 15.

World To Come: Essays On The Baltimore Uprising, Militant Racism, And History

West" as a white American frontier (uninhabited by native Indians) where it is expected that *anything goes*; and tacitly even in the contemporary landscape, that this violent behavior is normal. There was also a newer theme of rebel boldness that included the relationship between biker culture and the development of law enforcement motorcycle clubs (LEMCs). Still, in May, 2015, the bikers demonstrated that they possessed massive weaponry, as if they were prepared for a protracted suburban war campaign; and they were deemed responsible for the lives lost. Yet post-crisis media efforts supported their community-of-care endeavors. We had early reports of the shootout, but were not privy to the surveillance video and other evidentiary material that would miraculously emerge in the fall.[48] In the expansive Twin Peaks Restaurant and parking lot, there was an incredible crime scene, but few media outlets focused on the tactical vehicles, and there were no pervasive images of walled National Guardsmen. In addition, there was no curfew, and the actions of the bikers vis a vis their race and ethnicity was never an issue. There was no loss of life as a direct result of the Baltimore Uprising—but plenty of detentions and arrests for protesting, defying curfew, and the destruction of property. Public comment over the stark contradictions and media portrayal of the two spring events was swift and pointed. People understood that Waco, at the very least, was an honorary white emergency situation. One disparaging remark summed up the juxtaposition of the two events, "So I guess then it would be OK for the cops to stop every black kid in Baltimore wearing an oversized tee and saggy pants?"[49]

---

[48] Surveillance video showing the shootout from the inside of the Twin Peaks Restaurant was made public at the end of October, 2015. The video and other materials were procured by CNN. Ann O'Neill, Ed Lavandera and Jason Morris, "Knives, Guns, Blood and Fear: Inside The Texas Biker Shootout," CNN, October 30, 2015. http://www.cnn.com/2015/10/29/us/texas-biker-shootout-new-details/index.html, accessed October 30, 2015.

[49] Reader comments from Tom Dart and Jessica Glenza, "Waco Shootout: How a Friendly Sunday Get-Together Ended in a Biker Bloodbath," *The Guardian*, http://www.theguardian.com, May 20, 2015, http://www.theguardian.com/us-news/2015/may/20/waco-shootout-friendly-sunday-get-together-biker-bloodbath, accessed October 5, 2015.

CHAPTER 15

CONCLUSION—THE WORLD TO COME AND THE POST-MILLENNIAL REVOLUTION

> A nation or an individual may be at peace because all opponents have been killed or crushed; or, nation as well as individual may have found the secret of true harmony in the determination to live and let live.—
> Anna Julia Cooper[1]

The Pedagogy of Protest, Knowledge from Critical Public Discourse and Disruptive Activism

There is much that can be learned from the 2015 Baltimore Uprising. Several important lessons come to mind. *First*, that every event has a history. On its own, the death of Freddie Gray was tragic and unnecessary; but within the context of a pattern of police-encounter deaths, it is also an undeniable endemic social problem. When viewed through the history of African Americans, Gray's death represented the long struggle of blacks to be treated with the same care and respect that white and all other citizens expect. In combination with the accounts of Michael Brown, Eric Garner, Walter Scott and numerous other cases, we also learned that the immediate message of "Black Lives Matter" embodied a new rallying cry for an old theme linked to the historic extralegal killing of black people.

Second, we understood that countless voices have been raised. These included young articulate expressions of agency, those who used social media to take a stand against police brutality in the black community. We found voices that were not only powerful, but also intelligent and fully conscious of the importance of history, and not given to polite, but disingenuous euphemisms to describe social problems. As popular culture remained ahistorical and continued to push the outlandish myth of a post-racial America, the new activists were well aware of the fundamentals of racism and white supremacy and they, like the activists through the 1990s, were not afraid to use accurate terms and concepts. In addition, the modern activists usually organized with a smaller centralized base, and then reached out to a

---

[1] Anna Julia Cooper, *A Voice from the South*. New York: Oxford University Press, 1988.

World To Come: Essays On The Baltimore Uprising, Militant Racism, And History

larger audience—the world. They also organized within traditional institutions such as the black church, and they also consolidated their efforts just as effectively outside of religious institutions. The Black Lives Matter activists not only used social media dynamically, they leveraged social media—often causing the mainstream broadcasts to follow and react to them, rather than independently report. Social media connected the Black Lives Matter activist to his or her thoughts about history and social justice—increasing our ability to truly see the pervasive issues that affect black communities. It appeared that blacks nationwide were more involved in public message-making and the art of technological social network conservation. Activists then took this message to the people and the politicians.

Third, the Baltimore Uprising confirmed that the local policing system—across the nation—was pitifully broken, and in actuality, had never been repaired. One of the biggest challenges was that there were segments of society that did not know or chose not to believe that there was a problem—because it did not impact their communities. For them such an uprising signaled a prophetic racial apocalypse, not an indication of some of the failings of our municipalities. The voices for justice, demanding to be heard, had had enough. Therefore, activists not only lobbied for the immediate preservation of black lives, they were also conscious of the need to communicate with and educate all citizens on the issues.

Fourth, we continue to recognize that black people's lives, regardless of class and gender, are often truncated and objectified—viewed differently—in order to serve the demands of racism in society. The community felt that there was an obviously unfair double standard of behavior for police and the citizens. From the perspective of citizens, whose numbers overwhelmingly filled the criminal justice system's school-to-prison pipeline, the police in theory represented a higher standard of behavior because of their occupation, but in terms of their conduct did not have to (while they enjoyed the image) practice this higher standard in reality. Any documented criminal activity—no matter how petty—of a victim of a police-encounter shooting would be publically displayed and amplified to justify the shooting. Police with officially recorded complaints no matter how extensive or severe were often shielded. Thus we also understood that the police have a very high internal and formal community-of-care apparatus. Regardless of their conduct, they know that they are part of a very large and powerful community, which will always represent and protect the interest of its members. The dark side of this community-of-care system is that when

World To Come: Essays On The Baltimore Uprising, Militant Racism, And History

citizens seriously question the immediate post-killing actions, liberties, and activities of law enforcement, they often perceive potential cover-ups related to the killing of blacks, as well as concerted cooperation between police, city administrators, the mass media, prosecutors, medical examiners, and many others.

Fifth, another important lesson from the Baltimore Uprising was how the proactive community-based actions of blacks were overlooked or minimized in the mainstream media. Just as the media virtually ignored blacks who stayed up all night to guard businesses in an effort to stave off potential rioters, they gave little attention to the citizens who cleaned up the CVS; or area high school and college students (from HBCUs like Morgan and Coppin State Universities) who organized clean up campaigns in and around the Mondawmin Mall. During and after the Baltimore Uprising, citizens were engaged in organizing, self-policing, community clean up, and dialoguing about neighborhood revitalization. There were countless discussions about the direction of the city, led by the people as well as politicians. Ultimately, it was the citizens (along with coalitions of ministers and grass roots community leaders) that outlined the meaning of the Baltimore Uprising, and what the major issues would be moving forward.

Finally, the immediate aftermath of the Baltimore Uprising focused our attention on critical ideas and the development of programs designed to address the broad issues of police-community relations. Baltimore city leaders, especially mayor Stephanie Rawlings-Blake presented proposals for a number of projects to improve the quality of life for the residents. Though it was condemned by some, this included the request for the federal government to formally investigate the Baltimore City Police department. Recognizing the national import of all of this, President Obama's response was to launch a *White House Police Data Initiative* and to limit military grade weapons to the police.[2] These particular measures were announced by the middle of May 2015. The Baltimore Uprising has much more to teach us, and what we might glean from the event that is of transformative significance, will be revealed as we move further into the future. Yet, when all of the

---

[2]Recommendations Pursuant to Executive Order 13688 Federal Support for Local Law Enforcement Equipment Acquisition, *Law Enforcement Working Group*, May 2015. https://www.whitehouse.gov/sites/default/files/docs/le_equipment_wg_final_report_final.pdf, accessed May 19, 2015.

WORLD TO COME: ESSAYS ON THE BALTIMORE UPRISING, MILITANT RACISM, AND HISTORY

arguments about how to end police-encounter killings of citizens have been analyzed, what remains is a broad collective sense of shared humanity.

What Does It Mean To Be Human and Humane in the World?

As we move further into a post-millennial militaristic society, it is increasingly important to ask the question—what does it mean to be *human* and *humane* in the world? Neely Fuller, Jr. stated that, "A person who is human and/or humane knows and understands truth, and uses truth in such manner as to produce justice, and correctness, at all times, in all places, in all areas of activity."[3] Throughout American history, well-known public figures, especially black public intellectuals, have expanded and expounded on the idea that black humanity matters. This thought did not rest solely in the realms of philosophy and spirituality, but was at the core of the African American (and worldwide Africana) struggle for freedom. Thus, the questionable police killing of African Americans has been viewed as an intellectual crisis, and only part of the issues that compromise our "national survival"[4] as a people. Today the expression "Black Lives Matter" is no less palpable than "We shall overcome," "I am a Man," and "Black Power" were a half a century ago. This is a rational attempt to understand and articulate how austere policing turned into extralegal killings, and how black lives are further diminished when officers systematically attempt to dehumanize people, are supported by the media, police administrations and unions, and the vast judicial system in the process. The issue is one of racial justice, particularly the ability to be human and humane in the world.[5]

However, we cannot separate this essential concern—our expression of humanity and humaneness—from the common race relations discourse that negates the persistent crisis surrounding black lives, perennially suggesting that the conversation is "not just about black people." This is where the dialogue immediately changes

---

[3]Neely Fuller, Jr., *The United Independent Compensatory Codes/System/Concepts a Textbook/Workbook for Thought, Speech and/or Action for Victims of Racism (White Supremacy)*, Revised Edition. Washington, D.C.: Liberation Information Distributing Co., 1984, 267.
[4]Molefi Kete Asante, *Erasing Racism The Survival of the American Nation*, New York: Prometheus Books, 2003.
[5]"Human and humaneness" are fundamental core concepts in the Afrocentric paradigm/philosophy.

WORLD TO COME: ESSAYS ON THE BALTIMORE UPRISING, MILITANT RACISM, AND HISTORY

direction from the obliteration of black lives in order to deflate and refocus in order to engage another central idea or message. This is far from a critical comparative analysis of black issues and universal paradigms of struggle. The seemingly innocuous statement "not just about black people" uttered when blacks are *the* subject, fails to focus wholly and explicitly on the immediate, essential issues affecting black people. The phrase is a message in itself, suggesting a tacit acknowledgement of black suffering, in order to give way to an ostensively larger more meaningful discussion. In this space, the humanity and the crisis of a people are strategically dismissed. Too often, however the interjection, this is "not just about black people," is an unconscious flawed attempt to bond with black issues, without understanding that the discourse is meant to shift, and ultimately reject the criticality of the challenges. In assessing one of the main problems associated with the discourse, it can be said that the phrase "not just about black people" generally moves from blackness to the universal. However, blackness (as race, culture, art, or ethos) is often presented as essentialist and particular to the universal. Of course, the universal is translated as whiteness, and constantly asserted as common and all-inclusive. This idea is not only untrue it has dehumanized black people. It assumes that blackness is not a worthy universal construct for humanity—one in which the specificity and significance of Africanity is also sufficient to illuminate and explain worldwide issues, conditions, and themes.

In terms of how we develop as human and humane in world society, two important public figures—Bethune and DuBois— at the end of their lives, focused on what they learned from the expansive philosophy and experience of blacks. In 1955 human rights advocate and respected educator Mary McLeod Bethune (1875-1955) in her "Last Will and Testament," gave a thoughtful statement on the ethical values derived from the African American experience. As Bethune acknowledged her own life's work, she bequeathed to world society essential temporal gifts—love, hope confidence, a desire for education, a respect for power, faith, racial dignity, harmony, and a responsibility to the youth. Of all of these legacies, the respect for how power is used, coupled with racial dignity speaks to the humanity of black people. Bethune believed that "Power, intelligently directed, can lead to more freedom. Unwisely directed, it can be a dreadful, destructive force."[6] The bequeath of racial dignity is significant because in the face of

---

[6]Mary McLeod Bethune, "Last Will and Testament," *Ebony*, August 1955.

World To Come: Essays On The Baltimore Uprising, Militant Racism, And History

racism and white supremacy blacks are reminded of their own inherent dignity as a people, and that the operationalized prejudices that accompany a racist agenda do not diminish the essence of one's soul.

In 1963, scholar, historian, sociologist, and black rights activist, W.E.B. DuBois issued his "last message" to the world (written approximately seven years earlier) which presented one singular idea—that humanity can thrive. DuBois, who lived in multiple worlds and led many lives, was one of those rare individuals who not only studied and analyzed history—he was conscious of his ability to make history. DuBois offered the public the following declaration, "As you live, believe in life! Always human beings will live and progress to greater, broader and fuller life."[7] His idea appeared to be a deep rumination of the soul, a message from a black intellectual and activist pioneer, a public intellectual who nearly singlehandedly embodied these terms. DuBois had determined that mortality was a function of losing "...belief in this truth..."[8] To believe in truth offered immortality—as sense that eternally, humanity was great.

At the height of the Civil Rights movement in the 1960s, two voices for social justice, Martin Luther King, Jr. and James Baldwin, gave us their insights into pressing themes of racial equality, racism, civil disobedience, and the meaning of humanity. In 1964, Martin Luther King, Jr. minister, philosopher, and undisputed leader of the modern Civil Rights Movement, reminded the country that American racism was rooted in history, which caused a "schizophrenic personality on the question of race."[9] King had studied the black spiritual, philosophical, and cultural traditions and the legacy of nonviolent civil disobedience. To advance our sense of humanity, society needed to delve into the truth of racism, and understand that white supremacy was a much larger beast than what we were led to believe, and that racism operated solely to justify oppressive behavior. King eloquently advocated for non-violence activism in the pursuit of human rights. In his *Letter from a Birmingham Jail*, King shrewdly stated that "...we must see the need of having nonviolent gadflies to create the kind of tension in society that will help men rise from the dark depths of prejudice and racism to the majestic heights of understanding and brotherhood."[10]

---

[7]"The Last Message of Dr. W.E.B. DuBois to the World," *The Journal of Negro History*, Vol. 49, No. 2 (April 1964), 145.
[8]Ibid.
[9]Martin Luther King, Jr., *Where Do We Go From Here: Chaos or Community,* 1964 (2010).
[10]Martin Luther King, Jr., "Letter from a Birmingham Jail," April 16, 1963.

World To Come: Essays On The Baltimore Uprising, Militant Racism, And History

The Civil Rights movement had taught King that the collective was more important than the individual and that persistence in nonviolent engagement was essential to bringing about a more humane society.

Novelist, social critic and activist James Baldwin, in 1965, linked the overarching problem of racism to the distortions of history and humanity—specifically that white society, in valorizing their own history to the exclusion and demonization of other histories—had in fact "impaled"[11] itself upon this fallacy. It was the important argument that suggested that the oppressor ultimately oppresses himself. This means that a tyrannical society will delude and eventually destroy itself. No world society can call itself human if people are not treated humanely. Baldwin expanded his analysis to include not only the blind romance of European history, but also the attempt to diminish and deny white oppression in human history. The gulf that existed between blacks and whites in the Civil Rights years was a direct result of the inability to speak openly and honestly about race, and particularly about racism, thus rendering mutually beneficially human solutions impossible.

In the post-Civil Rights era, there were a number of significant thinkers speaking about the issue of race relations. Our understanding of race relations has helped us to appreciate exactly where our humanity is situated. Public scholar-intellectuals like Michael Eric Dyson, Cornell West and Angela Y. Davis have approached black humanistic studies with a searing honesty. Professor and author Michael Eric Dyson expounded upon the importance of controlling the ability to recognize racism in society and the notion of alternating experimental forms of racial justice. Dyson's analysis encapsulated both ideas in his statement "Americans take pride in shaping racial perception, fronting a house of pain with earnest conversation about how we can make things better by tinkering here and there."[12] It is an allusion to the façade of a high functioning interracial democratic society. One, like that voiced by James Baldwin and others, functions on self-deception. Scholar-activist and public intellectual Cornel West has offered a critical examination of the discursive nature of white supremacy, where he ultimately concluded "…the everyday life of black

---

[11]James Baldwin, "White Man's Guilt," *Ebony*, August, 1965.
[12]Tricia Rose, Andrew Ross, Robin DG Kelley, Joe Wood, Howard Winant, Jacquie Jones, Michael Eric Dyson et al. "Race And Racism: A Symposium." *Social Text* (1995): 1-52, 13.

people is shaped not simply by the exploitative (oligopolistic) capitalist system of production but also by cultural attitudes and sensibilities including alienating ideals of beauty."[13] As West has pointed out racism has a labor, economic and social function that is often overlooked in most popular analysis. Public intellectuals have consistently noted that our understanding of modern racism could not exist without this manifold dynamic. The political activist and scholar, Angela Y. Davis, in one of her critical examinations of race and the criminal justice system in 2010,[14] explored how and why racism as a social system is self-perpetuating. Davis surmised that it accomplished this by negating "the structural character of racism…"; and by linking the steady rise in the black prison population to crime and poverty in order to suggest normality (i.e. pathology) in the black community and to support the momentum of socially racist interests. As these scholars suggest, it comes down to an insidious form of race neutrality where ignoring intrinsic racism is the key to perpetuating it. This is also linked to the mechanisms that repeatedly convolute the efforts toward painstakingly honest discourse around issues of race and racism.

There are other important themes in considering what it means to be human and humane in the world—specifically resilience and civility as discussed by Maya Angelou and Pier Massimo Forni. In her 2013 interview with premier author and activist Maya Angelou about the education of children, Amy M. Azzam presented an interesting question about the burden of poor children. According to Azzam, "Resilience is obviously a good thing to have. But some kids—impoverished kids, kids from minority groups—are repeatedly called on to have more of it than others." It was an interesting question because embedded in it was deeper notions that poor people of color carry the burden of *accepting* their circumstances. It was a serious, anti-human expectation in modern world culture. In her inimitably succinct style, Angelou responded that it was "…the cruelty of poverty, the cruelty of ignorance."[15] That the poverty system, with all of its charitable efforts,

---

[13]Cornel West, "A Genealogy of Modern Racism," in *Race Critical Theories*, Philomena Essed and David Theo Goldberg, Blackwell, NY, 2002, 90-112, 109.
[14]Angela Y. Davis, "Race and Criminalization Black Americans and the Punishment System," in Wahneema Lubiano ed., *The House That Race Built: Original Essays by Toni Morrison, Angela Y. Davis, Cornel West, and Others on Black Americans and Politics in America Today*. New York: Vintage Books, 2010, 264-279.
[15]Amy M. Azzam, "Handle with Care: A Conversation with Maya Angelou," *Educational Leadership*, Vol. 71, No. 1, September 2013, 10-13.

WORLD TO COME: ESSAYS ON THE BALTIMORE UPRISING, MILITANT RACISM, AND HISTORY

is intrinsically harsh, and that people are dismissed because they are not deemed worthy of "being seen" as equally human. Resilience is an essential human virtue, but not when it is grafted to the human spirit in order to sustain perpetual suffering so others can prosper. Angelou's philosophy also linked humanness to the idea of innate dignity and worthiness. Until we unearth, uphold and appreciate human value as the core of world society (rather than religion, commerce, politics) we will be locked into erroneous and unproductive debates over who is human in the world.

To this extent, other public intellectuals have responded to the issue of human/humaneness as a search for fundamental modern Homo sapiens-sapiens values. Author, professor, and literary classicist Pier Massimo Forni founded the Johns Hopkins Civility Project and created a handbook on civility to discuss how humans can enhance their lives, if not minimize or eliminate conflicts and hostilities altogether. In a militaristic world where the very idea of civility is often misinterpreted and linked to human weakness, such an important discourse may be lost on generations who have learned that a cautious defense and a ready cynicism is the hallmark of savvy persons. Yet the irony is overwhelming, that civility would be fodder for public contempt, when we live in a *civilization*. Forni admitted that civility is a complex idea—because people define it in many different ways—still, it transcends our idea that it is merely about possessing "manners." Forni said that fundamentally civility is a function of consciousness, which means "…being constantly aware of others and weaving restraint, respect, and consideration…" into its meaning.[16] This is significant for our understanding of what it means to be human and humane in the world. It might be possible to imitate forms of civility, but genuine civility cannot be faked. It is a personal construct, which allows individuals to become self-aware, transcendent, introspective and consciously interactive in bringing about positive social change. Those who call for reforms within the criminal justice system, in all if its aspects, but particularly in the arrest and sentencing process, expect justice *and* respect, as seminal forms of civility.

Historically, African Americans have been subjected to various forms of extreme racial violence—psychological, symbolic, and physical. Just as significant as the position of being acted upon, blacks

---

[16] Pier Massimo Forni, *Choosing Civility The Twenty-Five Rules of Considerate Conduct*, New York: NY, 2002, 9.

World To Come: Essays On The Baltimore Uprising, Militant Racism, And History

have used their own cultural and intellectual resources to shape their lives as well as to create remarkable counter responses to racial oppression. Among the most important contributions to ideas that impact the black community as well as American public media are works which address the crisis within African American families by asserting that culturally-specific responses are necessary and that people in general should engage in genuine (and organically-grown solution-oriented) dialogue and activity. The early and recent work of Afrocentric scholar-pioneers like Molefi Kete Asante, Maulana Karenga, Ama Mazama, Ana Monteiro-Ferreira[17] and others indicates that a profound transition in the collective black consciousness has taken place.

This shift in thinking is undergirded by the Afrocentric philosophical paradigm—through its critique and rejection of the historically assigned racist victimization status of black people. This model advances Africana humanism, and provides a constructive cultural approach to African agency in black activist spheres. Prolific scholar, and founder of the Afrocentric scholarly movement, Molefi Kete Asante has maintained that the value of "humaneness or inhumaneness rises from a society's laws, religion, community, economics, organization, property, and technology."[18] This means that people decide, through their institutions, how to live or not live in harmony with one another—and that we cannot, for example, separate the legal issues surrounding inappropriate policing, and the dysfunctional economic dynamics of a community. Asante pointed out that those infrastructural facades, especially relics indicative of national state grandeur, like monuments for example—may give the impression of a high functioning and humane society, a civilization in fact, when the exact opposite is the reality.[19]

Further, structures that represent war are especially revealing about a society's sense and state of humaneness. Historic physical indicators of civilization often expose a lowered human-to-human

---

[17]Molefi Kete Asante, *Race, Rhetoric & Identity The Architecton of Soul*, New York: Humanity Books, 2005; Maulana Karenga, *Kawaida and Questions of Life and Struggle*, Los Angeles, CA: The University of Sankore Press, 2008; Ana Monteiro-Ferreira, *The Demise of the Inhuman Afrocentricity, Modernism, and Postmodernism*, New York: SUNY University Press, 2014; and Ama Mazama, ed., *The Afrocentric paradigm*, Trenton, NJ: Africa World Press, Inc., 2003.
[18]Molefi Kete Asante, 2005, 138.
[19]Molefi Kete Asante, 2005, 138-139.

WORLD TO COME: ESSAYS ON THE BALTIMORE UPRISING, MILITANT RACISM, AND HISTORY

perception of connectedness. Scholar-activist and Afrocentric culturalist Maulana Karenga, in his analysis of the 1964 murders of Chaney, Goodman and Schwerner in Mississippi, pointed out how racism reacts to black humanity: "James Chaney was murdered and mutilated for being Black and acting human; Goodman and Schwerner were murdered for their association with him and support for his cause."[20] This means that racism trumped all of humanity. In order to kill, and over kill the black body, whites would also be sacrificed in order to deny a black humanity. The failure to see and accept humanity is the real pathology; and the need to assert racial violence as a basic construct of humanity is not the mark of Homo sapiens-sapiens. Yet as we have seen, in the study of the western notion of human and humanness, black humanity in and of itself, is a death sentence.

Another scholar-activist and educator Ama Mazama reminds us of the importance of how language is organized in world societies, and specifically how the westernization of language shaped human conceptions of ideas such as racism—and thus control over African people.[21] Mazama would argue that it is the creation and control of one's own language, rather than reliance on the oppressors' tongue that produces a liberatory context. Language and cognitive intentionality are symbiotic; and how language is used reveals not only something of our thought processes—but what we choose to do life. The activists in the Baltimore Uprising strategically used language (particularly in protest signs and chants) in such a way as to focus and maintain the discussion of police-custody deaths centered on black people and on the issue of justice. Afrocentric scholar and theorist Ana Monteiro-Ferreira outlined the history of the ways in which people of African descent have been dehumanized in the world. Therefore, when the black nation asks the question: "What does it mean to be a human being?"[22] They know that they are definitively tied to an historical and contemporary struggle for freedom. According to Monteiro-Ferreira, blacks rescue themselves from existing systems of oppression by eliminating "…the insidious doctrines that dehumanized African existence."[23] The Afrocentric

---

[20] Maulana Karenga, *Kawaida and Questions of Life and Struggle*, Los Angeles, CA: The University of Sankore Press, 2008, 188.
[21] Ama Mazama, ed., *The Afrocentric paradigm*, Trenton, NJ: Africa World Press, Inc., 2003, 201-214.
[22] Ana Monteiro-Ferreira, *The Demise of the Inhuman Afrocentricity, Modernism, and Postmodernism*, New York: SUNY University Press, 2014, 75.
[23] Ibid., 75.

public intellectual-activist has demonstrated that community power is dynamic and essential to the liberation process. Decisively born out in the triumphs of black people, it is African agency that disrupts racism and white supremacy in order to bring about a more humane and just society.

Social Justice beyond Policing—Deconstructing Violent Racist Paradigms

Police-killing protest events like those in Oakland, Brooklyn, Ferguson, New York[24] and then Baltimore produced heightened attention to the issues of race, racism, white supremacy, and racial justice in the United States, if not around the world. One of the issues important to this focus was how citizens responded to militant racism in a traditional atmosphere of denial. For example on June 17, 2015 when nine African Americans were gunned down by a young white man during a Wednesday night prayer meeting in Charleston, South Carolina, one of the first mainstream responses was that even though it was being investigated as a hate crime—it was not legally a hate crime, and certainly not an act of domestic terrorism targeting African Americans. It was a conventional attempt to disavow what many believed to be the obvious; society's ability to read violent race crimes differently when blacks are the victims. During this timeframe, there had been the tragic shootings at a theater in Louisiana and at military sites in Tennessee (a recruitment and an operational support center). These were also horrendous acts displaying our preoccupation with domestic gun violence. However, as with acts of violence perpetrated at other religious sites, the killing of people in their sacred place of worship was, in the public's imagination, inviolate and incomprehensible. Among the nine who were killed at the Emanuel A.M.E. Church was a well-known and highly respected South Carolina state senator and the church's minister, Clementa Pinckney.[25] Senator Pinckney had been a life-long activist for human rights, including the protests over the police killing of Walter Scott, and he was instrumental in the state's bill requiring that police wear body cameras. One professor likened the attack on the Emanuel A.M.E. church to a

---

[24] 2009 Oakland, California (Oscar Grant), 2013 Brooklyn, New York (Kimani Gray), 2014 Ferguson, Missouri (Michael Brown), and 2014 New York (Eric Garner).
[25] In addition to Senator Clementa Pinckney, others killed on June 17 included: Cynthia Hurd, Susie Jackson, Ethel Lance, DePayne Middleton-Doctor, Tywanza Sanders, Daniel L. Simmons, Sr., Sharonda Coleman-Singleton, and Myra Thompson.

World To Come: Essays On The Baltimore Uprising, Militant Racism, And History

concerted act of terrorism which targeted Senator's Pinckney's long fight against white supremacy.[26]

To grasp some meaning of this specific massacre we must begin to understand the system of racism. In the history of science, medicine and technology Dr. Frances Cress Welsing has the distinction of being one of the few contemporary scholars of psychiatry to critically examine and analyze racism as a scientific construct. For more than forty years, Welsing (who died at the end of 2015) researched, studied and defined the behavioral underpinnings of racism and white supremacy as a global dynamic system of human survival, which she presented in the Cress Theory.[27] Welsing explicitly maintained that understanding the meaning of color is essential to our attempt to know racism. Her theories and sub-hypothesis were based on qualitative and quantitative research and observation. Color is more than a fascinating phenomenon; it is a controlling idea for the preservation of people who consider themselves white. It is no wonder then that white supremacists do not believe in colorblindness. Color, or the biogenetic impulse associated with melanin color creation (and recreation) is at the heart of the racial dynamic.

So philosophically speaking, the highest form of color supremacy in society is the idea of distinct white racial support groups and systems. This expression of militant racism exists to suggest that white people should control and dominate around the globe—and by force. Often the argument is based on the false idea that whites—due to the imposition of a multicultural society—have no genuine social, economic or political power; and that *they* have been systematically and brutally discriminated against by nonwhite people. It is a white militant movement—not a white ethnic expression—that, depending on the perceived success of the argument, is willing to claim such victimization. As surreptitious pseudo-victims of racial and cultural diversity, white supremacy adherents mock and deride those who have actually suffered systemic racial oppression. There is no question that people classified as white, have, can and do suffer horrid violent events that shape world society. When this happens, we see people acting inhumanely to other people. However, we do not see or even suggest

---

[26]Susanna Ashton, "Playing Hell in Charleston—Daniel Payne, Clementa Pinckney and the fight against White Supremacy," *TigerPrints*, Clemson University, June, 2015.
[27]Frances Cress Welsing, *The Isis Papers The Keys to the Colors*, Chicago: Third World Press, 1991, 1-16. Dr. Welsing presented the Cress Theory in the early 1970s.

white-on-white pathological crimes. We may want to believe that white supremacy is a function of contemporary pedestrian ignorance, but this is not true. It was "…created during the era of slavery…"[28] in order to rationalize human bondage. It is a highly intelligent arrangement of ideological oppression, which manages information for a specific end—the operationalization of racism.[29] The salient aspect of white supremacy ideology is that it is, fundamentally, a god-complex approach to collective self-worth in human relations, especially involving interracial interaction. This ideology encompasses the organized racial belief in omnipotence (all-powerful), omniscience (all seeing), Christologistic (belief that one is the embodiment of Jesus and is carrying out Christian teachings), and the divine right of sovereigns (the ancient idea of individual rule over the masses as mandated by God). The white supremacist god-complex approach to human relations involving people of color is ultimately, the ability to wield the power of life and death.

Therefore, the shooter at the Emanuel A.M.E. church in Charleston South Carolina, Dylann Storm Roof, a 21-year-old white male, apparently saw himself as a protector of white society. He was a young man on a mission concerned broadly about blacks "taking over our country," and citing that white women were being raped (by black men). Roof's racist beliefs were posted on social media, where he heralded the era of Apartheid in South Africa (the period before the 1950s through the mid-1990s), the old colonial holding of Rhodesia[30] (modern day Zimbabwe), and posed for a picture in which he brandished a gun and the Confederate Battle Flag. In what is thought to be his manifesto, Roof—who clearly believed all of the conventional racist ideology regarding blacks—including the most fundamental—that blacks as a race of people were somehow inferior to whites. Roof

---

[28]From An Interview with Bryan Stevenson, See Corey G. Johnson, "Bryan Stevenson on Charleston and Our Real Problem with Race, *The Marshall Project*, June 24, 2015, https://www.themarshallproject.org/2015/06/24/bryan-stevenson-on-charleston-and-our-real-problem-with-race#.hCPU6INst, Accessed February 8, 2016.
[29]See Neely Fuller, Jr., *The United Independent Compensatory Codes/System/Concepts a Textbook/Workbook for Thought, Speech and/or Action for Victims of Racism (White Supremacy)*, Revised Edition. Washington, D.C.: Liberation Information Distributing Co., 1984.
[30]Refers to the colonial settlement created in 1890 by the British South Africa Company to extract mineral wealth and labor, and extend the territory of the British Empire. The colony was named after Cecil Rhodes, considered the last of the British Imperialists. The Zimbabwean nationalist movement comprised of the African National Congress (ANC) fought to reclaim the country.

World To Come: Essays On The Baltimore Uprising, Militant Racism, And History

would appear on behalf of the white race and do something about his sense of racial power imbalance. While conservative pundits initially argued over whether the massacre of black people by a self-proclaimed white supremacist should continue to be pursued as a hate crime, those who merely evaluated the available cursory information on Roof were astonished. This was a master-narrative: Roof pre-selected the famed historic black A.M.E. church; participated in the prayer meeting for a time, and had identified Reverend Pinckney before he opened fire on the Bible study group members. He intentionally left one woman alive so that she could go back and tell the story of what happened and why he did it. To some debatable extent, Roof had made his sinister plans clear to others beforehand and his actions on June 17, 2015 confirmed his beliefs. He had articulated, not a generic cry for white power, but specifically for white supremacy. His ideology, a well-established global treatise, encompassed the essence of white supremacy. In this mind, the contemporary world was not as it should have been. In the targeted version of the doctrine, Senator Barack Hussein Obama should not have been elected president of the United States (for two terms), and blacks (as a people) were criminally suspect and deserving of white arbitrary summary judgement.

The high school dropout turned landscaper had some brushes with the law, yet Roof's community-of-care consistently painted him as a shy, quiet, and perhaps confused youth. At that time, few news outlets even intimated mental illness. Those who knew of his intentions said that they did not believe that he would act on them. This was the idea related by one of his friends Joseph Carlton Meek (who was later federally indicted for concealing and falsifying information about Roof's plans).[31] Though it was clear that the death penalty would initially be sought in the case, Roof's public network did not distance themselves from his actions; they largely defended his deeds as the work of a troubled "kid" or a human aberration. In fact, some of the public comments to the initial stories about the massacre at Emanuel A.M.E. church (the victims were being referred to as the Emanuel 9), were incredibly troubling—some citing that the manhunt, arrest (complete with a meal from Burger King), and pending trial of Roof, would only *empower blacks* towards criminality (a reference to racial

---

[31] *The United States of America v. Joseph Carlton Meek*, Grand Jury Indictment, United States District Court for the District of South Carolina, Columbia Division, September 15, 2015.

retaliation). What was clear is that the people he killed inside the historic Emanuel A.M.E. Church were highly educated, intelligent, caring, and accomplished citizens—people who were spiritually grounded and concerned about the human rights of all.

Yet there was the incredible sense of longing in the emerging Dylan Storm Roof story, one that connected his image holding the Confederate Battle Flag and a gun to the Old South, and the bygone days of the antebellum slave plantations. The profound pictures being drawn were associated with the enslavement of Africans, the colonial enterprise, and the Lost Cause. In essence, Roof took on a para-law enforcement role (vis a vis the public white supremacist ideology) when he committed this heinous act. He did this because he was bound to what Joe L. Kincheloe and Aaron Gresson have called the "recovery movement."[32] Not to oversimplify the complexity of their thesis, the concept involves the idea that the modern Civil Rights movement along with racial equality policy measures (regardless of their depth and breadth) has harmed whites; and this, coupled with a romantic view of the slave south, then justifies, in effect, a modern day white southern redemption crusade. Yet there is an appeal to an even older mythology as well, the white supremacists' popular affinity for ancient Aryan and Greek gods, and the lore and lure of twentieth century Nazism. All of these ideas serve an ideology of white supremacy intent on racial hate crimes as the highest expression of their human ethos.

Our traditional understanding of race relations, particularly overt racist acts has always been polemic. Generally, a larger number of whites' consistently believe that race is not an issue (or not their issue), that it does not matter, or that it is overemphasized. A majority of blacks regularly maintain that race is a predominant issue central to society and to black lives in particular. This impasse is instructive; but it sometimes leads us to believe that whites are race neutral (unbiased) and that blacks are race-obsessed (biased). Moreover, this conception is deeply flawed because, as anti-racism activist and scholar Tim Wise and others have pointed out, whites are not only highly racialized in their thinking—but they find race (black people) often and in genuinely nonaligned race issues.[33] Moreover, racial thinking is heightened in the

---

[32] Joe L. Kincheloe, "Southernication, Romanticization and the Recovery of White Supremacy" (Winter, 2006) *Souls: A Critical Journal of Black Politics, Culture, and Society*, 8, 1, 27-46.
[33] Tim Wise, *Color-Blind The Rise of Post-Racial Politics and the Retreat From Racial equity*, San Francisco, CA: City Lights Books, 2010, 140-152.

WORLD TO COME: ESSAYS ON THE BALTIMORE UPRISING, MILITANT RACISM, AND HISTORY

attempt to eliminate race from the discussion. This is demonstrated, in terms of who supports symbols like the Confederate Flag. The defense of the flag as a non-racial idea is largely conservative, white, and southern.[34] For them it is important to decouple white supremacy as an ideology and white supremacy as a structural mode of operation in society. Race was the only issue for Roof because he believed that blacks, as a group of people, were *the problem* in society.

On the other hand, there was another summer event that spoke to our ideas of humanity—especially the strength of humanness. In the midst of the national argument over the Confederate Flag, and ten days after Roof's murder of the Emanuel 9, Brittany "Bree" Newsome[35] (assisted by fellow activist James Tyson, a young white male—and supported by several other activists who converged upon the scene) scaled the pole and unhooked the flag on the state capitol grounds. A human rights activist and artist Newsome bravely climbed up a 30-foot pole and with historic resolve removed the Confederate Battle flag at the South Carolina Statehouse on June 27, 2015. The 30-year-old African American woman told the world, "You come against me with hatred and oppression and violence. I come against you in the name of God. This flag comes down today!" When Newsome reached the ground with the flag in hand, both she and Tyson were arrested, held on a $3,000 bond, and charged with defacing state property before they were released on bail. In the well planned protest, Newsome and Tyson understood that she could have been shot and even killed for the action. Mindful that social media is always watching, it was visually important to have Newsome escorted away coincidentally by a black officer—and later it was widely reported that she went before a black female judge. Notwithstanding what many regarded as one of the most important acts of contemporary Civil Rights heroism in the twenty-first century, the Confederate flag was replaced rather quickly (within an hour by black officers) and the devotees of the rebel flag continued their protests of support. However, Newsome claimed that the removal of the flag was simply "the right thing to do."

The Confederate Flag had long been regarded as a symbol of racial hatred, and a call to arms for those who wished to see a return to

---

[34]Christopher A. Cooper and H. Gibbs Knotts, "Region, Race, and Support for the South Carolina Confederate Flag." *Social Science Quarterly* 87, No. 1 (2006): 142-154.
[35]A community organizer and activist involved with the Occupy Movement, Moral Monday (Reverend Doctor William Barber, II), and The Tribe.

the days when blacks were legally regarded as second-class citizens in American society.[36] It was clear that given the pending national presidential election, the momentum of the Black Lives Matter movement and tragedies like the Emanuel A.M.E. Church massacre that state legislatures also had to address one the most recognizable contemporary symbol of the Lost Cause. Defenders of the confederate flag began with the notion that it was a misunderstood emblem—that it really was not about race at all. They denied that the flag was a symbol of racial hatred and asserted that it was merely a military insignia of American history—a history that many whites had regional and genealogical ties to and were very proud of—that is, the legacy of confederate soldiers fighting against the union. Mostly, the supporters of the Confederate flag asserted the same argument that has been used to suggest the Civil War had nothing to do with the enslavement of Africans in the United States. However, for many African Americans the flag was more than an old mark of racial hatred, it represented a warning to blacks and other people of color—that in certain parts of the country—they were not welcome, could be in physical jeopardy, and should be fearful. More than this, as journalist and award-winning author Ta-Nehisi Coates noted at the time, the Confederate flag meant "…the attempt to raise an empire in slavery."[37]

    The concerns and debate over the Confederate flag have always been present, but the flag in a sense reemerged as a symbol of racial hatred in the wake of law-enforcement shootings of blacks, and especially the massacre at the Emanuel A.M.E. church. As the nine church members were being buried, black citizens continued their protests in the south, and began criticizing legislators by stating that at the very least the Confederate flag should not be flown on the state grounds (especially during the June 26 funeral of a murdered African American state senator). However, after Newsome took down the flag (if only temporarily), the conversation got lost in the mass media—mainstream and social—and ludicrous ideas surfaced that somehow suggested that the goal was to ban the personal use of the flag. Yet several companies immediately pledged to remove the Confederate flag,

---

[36] James Forman Jr., "Driving Dixie Down: Removing the Confederate Flag from Southern State Capitols." *Yale Law Journal* (1991): 505-526; Juan Gonzales, "Confederate Flag is Finally Seen by Many People as Symbol of White Supremacy and Racism," *New York Daily News*, June 23, 2015.
[37] "Ta-Nehisi Coates on Police Brutality, The Confederate Flag and Forgiveness," NPR, Fresh Air, Interviewed by Terry Gross, July 13, 2015.

World To Come: Essays On The Baltimore Uprising, Militant Racism, And History

including Walmart, EBay, Sears, Target, Etsy, and Amazon. The move indicated that corporations understood and would not tolerate the Confederate flag as a symbol of racial hatred. In addition they also knew the buying power of citizens—especially African Americans— and how quickly social media can mount a crippling boycott. The main argument was that the Confederate flag should not be publically displayed on state or federal property—that for some meant that the flag was supported by peoples' tax dollars—thus, legislators and citizen defenders of the flag attempted to brand a new image for the banner. However, on July 9, 2015, the governor of South Carolina, Nimrata "Nikki" Randhawa Haley (R) sanctioned the removal of the Confederate Flag from the state capital. Two weeks later, on June 25, 2015, Rep. James E. Clyburn (D) introduced H.Res.344 in an effort to discourage the use of the Confederate flag altogether.

Dismantling Police-Encounter Killings and African Americans as a World Historical People

On July 7, 2015, Police Commissioner Anthony Batts called for an external independent review of the police during the Baltimore Uprising. He asked PERF, the Police Executive Research Forum, a nonprofit "…police research and policy organization …" based in Washington, D.C. to conduct an immediate investigation.[38] The next day (July 8, 2015) the Baltimore City Fraternal Order of Police Lodge #3 (the police union) released its own report on the riot, and the mayor in effect fired (a "termination without cause") the Police Commissioner. The FOP's report called the *After Action Review* gave the union's assessment of the police response to the Baltimore Uprising while at the same time excoriating both Mayor Rawlings-Blake and Police Commissioner Batts. The FOP report stated that the police did not have the overall resources or training to address the riot, and that the managerial "passive response"[39] led to chaos in the city. Generally, the FOP felt that the officers were victims of inadequate leadership, and all-but-called for Batts' termination in the report. Mayor Rawlings-Blake challenged the FOP report as "baseless," and denied that firing

---

[38] Police Executive Research Forum (PERF), http://www.policeforum.org/; Baltimore City Council, State of Emergency, "Police Commissioner Invites Outside Review," Baltimore, Maryland July 7, 2015.
[39] Baltimore City Fraternal Order of Police (FOP) Lodge #3 After Action Review, 32pp (undated, released July 8, 2015), 3.

WORLD TO COME: ESSAYS ON THE BALTIMORE UPRISING, MILITANT RACISM, AND HISTORY

Batts had any relationship to the *After Action Review*. Yet his firing appeared to be little more than a symbolic means toward addressing the issue of better policing in the city. Far from the disgrace associated with immediate dismissal, Batts left office as if he had resigned of his own volition. His firing was swift, and he was replaced by an interim appointment, Deputy Police Commissioner Kevin Davis. Davis, who headed the police department's Investigations and Intelligence Bureau, described Batts as a personal "friend and mentor."[40] Mayor Rawlings-Blake stated that Batts had done his job "with distinction," and many in Baltimore city government thanked him for his service.[41] Yet underneath the gracious high profile termination, there was an undercurrent of unanswered questions which suggested that the move was politically motivated.

For many years Batts served as a law enforcement officer in Long Beach and Oakland California and not without accolades, criticisms, and controversy. He officially began his term in Baltimore on September 26, 2012. Batts had only served as Police Commissioner in Baltimore for three years. His hire fulfilled at least one of Rawlings-Blake's main goals as mayor—crime reduction.[42] However, during this brief time, he did not appear to have earned any significant support or loyalty from the FOP, especially when he gave the impression that he was actually going to address racism in the ranks of the police force. Batts had some clear ideas about how to "...keep our country safe while reducing incarceration and racial injustices"[43] in the criminal justice system. While the media discussed any number of urban police issues, they rarely discussed racism, the overwhelming power of police unions, and particularly the Baltimore FOP. It was not unusual for ordinary citizens to confuse Baltimore's FOP with the Baltimore City Police Department. Given the acrimony between the two in the upper ranks, within days and weeks of the Baltimore Uprising, Commissioner

---

[40]Kevin Davis became interim Baltimore Police Commissioner.
[41]City of Baltimore, Mayor's Press Conference, Wednesday, July 8, 2015.
[42]City of Baltimore, Office of the Mayor, Press Release, "Mayor Rawlings-Blake and Commissioner Batts Release Strategic Plan for Baltimore Police Department, November 21, 2013; City of Baltimore, Office of the Mayor, Press Release, "Mayor Rawlings-Blake Announces Next Two Stops on Public Safety Town Hall Tour," March 18, 2014.
[43]Jessica Eaglin and Danyelle Solomon, "Reducing Racial And Ethnic Disparities In Jails: Recommendations for Local Practice," New York: Brennan Center for Justice at New York University of Law, 2015.

Batts had to remind the FOP: "The responsibility of the union is wages and working conditions, not day-to-day operations."[44]

However while some decried Batts' so-called low-key response to the open looting and lawlessness in the city during the Baltimore Uprising; others saw a lack of responsibility not to use traditional, or extreme, police force. Still, no matter their opinions regarding Batts' management style overall, others believed that in the moment of the uprising he (and the mayor) was truly concerned with the preservation of human life. The mayor's rationale for the firing was the issue of leadership, and that the public was "distracted" by his governing strategy, which was also interpreted as Batts' having lost (or never having gained) the support of the FOP. Ultimately, Batts, whose term as commissioner could have run through the year 2020,[45] became the first high profile political casualty of the Baltimore Uprising. One meant to energize the city's movement in a new direction. Intended or not, for the moment, Batts' firing gave the city, the BCPD and the FOP a necessary political scapegoat in the death of Freddie Gray, blame for the handling of the Baltimore Uprising, and for the post-uprising surge in the city's homicides.

Though Batts' termination served as an important symbol for the "city moving forward," the legal ramifications of the Baltimore Uprising appeared solely to be a battle between the city (the governing officials and the citizens) and the police (and/or the FOP). The two pre-trial hearings confirmed this challenge theory. The first pretrial hearing was held in early September and Baltimore Circuit court Judge Barry Williams ruled that the Baltimore 6 would stand trial for the charges as outlined by Marilyn Mosby; but they would be able to have separate trials. The position of the police, from the beginning, was that the six officers should have never been charged; and they attempted at every juncture, to have the charges dropped. They also argued vigorously in the public domain that Marilyn Mosby's involvement was flawed and that she (and her office) should be recused from the case. Further, they challenged—with varying degrees of intensity, the leadership and authority of both Police Commissioner Batts and Mayor

---

[44]Baltimore Police Department, Office of the Police Commissioner, Media Relations Section, "Baltimore Police Department Responds to FOP Lodge 3 June 16, 2015 Press Release," June 16, 2015.
[45]City of Baltimore Memo, From George A. Nilson, City Solicitor, To Honorable President and Members of the Board of Estimates, Subject Employment Agreement—Dr. Anthony W. Batts, September 5, 2012, 1.

World To Come: Essays On The Baltimore Uprising, Militant Racism, And History

Stephanie Rawlings-Blake. Judge Williams decided that Mosby and her office would not be removed from the case. Trying the group of officers separately would allow for better preservation of the image of police. As a group, they might be perceived and portrayed in the media as a "gang" or as mob of rogue cops. Separate trials also allowed for differing legal strategies; and allow for the officers to testify for and against each other. Severing the officers' cases made an immediate impact as the city anticipated the trials of the Baltimore 6.

The Baltimore Sun reported at the end of September 2015, that one of the defendants, William Porter informed the police van driver, defendant Caesar Goodson, Jr., that Freddie Gray might need medical help.[46] And this particular issue was at the crux of the indictments against the Baltimore 6. The second pretrial challenge, held the second week in September, addressed the issue of venue. Citizens waited with baited breath to hear if the trials would be moved outside of the city. One of the expressed fears was that the six officers would never be able to get a fair trial in Baltimore because of the pretrial media attention. The problem with this argument was that the trial, whether the city wanted it to be or not, was a national—and even international—media affair. Many believed that if the trial moved, the city would experience even more unrest. As the pretrial hearings got underway, the police made it known that they were anticipating rioting and as a result cancelled leave for the officers. There was also the insinuation that the predominately African American city (would yield a potentially bias jury pool) was not capable of delivering a fair verdict. However, Judge Barry Williams ruled that the trial would be held in Baltimore.

In the midst of the pretrial hearings, news came that the city of Baltimore would award the family of Freddie Gray 6.4 million dollars to preempt any future civil litigation. The settlement represented the largest payment for police-encounter misconduct in the city's history. Mayor Stephanie Rawlings-Blake made the announcement, indicating that the intent was to help support the healing of the city. Many believed that the monetary award would stave off citizen unrest if the officers in the case were found not guilty. The FOP circulated their condemnation of the Freddie Gray settlement widely, with one main

---

[46]Justin George and Kevin Rector, "Baltimore Officer said Freddie Gray asked for Help," *The Baltimore Sun*, September 26, 2015; Alex Dobuzinskis, "Baltimore Officer Warned Freddie Gray Needed Medical Help, Newspaper Reports," Reuters, September 27, 2015, http://www.reuters.com/article/2015/09/27/us-usa-police-maryland-idUSKCN0RR02Y20150927, accessed September 27, 2015.

idea, that the award was "obscene." Following these pivotal announcements, and two months after the termination of Police Commissioner Batts, the mayor held a press conference on September 11, 2015 (the day of the National 9/11 Memorial), stating that she would not seek reelection. The media immediately began to spin the story that "Freddie Gray" served as the death knell for her continued tenure as mayor. However, Rawlings-Blake said that she wanted to use her remaining time as mayor to focus on the needs of city, rather than on the "…distractions of running a campaign …."[47] As she cited her accomplishments during her term in office, Rawlings-Blake also noted that (among other endeavors), she would be working "…with the U.S. Department of Justice to reform our police department …."[48] This was something Rawlings-Blake was concerned about long before the Freddie Gray case.

As the events of the Baltimore Uprising (excluding the actual trials for the Baltimore 6) moved toward a conclusion of sorts, it remained clear that the city's police department possessed its own identity, or at least an embedded and powerful subculture. Coupled with the local and national strength of the FOP, the Baltimore police department continuously demonstrated that it was formidable. For Baltimore, as with many other cities across the nation it would be a supreme challenge to identify and unearth this subculture, engage in meaningful dialogue that included the communities directly impacted, and then to work to restructure the philosophy and operations of city policing. This arcane subculture theory seemed true when in the Fall, 2015—after months of news stories emphasizing the police-encounter deaths of blacks across the nation—mainstream media and bloggers gave considerably more attention and support to renewing 1970s and periodic headlines asserting that there was a domestic "war on police."[49]

After the Baltimore Uprising, there were countless discussions about how to address the questionable police shootings of Blacks, and improve city policing overall. Both citizens and police said that they wanted crime prevention and reduction in order to make communities

---

[47]"Mayor Rawlings-Blake Announces She Will Not Run for Reelection," City of Baltimore, Press Release, September 11, 2015.
[48]"Mayor Rawlings-Blake Announces She Will Not Run for Reelection," City of Baltimore, Press Release, September 11, 2015.
[49]Paul Takagi, "A Garrison State in 'Democratic' Society." *Crime and Social Justice*, Vol. 40, Nos. 1-2, (1974): 27-33.

safer. However, at the core of this discussion was the pressing idea that a complete change in society was necessary. This would be the kind of revolution that eradicated racism and elevated humane values. In the meantime—until the revolution came—there were calls for increased police training, mandating that all officers possess a minimum four-year college degree,[50] and expanding prosecutions for officers who shoot and kill citizens indiscriminately. There were also debates about enhanced community policing through mandating Body Worn Cameras (BWC) for officers, using the Restorative Justice Model in police-custody killings, and the truly revolutionary Dismantlement Model.

The national calls for police body worn cameras have suggested that if they are adopted: police misconduct would be reduced, citizens would complain less, trust between police and communities would be enhanced, dollars would be saved from several sources (litigation, settlements, man hours), and officers would be held accountable for their actions. Politicians, citizens and police agencies seemed to believe that these official video documents would "reveal the true story" behind questionable police-encounters and eventually render citizen journalist videos (at least legally) negligible evidence at best. The concerns about police body worn cameras were not entirely about citizens' privacy and their immediate use in the community either. In nearly all major U.S. cities, police have been using the extensive networks of CCTV cameras.[51] We are a society fixated on visual monitoring and ordinary citizens dwell in a participatory culture were recording their public and private existence (lifecasting) and uploading these videos to sites like *Facebook* and *YouTube* is commonplace. However, even these routine public displays of video documentation are very different then when police record citizens in their official capacity.

The main issues surrounding police body worn cameras were related to the many questions about standardized policies and procedures. Journalists, legal analysts, and activists wanted to know how, and under what circumstances, would police cameras be used? Where would police videos be stored (presumably in the Cloud) and by whom? Will police agencies retain all rights to the video data involving

---

[50]See John L. Hudgins, "Require College Degrees for Police," *The Baltimore Sun*, September 30, 2016.
[51]Benjamin J. Gold, "Public Area Surveillance and Police Work: The Impact of CCTV on Police Behaviour and Autonomy." *Journal of Surveillance and Society* 1, No. 2 (January 1, 2003): 191–203.

the general public? Who will have the right and responsibility to upload video from police body cameras? Will law enforcement officers (or others) be able to review and/or edit videos before they are uploaded? Who will have access to the video police officers capture during day-to-day contact with citizens, and for how long? Under what circumstances will video be purged or rendered inaccessible to the public in legal cases? Will police officers have mobile apps for the video they shoot using body cameras, and for what purpose? What state (i.e. Maryland Public Information Act) and federal (i.e. Freedom of Information Act) laws are currently in force and applicable, and what laws need to be discussed, developed, and enacted that will reasonably govern the use of police body-cameras?

Aside from universal police body worn cameras, probably the most controversial methods proposed to improve policing, are the restorative justice and the dismantlement models. In brief, the restorative justice model by definition is focused on "...repairing the harm caused by crime..."[52] rather than the authoritarian law and order system. Restorative justice presumes a heightened community role in the resolution of crime. In general, it has been seen as an instrument of law enforcement, not an application for the failures of law enforcement. Since the emphasis is on the harm done to individuals and communities, restorative justice transcends our traditional views. If this model were adopted, there would have to be a transformation of police-law enforcement culture and philosophy about crime and punishment. It means that police would not be seen as automaton overseers or superior to the community, but would be thought of as equal and integral members of the community. This would eliminate the power imbalance that currently exists, one that focuses on arrest analytics and prosecutions. Since restorative justice models focus on attempting to mend harm done to the communities,[53] police would have to recognize their fallibility beyond the occasional admission of a "bad seed" in egregious cases, engage in direct dialogue with the communities affected, and publically recognize (admit and atone) their criminal responsibility as an offender.

---

[52]Restorative Justice Online, Prison Fellowship International Centre for Justice and Reconciliation, http://www.restorativejustice.org/, accessed July 9, 2015.
[53]Nicholl, Caroline G. *Toolbox for Implementing Restorative Justice and Advancing Community Policing*. Washington, DC: U.S. Department of Justice, Office of Community Oriented Policing Services, 1999, 10.

World To Come: Essays On The Baltimore Uprising, Militant Racism, And History

Far beyond restorative justice, the dismantlement model is the most radical idea. Police dismantlement asserts that because officers are civil servants and work on behalf of the entire community, every aspect of policing—hiring credentials, training, practices, policies, and procedures—must be completely overhauled. This is beyond the standard community civilian review boards that already exist in many police districts. If not utopian, the idea of dismantlement is a revolutionary approach. It seeks to remove the counterfeit policing tactics of officers, topple the age-old embedded code of silence, and shatter the shield that protects criminal police behavior. It is a broad transformative model that assumes a dynamic reconstruction of policing where citizens have direct, sustained, and meaningful input.■

There is a distinctive cultural lens with which to view the police-encounter deaths of blacks that also goes beyond the focus on the apparatus and aegis of systemic racism. While the perception informs the issues of contemporary policing—it is a clarification about how African American people (as diverse as we are) see ourselves, and are seen, in America and within other world societies. At the core this idea rests two opposing decisions—the acceptance of racism and white supremacy and the actualization of African agency. This position encompasses and is expressed briefly through these two selected ideas—the fusion of dysconscious racism and the Black Radical Tradition.[54]

The "dysconscious racism" concept of endowed professor and educational scholar Joyce E. King is the "…uncritical habit of mind (including perceptions, attitudes, assumptions, and beliefs) and justifies inequity and exploitation by accepting the existing order of things as given."[55] In American society, racism and white supremacy exists as accepted inherited social difficulties —, which are thought of as "too big" to end. Using the root of the dysconscious paradigm, black Americans are denied the assertion of racial autonomy, have their ancestral affiliation negated, and are routinely denied genuine rights of nationality. In sum, blacks are treated as citizen aliens. To use Frederick Douglass' summation and critique of the black experience at the 1893 World's Columbian Exposition, African Americans "…are deemed by

---

[54]Reiland Rabaka. *Africana Critical Theory: Reconstruction the Black Radical Tradition, From W.E.B. DuBois and C.L.R. James to Frantz Fanon and Amílcar Cabral.* Lanham, MD: Lexington Books, 2009, 2-10.
[55]Joyce E. King, "Dysconscious Racism: Ideology, Identity, and the Miseducation of Teachers," *The Journal of Negro Education*, Vol. 60, No. 2, Spring, 1991, 133-146, 135.

World To Come: Essays On The Baltimore Uprising, Militant Racism, And History

Americans not within the compass of American law and of American civilization."[56] Ida B. Wells-Barnett, in her documentary protest against the lynching of blacks in 1900, stated that while the country routinely engaged in the "lynching bees" of African Americans, the nation paid compensatory fees for the murders of Chinese and Italian people.[57]

The display of dysconscious racism as a national dilemma reflected the conflict of a people who, recognized themselves as American citizens, and fought and died vigorously for this status. Ultimately, it was the understanding that historically African Americans have been treated as a foreign people, and at times like hostile extraterritorial invaders that somehow prevailed. This is in addition to the reality that we were a conquered people, forced to migrate for the purposes of slave labor, and held in a perpetual condition of servitude. In the United States, that African Americans struggled to be recognized as equal citizens has been consistently and forcefully challenged. However, long after the enslavement of Africans ended in the United States, black people were characterized as a national "question" or more often as a "problem" for society. Blacks have with equal consistency, reasserted their nebulous sense of "Americanness." However, history (without fail) has advised blacks that they were, at best, an uncertain "nation within a nation." There have been numerous examples of the country's declarations surrounding ancestral lineage and black nativity. As noted previously, the Supreme Court's *Dred Scott v. Sandford* (1857) and the *Plessy v. Ferguson* (1896) decisions confirmed that sense of separateness, difference, and asserted black inferiority, while maintaining white supremacy. Over subsequent generations, these ideas would continue to be reinforced through legal and social edicts; but particularly through the polemic public debates over paying reparations to African American people. Blacks must always choose as to whether they will be willing or unwitting partners to racism and white supremacy.

For many African Americans this dialogue was a much larger issue than nationality—it was the historical, racial, cultural, *and* affirmative sense of Pan-African identity, an ascendant awareness of human unity. This assertion of autonomy through the Black Radical

---

[56] Frederick Douglass, "Address by Hon. Frederick Douglass, Delivered in the metropolitan A.M.E. Church, Washington, D.C., Tuesday, January 9th, 1894," Baltimore: Press of Thomas & Evans, 1894, 20.
[57] Ida B. Wells-Barnett, "Lynch Law in America," January, 1900.

WORLD TO COME: ESSAYS ON THE BALTIMORE UPRISING, MILITANT RACISM, AND HISTORY

Tradition, is a "… often-despised, routinely overlooked, and frequently unengaged tradition of radicalism has, and continues to provide viable solutions to many of the problems confronting the contemporary world."[58] The thrust of the Black Radical Tradition is often only publically grasped when racial oppression is most brutal. Reiland Rabaka, professor, author, and founder of Africana Critical Theory, has maintained that the expression is central, and essential, to the liberation of Africans in the diaspora. This means that Africana people have a distinct radical history in the global effort to realize liberation. This tradition has been advanced by key activists, intellectuals, and even organizations.

We have models of this tradition through the lives of blacks like W.E.B. DuBois and Malcolm X and groups like the Black Panther Party; therefore, we can speak of DuBoisian and Shabazzian direct forms of social action and activist philosophical thought as well as a Panther ideology and theory of agency. This regard for national autonomy, the Black Radical Tradition, and institutionalized racial oppression has caused blacks to appeal to world bodies—through the early Pan-African congresses, and the United Nations for international recognition and assistance. Blacks have appealed to the United Nations for more than a half century. In 1947, under the editorial guidance of W.E.B. DuBois, the NAACP submitted "An Appeal to the World: A Statement on the Denial of Human Rights to Minorities in the Case of Citizens of Negro Descent in the United States of America and an Appeal to the United Nations for redress." Malcolm X appealed to the United Nations through the Organization of African Unity (OAU) in 1964.[59] Reflecting their demand for sovereignty, the Black Panther Party, in their "Ten-Point Platform and Program," called for a "United Nations-supervised plebiscite…" in which African Americans would vote on matters central to "their national destiny."[60] Citing police brutality and genocide, the Black Panther Party submitted a signed

---

[58] Reiland Rabaka. *Africana Critical Theory: Reconstruction the Black Radical Tradition, From W.E.B. DuBois and C.L.R. James to Frantz Fanon and Amílcar Cabral.* Lanham, MD: Lexington Books, 2009, 3.
[59] Fritz H. Pointer, "Marxism and Nationalism in Black Revolutionary Movements–U.S.A.," *Ufahamu: A Journal of African Studies*, 2(2), 1971, 41-56, 52.
[60] Philip S. Foner (ed.) *The Black Panthers Speak.* Philadelphia: J. B. Lippincott Company, 1970, 2-4.

petition to the United Nations.[61] Led by Bobby Seale and Huey P. Newton, the petition drew attention to the struggles of African Americans and other oppressed people in the United States,

> The racist planned and unplanned terror suffered by more than 40 millions of black, brown, red and yellow citizens of the United States cannot be regarded solely as a domestic issue. The continuance of these practices threatens the struggle of mankind throughout the world to achieve peace, security and dignity.[62]

In recent history, probably the most significant example of human rights abuses was in the response to Hurricane Katrina—where thousands of predominately-black citizens felt abandoned, displaced, threatened, and exploited. Activists on behalf of the citizens of New Orleans have appealed to the United Nations for human rights protections.[63] Other important examples of issues taken directly to the United Nations include Reparations, historic lynching, the mass incarceration of blacks (as a result of the War on Drugs), the school-to-prison pipeline, and the police-encounter deaths of people of African descent in the United States. African Americans today, as in the days of Douglass, Wells, DuBois and many others over the centuries, affirmed their nationality as a people of African descent, and as world historical people, who like other displaced and abused nations turned to the world for justice. For African Americans this meant that the United States could not have natal citizens who did not have the rights of citizenship. What remains, still, is a nation-within-a-nation, which must constantly battle for the rights of nationality, equality, *and* sovereignty. The Black Lives Matter movement reminded the country and the world, that through their agitational rhetoric, that when it came to the police-encounter deaths of black people, the United States could not have it "both ways." This meant that history informs agency; and agency ensures liberation. ■

---

[61]T. T. B. Koh and William T. Coleman, "United Nations Law on Racial Discrimination," *American Journal of International Law* (1970): 119-130; Philip S. Foner (ed.) *The Black Panthers Speak*. Philadelphia: J. B. Lippincott Company, 1970, 254-255.
[62]Philip S. Foner (ed.) *The Black Panthers Speak*. Philadelphia: J. B. Lippincott Company, 1970, 254-255.
[63]Monique Harden, Nathalie Walker and Kali Akuno, "Racial Discrimination and Ethnic Cleansing in the United States in the Aftermath of Hurricane Katrina: A Report to the United Nations' Committee for the Elimination of Racial Discrimination," November 30, 2007, 10pp.

World To Come: Essays On The Baltimore Uprising, Militant Racism, And History

Black Lives Matter in the New Millennium, where the life and death of Freddie Gray, and innumerable other black men, women, and children reverberates around the world. This movement has a moral-philosophical foundation, as professor Greg Carr noted, an old humanistic idea among blacks: "…once you cross that line of death, particularly with young women and young men, which we've seen (in) this spate of violence…we draw the line and say that's it, we won't take this anymore."[64] Black Lives Matters was the response and it is a worthy freedom movement, one dynamic response to the national crisis in police-encounter deaths. The movement serves to illustrate how the actions of multitudes of people serve to dismantle archaic, unproductive, and destructive thinking. The cries of activists give rise to citizens to speak and act up—to empower those who craft media advocacy and disrupt racism through social media—over ineffective and abusive community policing which routinely involve "patterns or practice of unlawful conduct" in black communities. We are only at the beginning of the Baltimore Uprising story—and why more of us did not see the strange and questionable deaths of countless blacks in the company of police as part of the long history of racial violence and militarization in America. For the exegeses of twenty-first century activism, there is no place for visionless hope or naïve optimism. There is however, an abiding faith in our ancestors, and in their assurances from the past, like that offered by Fredrick Douglass who understood, "Power concedes nothing without a demand. It never did, and it never will." Human life is irreplaceable and it is a right in the world to come.

---

[64]"Dr. Greg Carr Details the History of Abuse and Resistance in Baltimore and America," Interviewed by Ray Baker, *NewsOne Now*, TVOne, May 1, 2015.

Epilogue—The Past Catches All Of Us

> History has thrust something upon me from which I cannot turn away.—The Reverend Dr. Martin Luther King Jr.[1]

Maroons in the Mountains

In the 1990s, I held a joint teaching and administrative position at a large university in a small and rather bucolic mountainous college town. Shortly after my arrival, particularly after having been misidentified on the street as a "messiah" for the black community, among other interesting experiences, I received a curious note in the campus mail. It was brief, threatening, and to the point. It contemptuously depicted African Americans through a crude drawing, insulted blacks as a people, and cryptically warned me not to engage in that "black" business—, which was the basis for my employment (specifically to assist black students, faculty, and the community). It was an intelligible and highly credible threat issued by a well-known white supremacist militia group. I immediately took this message to my supervisor who at the time was a respected executive officer of the university. This person was an absolutely amiable and kind white person who saw no racist threat whatsoever. To this day, I believe that it would not have mattered what evidence I provided to the administrative officer, or the many others who imagined themselves as democratic social liberal progressives or racially benevolent republicans. When I pressed the issue—instead of contacting campus police, city police, or even the FBI—they faithfully consulted the local black oracle, an admittedly overall mischievous individual; and the one person who could always be counted on to confirm and support their view of the world whenever black faculty, staff and students complained about racial discrimination. This was the one person who always saw blackness—including and especially their own—as a flawed human experience. With seasoned political adeptness, the oracle had learned to exert some semblance of influence and authority in the small white town by instilling fear, jubilantly serving as *the* archaic token black, and by pandering to the basest needs of racism and white supremacy. For

---

[1] "Why Rev. M. L. King Is Leaving Montgomery: Leader Says Time Is Ripe to Extend Work in Dixie," *Jet Magazine*, December 17, 1959, 15.

World To Come: Essays On The Baltimore Uprising, Militant Racism, And History

the oracle, the enemy was never historic racism and white supremacy—the enemy was other blacks who did not have the wherewithal to "silently serve and suffer" under its power.

The truth is that it was highly unlikely that either of them would have been successful had they bothered to report this threat. There was no question whether local law enforcement agencies, designed to protect and serve, would have listened to me—such concerns from blacks was not a priority at the time. With that, my enlightened multicultural staff organized themselves and remained vigilant and supportive for years in order to protect our students (and unknown to me at the time, they made a hidden but concerted effort to keep me safe and sane). We had a number of documented and unrecorded experiences including vandalism, graffiti, racial slurs spray-painted on our building, trash routinely dumped at the door, and a host of other collegiate "pranks" (including an periodic orgy of empty beer cans littering the office grounds). To be sure, most of these incidents contained harsh and unmistakable racial overtones. In addition, and while I cannot forensically prove it, my house was shot at in the middle of the night, and I was sprinkled with some very familiar racial epithets. There is no video, no bullet casings recovered, and no audio of the liberal utterances of "nigger bitch" in the green pristine darkness. Nonetheless, I have not slept soundly for years. Those who I depended on for safety chose not to act. They decided to blind themselves, and simply ignored the situation. Still, there were among us, within the small group of blacks who lived and worked in this pastoral college town, an even smaller troupe of negroes—adepts and sycophants of the oracle—who constantly reminded the rest of us that *they* had—at one time or another—received such threats from the self-proclaimed and organized state-based racists—and *they* never complained. Suffice to say, we were maroons in the mountains and some of us preferred to act as if we did not know it. In those days the old Jamaican idiom was true, "Mischiff kum by de poun' an' go by de ownse" (Mischief comes by the pound and goes by the ounce). Within this disturbing atmosphere, I became a different person. I gave up passivism.

A Colleague's Hidden Fear and the Forces of History in an Ahistorical World

Not long after completing the draft of this motley collection of essays, and discussing it with several colleagues, a few of them asked bluntly, "Aren't you afraid?" For some reason the question struck me as odd every time. It never occurred to me to feel fear. The anxiety I

World To Come: Essays On The Baltimore Uprising, Militant Racism, And History

felt in the 1970s police traffic stop was more akin to anger—resentment, shock, and a youthful righteous indignation. However, the absence of fear does not mean one should not be deeply concerned. My colleagues said that given the information available in this technological day and age, and the polemic racial spotlight on the extralegal killings of blacks—that writing or saying anything publically (including on Facebook, Twitter, etc.) about law enforcement—even about members who proudly defile the badge—will have repercussions. They believed *any criticism* of the American police system that could be remotely construed as less than complimentary might cause a person serious—even life threatening—peril.

Then there was the one old friend, albeit the odd man out, but a professional colleague with keen insight, who often peered at me over large round glasses—and alluded to an even greater conspiracy. Kofi Ogungbende (an alias) was not given to traditional conspiracy theories (i.e. The Illuminati, The Philadelphia Experiment, Extraterrestrials, and the Birthers) so I listened. He said that it didn't make sense—nothing involving the police-encounter killings of blacks possessed any intelligible logic. He noted the numbers of black people killed, the frequency with which they are killed, the use of excessive or deadly force in nearly every single case, the lack of reliable data even on the federal level, the habitual clearing of officers involved in the majority of the cases, and the collective liaise faire attitude about taking black lives. As Kofi talked, a picture formed in my head; one so insidious that even with all of the evidence before us—it had not crossed my mind before. He had considered that perhaps it wasn't about individual police officers (the "bad apples" theory)—or even the traditional policing culture of American law enforcement, or their unions. Kofi surmised the existence of clandestine extralegal police agencies (secret police) feeding a consistent kill order—either directly or stealthily to police officers in external support organizations, ancillary officer associations, para-military groups, para-police, and even planting the insipient blue seed in associated police youth groups and summer camps.

For a time Kofi speculated about the operational ease for such an endeavor (cross-agency connections, inter-personal get-togethers, police training camps and educational centers, media and periodicals, the incestuously racist nature of police hiring); and how simple it would be to limit or exclude blacks altogether. For my friend and sometimes frenetic colleague it all made perfect sense. Before and after the turn of the century 1900, untold numbers of blacks were lynched in the United States with law enforcement disregard or cooperation *and* public approval and participation; and since the 1950s the incidence of black extralegal killings in the south has yielded recent federal, scholarly and popular interest in Civil Rights cold cases and the preponderance of lynching.[2] An original definition of lynching was that it was the act of forcibly taking a person from legal custody for the purposes of public murder. In addition, had they not called the Ku Klux Klan (KKK) the "invisible empire" for a reason? In our not so distant history that surreptitious terrorist organization was filled with state public servants, police, ex-soldiers, militants, and even government supporters and sympathizers. Kofi was trying hard to convince me of the gruesome possibility of something akin to but more sinister than this, perhaps a more formal group, but my research didn't reveal any such clandestine organization today.

Then I remembered reading an article by journalist Rubén Rosario. Rosario reported on a racial discrimination lawsuit that had been filed by black police officers in Minneapolis Minnesota. The officers claimed that from the early 1990s they had been subjected to unrelenting racist attacks on the job, and their lives had been threatened. It appeared that all levels of authority had dismissed, rationalized, or otherwise ignored the officers' complaints, and this even included side attacks on Rep. Keith Ellison (D-MI). Rosario indicated that at the crux of the issue was the Twin Cities chapter of a Chicago-based motorcycle club called City Heat. Some members of the police force belonged to the biker group and spent some of their off-duty time engaged in club activities. According to Rosario, the group and others like the Iron Brotherhood and the Blue Knights, represented "…just one of an increasing number of off-duty law-enforcement motorcycle clubs (LEMCs) sprouting across the country

---

[2] See Rachel Pollack, "Cold Case Justice." *Syracuse University Magazine* 25, No. 3 (2008): 19-23; Renee C. Romano, *Racial Reckoning: Prosecuting America's Civil Rights Murders*. Harvard University Press, 2014; Barbara A. Schwabauer, "Emmett Till Unsolved Civil Rights Crime Act: The Cold Case of Racism in the Criminal Justice System," *Ohio St. LJ* 71 (2010): 653; and Mark C. Simpson, *In Search of Justice: Examining Efforts to Obtain Convictions in Unsolved Civil Rights Era Murders in Mississippi*. iUniverse, 2006; in the television medium see also Keith Beauchamp, Executive Producer and Host, Investigation Discovery (ID) (television series), *The Injustice Files* (2013).

World To Come: Essays On The Baltimore Uprising, Militant Racism, And History

and blurring the lines…"[3] There was a correlation between some of the clubs racist icons and those used to terrorize the black cops.[4]

We grappled with the logic and the logistics of the implications of this idea. Racist thought was prevalent but it still did not explain what Kofi cautiously alluded to. Of course he reminded me that such a group would be subversive for a reason. But you didn't need a dedicated secret group or even a handful of devoted organizations. All you needed was a pervasive, persistent, and embedded racist ideology capable of being renewed—like The Ouroboros[5]—by its own history. So, Kofi again insisted, invoking the collective, "are *we* not afraid?" … and then astutely added "how much evidence do *we* need?" Kofi never feared anything, but if he had anything more to tell me he kept it to himself. Now I think he was troubled at that moment—like everyone truly concerned about black lives and the trajectory of all humanity. However, we as a people are already in jeopardy. We have been for a very long time. Our cultural legacy—the Africana tradition—teaches us to be more afraid of not doing what needs to be done. This was so for the many people who gave their lives for our freedom—men like Marcus Garvey, Martin Luther King, Jr., Malcolm X, Kwame Toure, an endless recitation of ancestral names. There were so many heroes inside of the old men and women who prayed at the church of my youth, people who would say with deep-down humility, courage and conviction, "Dey (there) is work to be done." There was enormous valor in the work, the struggle, and deeds of so many heroines like Harriet Tubman, Ida B. Wells-Barnett, Fannie Lou Hamer, and Audre Lorde. Still, there are many names we could add here—but we know that the list is vast. In the black world experience, how many people paused within their defining moment—and then did it anyway.

They did so because activism, philosophy, intellectuality, and historicity converged. But without the latter, historicity—our sense of the actuality of past events—nothing that we do has any real meaning. It is doubtful that we can achieve anything honest at all. Notwithstanding the local and national rhetoric supporting historical preservation advocacy and education—*Americans constantly hide from history*. So what also caused me great concern was the realization (some time ago) that it

---

[3] Rubén Rosario, "Rubén Rosario: Then Blue Line Appears Blurred In Biker Clubs," *TwinCities.com Pioneer Press*, January 11, 2009.
[4] Rubén Rosario, "Rubén Rosario: Cop's off-duty Club Questioned in Lawsuit," *TwinCities.com Pioneer Press*, January 11, 2009.
[5] The mythological symbol of the snake eating its own tail forever.

had, almost under the radar, become fashionable—a mark of pseudo-intellectual elevation —to degrade, ridicule and dismiss the formal study of history. It seemed more than coincidental that the rise of the internet and the nation's ultra-privileging of STEM in education were concomitant to the decline of historical studies. What created a sense of trepidation in me was the knowledge that inside of the current issues that deeply touch our lives, we seem completely oblivious to the genuine (yet concerted) demise of the study of history. I tremble for ahistorical students; and people who cannot think critically for themselves. I am concerned about those who do not ask analytical questions; those who choose "hate mob" discourse, over respectful divergent exchange. We are always mindful of those who choose cruelty, bullying, manipulation, and oppression over justice, fairness and peace. The *absolute importance of the study of history* seems to have faded into the recesses of our national consciousness; and history as a foundational knowledge concept has been relegated to truncated conversations over whether public schoolteachers *should* impart "difficult" or "traumatic" histories mostly involving people of color (i.e. slavery, colonialism, imperialism, and holocaust)—histories which challenge the uncritical and arrogant valorization of western civilization. These are queries that are never asked of historic white-on-white humanity crimes (should we dispense with the teaching of warfare and slavery in ancient Greece and Rome?). While the mere quest for historical knowledge is stealthily being removed from the masses, it remains readily available inside of the elite educational hollows of future world leaders. They know that history is like air and water; too often we fail to observe how important it is to know and appreciate. This is true for those who value the power of an historical consciousness. Those who truly understand the facets of history know that it is the elegant and at times profoundly flawed memory of all humanity. They know that this memory, among other necessary intellectual commitments, is instructive for living, growing, moving, thinking—the act of definitively consciously being. Only the passionately ignorant—no matter how ingenious they are perceived to be—eschew the importance and function of history. Ordinary leaders might sheepishly declare to the public "let us not dwell on the past" for political expediency. However, great leaders operate with a formidable understanding of history. It has been said many times that if you do not know what happened yesterday, you cannot possibly understand the present—and you certainly cannot gain a credible glimpse into a future of your own making. Collectively, Black lives represent one of the

WORLD TO COME: ESSAYS ON THE BALTIMORE UPRISING, MILITANT RACISM, AND HISTORY

greatest histories ever chronicled. In order to gauge its importance and longevity among the masses, persistent structural racism constantly tests our knowledge, understanding, *and* appreciation of the past. Historian Lerone Bennett, Jr. said it differently, "history does not forgive those who lose their way."[6]

On Research and the Upwelling of Souls

Research of any kind involves an incredibly intimate relationship with a wide range of information. Spending time with research material asks initially for only one outcome—that we learn something meaningful—gain valuable knowledge. I was particularly affected by some of the revelations that emerged from this research. Because we are compelled to look critically at the issue of hostile police-encounters, we are surrounded by needless death. At times, the work was a sad and desolate endeavor. At the same time, it was also an obsessively empowering pursuit. The exploration was passionately and curiously energizing, laden with important knowledge and information. Every issue encompassing questionable police-custody deaths pointed to some aspect of the institutional failures of a culturally diverse and multiracial society operating under static racial aggression. The work also exposed a number of opportunities for critical dialogues about improving human relations and systems. These possibilities ultimately involve our ability to conceptualize new worlds, a greater sense of humanness, and to act humanely. The material in this manuscript laid bare some thought-provoking insights: 1) the *upwelling of police-encounter deaths;* 2) the cursory study of rudimentary *military philosophy*; 3) understanding the nature of *public comment in cyberspace;* 4) the *militant racial defiance to President Obama*; and 5) the *unrelenting display of hope* in the city of Baltimore.

While preparing this manuscript, one of the most disconcerting aspects was in researching the public information on police-encounter shootings, there was the ever-increasing preponderance of black mortality. First, consider this analogy: oceanographers have a term to describe how cold water moves from the ocean's depths to the top. As the wind pushes the warm water along the surface, this allows for the continuous rise of deep cold water from the bottom. This hypnotic

---

[6]Lerone Bennett, Jr., *The Challenge of Blackness*, Chicago: Johnson Publishing Company, 1972.

process is known as upwelling. It seemed that every fatal police-encounter reviewed revealed the existence of another incident, a veritable upwelling of corpses. This is not to mention the emergence of new (through the end of 2015) police-custody death cases of ordinary citizens—and the attempt of law enforcement agencies across the country to effectively manage public disclosers of these deaths (especially the suppression of videos). Because of the Freddie Gray case, the death of African Americans was the center focus for a diverse group of local and national activists. Within months of the Baltimore Uprising, police organizations became hypersensitive to the overwhelming numbers of in-custody deaths questioned by the community, government leaders, and prominent organizations such as the NAACP, the ACLU, and Amnesty International. Police agencies immediately secured public information and moderated open communication. More often than not, citizens who questioned the police were reminded that they "didn't have all the facts," and were cautioned not to rush to judgement, even though the facts were largely controlled by internal police administrations or through city government. By the end of April 2015, there were thousands of documented police-encounter death cases, and seemingly hundreds of incidents being actively examined by the Department of Justice, and by concerned citizens across the nation. This research selected only a small number of these cases (150) for review. It was no less disheartening to continuously uncover the police shootings of black citizens that were underreported, deracinated, and/or did not make any of the innumerable blogs and cyber lists. It is also important to note that deracinating the cases (purposely excluding the race of the victim) in the media (on the part of police agencies and news outlets) meant less condemnation and scrutiny of police actions within the context of the burgeoning Black Lives Matter movement.

    We know that America's popular embrace of and desensitivity to violence is nothing new. Mainstream film, television, literature, video games, and news programs rely heavily on violent content ostensively to capture and hold the attention of the robotic consuming masses—people who must be constantly traumatized into engagement. However, there is nothing more chilling than reading volumes of historical military reports and scholarly articles on the philosophy and strategy of killing, and of the tactical operations involved in urban (foreign and domestic) warfare. Many erudite military scholars can be found casually

World To Come: Essays On The Baltimore Uprising, Militant Racism, And History

discussing, not only "sweeping" (killing) tactics,[7] but also why they think it is necessary to target non-combative civilians. In response to this, Americans have convinced themselves that race, more precisely, is not real—it is an anthropomorphized beast. That this relatively benign monster hides, and only rears its ugly head when people talk about it. Simply put, if we learn not to talk about racism, then it will simply go away. However, this stubborn and dangerous naiveté has never been the true nature of racism. Racism exists and insinuates itself into the lives of the masses of people every day, whether we choose to talk about it or not. Americans have gone to great lengths to convince themselves that racism does not really exist, except in the minds of blacks, Latinos, Native Americans, and Asians, that they must go deep into the psyche of racism in order to find its lair. When law enforcement agencies want to deal with pressing racial issues among their ranks they usually hire psychologists and criminal justice trainers. These experts may test for racial bias, generally through the administration of a survey, or more popularly, they use online game simulation. When it is found that overwhelmingly police officers have been preprogrammed to target, employ aggression, and/or use deadly force primarily against nonwhite people, everyone is amazed. Mostly at how the experts found racial bias in their collective consciousness, rather than how it got there in the first place; or by plainly admitting that it had always been there. When race, gender, ethnicity, or religion (when factored as negative social determinants) is bound to bias, violence, and a militaristic code of conduct—it produces an ideological concoction that is easily exploited to eliminate people. This represents the philosophical groundwork for genocide.

It was disconcerting, though not unexpected, to see the increasing visceral nature and volume of random public blogs and comments (including remarks posted to digital newspaper articles as well as through social media). However, based on the content accessed through 2015, the material that was transmitted by high school students during the Baltimore Uprising should never have been regarded as credible threats against the city or state. Yet cyber meanness and random condemnation abounds; and some believe that the online "hate

---

[7] The term *sweep/sweeping* in generic military parlance is used to describe basic maneuvers designed *to uncover*. It can specifically mean *the discovery* of surveillance devices or other material. Generally, the term refers to the process of physically inspecting inhabitants and/or terrain—*to search*. However, sweeping in its punitive form, means *to remove or kill people*.

mob" mentality is just one aspect of a communal pessimism born of youth culture poised to embrace a dystopic future. If this is true, and America is a nation of cynics and narcissists, the youth are merely adroit students in this regard. The public comment process should freely allow for vigorous political speech *and* angry rants that are neither an anomaly or unconstitutional. Yet I was struck by the intensity of cyberbullying within the "look at me" media culture, and the comfort with which hate speech is spewed, tolerated and defended. This is said to be a hallmark of social media engagement and the fuel of online fandom—individual commentators self-possessed in the issuance of scatological diatribes and threats veiled or otherwise.

 One example included Reddit's[8] 2015 battle over "…overt racist subreddits mired in hate speech."[9] Nearly 70 million people use Reddit every month. Some racist communities on Reddit found the site ideal—not just for sharing their hateful, bigoted and stereotypic racial thoughts with like-minded readers—but because some of these groups (r/niggers) existed solely for the purpose of enraging the groups they targeted. This included harassment, and name calling. The situation became so serious that the site was forced to address the racist material by updating its content policy in August 2015—effectively quarantining and banning some Reddit communities that deliver racist speech. In another example, it was reported that Mayor Rawlings-Blake was doused with a cup of water at an OneBaltimore public event at the Mondawmin Mall on July 12, 2015, more than two months after the Baltimore Uprising. The most telling aspect of the incident was that it was widely circulated as news, and for the public comments that were generated. If news outlets did indeed believe that a cup of water thrown in the face of the mayor was news worthy, the question should have been *why*—given all of the complexities of the Baltimore Uprising— why was it news; and why did she not have increased personal security? *Fox Nation*, among other news outlets, posted the water-throwing incident and hosted public remarks that included many racist comments and statements that could only be interpreted as death

---

[8]An online social networking bulletin board.
[9]Jason Mick, "Editorial: Reddit Allows Itself to be Hijacked as a hate platform or Racist Bigots," *Daily Tech*, July 21, 2015, http://www.dailytech.com/Editorial+Reddit+ Allows+Itself+to+be+Hijacked+as+a+Hate+Platform+For+Racist+Bigots/article37 446.htm, accessed August 2, 2015.

threats.[10] Yet most of these kinds of public comments were unmediated, had semi- or unrestricted comment periods, and provided for a certain amount of screen anonymity. Even so there is considerable power (and high quality content) in the digital spaces afforded by social media. The online, often pseudonymous, comment process fosters an expansive exchange of ideas, along with the opportunity to publicly condemn anyone for anything. Fortunately, critical thinkers and reflective readers decide the worth and value of these ideas.

Race, as racism, is a mind-blowing western concept that never ceases to be a dynamic challenge. Racism is completely abhorrent, and at the same time, is the embodiment of an incredibly curious social creation. Racism is *the* defining feature in the history of the robust development of global empire. While the fundamental nature and power of the concept does not change, it is only how we choose to interpret and react to it that is mutable. Much of the public discussion (directly or indirectly) related to the Baltimore Uprising, and the issue of militant racism, reflected extreme racial perceptions about the election (and reelection) of President Obama. There was a clearly articulated militant racial insurgency, largely expressed in the idea of "taking the country back." This notion of redemption would be an important theme in the 2016 presidential election campaign. President Obama's election and term as the American commander-in-chief demonstrated—far beyond the associative labels of neocon, leftist, progressive, neo-Nazi, liberal, rightwing, or white supremacist—that there has been a seething disdain that a black man (irrespective of his biracial antecedents) held the highest office in the land. From the beginning, in 2008 there were racialized fears seemingly hidden in the idea of protecting the Second Amendment to the Constitution. Gun sales (along with applications, licenses, background checks, and gun company stock) rose sharply one week after he was elected president in 2008; and again in 2012. The broad online discussion was that gun sales represented intense (white) panic that President Obama would ban or at the very least significantly restrict gun ownership.[11] This was a surface concern, one that barely hid embedded fears of blackness.

---

[10]See Amy Yensi, "Bystander Throws Water on Baltimore Mayor Stephanie Rawlings-Blake," CBS Baltimore, July 12, 2015, http://nation.foxnews.com/2015/07/12/bystander-throws-water-baltimore-mayor-stephanie-rawlings-blake, accessed August 2, 2015.
[11]Kevin Bohn, "Gun Sales Surge After Obama's Election," *CNN News*, November 11, 2008, http://www.cnn.com/2008/CRIME/11/11/obama.gun.sales/, accessed June 7,

WORLD TO COME: ESSAYS ON THE BALTIMORE UPRISING, MILITANT RACISM, AND HISTORY

However, the subtext included anxiety over crime and the coded messages persistently connecting the image of a black face to the threat of crime. I would have to write another, different book, about this and certainly, there are a number of scholarly works encompassing this thought[12]—but the idea that all of the ills of the country—If not white western civilization—can be placed at the feet of America's first black President is very real. These caustic attitudes transcend our labels and euphemisms about who is simply racially biased in this country. Unmediated public comments in the vast realm of cyberspace were particularly critical of the President each time he made any kind of constructive statement—no matter how benign—related to race, racism and race relations. There was extensive public critique when his comments were more specific to African Americans being killed in law enforcement-encounters, i.e. about Trayvon Martin, Michael Brown, Freddie Gray and events like the Ferguson and Baltimore Uprisings, etc. One commentator surmised in 2009, in support of Obama, that "This type of madness did not and would not have happened under the last president."[13] Even the First Lady, Michelle Obama, who used the President's two terms to improve the lives of children, advocated for better health and nutrition, and made appeals for human rights, literally could not been seen in public without cyber racist and sexist trolls attacking nothing more than her very existence as a black woman. We should make no mistake that there are angry and embittered voices in this land; people who deeply believe in old-fashioned racial subjugation. They cherish and vigorously uphold the negative racial stereotypes and views of African Americans (and all black people for that matter) and

---

2009; Perry Chiaramonte, "Gun Sales Explode as Election Looms," *FoxNews.com*, http://www.foxnews.com/us/2012/03/22/gun-sales-off-to-bang-for-election-year/, accessed June 7, 2009.

[12]See Tim Wise, *Between Barack and a hard place: Racism and white denial in the age of Obama*. City Lights Books, 2013; Kristin A. Lane, John T. Jost, Gregory S. Parks, and Matthew W. Hughey, "Black Man in the White House: Ideology and Implicit Racial Bias in the Age of Obama." *The Obamas and a (post) Racial America* (2011): 48-69; Wingfield, Adia Harvey, and Joe R. Feagin. *Yes We Can?: White Racial Framing And The Obama Presidency*. Routledge, 2013; Lopez, Ian Haney. *Dog Whistle Politics: How Coded Racial Appeals Have Reinvented Racism And Wrecked The Middle Class*. Oxford University Press, 2013; and Unnever, James D., and Shaun L. Gabbidon. *A Theory Of African American Offending: Race, Racism, And Crime*. Taylor & Francis, 2011.

[13]"Pres. Carter: Racism Plays Role In Opposition to Obama," CNN Newsroom, Tony Harris, http://newsroom.blogs.cnn.com/2009/09/16/pres-carter-racism-plays-role-in-opposition-to-obama/, Comments by K E Dyson, September 16, 2009, accessed October 12, 2015.

no amount of evidence to the contrary or moral suasion will convince them otherwise.■

Hope for the residents of black Baltimore has always been transformed into concerted action. Long before the Baltimore Uprising appeared and then subsided, the Leaders of a Beautiful Struggle (LBS) had been in the forefront of a new black activism in the city. LBS succinctly informed everyone that they were "...a grassroots think-tank which advances the public policy interest of Black people, in Baltimore, through: youth leadership development, political advocacy, and autonomous intellectual innovation."[14] By 2015 their board of directors included Adam J. Jackson, Dayvon Love, Lawrence Grandpre, Deverick Murray, and (Lady) Brion Gill. They represent a uniquely courageous collective of college graduates, artists, social justice advocates, intellectuals—and foremost black activists in the city of Baltimore. There was no mainstream news outlet that could rival the reporting and commentary fueled by activists like the LBS. While their info-streams on the internet and through social media included a wealth of local and national issues and events, they were among the first to independently report on the protest movements in the city. They used Twitter to keep thousands of people informed about the Baltimore Uprising, and the issue of police misconduct, including the legal disposition of the Baltimore 6. They were also astute in analyzing the battles between the police and the citizens which they knew began on the city's streets and continued in the courtroom.

The LBS was singularly critical of how the city and the police shaped the idea that the *activists were always the problem*, and thus they had to thwart the protests of citizens. The LBS condemned the city's initial response to the death of Freddie Gray, which was to brace for violence from black people, in addition to attempting to curtail peaceful protests. While the LBS was not alone in their scrutiny of Baltimore's police operations, they observed that too often it seemed that the police have policies that may or may not be fully communicated to, or even followed by, the officers. Once again, confirming the idea that they are above the law and everyone else is below it. Moreover, they knew that the pending trials of the Baltimore 6 and the legal labyrinth that would follow (their trials were scheduled from November 2015 through June 2016) would last for months, perhaps even more than a year. Many

---

[14]Leaders of a Beautiful Struggle (LBS) website, http://lbsbaltimore.com/ accessed May 8 and December 11, 2015.

World To Come: Essays On The Baltimore Uprising, Militant Racism, And History

believed that the justice system through the courts would run its course—and that whatever verdicts were delivered, the rulings would reflect the will of the people. The trials of the Baltimore 6 were postponed. LBS held out little hope that there would be convictions for the Baltimore 6 or actual justice for Freddie Gray and citizens of Baltimore. They were young, but they knew history. They studied history. They had been here before. For the Leaders of a Beautiful Struggle, like so many activists everywhere, what remained was the work of the brilliant movement, that great auspicious social justice and human rights legacy of black people.

    Baltimoreans have a tremendous amount of hope for the future of city and its citizens. Though many would assert that it was unrealized, Mayor Rawlings-Blake's message from 2013 was important because so many still shared this lofty vision for the city of Baltimore: "…we have the power to create the future that we want for Baltimore's families. We have the power to overcome the difficulties of economic and budget pressures…Our charge is to grow Baltimore, to rebuild a thriving city where more families choose to live–a place where children find educational opportunity, where neighbors live in safety without abandoned blight, and where businesses make new investments, creating jobs for our people."[15] But this was more than traditional political rhetoric, it was also a vision born of a generation who experienced great hopes and dreams—people who were raised to believe in infinite possibilities for the future, rather than dire austere limitations. However, two years later as the vision languished and the drama of the 2015 Baltimore Uprising unfolded, one of the first themes was that the anger people felt—about policing, city administration, housing, education, jobs—was born out of an intense love and pride for the city. The peaceful protests in the city encompassed this idea. The emblematic signs of marchers spoke to a deep affection for Baltimore, and included the messages "Baltimore Rising Out of the Flames," "Bmore United," "I love my city! Bmore" and "We Love our City." Many of the signs that people carried expressed unity, such as "One Baltimore" and "We are One Baltimore." Citizens also carried those messages reminiscent of the 1960s counter culture protests, "Peace," "Keep Loving Keep Fighting," "Make Love not Hate," and "No Violent Actions, Be Peaceful." As the protest signs indicated

---

[15]"The Mayor's State of the City Address," *Journal City Council of Baltimore*, Second Councilmanic Year—Session of 2011-2016, February 11, 2013, 976.

World To Come: Essays On The Baltimore Uprising, Militant Racism, And History

Baltimoreans, especially younger generations, are neither completely jaded, nor are they a deluded people. They temper their solid filiality and affection for the city with an equally strong candor about justice. Academics tend to call this skill *constructive criticism*. For Baltimoreans it is the ability to tell truths without the entrepreneurial "spin."

Baltimore photographer Glenford Nunez summed up a familiar personal feeling of love toward the city as well as his critique of the media during Baltimore's uprising. He told *Al Jazeera America*, "Baltimore is grungy, raw, dangerous and in denial, but there is no place like home. I have traveled all over, and still there is no place like Baltimore."[16] Many of Nunez' iconic photographs captured the realities of Baltimore's Penn and North area—ground zero for the Baltimore Uprising. He observed the media manipulations, including: "…how the media will skip over an educated person who is making sense in order to speak to a seemingly uneducated person who is talking crazy. The media tailor their story to fit the narrative that they want to tell, not what is really happening."[17] In addition, author, activist and university lecturer D. Watkins lambasted the variety of Baltimore Uprising "opportunists," those who emerged camera-ready for "…the circus of cable news reporters…" the people that flocked to the scene to be seen. Watkins determined that truth and genuine economic opportunity could save Baltimore. Watkins stated: "The solution is simple. Stop selling the illusion of social mobility to people in neighborhoods with schools and conditions that prohibit growth; abandon the greed by sharing the wealth and opportunity—watch the murders stop and lose the fears of future unrest."[18] Watkins' idea echoed the sentiments of many Baltimoreans, people who were tired of grand promises and lofty development plans, those who had witnessed (many times) the political sleight of hand. A better future for the city of Baltimore, the optimism and goodwill expressed by the people, rests on deep-rooted ideas of truth, inclusion, universal equality, respect for humanity and justice.

---

[16]"Life After Michael Brown and Freddie Gray," *Al Jazeera America*, August 3, 2015, Produced by Lam Thuy Vo, Edited by Danielle Zalcman, Vaughn Wallace, Lam Thuy Vo, and Jayati Vora, August 3, 2015, http://projects.aljazeera.com/2015/07/ferguson-baltimore-echosight/, accessed November 3, 2015.
[17]Ibid; this included truncating educated persons. Baltimore resident Kenneth Jackson's May 1, 2015 *Fox News* interview was heavily edited to craft a city-in-chaos narrative.
[18]D. Watkins, "Opportunity Quells Unrest: To Avoid Another Uprising, Baltimore Needs To Give Its Residents Real Prospects For Success," *The Baltimore Sun*, September 13, 2015.

World To Come: Essays On The Baltimore Uprising, Militant Racism, And History

A Movement Reborn, or the Past Catches all of Us

Profound changes can take place in the world and some of these changes are fueled by movements—powerful human forces for social transformation. Depending on the objective, movements can fill us with awe and dread. However, we gain valuable knowledge about the changes they can produce by assessing a good measure of history. There were specific domestic events fostered by human (and to some extent natural) power that I in no way thought to witness in my lifetime. These events included the exploitation of fears and the fanaticism over Y2K,[19] the September 11, 2001 terrorist attack, and the immediate transformation of the United States national security infrastructure. This also included in 2005 Hurricane Katrina in the Gulf Coast; the bitter experience of thousands of American people who were in crisis. Citizens in the historic city of New Orleans, Louisiana sustained governmental negligence and local abuse at a time when they needed the most help. In addition, others surely more astute, but I would have never predicted the election of the first African American president of the United States in 2008; or in that same year that we would experience a global economic crisis. Nor could I foresee that state and federal agencies would condemn and remove the Confederate Battle Flag from many public sites in 2015. Given the longstanding embargo against Cuba, other than those in the political inner circle, who predicted that the United States' would officially recognize Cuba and in doing so prove the nation's former leader Fidel Castro correct when he said sixty-two years ago "history will absolve me."[20] We see that like the past, the present is full of surprises. Of course these two latter events of 2015 might have been eclipsed altogether by the highly anticipated and controversial six-day visit (September 22-27) of the first Latin American Pope, Francis. He was the first sitting Catholic pontiff to address the United States Congress. During his world wind tour, Pope Francis canonized the 18th century Spanish Franciscan monk, Junipero Serra (1713-1784). And it is here, as I close, in the archaic

---

[19] The "year 2000" (or 2001), the turn of the millennium, which included a host of mass media fueled fears, including but not limited to, concerns that financial markets and other systems which rely on computers would immediately malfunction and crash and significantly disrupt (or even destroy) society.
[20] Fidel Castro's 1953 speech about the meaning of the Cuban revolution was translated and appeared in Benjamin Keen's *Latin American Civilization: History and Society, 1492 to the Present,* Boulder, CO: Westview Press, 1986, 364-370.

WORLD TO COME: ESSAYS ON THE BALTIMORE UPRISING, MILITANT RACISM, AND HISTORY

narrative of colonization that we find the prevailing paradox of racial history in contemporary society.

Serra, who founded the mission system in California in the mid to late 1700s, was part of the wave of Spanish conquistadors and missionary monks who came to colonize the Americas. Serra has been praised for his criticisms of the colonial military, and condemnation of the local governors of the Spanish Crown. He has also been cited for overseeing the aggressive conversion of the indigenous Indian people to Christianity. Conversely, Serra has been denounced for his role in the much less discussed history of Native American genocide, and the exploitation, enslavement and displacement of Indian peoples. Critics called the whole canonization affair "Serra-gate," as vandals decapitated the granite statue of Serra at the Monterey California Presidio in October 2015. Months later, the Stanford University faculty senate approved a resolution for new policies which would oversee the removal of Serra's name from campus buildings.[21] Though this was troublesome for some, there were strange mixed-messages to the world community. This included Pope Frances' unprecedented apology for the crimes associated with European colonization. However, this apology was coupled with the contemporaneous need to uphold, preserve, and celebrate colonization, enslavement, and the other vestiges of imperial conquest. In ways oblivious to supporters of Serra's legacy, the act of canonization justified dehumanizing indigenous nations in particular, and denied the world-altering outcomes of colonization. Within this current context, the crisis of police-encounter deaths was prescient in the black community—absolutely stunning. But seemingly (like Native American genocide), not of paramount importance to world society at large. Still, the national spotlight surrounding the police-custody deaths of African American citizens demanded that people seriously discuss the history of the issue. In the current conversation we began intense public debates about the terms racism, white supremacy, mass incarceration, and the police-state— concepts which are usually avoided in the national discussion. Though, at the same time, as in Serra-gate, the fervent justifications for the police-encounter killings of blacks mounted—and seemed to have no

---

[21]"ASSU Resolution In Support Of Reaffirming Stanford's Commitment To Indigenous And Native American Community, Identity, Dignity, And Space," Meeting Of The Forty-Eight Senate Of The Academic Council, Stanford University Faculty Senate, Meeting Agenda, March 3, 2016.

end. This means that even the most heartfelt admission of past wrongdoing, in the midst of continuing crimes against humanity, unfortunately does little more than negate the apology—and, in many ways, defends historical misdeeds as well as present-day cruelties.

While it is true that we cannot change the past, we can alter the future. Within the important events and concerns surrounding black lives lay a profound philosophical and intellectual foundation to our social movement. The motives and aims of this powerful movement are clear—black lives matter—yet it is certain that portions of the population remain oblivious to the historical moment. Those who think deeply about, and endeavor to understand history within the context of constructive social change also tend to be a part of worthwhile movements. And this effort involves the people of the world. We are witness to the incredible energy emanating from courageous activists—spanning all generations—in the quest for social justice and human rights, especially when trying to fathom events like the Baltimore Uprising. The seasoned as well as the up-and-coming activists of today, as Black Lives Matter, or under another perceptive banner, are involved in a highly capable yet often leaderless (i.e. resistant to singular charismatic personas) network. At the same time, modern activism is seriously committed to multiple and inter-organizational alliances. Activists are creative and expressive about the art and science of civil disobedience—not in an effort to destroy society, but to improve humanity. Today, everyone is a #hashtag away from being a cause unto him or herself—and sometimes becomes a catalyst that galvanizes people from around the globe. This means that the world to come is of our own making—and continues to exist in our determined ability to define, defend and work together for positive change. This is the kind of movement that compels everyone to do something just and good. We have a responsibility to "speak truth to life."[22]

---

[22] The quote is from former judge DeWayne Charleston over the death of Sandra Bland in Waller County Texas. Charleston was interviewed by Amy Goodman, *Democracy Now*, aired July 27, 2015.

APPENDICES

Appendix A: Timeline of the 2015 Baltimore Uprising—327

Appendix B: Baltimore Uprising Protest Signs—343

Appendix C: A Compendium of African Americans Who Died In Police-Encounters, 1994—2015—349

Appendix D: Grand Jury Charges Against The Baltimore 6 In The Death Of Freddie Gray, May 21, 2015—391

Appendix E: Domestic Riot/Civil Disobedience and Protest Events Related To Race In The United States, 1863—2015—393

World To Come: Essays On The Baltimore Uprising, Militant Racism, And History

Appendix A: Timeline Of The 2015 Baltimore Uprising[1]

SUNDAY, APRIL 12, 2015
- Twenty-five-year old Baltimore resident Freddie Gray attempted to run when he made eye contact with police officers. He was chased, subdued and arrested for possessing an illegal knife. The arrest was videotaped by Kevin Moore and others.

MONDAY, APRIL 13, 2015
- The Baltimore City Police department held a news conference about the arrest of Freddie Gray and defended the actions of the six police officers involved.

THURSDAY, APRIL 16, 2015
- The U.S. Department of Justice held a community forum on police brutality at Coppin State University in Baltimore, Maryland.

SATURDAY, APRIL 18, 2015
- The first major protest over the arrest of Freddie Gray was held. Hundreds of people converged on the Western District police station, put their hands up in the air, and turned their backs to police officers.
- Baltimore resident Dawan Hawkins was shot five times by Baltimore City Police during the Freddie Gray protests. Police said that he was armed and shot at them. Hawkins said he was unarmed.

SUNDAY, APRIL 19, 2015
- Freddie Gray was pronounced dead at the hospital at 7 a.m. As protests resumed, the Gray family released a statement: "His take-down and arrest without probable cause occurred under a police video camera, which taped everything including the police dragging and throwing Freddie into a police vehicle while he screamed in pain."

MONDAY, APRIL 20, 2015
- At a news conference, Baltimore officials announced that six police officers involved in Gray's arrest were suspended (with pay) but that they denied using excessive force during arrest.

TUESDAY, APRIL 21, 2015
- Baltimore City Council President Bernard C. "Jack" Young requested that Governor Larry Hogan have the Maryland Attorney General "…conduct an independent investigation into the events surrounding the death of Mr. Gray." ■At the request of Maryland senators and congressmen, The U.S. Department of Justice announced a federal civil

---

[1] The state of Maryland established the period of the Baltimore Uprising from April 25-May 1, 2016 in the governor's request for federal assistance from FEMA.

World To Come: Essays On The Baltimore Uprising, Militant Racism, And History

rights investigation into Gray's death. ▪Protests in the city continued. Baltimore Police Commissioner Anthony Batts remarked that the protests had been peaceful, noting: "I think that they're sharing their thoughts, they're sharing their concerns, and I hear them and I understand."

WEDNESDAY, APRIL 22, 2015

▪Protests continued outside of the police station. ▪The United States Senate held hearings on the use and implementation of Police Body Worn Cameras.

THURSDAY, APRIL 23, 2015

▪Protests persisted, and there was a march to Baltimore's City Hall.
▪Maryland Governor Hogan deployed the state police to Baltimore as protests grew. At least two protesters were arrested in the afternoon.

FRIDAY, APRIL 24, 2015

▪Approximately 200 Paul Laurence Dunbar High School students staged a sit-in to protest budget cuts and the loss of teachers and classes. ▪City officials held a news conference, and Police Commissioner Batts acknowledged that the officers should have given Gray care sooner (instead of waiting more than 40 minutes after his arrest for medical assistance to arrive): "We know our police employees failed to get him medical attention in a timely manner multiple times." Batts also stated that Gray was not wearing a seat belt while he was transported. ▪Baltimore Mayor Stephanie Rawlings-Blake met with protesters earlier in the day over their concerns and in anticipation of more demonstrations the next day. ▪Religious leaders met with Mayor Rawlings-Blake about how to address the mounting community protests over the death of Freddie Gray. The ministers also called for reforms of the BCPD.

SATURDAY, APRIL 25, 2015

▪More than 1,000 people gathered for a protest march toward Baltimore's City Hall. ▪Police stated they arrested 12 people and suffered minor injuries, from "pockets of individuals causing disturbances," after rocks were thrown and windows smashed near Camden Yards.

SUNDAY, APRIL 26, 2015

▪Freddie Gray's wake was held. Inside the coffin there was a pillow embossed with his picture and a quotation that read, "Peace, Y'all."
▪Baltimore City Council President Bernard C. "Jack" Young issued an "Appeal for Peace" after disruptions of peaceful protests took place.
▪Baltimore's faith-based community leaders, along with the office of the mayor, issued a formal "Call for Peace."

WORLD TO COME: ESSAYS ON THE BALTIMORE UPRISING, MILITANT RACISM, AND HISTORY

MONDAY, APRIL 27, 2015

■Freddie Gray's funeral was held. Mourners at New Shiloh Baptist Church jammed into a second-floor balcony, which prompted the church to open an overflow room with a live feed of the funeral. ■Official reports circulated that local gangs—the Bloods, Crips, and The Black Guerilla Family (BGF)—had formed an alliance to kill BCPD officers; also, a planned local high school "purge" activity was leaked and police mobilized on the streets of Baltimore. ■In the afternoon and into the night police clashed with protesters; Baltimore exploded into violence. Cars were set on fire, cinder blocks were thrown at police, and stores were looted across the city. ■Baltimore police began posting Tweets informing the community that officers were being attacked with bricks, bottles and rocks. ■With no access to public transportation, school youth congregated and encountered police in the Mondawmin Mall area. ■Coppin State University student leaders Shaquille Carbon, Damien Poole, and Khadijah Butler were among the peaceful protesters assailed by police. Carbon, CSU SGA President was maced severely by police "…from head to toe." ■The CVS pharmacy closed, and was later entered. Looting took place at the CVS and smoke engulfed the store. ■Camden Yards, home field of the Baltimore Orioles, consulted with the BCPD, closed its gates, and cancelled the scheduled game. ■Governor Hogan cancelled his scheduled events. ■Governor Hogan declared a state of emergency. The state police and the National Guard were called in. ■At a press conference, Baltimore Mayor Rawlings-Blake announced that a citywide, nightly curfew would be imposed starting Tuesday from 10 p.m. to 5 a.m. It would be in effect for one week. ■The Maryland State Police announced that up to 5,000 law enforcement officials were requested from the mid-Atlantic region to help quell the violence in Baltimore. ■One of the first Baltimore residents arrested in the Baltimore Uprising was Branden Owens. Owens, not a protestor, was en route to Mondawmin Mall to buy groceries. When he asked police what was happening, he was hit with a baton. Owens demanded the officer's badge number, and was told that it was "666." Owens was beaten, arrested, and transported to Central Booking, and held for two days without charges.

TUESDAY, APRIL 28, 2015

■Public schools closed. Some universities modified their hours of operation. ■Baltimore state and federal offices were closed or administrative leave was instituted. ■The Baltimore Branch of the NAACP held a press conference on complaints of racial profiling and police abuse; and announces a new satellite office in Freddie Gray's West Baltimore Neighborhood. ■President Barack Obama spoke on the events taking place in Baltimore[2] during a press conference (a meeting in support of the TPP [Trans-Pacific Partnership]) with the Japanese Prime Minister, Shinzo Abe. ■Mayor Rawlings-Blake announced a weeklong citywide curfew beginning at 10 o'clock each night until 5 o'clock the following morning.

WEDNESDAY, APRIL 29, 2015

■Police said their initial report on Gray's death would not be released publicly to protect the integrity of the inquiry but would be handed over to the state's attorney for Baltimore, Marilyn Mosby. ■Dozens of people who were arrested during the week's unrest were released because police were unable to complete paperwork. ■*The Washington Post* published a story that stated another prisoner in the van with Freddie Gray told police that Gray might have been trying to harm himself. *WBAL* of Baltimore reported that the medical evidence available did not indicate that Gray was able to harm himself while in police-custody. ■Protests began in several cities nationwide, including Denver, San Diego and New York City.

THURSDAY, APRIL 30, 2015

■Baltimore police department completed their internal investigation and submitted their investigative report to the Baltimore City State's Attorney. ■Kevin Moore, one of the citizens who videotaped Freddie Gray's arrest, was arrested by Baltimore police and released within hours. ■Police Commissioner Batts said the police investigation of Gray's death has been given to the state's attorney. He praised and thanked Baltimoreans for observing the curfew peacefully but said it will remain in place through the following weekend. ■Donte Allen, the second man in the police van with Freddie Gray, told *WBAL* "…all I heard was a little banging for like four seconds…" from the other side of the barrier separating them on April 12. His account differed from the one attributed to him in the *Washington Post* report. ■Nationwide rallies continued, with notable protests in Baltimore, Philadelphia and Cincinnati. ■Reverend Al Sharpton's National Action Network hosted a community summit at New Shiloh Baptist Church. In addition to Sharpton, the summit was led by Mayor Rawlings-Blake. Other leaders in attendance included: Cornell Williams Brooks (NAACP), Marc

---

[2]"President on the Situation in Baltimore," Whitehouse.gov, http://t.co/T3t6ptxmaZ, April 28, 2015, accessed May 19, 2015.

World To Come: Essays On The Baltimore Uprising, Militant Racism, And History

Morial (National Urban League), and Kevin Lyles (Media/Music Executive). ■The University of Maryland School of Law (with the College of Arts and Humanities, and the Center for Synergy) and the Greater Baltimore Cultural Alliance held a "Think-a-Thon," discussions addressing the issues in the city emanating from the Baltimore Uprising.

FRIDAY, MAY 1, 2015

■Baltimore City State's Attorney Marilyn Mosby held a press conference and announced that criminal charges would be filed against 6 BCPD officers. Gray's death was ruled a homicide. The charges included second-degree murder, manslaughter, assault, and misconduct. She also said that the switchblade knife that police found on Gray was not a switchblade but a type of knife legal under Maryland law. ■ Governor Hogan announced the "Maryland Unites" program effort "...to provide assistance, food, and donations to those directly affected by the week's events." ■The ATF announced they would give up to $10,000 for information about riot related fires. They also announced the establishment of an anonymous website for uploading fire videos. ■The Baltimore FOP created a *GoFundMe* page (with a fundraising goal of $600,000) for the 6 police officers charged in the death of Freddie Gray. In less than an hour, and after having received $1,135.00, the site was suspended.

SATURDAY, MAY 2, 2015

■A major protest at the War Memorial Plaza took place. Baltimore activist Kwame Rose led a crowd to the CVS at Pennsylvania and North Avenue. Rose spoke to the crowd encouraging peaceful protests, black unity, and for self-determination in the black community. He led the chant "Take back Baltimore."

SUNDAY, MAY 3, 2015

■Baltimore Mayor Rawlings-Blake cancelled the citywide curfew.

TUESDAY, MAY 5, 2015

■The Baltimore City Council, led by its President Bernard C. "Jack" Young, requested that the Department of Justice open a civil rights investigation into the Baltimore City Police Department.

WEDNESDAY, MAY 6, 2015

■Maryland Governor Hogan rescinded the state of emergency and dismissed all troops. ■Baltimore Mayor Rawlings-Blake requested a federal civil rights investigation into policing practices (in addition to the Justice department's preceding probe into whether Gray's civil rights were violated). She also announced that by the end of the year police would have body worn cameras.

World To Come: Essays On The Baltimore Uprising, Militant Racism, And History

THURSDAY, MAY 7, 2015
- Baltimore city Mayor Rawlings-Blake announced a new initiative, #OneBaltimore, a "Public-private partnership will focus on short term recovery and deeper systemic change."

FRIDAY, MAY 8, 2015
- Attorney General Loretta Lynch announced that the U.S. Justice Department would open an investigation into the Baltimore City Police Department.
- The lawyers for the Baltimore 6 filed a motion in Baltimore district court to dismiss the case and requested that Mosby recuse herself.

SATURDAY, MAY 9, 2015
- Mothers for Justice United led a Millions Moms March at the U.S. Department of Justice to protest police brutality and the law enforcement shootings of African Americans.

SUNDAY, MAY 10, 2015
- Prince's *Rally 4 Peace* Concert at the Royal Farms Arena in Baltimore took place.

MONDAY, MAY 18, 2015
- President Obama announced the White House Police Data Initiative (part of the recommendations from the Task Force on 21st Century Policing, launched December, 2014)

THURSDAY, MAY 21, 2015
- The Grand Jury indicted the Baltimore 6 (which included original and revised charges) in the death of Freddie Gray. The most extensive charges were against Officer Caesar Goodson. In addition to Second-degree depraved heart murder, he was charged with six other criminal violations. All of the officers were charged with reckless endangerment.
- Maryland Governor Hogan requested that FEMA declare the state a major disaster area as a result of the Baltimore Uprising.

WEDNESDAY, MAY 26, 2015
- The city of Cleveland announced an agreement with the Department of Justice that held the city's police department to a consent decree which would strongly reform police conduct.

SATURDAY, MAY 30, 2015
- Former Maryland Governor, Martin O'Malley announced his bid for President of the United States at Federal Hill Park in Baltimore, MD.
- The Black and Missing Foundation held its third annual Hope Without Boundaries Walk/Run at the National Harbor in Baltimore to call attention to missing people of color and their families.

World To Come: Essays On The Baltimore Uprising, Militant Racism, And History

TUESDAY, JUNE 2, 2015
■Senator Barbara Boxer introduced bill S. 1476 into the U.S. Senate, "To require States to report to the Attorney General certain information regarding shooting incidents involving law enforcement officers, and for other purposes." This was known as the "Police Reporting Information, Data, and Evidence Act of 2015" and the "PRIDE Act."

WEDNESDAY, JUNE 3, 2015
■Police Commissioner Anthony Batts held a press conference, which linked the rise in the city's murders to the looting of pharmacies during the uprising.

SUNDAY, JUNE 7, 2015
■Keith Davis, Jr. was shot twice (once in the face) by BCPD. Police maintained that Davis robbed an unlicensed cab driver; Davis said he was in a group at the scene of a hit-and-run accident when officers confronted him with a hail of gunfire. The case is considered one of the first highly contested police shootings in the city of Baltimore since the arrest of Freddie Gray. Davis was arrested and charged.

FRIDAY, JUNE 12, 2015
■FEMA rejected the state of Maryland's request to be designated a major disaster site as a result of the Baltimore Uprising.

THURSDAY, JUNE 25, 2015
■Representative James E. Clyburn (D-SC) Introduced House Resolution 344 "Urging the discontinued use of the Confederate battle flag, which represents pain, humiliation, torture, and racial oppression, in remembrance of the Emanuel 9." The bill urges the banning of the display of the Confederate Flag in public, state, and federal facilities.

THURSDAY, JUNE 30, 2015
■Baltimore activist and scholar Dr. Marvin L. "Doc" Cheatham and the Matthew A. Henson Neighborhood Association called for the Robert E. Lee and Stonewall Jackson Monuments to be taken down.

TUESDAY, JULY 7, 2015
■Police Commissioner Batts called for an independent review of the Baltimore Uprising to be conducted by the Police Executive Research Forum (PERF). ■Congressman Elijah Cummings, Mayor Stephanie Rawlings-Blake, and the Obama Administration announce the creation of a solar energy and employment training initiative for the city of Baltimore.

World To Come: Essays On The Baltimore Uprising, Militant Racism, And History

WEDNESDAY, JULY 8, 2015
■The Baltimore City Fraternal Order of Police released its "After Action Review," a "Review of the Management of the 2015 Baltimore Riots." ■Mayor Rawlings Blake fired police commissioner Anthony Batts and immediately appointed deputy-police commissioner Kevin Davis to the post as an interim promotion.

TUESDAY, JULY 11-15, 2015
■The 106th annual NAACP Convention was held in Philadelphia, PA. The theme was "Pursuing Liberty In the Face of Injustice."

SUNDAY, JULY 12, 2015
■Mayor Rawlings-Blake and Police Commissioner Davis announced the creation of an interagency "War Room" to address the issue of crime in Baltimore.

THURSDAY, JULY 16, 2015
■President Obama became the first sitting president of the United States to visit a federal correctional facility—El Reno Correctional Institution near Oklahoma City. The visit was intended to highlight the injustices in the American criminal justice system.

MONDAY, JULY 27, 2015
■*The Baltimore Sun* reported that the city released more than 7,000 emails and other documents related to the Baltimore Uprising.

THURSDAY, JULY 30, 2015
■Governor Hogan announced the immediate closing of the Baltimore Detention Center.

SUNDAY, AUGUST 2, 2015
■Federal agents from the FBI, DEA, ATF, the U.S. Marshall and the Secret Service began a two month assignment inside of the Baltimore homicide unit. The federal support came to assist the police in addressing the rise of homicides and the resolution of cold cases.

MONDAY, AUGUST 3, 2015
■*Al Jazeera America* published "Life After Michael Brown and Freddie Gray," highlighting the interactive/integrated images and interviews with resident photographers of Ferguson, Missouri (Michael Thomas) and Baltimore, Maryland (Glenford Nunez).

WEDNESDAY, SEPTEMBER 2, 2015
■The first of two pretrial hearings was held in the Freddie Gray case. The hearing determined that the Baltimore 6 would be tried for the charges levied, and that they could be tried separately.

World To Come: Essays On The Baltimore Uprising, Militant Racism, And History

THURSDAY, SEPTEMBER 3, 2015
■Surf City, N.C. Police Chief M. Halstead issued, using his personal Facebook page, a statement that called Black Lives Matters protesters "terrorists." Halstead was immediately forced to retire.

MONDAY, SEPTEMBER 7, 2015
■The City of Baltimore announced that on September 2, it agreed to pay the family of Freddie Gray $6.4 million dollars in a civil settlement.

WEDNESDAY, SEPTEMBER 9, 2015
■The second of two pretrial hearings was held in the Freddie Gray case. The hearing determined that the venue of the trial would be the city of Baltimore. ■Former tennis champion James Blake stated that he was subjected to an excessive force arrest in New York City. He was mistaken for a suspect in a credit card fraud investigation. The arrest of Blake was videotaped. Blake vowed to use his public status to speak out against the use of excessive force by police.

FRIDAY, SEPTEMBER 11, 2015
■Mayor Rawlings-Blake announced she would not seek a second term as mayor of the city of Baltimore.

WEDNESDAY, SEPTEMBER 16—20, 2015
■The 45th Congressional Black Caucus (CBC) Annual Legislative Conference was held in Washington, D.C. with the theme: "Liberty and Justice for All."

FRIDAY, SEPTEMBER 18, 2015
■Governor Hogan published an online op-ed piece in the *Baltimore Sun* pledging his commitment to focus on improving the challenges faced by the city of Baltimore.

TUESDAY, SEPTEMBER 22, 2015
■In Texas, the Prairie View City Council voted to retain the "Sandra Bland Parkway" road. The street, formally known as University Parkway, was renamed in honor of Bland who died in a jail cell after being arrested during a routine traffic stop. It was the road on which she was arrested.

SATURDAY, OCTOBER 10, 2015
■The "Justice or Else" rally was held at the National Mall in Washington, D.C. The event was held in commemoration of the 20th anniversary of the Million Man March. One of the main platforms of the rally was the police-encounter deaths of African Americans.

TUESDAY, OCTOBER 13, 2015
■Judge Barry Williams ruled that statements made by police officer William G. Porter and Sgt. Alicia D. White (two of six officers charged in the death of Freddie Gray) would be admissible in their pending

trials. White's legal counsel maintained that her legal rights were violated when she was questioned by the BCPD.

WEDNESDAY, OCTOBER 14, 2015

■Baltimore activists (including the Baltimore Uprising Coalition) against interim police Commissioner Kevin Davis becoming permanent in the position, staged an overnight sit-in at City Hall. Out of the larger group, police arrested sixteen protesters Thursday morning and charged them with trespassing. Access to and security at city hall was increased.

SATURDAY, OCTOBER 24, 2015

■The "Rise Up October" rally was held in New York City to protest police brutality in the United States. Thousands attended the three-day event (October 22-24, 2015) that culminated in the Saturday march, and included at least a dozen arrests. The event, initiated by Cornell West and Carl Dix (along with Quentin Tarantino, Eve Ensler, Michael Rappaport and others), was endorsed by activists, scholars, journalists, celebrities, and families who suffered the consequences of police violence. Rally speakers included Kadiatou Diallo (mother of Amadou Diallo) and journalist Chris Hedges.

SUNDAY, OCTOBER 25, 2015

■Councilman Nick Mosby officially announced his plan to run for mayor of the city of Baltimore.

MONDAY, OCTOBER 26, 2015

■In a press conference, the Baltimore City Police Department announced that 155 officers (mostly volunteers) will begin testing body-worn cameras in a two-month (54-day) pilot program (prior to awarding a fulfillment contract to a vender).[3] Policies and procedures for the use of the body worn cameras were drafted but not made available at the press conference. For the pilot program, police were instructed, "when in doubt record it." However, citizens can ask not to be recorded. Within two years, the BCPD expected that all officers would be equipped with body-worn cameras.

MONDAY, NOVEMBER 2, 2015

■President Obama made remarks on "Criminal Justice Reform" at the Rutgers University Center for Law and Justice in Newark, New Jersey. (In the fall of 2015 the president gave several talks on criminal justice reform, including one in his weekly address, October 21, 2015)

---

[3]Baltimore Police, Press Conference, "BPD Announces Body Camera Pilot Program," October 26, 2015.

WORLD TO COME: ESSAYS ON THE BALTIMORE UPRISING, MILITANT RACISM, AND HISTORY

THURSDAY, NOVEMBER 5, 2015

▪In support of other police unions nationwide, The Baltimore Police Union announced that they would boycott Filmmaker Quentin Tarantino's new film "The Hateful Eight," because of brief comments he made at the October 24, 2015 "Rise Up October" rally held in New York City to protest police brutality in the United States.

MONDAY, NOVEMBER 9, 2015

▪President Tim Wolfe and Chancellor R. Bowen Loftin of the University of Missouri resigned their positions after student protests over racism at the institution. The next day racist death threats were issued on the social media app Yik Yak. Two University of Missouri students were arrested for making online threats against black people. The student behind the threat was charged with taking a terrorist threat. On Thursday, African American alumni, former civil rights attorney, and administrator of UM, Michael Middleton, was immediately appointed interim president. By the end of the week head football coach, Gary Pinkel (who publically supported the athletes in the student protests) resigned for medical reasons. The events at University of Missouri sparked protests from African Americans students at other universities across the nation including Yale University; and other anonymous threats were issued against blacks, including one which targeted Howard University in Washington, D.C.

FRIDAY, NOVEMBER 13, 2015

▪3 males, self-identified white supremacists, were arrested by the FBI and charged with planning a terrorist attack on African American churches and Jewish Synagogues.

SATURDAY, NOVEMBER 14, 2015

▪The city of Baltimore reached a homicide rate of 300—the highest since 1999.

MONDAY, NOVEMBER 16, 2015

▪The Police Executive Research Forum (PERF) released a report, "Lessons Learned from the 2015 Civil Unrest in Baltimore." The report examined law enforcement's role in the Baltimore Uprising from April 25 to May 3. It is called the first independent analysis of the event.

TUESDAY, NOVEMBER 17, 2015

▪Black students at Princeton University launched a protest and occupation of the President's office challenging racism at the institution and demanding that a building that honors President Woodrow Wilson be renamed. After the president and students reached an agreement, an anonymous bomb threat was issued via email citing student protests;

WORLD TO COME: ESSAYS ON THE BALTIMORE UPRISING, MILITANT RACISM, AND HISTORY

■A death threat was issued against blacks at Kean University in New Jersey. The anonymous Twitter threat came from @keanuagainstblk. Students at Kean had mounted protests over issues of racism and in support of the students at the University of Missouri. The threat was proven to be false, initiated by one of the protesters at the University.

WEDNESDAY, NOVEMBER 18, 2015

■Major protests were conducted by black students at colleges and universities (including Purdue, Emory, Yale, Harvard, Princeton, UC-Berkley, Tufts, Stanford and many other institutions of higher education) across the United States under the banner the Black Liberation Collective's #studentblackout.

THURSDAY, NOVEMBER 19, 2015

■Portraits of black Harvard law school professors were defaced. The university deemed the act a hate crime.

MONDAY, NOVEMBER 23, 2014

■Black Lives Matter protesters, demonstrating over the shooting of Jamar Clark in Minneapolis, were assaulted by three white males who open fired on the group. 5 people sustained injuries from the shooting attack. Police purportedly used mace and berated protesters. The shooters, allegedly white supremacists, were arrested.

TUESDAY, NOVEMBER 24, 2015

■Western Washington University cancelled classes over a violent racist threat made against an African American female student (student body president, Belina Seare). Tyson Campbell (19-years-old) was arrested and later allowed to post a $10,000 bond. The threat was made on Yik Yak, an anonymous social media site.

MONDAY, NOVEMBER 30, 2015

■The Trials of the Baltimore 6. The trial of Officer William G. Porter began.

TUESDAY, DECEMBER 8, 2015

■The FBI announced that it would expand its data collection on police-custody death encounters beyond shootings. Their reformed data base would also include other ways people die at the hands of police; and this information would be immediately provided to the public.

THURSDAY, DECEMBER 10, 2015

■Baltimore City Council Resolution 15-250R, introduced in August by Nick Mosby, would move the Baltimore City Police Academy to the Campus of Coppin State University, located in West Baltimore.

FRIDAY, DECEMBER 11, 2015

■In a victory for the "Say Her Name" Campaign of the Black Lives Matter movement, former police officer Daniel Holtzclaw was found

World To Come: Essays On The Baltimore Uprising, Militant Racism, And History

guilty of sexually assaulting 8 of 13 black women in the Oklahoma City area. It was the first high profile serial rape case involving police and African American women. ■MSNBC aired a special report, "All In—Back to Baltimore," hosted by Chris Hayes, and featured commentary on the Baltimore Uprising by Kweisi Mfume, D. Watkins, and Sherrilyn Ifill.

MONDAY, DECEMBER 14, 2015

■Baltimore City and Baltimore County schools issued urgent communications to staff, parents and the community in anticipation of civil unrest pending the verdict in the trial of Officer William Porter.[4] ■ The National Endowment for the Humanities (NEH) awarded a $225,000.00 grant to the University of Maryland College of Arts and Humanities and the Maryland Humanities Council, to present a public program series, entitled, "Baltimore Stories: Narratives and the Life of an American City."

WEDNESDAY, DECEMBER 16, 2015

■When the jury could not reach a verdict in the case of William G. Porter on Tuesday December 15, 2015, judge Barry Williams ordered continued deliberations. The trial ended in a hung jury, and Judge Williams declared a mistrial. A retrial for Officer Porter was scheduled for June 13, 2016.

THURSDAY, DECEMBER 17, 2015

■The New Orleans City Council voted to remove monuments erected to the Confederacy.

WEDNESDAY, DECEMBER 23, 2015

■Black Lives Matter protestors attempting to draw attention to the police shooting of Jamar Clark, shut down the Minneapolis Mall of the Americas, the largest shopping mall in the United States.

SUNDAY, DECEMBER 31, 2015

■The city of Baltimore ended the year with 344 homicides.

TUESDAY, JANUARY 5, 2016

■Governor Hogan and Mayor Rawlings-Blake announced a $700 million dollar redevelopment plan for West Baltimore. Part of the plan includes demolishing approximately 4,000 vacant housing units and relocating residents. Questions and condemnations were swift on social

---

[4]Baltimore City Schools, Gregory E. Thornton, Chief Executive Officer, Letter to Parents, Families and Community Members, December 14, 2015; and Baltimore County Public Schools Emergent Bulletin, Vol. IV, No. 5, Cancellation/Postponement of BCPS activities/Events, December 14, 2015.

media, Adam J. Jackson CEO of LBS surmised, "…the goal is gentrification, displacement and divestment in the people of the community."[5]

WEDNESDAY, JANUARY 6, 2016

■ The Trials of the Baltimore 6. The trial of Officer Caesar Goodson (the police van driver) began. The trial (jury selection) was moved to January 11, 2016; and then postponed by the Court Of Special Appeals, in part because of Officer Porter's refusal to testify in Goodson's case.

THURSDAY, JANUARY 14, 2016

■ The Delaware House of Representatives passed a bill (with one abstention) HJR 10, "Apologizing for the Wrongs of Slavery and Expressing Delaware's Profound Regret for Its Role in Slavery." The bill passed in the Senate on January 21, 2016; and was introduced by Representative Stephanie T. Bolden.

MONDAY, JANUARY 18, 2016

■ The Reverend Dr. S. Todd Yeary (of the Maryland NAACP) led a group of activists to the Annapolis Legislature to protest for law enforcement reforms.

WEDNESDAY, JANUARY 20, 2016

■ Black Lives Matters protestors (lead by April Goggins), during the remarks of Baltimore Mayor Stephanie Rawlings-Blake, interrupted the U.S. Conference of Mayors meeting held in Washington, D.C. ■ Dr. Zackery Berger, a Johns Hopkins University physician was handcuffed and searched (but not arrested) on his way to a North Baltimore CVS pharmacy. Dr. Berger said that he was stopped by Baltimore City Police for no reason; the police stopped Dr. Berger for allegedly talking to, or receiving a pill bottle from a man on the street.

MONDAY, JANUARY 25, 2016

■ The Trials of the Baltimore 6. The trial of Sergeant Alicia White was scheduled to begin. White's trial was pushed to February 8, 2016.

MONDAY, FEBRUARY 1, 2016

■ Martin O'Malley ended his campaign for President of the United States.

---

[5] Adam J. Jackson, [SmartBlackMan], (2016, Jan 5). Retrieved from https://twitter.com/SmartBlackMan/status/

World To Come: Essays On The Baltimore Uprising, Militant Racism, And History

WEDNESDAY, FEBRUARY 3, 2016

■DeRay McKesson, 30-year-old local and national community Black Lives Matter movement activist and organizer, officially declared his intention to run for mayor of the city of Baltimore.[6]

SATURDAY, FEBRUARY 6, 2016

■Beyoncé released the music video for her song *Formation*, called a homage to New Orleans Louisiana, Hurricane Katrina, ahead of her halftime show performance at Super Bowl 50. Less than a week later (Friday, February 10, 2015) Beyoncé announced plans to perform at Baltimore's M&T Bank Stadium on her summer *Formation* tour. ■Imani Perry, a professor of African American Studies at Princeton University, was arrested for a "…single parking ticket (issued) three years ago…"[7] She contextualized her experience within the police-encounter narrative targeting black people in the United States.

MONDAY, FEBRUARY 8, 2015

■23-year-old Black Lives Matter activist Marshawn McCarrell was found dead with a gunshot wound to the head on the steps of the Ohio Statehouse. Because of his Facebook and Twitter feeds, his death was presumed a suicide by police.

TUESDAY, FEBRUARY 9, 2016

■The Trials of the Baltimore 6. The trial of Officer Garrett Miller was scheduled to begin; his trial was pushed to March 7, 2016. ■The Maryland legislature upheld a bill (by vetoing Governor Hogan) extending voting rights to ex-felons.

WEDNESDAY, FEBRUARY 10, 2016

■The U.S. Department of Justice filed a lawsuit against the city of Ferguson, Missouri, citing a pattern and practice of unlawful police conduct. The government found in 2015, racial discrimination and civil rights violations, promulgated by the death of Michael Brown.

---

[6]By February 3, 2016, in addition to DeRay McKesson, declarations for the Baltimore mayor's race included: Cindy Walsh, Gersham Cupid, Richard Black, Mack Clifton, Sheila Dixon, Elizabeth Embry, Mike Maraziti, Connor Meek, Nick Mosby, Collins Ottona, Catherine E. Pugh, Carl Stokes, David Warnock, Calvin Allen Young, Patrick Gutierrez, Alan Walden, Brian Charles Vaeth, Joshua Harris, Emanuel McCray, and David Marriott.
[7]Imani Perry, Twitter, (@imaniperry) February 7, 2016.

World To Come: Essays On The Baltimore Uprising, Militant Racism, And History

FRIDAY, FEBRUARY 12, 2016
■Baltimore City Police Commissioner Kevin Davis announced a plan to reform the police department, called "Duty to Intervene." The objectives include, among the ideas proposed (i.e. History of Baltimore seminar, "Pizza and a Precinct"), a policy effort to target police officers whose excessive force against citizens.

THURSDAY, FEBRUARY 18, 2016
■The Maryland Court of Appeals delayed the trials of the Baltimore 6 because of the dispute over the admission of Officer William Porter's testimony. ■President Barack Obama met with a diverse inter-generational group of civil rights activists and leaders at the White House. The group discussed the issue of criminal justice and policing. One of the leaders in the Black Lives Matter movement declined the invitation citing that it would represent little more than a photo opportunity.

MONDAY, FEBRUARY 22, 2016
■The Trials of the Baltimore 6. The trial of Officer Edward Nero was scheduled to begin.

WEDNESDAY, FEBRUARY 24, 2016
■President Obama selected Carla D. Hayden as a nominee for the next Librarian of Congress. Dr. Hayden is the CEO of the Enoch Pratt Free Library in Baltimore, MD.

SATURDAY, FEBRUARY 27, 2016
■In Oakland, California, the National Victims of Police Terror held panels of parents across the nation whose children were killed in police-encounters. The event was part of a birthday memorial celebration for Oscar Grant, killed by Bay Area Rapid Transit Police in January 2009.

TUESDAY, MARCH 8, 2015
■The Maryland Court of Appeals ruled that Officer Porter is compelled to testify in the Baltimore 6 trials.

WEDNESDAY, MARCH 9, 2016
■The Trials of the Baltimore 6. The trial of Lieutenant Brian Rice was scheduled to begin.

TUESDAY, APRIL 26, 2016
■The primaries for Baltimore city offices, including the mayoral election.

WEDNESDAY, APRIL 27, 2016
■The first anniversary of the Baltimore Uprising.

World To Come: Essays On The Baltimore Uprising, Militant Racism, And History

Appendix B: Baltimore Uprising Protest Signs[1]

1. Abolish the Police
2. Aiyanna was 7! Black Girls Matter[2]
3. All Black Lives Matter
4. All Night All Day We're Gonna fight for Freddie Gray
5. Am I Next?
6. Are you helping? Or are you hurting?
7. Arrest, Prosecute & Jail Cops Guilty of Police Brutality

8. Baltimore Rising Out of the Flames
9. BCPD You're in for a rough ride
10. Being Black is not a crime
11. #Blackgirlsmatter
12. #Blacklivesmatter
13. #Blacklivesmatter #JusticeforFreddieGray
14. Black Lives Matter
15. Black lives matter more than Property
16. Black Lives Matter More than White Supremacy
17. Black Power
18. Black Power! Stop Police Brutality
19. Black Rage is Political
20. Black Youth are not Thugs
21. Bmore United
22. By any means necessary

23. Cincy Stands with Baltimore
24. Class Warfare Kills
25. Community control of Police Now!
26. Cops are people too indict them

27. D.C. Cops Out of Baltimore!
28. Don't Forget Freddie Gray

29. End Police Terror! Racism is the Disease, Revolution is the Cure!
30. End Police Terror!
31. End Police Brutality

---

[1] Protest signs used in the Baltimore Uprising and in Freddie Gray protests across the nation, April/May 2015.
[2] Refers to the death of 7-year-old Aiyanna Jones in her home, while she slept by Detroit police 2010.

World To Come: Essays On The Baltimore Uprising, Militant Racism, And History

32. End Police Killings of black lives now
33. End Systemic Racism
34. End Racism Now
35. End Racist Police Violence
36. End the Curfew
37. End the Police state Justice for Freddie Gray
38. End the War on Black + Brown Lives + Livelihoods
39. Equal
40. Equal Opportunity And Human Dignity

41. Ferguson, Missouri Standing in Solidarity with Baltimore!
42. Fight Another Day!
43. Freddie Didn't Die In Vain, Civil Rights Today
44. Freddie Gray (with Photograph)
45. Freddie Gray, (Akai) Gurley, Trayvon Martin, Ramarley Graham, Sean Bell and too many others...
46. Freddie Gray We Love You
47. Fund State Schools Not a Police State

48. Get Up Stand Up For Your Rights Don't Give Up The Fight!!![3]
49. Go Home!
50. Government and mayor want to sweep another murder under the rug we want justice

51. Hands Up, Don't Shoot
52. Honk for Justice
53. Human Rights

54. I am A Man
55. I am not a Threat
56. I can't Breathe
57. I'd Love a Job. Got One?
58. I do not mourn broken windows. I mourn broken necks
59. I love my city! Bmore
60. I Will not be silent
61. If all loves matter then why are black lives taken so easily?
62. Imperial War Abroad = Racist Repression at Home

---

[3] From Bob Marley and Peter Tosh's (The Wailers) 1973 Reggae anthem, "Get Up, Stand Up."

World To Come: Essays On The Baltimore Uprising, Militant Racism, And History

63. Indict Killer Cops
64. Indict the System
65. "Injustice Anywhere is a threat to Justice Everywhere"[4]
66. Is Life a White Privilege?
67. Is my life worth more than theirs?
68. It's Time for Good Cops to do something about bad cops

69. Jail Killer Police
70. Jobs & Education Not Youth Jails!
71. Justice
72. Justice 4 Black Lives
73. Justice for All
74. Justice for Black Men
75. Justice For Freddie Gray
76. Justice for Freddie Gray Indict and Jail Killer Cops Now!
77. Justice for Freddie Gray, Walter Scott, Eric Garner, Michael Brown, Akai No Justice, No Peace
78. Justice Through Solidarity

79. Keep Loving Keep Fighting
80. Kill Racism not Me
81. Killer Cops in cell blocks

82. Let Me Guess He Feared for His Life Too?!?! Unacceptable!!!
83. Let's Bring Back Black Wallstreet
84. Love has no color say no to racism

85. Make Love Not Hate
86. Marilyn Mosby for Mayor
87. My 2 white nephews have white privilege in USA my 3 black nephews are Freddie Gray!!!

88. Nice Day for a Revolution
89. No good cops in a racist system
90. No Justice for Gray Brown Garner Grant Nieto Zambrano-Montes[5] No Peace

---

[4] Quote on protest poster attributed to Martin Luther King, Jr.
[5] 35-year-old Antonio Zambrano-Montes was the Mexican immigrant killed by police in Pasco, Washington on February 10, 2015 for throwing rocks at the police.

World To Come: Essays On The Baltimore Uprising, Militant Racism, And History

91. No Justice, No Peace, No Racist Police
92. No Violent Actions, Be Peaceful

93. Oink Oink Bang Bang Every day the same old Thing
94. One Baltimore
95. Our city Our Lives Our Freedom
96. Our inalienable rights to: life liberty and the pursuit of happiness should never be subject to the whim of law enforcement

97. Peace
98. Police Brutality
99. Police Brutality is a systematic problem
100. Preach peace to the Police Black Lives Matter
101. Psalms 59 O God, save me from my enemies. Protect me from these who have come to destroy me. Preserve me from these criminals, these murderers…

102. Racism is a Disease
103. #Rebel
104. Reparations Now
105. Respect for All
106. Respect Human Rights
107. Rights not Fights
108. R.I.P. Freddie Gray

109. Say No to Racism Justice Now!
110. Shut Down Baltimore Shut Down Amerikkka
111. Shut Em Down!
112. Silence the Violence
113. Silence = Violence
114. Six is a good start!
115. Six down 3000 to go!
116. Solutions:
    Indictments
    Training
    Reform Legislation
    Civilian Review
    Body Cameras
    Leadership
    Jobs
117. Spines Don't Get Severed When You Serve and Protect

World To Come: Essays On The Baltimore Uprising, Militant Racism, And History

118. Still Waiting for Justice
119. Stop Calling For Peace When You Really Mean Silence
120. Stop Killer Cops
121. Stop Killing Our Brothers!!!
122. Stop Killing Our Fathers!!!
123. Stop Killing Us!
124. Stop Killing Black People
125. Stop Lethal Force
126. Stop Police Brutality and Murder
127. Stop Police Militarization
128. Stop Police Terror
129. Stop Racism and Police Brutality!
130. Stop Racist Police Terror
131. Stop the Hate
132. Stop the war on Black America
133. Stop Murder by Police

134. The People United Will Never Be Defeated
135. The Police are the Government's Gang! They used to be called 'Slavecatchers' Its deeper than Black and White in Baltimore!
136. The Power is Ours
137. The rich get old & the poor die Silent!
138. The Whole Damn System is Guilty as Hell
139. "To be black and conscious in America is to be in a constant state of Rage"[6]
140. Truth is: We are all 1 Bullet Away From Being a #Hashtag

141. Voice not Violence

142. Wake Up! We Live in a Police State
143. We are Praying with our Feet
144. We are Not Thugs
145. We are not Thugs and Neither are our children
146. We are One Baltimore
147. We can't Breathe
148. We Love Our City
149. We Need Results
150. We Praying for an Indictment!

---

[6] Quote on protest poster attributed to James Baldwin.

World To Come: Essays On The Baltimore Uprising, Militant Racism, And History

151. We remember Freddie
152. We see our Power
153. We Want Justice
154. We want real justice
155. What happened to Freddie?
156. "When Injustice becomes law, resistance becomes duty"[7]
157. White Silence is Violence
158. White Silence = White consent
159. Who Are they Protecting?
160. Work Together

161. You want peace? I want Justice!!

---

[7] Quote on protest poster attributed to Thomas Jefferson.

World To Come: Essays On The Baltimore Uprising, Militant Racism, And History

Appendix C: A Compendium Of African Americans Who Died In Police-Encounters, 1994—2015

(Or Whose Deaths Were Questioned As The Result Of Law Enforcement Or Para-Police Contact; ☉=indicates known personal, or police cameras [released or public] were identified in the case)[1]

	Name/Age	Place/Date	Abstracts of Police-Encounter Death Cases[2]
1.	AJIBADE Matthew 21	Savannah, GA January 1, 2015	BRIEF: Ajibade, a college student, was arrested for a domestic disturbance complaint involving his girlfriend. Police say that during the booking of Ajibade, he became violent. Ajibade was restrained in a chair, and placed inside of an isolation cell. He was found dead this way on January 1, 2015.† Ajibade was determined to have died of blunt force injuries. Months passed before information about his death was disclosed. His parents discovered that the May 8 death certificate had been filed when it was posted online. LEGAL STATUS: 9 deputies were fired; the case was sent to a grand jury for indictment. MAIN CONCEPTS/ THEMES: Mysterious Deaths, Domestic Disturbance, Mental Illness, Excessive Use-Of-Force. †Note: Ajibade's Death certificate listed his DOD as May 8, 2015.
2.	ALCIS Carlos 43	New York, NY August 15, 2013	BRIEF: The police mistakenly raided Alcis' home to search for a stolen cell phone. Alcis died of a heart attack thereafter. LEGAL STATUS: Alcis' family filed a wrongful death suit against the city and the NYPD for $10 million. MAIN CONCEPTS/THEMES: Accidental Entry/Raid, Cellphone, Heart Attack
3.	ALLEN Raymond, 34	Galveston, TX February 27, 2012	BRIEF: The police responded to a complaint that Allen was repeatedly jumping from the second story of a hotel. The two officers on the scene tased him. Allen stopped breathing, and later died in the hospital. LEGAL STATUS: Allen's wife filed a lawsuit against

---

[1]This compendium is a random list that includes black men, women and children (with two Hispanic/Latino entries), and is not meant to be exhaustive. The record is illustrative of the wide variety of questionable police-encounter deaths, some of which have garnered national and international media attention. The document also includes para-police incidents (security guards, volunteer police, and self-appointed community watchmen, etc.). The compendium does not include the suspicious deaths of those who have been convicted of crimes and died while serving adjudicated sentences in state or federal institutions. Note that the legal status frequently changes for many of the recent cases and up-to-date briefs may not have been available at the time of this manuscript's printing. Finally, the featured case briefs of people who died in police-encounters are not meant as an endorsement of any alleged or actual crimes committed by those listed here.

[2]Case brief information comes from print and internet news sources, public records, press releases, police reports, charging documents, interviews, and legal case briefings.

World To Come: Essays On The Baltimore Uprising, Militant Racism, And History

			Galveston county and the company that manufactured the taser weapon. MAIN CONCEPTS/THEMES: Mental Disorders, Tasers, Asphyxiation
4.	ALLEN Wendell 20	New Orleans, LA March 7, 2012	BRIEF: Allen was shot and killed by New Orleans police officer Joshua Colclough who was executing a search warrant of Allen's home for marijuana. Allen was unarmed, dressed only in jeans and sneakers. LEGAL STATUS: Officer Colclough pleaded guilty to manslaughter and was sentenced to four years in prison. MAIN CONCEPTS/THEMES: Narcotics, Shooting, Unarmed Citizens, Search Warrant
5.	ANDERSON, Sr. Anthony 46	Baltimore, MD September 21 2012	BRIEF: Anderson was arrested as he returned from a neighborhood store. Officer Strohman arrested him, and while he was restrained and on the ground (and cuffed), Anderson was beaten by officers. He later died from these injuries. LEGAL STATUS: The family filed a wrongful death lawsuit against the officers, and the Baltimore police department. In March 2014, a district court judge dismissed the case. MAIN CONCEPTS/ THEMES: Police Brutality
6.	ANDERSON Tanisha 37	Cleveland, OH November 12, 2014	BRIEF: Police responded to two domestic disturbance calls at Anderson's home. She was believed to be mentally ill which was controlled through medication. Anderson eventually agreed to be taken to the hospital, but changed her mind. Anderson, who was handcuffed behind her back by police, and according to family, wrestled to the ground, and then suffocated as police "took her down." Family members said she recited the Lord's Prayer before she died. Anderson was unarmed and not considered violent. LEGAL STATUS: Pending. MAIN CONCEPTS/ THEMES: Domestic Disturbance, Mental Disorders (bipolar and schizophrenia), Asphyxiation, African American/Black Women
7.	ASHLEY Alonzo 29	Denver, CO July 18, 2011	BRIEF: Denver Zoo security officers called police when they became concerned over Ashley's behavior. The police confronted Ashley and then tasered him. Ashley began convulsing and subsequently stopped breathing. LEGAL STATUS: The coroner determined that Ashley's death was a homicide. However, the officers were not charged in the case. Ashley's family filed a lawsuit naming the city of Denver and the zoo. MAIN CONCEPTS/THEMES: Security Officers, Tasers
8.	BAKER Jordan 26	Houston, TX January 16, 2014	BRIEF: An off-duty police officer believed Baker fit the description of robbery suspects (wearing black hooded sweatshirts). An unarmed Baker was fatally shot after an altercation and foot chase. LEGAL STATUS: Officer J. Castro was placed on administrative leave pending an investigation. Other legal action is pending. MAIN CONCEPTS/THEMES: Off-Duty Police Officer

World To Come: Essays On The Baltimore Uprising, Militant Racism, And History

9.	BARLOW Orlando 28	Las Vegas, NV February 28, 2003	BRIEF: Barlow was hired to babysit seven children. After an argument with the children's mother, the police were called and told the children were being held hostage with a gun. Police responded; and an unarmed Barlow was shot while surrendering. LEGAL STATUS: The coroner determined that the shooting was excusable. The FBI investigated. The shooting was ruled a justifiable homicide. The officers involved were fired for printing T-shirts with the abbreviation 'BDRT'—'Baby's Daddy Removal Team.'" MAIN CONCEPTS/THEMES: Domestic Disturbance, Adolescents/Juveniles/Children, Racial Mockery
10.	BEASLEY Ronald 36	Dellwood, MO June 12, 2000	BRIEF: (See also Earl Murray) Beasley and Murray were called in the media, small-time drug dealers. Murray, Beasley and another passenger, were shot and killed in a "hail of bullets" during an attempted drug bust in a restaurant parking lot. Officers claimed Murray's car moved towards them and that they were in danger; other officers said the car was not moving forward. Another perspective was that the car was in reverse attempting to flee officers. One officer purportedly called the killings "unintended, but not a mistake." An officer also referred to Beasley and Murray as "bums." All of the men were unarmed. LEGAL STATUS: The officers were cleared of wrongdoing after a yearlong investigation. A Grand Jury did not indict. Authorities felt there was not enough evidence to file federal charges. MAIN CONCEPTS/THEMES: Narcotics.
11.	BEATY Kawanza Jamal 23	Newport News, VA July 4, 2015	BRIEF: Police officers stated they came upon Beaty walking on the street and attempted to talk to him. He ran and the police chased. They said that they could see a gun, and that the gun was pointed at them. The police fired on Beaty. He was shot in the back of the head, and pronounced dead at the scene. The fingerprints and DNA found on the gun at the scene was not Beaty's. LEGAL STATUS: Beaty's family requested a federal investigation and held a press conference indicating they would file a lawsuit against the city and police department. MAIN CONCEPTS/THEMES: Police Chase, Wrongful Death, Excessive Use-Of-Force
12.	BELL Sean 23	New York, NY November 25, 2006	BRIEF: The night before his wedding, Bell and his friends attempted to flee the scene of a confrontation with police. Officers fired approximately 50 rounds into Bell's car, killing him. LEGAL STATUS: The three officers involved were acquitted on all charges. However, they and their commanding officer were fired or forced to resign. New York City agreed to pay the Bell family $3.25 million to settle a wrongful death suit. MAIN CONCEPTS/THEMES: Excessive Use-Of-Force, Wrongful Death

World To Come: Essays On The Baltimore Uprising, Militant Racism, And History

13.	BLAND Sandra 28	Waller County, TX July 13, 2015 ⊙	BRIEF: Bland was forcibly removed from her car after a routine traffic stop by Officer Brian Encinia. She was arrested on specious charges, held on $5,000 bond, and three days later, she was found dead in her jail cell. Police maintained that Bland told them that she suffered from depression and that she hung herself in her jail cell with a plastic trashcan liner. Her death was ruled a suicide. Bland's family disputed this account; and major protests about the police-custody deaths of African American women took place. LEGAL STATUS: There has been a request for a federal investigation into the death of Bland. Within weeks, the Bland family filed a wrongful death suit against Waller County, Texas; in early 2016 Officer Encinia was indicted on a perjury charge in connection to her case and was fired by the Texas Department of Public Safety several months later. MAIN CONCEPTS/ THEMES: In-Custody Deaths, Suicide, African American/Black Women, Traffic Stops
14.	BOYD Rekia 22	Chicago, IL March 21, 2012	BRIEF: Off-duty officer Dante Servin believed he saw a man brandish a gun in an alleyway where four people were standing. The officer fired an unregistered firearm at the group. One of the bullets hit Boyd in the back of the head. She died the next day. LEGAL STATUS: The city of Chicago paid Boyd's family $4.5 million to settle a wrongful death suit. Officer Servin was charged with involuntary manslaughter, reckless discharge of a firearm, and reckless conduct. MAIN CONCEPTS/ THEMES: Off-Duty Police Officer, Accidental Death
15.	BRINSON Kelly 45	Cincinnati, OH January 24, 2010	BRIEF: Brinson, who was a mental patient undergoing treatment, was tased by University of Cincinnati Police officers (who were also involved in the 2015 DuBose shooting). LEGAL STATUS: Pending. MAIN CONCEPTS/THEMES: Campus Police, Mental Disorders
16.	BRISBON Rumain 34	Phoenix, AZ December 2, 2014	BRIEF: Brisbon, who was unarmed, was shot to death when a police officer apparently thought his bottle of pills was a gun. LEGAL STATUS: Pending. MAIN CONCEPTS/THEMES: Fallacious Weapon
17.	BRISETTE James 17	New Orleans, LA September 4, 2005	BRIEF: (See also Ronald Madison) Days after Hurricane Katrina, police received a call saying that there was gunfire on the Danziger Bridge. They opened fire upon arriving in a Budget Rental Truck. Brisette was struck; Madison (thought to be developmentally disabled), ran from the scene and was chased by police. Officer Faulcon, shot him; and Sgt. Bowen, stomped Madison on the back before he died. LEGAL STATUS: Sgt. Bowen was convicted in Madison's death; that conviction was later overturned. The case involved elements of a cover-up. Eventually five officers were found guilty of various charges. Faulcon was

sentenced to 65 years' imprisonment, Bowen and Sgt. Robert Gisevius received 40 years. Officer Villavaso received 38 years. Arthur "Archie" Kaufman, who served as the investigator for the case was eventually found guilty of conspiring to conceal evidence, and he received 6 years. A month later, the judge that convicted them (Kurt Engelhardt) vacated their convictions and ordered new trials. MAIN CONCEPTS/THEMES: Excessive Use-Of-Force

18.	BROWN Aaron 18	Alexandria, VA February, 2006	BRIEF: An Off duty police officer shot into the SUV (which included Brown, a Freshman at Northern Virginia Community College, and 5 other passengers) because the teens were attempting to leave the IHOP restaurant without paying a $26 bill. Officer Stow said that he feared that the SUV would run over him, so he fired six rounds into the vehicle, one of which hit Brown. There were widely different accounts about the incident. LEGAL STATUS: A three-month investigation of the case took place. Officer Stow was not charged in Brown's death. MAIN CONCEPTS/THEMES: Off-Duty Police Officer, Frightened Police
19.	BROWN Chris 17	Randallstown, MD June 13, 2012	BRIEF: An off-duty Baltimore County police officer had an exchange with the teenager, after he heard a crash near his home about 10:30 PM. Thereafter he heard people running away and gave chase. At some point he found Brown in a bush and when he refused to come out a fight began. In the confrontation, Brown became unconscious. Purportedly, the officer placed Brown in a chokehold, and thereafter performed CPR. The teen died at the hospital. The determination of death was asphyxiation. LEGAL BRIEF: the officer was placed on paid administrative leave. The police conducted an internal investigation. MAIN CONCEPTS/THEMES: Off-Duty Police Officer, Police Chase, Unarmed Citizens, Excessive Use-Of-Force, Adolescents/Juveniles/Children, Hospitalization
20.	BROWN Michael 18	Ferguson, MO August 9, 2014	BRIEF: Brown was shot by Ferguson, Missouri police officer Darren Wilson after an altercation that began on the street and then inside Wilson's patrol car. Wilson reported that Brown "looked like a demon" and fired several shots into Brown, including a head shot. Browns body lay in the street for hours. Weeks of protest ensued. LEGAL STATUS: Wilson was not indicted by a grand jury. He resigned from the Ferguson police force. THE DOJ launched a comprehensive review of the case. The Brown family filed a civil lawsuit. MAIN CONCEPTS/THEMES: Frightened Police, Investigative Stops, Excessive Use-Of-Force.

World To Come: Essays On The Baltimore Uprising, Militant Racism, And History

21.	BROWN Raheim 20	Oakland, CA January 22, 2011	BRIEF: Brown was shot five times, including twice in the head, during an altercation with the police. The police alleged that Brown was trying to stab an officer with a screwdriver. LEGAL STATUS: There was no indictment for Officer Barhin Bhatt. However, The Oakland Unified School District settled with Brown's parents for $995,000. MAIN CONCEPTS/THEMES: Excessive Use-Of-Force
22.	CAMPBELL Aaron 25	Portland, OR January 29, 2010	BRIEF: Police received a call that Campbell was suicidal and that he had a gun. Campbell, who was unarmed, in front of his apartment complex, walked backwards with his hands positioned behind his head. Officer Frashour shot Campbell when he refused to place his hands in the air. LEGAL STATUS: The officer was not indicted. However, he was fired for not adhering to police procedure; then he was rehired. The city of Portland decided to pay the Campbell Family more than one million dollars to settle their lawsuit against the city. MAIN CONCEPTS/ THEMES: Unarmed Citizens
23.	CAREY Miriam 34	Washington, DC October 3, 2013	BRIEF: Carey drove from her home in Connecticut to Washington, D.C. When she attempted to make a U-turn at an outer White House security checkpoint, she was ordered to stop. She did not stop. She tried to make a U-turn. An unidentified plainclothes off duty Secret Service agent attempted to blockade her effort to leave the area. In the effort to leave, Carey hit the makeshift gate trying to get away. A chase ensued and near the Capital Reflecting Pool, she is surrounded by law enforcement. She attempted to flee again, and they opened fire on her vehicle. The chase continued, eventually Carey was shot and killed by law enforcement officers (Secret Service and U.S. Capitol Police). She was shot at 26 times, and she received 5 bullets. Carey was unarmed; and she had her year old infant with her. The baby was unharmed. The House of Representatives believed this event represented a great threat against the capitol. After her death, public information was released alleging that she had experienced post-partum depression. The family believes that after the incident, false information was distributed about Carey. LEGAL STATUS: The U.S. Attorney's Office declined to press charges. The family is looking for full disclosure of information related to this case. A wrongful death lawsuit is being filed by Carey's family. Judicial Watch filed a complaint to uncover documents relevant to the case. MAIN CONCEPTS/THEMES: Excessive Use-Of-Force, Unarmed Citizens, National Security

24.	CARR Dewayne 45	Scottsdale, AZ January, 2015	BRIEF: Carr and three others were being surveilled by police for credit card fraud. Police claimed that Carr used the Mercedes Benz car he was driving as a weapon against police. As a result, the police fired at Carr, who later died in the hospital. The three others were arrested. LEGAL STATUS: Pending. MAIN CONCEPTS/THEMES: Surveillance, Automobile-As-A-Weapon, Hospitalization.
25.	CARRINGTON Kiwane 15	Champaign, IL October 9, 2009	BRIEF: When police responded to a break-in, they found Carrington. A conflict followed. Police maintain that the officer's gun accidentally discharged and killed Carrington. LEGAL STATUS: The officer involved, was not indicted. He received disability and worker's compensation payments. The Carrington family filed a wrongful death lawsuit and received a settlement of nearly one half million dollars. MAIN CONCEPTS/THEMES: Accidental Shooting.
26.	CARTER Jr., Byron 20	Austin, TX May 30, 2011	BRIEF: Police officer Wagner (and officer J. Rodriguez), believed that Carter (and his friend in the driver's seat, 16-year-old Leyumba Webb) looked suspicious so he followed them. They were on foot. The two got into a car, and according to police, headed the vehicle directly towards them. Wagner believed his partner was hit by the car and open fired. He hit Carter 5 times and killed him. LEGAL STATUS: Webb was charged with assault of the officer, among other charges, but was not indicted. The administrative investigation cleared Wagner. Carter's family filed a federal civil rights suit against Wagner. The Grand Jury refused to indict Wagner. The case has been heavily debated and the official record of events has been disputed in the Austin media, including by investigative journalists. One of the key issues was the inability of lawyers to obtain evidence important to the case. MAIN CONCEPTS/THEMES: Suspicious Persons/Citizens, Automobile-As-Weapon.
27.	CARTER Chavis 21	Jonesboro, AR July 29, 2012	BRIEF: Carter was being detained for possession of marijuana. According to police, they did not discover a concealed weapon at the time of his arrest. Carter purportedly committed suicide while he was handcuffed in the back of a police cruiser. Carter's mother has stated that he was left-handed, and could only have shot himself with his right hand. LEGAL STATUS: The officers involved were placed on administrative leave. The FBI "monitored and assessed" the case. The Carter family filed a wrongful death lawsuit. MAIN CONCEPTS/THEMES: Narcotics, Suicide, Concealed Weapon.

28.	CHAMBERLAIN, Sr. Kenneth 68	White Plains, NY November 19, 2011	BRIEF: Chamberlain's medical emergency necklace was activated by mistake. When police responded, Chamberlain refused to come to the door. Chamberlain told police that he did not need any assistance. Police officers knocked down the door to his apartment. An Officer Hart referred to Chamberlain as a "nigger" and there were other taunts, and slurs utter by police. The police maintained that Chamberlain came at them with a butcher knife. They tasered and eventually shot him twice. LEGAL STATUS: The officer who shot Chamberlain (A. Carelli) was not indicted. The Chamberlain family filed a $21 million wrongful death lawsuit. MAIN CONCEPTS/THEMES: Wellness Check, Excessive Use-Of-Force, Fallacious Weapon, Knife-Wielding.
29.	CHAPMAN Jesse 30	Baltimore, MD July 2, 1994	BRIEFS: Chapman was in police-custody, being transported, when he lost consciousness and died suddenly. The autopsy stated that Chapman died of complications from cocaine and an asthma attack. Witnesses and other members of the community were skeptical and maintained that he had been beaten by police. LEGAL STATUS: The grand jury did not indict the officers in this case. MAIN CONCEPTS/THEMES: Sudden Death, Pre-Existing Condition.
30.	CHAPMAN Kindra 18	Homewood, AL July 14, 2015	BRIEF: Chapman was arrested on July 14 for allegedly stealing a cell phone. She was later found dead hanging in a jail cell. LEGAL STATUS: Pending. MAIN CONCEPTS/THEMES: Suicide, Suspicious Persons/Citizens.
31.	CLARK Jamar 24	Minneapolis, MN November 15, 2015 ⊙	BRIEF: According to police, Clark was suspected in an assault. When police and paramedics arrived, Clark purportedly interfered with the medical workers attempt to treat the victim. There was some altercation and Clark was shot in the head by police. Initial reports gave only the police version of events, which were vague. There was a dispute as to whether Clark was shot while he was handcuffed by police or not. Witnesses say he was handcuffed when he was shot. The videos collected by police were not released to the public because of fears they would taint the investigation. City and nationwide protests ensued. LEGAL STATUS: an outside investigation by the Bureau of Criminal Apprehension, and the FBI Civil Rights Division was launched. MAIN CONCEPTS/THEMES: Handcuffs, Custody, Restraint, Assault
32.	COCHRAN, McKenzie 25	Southfield, MI January 28, 2014	BRIEF: Inside of the Northland Mall, a storeowner called security to report that he feared a black male who stared at him and threatened to kill "someone." Because he was wearing a puffer coat, it he also thought that Cochran might be armed. Mall security told Cochran to

leave, when he did not they pepper-sprayed, wrestled him to the ground. At least 4 officers restrained his arms, back, shoulder, legs, and a knee is forced into his back. Though not resisting, he is restrained for several minutes. It was determined that Cochran died of asphyxiation. He purportedly told the police that he could not breathe and asked bystanders to call 911 for help. The medical examiner ruled his death an accident. LEGAL STATUS: The security guards were not indicted. MAIN CONCEPTS/THEMES: Excessive Use-Of-Force, Restraint, Security Officers, Accidental Death, Unarmed Citizens, Asphyxiation

#	Name	Location	Date	Brief
33.	COPPIN Khiel 18	Brooklyn, NY	November 13, 2007	BRIEF: In a 911 call a woman reported that her son threatened her. The voice of the son could be heard saying he had a gun. However, the mother told 911 and the police that he had no gun. When police arrived, Coppin refused to show his hands and was shot at 20 times, and struck 10 times. Coppin died later at the hospital. It was discovered that he had a hair brush. LEGAL STATUS: The case was investigated by the police and the Brooklyn district attorney's office. MAIN CONCEPTS/THEMES: 911 Callers, Suicide-By-Cop, Unarmed Citizens, Mental Illness, Domestic Disturbance
34.	CRAWFORD, III John 22	Beavercreek, OH	August 5, 2014	BRIEF: A 911 caller reported that a man pointed a gun at people in the Walmart store. Crawford held a pellet gun, which was for sale, inside the Walmart. He was fatally shot by police. The pellet gun had been removed from the original packaging. The 911 caller later admitted that Crawford did not point the gun at people. LEGAL STATUS: The officers were not indicted. The Crawford family filed a lawsuit against the police department and Walmart. MAIN CONCEPTS/ THEMES: Public Threat, Retail Weapons, Consumers, 911 Callers
35.	CUEVAS Reynaldo 20 (Hispanic/ Latino)	New York, NY	September 7, 2012	BRIEF: Three gunmen attempted to rob the bodega Cuevas worked in. A passerby who noticed the robbery called 911. When the robbers moved to the rear of the store, Cuevas took the opportunity to effort an escape. Cuevas was mistaken for a robber, and was killed by police. LEGAL STATUS: The officer was not found to have engaged in any wrongdoing in the shooting of Cuevas, and was not subject to a grand jury indictment. The Cuevas family filed a $25 million wrongful death claim against the city. MAIN CONCEPTS/THEMES: Accidental Death, 911 Callers.
36.	DASRATH Rexford 22	Bushwick, NY	November 18, 2013	BRIEF: Neighbors and officials stated that Dasrath was learning-disabled. Police responded to a landlord-tenant dispute at Dasrath's Hart Street apartment. They reported that Dasrath lunged at them with a knife. Dasrath was shot five times in the chest and arm and

37.	DAVIS Shantel 23	New York, NY June 14, 2012	killed by police. LEGAL STATUS: Pending. MAIN CONCEPTS/THEMES: Mental Disabilities (Learning), Knife-Wielding, Excessive Use-Of-Force, Domestic Disturbance. BRIEF: Plainclothes police attempted to stop Davis, who was allegedly driving erratically through red lights. The police chased Davis through East Flatbush and she crashed into a parked vehicle. In the crash the airbags deployed trapping Davis in the car. The widely reported struggled with police occurred when Davis refused to exit the vehicle at the officer's command. As Davis begged for her life, the officers dragged her from the vehicle and then one officer fired a shot into her chest, killing Davis. She was pulled out of the car and handcuffed face down in a pool of her own blood. It was immediately circulated that Davis stole the car she was driving, and that she was due in court the next day on charges of kidnapping and robbery. Others disputed that she stole the car; that at the time there was no evidence that officers knew the car they were chasing was stolen, and state that Davis had never been convicted of a crime, and was trying to change/improve her life. Protesters reminded the Brooklyn community that the police in question regularly terrorized the predominately black and brown neighborhood and that at the time Davis was unarmed. LEGAL STATUS: The police were said to have confiscated all of the retail video that might have captured the event. The officers involved were placed on administrative duty; and thereafter returned to routine service. MAIN CONCEPTS/THEMES: Police Chase, Excessive Use-Of-Force, Unarmed Citizens, Plainclothes Police.
38.	DECKARD Monique Jenee 43	Anaheim, CA March 8, 2015 ⊙	BRIEF: When Deckard's family could not locate her, expressed that she had been acting strangely, and was looking to acquire a gun (noting she had a history of mental health behaviors), they asked police to check on her. Police gained information that she might have stabbed a woman at a laundromat. Police went to Deckard's apartment, and when she refused to talk to police, they got a negotiator. Deckard allegedly came out of her apartment "armed with two knives," lunged at officers, and officers shot her. LEGAL STATUS: Some of the police on the scene wore body cameras. The videos were given to the Orange County District Attorney. MAIN CONCEPTS/ THEMES: Mental Disorders, Wellness Check, Knife-Wielding, African American/Black Women.

World To Come: Essays On The Baltimore Uprising, Militant Racism, And History

39.	DIALLO Amadou 23	New York, NY February 4, 1999	BRIEF: Police officers initially approached Diallo because he allegedly matched the description of a prolific serial rapist they were seeking. In the encounter which occurred outside of his Bronx apartment, four plainclothes officers stopped Diallo demanding he show them his hands. Diallo, who possessed a wallet, pulled it out of his pocket and held it for the officers to see, when one officer mistook it for a gun. They fired 41 shots at Diallo. He was struck nineteen times. LEGAL STATUS: The officers were acquitted of all charges. Diallo's mother and stepfather filed a $61 million wrongful death suit against the officers and the City of New York. They settled for $3 million. MAIN CONCEPTS/THEMES: Plainclothes Officers, Excessive Use-Of-Force, Fallacious Weapon, Suspicious Persons/Citizens, Police Task Force.
40.	DILLARD Nehemiah 29	Gainesville, FL March 5, 2012	BRIEF: Dillard, who was cited as behaving strangely in a neighbor's yard, was admitted to Meridian Behavioral Healthcare center. At the center he allegedly hit a hospital staff member. The police were called. Police maintain that Dillard attacked them prompting their use of tasers. Dillard was handcuffed and according to the *Tampa Bay Times*, "a staffer at the facility injected him with drugs." Thereafter Dillard died of cardiac arrest. LEGAL STATUS: Pending. MAIN CONCEPTS/THEMES: Tasers, Mental Disorders, Hospitalization.
41.	DOUCET Reginald 25	Los Angeles, CA January 14, 2011	BRIEF: Doucet got into an argument with a taxi driver. Police were called to the site in an effort to respond to a "disturbing the peace" complaint. According to police, Doucet resisted arrest, and ran from police. They chased him. They claim that a violent confrontation with an unarmed Doucet took place, and he was fatally shot. LEGAL STATUS: The Los Angeles Police Commission ruled that the officer was justified in the shooting. The Doucet family filed wrongful death lawsuit which was dismissed. MAIN CONCEPTS/THEMES: Domestic Disturbance, Police Chase, Resisting Arrest, Unarmed Citizens.
42.	DORISMOND Patrick 26	New York, NY March 16, 2000	BRIEF: Dorismond and his friend, Kevin Kaiser, were standing outside of a lounge (trying to find a taxi to leave) when they were approached by three undercover cops. One officer asked Dorismond where he could buy drugs (marijuana, crack cocaine). Purportedly a physical altercation took place when Dorismond became offended and angrily insisted that he didn't have drugs for sale. At that point one of the undercover cops Detective Anthony Vasquez' came to assist his partner. Detective Vasquez' shot Dorismond. He claimed that Dorismond grabbed his gun and accidently shot himself in the chest. The other officer claimed that he attempted

to remove Dorismond from the situation. Kaiser said that the officers physically assaulted Dorismond and never identified themselves as police officers. LEGAL STATUS: Mayor Giuliani authorized the release of Dorismond's sealed juvenile arrest record. Vasquez was not indicted in the case. The city of New York paid the Dorismond family $2.25 million in a wrongful death lawsuit. MAIN CONCEPTS/THEMES: Undercover Police/Operation, Narcotics, Unarmed Citizens.

43.	DUBOSE Samuel 43	Cincinnati, OH July 19, 2015	BRIEF: DuBose was subject to a traffic stop by a University of Cincinnati campus police officer Ray Tensing for not having a front license plate displayed on his car. The stop occurred off the University's campus. DuBose, who was unarmed, was fatally shot by the officer when he refused to leave the car. The officer claimed that the DuBose dragged him with the car thus posing a threat to his life. The police body camera evidence released within days of the shooting revealed that the officer was not dragged, and that he shot DuBose in the head. Other officers have been implicated in supporting Tensing's story. LEGAL STATUS: The officer was indicted by the Grand Jury, for the murder of DuBose. This was the first time in the county's history that a police officer has been indicted for murder. Officer Tensing pleaded not guilty and was later released on a 1 million bail. The DuBose family received a 5.3 million settlement in January 2016. MAIN CONCEPTS/THEMES: Campus Police, Traffic Stop, Excessive Use-Of-Force, Automobile-As-Weapon.
44.	EDWARDS Sharmel 49	Las Vegas, NV April 21, 2012	BRIEF: The police suspected Edwards of car theft and they chased her. When they reached Edwards, they said that she fired on them, and they in return opened fire. Witnesses stated that Edwards was unarmed. LEGAL STATUS: The DA's office absolved the officers of any wrongdoing. MAIN CONCEPTS/THEMES: Disputed Accounts, Suspicious Persons/Citizens.
45.	FARROW DeAunta Terrel 12	West Memphis, AK July 22, 2007	BRIEF: Farrow and his 14-year-old cousin were out walking when he was killed by officer Erik Sammis. The officer claimed that he shot Farrow unaware that the boy's gun was a toy. LEGAL STATUS: Officer Sammis was not indicated in the case, but he did resign from the police force, believing that he was a victim of racial hatred. Neither Sammis nor his partner Officer Evans was found guilty in the civil lawsuit that the Farrow family filed. MAIN CONCEPTS/THEMES: Toy Guns/Weapons/BBs, Adolescents.
46.	FERGUSON Malcolm 23	New York, NY March 1, 2000	BRIEF: NYC plainclothes street narcotics officers were patrolling a public housing building suspected of drugs. The police-encountered three men in the hallway of the building. Ferguson ran up the stairs and one drug officer

chased him. Ferguson resisted arrest, a struggle occurred and Officer Louis Rivera shot Ferguson who he knew was unarmed. Ferguson was shot at close range in the head, and was dead on the scene. Police said they found heroin on Ferguson's body. Ferguson was on parole for selling drugs. A week before Ferguson was arrested for participating in protests over the acquittals in the Amadou Diallo shooting. LEGAL STATUS: Officer Rivera was cleared of any wrongdoing. Juanita Young, Ferguson's mother, filed a wrongful death lawsuit against the NYPD and the city, and was awarded $10.5 million. MAIN CONCEPTS/THEMES: Unarmed Citizen, Accidental Shooting, Plainclothes Police, Narcotics.

47. FERRELL Jonathan 24

Bradfield Farms, NC

September 14, 2013

BRIEF: Ferrell had a car crash and knocked on the door of a nearby house. The woman inside called the police. There was an attempt to arrest Ferrell. Police said that when Ferrell was apprehended, they were forced to shoot him ten times. LEGAL STATUS: After two grand juries, Officer Randall Kerrick was indicted for voluntary manslaughter. MAIN CONCEPTS/THEMES: Excessive Use-Of-Force.

48. FISHER, III Winfield Carlton 32

Salisbury, MD

March 18, 2014

BRIEF: Fisher went to the Salisbury Police Barrack for a routine rear tag light inspection for his car. The official story suggested that one of the troopers went with Fisher to conduct the inspection and "something" happened that left the officer in fear for his life. Police said that Fisher hit the officer with his car and perhaps dragged him. Two state troopers fired on Fisher which caused him to crash his car. Fisher was DOA at the hospital. LEGAL STATUS: Pending. The state troopers involved were placed on administrative leave. MAIN CONCEPTS/THEMES: Excessive Use-Of-Force, Vehicle Inspection, Unarmed Citizens, Weaponized Vehicles.

49. FLUDD Deion 17

New York, NY

May 5, 2013

BRIEF: Police chased Fludd for dodging a subway fare. They say a train hit Fludd as they chased him. Fludd's mother says that he, on his deathbed, denied the police account. LEGAL STATUS: Fludd's mother filed a lawsuit against the NYPD and the MTA. MAIN CONCEPTS/THEMES: Police Chase, Disputed Account, Hospitalization.

50. FONVILLE Janisha 20

Charlotte, NC

February 18, 2015

BRIEF: Police was called to a domestic disturbance involving Fonville and her girlfriend by an anonymous 911 caller. When the officers approached Fonville, they say she was armed with a knife, refused to drop it, and then lunged at them. Fonville was purported shot in the hand and shoulder. She was taken to the medical center and pronounced dead. LEGAL STATUS: Officer Holzhauer was placed on administrative leave until the

51.	FORD Ezell 25	Los Angeles, CA August 12, 2014	full investigation is completed; and he will have to undergo psychological counseling before resuming regular duties. The officer was not charged. Neighbors and others in the community questioned the death. MAIN CONCEPTS/THEMES: Domestic Disturbance, LGBT, 911 Callers, Knife-Wielding. BRIEF: According to police, Ford was being detained for behaving suspiciously on the street for issues related to mental illness. Police say there was a struggle. Ford allegedly reached for one police officer's guns and was shot three times. He was shot in the chest, abdomen and back. Ford was taken to the hospital and died during surgery. Ford's family maintained that he was lying down when shot; that he walked away from police; and that he had the mental capacity of a 10-year-old. LEGAL STATUS: The LAPD placed an indefinite investigative hold on the autopsy report (it was released December 29). The LAPD ruled that the officers engaged in no wrongdoing. The LAPD Commission conducted an investigation. One of the officers involved was deemed justified in the shooting while the other was determined to be unjustified. The LAC DA's office launched its investigation. Ford's family filed lawsuits. MAIN CONCEPTS/THEMES: Investigative Stops, Mental Disorder, Unarmed citizens, Hospitalization.
52.	FRANCIS Shereese 30	New York, NY March 15, 2012	BRIEF: Francis' family called 911 for an ambulance to transport her to the hospital for psychiatric evaluation. Four police officers came to the home instead of the ambulance. The police approached her in her bedroom with guns drawn. Francis was confused and refused to go to the hospital. They chased Francis, tackled, and held her down attempting to handcuff her. They purportedly beat her about the head and then tasered her. When EMS arrived the officers would not allow them to treat Francis. Francis eventually stopped breathing. She was taken to the hospital and then pronounced dead. LEGAL STATUS: Her family filed a lawsuit charging the police with in her death, and citing their belief that a police cover-up took place. MAIN CONCEPTS/ THEMES: 911, Mental Disorder, Excessive Use-Of-Force, African American/Black Women, Hospitalization, Asphyxiation, Tasers.
53.	FRANKLIN, JR. Dominique 23	Chicago, IL May 20, 2014	BRIEF: Franklin was suspected of trying to steal a bottle of vodka from Walgreens. Police were called, a struggle ensued, and Franklin ran. Police chased Franklin and tased him. Franklin then hit a light pole and the ground. Franklin lay in the streets more than 15 minutes before he received any medical assistance. LEGAL STATUS: an independent Police Review Authority launched an investigation. Franklin's father,

World To Come: Essays On The Baltimore Uprising, Militant Racism, And History

54.	GARNER Eric 43 ⊙	New York, NY July 17, 2014	Dominique Franklin, Sr., filed a lawsuit against the city of Chicago. MAIN CONCEPTS/THEMES: Police Chase, Tasers, Car Crash BRIEF: Plainclothes police maintained that they noticed Garner on the street breaking the law by selling illegal loose untaxed cigarettes as a vender. Others state that police attempted to arrest Garner because he tried to break up a fight. When the police and Garner argued, Officer Daniel Pantaleo placed Garner in a chokehold. Four officers wrestled Garner to the ground, and three other officers came to assist. Garner was restrained and choked and he is heard telling the police, "I can't breathe," and later (after laying on the side walk for 5 minutes) pronounced dead at the hospital. Ramsay Orta videotaped the scene. His death launched city and nationwide protests against lethal force used by police. LEGAL STATUS: Garner's death was ruled a homicide. The Grand Jury did not indict Pantaleo. Another officer, Sergeant Kizzy Adonis was stripped of her shield and gun, charged for failing to supervise the arrest scene. The family filed a 75 million dollar lawsuit against the city of New York. A year after his death, the Garner family was awarded a 5.9 million dollar pre-trial settlement by the city. Thereafter, Richmond University Medical Center entered into a confidential settlement agreement to pay Garner's family 1 million dollars. MAIN CONCEPTS/THEMES: Excessive Use-Of-Force, Asphyxiation, Video tapes
55.	GLOVER Henry 31	New Orleans, LA September 2, 2005	BRIEF: On September 2, 2005 Glover was shot in the chest by NOPD Officer David Warren behind a strip mall on the Sunday after Hurricane Katrina sweep through the city of New Orleans. Glover was riding his bicycle and the officer shot him with his personal firearm. With the help of a friend, and his brother, a wounded Glover, attempted to get help near a gas station. At the gas station they encountered William Tanner (who stopped for gas) and solicited his help. The men put Glover in the back seat of Tanner's car and then drove to Paul B. Habans Elementary School because they believed that they would find police there and seek their assistance. When they got there, law enforcement officers accused them of looting and handcuffed the men, including the wounded Glover in the back seat of Tanner's car. The officers beat the men, verbally abused them, and refused to get medical help for Glover. Glover died. One of the officers commandeered Tanner's car and drove away. NOPD Officer Greg McRae set fire to Glover's body in Tanner's car. Tanner was not successful in finding out what happened to the vehicle. The car was found weeks

later with Glover's remains inside. The car was abandoned near a levee blocks away from the police department's 4th District Station. The Glover Family, *Times-Picayune* and *ProPublica* essentially broke the case. Thereafter, in 2009, The U.S. Department of Justice investigated Glover's death. LEGAL STATUS: Five officers (two were SWAT) were charged and trials began in 2010. Officer David Warren was charged with manslaughter, convicted and sentenced to 25 years. Warren's conviction was later overturned by the Fifth Circuit Court of Appeals and when retried, he was acquitted. Officer Greg MacRae received 17 years for obstruction of justice. The Fifth Circuit Court of Appeals vacated two of MacRae's convictions and ordered new trials. Officer Travis McCabe was found guilty of covering-up the case. MAIN CONCEPTS/THEMES: Hurricane Katrina, Police Cover-Up, Arson, Unarmed Citizens.

56. GRAHAM Ramarley, 18 — New York, NY — February 2, 2012

BRIEF: Graham was shot and killed by police in the Bronx New York. Officers chased him into his home without a warrant, and shot him in front of his younger brother and grandmother. Graham, purportedly in the act of getting rid of marijuana, was unarmed. LEGAL STATUS: The officer involved, Richard Haste, was initially indicted in 2012; however, the case was later overturned on a technicality. A second grand jury would not indict Haste. The Department of Justice launched an investigation. MAIN CONCEPTS/THEMES: Unarmed Citizens, Police Chase, Excessive Use-Of-Force.

57. GRANT Oscar, 22 — Oakland, CA — January 1, 2009

BRIEF: After reports of a fight at the BART (Bay Area Rapid Transit) train station, police detained Grant and some of his friends at the Fruitvale station. While Grant was lying face down, a transit police officer named Johannes Mehserle shot him. The officer claimed he meant to use a taser gun on Grant. Grants killing set off one of the largest protests in the area. A film based on Oscar Grant's last day of life, *Fruitvale Station*, was released in 2013. LEGAL STATUS: Mehserle was found guilty of involuntary manslaughter and not guilty of second-degree murder and voluntary manslaughter. He was sentenced to two years in prison. BART paid Grant's mother and daughter $2.8 million to settle the civil suit they filed. Grant's father lost a civil case against Mehserle. MAIN CONCEPTS/THEMES: Taser, Accidental Shooting.

World To Come: Essays On The Baltimore Uprising, Militant Racism, And History

58.	GRAY Freddie 25	Baltimore, MD April 19, 2015 ⊙	BRIEF: When Gray made "eye contact" with officers in the early morning, he ran. Gray was arrested (for having a pocketknife in his possession); and despite asking for medical assistance, he was placed in a police transport vehicle without a seat belt. He was eventually taken to the hospital, lapsed into a coma and died. His death was the catalyst for the Baltimore Uprising. LEGAL STATUS: 6 Officers were indicted in the case. In September 2015, the city of Baltimore agreed to pay the Gray family 6.4 million dollars in a civil settlement. CONCEPTS/THEMES: Suspect, Medical Assistance, Excessive Use-Of-Force, Police Transport Injury.
59.	GRAY Kimani 16	New York, NY March 9, 2013	BRIEF: Police accounts suggested that when they tried to question Gray he pulled a gun on them. In response, the police fired on Gray. They fired 11 rounds, which killed Gray instantly. Grays family stated that he did not possess a gun. LEGAL STATUS: The police involved were not indicted. MAIN CONCEPTS/THEMES: Excessive Use-Of-Force.
60.	GURLEY Akai 28	Brooklyn, NY November 20, 2014	BRIEF: Officer Peter Liang shot Gurley in a dark stairwell in an east New York housing project. Witnesses do not know how the shooting occurred. Gurley did not possess a weapon; and did not receive medical assistance. LEGAL STATUS: An investigation took place. The officer involved was initially found not liable for the shooting. However, he later faced a trial on second degree manslaughter charges in January 2016. Officer Liang was found guilty, but the Brooklyn district attorney decided not to seek any prison time. MAIN CONCEPTS/THEMES: Unarmed Citizens.
61.	HAGGERTY LaTanya 26	Chicago, IL June 4, 1999	BRIEF: Haggerty was a passenger in a car was subjected to a traffic stop by Officer Serena Daniels. When the driver of the car seemingly ignored the officer and failed to pull over, Daniels shot Haggerty. Officer Daniels maintained that she thought Haggerty had pulled a gun on her. Haggerty was talking on her cell phone at the time she was shot. No weapon was found at the scene. LEGAL STATUS: Three of the officers involved were fired, and one officer was suspended from the force. Haggerty's family was awarded $18 million in a settlement from the City. MAIN CONCEPTS/THEMES: Traffic Stop, Mistaken Gun.
62.	HALL Lavall 25	Miami Gardens, FL February 15, 2015 ⊙	BRIEF: Hall's mother contacted 911 seeking help for her son, who was schizophrenic. Miami Gardens Police claim that Hall attacked them with a broomstick. They opened fire on him. A video discounts the officer's interpretation of the shooting. LEGAL STATUS: The family filed a lawsuit against the police and the city. MAIN CONCEPTS/THEMES: Mental Disorders (Schizophrenia), Excessive Use-Of-Force, 911 Callers.

World To Come: Essays On The Baltimore Uprising, Militant Racism, And History

63.	HALL Mya 27	Baltimore, MD March 30, 2015	BRIEF: When Hall turned into the NSA property and attempted to make a U-turn she hit a security gate and police car. She was shot on National Security Agency (NSA) grounds. Because, among other things, she was a transgender woman, the immediate media stories made an effort to link Hall to Jihadism. They also suggested that she struggled with a mental illness and had stolen a car. LEGAL STATUS: Pending. MAIN CONCEPTS/THEMES: High Security Facility, National Security, African American/Black LGBTQ, Islamophobia.
64.	HAMILTON Dontre 31	Milwaukee, WI April 30, 2014	BRIEF: Starbucks employees called 911 to report a homeless man sleeping near their retail Kiosk in Red Arrow Park. Police initially determined and reported to Starbucks employees that Hamilton had committed no crime. The employees called back. When other officers converged on the scene, one in particular took exception to this. Police claimed that Hamilton took his baton and tried to hit him with it. Hamilton was fired upon 14 times, including one shot in the back. He also appeared to have been beaten in the face, neck and arm (evidence of "blunt force injuries"). LEGAL STATUS: Hamilton's mother formed the Coalition for Justice. The group exposed the name of the officer who killed Hamilton. The Milwaukee County District Attorney's office decided not to file charges against Officer Christopher Manney in the shooting death of Hamilton. Christopher Manney was fired from the Milwaukee police department. The DOJ, a year later, announced that they did not have enough evidence to open an investigation. MAIN CONCEPTS/THEMES: 911 Callers, Excessive Use-Of-Force, Mental Disorders (Schizophrenia), Unarmed Citizens
65.	HANNA, Darrin 45	North Chicago, IL November 13, 2011 ⊙	BRIEF: Police responded to a domestic disturbance call that Hanna was beating his pregnant girlfriend. The police stated that Hanna refused to leave, fought with the officers on the scene and that they beat and used a taser (purportedly for 20 minutes) in order to handcuff him. Hanna died a week later of multiple organ failure and complications associated with his sickle cell trait. An audio tape revealed that police had subdued Hanna, but continued to beat him, and that he begged for his life. With an autopsy image reminiscent of Emmett Till, numerous protests were launched. LEGAL STATUS: An internal investigation was conducted. One officer was fired, another officer was suspended. Officers were not found to be liable for any wrong doing in the case. The family filed a lawsuit for 3 million dollars in 2015. MAIN CONCEPTS/THEMES: Domestic Disturbance, Excessive Use-Of-Force, Tasers

World To Come: Essays On The Baltimore Uprising, Militant Racism, And History

66.	HARDING Kenneth 19	San Francisco, CA July 16, 2011	BRIEF: Thousands of people ride Muni (The San Francisco Municipal Transportation Agency) every day. Muni has said that it loses millions annually because of the people who evade the fare. Full time Fare inspectors are assigned to catch people who have not paid. According to media reports, Harding fled a Muni fare inspection. The police stated that a shootout with Harding took place. Witnesses at the scene said that Harding did not have a weapon. The police department went on to state that, using ballistics, that Harding killed himself. LEGAL STATUS: The Harding family filed federal wrongful death and civil rights lawsuits against the city of San Francisco. MAIN CONCEPTS/THEMES: Public Transportation, Questionable Suicide.
67.	HARRIS Eric 44	Tulsa, OK April 2, 2015	BRIEF: Harris ran from Tulsa Oklahoma police officers when he realized he was the target of a sting operation. Harris was tackled and restrained by the officers. Volunteer deputy reserve officer Robert Bates with his personal handgun, shot Harris in the back. He said that he confused it with his stun gun (taser). The police maintained that Harris was trying to sell an illegal gun to an undercover officer. Bates can be heard apologizing on tape for shooting Harris. LEGAL STATUS: Bates was charged with second-degree manslaughter, and he pleaded not guilty. A grand jury charged sheriff Stanley Glanz with two misdemeanors, and called for his removal. Glanz resigned from the Tulsa OK police force. MAIN CONCEPTS/THEMES: Undercover Police/Operation, Police Chase, Taser, Accidental Shooting, Sting Operation, Volunteer Police, Police Training.
68.	HENRY Danroy 20	Thornwood, NY October 17, 2010	BRIEF: Henry, a Pace University student, and others were leaving a bar in his car where a disturbance had occurred. Officer Aaron Hess shot Henry through the windshield. The police said that Henry tried to run him over. Witnesses state this was not true. Henry's body lay in the street for 3 minutes before he was attended. LEGAL STATUS: Officer Hess was not indicted. Henry's family filed a wrongful death suit. MAIN CONCEPTS/THEMES: Automobile-As-Weapon.
69.	HICKS Linda 62	Toledo, OH December 13, 2009	BRIEF: Police were called to Hicks' group home where she was purportedly off medication and acting out of control. They say, Hicks had a pacemaker, approached the police ("charged") with a pair of scissors and threatened them. When one officer attempted to taser her and the device malfunctioned, the other officer shot Hicks two times in the head. LEGAL STATUS: A grand jury cleared the officer that killed Hicks of murder. The family has maintained that there are too many unanswered questions in the case. MAIN

World To Come: Essays On The Baltimore Uprising, Militant Racism, And History

CONCEPTS/THEMES: Knife-Wielding (Scissors), Lethal Force, African American/Black Women, Tasers, Mental Illness.

70.	HILL Anthony 27	Chamblee, GA March 9, 2015	BRIEF: Hill, a veteran who believed he was bipolar and was going VA treatment, was outside his apartment complex in his shorts (other accounts suggested that at some point he was naked), unarmed, laying on the ground. Rental office staff called 911. When the police arrived, hill stood up, walked toward the officer with his hands raised. The officer told him to stop. He proceeded to shoot hill. There were several witnesses, and those who were on the scene of the shooting. There was also the intimation that the officer had intended to use a taser. LEGAL STATUS: Pending. MAIN CONCEPTS/ THEMES: Mental Disorders (Bi-Polar), 911 Callers, Excessive Use-Of-Force.
71.	HOPKINS, Jr. Gary A. 19	West Lanham Hills, MD November 27, 1999	BRIEF: After leaving a late-night party with a carload of friends, Hopkins a college student was shot and killed in a parking lot at the West Lanham Hills fire station. Police stated that they proceeded to stop the car after someone reported a passenger was in possession of a gun. Authorities stated that Hopkins exited the vehicle and attempted to grab an officer's gun out of his hand. According to the police report a second officer, Brian C. Catlett, shot Hopkins once in the chest after a struggle for the weapon ensued. Witnesses maintained that Hopkins was shot without provocation and that prior to the shooting the same officers had harassed Hopkins and his friends. LEGAL STATUS: After an indictment on manslaughter charges, Catlett became the first Prince George's officer to face criminal charges for killing someone while in uniform. Ultimately, Catlett was acquitted after a Circuit Court judge found him not guilty. MAIN CONCEPTS/THEMES: Suspected Weapons Possession (SWP).
72.	HOWARD, Jr. Everette 18	Cincinnati, OH August 6, 2011	BRIEF: Howard was an Upward Bound program student at the University of Cincinnati. His early morning encounter with campus police officer Richard Haas ended in Howard being tasered. Howard died thereafter. LEGAL STATUS: The University and the officer never admitted any wrongdoing in this case. The Howard family filed a civil rights lawsuit, and was awarded two million dollars. However, among the non-monetary conditions, the Howard's parents also received a letter of sympathy from the university; tuition fee waivers for the undergraduate education of both Howard's younger brother and sister; stipulations about the training of law enforcement with tasers; and a memorial area at the University. MAIN CONCEPTS/ THEMES: Taser Death.

World To Come: Essays On The Baltimore Uprising, Militant Racism, And History

73.	HUNT Darrien 22	Sarasota Springs, UT September 10, 2014	BRIEF: A person made a 911 call to the Saratoga Springs police to report a "suspicious person." According to the caller the person was carrying a sword (part of an anime costume) and walking through a middle class neighborhood. Police said that when they approached Hunt, he had been cooperative. However, suddenly he became violent. He refused to relinquish the sword and then swung it at them. The officers shot Hunt as he ran from the scene. Hunt's body was found with multiple bullet wounds, most in his back. Hunt's family disputed the police version of the story. LEGAL STATUS: Hunt's family filed lawsuits (civil rights and wrongful death). MAIN CONCEPTS/THEMES: 911 Callers, Suspicious Persons/Citizens.
74.	IVY Donald "Dontay" 39	Albany, NY April 2, 2015	BRIEF: Ivy was approached by three officers for "suspicious activity." Ivy, described as a paranoid schizophrenic and unarmed, was cited for aggressive behavior. He purportedly ran away, was tackled and tasered by officers. Ivy died shortly thereafter. LEGAL STATUS: Investigations into the death of Ivy were initiated. The officers were placed on leave pending investigation outcomes. MAIN CONCEPTS/THEMES: 911 Callers, Suspicious Persons/Citizens.
75.	JACKSON, Jr. Larry Eugene 32	Austin, TX July 26, 2013	BRIEF: In one version of the story Jackson was chased before an altercation with Det. Charles Kleinert as he tried to stop him from committing fraud. Kleinert shot Jackson. It was also reported that Jackson tried to enter a bank that was closed. The bank had been robbed earlier. The detective questioned Jackson, and chased him, before shooting him. LEGAL STATUS: Detective Charles Kleinert was indicted on manslaughter. MAIN CONCEPTS/THEMES: Police Chase.
76.	JEFFERSON Ervin 18	Atlanta, GA March 24, 2012	BRIEF: Two African American security guards shot Jefferson to death outside of an apartment complex. The officers ostensibly shot Jefferson because he walked toward them aggressively, shouting threats because he believed his sister was in danger. LEGAL STATUS: The security guards, Curtis Scott and Gary Jackson, were arrested and charged with impersonating police. MAIN CONCEPTS/THEMES: Para-Police, Security Guards.
77.	JOHNSON, Sr. Dondi 43	Baltimore, MD December 7, 2005	BRIEF: The Baltimore Police department arrested Johnson for urinating in public. Johnson was handcuffed and placed inside of a police transport vehicle. When Johnson emerged from the vehicle he was badly injured. His spine was crushed and he died weeks later. LEGAL STATUS: The Johnson family filed a wrongful death suit. They were finally awarded $200,000. MAIN CONCEPTS/THEMES: Police Transport Injury, Public Urination Laws.

78.	JOHNSON Ronald 25	Chicago, IL October 12, 2014 ⊙	BRIEF: Johnson was suspected in a random south side shooting and fled from police when approached. Police-encountered him and said that Johnson was armed and refused to comply. They said he pointed a gun at the officers as he ran away, so they shot him. The family disagreed and believed the gun found at the scene was planted. LEGAL STATUS: the family filed a federal suit and a public records complaint in order to have the police dash cam video publically released. Charges were not filed against the officers. MAIN CONCEPTS/THEMES: Police Chase
79.	JONES Aiyana 7	Detroit, MI May 16, 2010	BRIEF: 7-year-old Aiyana Jones was shot when a Special Response Team raided her family's duplex. Officers tossed a grenade into the apartment. Officer Joseph Weekley claimed Jones's grandmother seized his gun, and this caused Jones to be shot. LEGAL STATUS: Weekley was charged with involuntary manslaughter. His legal proceedings ended in mistrials. MAIN CONCEPTS/THEMES: Adolescents/Juveniles/Children, SWAT, Accidental Shooting.
80.	JONES Corey 31	Palm Beach, FL October 18, 2015	BRIEF: Jones' car broke down on highway I-95 in the early morning. He called for automotive assistance. Officer Nouman Raja, who was plain clothed and in an unmarked police car investigated Jones' car, believing it to be an abandoned. Reports differ thereafter. One suggested that Raja was confronted by an armed Jones; and other reports state Jones was on the phone with roadside assistance when he was shot. LEGAL STATUS: Officer Raja was placed on administrative leave pending investigation. MAIN CONCEPTS/THEMES: Plainclothes Police, Legal Firearms.
81.	JONES Derrick 37	Oakland, CA November 8, 2010	BRIEF: One of Jones' neighbors accused him of assault. When officers responded (Perez-Jones and Daza-Quiroz) Jones ran and they chased. According to officers when they caught up to Jones they thought he was reaching for a gun in his waistband. Both officers' fired on Jones, who was unarmed, and he was hit six times. Jones carried a small silver colored scale in his waistband. The case also involved officers handcuffing/taking a woman to police headquarters for questioning. Both officers' had misconduct complaints; and one purportedly admitted that he wanted to use lethal force on Jones. LEGAL STATUS: Police Chief Anthony Batts asked the FBI to investigate. The DA would not indict the officers. The city of Oakland settled with Jones' family for $225,000. In a federal suit the officers were cleared of wrongdoing. MAIN CONCEPTS/THEMES: Domestic Disturbance, Police Chase, Suspected Weapon, Unarmed Citizens, Excessive Use-Of-Force, Police Intimidation.

82.	JONES Prince 25	Fairfax County, VA September 1, 2000	BRIEF: The officer-involved shooting of Jones (who was a Howard University student) was caste initially in the media as one of mistaken identity. Jones was purportedly seen driving through a drug ridden neighborhood by Officer Carlton Jones. He was driving a vehicle that fit the description police were looking for. The undercover officer followed Jones and when they stopped near his girlfriend's house, Jones got out of his car and confronted the officer who brandished a gun (not a badge). Jones then ran; or; the officer fired 16 shots at him in his Jeep. Eight of the gunshots hit Jones. The Jones family did not agree with the official police statement. They believe he was driving away when he was fired upon. LEGAL STATUS: Authorities declined to file charges against the Officer Carlton Jones. Years later the Jones family was awarded $3.7 million in a wrongful death lawsuit. MAIN CONCEPTS/ THEMES: Undercover Police/Operation, Excessive Use-Of-Force, Unarmed Citizens, Mistaken Suspect.
83.	JONES Ralkina 37	Cleveland Heights, OH July 26, 2015	BRIEF: Jones was involved in a domestic violence incident with her ex-husband on a Friday. Police were called and she was arrested. By Sunday morning she was found "unresponsive in her jail cell. Jones was taken to the hospital on Sunday morning for conditions associated with diabetes and high blood pressure. When it was determined that Jones was dead, the police were confused about why she had been arrested and jailed and didn't know how she died. Police maintained however that her death was not suspicious. When Jones' sister visited her on that Saturday Ralkina Jones appeared to be in good health. LEGAL STATUS: Pending. MAIN CONCEPTS/THEMES: Domestic Disturbance, Medical Health, In-Custody Death, African American/Black Women.
84.	LAMBERT, Jr. Linwood R. 46	South Boston, VA May 4, 2013	BRIEF: Police were called for a noise complaint in the hotel Lambert was staying in. He was taken to the emergency room as "delusional" when he purportedly became agitated, tried to run, and was tased. Over the course of thirty minutes Lambert was tased 20 times. His cause of death was listed as cocaine intoxication. LEGAL STATUS: Lamberts death is under investigation. His family has filed a wrongful death lawsuit for $25 million dollars. MAIN CONCEPTS/ THEMES: Narcotics, Tasers, Mental Disabilities
85.	LANEY Michael Deangelo 28	Charlotte, NC July 2, 2015	BRIEF: Officers tried to stop Laney who was riding a scooter. According to police the scooter matched the description of one used in a robbery. Laney did not stop, left the scooter and ran to his home. The officers caught and struggled with Laney on the front yard of his home. There are varying accounts of the story. Police

#	Name	Location / Date	Details
			claim he reached for a handgun. Another account says that he had a gun in his pocket, and was holding the gun clip. He was shot in the head, by Anthony Holzhauer. LEGAL STATUS: The officer was placed on administrative leave. MAIN CONCEPTS/THEMES: Police Chase, Resisting Arrest.
86.	LINYARD Richard Lamar 23	Oakland, CA July 19, 2015	BRIEF: When police stopped Linyard, he purportedly ran into a neighborhood, where at some point, he became "wedged" between two buildings in a space less than 2 inches wide—and choked. Police stated that they did not pursue Linyard immediately, but called for backup. Thirty minutes later, they found Linyard, performed CPR, and called paramedics. Linyard died at the hospital. Police maintain that they did not pursue Linyard or use any force against him; and that Linyard's car had one pound of marijuana, and that he was wanted for a $10,000 (undisclosed) warrant. Family members have found his death "unacceptable" and have many questions about the condition of his body, information, and post-incident police conduct; a *GoFundMe* account was set up to assist with his funeral/burial fees. LEGAL STATUS: Pending. MAIN CONCEPTS/THEMES: Mysterious Deaths
87.	LOGGINS, Jr. Sgt. Manuel 31	Orange County, CA February 7, 2012	BRIEF: Loggins was said to have been on a religious fast and thus off of his ADHD medication. Loggins purportedly crashed into an Orange County high gate. At the time his two daughters was with him. Loggins while walking through the school's athletic field holding his Bible, returned to his car, and was approached by a police officer. The officer shot Loggins, who was unarmed, through his car window three times, killing him. LEGAL STATUS: The Loggins family received a settlement of $4.4 million from Orange County. MAIN CONCEPTS/THEMES: Unarmed Citizens.
88.	LOPEZ Andy 13 (Hispanic/Latino)	Santa Rosa, CA October 22, 2013	BRIEF: Lopez was carrying a pellet/toy gun headed to a friend's house. Police who were on patrol in the area allegedly asked Lopez to drop the gun. When Lopez turned towards the police offices, they fired on him. The police stated that the toy gun looked like an AK-47 assault rifle. The officer was in fear for his life. LEGAL STATUS: There was no indictment in Lopez' case. MAIN CONCEPTS/THEMES: Latinos, Adolescents/Juveniles/Children, Toy Guns/Weapons/BBs.
89.	MADISON Ronald 40	New Orleans, LA September 4, 2005	BRIEF: (See James Brisette) Days after Hurricane Katrina, police received a call saying that there was gunfire on the Danziger Bridge. They open fired upon arriving in a Budget Rental Truck. Brisette was struck; Madison (thought to be developmentally disabled), ran from the scene and was chased by police. Officer Faulcon, shot him; and Sgt. Bowen, stomped Madison

on the back before he died. LEGAL STATUS: Sgt. Bowen was convicted Madison's death, and that conviction was later overturned. The case involved elements of an attempted cover-up. Eventually five officers involved in the shooting were found guilty of various charges. Faulcon was sentenced to 65 years' imprisonment, Bowen and Sgt. Robert Gisevius received 40 years. Officer Villavaso received 38 years. Arthur "Archie" Kaufman, who served as the investigator for the case was eventually found guilty of conspiring to conceal evidence, and he received 6 years. A month later, the judge that convicted them (Kurt Engelhardt) vacated their convictions and ordered a new trial. MAIN CONCEPTS/THEMES: Excessive Use-Of-Force

90.	MANYOUN Deng 35 ⊙	Louisville, KY June 14, 2015	BRIEF: An officer pulled up in his cruiser and approached Manyoun on the street. Manyoun appeared to be dazed and confused and/or intoxicated. The officer engaged Manyoun in a conversation, who may not have understood English. Manyoun seemingly became more agitated at the questions walked away from the officer. Shortly after, Manyoun grabbed a flag pole and walked towards the officer swinging it and hitting the squad car. The officer shot Manyoun who was later pronounced dead at the University of Louisville hospital. LEGAL STATUS. The officer was placed on administrative leave; a departmental investigation was initiated. MAIN CONCEPTS/THEMES: Mental Illness, Unarmed Citizens, Weaponized Objects, Weapons-Of-Convenience, Lethal Force, Investigative Stops.
91.	MARTIN Trayvon 17	Sanford, FL February 26, 2012	BRIEF: Martin was visiting Sanford Florida with his father when he was fatally shot by George Zimmerman. Zimmerman, a neighborhood watch volunteer, called the police indicating that Martin, who was returning from a convenience store, looked suspicious. Zimmerman followed Martin (even though the police advised him not to); an altercation occurred and Martin, who was unarmed, was shot in the chest. LEGAL STATUS: Zimmerman was not immediately charged and it was assumed that he was defending himself against Martin. He was eventually charged with second-degree murder and manslaughter, claimed self-defense, and was acquitted July 13, 2013. Nation-wide protests took place. The Justice Department declined to charge Zimmerman of a Civil Rights violation. The Martin family filed a wrongful death lawsuit against the HOA and settled the case. Post-acquittal, Zimmerman was charged with aggravated assault with a weapon, has had domestic assault charges filed against him (which were

92.	MCCAIN Spencer Lee 41	Owings Mill, MD June 25, 2015	dropped), and he has also been involved in a road rage altercation. MAIN CONCEPTS/THEMES: Para-Police, Neighborhood Watch, Adolescents/Juveniles/Children, Suspicious Persons/Citizens. BRIEF: On a domestic disturbance call, three officers shot McCain. They claim that they heard screams coming from the home; found McCain in a "defensive Position," and believing he had a gun, all fired on him. He was pronounced dead at Sinai Hospital. LEGAL STATUS: Pending. MAIN CONCEPTS/THEMES: Unarmed Citizens, Domestic Disturbance.
93.	MCDADE Kendrec 19	Pasadena, CA March 24, 2012	BRIEF: McDade was on his way to visit his girlfriend, and then spend the night with his father. A 911 caller reported that he had been robbed of his backpack and a laptop computer at gunpoint by two black men. He later admitted that he was robbed but not at gunpoint. McDade was in the area where the theft occurred. The police approached McDade as one of the suspects in the robbery and he ran. Police gave chase in their patrol car. When they caught up to him, one of the officers chased him on foot. They said they feared for their lives. When McDade ran toward the police car the other officer, Griffin, believed that he had a gun and that he was reaching for it. Officer Griffin then shot McDade. Officer Newlen shot McDade from behind as well. McDade was shot a total of seven times. They proceeded to handcuff him. He later died at the hospital. The police did not find the stolen items or a weapon. His mother found out about the shooting in the newspaper, but didn't know it was her son until later. LEGAL STATUS: The LA police department and the District Attorney's Office cleared the officers of any wrongdoing. Investigations by the Office of Independent Review and the FBI agreed with the findings. The city settled out of court with the family for $850,000. MAIN CONCEPTS/THEMES: Police Chase, 911 Callers, Unarmed Citizens.
94.	MCDOLE Jeremy 28	Wilmington, DE September 23, 2015 ⊙	BRIEF: Four officers responded to a 911 call stating that McDole, who was paralyzed and wheel chair bound, had committed suicide with a gun. Officers found McDole "shuffling" in the wheel chair and ordered him to put his hands up. When McDole did not comply, they open fired, killing him. The police state that a weapon was found. The family disputed that McDole possessed a weapon. A cellphone video captured part of the encounter. LEGAL STATUS: Officers were placed on administrative leave. The Delaware DOJ (Civil Rights and Public Trust) launched an investigation. MAIN CONCEPTS/THEMES: Wheel Chair, 911 Callers, Disabilities

World To Come: Essays On The Baltimore Uprising, Militant Racism, And History

| 95. | MCDONALD Laquan 17 | Chicago, IL

October 20, 2014

⊙ | BRIEF: Police received a 911 call that a man was carrying a knife. McDonald refused to drop the knife and walked away from officers. McDonald was shot 16 times, including after he had fallen to the ground. Police maintained that McDonald was erratic and came toward them with the knife. Chicago activists called for release of the police-cam video of the shooting for over a year. The video of the shooting was not released until after a judge's order on November 19, 2015. Protests in the city mounted and criticisms were leveled against city government, with criticisms particularly citing Mayor Rahm Emmanuel's office. LEGAL STATUS: The officer was placed on desk duty. Weeks later, pending release of the video, he was charged with first degree murder and denied bail. The FBI and Cook County State's attorney's office initiated investigations. The family of McDonald was paid a $5 million dollar pre-trial settlement. MAIN CONCEPTS/THEMES: Knife-Wielding, 911 Callers, Excessive Use-Of-Force |
|---|---|---|---|
| 96. | MCGILL Travares 16 | Sanford, FL

July 18, 2005 | BRIEF: McGill, 16, sat in a car at an apartment complex. A bright light was directed into the car. McGill tried to back out and leave. The two security guards did not identify themselves. The guards, Bryan Ansley and William Patrick Swofford, stated that Travares tried to hit them with the car. They feared for their lives and open fired. Travares was struck in the back and died. LEGAL STATUS: the guards were indicted by a grand jury. The case went to trial, and was dismissed by the judge. MAIN CONCEPTS/THEMES: Security Guards, Para-Police, Adolescents/Juveniles/Children, Automobile-As-Weapon |
| 97. | MCLEOD Keith Harrison 19 | Reisterstown, MD

September 25, 2015

⊙ | BRIEF: A Baltimore County police officer shot McLeod whom he believed was armed and intending to shoot. The officer shot McLeod three times. The police released a video to defend the shooting (there is no audio); news articles included statements from unidentified witnesses suggesting that the officer pleaded with McLeod, and that McLeod threatened to kill him. LEGAL STATUS: Pending. MAIN CONCEPTS/THEMES: Unarmed Citizens. |
| 98. | MILLER Adaisha 24 | Detroit, MI

July 8, 2012 | BRIEF: Miller attended a party given by officer Isaac Parrish. As she danced with Parrish his police-issued service weapon discharged. Miller was shot in the lung and heart. She died at the hospital. LEGAL STATUS: The Detroit Police Department and Wayne County prosecutor ran investigations. Officer Parrish was assigned to temporary desk duty. The family wanted the case reopened; and started a petition at *Change.org*. MAIN CONCEPTS/THEMES: Accidental Shooting, Off-Duty Police Officer. |

World To Come: Essays On The Baltimore Uprising, Militant Racism, And History

99.	MITCHELL Robert 16	Detroit, MI April 10, 2009	BRIEF: Mitchell was a passenger in a car with two other relatives when stopped by Warren, Michigan police for an expired license plate. Mitchell ran from police and they chased him into an abandoned house in Detroit. Police say that Mitchell resisted arrest by three officers, so they tasered him. In another account, Mitchell raised his hands and surrendered to police, and he was held by the wrist before being tasered. Mitchell stopped breathing. Mitchel died of heart failure. LEGAL STATUS: The Mitchell family filed a wrongful death suit against the police. MAIN CONCEPTS/THEMES: Unarmed Citizens, Taser Deaths, Excessive Use-Of-Force, Adolescents, Police Chase.
100.	MOORE Bernard 62	Atlanta, GA March 6, 2015	BRIEF: Moore was hit by a police car said to be on routine patrol, and thus not displaying lights, sirens, or responding to a call. He died after being taken to the hospital. Some witnesses have suggested that the police vehicle was speeding. LEGAL STATUS: Pending. MAIN CONCEPTS/THEMES: Automobile Homicide, Hospitalization.
101.	MORRISON Bo 20	Slinger, WI March 3, 2012	BRIEF: Morrison had attended a party with about twenty other people. The party included loud music, alcohol and marijuana. Police received a noise complaint from one of the neighbor's adjacent to the party. When party-goers heard that the police had arrived and had "surrounded" the place, several partyers ran, including Morrison. Morrison purportedly ran toward a homeowner's residence, the homeowner claimed he came inside of his porch. The armed homeowner detected Morrison in the dark porch. When Morrison moved toward him he shot him in the chest through the heart. The homeowner's wife called 911 and "…The homeowner followed all directions to place the gun down, and to keep his hands up when officers arrived on scene."[3] Police, ambulance and EMTs were unable to save Morrison. LEGAL STATUS: No criminal charges were filed against the homeowner. Morrison's mother filed a wrongful death lawsuit in the Milwaukee County Circuit Court. MAIN CONCEPTS/THEMES: Domestic Disturbance, Home Defense, Self-Defense, Castle Doctrine.
102.	MYERS, Jr. VonDerrit 18	St. Louis, MO October 8, 2014	BRIEF: An off duty police officer, working as a security guard, saw Myers (a high school student) with two other males on the street, one of them ran. Myers allegedly pulled a gun and fired and the gun jammed. The officer

---

[3] Report of the Washington County District Attorney's Office Regarding the Shooting of Mr. Bo Morrison On March 3, 2012, 13.

103. MURPHY Andre Larone 42 — Norfolk, NE — July 1, 2015

fired his gun 17 times. In another version of the story, Myers and friends were purchasing food from a local market and he was not armed. Meyers was killed two months after Michael Brown, and ten miles south of Ferguson in south St. Louis, Missouri. Within hours of the shooting, the police began Tweeting their narrative. LEGAL STATUS: Pending. MAIN CONCEPTS/THEMES: Off-Duty Police Officer, Security Guards.

BRIEF: Police responded to 911 calls at a motel where Murphy was located. There was a struggle with an officer and Murphy was arrested and taken to an emergency room. He died later. They found no weapons. The officer may or may not have used a taser. LEGAL BRIEF: Pending. MAIN CONCEPTS/THEMES: 911 Callers, Hospitalization, Unarmed Citizens.

104. MURRAY Earl 36 — Dellwood, MO — June 12, 2000

BRIEF: (See also Ronald Beasley) Murray and Beasley, were called in the media, small-time drug dealers. Murray, Beasley and another passenger, were shot and killed in what has been described as a "hail of bullets" during an attempted drug bust in a restaurant parking lot. Some officers claimed that Murray's car was moving towards them and that they were in danger; other officers say that the car was not moving forward. Another perspective was that the car was in reverse in an effort to flee the officers. One officer purported called the killings "unintended, but not a mistake." An officer also revered to Beasley and Murray as "bums." All of the men were unarmed. LEGAL STATUS: The officers were cleared of wrongdoing after a yearlong investigation. A Grand Jury did not indict. Authorities felt there was not enough evidence for federal charges to be filed. MAIN CONCEPTS/THEMES: Narcotics.

105. NICHOLS Jacqueline 64 — Flint, MI — July 3, 2014

BRIEF: Nichols was riding as a passenger in a vehicle that was struck and killed in an accident involving a state trooper. The trooper was engaged in a police chase with a car for a possible traffic violation. It has been disputed in this case, whether the officer used a siren and flashing lights. LEGAL STATUS: There are various court cases and lawsuits pending. The state of Michigan approved a 7.7 million dollar settle, pending legislative approval. MAIN CONCEPTS/THEMES: Police Chase, Car Crash, Collateral Damage.

106. OKUTUGA Emmanuel 26 — Silver Spring, MI — February 19, 2011

BRIEF: Police received reports that a City Place Mall security guard had been assaulted. An officer encountered Okutuga outside of the mail "wielding an ice pick." Police state that Okutuga refused to drop the ice pick, and was shot twice. LEGAL STATUS: The officer was placed on paid administrative leave; and an investigation was launched. The family of Okutuga filed

World To Come: Essays On The Baltimore Uprising, Militant Racism, And History

			a wrongful death lawsuit against the police; and they set up a "Justice for Emmanuel" fund. MAIN CONCEPTS/THEMES: Knife-Wielding ("Ice Pick"), Lethal Force, Mentally Challenged, Security Guards.
107.	PARKER Dante 36	San Bernardino County, CA August 12, 2014	BRIEF: Police responded to a 911 call about an attempted break-in. The suspect in the break-in fled on a bicycle. The police later found Parker nearby riding his bike. Parker was unarmed. A struggle resulted when he resisted arrest. The police used a taser on him and he died. LEGAL STATUS: Pending. The NAACP called for a federal investigation. MAIN CONCEPTS/THEMES: Police Chase, Unarmed Citizens, Taser Death.
108.	PAUL Jonathan Ryan 42	Arlington, TX March 13, 2015	BRIEF: A domestic disturbance call led police to Paul who was arrested on misdemeanor warrants. Paul was processed and placed in a jail cell. The next day he was moved to an isolation cell. Paul was found unresponsive in the isolation cell. He was hospitalized and pronounced dead. LEGAL STATUS: Pending. MAIN CONCEPTS/THEMES: Domestic Disturbance, Jail Cell Death.
109.	PIKES Baron 21	Winnfield, LA January 17, 2008	BRIEF: Police approached Pikes on the street, and tried to arrest him on drug possession charges. Pikes then ran from police. They said that Pikes resisted arrest when he was finally captured, and was tasered. Pikes became ill (the police said that Pikes admitted having cocaine in his system) and was taken to the hospital where he died. This account differed remarkably from other reports. It is also believed that Pikes did not resist arrest, that he was forced to the ground, handcuffed, and then tased by police nine times. In addition, Pikes had no cocaine in his system. Pikes was most likely unconscious during the remaining taser shots.[4] LEGAL STATUS: The Louisiana State Police investigated. One officer was fired from the police force. MAIN CONCEPTS/THEMES: Police Brutality, Excessive Use-Of-Force, Police Chase, Tasers.
110.	PINEX Darius 27	Chicago, IL January 7, 2011	BRIEF: Pinex was killed after a routine traffic stop because police believed that his car that matched the description of a vehicle involved with gunshots. The police stated that he hit and dragged a police officer with his car. Other sources stated that Pinex backed away into a light pole and then moved forward to escape the police. He was shot trying to drive away. The officers were masked. LEGAL STATUS: The officers

---

[4] Howard Witt, "Taser Death Spotlights Town's Corrupt History Handcuffed Man, 21, Was Stunned 9 Times by Officer," *Chicago Tribune*, July 19, 2008.

World To Come: Essays On The Baltimore Uprising, Militant Racism, And History

			were found not guilty and retried. Information surfaced indicating a potentially major cover-up in the case (there was no police call about an armed driver), including the actual reasons Pinex was pulled over; police colluded to cover the murder.[5] MAIN CONCEPTS/ THEMES: Traffic Stops, Police-Cover-Up, Unarmed Citizens.
111.	POPE Aaron 34	Toledo, OH March 27, 2015	BRIEF: Pope was arrested after police received a 911 domestic disturbance call. Police, believing Pope was influenced by drugs, was taken to the hospital, and pronounced dead. Members of the family and community were concerned because he was taken to the hospital in a police wagon rather than an ambulance. LEGAL STATUS: Pending. MAIN CONCEPTS/ THEMES: 911 Callers, Domestic Disturbance, Narcotics, Hospitalization.
112.	POWELL Kajieme 25	St. Louis, MO August 19, 2014 ⊙	BRIEF: The police received a 911 call stating that Powell was stealing energy drinks and pastries. The police shot Powell within seconds of arriving on the scene. The police maintained that Powell approached them holding a knife. A video of the incident contradicted the account. Powell did not close in on police; his hands were by his side. LEGAL STATUS: The Powell family filed a wrongful death suit against the St. Louis police chief and the officers. MAIN CONCEPTS/THEMES: 911 Callers, Petty Theft, Knife Wielding, Excessive Use-Of-Force.
113.	PRICE Dante 25	Dayton, OH March 1, 2012	BRIEF: Two Ranger Security guards ordered Price out of an apartment complex because they believed he was trespassing. Price, who was visiting his girlfriend and 1-year-old son, refused to leave and waited for police. The two security guards ordered him from his car repeatedly, and one peppered-sprayed him. Price decided to drive away. They fired 17-20 shots at him. They claimed that Price attempted to run them over with his car. When a fire started in the car, the two purportedly yelled, "let the nigger burn." LEGAL STATUS: The Southern Christian Leadership Conference (SCLC) was one of the groups leading rallies protesting the murder of Price. Justin Wissinger and Christopher Tarbert were charged, and pled guilty to involuntary manslaughter and abduction. One had been allowed home monitoring before sentencing. They were sentenced 4 years in prison. Both were also fined $4,000 each. MAIN CONCEPTS/THEMES: Security Guards, Para-Police, Excessive Use-Of-Force, Lethal Force.

---

[5]Shaun King, "Chicago Police and Prosecutors Caught Lying As They Cover Up Their Murder Of Darius Pinex," *Daily Kos*, October 2, 2015.

114.	QUARLES Jamie 22	Baltimore, MD August 9, 1997 ⊙	BRIEF: Near Baltimore's famed Lexington Market, police-encountered Quarles holding a knife. Police surrounded him with their weapons drawn. Onlookers begged the police not to shoot Quarles. When he refused to drop the knife at the police officers command they shot him. Quarles was dead upon arrival at the Maryland Shock Trauma Center. The incident, which was videotaped, differed from the police narrative of the event. LEGAL BRIEF: The officer who shot Quarles was placed on administrative duty and an investigation was launched by the police. Despite an earlier domestic violence conviction, the officer was later allowed to resume patrol duty. In 1999 the police settled the $200 million dollar lawsuit against them, but the actual amount was not disclosed until the next year. The Quarles settlement was 500,000. MAIN CONCEPTS/THEMES: Knife-Wielding, Excessive Use-Of-Force.
115.	REID Jerame 36	Bridgeton, NJ December 30, 2014 ⊙	BRIEF: Leroy Tutt, the driver of a vehicle in which Reid was a passenger was subjected to a traffic stop after he went through a stop sign. Both men were ordered to "show their hands." One of the officers believed that he saw a gun in the car and they demanded that Tutt and Reid raise their hands and also tell them that they should not reach for a weapon. Officer Days addressed Reid personally, warning him that he would shoot him if he reached for anything. Reid said he had no reason to reach for anything. As an officer attempted to retrieve a gun, Reid got out of the car with his hands raised and was shot repeatedly. The police dash cam video captured the encounter. Police found no weapons in Reid's possession. One of the officers knew Reid. As a teen Reid, was charged with and convicted of shooting at NJ state police troopers and spent 13 years in prison. Officer Days was listed as one of the arresting officers on a drug possession charge against Reid. Community protests over the shooting took place. LEGAL STATUS: Officer Days was placed on leave pending investigation. MAIN CONCEPTS/THEMES: Unarmed Citizens, Traffic Stops, Convicted Felons.
116.	RICE Tamir 12	Cleveland, OH November 22, 2014 ⊙	BRIEF: Rice and his teen sister were visiting the park. Rice was playing with a toy/BB gun. A 911 caller informed dispatch that a black male was in the park pointing a gun at people. When the police arrived on the scene, Officer Tim Loehmann shot and killed Rice, within seconds after spotting him. LEGAL STATUS: The shooting was ruled as justified by authorities. The Rice family filed a wrongful death lawsuit against the city of Cleveland. In February 2016, the city of Cleveland billed the "estate of Tamir Rice," $500.00 for

			ambulance services, that included mileage and advanced life support. The mayor later apologized. MAIN CONCEPTS/THEMES: Toy Guns/Weapons/ BBs, Adolescents/ Juveniles/Children, Excessive Use-Of-Force.
117.	RICKS Robert 23	Alexandria, LA February 5, 2011	BRIEF: Ricks, who was unarmed when he was taken into police-custody was tased (a second time) to death while handcuffed when he refused to comply with a police order. Ricks was said to have died of "excited delirium." Ricks suffered from mental illness and authorities stated that at the time of his arrest, he had lethal doses of cocaine in his system. LEGAL STATUS: Rick's father filed a wrongful death suit. MAIN CONCEPTS/THEMES: Taser Death, Unarmed Citizens, Excessive Use-Of-Force, Mental Illness, Narcotics.
118.	ROBERTS Askari 35	Floyd County, GA March 16, 2015	BRIEF: Police responded to a family's domestic complaint call, and in an effort to restrain Roberts with handcuffs (who was cited as attempting to hurt family members), he became unconscious, CPR was performed, and Roberts was taken to the hospital where he was pronounced dead. LEGAL STATUS: The GBI took over the investigation of the case. MAIN CONCEPTS/THEMES: Domestic Disturbance, Hospitalization, DOA, Police Restraint.
119.	ROBINSON Tamon 27	New York, NY April 18, 2012	BRIEF: Police responded to a call that Robinson was stealing paving stones. When confronted by the police, Robinson, who was unarmed, ran toward the building where his mother lived. The police officers chased him by car and hit him in the process. LEGAL STATUS: The Robinson family received a $2 million settlement in a wrongful death suit they filed against the city. MAIN CONCEPTS/THEMES: Unarmed Citizens, Police Chase, Automobile Homicide.
120.	ROBINSON, Jr. Tony 19	Madison, WI March 6, 2015	BRIEF: The police responded to a domestic disturbance call concerning a mental wellness check. Robinson, who was unarmed, was shot seven times by a Madison Police Officer who forced his way into an apartment. LEGAL STATUS: The district attorney announced that charges would not be filed against the officer. MAIN CONCEPTS/THEMES: Domestic Disturbance, Mental Health, Unarmed Citizens, Wellness Check.
121.	ROSSER Aura 40	Ann Arbor, MI November 9, 2014	BRIEF: Police (Officers Reid and Mark Raab) responded to a domestic disturbance call at the home of Rosser shared with her boyfriend Victor Stephens. Officer Reid claimed that Rosser came at them with a knife. Officer Raab tasered Rosser and Officer Reid shot her. Stephens questioned the need for the police to shoot her. He challenged the police statement that they shot her only once. Stephens stated that she was shot

			twice—in the head as well as the chest. LEGAL STATUS: The officers did not face charges in the death of Rosser. Her death was ruled a justifiable homicide. A civil lawsuit is pending. MAIN CONCEPTS/ THEMES: African American/Black Women, Knife-Wielding, Domestic Disturbance.
122.	RUSS Robert "Bobby" 22	Chicago, IL June 5, 2009	BRIEF: Russ (a Northwestern University football star slated to graduate) was subjected to a routine traffic stop. Russ was shot because he allegedly attempted to grab the officer's gun. Three officers were implicated in the shooting, and cited for falsifying the accounts of the report. LEGAL STATUS: The shooting was ruled a justified homicide. In 2003 the Russ family was awarded 9.6 million from their lawsuit. MAIN CONCEPTS/ THEMES: Traffic Stop, Disputed Accounts.
123.	RUSSELL Timothy 43	Cleveland, OH November 29, 2012	BRIEF: (See also Malissa Williams) An officer reported that gunshots had been fired from (like the one Russell and Williams were driving) the Justice Center. Russell and Williams were chased by 62 police cars. Officers fired 137 rounds of ammunition into the car killing Russell and Williams. Both were unarmed. One officer stood on the hood of the car and fired into the windshield. In the confusion, police said they believed that gunfire was coming from the car. LEGAL STATUS: A settlement between the city and the two's families—was reached for $1.5 million each. Brelo was indicted in May 2014 for voluntary manslaughter and found innocent of the charge. Police supervisors were also accused of failing to perform their duties. MAIN CONCEPTS/THEMES: Police Chase.
124.	SATTER-WHITE Ernest 68	North Augusta, SC February 9, 2014	BRIEF: Satterwhite led Officer Justin Craven on a low-speed chase after he refused to pull over for a routine traffic stop. Officer Craven chased Satterwhite into his own driveway which was I another county. Despite heeding Edgefield county police's instructions to leave the matter to them, Officer Craven approached Satterfield parked in his own driveway, and fired five times. Satterwhite was hit four times and shot twice in the chest. Thereafter, officers pulled Satterwhite out of his car, placed him in handcuffs and left him on the ground until EMS arrived. LEGAL STATUS: The prosecutor, attempted to charge Craven with voluntary manslaughter. A grand jury indicted him on a misdemeanor. A lawsuit was filed against Craven and his trial was scheduled for 2016. The family of Satterwhite received a $1.2 million dollar settlement. MAIN CONCEPTS/THEMES: Police Chase, Older Citizens, Traffic Stops, Police Chase.

World To Come: Essays On The Baltimore Uprising, Militant Racism, And History

125.	SCOTT Walter 50	North Charleston, SC April 8, 2015 ⊙	BRIEF: The police pulled Scott, who was unarmed, over in a routine traffic stop for a broken taillight. Officer Slager maintained that he shot Scott in self-defense. A bystander, Feidin Santana, videoed the shooting and gave it to the Scott's family. In the video, Scott attempted to flee the taser gun. Officer Slager took his gun and shots Scott 8 times. LEGAL STATUS: A formal complaint was filed against Officer Slager. Slater was fired, charged with murder, and jailed after the video emerged. The FBI and the Justice Department opened a Civil Rights investigation into the case. In the fall of 2015, the family of Walter Scott was awarded a settlement of 6.5 million. MAIN CONCEPTS/ THEMES: Traffic Stop, Unarmed Citizens, Taser, Excessive Use-Of-Force.
126.	SHAW Ananias 74	Selma, AL December 4, 2013 ⊙	BRIEF: police received a call to come to the Church's Chicken because Shaw was acting erratically. When the police arrived at the restaurant, Shaw was gone. The police found Shaw later in an abandoned building. They maintain that when he left the abandoned building, he was "wielding an axe." They say he insulted the officers and refused to comply with their orders to drop the axe. The police said that Shaw came at then with the axe. They shot and killed him. LEGAL STATUS: Pending. MAIN CONCEPTS/ THEMES: 911 Callers, Older Citizens, Excessive Use-Of-Force, Knife-Wielding ("Axe").
127.	SMITH Yvette 47	Bastrop, TX February 16, 2014	BRIEF: Police officer Deputy Daniel Willis responded to a domestic disturbance call at Smith's home. When Smith opened the front door to him he shot her. Willis maintained that Smith possessed a weapon. The next day that claim was denied by the police department. LEGAL STATUS: Deputy Daniel Willis was indicted for murder. The Smith family filed a wrongful death lawsuit asking for 5 million dollars. MAIN CONCEPTS/THEMES: Domestic Disturbance, Unarmed Citizens.
128.	SPRUILL Alberta 57	New York, NY May 16, 2003	BRIEF: Law enforcement officers, seeking drugs and guns, knocked down Spruill's apartment door. In their tactical assault, they tossed a concussion grenade into her home. Spruill died of a heart attack. Apparently, the officers received incorrect information, and entered the wrong apartment. LEGAL STATUS: The Spruill family filed a wrongful death lawsuit. The city paid the Spruill's a settlement of $1.6 million. MAIN CONCEPTS/ THEMES: Accidental Entry/Raid, Heart Attack.
129.	STANSBURY, Jr. Timothy 19	New York, NY January 24, 2004	BRIEF: Officer Richard S. Neri, Jr. was patrolling a building on his beat. When Stansbury, who was unarmed, pushed open the rooftop door of the building Officer Neri shot him by accident. LEGAL STATUS:

World To Come: Essays On The Baltimore Uprising, Militant Racism, And History

			Officer Neri was suspended from duty with pay, but permanently stripped of his firearm. He was not indicted. The family of Stansbury filed a wrongful death lawsuit. The NYPD settled the suit for 2 million dollars. MAIN CONCEPTS/THEMES: Shooting, Unarmed Citizens.
130.	STEEN Victor 17	Pensacola, FL October 3, 2009 ⊙	BRIEF: Officer Jerald Ard attempted to question Steen after seeing him on his bicycle at an empty construction site. Steen fled and the officer chased him in his police cruiser. The officer, from the window of the moving cruiser, discharged the taser gun at Steen. Steen fell from his bike and was struck and dragged by the officer, killing him. Ard also may have planted a gun on Steen after his death. The incident was captured on video. LEGAL STATUS: Officer Ard was placed on paid administrative leave. A judge ruled that no crime had been committed. The city paid Steen family a $500,000 settlement. MAIN CONCEPTS/THEMES: Police Chase, Taser, Automobile Homicide.
131.	STINGLEY Corey 16	Milwaukee, WI December 29, 2012 ⊙	BRIEF: When a convenience store employee and three customers believed that Stingley had shoplifted alcohol, the three customers tackled him to the ground and the police were called. One of the men placed in a chokehold. The three men claimed "citizen's arrest." The men piled on top of him restricting blood and air, ultimately choking Stingley to death. LEGAL STATUS: the District Attorney's office declined to charge the men; and the DOJ reviewed the case but found no evidence for prosecution. MAIN CONCEPTS/THEMES: Para-Police, Vigilantism, Adolescents/Juveniles/Children.
132.	TAYLOR Christian 19	Arlington, TX August 7, 2015	BRIEF: Police officer Brad Miller, who was on a call suspecting burglary, said he found Taylor (a college athlete) wondering around a car dealer-ship. He said Taylor refused to comply with the officer's commands, tried to escape, and Miller shot at him 4 times, striking struck him once; the other officer used a taser on him. Taylor was unarmed. LEGAL STATUS: Deeming his actions as one on an inexperienced "rookie" Officer Miller was fired. MAIN CONCEPTS/THEMES: Unarmed Citizens, Taser.
133.	THOMAS Timothy 19	Cincinnati, OH April 7, 2001	BRIEF: Two off duty police officers recognized Thomas as a person wanted for outstanding warrants (mostly traffic violations). The officers pursued Thomas and they were joined twelve other law enforcement officers. As Thomas ran he was shot by Patrolman Stephen Roach in the chest. Officer Roach requested an ambulance. Roach maintained that Thomas reached for a gun; when he pulled up his pants. Thomas was taken to the hospital and pronounced dead. Thomas did not possess a weapon. Officer Roach said he killed Thomas

World To Come: Essays On The Baltimore Uprising, Militant Racism, And History

in self-defense. Thomas' death sparked massive protests, along with aggressive community policing, and riots. A state of emergency was declared and a curfew was enacted. During the protests, over 800 people were arrested (mostly for curfew violations). Over 2000 people attended Thomas' funeral services, during which witnesses say police cars rushed the scene and police fired into the crowd (bean bag rounds). LEGAL STATUS: a video was suppressed. Several investigations were launched. Roach was acquitted on the charge of negligent homicide. An investigation conducted later revealed that Roach lied on the incident report and ignored police protocol. MAIN CONCEPTS/THEMES: Police Chase, Traffic Warrants, Shooting, Falsified Accounts.

134.	TILLMAN Cameron 14	Houma, LA September 23, 2014	BRIEF: Police received a 911 call that six juveniles had guns and entered an abandoned house. The deputy, Preston Norman, stated that Tillman "flung open the door" and came toward him with a "semi-automatic pistol" pointed directly at him. He fired four times at Tillman. The police found two BB guns at the scene. The teens say law enforcement did not identify themselves; and that they thought it was neighbors trying to scare them. They say Tillman was struck as soon as he opened the door, and that he was not carrying one of the BB guns. LEGAL STATUS: the State police conducted an investigation supporting the deputy's account. A grand jury decided not to indict deputy Preston Norman, and he was returned to patrol duty. Tillman's mother, Wyteika Tillman, stated that she intends to file a federal lawsuit; the FBI also launched an independent investigation. MAIN CONCEPTS/THEMES: 911 Callers, Juveniles, Toy Guns/Weapons/BBs, Excessive Use-Of-Force.
135.	TRAVIS Deshone Lamar 20	Port Wentworth, GA June 26, 2012	BRIEF: Four police officers made an early morning call to Travis' home in order to question him about an armed robbery at a Wendy's restaurant. They maintained that Travis was uncooperative in the interview. The police returned Travis' car keys to him. Travis assumed that he was free to leave his home. At this point the police said that they feared (were in "imminent danger") for their lives as Travis backed-up his car out of the drive way towards one of them. The officers open fired and killed him. News reports suggested that Travis was attempting to escape from the officers. Witnesses suggest that Travis was barely driving 5 mph, and was not trying to flee the police. His father said that one officer attempted to break the glass on the passenger side of Travis' car window while the other officers fired. His father disputed the entire police

			account, and maintained that "deadly force was not warranted"; stated that as an eyewitness, no one spoke with him, and that the police threatened to arrest him because he would not "be quiet." Travis' body lay in the car for ten minutes. LEGAL STATUS: GBI conducted an investigated the case and there were reports of multiple arrests. The grand jury would not indict the two officers involved. MAIN CONCEPTS/THEMES: Excessive-use-of-force, Unarmed citizens
136.	TURNER Raynetta 43	Mount Vernon, NY July 27, 2015	BRIEF: Turner was arrested for allegedly stealing from a food store On Saturday July 25, 2015. Turner told police that she had multiple medical problems. At that point she was taken to a hospital and treated for hypertension. She was then returned to jail. By Monday afternoon she was found unresponsive in her jail cell. EMS was called and she was pronounced dead. Officers maintained that Turner was thought to have been asleep the entire day. Turner's husband stated that law enforcement has not released all of the information in the death of his wife. LEGAL STATUS: Multiagency investigations of her death are taking place. MAIN CONCEPTS/THEMES: African American/Black Women, Mysterious Deaths, In-Custody Death, Hospitalization.
137.	VINZANT Naeschylus 37	Aurora, CO March 6, 2015	BRIEF: Members of a SWAT team, while attempting to arrest Vinzant, shot him. He was taken to the hospital and died. Vinzant had removed an ankle bracelet, violating his parole, and was also wanted for a "…alleged domestic violence incident…"[6] Vinzant was unarmed. LEGAL STATUS: Pending. MAIN CONCEPTS/THEMES: Parole Violation, SWAT, Hospitalization, Unarmed Citizens.
138.	WALKER Shem 49	New York, NY July 11, 2009	BRIEF: A NYC undercover police officer was participating in a drug buy when he encountered Walker on the porch of his home. It is believed that Walker thought the man was a drug dealer or someone trying to invade his home. Walked told the man to leave, and tried to remove the man from his porch; when he did so he was shot by the officer. Walker was unarmed. LEGAL STATUS: The office was not indicted. The city of New York settled with Walker's family for 2.25 million. MAIN CONCEPTS/THEMES: Undercover Police/Operation, Unarmed Citizens, Shooting

---

[6]Angela Bronner Helm, "Aurora, Colorado Police Shoot & Kill Yet Another Unarmed Black Man," *Newsone for Black America*, March 10, 2015, http://newsone.com/3097058/naeschylus-vinzant-killed-by-aurora-colorado-police/, accessed May 28, 2015.

WORLD TO COME: ESSAYS ON THE BALTIMORE UPRISING, MILITANT RACISM, AND HISTORY

139.	WARD Dewayne DeShawn 29	Antioch, CA March 2, 2015	BRIEF: Police killed Ward in a barrage of gunfire while trying to serve a restraining order issued by his mother. The police say Ward had a knife and came at police. LEGAL STATUS: Pending. MAIN CONCEPTS/ THEMES: Restraining Order, Knife-Wielding, Shooting.
140.	WARREN Johnnie Kamahi 43	Dotham, AL December 10, 2012	BRIEF: Warren was in an altercation with three other men outside a bar. A Houston County Sheriff's deputy noticed the scene and approached Warren. He used his taser gun on Warren twice. Thereafter, several other offices arrived on the scene and arrested Warren. Warren became unconscious. He later died at the Hospital. LEGAL STATUS: the Alabama Bureau of Investigation started an investigation. The sheriff's deputy who tased Warren was placed on paid leave. MAIN CONCEPTS/THEMES: Disorderly Conduct, Tasers, Hospitalization.
141.	WASHINGTON Steven Eugene 27	Los Angeles, CA March 10, 2010	BRIEF: Police Officers Allan Corrales and George Diego noticed Washington on a Los Angeles street in Koreatown after they heard a loud boom noise. They approached Washington. Washington gave them a look and then appeared to be removing something from his waistband. They say he did not comply with their instructions. Washington was shot in the head and killed. No weapon was found on him. Washington's family made it known that he was autistic. LEGAL STATUS: The Department recommended that the Officers involved be cleared of all charges. The civilian commission disagreed. Washington's mother received $950,000 in a settlement. MAIN CONCEPTS/ THEMES: Autism, Shooting, Unarmed Citizens.
142.	WEST Tyrone 44	Baltimore, MD July 21, 2013	BRIEF: West (and a female passenger) was subject to a routine traffic stop. Within minutes police say West resisted arrest. Witnesses said that West was severely beaten by police. West was beaten with batons, fists, and he was pepper sprayed. He died as they forced him to the ground. LEGAL STATUS: The medical report was inconclusive—it was thought that West had a heart condition and was dehydrated. The autopsy did not link the beating of West to his death. An internal review was launched. After an investigation, the police department determined that "objectively reasonable force" for used by the officers. The State's attorney's office found that the nine officers involved did nothing wrong. Baltimore activist Tawanda Jones, sister of Tyrone West, has advocated for families who have suffered from fatal police-encounters; and called for federal criminal charges to be filed against the officers who killed her brother. MAIN CONCEPTS/ THEMES: Traffic Stop, Resisting Arrest, Police Brutality.

World To Come: Essays On The Baltimore Uprising, Militant Racism, And History

143.	WHITE Phillip 32	Vineland, NJ March 31, 2015	BRIEF: The Police in Vineland, New Jersey arrested and handcuffed White for disorderly conduct. The officer stated that White tried to take his weapon. One witness said White resisted arrest. Other witnesses said police assaulted White while he was handcuffed and eventually lost consciousness. This included using a police dog on him. White was taken to the hospital and pronounced dead. LEGAL STATUS: The Cumberland County Prosecutor's office launched an investigation and the autopsy is still being processed. The two officers were placed on administrative leave. When the police received critical remarks on Facebook, they hid the comments, but later returned the critical comments to the page. MAIN CONCEPTS/THEMES: Disorderly Conduct, Police Brutality, Hospitalized.
144.	WHITE, III Victor 22	Iberia Parish, LA March 22, 2014	BRIEF: Police officers stopped White and his friend Isaiah Lewis. The two allegedly consented to a pat-down search. It was then that they discovered marijuana. The officers were joined by others and White and Lewis were searched further. Both were handcuffed. Lewis was eventually released. White was read his rights and put in a police cruiser. Police maintained that when they reached the processing office, White was uncooperative and refused to get out of the police car. The deputy in question requested assistance in removing White from the car. White then, while handcuffed behind his back, drew a weapon from his person and shot himself in the back. Police theorized that White was somehow in possession of a gun and that he killed himself in the police cruiser, even though he was searched more than once. The coroner agreed with this explanation. Police were also said to have visited White's home, spoken with his father, but did not inform him that his son had been shot. There was also conflicting forensic evidence. The White family disagreed. LEGAL STATUS: Pending. MAIN CONCEPTS/THEMES: Suicide, In-Custody Death.
145.	WILLIAMS Derek 22	Milwaukee, WI July 6, 2011	BRIEF: The police maintained that when they saw Williams wearing a white mask, he was in the process of committing a street robbery. Williams ran when he saw the police cruiser. The police found Williams without a shirt or shoes, and they said he resisted arrest. The police restrained Williams; and it was at that point that they said that he attempted to reach inside of his waistband. The officer was afraid that it was a weapon. They then handcuffed and searched Williams. When officers tried to stand him upright, he became limp. They assumed that he was feigning illness. They put Williams in the back of the squad car. Williams complained that he could not breathe, and eventually he

lost consciousness. CPR was rendered by police and fire paramedics, however, Williams died. It was suggested that Williams died of a sickle cell anemia crisis. Later, it was determined that Williams was suffocated and his neck was broken. LEGAL STATUS: The Milwaukee county district attorney's office launched an independent investigation. The ultimately cleared the officers of any wrongdoing. The police also conducted a review and reported the same findings. The DOJ did not have enough evidence to pursue federal charges. The community pressure advanced a federal inquest and revealed inconsistent evidence. The three officers involved were charged in 2013. MAIN CONCEPTS/THEMES: Police Chase, Unarmed Citizens, Robbery Suspects, Negligence.

146. WILLIAMS Malissa 30 — Cleveland, OH — November 29, 2012 — BRIEF: (See also Timothy Russell) An officer reported that gunshots had been fired from (like the one Russell and Williams were driving) the Justice Center. Russell and Williams were chased by 62 police cars. Officers fired 137 rounds of ammunition into the car killing Russell and Williams. Both were unarmed. One officer stood on the hood of the car and fired into the windshield. In the confusion, police said they believed that gunfire was coming from the car. LEGAL STATUS: A settlement between the city and the two's families—was reached for $1.5 million each. Brelo was indicted in May 2014 for voluntary manslaughter and found innocent of the charge. Police supervisors were also accused of failing to perform their duties. MAIN CONCEPTS/THEMES: Police Chase.

147. WILSON Tarika 26 — Lima, OH — January 4, 2008 — BRIEF: Wilson was at home with her companion when SWAT invaded the home. They were there to arrest the companion for drug dealing. SWAT opened fire and killed Wilson. LEGAL STATUS: The officer who shot Wilson, Sgt. Joe Chavalia, was acquitted of negligent homicide and assault. The Wilson family filed a wrongful death lawsuit. The family received $2.5 million in a settlement. MAIN CONCEPTS/THEMES: Narcotics, SWAT.

148. WOODS Mario 26 — San Francisco, CA — December 2, 2015 — BRIEF: Police, attempted to get Woods to drop a knife in his possession. They fired beanbag rounds and they also pepper sprayed him. When this failed, the police open fired on Woods. The officers used 15 rounds. Members of the community were outraged and did not believe that Woods raised a knife to officers. LEGAL BRIEF: Pending. MAIN CONCEPTS/THEMES: Knife-Wielding, Excessive-Use-Of-Force

World To Come: Essays On The Baltimore Uprising, Militant Racism, And History

149.	WOODSON Tyree 38	Baltimore, MD August 2, 2014	BRIEF: Woodson was brought into the police station for several open warrants. Police maintained that Woodson committed suicide inside of the station. The police theory was that he was able to bring in an undetected weapon; and then decided to shoot himself. LEGAL STATUS: Pending. MAIN CONCEPTS/THEMES: Suicide.
150.	ZONGO Ousmane 43	New York, NY May 22, 2003	BRIEF: Officer Bryan Conroy was conducting a police raid on a storage facility suspected of CD/DVD piracy where Zongo worked. Zongo was unarmed and his business had nothing to do with the police investigation. Zongo was shot four times (twice in the back) and killed. LEGAL STATUS: Officer Bryan Conroy was convicted of criminally negligent homicide. He received five years' probation, and lost his position. The Zongo family filed a wrongful death lawsuit. They received $3 million in a settlement. MAIN CONCEPTS/THEMES: Unarmed Citizens, Police Raid.

World To Come: Essays On The Baltimore Uprising, Militant Racism, And History

Appendix D: Grand Jury Charges Against The Baltimore 6 In The Death Of Freddie Gray, May 21, 2015[1]

Officer Caesar Goodson

1. Second degree depraved heart murder
2. Involuntary manslaughter
3. Second degree negligent assault
4. Manslaughter by vehicle—gross negligence
5. Manslaughter by vehicle—criminal negligence
6. Misconduct in office for failure to perform a duty regarding the safety of a prisoner
7. Reckless endangerment

Officer Edward Nero

1. Second degree intentional assault
2. Misconduct in office for an illegal arrest
3. Misconduct in office for failure to perform a duty regarding the safety of a prisoner
4. Reckless endangerment

Officer William Porter

1. Involuntary manslaughter
2. Second degree negligent assault
3. Misconduct in office for failure to perform a duty regarding the safety of a prisoner
4. Reckless endangerment

Officer Garrett Miller

1. Second degree intentional assault
2. Misconduct in office for an illegal arrest
3. Misconduct in office for failure to perform a duty regarding the safety of a prisoner
4. Reckless endangerment

Lt. Brian Rice

1. Involuntary manslaughter
2. Second degree negligent assault
3. Misconduct in office for failure to perform a duty regarding the safety of a prisoner
4. Illegal arrest
5. Reckless endangerment

Sgt. Alicia White

1. Involuntary manslaughter
2. Second degree negligent assault
3. Misconduct in office for failure to perform a duty regarding the safety of a prisoner
4. Reckless endangerment

---

[1] The revised charges against the Baltimore 6, reflecting the indictment by the Grand Jury on May 21, 2015.

World To Come: Essays On The Baltimore Uprising, Militant Racism, And History

Appendix E: Domestic Riot/Civil Disobedience And Protest Events Related To Race In The United States, 1863—2015[1]

	DATE[2]	EVENT[3]
1.	July 13, 1863	New York Draft Riots New York
2.	May 1, 1866	Memphis Riot Tennessee
3.	July 30, 1866	New Orleans Riot Louisiana
4.	April 13, 1873	Colfax Massacre, Louisiana
5.	July 8, 1876	Hamburg Massacre, South Carolina
6.	November 10, 1898	Wilmington Race Riot North Carolina
7.	November 8, 1898	Phoenix Riot South Carolina
8.	August 13, 1900	"Promised Land" Riots Harlem, New York
9.	July 23, 1900	New Orleans Riot Louisiana
10.	August 13, 1906	Brownsville Riot Texas
11.	November 24, 1906	"Atlanta Revolution" Riot Georgia
12.	May—September, 1907	The Pacific Coast Race Riots California, Washington

---

[1] These are selected examples of prominent civil disobedience, riot and protect activity in the United States from 1863-2015. The list does not include the antebellum revolts, rebellions and uprisings of enslaved Africans.
[2] Approximate start date of the event; multiple city riots include approximate start and end dates.
[3] City or popular name of the event is provided.

WORLD TO COME: ESSAYS ON THE BALTIMORE UPRISING, MILITANT RACISM, AND HISTORY

13.	August 14-15, 1908	Springfield Riot Illinois
14.	July 2, 1917	East St. Louis Illinois
15.	July 25, 1917	Chester, Pennsylvania
16.	August 26, 1917	Houston, Texas
17.	July 26, 1918	Philadelphia, Pennsylvania
18.	May 10—October 3, 1919	The "Red Summer" Riots: Charleston, South Carolina Gregg and Longview County, Texas Washington, D.C. Chicago, Illinois Elaine, Arkansas
19.	November 2, 1920	Ocoee, Florida
20.	May 31—June 1, 1921	Tulsa Race Riot and Massacre Oklahoma
21.	January 1, 1923	Rosewood Massacre
22.	March 19, 1935	The Harlem Riot of 1935 New York
23.	May 25, 1943	Mobile Alabama Race Riot
24.	June 20, 1943	Belle Isle Riot
25.	August 27, 1949	Peekskill riot, New York
26.	May 11, 1963	Birmingham, Alabama
27.	July 18, 1964	Harlem, New York
28.	1964	1964 Nationwide Race Riots: Brooklyn, New York Chicago, Illinois Cleveland, Ohio Elizabeth, New Jersey Jacksonville, Florida

World To Come: Essays On The Baltimore Uprising, Militant Racism, And History

		Patterson, New Jersey Philadelphia, Pennsylvania Jersey City, New Jersey Rochester, New York St. Augustine, Florida
29.	August 11, 1965	The Watts Riot Los Angeles California
30.	June 12, 1966	Chicago, Illinois
31.	July 15, 1966	Dayton, Ohio
32.	July 18, 1966	Hough Riots Cleveland, Ohio
33.	April 30-October 18, 1967	1967 Nationwide Race Riots: Atlanta, Georgia Cincinnati, Ohio (Avondale) Detroit, Michigan Elizabeth, New Jersey Englewood, New Jersey Houston, Texas Jackson, Mississippi Jersey City, New Jersey Nashville, Tennessee Newark, New Jersey New Brunswick, New Jersey Plainfield, New Jersey Tampa, Florida
34.	February 8, 1968	Orangeburg Massacre, South Carolina
35.	February 12, 1968	Memphis Sanitation Strike, Memphis, Tennessee
36.	April 4-5, 1968	1968 Nationwide Race Riots (The "King Assassination Riots"): Cincinnati, Ohio (Avondale) Baltimore, Maryland Chicago, Illinois Cleveland, Ohio Detroit, Michigan Kansas City, Missouri

WORLD TO COME: ESSAYS ON THE BALTIMORE UPRISING, MILITANT RACISM, AND HISTORY

        Louisville, Kentucky (May 27-29, 1968)
        Pittsburgh, Pennsylvania
        Washington, D.C. (April 4-8, 1968)
        Wilmington, Delaware (April 9-10, 1968)

37. August 25-29, 1968 — Democratic National Convention, Illinois

38. August 7, 1968 — Liberty City, Miami, Florida

39. May 21, 1969 — Greensboro Uprising, North Carolina

40. May-December, 1969 — Cairo Riots, Illinois

41. July 17, 1969 — Sacramento, California

42. July 17, 1969 — York Race Riot, Pennsylvania

43. May 14, 1970 — Jackson State, Mississippi

44. September 9, 1971 — Attica Prison Revolt, New York

45. November 16, 1972 — Baton Rouge, Louisiana

46. April 5, 1976 — Boston Bussing Riot, Massachusetts

47. February 5, 1976 — Escambia High School Riots, Pensacola, Florida

48. November 3, 1979 — Greensboro Massacre, North Carolina

49. May 8, 1980 — Miami Riot, Florida

50. December 30, 1982 — Overtown Riot, Miami, Florida

51. August 6, 1988 — Tompkins Square Park Police Riot, New York

52. January 16, 1989 — Overtown Riot, Miami, Florida

53. August 9, 1991 — Crown Heights Brooklyn Riot, New York

54. April 29, 1992 — Los Angeles/Rodney King Riot, California

55. April 9, 2001 — Cincinnati Riots, Ohio

WORLD TO COME: ESSAYS ON THE BALTIMORE UPRISING, MILITANT RACISM, AND HISTORY

56.	August 30, 2003	Benton Harbor Riot, Michigan
57.	August 29, 2005	Hurricane Katrina Civil Catastrophe and Unrest, New Orleans, Louisiana
58.	October 15, 2005	Toledo Riot, Ohio
59.	January 7, 2009	BART/Oakland Riot/Oscar Grant Killing California
60.	July 8, 2010	BART/Oakland Riot/Oscar Grant Verdict California
61.	November 10, 2010	BART/Oakland Riot/Oscar Grant Verdict California
62.	September 17, 2011	Occupy Oakland (Occupy Wallstreet Protests)
63.	March 9, 2013	Brooklyn Riots (Kimani Gray) New York
64.	August 10, 2014	Ferguson Uprising (Michael Brown) Missouri
65.	July 17, 2014	New York (Eric Garner) New York
66.	April 27, 2015	Baltimore Uprising (Freddie Gray) Maryland

World To Come: Essays On The Baltimore Uprising, Militant Racism, And History

Bibliography

A Collection of Cases Decided By the General Court of Virginia, Chiefly Relating To the Penal Laws of the Commonwealth. Commencing In The Year 1789, And Ending In 1814, Philadelphia: James Webster, 1815.

Agar, Michael, and Heather Schacht Reisinger. "A Heroin Epidemic at the Intersection Of Histories: The 1960s Epidemic Among African Americans In Baltimore." *Medical Anthropology* 21, No. 2 (2002): 115-156.

Agrama, Hussein Ali. "Ethics, Tradition, Authority: Toward an Anthropology of the Fatwa." *American Ethnologist*, 37, No. 1 (2010) 2-18.

Akbar, Na'im, *From Miseducation to Education*, New Mind Productions, 1984.

Akerlof, George, and Janet L. Yellen. "Gang Behavior, Law Enforcement, and Community Values." Canadian Institute for Advanced Research, 1994.

Alcoff, Linda. "What Should White People Do?" *Hypatia* 13, No. 3 (1998): 6-26.

Alejandro, Roberto "Gang members discuss role in Baltimore's uprising," (Special to the AFRO http://www.afro.com/gang-members-role-in-baltimores-uprising/), New Pittsburgh Courier, May 7, 2015, http://newpittsburghcourieronline.com/2015/05/07/gang-members-discuss-role-in-baltimores-uprising/, accessed May 9, 2015.

Alexander, Michelle. *The New Jim Crow: Mass Incarceration in the age of Colorblindness*. The New Press, 2012.

Alford, Brittnee and Sarah Mott. "Baltimore City Police Department Academy Report Writing Manual." Baltimore: BCPDA-Towson University Writing Enhancement Initiative, u.d., 33pp.

"Alpha Kappa Alpha Sorority Expresses Concern about Death of Sandra Bland," Press Release, Chicago, Illinois, July 20, 2015.

Anderson, James F. Laronistine Dyson, and Tazinski Lee, "Ridding the African-American Community of Black Gant Proliferation," *The Western Journal of Black Studies*, Vol. 20, No. 2, 1996, 83-88, 85.

"Anti-Slavery in Virginia: Extracts from Thos. Jefferson, Gen. Washington and others Relative to the 'Blighting Curse of Slavery.' Debates on the 'Nat Turner Insurrection,' Queries by William Crane, &c." Baltimore: J. F. Weishampel, Bookseller and Stationer, 1865.

Alpert, Geoffrey P. *Helicopters in Pursuit Operations*. Washington, DC: National Institute of Justice, 1998.

Alpert, Geoffrey P. "Helicopters in Pursuit Operations." Research in Action, Washington, DC: National Institute of Justice, August 1998, 1-6.

Alvarez, Rafael (with an Introduction by David Simon), *The Wire: Truth Be Told*, New York: Pocketbooks, 2010.

Applegate, Rex. *Kill or Get Killed: Riot Control Techniques, Manhandling, and Close Combat, for Police and the Military*. Boulder, CO: Paladin Press, 1976.

Asante, Molefi Kete. *Race, Rhetoric & Identity The Architecton of Soul*, New York: Humanity Books, 2005.

Asante, Molefi Kete. *Erasing Racism: The Survival of the American Nation*. Amherst, NY: Prometheus Books, 2003.

Asante, Molefi Kete. *The Afrocentric Idea*. Philadelphia: Temple University Press, 1987.

Asante, Molefi Kete. *Kemet, Afrocentricity, and Knowledge*. Trenton: Africa World Press, 1990.

Asante Jr., M.K. "Enough Disrespect: Return Rap To Its Artistic Roots," *USA Today*, Pg. 13a, October 26, 2004.

Ashton, Susanna. "Playing Hell in Charleston—Daniel Payne, Clementa Pinckney And The Fight Against White Supremacy," *TigerPrints*, Clemson University, June, 2015.

"ASSU Resolution In Support Of Reaffirming Stanford's Commitment To Indigenous And Native American Community, Identity, Dignity, And Space," Meeting Of The Forty-Eight Senate Of The Academic Council, Stanford University Faculty Senate, Meeting Agenda, March 3, 2016.

"ATF Baltimore Fire," Dropbox, DriveHQ, http://www.atfbaltimorefire.com/, accessed May 15, 2015.

Asumah, Seth N. "Race, Immigration Reform, and Heteropatriarchal Masculinity: Reframing the Obama Presidency." *Wagadu: A Journal of Transnational Women's & Gender Studies* 13 (2015).

Azzam, Amy M. "Handle with Care: A Conversation with Maya Angelou," *Educational Leadership*, Vol. 71, No. 1, September 2013, 10-13.

Badger, Emily, Jonathan Rothwell, and Margery Turner. "Panel," "Place and Opportunity: What Now For Policy? A Conversation with Harvard's Raj Chetty," Proceedings, The Brookings Institution, *Policy*, Washington, D.C., June 1, 2015, 68pp.

World To Come: Essays On The Baltimore Uprising, Militant Racism, And History

Baldwin, James "An Open Letter to My Sister, Angela Y. Davis," in Angela Y. Davis, et al, *If They Come in the Morning*, New York: New America Library, 1971, 19-23.

Baldwin, James. *Notes of a Native Son*. New York: Beacon Press, 1955.

Baldwin, James "White Man's Guilt," *Ebony*, August, 1965.

Balfanz, Robert, and Nettie Legters. "Locating the Dropout Crisis. Which High Schools Produce the Nation's Dropouts? Where Are They Located? Who Attends Them?" Report 70. Center for Research on the Education of Students Placed at Risk CRESPAR (2004).

Balko, Radley. (2013). *Rise of the Warrior Cop: The Militarization of America's Police Forces* (First edition). New York: Public Affairs.

Balko, Radley. *Overkill: The Rise of Paramilitary Police Raids in America*. Washington, D.C.: The Cato Institute, 2006.

Baltimore, lyrics by Prince, NPG Records, copyright 2015.

Baltimore Association for the Improvement of the Condition of the Poor, and Charity Organization Society of Baltimore City. Housing Conditions in Baltimore: Report of a Special Committee of the Association for the Improvement of the Condition of the Poor and the Charity Organization Society. Arno Press, 1974.

Baltimore City Criminal Justice Coordinating Council, *Baltimore City Gang Violence Reduction Plan*, Baltimore, Maryland, November 15, 2006, 55pp.

Baltimore City Fraternal Order of Police (FOP) Lodge #3 After Action Review, 32pp (undated, released July 8, 2015), p. 3.

Baltimore City Schools, Gregory E. Thornton, Chief Executive Officer, Letter to Parents, Families and Community Members, December 14, 2015.

Baltimore County Public Schools Emergent Bulletin, Vol. IV, No. 5, Cancellation/Postponement of BCPS activities/Events, December 14, 2015.

Baltimore Police, Press Conference, "BPD Announces Body Camera Pilot Program," October 26, 2015.

Baltimore Police, (#BaltimorePolice), "Groups of Violent Criminals Are Continuing To Throw Rocks, Bricks, and Other Items at Police Officers." April 27, 2015, 9:28PM.

Baltimore Police Department, Office of the Police Commissioner, Media Relations Section, "Baltimore Police Department Responds to FOP Lodge 3 June 16, 2015 Press Release," June 16, 2015.

WORLD TO COME: ESSAYS ON THE BALTIMORE UPRISING, MILITANT RACISM, AND HISTORY

Baltimore Police Department, General Order J-16, "Video Recording of Police Activity," November 8, 2011, 7pp. https://ia801005.us.archive.org/3/items/291576-j-16-video-recording-of-police-activity/291576-j-16-video-recording-of-police-activity.pdf, accessed May 15, 2015.

Baltimore Police Department, Policy 1114, By Order of the Police Commissioner, "Persons in Police Custody," April 3, 2015, 15pp.

"Baltimore's Hasty Prosecutor," Baltimore Criminal Justice Blogger Page Croyder, May 4, 2015, http://pagecroyder.blogspot.com/, accessed May 6, 2015.

Bankole-Medina, Katherine, "History, Racial Stereotypes, and Social Network Conservation: The Legacy of Intolerable Blackness," *Africalogical Perspectives*, Vol. 6, No. 1, November/December 2009, 14-26.

Bankole, Katherine. *Slavery and Medicine: Enslavement and Medical Practices in Antebellum Louisiana.* New York: Garland Publishing, Inc., 1998.

Banks, Taunya Lovell. "Setting the Record Straight: Maryland's First Black Women Law Graduates." *Maryland Law Review* 63, No. 4, 752-772 (2004).

Barak, Gregg. "Between the Waves: Mass-Mediated Themes of Crime and Justice." *Social Justice* (1994): 133-147.

Barnes, David M. *The Draft Riots in New York July, 1863. The Metropolitan Police Their Services During Riot Week.* New York: Baker & Godwin, Printers and Publishers, 1863.

Bass, Sandra. "Policing Space, Policing Race: Social Control Imperatives and Police Discretionary Decisions." *Social Justice* (2001): 156-176.

Bassiouni, M. Cherif. "Terrorism, Law Enforcement, and the Mass Media: Perspectives, Problems, Proposals." *Journal of Criminal Law and Criminology* (1981): 1-51.

Batts, Anthony, "Police Commissioner's Message" Email to BCPD, April 26, 2015.

Batts, Anthony W., Sean Michael Smoot and Ellen Scrivner, "Police Leadership Challenges in a Changing World." *New Perspectives in Policing Bulletin.* Washington, DC: U.S. Department of Justice, National Institute of Justice, 2012. NCJ 238338.

Beaulac, Julie, Kristjansson, Elizabeth, and Cummins Steven. "A Systematic Review of Food Deserts, 1966-2007." *Preventing*

WORLD TO COME: ESSAYS ON THE BALTIMORE UPRISING, MILITANT RACISM, AND HISTORY

Chronic Disease 2009;6(3):A105.
http://www.cdc.gov/pcd/issues/2009/jul/08_0163.htm.
Beckles, Colin A. "Black Liberation and the Internet: A Strategic Analysis," *Journal of Black Studies,* Vol. 31, No. 3, Special Issue: Africa: New Realities and Hopes. (January 2001), 311-324.
Bell, Derrick A. *Silent Covenants: Brown v. Board of Education and the Unfulfilled Hopes for Racial Reform.* New York: Oxford University Press, 2005.
Bell, Derrick A. *Faces at the Bottom of the Well: The Permanence of Racism.* New York: Basic Books, 1992.
Bell, Derrick A. *And We Are Not Saved The Elusive Quest for Racial Justice.* New York: Basic Books, 1989.
Bennett, Jr., Lerone, *The Challenge of Blackness*, Chicago: Johnson Publishing Company, 1972.
Berger v. Battaglia, 779 F. 2d 992 (4th Cir. 1985).
Bethune, Mary McLeod "Last Will and Testament," *Ebony*, August 1955.
Bhabha. Homi K. *The Location of Culture.* London: Routledge, 1994.
Bice, Thomas W. *Medical Care for the Disadvantaged: Report on a Survey of Use of Medical Services in the Baltimore SMSA, 1968-1969.* Baltimore: Johns Hopkins University, Department of Medical Care and Hospitals, 1971.
Black Lives Matter website, http://blacklivesmatter.com/about/, accessed May 14, 2015.
Bolton, Kenneth, and Joe Feagin. *Black in Blue: African-American Police Officers and Racism.* Routledge, 2004.
Boukari, Safoura "20th Century Black Women's Struggle for Empowerment in a White Supremacist Education System: Tribute to Early Women Educators," (2005) Information and Materials from the Women's and Gender Studies Program, Paper 4.http://digitalcommons.unl.edu/wgsprogram/4.
Boone, Christopher G. "An assessment and explanation of environmental inequity in Baltimore." *Urban Geography* 23, No. 6 (2002): 581-595.
Born Suspect Stop-and-Frisk Abuses and the Continued Fight to End Racial Profiling in America, NAACP Report, Baltimore, MD: National Association for the Advancement of Colored People, September 2014, 81pp.
Bramall, Rebecca, and Ben Pitcher. "Policing The Crisis, Or, Why We Love *The Wire.*" *International Journal of Cultural Studies* 16, No. 1 (2013): 85-98.

WORLD TO COME: ESSAYS ON THE BALTIMORE UPRISING, MILITANT RACISM, AND HISTORY

Brandl, Steven G. "Back To the Future: The Implications of September 11, 2001 on Law Enforcement Practice and Policy." *Ohio State Journal of Criminal Law*. 1 (2003): 133.

Bright, Stephen B. "Discrimination, Death, and Denial: The Tolerance of Racial Discrimination in Infliction of the Death Penalty," in Charles J. Ogletree, Jr. and Austin Sarat's *From Lynch Mobs to the Killing State: Race and the Death Penalty in America*. New York: New York University Press, 2006, 211-259.

Browder, Anthony T. *Survival Strategies for Africans in America*. Washington, D.C.: The Institute of Karmic Guidance, 1996.

Brown, William Wells. *Narrative of William W. Brown a Fugitive Slave Written By Himself*, Boston: The Anti-Slavery Office, 1847.

Bruns, Axel, and Tim Highfield. "Blogs, Twitter, and Breaking News: The Produsage of Citizen Journalism" in *Produsing Theory in a Digital World: The Intersection of Audiences and Production*. New York: Peter Lang (2012): 15-32.

Bureau of Alcohol, Tobacco, Firearms and Explosives, U.S. Department of Justice, Press Release, "Man Arrested in Penn-North One Week After Baltimore Riots Sentenced to 42 Months in Prison for Federal Gun Charge," December 14, 2015.

Bureau of Alcohol, Tobacco, Firearms and Explosives (ATF), Baltimore Field Division, Reward Announcement, May 1, 2015.

Bureau of Alcohol, Tobacco, Firearms and Explosives (ATF), Baltimore Field Division, Press Release, May 1, 2015, https://www.atf.gov/news/pr/atf-offers-10000-reward-baltimore-fire-investigations, accessed, May 15, 2015.

Bureau of Alcohol, Tobacco, Firearms and Explosives (ATF), Facebook site, https://www.facebook.com/HQATF, May 1, 2015, accessed, May 15, 2015.

Bureau of Alcohol, Tobacco, Firearms and Explosives, Press Release, https://www.atf.gov/news/pr/atf-offers-10000-reward-baltimore-fire-investigations, May 1, 2015, accessed May 15, 2015.

Burke, Alafair S. "I Got the Shotgun: Reflections on *The Wire*, Prosecutors, and Omar Little." *Ohio State Journal of Criminal Law* 8 (2010): 447.

Bush, Melanie. "White World Supremacy And The Creation Of Nation: "American Dream" Or Global Nightmare?" *Critical Race and Whiteness Studies* 6, No. 1 (2010): 1-12.

Butler, Paul. "Racially Based Jury Nullification: Black Power in the Criminal Justice System." *Yale Law Journal* (1995): 677-725.

Butz, Arthur R. *The Hoax of the Twentieth Century: The Case Against The Presumed Extermination Of European Jewry.* Torrance, CA: Institute for Historical Review, 1985.

Bzdak, David, Joanna Crosby and Seth Vannatta, *The Wire and Philosophy: This America, Man,* Chicago: Open Court Publishing, 2013.

Capers, I. Bennett. "Crime, Legitimacy, Our Criminal Network, and *The Wire.*" *Ohio State Journal of Criminal Law* 8 (2011): 10-34.

Carby, Hazel V. "White Woman Listen! Black Feminism and the Boundaries of Sisterhood," in Heidi Safia Mirza, (ed.), *Black British Feminism: A Reader,* London: Routledge, 1997.

Carpenter, Serena, "A Study of Content Diversity in Online Citizen Journalism and Online Newspaper Articles," *New Media and Society,* 12(7), November 2010, 1064-1084, 1064.

Chaddha, Anmol, and William Julius Wilson. "Why we're Teaching 'The Wire' at Harvard." *The Washington Post* 12 (2010).

Chaney, Cassandra and Ray V. Robertson, Armed and Dangerous? An Examination of Fatal Shootings of Unarmed Black People by Police, *The Journal of Pan-African Studies,* Vol. 8, No. 4, September 2015, 45-78.

Chaudhry, Irfan. #Hashtagging Hate: Using Twitter To Track Racism Online. First Monday, [S.l.], February 2015. ISSN 13960466. Available at: <http://uncommonculture.org/ojs/index.php/fm/article/view/5450/4207>. Date accessed: 04 August. 2015. doi:10.5210/fm.v20i2.5450.

Cheatwood, Derral. "Black Homicides in Baltimore 1974-1986: Age, Gender, and Weapon Use Changes." *Criminal Justice Review* 15, No. 2 (1990): 192-207.

Chen, Rui, Raj Sharman, H. Raghav Rao, and Shambhu J. Upadhyaya. "Coordination in Emergency Response Management." *Communications of the ACM* 51, No. 5 (2008): 66-73.

Chomsky, Noam. *9-11*, New York: Seven Stories Press, 2002.

Christian, Mark. "An African-Centered Perspective on White Supremacy," *Journal of Black Studies,* Vol. 33, No. 2, 13th Cheikh Anta Diop Conference Selected Proceedings. (November 2002), 179-198.

Churchill, Ward. *Agents of Repression: The FBI's Secret War Against the Black Panther Party and the American Indian Movement.* Boston, MA: South End Press, 1988.

Cipollone, Diane W. "Gambling On a Settlement: The Baltimore City Schools Adequacy Litigations." *Journal of Education Finance* (1998): 87-107.

"City Desk: Malcolm X," WMAQ-TV (Chicago, IL), March 1, 1963.

"City of Baltimore Adds Pictometry to Enterprise GIS Program," *Directions Magazine*, September 14, 2004.

City of Baltimore, Mayor's Office of Emergency Management, Situation Report #13, "Civil Unrest," May 1, 2015.

City of Baltimore Memo, From George A. Nilson, City Solicitor, To Honorable President and Members of the Board of Estimates, Subject Employment Agreement—Dr. Anthony W. Batts, September 5, 2012.

City of Baltimore, Office of the Mayor, Press Release, "Mayor Rawlings-Blake and Commissioner Batts Release Strategic Plan for Baltimore Police Department, November 21, 2013.

City of Baltimore, Office of the Mayor, Press Release, "Mayor Rawlings-Blake Announces Next Two Stops on Public Safety Town Hall Tour," March 18, 2014.

City of Baltimore, Baltimore Police Department, Press Conference, June 3, 2015.

City of Baltimore, Social Media Tracking Spreadsheet, April 27, 2015 ("Emails from the Baltimore Unrest: Explore Documents and Findings," "Finding: Monitoring Social Media," *The Baltimore Sun*, July 30, 2015, http://www.baltimoresun.com/news/maryland/freddie-gray/bal-emails-from-the-unrest-20150730-htmlstory.html, accessed July 30, 2015.

Clarke, John Henrik. *African People in World History*, Baltimore: Black Classics Press, 1993.

Clawson, James G., and Gerry Yemen. "Edward Norris and the Baltimore Police Department (A)." (Case) Darden School of Business, University of Virginia, 2003, 27pp.

Cleaver, Kathleen Neal. "Women, Power, and Revolution." *New Political Science* 21, No. 2 (1999): 231-236.

Clifton, Derrick "11 Stunning Images Highlight the Double Standard of Reactions to Riot Like Baltimore," The Mic.com, http://mic.com/articles/116680/11-stunning-images-highlight-the-double-standard-of-reactions-to-riots-like-baltimore, April 27, 2015, accessed May 13, 2015.

Cole, David. "The new McCarthyism: Repeating History in the War on Terrorism." *Harvard Civil Rights-Civil Liberties Law Review* 38 (2003).

Collins, Reed. "Strolling While Poor: How Broken-Windows Policing Created A New Crime In Baltimore." *Georgetown Journal on Poverty Law. & Policy* 14 (2007): 419.

Collins, William J. "The Housing Market Impact of State-Level Anti-Discrimination Laws, 1960–1970." *Journal of Urban Economics* 55, No. 3 (2004): 534-564, 534.

Cooper, Anna Julia. *A Voice from the South*. New York: Oxford University Press, 1988.

Cooper, Christopher A., and H. Gibbs Knotts, "Region, Race, and Support for the South Carolina Confederate Flag." *Social Science Quarterly* 87, No. 1 (2006): 142-154.

Copwatch Handbook An Introduction to Citizen Monitoring of the Police, n.p., n.d., Berkeley, California.

Cordner, G. W. "The Baltimore County Citizen Oriented Police Enforcement (COPE) Project: Final Report to the Florence v. Burden Foundation." (1985).

Correll, Joshua, Bernadette Park, Charles M. Judd, Bernd Wittenbrink, Melody S. Sadler, and Tracie Keesee. "Across The Thin Blue Line: Police Officers And Racial Bias In The Decision To Shoot." *Journal of Personality and Social Psychology* 92, No. 6 (2007): 1006.

"Corruption in Baltimore City DPW," The P.O.T.E. Channel, https://www.youtube.com/watch?v=NLUGL-MHS3Y, accessed May 9, 2015.

Costa, Dora L. "Race and Pregnancy Outcomes in the Twentieth Century: A Long-Term Comparison." *The Journal of Economic History* 64, No. 04 (2004): 1056-1086.

Council, City. "City of Baltimore." (2011).

Cowper, Thomas J. "The Myth of the 'Military Model' Of Leadership in Law Enforcement." *Police Quarterly* 3, No. 3 (2000): 228-246.

Cox, Rachel. "Unethical Intrusion: The Disproportionate Impact of Law Enforcement DNA Sampling on Minority Populations." *American Criminal Law Review*. 52 (2015): 155-177.

Crenshaw, Kimberle´ Williams and Andrea J. Ritchie (with Rachel Anspach, Rachel Gilmer, and Luke Harris), "Say Her Name: Resisting Police Brutality against Black Women," African American Policy Forum, Center for Intersectionality and Social Policy Studies, 48pp.

Croyder, Page "Police Charges in Freddie Gray case are Incompetent at Best," *The Baltimore Sun*, May 5, 2015, http://www.baltimoresun.com/news/opinion/oped/bs-ed-freddie-gray-mosby-20150505-story.html, accessed May 6, 2015.

Currie, Elliott. *Crime and Punishment in America*. New York: Macmillan, 2013.

Curry, Aaron, Carl Latkin, and Melissa Davey-Rothwell. "Pathways To Depression: The Impact Of Neighborhood Violent Crime On Inner-City Residents in Baltimore, Maryland, USA." *Social Science & Medicine* 67, No. 1 (2008): 23-30.

Cuyahoga County Sheriff's Department, File #: 15-00004, "Synopsis of CCSD Case #15-004 Use of Deadly Force Incident," June 2, 2015.

Daniels, Cora. *Ghettonation A Journey into the Land of Bling and the Home of the Shameless*. New York: Doubleday, 2007.

Davis, Angela Y. *Freedom is a Constant Struggle: Ferguson, Palestine, and the Foundations of a Movement*. Chicago: Haymarket Books, 2016.

Davis, Angela Y. "Race and Criminalization Black Americans and the Punishment System," in Lubiano, Wahneema, ed. *The House That Race Built: Original Essays by Toni Morrison, Angela Y. Davis, Cornel West, and Others on Black Americans and Politics in America Today*. New York: Vintage Books, 2010, 264-279.

Davis, Angela Y. et al, *If They Come in the Morning*, New York: New America Library, 1971.

Davis, Jessica L. and Oscar H. Gandy, Jr., "Racial Identity and Media Orientation: Exploring the Nature of Constraint," *Journal of Black Studies*, Vol. 29, No. 3 (January 1999), 367-397.

Davis, Mike. "Fortress Los Angeles: The Militarization of Urban Space." Variations on a Theme Park (1992): 154-180.

Dean, Patricia (Patty), "Punk Funk Rock Pop," *Minnesota History Magazine*, Minnesota Historical Society, MHS Collections, Vol. 58, Issue 1, 29-39, 2002.

Department of Justice, "Federal Officials Close Review into the Death of Dontre Hamilton," Press Release, November 10, 2015.

Department of Justice, U.S. Attorney's Office, District of Maryland," Press Release, "Defendant Charged in Federal Court for Possessing Medication Stolen From a CVS Pharmacy During the Baltimore Riots," September 9, 2015.

Department of Justice, U.S. Attorney's Office, District of Maryland," Press Release, "Baltimore Man Charged with Arson of CVS Pharmacy," July 2, 2015.

Department of Justice, U.S. Attorney's Office, District of Maryland," Press Release, "Suspect Charged for Arson of Liquor Store During the Baltimore Riots," October 1, 2015.

District Court of Maryland for Baltimore City, *State of Maryland vs. Grey, Freddie Carlos Jr.*, Case No. 6B02294074, April 12, 2015

Dominguez, Silvia, and Celeste Watkins. "Creating Networks For Survival And Mobility: Social Capital Among African-American And Latin-American Low-Income Mothers." *Social Problems* 50, No. 1 (2003): 111-135.

Donner, Frank. 1990. *Protectors of Privilege: Red Squads and Police Repression in Urban America.* Berkeley: University of California Press.

Douglass, Frederick. *Narrative of the Life of Frederick Douglass, an American Slave: Written by Himself.* Edited by Benjamin Quarles. Cambridge, MA: Harvard, 1960.

Douglass, Frederick. "Address by Hon. Frederick Douglass, Delivered in the Metropolitan A.M.E. Church, Washington, D.C., Tuesday, January 9th, 1894," Baltimore: Press of Thomas & Evans, 1894.

Dowler, Kenneth. "Job Satisfaction, Burnout, and Perception of Unfair Treatment: The Relationship Between Race And Police Work." *Police Quarterly* 8, No. 4 (2005): 476-489.

Drabble, John. "From White Supremacy to White Power: The FBI, COINTELPRO-WHITE HATE, and the Nazification of the Ku Klux Klan in the 1970s." *American Studies* 48, No. 3 (2007): 49-74.

Dreier, Peter, and John Atlas. "*The Wire*–Bush-Era Fable about America's Urban Poor?" *City & Community* 8, No. 3 (2009): 329-340.

Dreutz, Liz (via Good Morning America), "Amid Baltimore Violence, Hillary Clinton Calls for End to 'Era of Mass Incarceration,'" ABC News, April 29, 2015, http://abcnews.go.com/Politics/amid-baltimore-violence-hillary-clinton-set-unveil-plan/story?id=30664649, accessed July 26, 2015.

Du Bois, William Edward Burghardt, edited by Nathan Irvin Huggins. *W.E.B. DuBois Writings.* Vol. 34. New York, NY: The Library of America, 1986.

Durham, Rachel E., Marc L. Stein, and Faith Connolly, "College Opportunities and Success: Baltimore City Graduates through the Class of 2014," Baltimore: BERC, November, 2015, 41pp.

Dyson, Michael Eric. *Reflecting Black: African-American Cultural Criticism*, Minneapolis, MN: The University of Minneapolis Press, 1993.

Eaglin, Jessica, and Danyelle Solomon. "Reducing Racial and Ethnic Disparities in Jails: Recommendations for Local Practice." New York: Brennan Center for Justice at New York University of Law, 2015.

Eck, John E., and William Spelman. "Who Ya Gonna Call? The Police as Problem-Busters." *Crime & Delinquency* 33, No. 1 (1987): 31-52.

Enck-Wanzer, Darrel. "Barack Obama, The Tea Party, And The Threat Of Race: On Racial Neoliberalism and Born Again Racism." *Communication, Culture & Critique* 4, No. 1 (2011): 23-30.

Ehrenreich, Barbara, and Dedrick Muhammad. "The Recession's Racial Divide." *The New York Times* 12 (2009): 1-2.

Ehrlinger, Joyce, E. Ashby Plant, Richard P. Eibach, Corey J. Columb, Joanna L. Goplen, Jonathan W. Kunstman, and David A. Butz. "How Exposure To The Confederate Flag Affects Willingness To Vote for Barack Obama." *Political Psychology* 32, No. 1 (2011): 131-146.

Ellsworth, Scott. *The Tulsa Race Riot. Tulsa Race Riot: A Report*, 2001.

Ellsworth, Scott. *Death In A Promised Land: The Tulsa Race Riot Of 1921*. Baton Rouge, LA: LSU Press, 1992.

Erickson, Jr. Edward and Evan Serpick, "Enough Narcotics to Keep the City Intoxicated For a Year? Checking Batts' Fuzzy Drug Math," *Baltimore City Paper*, June 4, 2015, http://www.citypaper.com/blogs/the-news-hole/bcpnews-checking-batts-fuzzy-drug-math-20150604,0,5269132.story, accessed June 4, 2015.

Ervin, Kelly S. and Geoff Gilmore, "Traveling the Superinformation Highway: African Americans' Perceptions and Use of Cyberspace Technology," *Journal of Black Studies*, Vol. 29, No. 3. (January 1999), 398-407.

"Facts and Figures" Bureau of Alcohol, Tobacco, Firearms and Explosives Factsheet, "Budget," February 1, 2015, https://www.atf.gov/resource-center/pr/facts-and-figures, accessed 1/10/2016.

Falkner, Scott. "Baltimore Arrest Report Says Thousands of Suspects Too Injured to Enter Jail," Inquisitr, http://www.inquisitr.com/2080983/baltimore-arrest-report-says-thousands-of-suspects-too-injured-to-enter-jail/, May 11, 2015, accessed May 11, 2015.

Fanon, Franz, *The Wretched of the Earth*. New York: Grove Press, Inc., 1963.

Farrow, Edward S. Farrow's *Military Encyclopedia A Dictionary of Military Knowledge Illustrated with Maps and About Three Thousand Wood Engravings*, Vol. 1, New York: Published by the Author, 1885.

FBI Memorandum To SAC, Albany, Counterintelligence Program, Black Nationalist—Hate Groups, Racial Intelligence, March 4, 1968.

Feagin, Joe. "Slavery Unwilling to Die: The Background of Black Oppression in the 1980s," *Journal of Black Studies*, Vol. 17, No. 2, The Economic State of Black America. (December 1986), 173-200.

Fellner, Jamie. "Race, Drugs, and Law Enforcement in the United States." *Stanford Law & Policy Review* 20 (2009): 257.

Fernandez-Kelly, Patricia, *The Hero's Fight: African Americans in West Baltimore and the Shadow of the State*, Princeton, NJ: Princeton University Press, 2015.

Finnegan, James C. "A Study of Relationships Between College Education And Police Performance In Baltimore, Maryland." *Police chief* 43 (1976): 60-62.

Fischer, Pamela J. "Criminal Activity Among The Homeless: A Study Of Arrests in Baltimore." *Psychiatric Services* 39, No. 1 (1988): 46-51.

Fisher, Linda. "Target Marketing Of Subprime Loans: Racialized Consumer Fraud & Reverse Redlining." *Brooklyn Journal of Law and Policy* 18, No. 1 (2009).

Foner, Philip S. (ed.) *The Black Panthers Speak*. Philadelphia: J. B. Lippincott Company, 1970, 254-255.

Foote, Caleb. "Law and Police Practice: Safeguards in the Law of Arrest." *Northwestern University Law Review*. 52 (1957): 16.

Forman Jr, James. "Driving Dixie Down: Removing the Confederate Flag from Southern State Capitols." *Yale Law Journal* (1991): 505-526.

Forni, P.M. *Choosing Civility The Twenty-Five Rules of Considerate Conduct*, New York: NY, 2002.

Frank, James, Steven G. Brandl, Francis T. Cullen, and Amy Stichman. "Reassessing The Impact Of Race On Citizens' Attitudes Toward The Police: A Research Note." *Justice Quarterly* 13, No. 2 (1996): 321-334.

Freeman, John. *Brewer's Dictionary of Phrase and Fable*. New York: Harper & Row, 1963.

Friedman, Michael T., David L. Andrews, and Michael L. Silk. "Sport and the Façade Of Redevelopment In The Postindustrial City." *Sociology of Sport Journal.* 21 (2004): 119-139.

Fuller, Jr., Neely, *The United Independent Compensatory Codes/System/Concepts a Textbook/Workbook for Thought, Speech and/or Action for Victims of Racism (White Supremacy),* Revised Edition. Washington, D.C.: Liberation Information Distributing Co., 1984.

Furstenberg, Frank F., and Charles F. Wellford. "Calling The Police: The Evaluation Of Police Service." *Law and Society Review* (1973): 393-406.

Gabrielson, Ryan, Ryann Grochowski Jones, and Eric Sagara. "Deadly Force, in Black and White." *Pro Publica*, October 10, 2014, https://www.propublica.org/article/deadly-force-in-black-and-white.

Garofalo, James. *Public Opinion About Crime: The Attitudes Of Victims And Nonvictims In Selected Cities.* Vol. 1. US Department of Justice, Law Enforcement Assistance Administration, National Criminal Justice Information and Statistics Service, 1977.

Geberth, V. "Suicide by cop." *Law and Order* 41, No. 7 (1993): 105-109.

Genet, Jean. *Soledad Brother: The Prison Letters of George Jackson.* Chicago: Lawrence Hill Books, 1994.

George, Justin and Justin Fenton, "Man Says Gang Told Him to Take Gun Into Baltimore Police Station, Police Say," *The Washington Post,* January 6, 2015.

Gil, Ricard, and Mario Macis. "'Ain't No Rest for the Wicked': Population, Crime, and the 2013 Government Shutdown." Discussion Paper No. 8864, Bonn Germany: IZA Institute for the Study of Labor, February 2015, 23pp.

Gilens, Martin. "How the Poor Became Black." *Race and the Politics of Welfare Reform* (2003): 101.

Gitari, Njagi Dennis, Zhang Zuping, Hanyurwimfura Damien, and Jun Long. "A Lexicon-based Approach for Hate Speech Detection." (2015).

Gold, Benjamin J. "Public Area Surveillance and Police Work: The Impact of CCTV on Police Behaviour and Autonomy." *Journal of Surveillance and Society* 1, No. 2 (January 1, 2003): 191–203.

Goldberg, Louis C. "Ghetto Riots and Others: The Faces of Civil Disorders in 1967," in Gary T. Marx, *Racial Conflict Tension and Change in American Society*, Boston: Little, Brown and Company, 1971, 273-285.

Gonnerman, Jennifer. "The Wrong Way: Miriam Carey Drove through a White House Checkpoint and Died In A Hail of Bullets, Her Infant in the Back Seat. Was A Secret Service Screwup To Blame? *Mother Jones*, March, 2015, http://www.motherjones.com/politics/2015/03/miriam-carey-whitehouse-rammer-police-death, accessed August 5, 2015.

Gonzales, Juan. "Confederate Flag Is Finally Seen By Many People As Symbol Of White Supremacy And Racism," *New York Daily News*, June 23, 2015.

Government of the District of Columbia, Office of the Chief Medical Examiner, Autopsy Report, Case No. 13-02470, October 4, 2013.

Graham, Hugh Davis. "On Riots and Riot Commissions: Civil Disorders in the 1960s." *The Public Historian* (1980): 7-27.

Grand Jury Report, September Term 1965, Baltimore City, The Special Collections Department, Langsdale Library, University of Baltimore.

Gray, Herman. *Watching Race: Television and the Struggle for Blackness*. Minneapolis, MN: University of Minnesota Press, 1995.

Grayson, Sandra M. Black Women in the Antebellum America: Active Agents in the Fight for Freedom, Occasional paper, William Monroe Trotter Institute, University of Massachusetts at Boston, 1996, 32pp.

Grossman, Dave. *On Killing: The Psychological Cost Of Learning To Kill In War And Society*. Boston: Back Bay Books, 1995.

Hackel, Steven W. *Junipero Serra, California's Founding Father*, New York: Hill and Wang, 2013.

Hagedorn, John M. "Race not Space: A Revisionist History of Gangs in Chicago." *The Journal of African American History* (2006): 194-208.

Halpin, Dennis P. "'The Struggle for Land and Liberty' Segregation, Violence, and African American Resistance in Baltimore, 1898-1918." *Journal of Urban History* (2015).

Hanania-Freeman, Debra, T. Mitchell, L. Young, and C. Mitchell. "Baltimore Coalition Mobilizes Against Hit Squad in the DOJ." *Executive Intelligence Review* 25 (1998): 26-31.

Hanlon, Bernadette, and Thomas J. Vicino. "The Fate of Inner Suburbs: Evidence from Metropolitan Baltimore." *Urban Geography* 28, No. 3 (2007): 249-275.

Harden, Monique, Nathalie Walker and Kali Akuno, "Racial Discrimination and Ethnic Cleansing in the United States in the Aftermath of Hurricane Katrina: A Report to the United Nations' Committee for the Elimination of Racial Discrimination," November 30, 2007, 10pp

Harvard Public Health Review Editorial Board, "HPHR Editorial: Racism Is a Public Health Problem," *Harvard Public Health Review*, Vol. 3, January 2015, http://harvardpublichealth review.org/hphr-editorial-racism-is-a-public-health-problem/, accessed May 15, 2015.

Harwell, Fred. *A True Deliverance: The Joan Little Case*, New York: Alfred A. Knopf, 1980.

Haskins, James. "New Black Images in the Mass Media—How Educational is Educational TV?," *Freedomways*, 14, 3, 200-208, 1974.

Helm, Angela Bronner. "Aurora, Colorado Police Shoot & Kill Yet Another Unarmed Black Man," *Newsone for Black America*, March 10, 2015, http://newsone.com/3097058/ naeschylus-vinzant-killed-by-aurora-colorado-police/, accessed May 28, 2015.

Henderson, Errol A. "Black Nationalism and Rap Music," *Journal of Black Studies*, Vol. 26, No. 3 (January 1996), 308-339.

Henderson, J. Howard, Battle, Stanley F., et al., *The State of Black Baltimore, Baltimore*. Baltimore: Coppin State University, 2004.

Hess, Kären, Christine Hess Orthmann, and Henry Cho. *Introduction To Law Enforcement And Criminal Justice*. Cengage Learning, 2014.

"High School Graduation Rates in Maryland," Maryland Equity Project, Data Brief, January 2014.

Hirokawa, Keith H., and Ira Gonzalez. "Regulating Vacant Property." *The Urban Lawyer* (2010): 627-637.

Hochschild, Jennifer L., Vesla M. Weaver, and Traci Burch. "Destabilizing the American Racial Order." *Daedalus* 140, No. 2 (2011): 151-165.

Holly, Ellen. "The Role of Media in the Programming of an Underclass." *Black Scholar*, Vol. 10, No. 5, January-February 1979, 31-37.

Howell, Anthony T. Proven in War: The American Expeditionary Force and the Effort to Establish a Permanent Military Police Corps. Army Command and General Staff College Fort Leavenworth KS, 2014.

Howell, Babe. "Broken Lives from Broken Windows: The Hidden Costs of Aggressive Order-Maintenance Policing." *New York University Review of Law & Social Change* 33 (2009): 271.

H.R. 1933, "End Racial Profiling Act of 2015," the House Committee on the Judiciary, April 22, 2015.

Hrabowski III, Freeman A., Kenneth I. Maton, and Geoffrey L. Greif. *Beating The Odds: Raising Academically Successful African American Males*. Oxford University Press, 1998.

Hrabowski, III, Freeman A., Kenneth I. Maton, Monica L. Greene, and Geoffrey L. Greif. *Overcoming The Odds: Raising Academically Successful African American Young Women*. Oxford University Press, 2002.

Hudgins, John L. "Require College Degrees for Police," *The Baltimore Sun*, September 30, 2016.

Hudson-Weems, Clenora. *Emmett Till: The Sacrificial Lamb of the Civil Rights Movement*. Bloomington, IN: Authorhouse, 2006.

Hudson-Weems, Clenora. *Africana Womanist Literary Theory*. Trenton, NJ: Africa World Press, 2004.

Hurston, Zora Neale. "Characteristics of Negro Expression," in *Signifyin (g), Sanctifyin', and Slam Dunking: A Reader in African American Expressive Culture* (1934): 293-308.

Ifill, Sherrilyn. "Statement by the NAACP Legal Defense and Educational Fund, Inc. Before the President's Task Force on 21st Century Policing." (2015).

In The Matter Of Charges Filed Against Detective Timothy McDermott, No. 14 PB 2855 STAR No. 21084, Department Of Police, City Of Chicago, (CR No. 1061847) Respondent. Findings and Decision, 2014.

"Insurrection of the Blacks," *Niles' Register*, September 10, 1831.

"Insurrection of the Blacks," *Niles' Register*, September 3, 1831.

Introna Jr, Francesco and John E. Smialek. "The" Mini-Packer" Syndrome: Fatal Ingestion of Drug Containers in Baltimore, Maryland." *The American Journal of Forensic Medicine and Pathology* 10, No. 1 (1989): 21-24.

Jameson, Fredric. "Realism and Utopia in *The Wire*." *Criticism* 52, No. 3 (2010): 359-372.

Jernigan, Maryam M., Carlton E. Green, Leyla Pérez-Gualdrón, Marcia Liu, Kevin T. Henze, Cynthia Chen, Kisha N. Bazelais, Anmol Satiani, Ethan H. Mereish, and Janet E. Helms. "Alumni Advisory Group Institution for the Study and Promotion of Race and Culture." (2015).

Jasinski, Donald R., Jack E. Henningfield, John E. Hickey, and Rolley E. Johnson. "Progress report of the NIDA Addiction Research

Center, Baltimore, Maryland, 1982." *Problems of Drug Dependence* (1982): 92-98.

Jealous, Ben. Toward Trust Grassroots Recommendations for Police Reform in Baltimore, Washington, D.C.: Center for American Progress, October 2015, 24pp.

Jeffries, Judson L. "Black Radicalism and Political Repression in Baltimore: The Case of the Black Panther Party." *Ethnic and Racial Studies* 25, No. 1 (2002): 64-98.

Jenkins, Brian Michael. *Soldiers Versus Gunmen: The Challenge of Urban Guerrilla Warfare*. Rand Corporation, 1974.

Jernigan, Maryam M., Carlton E. Green, Leyla Pérez-Gualdrón, Marcia Liu, Kevin T. Henze, Cynthia Chen, Kisha N. Bazelais, Anmol Satiani, Ethan H. Mereish, and Janet E. Helms10. "Alumni Advisory Group Institution for the Study and Promotion of Race and Culture." (2015).

Johnson, Erika L. "Menace to Society: The Use of Criminal Profiles and Its Effects on Black Males, A." *Howard Law Journal* 38 (1994): 629-674.

Johnson, John. "Cop Rants About Killing Black Man, Covering it Up," *Newser*, August 4, 2015, http://www.newser.com/story/210812/cop-rants-about-killing-black-man-covering-it-up.html, accessed August 4, 2015.

Jones, Charles E. "The Political Repression of the Black Panther Party 1966-1971: The Case of the Oakland Bay Area." *Journal of Black Studies* (1988): 415-434.

Jones, Cynthia E. "'Give us Free': Addressing Racial Disparities in Bail Determinations," *Legislation and Public Policy*, Vol. 16, 919-961, 2013.

Joseph Crystal v. Anthony W. Batts, Robert Amador, and the Baltimore City Police Department, Case 1:14-cv-03989-JKB, Filed December 22, 2014.

Joseph, George. "Exclusive: Feds Regular Monitored Black Lives Matter Since Ferguson," *The Intercept*, July 24, 2015, accessed https://theintercept.com /2015/07/24/documents-show-department-homeland-security-monitoring-black-lives-matter-since-ferguson/.

Joseph, Peniel E. "The Black Power Movement: A State of the Field." *The Journal of American History* 96, No. 3 (2009): 751-776.

Joseph, Philip. "Soldiers in Baltimore: *The Wire* and the New Global Wars," *CR: The New Centennial Review*, Vol. 13, No. 1, Spring, 2013, 209-240.

Kaczorowski, Robert J. "The Enforcement Provisions of the Civil Rights Act of 1866: A Legislative History in Light of *Runyon v. McCrary*." *Yale Law Journal* (1989): 565-595.
Kaminski, Robert J., Steven M. Edwards, and James W. Johnson. "Assessing the Incapacitative Effects of Pepper Spray During Resistive Encounters With The Police." *Policing: An International Journal of Police Strategies & Management* 22, No. 1 (1999): 7-30.
Kane, P. S. "Why Have You Singled Me Out? The Use of Prosecutorial Discretion for Selective Prosecution." *Tulane Law Review*. 67 (1993): 2293-2371.
Karenga, Maulana, *Kawaida and Questions of Life and Struggle*, Los Angeles, CA: The University of Sankore Press, 2008.
Karenga, Maulana. *Introduction to Black Studies*. Los Angeles: University of Sankore Press, 2002.
Karenga, Maulana. Interview, *The Source*, February 1996.
Keeble, Arin and Ivan Stacy, *The Wire and Post-9/11 America Critical Essays* (2015).
Keen, Benjamin. *Latin American Civilization: History and Society, 1492 to the Present*, Boulder, CO: Westview Press, 1986.
Kelling, George. "Don't Blame my 'Broken Windows' Theory for Poor Policing," *Politico*, August 11, 2015.
Kelley, Robin D.G., *Freedom Dreams: The Black Radical Imagination*. Boston: Beacon Press, 2002.
Kennedy, Liam, and Stephen Shapiro. *The Wire: Race, Class, and Genre*. University of Michigan Press, 2012.
Keto, C. Tsehloane. *The Africa Centered Perspective of History*. Blackwood, NJ: K. A. Publications, 1989.
Khalek, Rania "Israeli-Trained Police Invade Baltimore In Crackdown on Black Lives Matter," The Electronic Intifada, http://electronicintifada.net/blogs/rania-khalek/israeli-trained-police-invade-baltimore-crackdown-black-lives-matter, May 7, 2015, accessed May 9, 2015.
Kianga Mwamba v. Baltimore City Police and Mayor and City Council of Baltimore et al, Circuit Court for Baltimore City, 2014.
Kiker III, Cadman R. "From Mayberry to Ferguson: The Militarization of American Policing Equipment, Culture, and Mission." *Washington and Lee Law Review Online* 71, No. 4 (2015): 282-298.
Kincheloe, Joe L. "Southernication, Romanticization and the Recovery of White Supremacy" *Souls: A Critical Journal of Black Politics, Culture, and Society*, (Winter, 2006) 8, 1, 27-46.

Kinder, Marsha. "Re-wiring Baltimore: The Emotive Power of Systemics, Seriality, and the City." *Film Quarterly*, Vol. 62, No. 2 (Winter 2008): 50-57.

King, Joyce E. "Dysconscious Racism: Ideology, Identity, and the Miseducation of Teachers," *The Journal of Negro Education*, Vol. 60, No. 2, Spring, 1991, 133-146.

King Jr., Martin Luther. "Beyond Vietnam: A Time To Break Silence." Speech, Riverside Church, New York, NY, April 4, 1967.

King, Jr., Martin Luther. *Where Do We Go From Here: Chaos or Community*, 1964. New York: Beacon Press, 2010.

King, Jr., Martin Luther. "Letter from Birmingham Jail," April 16, 1963, in Martin Luther King, Jr., *Why We Can't Wait*, 1963." Reprint. New York: Signet Classic (2000).

King, Shaun. "Chicago Police and Prosecutors Caught Lying As They Cover Up Their Murder Of Darius Pinex," *Daily Kos*, October 2, 2015.

King, Yvonne. "Philadelphia Panthers Reflect on the BPP." Unpublished paper, http://www. itsabouttimebpp.com/Chapter_History/pdf/Philadelphia/Philadelphia_Panthers_Reflect_BPP. pdf (accessed 27 July 2015) (2004).

Koh, T. T. B., and William T. Coleman. "United Nations Law on Racial Discrimination." *American Journal of International Law* (1970): 119-130.

Kotkin, Joel. The Future of the Center: The Core City In The New Economy. Reason Public Policy Institute, 1999.

Kraska, Peter B. "Enjoying Militarism: Political/Personal Dilemmas In Studying US Police Paramilitary Units." *Justice Quarterly* 13, No. 3 (1996): 405-429.

Krieger, Nancy, Mathew V. Kiang, Jarvis T. Chen, and Pamela D. Waterman, "Trends In US Deaths Due To Legal Intervention Among Black And White Men, Age 15-34 Years, By County Income Level: 1960-2010," *Harvard Public Health Review*, Vol. 3, January 2015, 1-5.

Krieger, Nancy. "Police Killings, Political Impunity, Racism and the People's Health: Issues for our Times," *Harvard Public Health Review*, Vol. 3, January 2015, 1-3, http://harvardpublichealth review.org/wp-content/uploads/2015/01/HPHRv3-Krieger-Police-Killings.pdf, accessed May 15, 2015.

Krug, Etienne G., James A. Mercy, Linda L. Dahlberg, and Anthony B. Zwi. "The World Report On Violence And Health." *The Lancet* 360, No. 9339 (2002): 1083-1088.

Lageson, Sarah, Kyle Green, and Sinan Erensu. "*The Wire* Goes To College." *Contexts* 10, No. 3 (2011): 12-15.

Lamberth, John. "Driving While Black; A Statistician Proves That Prejudice Still Rules the Road," The *Washington Post*, August 16, 1998; C01.

Lane, Kristin A., John T. Jost, Gregory S. Parks, and Matthew W. Hughey. "Black Man in the White House: Ideology and Implicit Racial Bias in the Age of Obama." *The Obamas and a (post) racial America* (2011): 48-69.

Langan, Patrick A. The measurement of robbery in Baltimore: a study of citizen discretion in the reporting of noncommercial predatory robbery to the Baltimore City Police Department. No. 78-24018 UMI. University of Maryland, 1978.

Lazare, Daniel. "Why US Police are out of Control," *Consortiumnews.com*, August 20, 2015. https://consortiumnews.com/2015/08/20/why-us-police-are-out-of-control/, accessed September 28, 2015/.

Lee, Felicia R. "Network for Blacks Broadens Its Schedule," *The New York Times*, July 9, 2007.

Lerner, Gerda. *Why History Matters: Life and Thought*. New York: Oxford University Press, 1997.

"Lessons Learned from the 2015 Civil Unrest in Baltimore," Police Executive Research Forum (PERF), Washington, D.C., September 2015, 79pp.

Lewis, Thabiti. "How Much Has Changed for Black Men? An Interview with Haki R. Madhubuti." *AmeriQuests* 6, No. 1 (2008).

LiDAR USA, http://www.lidarusa.com/company.php, accessed May 21, 2015.

Lieutenant Arthur Doyle (Retired), "From the inside Looking Out: Twenty-nine Years in the New York Police Department," in Jill Nelson's (ed.) *Police Brutality an Anthology*. New York: W.W. Norton & Company, 2000, 171-186.

Lieutenant General Jubal Anderson Early, C.S.A. Autobiographical Sketch and Narrative of the War Between the States. Philadelphia: J.B. Lippincott, 1912.

"Life After Michael Brown and Freddie Gray," *Al Jazeera America*, August 3, 2015, Produced by Lam Thuy Vo, Edited by Danielle Zalcman, Vaughn Wallace, Lam Thuy Vo, and Jayati Vora, August 3, 2015, http://projects.aljazeera.com/2015/07/ferguson-baltimore-echosight/.

Links, Jonathan, Katie O'Conor, and Lauren Sauer, "Recommendations for Enhancing Baltimore City's Preparedness and Response to Mass Demonstration Events Based on a Review and Analysis of the Events of April 2015," Baltimore, Maryland: The Johns Hopkins University, December 4, 2015, 73pp.

Linton. Ralph (ed.) *The Science of Man in the World Crisis*. New York: Columbia University Press, 1945.

Lochner, Kimberly, Ichiro Kawachi, and Bruce P. Kennedy. "Social Capital: A Guide to Its Measurement." *Health & Place* 5, No. 4 (1999): 259-270.

Loftin, Colin. "The Validity of Robbery-Murder Classifications in Baltimore." *Violence and Victims* 1, No. 3 (1986): 191-204.

Logue, Cal M. "Racist Reporting During Reconstruction," *Journal of Black Studies*, Vol. 9, No. 3. (March., 1979), 335-349.

Lonsway, Kim, Michelle Wood and Megan Fickling et al, "Men, Women, and Police Excessive Force: A Tale of Two Genders: A Content Analysis of Civil Liability Cases, Sustained Allegations and Citizen Complaints," The National Center for Women and Policing, a Division of the Feminist Majority Foundation, Los Angeles, CA, 2002, 11pp.

Lopez, Ian Haney. *Dog Whistle Politics: How Coded Racial Appeals Have Reinvented Racism And Wrecked The Middle Class*. New York: Oxford University Press, 2013.

Lutz, Catherine. "Making War At Home in the United States: Militarization and the Current Crisis." *American Anthropologist* (2002): 723-735.

Madhubuti, Haki R. (Ed.). (1993). *Why LA Happened: Implications of the '92 Los Angeles Rebellion*. Chicago: Third World Press.

Madhubuti, Haki R. (1990). *Black Men: Obsolete, Single, Dangerous?: Afrikan American Families In Transition: Essays In Discovery, Solution, And Hope*. Chicago: Third World Press.

Major, Reginald. *A Panther is a Black Cat*, New York: William Morrow & Co., Inc. 1971.

Malcolm, John G. "Operation Fast and Furious: How a Botched Justice Department Operation Led to a Standoff Over Executive Privilege," The Heritage Foundation, Washington, D.C. No. 83, July 25, 2012.

Mander, Jerry. *Four Arguments for the Elimination of Television*, New York: Quill, 1978, 31-33.

Marable, Manning. *The Great Wells of Democracy*, New York: BasicCivitas Books, 2002.
Mark, Puente and Meredith Cohn, "Freddie Gray Among Many Suspects Who Do Not Get Medical Care From Baltimore Police," *The Baltimore Sun*, May 9, 2015.
Marshall, Barbara. "Working While Black: Contours of an Unequal Playing Field," *Phylon*, Vol. 49, No. 3/4 (Autumn-Winter, 2001), 137-150, 138.
Martin, Brett. *Difficult Men: Behind the Scenes of a Creative Revolution: From The Sopranos and The Wire to Mad Men and Breaking Bad.* New York: Penguin Press, 2013.
Marx, Gary T. *Racial Conflict Tension and Change in American Society*, Boston: Little, Brown and Company, 1971.
Maryland Coordination and Analysis Center, "(U) Warning of Possible Incitement in Baltimore, Maryland," *Officer Safety Bulletin*, No.: 2015-0138, May 1, 2015.
Maryland House Bill 713, Chapter 496, "Maryland Gang Prosecution Act of 2007," May 17, 2007.
Maryland Statistical Analysis Center, Governor's Office of Crime Control and Prevention, Eleventh Report to the State of Maryland under TR 25-113 2013 Race-Based Traffic Stop Data Analysis MSAR #8801, September 2, 2014, 28pp.
"Massacre at Newark," *Freedomways, A Quarterly Review of the Negro Freedom Movement*, Vol. 7, No. 3, Summer 1967 (Third Quarter).
Mazama, Ama, ed., *The Afrocentric Paradigm*, Trenton, NJ: Africa World Press, Inc., 2003
McCabe, Bred. "Was '*The Wire*' Just Another Obstacle Standing in the Way of the City?" *Baltimore City Paper*, June 2, 2015. http://www.citypaper.com/news/features/bcpnews-was-the-wire-just-another-obstacle-standing-in-the-way-of-selling-the-city-20150602,0,1003317.story, accessed June 4, 2015.
McConahay, J., Mullin, C. & Frederick, J. "The Uses of Social Science in Trials with Political and Racial Overtones: The Trial of Joan Little," 41 *Law and Contemporary Problems*, 1977, 204-229.
McDougall, H. Black Baltimore: *A New Theory of Community*. Philadelphia: Temple University Press, 1993.
McFarlane, Audrey. "The New Inner City: Class Transformation, Concentrated Affluence and the Obligations of the Police Power." *University of Pennsylvania Journal of Constitutional Law* 8 (2005).
MD Criminal Law Code §9-801 (2013).

WORLD TO COME: ESSAYS ON THE BALTIMORE UPRISING, MILITANT RACISM, AND HISTORY

Media Matters for America, "Imus Called Women's Basketball Team 'Nappy-Headed Hos,'" April 4, 2007, http://www.media matters.org/research/2007/04/04/imus-called-womens-basketball-team-nappy-headed/138497, accessed April 13, 2007 and October 6, 2015.

Mediratta, Kavitha, and Norm Fruchter. "Mapping the field of organizing for school improvement: A report on education organizing in Baltimore, Chicago, Los Angeles, the Mississippi Delta, New York City, Philadelphia, San Francisco, and Washington DC." (2001).

Mejia, Sebastian C. *"Big Brother is Watching': The Fundamental Rights and Fourth Amendment Implications of Chicago's City-Wide Surveillance Network."* (July 28, 2014). Available at SSRN: http://ssrn.com/abstract=2473303 or http://dx.doi.org/10.2139/ssrn.2473303, accessed April 28, 2015.

Meranto, Philip. The Kerner Report Revisited, Final Report and Background Papers, Illinois: University of Illinois Institute of Government and Public Affairs, 1970, 155.

Mick, Jason. "Editorial: Reddit Allows Itself to be Hijacked as a hate platform or Racist Bigots," Daily Tech, July 21, 2015, http://www.dailytech.com/Editorial+Reddit+Allows+Itself+to+be+Hijacked+as+a+Hate+Platform+For+Racist+Bigots/article37446.htm, accessed August 2, 2015.

Miller, Jerome G. *Search And Destroy: African-American Males In The Criminal Justice System.* Cambridge University Press, 1996.

Mills, Charles W. *The Racial Contract.* Ithaca: Cornell University Press, 1997.

Mmari, Kristin, et al., "A Global Study on the Influence of Neighborhood Contextual Factors on Adolescent Health," Journal of Adolescent Health, Vol. 55, No. 6, Supplement, December 2014, pp. S13-S20. http://www.jahonline.org/article/S1054-139X%2814%2900355-3/fulltext Accessed May 2, 2015.

Monteiro-Ferreira, Ana *The Demise of the Inhuman Afrocentricity, Modernism, and Postmodernism,* New York: SUNY University Press, 2014.

Montgomery, David "Her Name Was Miriam Carey. She Drove To D.C. From Connecticut with Her Baby Daughter. A U-Turn At A Checkpoint Led To Her Being Killed—And A Slew Of Unanswered Questions." *The Washington Post,* November 26, 2014.

WORLD TO COME: ESSAYS ON THE BALTIMORE UPRISING, MILITANT RACISM, AND HISTORY

Montgomery, David. "Official Silence on Capitol Hill Shooting Draws Watchdog Lawsuit," *The Washington Post*, April 15, 2015.

Moore, Andrew. "Teaching HBO's *The Wire*." *Transformative Dialogues: Teaching & Learning Journal* 5, No. 1 (2011).

Moore, Jim. *Very Special Agents: The Inside Story Of America's Most Controversial Law Enforcement Agency--The Bureau Of Alcohol, Tobacco & Firearms*. University of Illinois Press, 1997.

Moyo, Dumisani. "Citizen Journalism and the Parallel Market of Information in Zimbabwe's 2008 Election." *Journalism Studies* 10, No. 4 (2009): 551-567.

Mosby, Marilyn. "Marilyn Mosby's Announcement Speech for the Office of Baltimore City State's Attorney," June 24, 2013, accessed May 14, 2015.

Moses, Greg. *Revolution of Conscience: Martin Luther King, Jr., and the Philosophy of Nonviolence*. New York: The Guilford Press, 1997.

Moynihan, Daniel Patrick, Lee Rainwater, and William L. Yancey. *The Negro family: The Case for National Action*. Cambridge, MA: MIT Press, 1967.

Mullings, Leith. *On Our Own Terms: Race, Class, and Gender in the Lives of African American Women*. New York: Routledge, 1997.

Murphy, Laura W. "Preventing the Next Death in Police Custody," Op-Ed, *The Baltimore Sun*, April 24, 2015, http://www.baltimoresun.com/news/opinion/oped/bs-ed-police-custody-deaths-20150425-story.html, accessed May 15, 2015.

Murray, Nancy, and Sarah Wunsch. "Civil Liberties in Times of Crisis: Lessons from History." *Massachusetts Law Review* 2013 (2014): 2012.

Musgrove, George Derek. *Rumor, Repression, and Racial Politics: How the Harassment of Black Elected Officials Shaped Post-civil Rights America*. Athens: University of Georgia Press, 2012.

Najdowski, Cynthia J., Bette L. Bottoms, and Phillip Atiba Goff. "Stereotype Threat and Racial Differences in Citizens' Experiences of Police Encounters." (2015).

Narrative of the Life of Frederick Douglass An American Slave Written By Himself. Edited with an Introduction by David W. Blight. New York: Bedford/St. Martin's, 1993.

Neal, Anthony. "The Naming: A Conceptualization of an African American Connotative Struggle," *Journal of Black Studies*, Vol. 32, No. 1. (September 2001), 50-65, 51.

Needleman, Herbert L. "Childhood Lead Poisoning: The Promise And Abandonment Of Primary Prevention." *American Journal of Public Health* 88, No. 12 (1998): 1871-1877.

Nelson, Arthur C., Thomas W. Sanchez, and Casey J. Dawkins. "The Effect of Urban Containment and Mandatory Housing Elements on Racial Segregation in US Metropolitan Areas, 1990-2000." *Journal of Urban Affairs* 26, No. 3 (2004): 339-350.

Nelson, Jill (ed.) *Police Brutality an Anthology.* New York: W.W. Norton & Company, 2000.

Newkirk, Anthony Bolton. "The Rise of the Fusion-Intelligence Complex: A Critique of Political Surveillance after 9/11." *Surveillance & Society* 8, No. 1 (2010): 43-60.

New York Civil Liberties Union Letter to Raymond Kelly, Commissioner, New York City Police Department, Re: Sean Bell Shooting and Stop-and-Frisk Reports, November 30, 2006.

New York Civil Liberties Union v. New York City Police Department et al, November 12, 2009.

Nicholl, Caroline G. *Toolbox for Implementing Restorative Justice and Advancing Community Policing.* Washington, DC: U.S. Department of Justice, Office of Community Oriented Policing Services, 1999.

Niedt, Christopher, Greg Ruiters, Dana Wise, and Erica Schoenberger. *The Effects of the Living Wage in Baltimore.* Economic Policy Institute, 1999.

Noel, Crista E. and Olivia Perlow. "American Police Crimes Against African Women and Women of Color." Chicago, IL: *The Women's All Points Bulletin,* 2014.

Northup, Solomon. *Twelve Years A Slave. Narrative of Solomon Northup, a Citizen of New York, Kidnapped In Washington City in 1841, And Rescued In 1853, From A Cotton Plantation Near The Red River, in Louisiana,* London: Sampson Low, Son & co, 1853.

O'Connor, Sandra Day. "Thurgood Marshall: The Influence of a Raconteur." *Journal of Supreme Court History.* 1992 Dec. 1; 17(1):9-14.

Office of the State's Attorney for the City of Baltimore, Press Release, "Statement from State's Attorney Mosby on Freddie Gray Case," May 5, 2015. http://www.stattorney.org/media-center/press-releases/716-statement-from-state-s-attorney-mosby-on-freddie-gray-case, Accessed May 16, 2015.

Ogletree, Charles and Sarat, Austin, (eds.). *From Lynch Mobs to the Killing State: Race and the Death Penalty in America.* New York: NYU Press, 2006.

Oliver, William "'The Streets' an Alternative Black Male Socialization Institution," *Journal of Black Studies*, Vol. 36, No. 6, July 2006, 918-937.

Olmstead, Kathleen. *The Wire: The Untold History of Television*, New York: HarperCollins, 2011.

Olson, Sherry H. *Baltimore: The Building of an American City.* Baltimore: Johns Hopkins University Press, 1997.

Operation Ghetto Storm, 2012 Annual Report on the Extrajudicial Killings of 313 Black People by Police, Security Guards and Vigilantes, with a Preface by Kali Akuno, Produced by the Every 36 Hours Campaign, Issued by Malcolm X Grassroots Movement, April 2013.

O'Reilly, Bill. "The Baltimore Rioting Now Leading to Madness," *Fox News*, FoxNews.Com, May 1, 2015 (Interview with Kenneth Jackson).

O'Reilly, Kenneth. *"Racial Matters": The FBI's Secret File on Black America.* New York: Free Press, 1989.

Over Policed, Yet Underserved: The People's Findings Regarding Police Misconduct in West Baltimore, Baltimore, MD: No Boundaries Coalition and the West Baltimore Commission on Police Misconduct, March 8, 2016, 32pp.

Painter, Nell Irvin. "Soul Murder and Slavery: Toward a Fully Loaded Cost Accounting," in *U.S. History as Women's History: New Feminist Essays*, ed. Linda K. Kerber, Alice Kessler-Harris, and Kathryn Kish Sklar, Chapel Hill: University of North Carolina Press, 1995.

Pancoast, Elinor. The Report of a Study on Desegregation in the Baltimore City Schools. The Commission, 1956.

Paoline, Eugene A., and William Terrill. "Women Police Officers and the Use of Coercion." *Women & Criminal Justice* 15, No. 3-4 (2005): 97-119.

Parker, Simon. "From Soft Eyes To Street Lives: *The Wire* And Jargons Of Authenticity." *City* 14, No. 5 (2010): 545-557.

Parenti, Christian, *Lockdown America: Police and Prisons in the Age of Crisis.* New York, NY: Verso, 2000.

Pate, Antony M., Sampson Annan, Police Foundation, and United States of America. "The Baltimore Community Policing Experiment." Washington, DC: Police Foundation (1989).

Pate, Antony M., Sampson O. Annan, Police Foundation, and United States of America. "Baltimore Community Policing Experiment: Summary Report." Washington, DC: Police Foundation (1989).

Peake, Bethany J. "Militarization of School Police: One Route on the School-to-Prison Pipeline." *Ark. L. Rev.* 68 (2015): 195.

Pendall, Rolf, Jonathan Martin, and William B. Fulton. *Holding the line: urban containment in the United States*. Center on Urban and Metropolitan Policy, the Brookings Institution, 2002.

Penfold-Mounce, Ruth, David Beer, and Roger Burrows. "*The Wire* as Social Science-Fiction?" *Sociology* 45, No. 1 (2011): 152-167.

Peterson, James Braxton "America's Mass Incarceration System: Freedom's Next Frontier," *Reuters*, July 24, 2015, http://blogs.reuters.com/great-debate/2015/07/23/americas-mass-incarceration-system-freedoms-next-frontier/, accessed August 3, 2015.

Petras, James. "Signs Of A Police State Are Everywhere." *Z Magazine* 15, No. 1 (2002): 10-12.

Phillips, Christopher. *Freedom's Port: The African American Community of Baltimore, 1790-1860*. University of Illinois Press, 1997.

Pietila, Antero. *Not in My Neighborhood: How Bigotry Shaped a Great American City*, Chicago: Ivan R. Dee, 2010.

Pitts, Jr., Leonard, "No Accountability for take-down of James Blake," *Sun Journal*, September17, 2015, http://www.sunjournal.com/news/columns-analysis/2015/09/17/leonard-pitts-no-accountability-take-down-james-black/1783276, accessed September 21, 2015.

Pointer, Fritz H. "Marxism and Nationalism in Black Revolutionary Movements—U.S.A.," *Ufahamu: A Journal of African Studies*, 2(2), 1971, 41-56.

Poe, Zizwe. "The Construction of an Africalogical Method to Examine Nkrumahism's Contribution to Pan-African Agency," *Journal of Black Studies*, Vol. 31, No. 6. (July 2001), 729-745, 738.

Pollack, Rachel. "Cold Case Justice." *Syracuse University Magazine* 25, No. 3 (2008): 19-23.

Porter, Tracie R. "School-to-Prison Pipeline: The Business Side of Incarcerating, Not Educating, Students in Public Schools." *Arkansas Law Review* 68 (2015): 55.

Potter, Tiffany and C.W. Marshall, *The Wire: Urban Decay and American Television* (2009).
Power, Garrett. "Apartheid Baltimore style: The Residential Segregation Ordinances of 1910-1913." *Maryland Law Review* 42 (1983): 289.
"President on the Situation in Baltimore," Whitehouse.gov, http://t.co/T3t6ptxmaZ, April 28, 2015, accessed May 19, 2015.
Price, Barbara Raffel. "Female Police Officers in the United States." Policing In Central and Eastern Europe: Comparing Firsthand Knowledge with Experience from the West. Ljubljana, Slovenia: College of Police and Security Studies (1996).
Prokos, Anastasia, and Irene Padavic. "'There Oughtta Be A Law Against Bitches': Masculinity Lessons In Police Academy Training." *Gender Work and Organization* 9 (2002): 439-459.
Pulido, Laura. "Rethinking Environmental Racism: White Privilege and Urban Development in Southern California." *Annals of the Association of American Geographers* 90, No. 1 (2000): 12-40.
Rabaka, Reiland. *Africana Critical Theory: Reconstruction the Black Radical Tradition, From W.E.B. DuBois and C.L.R. James to Frantz Fanon and Amílcar Cabral.* Lanham, MD: Lexington Books, 2009.
Rabaka, Reiland "Malcolm X and/as Critical Theory: Philosophy, Radical Politics, and the African American Search for Social Justice," *Journal of Black Studies*, Vol. 33, No. 2, 13th Cheikh Anta Diop Conference Selected Proceedings. (November 2002), 145-165.
"Racist German Army Clip Targets NY Blacks: German Military Instructor Tells Soldier to Envision Black Bronx Residents, Yell Obscenity and Fire Gun," ABC News Now, Show: Inside the Newsroom #1 6:08 AM EST, April 16, 2007.
Randall, Vernellia R. *Dying While Black: An In-Depth Look at a Crisis in the American Healthcare System.* Dayton, OH: Seven Principles Press, 2006.
Rao, Anupama. "Value, Visibility and the Demand for Justice." *Economic and Political Weekly* 50, No. 36 (2015): 37-42.
Rector, Kevin. "Ex-Cop and Blackface Performer's Fundraiser For Officers In Freddie Gray Case Canceled," *The Baltimore Sun*, July 22, 2015.
Redden, Molly and Lauren Gambino, "Attorney Defends Alleged Serial Rapist Cop By Attacking The Credibility Of Vulnerable Black Women," *The Guardian*, November 27, 2015.

Reid, Randall, "Ferguson, Baltimore, and the Search for Civic Health Metrics: Addressing the Lingering Problems," *Public Health*, Vol. 97, Issue 8, September 2015, p. 12, 4pp.

Relman, John P. "Foreclosures, Integration, and the Future of the Fair Housing Act." *Indiana Law Review*. 41 (2008): 629.

"Remarks by the President on Trayvon Martin," Press Release, The White House, Office of the Press Secretary, July 19, 2013.

Report of the Washington County District Attorney's Office Regarding the Shooting of Mr. Bo Morrison On March 3, 2012, 13.

Report on the Officer Involved Fatality Involving Milwaukee Police Officer Christopher Manney and Dontre Hamilton, December 20, 2014, 30pp.

Report to Congress, "Access to Affordable and Nutritious Food, Measuring and Understanding Food Deserts and Their Consequences," United States Department of Agriculture, June 2009.

Request for Presidential Disaster Declaration Governor's Request Cover Letter Major Disaster, State of Maryland, Office of the Governor, May 21, 2015, 6pp.

Reston, Jr., James. *The Innocence of Joan Little a Southern Mystery*, New York: Times Books, 1977.

Restorative Justice Online, Prison Fellowship International Centre for Justice and Reconciliation, http://www.restorativejustice.org/, accessed July 9, 2015.

Reuss-Ianni, Elizabeth. *Two Cultures of Policing: Street Cops and Management Cops*. Transaction Publishers, 1993.

Reynolds, William L. "Legal History of the Great Sit-in Case of *Bell v. Maryland*," *Maryland Law Review*. 61 (2002): 761.

Ridgeway, Greg, "Analysis Of Racial Disparities In The New York Police Departments Stop, Question, And Frisk Practices," Sponsored by the New York City Police Foundation, Santa Monica, CA: RAND Corporation, 2007.

Rinder, Irwin D. "Minority Orientations: An Approach to Intergroup Relations Theory through Social Psychology," *Phylon*, XXVI (Spring, 1965), 5-17.

Roberts, Dorothy E. "The Value of Black Mothers' Work." *Connecticut Law Review*. 26 (1993): 871.

Roberts, Randy. *Papa Jack: Jack Johnson and the Era of White Hopes*, London: Collier Macmillan, 1983.

Robeson, Paul. *Here I Stand*. Boston: Beacon, 1971.

Robinson, Christine Renee. "Black Women: A Tradition of Self-Reliant Strength." *Women & Therapy* 2, No. 2-3 (1983): 135-144.

Romano, Renee C. *Racial Reckoning: Prosecuting America's Civil Rights Murders*. Harvard University Press, 2014.

Rose, Tricia, Andrew Ross, Robin DG Kelley, Joe Wood, Howard Winant, Jacquie Jones, Michael Eric Dyson et al. "Race And Racism: A Symposium." *Social Text* (1995): 1-52.

Rose, T. "'Fear Of a Black Planet': Rap Music and Black Cultural Politics in the 1990s." *Journal of Negro Education*, 60, 276-290, 1991.

Rose, T. *Black Noise: Rap Music and Black Culture in Contemporary America*. Hanover, NH: Wesleyan University Press, 1994.

Rosen, Jeffrey, "Excessive Force: Why Patrick Dorismond didn't Have to Die," *The New Republic*, April 20, 2000.

Rubinowitz, Leonard S. and Imani Perry, "Crimes without Punishment: White Resistance to Black Entry," *Journal of Criminal Law and Criminology*, Vol. 92, No. 2, Fall, 2001, 335-428.

Rudovsky, David. "Law Enforcement by Stereotypes and Serendipity: Racial Profiling and Stops and Searches Without Cause." *University of Pennsylvania Journal of Constitutional Law*. 3 (2001): 296.

Rugh, Jacob S., Len Albright, and Douglas S. Massey. "Race, Space, And Cumulative Disadvantage: A Case Study Of The Subprime Lending Collapse." *Social Problems* (2015): spv002.

Runcie, John. "'Hunting the Nigs' in Philadelphia: the Race Riot of August 1834." *Pennsylvania History* (1972): 187-218.

Rushton, J. Philippe *Race, Evolution, and Behavior: A Life History Perspective*, 2nd Special Abridged Edition, Port Huron, MI: Charles Darwin Research Institute, 2000.

Russell-Brown, Katheryn. *The Color of Crime: Racial Hoaxes, White Fear, Black Protectionism, Police Harassment, and Other Macroaggressions*. New York: New York University Press, 1998.

Sahar, Khamis, and Katherine Vaughn. "Cyberactivism In The Egyptian Revolution: How Civic Engagement And Citizen Journalism Tilted The Balance." *Arab Media and Society* 14, No. 3 (2011): 1-25.

Sampson, Robert J., and Stephen W. Raudenbush. "Seeing Disorder: Neighborhood Stigma and the Social Construction of "Broken Windows." *Social Psychology Quarterly* 67, No. 4 (2004): 319-342.

Sanford Police Department, 911 Event Report, George Zimmerman, August 12, 2004—February 26, 2012.

Sanford Police Department, 911 Event Report, George Zimmerman, February 26, 2012.
Sanford Police Department, Partial Report, February 26, 2012.
Scales Jr., Robert H. The Indirect Approach: How US Military Forces Can Avoid the Pitfalls of Future Urban Warfare. Center For Army Lessons Learned Fort Leavenworth KS Virtual Research Library, 1998.
Scharf, John Thomas. *The Chronicles of Baltimore: Being a Complete History of "Baltimore Town" and Baltimore City from the Earliest Period to the Present Time.* Turnbull brothers, 1874.
Schaub, Joseph Christopher. "*The Wire*: Big Brother Is Not Watching You In Body-More, Murdaland." *Journal of Popular Film and Television* 38, No. 3 (2010): 122-132.
Schwabauer, Barbara A. "Emmett Till Unsolved Civil Rights Crime Act: The Cold Case of Racism in the Criminal Justice System, The." *Ohio State Law Journal* 71 (2010): 653.
Schwartzman, Paul Ovetta Wiggins and Cheryl W. Thompson (with contributions from John Wagner), "In the Crucial Hours in Baltimore, a Communication Breakdown," *The Washington Post*, May 11, 2015.
Schnabel, Albrecht, Centre Pour Le Contrôle Démocratique Des Forces Armées (Genève), and Marc J. Krupanski. Mapping Evolving Internal Roles of the Armed Forces. DCAF, 2012.
"Scott Statement on the Signing of Death In Custody Reporting Act of 2013 into Law by President Obama," Press Release, December 18, 2014, Congressman Bobby Scott Representing the 3rd District of Virginia, http://bobbyscott.house.gov/media-center/press-releases/scott-statement-on-the-signing-of-death-in-custody-reporting-act-of-2013, accessed May 15, 2015.
Scriven, Darryl. "Blue on Black Violence: Freddie Gray, Baltimore, South Africa, & the Quietism of Africana Christian Theology." *Journal of Pan African Studies* 8, No. 3 (2015): 119-126.
Scully, Judith A.M. "Rotten Apple or Rotten Barrel?: The Role of Civil Rights Lawyers in Ending the Culture of Police Violence." *National Black Law Journal.* 21, 137-172, 2008.
Seale, Bobby. *Seize The Time: The Story Of The Black Panther Party And Huey P. Newton.* New York, NY: Random House, 1970.
Shakur, Assata. "An Open Letter from Assata Shakur." (1998).
Sharpton, Al. "Statement by Reverend Al Sharpton on Criminal Charges of Six Baltimore Police Officers in Death of Freddie Gray," May 1, 2015, the National Action Network (NAN),

http://nationalactionnetwork.net/press/statement-by-reverend-al-sharpton-on-criminal-charges-of-six-baltimore-police-officers-in-death-of-freddie-gray/, accessed May 31, 2015.

Sheehan, Helena, and Sheamus Sweeney. "*The Wire* And The World: Narrative and Metanarrative." *Jump Cut 51*, No. Spring 2009 (2009).

Shuck, Johari R., and Robert J. Helfenbein. "Civic Identity, Public Education, and the African-American Community in Indianapolis: Mending the Fracture." *Journal of Civic Literacy* 2, No. 1 (2015): 24-42.

Sidhu, Dawinder S. "Wartime America and *The Wire*: A Response to Posner's Post-9/11 Constitutional Framework." *George Mason University Civil Rights Law Journal* 20 (2009): 37.

Simpson, Mark C. *In Search of Justice: Examining Efforts to Obtain Convictions in Unsolved Civil Rights Era Murders in Mississippi*. iUniverse, 2006.

Singh, Karan R. "Treading The Thin Blue Line: Military Special-Operations Trained Police SWAT Teams and the Constitution." *William and Mary Bill of Rights Journal*. Vol. 9, No. 3 (2000): 673-717.

Sklansky, David Alan. "Confined, Crammed, And Inextricable: What *The Wire* Gets Right." *Ohio State Journal of Criminal Law* 8, No. 2 (2011): 473.

Smith, McKay M. "Occupy Wall Street and the US Army's 82nd Airborne Division: A Hypothetical Examination of the Slippery Slope of Military Intervention during Civil Disturbance." *George Mason University Civil Rights Law Journal*. 22 (2011): 295.

Smith-Shomade, Beretta. *Pimpin' Ain't Easy: Selling Black Entertainment Television*, Taylor and Francis, Inc., 2007.

Snow, Nancy. *Information War American Propaganda, Free Speech and Opinion Control since 9-11*, New York: Seven Stories Press, 2003.

Southall, Pamela, Jami Grant, David Fowler and Shauna Scott, "Police Custody Deaths in Maryland, USA: an Examination of 45 Cases, *Journal of Forensic and Legal Medicine*, Vol. 15, Issue 4, 227-230, May, 2008.

South Carolina Department of Public Safety, Press Release, "SCDPS Releases Statement Regarding Trooper-Involved Shooting," September 4, 2014.

South Carolina Department of Public Safety, Press Release, "Second Follow up: Trooper-Involved Shooting in Richland County on September 4, 2014," September 19, 2014.

St. Pierre, Maurice A. Reaganomics and Its Implications for African-American Family Life, *Journal of Black Studies*, Vol. 21, No. 3. (March, 1991), 325-340.

Sanford Police Department, 911 Event Report, George Zimmerman, August 12, 2004—February 26, 2012.

Stanley, Eugene. "Educational Desegregation in Baltimore: A Status Report." *Journal of Negro Education* (1955): 71-77.

Stewart, Gary. "Black Codes and Broken Windows: The Legacy of Racial Hegemony in Anti-Gang Civil Injunctions." *Yale Law Journal* (1998): 2249-2279.

Stolberg Sheryl Gay and Stephen Babcock, "Scenes of Chaos in Baltimore as Thousands Protest Freddie Gray's Death," The New York Times, April 25, 2015, http://www.nytimes.com/2015/04/26/us/baltimore-crowd-swells-in-protest-of-freddie-grays-death.html?_r=0, accessed August 2, 2015.

Strausbaugh, John. *Black Like You: Blackface, Whiteface, Insult and Imitation in American Popular Culture*, New York: Penguin Group, 2006, 147.

Strayer, George Drayton. Report of the Survey of the Public School System of Baltimore, Maryland. Vol. 1. 1921.

Subhas, Nital, and Anita Chandra. "Baltimore City Police Athletic League Assessment Study," 2004.

Sudarkasa, Niara. African American Families and Family Values. In H. P. McAdoo (Ed.), *Black Families* (3rd ed., pp. 9-40). Thousand Oaks, CA: Sage, 1997.

Sudarkasa, Niara. *Strength of Our Mothers: African and African-American Women and Families: Essays and Speeches*, Trenton: Africa World Press, 1996.

Sudarkasa, Niara. "Female-headed African American Households: Some Neglected Dimensions." *Family Ethnicity: Strength In Diversity* (1993): 81-89.

"Summary of a Report on the Race Riots in the Alabama Dry Dock and Shipbuilding Company Yards in Mobile, Alabama," New York: National Urban League for Social Service Among Negroes, June, 1943.

Summers, Alicia. "Racial Disparity Begins In Childhood: How Disproportionality in Child Abuse Cases Impacts Adult Justice

System Inequities," *Critical Issues in Justice and Politics*, Vol. 1, No. 1, March 20008, 47-62.

"Surveillance Planes Spotted in the Sky for Days after West Baltimore Rioting," Craig Timberg, May 5, 2015, *The Washington Post*, http://www.washingtonpost.com/business/technology/surveillance-planes-spotted-in-the-sky-for-days-after-west-baltimore-rioting/2015/05/05/c57c53b6-f352-11e4-84a6-6d7c67c50db0_story.html.

Sutherland, Marcia E. "Individual Differences in Response to the Struggle for the Liberation of People of African Descent," *Journal of Black Studies*, Vol. 20, No. 1. (September 1989), 40-59, 43.

Swaine, Jon, "Alabama Officer Kept Job after Proposal to Murder Black Man and Hide Evidence," *The Guardian*, August 4, 2015.

Takagi, Paul. "A Garrison State in "Democratic" Society." *Crime and Social Justice*, Vol. 40, Nos. 1-2, (1974): 27-33.

"Ta-Nehisi Coates on Police Brutality, The Confederate Flag and Forgiveness," NPR, Fresh Air, Interviewed by Terry Gross, July 13, 2015.

Taylor, Keeanga-Yamahtta. *From #BlackLivesMatter to Black Liberation*. Chicago: Haymarket Books, 2016.

Taylor, Ralph B. *Breaking Away From Broken Windows: Baltimore Neighborhoods and the Nationwide Fight against Crime, Grime, Fear, and Decline*. Boulder, CO: Westview Press, 2001.

Teun A. van Dijk, New(s) "Racism. A Discourse Analytical Approach," In: Simon Cottle (Ed.), *Ethnic Minorities and the Media*. Milton Keynes, UK: Open University Press, 2000, 33-49.

The Case of Mumia Abu-Jamal Information Booklet, Philadelphia, PA: International Concerned Family and Friends of Mumia Abu-Jamal, November, 2005, 26pp, 2.

The Emmett Till Unsolved Civil Rights Crime Act of 2007, Public Law 110-344, 110th Congress, October 7, 2008.

The Forty Acres Documents, with an Introduction by Amílcar Shabazz. Baton Rouge, LA: The House of Songhay, 1994.

"The Joanne Little Case," *CBC For the People*, Vol. 1, No. 2, May, 1975.

The Last Poets, "This is Madness," *This is Madness*, Douglass, 1971.

The Office of Governor Larry Hogan, "Inaugural Address—Governor Larry Hogan," January 21, 2015, Maryland.gov, http://governor.maryland.gov/2015/01/21/inaugural-address-governor-larry-hogan/, accessed May 15, 2015.

The Pew Research Center, "Multiple Causes seen for Baltimore Unrest," May 4, 2015, http://www.people-press.org/2015/05/04/multiple-causes-seen-for-baltimore-unrest/, accessed May 11, 2015.

The Retreat at Twin Lakes HOA Newsletter, *Retreat Reflections*, Vol. 5, Issue 1, February 2012.

The State of Maryland, Executive department, Executive Order 01.01.2015.16, "Declaration of Emergency," April 27, 2015.

The State's Attorney for the City of Baltimore, Press Conference, May 1, 2015, Baltimore, Maryland.

The United States Conference of Mayors, Press Release, "Statement By U.S. Conference Of Mayors President Sacramento Mayor Kevin Johnson On The Baltimore State's Attorney's Announcement In The Freddie Gray Case And Baltimore Mayor Stephanie Rawlings-Blake's Response Following It," Washington, D.C., May 1, 2015.

Thelen, D.P. (1990). *Memory and American History*. Bloomington: Indiana University Press.

Thompkins, Stephen G. "Army Feared King, Secretly Watched Him." *Commercial Appeal* (1993).

Till, Rupert. "Pop Stars and Idolatry: An Investigation of The Worship Of Popular Music Icons, And The Music And Cult Of Prince." *Journal of Beliefs & Values* 31, No. 1 (2010): 69-80.

Tillotson, Michael. *Invisible Jim Crow: Contemporary Ideological Threats to the Internal Security of African Americans*, Trenton, NJ: Africa World Press, 2011.

Trier, James. "Representations of Education in HBO's *The Wire*, Season 4." *Teacher Education Quarterly* (2010): 179-200.

Trotta, Joe, and Oleg Blyahher. "Game Done Changed: A Look At Selected AAVE Features In The TV Series *The Wire*." *Moderna språk* 105, No. 1 (2011): 15-42.

Tulsa Race Riot: A Report by the Oklahoma Commission to Study the Tulsa Race Riot of 1921," Final Report of Findings and Recommendations of the 1921 Tulsa Race Riot Commission, February 28, 2001.

United States Department of Justice, Civil Rights Division, *Investigation of the Ferguson Police Department*, March 4, 2015.

United States Department of Justice, Office of the Inspector General, A Review of ATFs Operation Fast and Furious and Related Matters (Redacted), November, 2012.

WORLD TO COME: ESSAYS ON THE BALTIMORE UPRISING, MILITANT RACISM, AND HISTORY

United States District Court, *Travonna Howard v. Richard Hass*, Settlement Agreement, Full Release and Covenant Not to Sue, Richard Haas and The University of Cincinnati with Travonna Howard and Everette Howard, January 7, 2013.

Unnever, James D., and Shaun L. Gabbidon. *A Theory of African American Offending: Race, Racism, And Crime.* Taylor & Francis, 2011.

Van Dyke, Nella, and Sarah A. Soule. "Structural Social Change And The Mobilizing Effect Of Threat: Explaining Levels Of Patriot And Militia Organizing In The United States." *Social Problems* 49, No. 4 (2002): 497-520.

Vetter, Drew, BCPD, "Situation Update," Email to The City, April 28, 2015.

Visher, Christy, Nancy LaVigne, and Jeremy Travis. "Returning Home: Understanding the Challenges of Prisoner Reentry: Maryland Pilot Study: Findings from Baltimore." Washington, D.C.: Urban Institute Justice Police Center, 2004, 240pp.

Wacquant, Loïc, "The New 'Peculiar Institution': On the Prison as Surrogate Ghetto," *Theoretical Criminology*, Vol. 4 (3), 377-389, 2000.

Wallace, Michelle. *Black Macho and the Myth of Superwoman*, New York: Verso, 1999.

Walmsley, Roy. *World Prison Population List* (tenth edition), International Centre for Prison Studies (ICPS), London: The University of Essex, 2003.

Walsh, William F. "COMPSTAT: An Analysis of an Emerging Police Managerial Paradigm." *Policing: An International Journal of Police Strategies & Management* 24, No. 3 (2001): 347-362.

Ward, Churchill and Jim Vander Wall, *The COINTELPRO Papers Documents from the FBI's Secret Wars Against Domestic Dissent*, Boston: South End Press, 1990.

Watkins, D. "Black History Bulldozed For another Starbucks: Against the New Baltimore," *Salon*, March 23, 2015.

Weisburd, David, and John E. Eck. "What Can Police Do To Reduce Crime, Disorder, And Fear?." *The Annals of the American Academy of Political and Social Science* 593, No. 1 (2004): 42-65.

Welsh, Brandon C., Anthony A. Braga, and Gerben Bruinsma. "Reimagining Broken Windows from Theory to Policy."*Journal of Research in Crime and Delinquency* 52, No. 4 (2015): 447-463.

Welch, Kelly. "Black Criminal Stereotypes and Racial Profiling," *Journal of Contemporary Criminal Justice* 23, No. 3 (2007): 276-288.

Wells-Barnett, Ida B. "Lynch Law in America." *The Arena* 15 (1900).
Wells-Barnett, Ida B. *A Red Record: Tabulated Statistics and Alleged Causes of Lynchings in the United States, 1892-1893-1894*. Chicago: Donohue and Henneberry, 1895.
Welsing, Frances Cress. *The Isis Papers The Keys to the Colors*, Chicago: Third World Press, 1991.
Wemple, Erik. "Comedy Central's Larry Wilmore: 'Let Me Be the First to Call [Waco] Bikers Thugs'" *The Washington Post*, May 27, 2015, accessed May 30, 2015.
Wen, Leana S., Katherine E. Warren, Shirli Tay, Joneigh S. Khaldun, Dawn L. O'Neill, and Olivia D. Farrow, "Public Health In The Unrest: Baltimore's Preparedness And Response After Freddie Gray's Death," *American Journal of Public Health*, October 2015, Vol. 105, Issue 10.
West, Cornel. "A Genealogy of Modern Racism," in *Race Critical Theories*, edited by Philomena Essed and David Theo Goldberg, Malden, MA: Blackwell Publishers, 2002, 90-112.
Whitman, T. Stephen. *The Price of Freedom: Slavery and Manumission In Baltimore And Early National Maryland*. London: Psychology Press, 1999.
"Why Rev. M. L. King Is Leaving Montgomery: Leader Says Time Is Ripe to Extend Work in Dixie," *Jet Magazine*, December 17, 1959.
Wilkins, Roy. "Riots of 1964: The Causes of Racial Violence." *Notre Dame Law*. 40 (1964): 552.
Williams, Joseph J.E. *The Principles of American Slavery: An Interesting and Authentic Pamphlet Giving a Full and Satisfactory Description of the Principles of the Slave Code of the South, with the Morals and Improvements of the Colored People of Canada, of the Elgin Association*. Hamilton, Ontario: Christian Advocate Office, 1858.
Williams, Yohuru and Jama Lazerow, *Liberated Territory Untold Local Perspectives on The Black Panther Party*, Durham, NC: Duke University Press, 2008.
Wilson, Amos N. *The Falsification of Afrikan Consciousness: Eurocentric History, Psychiatry, and the Politics of White Supremacy*. Afrikan World InfoSystems, 1993.
Wilson, Amos N. *Black-On-Black Violence: The Psychodynamics of Black Self-Annihilation in Service of White Domination*. Afrikan World Infosystems, 1990.
Wilson, David. *Inventing Black-On-Black Violence: Discourse, Space, and Representation*. Syracuse University Press, 2005.

Wilson, David. "Constructing a 'Black-on-Black' Violence: The Conservative Discourse." *ACME: An International E-Journal for Critical Geographies* 1, No. 1 (2002): 35-54.

Wilson, James Q., and George L. Kelling. "Broken Windows." *Atlantic Monthly* 249, No. 3 (1982): 29-38.

Wingfield, Adia Harvey, and Joe R. Feagin. *Yes We Can?: White Racial Framing And The Obama Presidency*. Routledge, 2013.

Winkler, Adam. "The Secret History of Guns." *Atlantic Magazine* (2011).

Winslow, Barbara. *Shirley Chisholm*. Boulder, CO: Westview Press, 2014.

Wise, Tim. *Between Barack and a Hard Place: Racism and White Denial in the Age of Obama*. San Francisco, CA: City Lights Books, 2013.

Wise, Tim. *Color-Blind The Rise of Post-Racial Politics and the Retreat From Racial equity*, San Francisco, CA: City Lights Books, 2010.

Witt, Howard. "Taser Death Spotlights Town's Corrupt History Handcuffed Man, 21, Was Stunned 9 Times by Officer," *Chicago Tribune*, July 19, 2008.

Wolfers, Justin, David Leonhardt and Kevin Quealy, "1.5 Million Missing Black Men," *The New York Times*, April 20, 2015.

Wright, Bobby E. *The Psychopathic Racial Personality and Other Essays*. (Second Edition) Chicago: Third World Press, 1997.

Yan, Holly and Dana Ford, "Baltimore Riots: Looting, Fires Engulf City after Freddie Gray's Funeral," CNN, April 28, 2015. http://www.cnn.com/2015/04/27/us/baltimore-unrest/, accessed May 27, 2015.

Yensi, Amy. CBS Baltimore, "Bystander Throws Water on Baltimore Mayor Stephanie Rawlings-Blake," July 12, 2015, http://nation.foxnews.com/2015/07/12/bystander-throws-water-baltimore-mayor-stephanie-rawlings-blake, accessed August 2, 2015.

Yette, Samuel F. *The Choice: The Issue of Black Survival in America*, Silver Spring, MD: Cottage Books, 1996.

Young, Jean Childs "The Black Child," in *Proceedings, Conference On The Black Family*, edited by Janice Hale-Benson, Cleveland, Ohio, September 25-28, 1985, 44-48.

Zimring, Franklin E. "Firearms and Federal Law: the Gun Control Act of 1968." *The Journal of Legal Studies* (1975): 133-198.

WORLD TO COME: ESSAYS ON THE BALTIMORE UPRISING, MILITANT RACISM, AND HISTORY

ABOUT THE AUTHOR

KATHERINE BANKOLE-MEDINA is a Professor of History (and former history department chairperson) at Coppin State University in Baltimore, Maryland. She has worked in faculty and administrative positions at Kean University, the University of Virginia, Xavier University (New Orleans), and West Virginia University. She is a scholar of African American and United States history, African American Studies, Africalogy, Race Relations, Black Women, and Slavery and Medicine Studies. Dr. Bankole-Medina has published numerous scholarly articles on these subjects, including her book, *Slavery and Medicine: Enslavement and Medical Practices in Antebellum Louisiana*. Her research and scholarship has appeared in the *Journal of Black Studies, Plantation Society and Race Relations* (edited by Thomas J. Durant and J. David Knottnerus), *Afrocentricidade: Uma Abordagem Epistemologica Inovadora* (edited by Elisa Larkin Nascimento); *Handbook of Black Studies* (edited by Molefi Kete Asante and Maulana Karenga) and *Malcolm X A Historical Reader* (edited by James L. Conyers, Jr. and James Smallwood). She served on the Editorial Board of *The Encyclopedia of Black Studies* (edited by Molefi Kete Asante and Ama Mazama, Los Angeles: Sage, 2005). Since 2004 she has worked as the founding editor of *Africalogical Perspectives: Historical and Contemporary Analysis of Race and Africana Studies*. She is also co-editor of the series *Women of African Descent and Justice and World Societies* (with Abena Lewis-Mhoon and Stephanie Yarbough). Her most recent publications include an article on African American women's studies, the life and legacy of Fannie Jackson Coppin, and on Charles Hamilton Houston. Her current research focuses on antebellum medical racism; and a contemporary analysis of the 2015 Baltimore Uprising. The recipient of numerous scholarship, teaching and service awards, Dr. Bankole-Medina was twice named *most influential person* in the state of West Virginia. She is a recipient of the Judith Stitzel Endowment Award for teaching and research, The Martin Luther King, Jr. Award for Scholarship, The Cheikh Anta Diop International Conference Award for Editorial Excellence, and she was selected for the first Distinguished Senior Faculty Research grant awarded by Coppin State

University. Dr. Bankole-Medina's additional training includes certification in Conflict Mediation (Racial/Ethnic Conflict); and she was also awarded the Certificate in Online Teaching and Learning from the Online Learning Consortium OLC (formerly the Sloan-C Consortium). Dr. Bankole-Medina currently teaches a variety of university courses/seminars (face-to-face and online) including World History, U.S. History, African American History, African American Intellectual History, Introduction to Latin American History, History of the Middle East, Methods of Historical Research, and the History of Science, Medicine and Technology. Dr. Bankole-Medina's occasional Blog and YouTube channel *History is a State of Mind* engages students and the general public. She is an Executive Board member of the Diopian Institute for Scholarly Advancement, a life member of the Association of Black Women Historians (ABWH) and the Association for the study of African American Life and History (ASALAH), and a fellow of the Molefi Kete Asante Institute (MKAI) in Philadelphia. Dr. Bankole-Medina has been interviewed by numerous radio stations, print news outlets (the *Baltimore Sun*, the *Times-Picayune*, and the *Dominion Post*), and on television (*CNN* [Fox and Friends] and *NBC* and *CBS* news affiliates). She is a graduate of Howard University in Washington, D.C. (BA) and Temple University in Philadelphia (MA and PhD). For more information, Dr. Bankole-Medina can be contacted at drkatherinemedina@outlook.com.

WORLD TO COME: ESSAYS ON THE BALTIMORE UPRISING,
MILITANT RACISM, AND HISTORY

GENERAL INDEX

A
Abu-Jamal, Mumia, 51-52
African Americans who Died in Police-Encounters, 1994-2015, A
    Compendium of, 349-389
Afro-American, The, 118, 125
Afrocentric Philosophical Paradigm, 286
Afrocentric scholarship, 87, 98, 176, 286-287
Afrofemiphobia, 41, 240-243, 244
Al Jazeera America, 118, 161, 321, 334
American Civil Liberties Union (ACLU), 47, 204, 314
Amnesty International, 55
Angelou, Maya, 284-285
Apartheid Schools, 30, 127, 166
Arab Spring, 110, 219, 221
Asante, Molefi Kete, 90, 114, 123, 286
ATF (Bureau of Alcohol, Tobacco, Firearms and Explosives), 40, 192-
    196, 332, 335, 404
Attica Prison Revolt, 1971, 141-142, 396

B
Bail/Bond (see Money Bail), 41, 117, 201, 225, 229, 230, 265, 271, 293
Baldwin, James, 63, 166, 178, 282, 283
Baltimore 6, The, 28, 41, 56, 193, 197, 208, 224, 225, 237, 243, 244,
    271, 297, 298, 299, 319, 325, 342
Baltimore City Fraternal Order of Police (FOP), 57, 244, 295, 296, 297,
    298, 299
Baltimore City Police Department, 117, 125, 153, 162, 164, 183, 186,
    189, 190, 207, 213, 222, 237, 238, 279, 296
Baltimore City Paper, The, 118, 130, 252
Baltimore Sun, The, 118, 125, 186, 208, 222, 223, 298
Baltimore Uprising Protest Signs, 28, 35, 39, 164, 177, 246, 287, 320,
    343-348
Batts, Anthony, 34, 57, 130, 163, 207, 213, 241, 243, 295-297, 299, 370
Bell, Sean, 143, 144f, 351
Belle Isle Riot, 139, 394
Bethune, Mary McLeod, 281
Beyoncé, 341
Black Codes, 75
Black Entertainment Television (B.E.T.), 96-97
Blackface, 208-209, 317

441

WORLD TO COME: ESSAYS ON THE BALTIMORE UPRISING, MILITANT RACISM, AND HISTORY

Black Guerrilla Family (BGF), 152, 153, 160, 162, 329
Black Information Gateways (BIG), 112
Black Lawyers for Justice, 190
Black Lives Matter (BLM), 19, 21, 23, 29, 37, 39, 41, 42, 57, 99, 100, 104, 110, 119, 150, 165, 169, 176, 178, 189, 202, 209, 216, 217, 218, 232, 246, 248, 260, 277, 278, 280, 294, 305, 314, 323, 343
"Black-on-Black" Crime, 41, 272-275
Black Panther Party, 181, 190, 257, 259, 304
Black Radical Tradition, 302-303, 304
Black Tax, 205
Blactivist, 48
Bland, Sandra, 247-248, 352
Bloods, 152, 153, 154, 160, 161, 162, 329
Blue Line, 204
Boxer, Senator Barbara (D-CA), 333
Brown v. Board of Education, 137, 220
Brown, H. Rap (Jamil Abdullah Al-Amin), 190
Brown, Michael, 21, 32, 35, 49, 53-54, 55, 56, 57, 58, 105, 108, 164-165, 174, 185, 201, 202, 237, 238, 269, 277, 318, 335, 342, 345, 377, 397
Broken Windows, 41, 260-262, 344
Bryant, Reverend Dr. Jamal, 57, 241
Bullock, Alan, 229-230

C
Camden Yards, 191, 328-329
Cardin, Senator Ben (D-MD), 107
Carter, Jill P., 221,
Carter, Walter P., 221
Carter Sr., Reverend Harold A., 57
Carter Jr., Reverend Harold A., 58
Chaney, Goodman and Schwerner, 287
Chisholm, Congresswoman Shirley (D-NY), 183
Choice, The, 37, 119-122
Christian, Mark, 114, 405
Citizen Journalism, 106, 110, 115, 118
Civil Disobedience, 32, 38, 39, 41, 42, 46, 51, 139, 140, 147, 159, 190, 219, 220, 232, 282, 324, 325, 393
Civility, 216, 284, 285,
"Clean" Person, 102
Clinton, Secretary of State Hillary Rodham, 215

Clinton, President Bill, 236
Civil Rights Era Cold Cases, 310
Clyburn, Representative James E. (D-SC), 210, 295, 333
Coates, Ta-Nehisi, 294
COINTELPRO, 39, 181, 182, 183, 184,
Colored Orphan Asylum, 133
Community-of-Care (COC), 35, 51-53, 268
Community Policing, 209, 226, 269, 300, 306, 385
Confederate Flag, 42, 293, 294, 295, 334,
Contested Territory, 41, 269, 275
Conyers, Representative John (D-MI), 49, 50, 183, 245
Cooper, Anna Julia, 277
Coppin State University, 152, 279, 327, 339
Cress Theory, 289,
Crips, 152, 153, 154, 161, 162, 329
Cuba, 322
Cummings, Representative Elijah (D-MD), 58, 213, 215, 334
Curfew, 58, 140, 147, 151, 155, 158, 164, 165, 177, 188, 230, 231, 232, 233, 276, 330, 331, 332, 344, 385
CVS, 38, 39, 159, 160, 163, 193, 194, 195, 228, 279, 329, 332, 341, 408

D
Davis, Angela Y., 22, 166, 283, 284
Davis, Kevin, 296, 333, 334 336, 341, 342
Death-by-cop, 103, 104
Detroit Riot, 1968, 139, 140, 395
Dismantlement, 300, 301, 302
Domestic Riot/Civil Disobedience and Protest Events Related to Race in the United States, 1863-2015, 393
Douglass, Frederick, 65, 73-74, 306
Doyle, Arthur, 204-206
Dred Scott v. Sandford, 70, 303
DuBois, W.E.B., 282
Dyconscious Racism, 302, 303
Dyson, Michael Eric, 58, 97, 283

E
Early, Jubal Anderson, 85-86
Ellison, Representative Keith (D-MI), 310
Emanuel A.M.E. Church, 42, 208, 288, 290, 291, 292, 293, 294, 334
Emmett Till Unsolved Civil Rights Crimes Act of 2007, 107

WORLD TO COME: ESSAYS ON THE BALTIMORE UPRISING, MILITANT RACISM, AND HISTORY

F

Facebook, 111, 117, 149, 189, 193, 202, 215, 300, 309, 335, 387
Families United for Justice, 58
Fatwa, 152, 153, 158
"Ferguson Effect, The"
Ferguson, Missouri, 29, 33, 35, 54, 55, 56, 57, 59, 118, 146, 164, 165, 185, 190, 192, 201, 202, 219, 231, 237, 238, 263, 270, 288, 318, 335, 342, 344, 353, 377, 397
Freedom of Information Act, 301
Freedmen's Bureau, 76

G

Gangs, 152, 153, 154, 157, 161, 162, 163, 249, 269, 270, 271, 329
Garner, Eric, 49, 117, 165, 185, 238, 277, 345, 362-363, 397
Gates, Jr., Henry Louis, 226-227
Grand Jury Charges Against the Baltimore 6 in the Death of Freddie Gray, May 21, 2015, 391
Gray, Freddie, 21, 28, 31-33, 34, 35, 37, 40, 47, 49, 53, 56-59, 100, 105, 107, 108, 116, 118, 123, 125, 126, 128, 131, 146, 147, 149, 151, 153, 154, 156, 159, 165, 174, 177, 178, 187, 190, 195, 197, 198, 199, 207, 208, 209, 211, 214, 215, 222, 223, 224, 225, 229, 230, 231, 236, 237, 238, 240, 243, 244, 263, 269, 272, 277, 297, 298, 299, 306, 314, 318, 319, 327, 328, 333, 334, 335, 336, 343, 344, 345, 346, 391, 397
Gregory, Dick, 58

H

Haley, Governor Nimrata "Nikki" Randhawa (R-SC), 295
Harvard Public Health Review, 49
Hill-Aston, Tessa, 244
Hogan, Larry, 58, 155-156, 157, 193, 238, 327, 328, 329, 332, 333, 335, 336, 340, 342
Holder, Attorney General Eric, 54, 55, 213, 235
Homan Square, 233
Horner, Senator Maxine (D-OK), 135
Houston, Charles Hamilton, 220
Human/Humane, 41, 42, 66, 280-288
Hurricane Katrina, 239, 305, 322, 341, 352, 363, 372, 397

I

Ifill, Sherrilyn, 339
IGens, 38, 149, 151

Immigrant/Immigration, 99, 168, 169, 220, 263, 269
Inspectional Services Division (IDS), 183
Intolerable blackness, 36, 81, 85, 88, 89, 90, 91, 92, 93, 113
Involuntary segregation, 86, 88
Islamophobia, 366

J
Jackson, Adam J., 319, 340
Jackson, Jr., Reverend Jesse, 58
Jailitis, 230
Jay Z, 240
Jena 6, 115
Johnson, Jack, 88-89
Johnson, President Lyndon Baines, 121, 140, 141, 220

K
Kent, Joseph, 40, 231-233
Kerner Commission, 141
Killology, 39, 167, 172, 173
King, Jr., Martin Luther, 45, 46, 51, 120, 140, 146, 176, 178, 183, 193, 282, 307, 311
Ku Klux Klan, 135, 310
Kwanzaa, 113, 176

L
Lamar, Kendrick, 19
Law Enforcement Bill of Rights (LEOBOR), 16, 268, 268f
Law Enforcement Motorcycle Clubs (LEMCs), 16, 276, 310
Leaders of a Beautiful Struggle (LBS), 110, 318, 319, 340
Lee, Spike, 61-62, 139f
Lewis, Representative John (D-GA), 107
Liberation (Yette Hypothesis), 120, 121, 122
Liquidation (Yette Hypothesis) 120, 121, 122
Little, Joan, 245
Los Angeles/Rodney King Riot, 1992, 101, 143, 206, 396
Lynch, Loretta, 213, 235, 332
Lynching, 303, 305, 310

M
Malcolm X, 22, 45, 113, 114, 120, 139, 178, 304, 311
Marshall, Thurgood, 220
Martin, Trayvon, 35, 56f, 165, 209, 210, 211, 318, 344, 373

Maryland Gang Prosecution Act, 161
Maryland Public Information Act, 301
Maryland Unites, 193, 238, 331
Mass Incarceration, 30, 131, 132, 215, 222, 305, 323
Maximum Discomfort, 177-179
Mfume, Kweisi, 58
Mikulski, Senator Barbara (D-MD), 107
Militant racism, 29, 59, 288, 289, 317
Millennials, 38, 149, 150, 151,
Mitchell, Juanita Jackson, 220-221,
Mitchell, Congressman Parren (D-MD), 183
Moynihan, Senator Daniel Patrick, 79, 243
Mondawmin Mall, 151, 152, 160, 228, 231, 241, 270, 279, 316, 329, 330
Money Bail, 229, 230, 266, 271, 293, 360, 375
Moore, Kevin, 37, 115, 117, 327, 331
Morgan State University, 119, 231, 279
Mosby, Marilyn, 40, 131, 193, 198, 213, 222, 223, 224, 225, 240, 243, 297, 330, 331, 345
Mosby, Nick, 240, 337, 339
Murphy, William "Billy", 58, 223

N
NAACP, 16, 28, 51, 77, 132, 202, 203, 208, 220, 244, 304, 314, 330, 331, 340, 378
Nation of Islam (NOI), 114, 182, 250
National Action Network (NAN), 58, 331
National Guard, 41, 46, 55, 140, 151, 156, 157, 160, 164, 230, 276, 329
Netroots Nation, 216, 217
New Black Panther Party, The, 190
New Jim Crow, The, 132
New Media, 37, 109-110
New Shiloh Baptist Church, 57, 329, 331
Newsome, Bree, 42, 293, 294
Niagara Movement, 77
Non-violence, 282

O
#OneBaltimore, 332
Obama, Michelle, 318
Obama, President Barrack, 23, 36, 55, 58, 95, 132, 157, 202, 210, 213, 214, 215, 227, 236, 279, 291, 311, 313, 317, 318, 330, 333, 334, 337, 342

Occupy Wallstreet, 166, 263, 397
O'Malley, Martin, 162, 216, 217, 333, 341
Operation Fruehmenschen, 184
Operation Ghetto Storm, 274
Orta, Ramsay, 117, 363
Overcompensation, 41, 262-269

P

Pacification (Yette Hypothesis), 120, 121, 122
Pan-African(ism), 22, 112, 113, 221, 241, 303, 304
Parks, Rosa, 51
Para-Police, 209, 309, 349, 369, 373, 375, 380, 384
Patrollers, 35, 69-70, 72, 75, 209
Pinckney, Clementa, 42, 208, 288-289, 291
Plessy v. Ferguson (1896), 303
Poe, Zizwe, 114
Police Executive Research Forum (PERF), 333, 337
Political Prisoners, 52, 142
Pope Frances, 322, 323
PRIDE Act, 107f, 333
Prince, 41, 239, 240, 333
Pugh, Senator Catherine (D-MD), 213
Purge, The, 38, 151, 154, 329

R

Rabaka, Reiland, 19-23, 113, 114, 304
Race Riots, 78, 79, 133, 135, 136, 137, 139, 153, 393-397
Racial Profiling, 33, 34, 48, 49, 62, 89, 132, 143, 166, 199, 210, 247, 262, 330
Racial Stereotypes, 36, 48, 60, 62, 81, 92, 93, 96, 99, 104, 171, 242, 246, 250, 271, 318
Racism, 19, 22, 29, 30, 32, 35, 36, 39-45, 49, 59, 64, 65, 66, 71, 74, 76, 79, 83, 85-93, 106, 119, 120, 121, 122, 123, 132, 133, 134, 138, 141 (White Racism), 142, 143, 146, 150, 153, 165, 167, 169, 170, 171, 172, 173, 174, 177, 197, 198, 199, 200, 209, 214, 220, 225, 227, 235, 242, 244, 246, 250, 253, 263, 273, 275, 277, 278, 282, 283, 284, 287, 288, 289, 290, 292, 296, 300, 302, 303, 306, 307, 308, 313, 315, 317, 318, 323, 337, 338, 343, 344, 345, 346, 347
Rawlings-Blake, Stephanie, 58, 156-157, 158, 163, 164, 213, 214, 230, 237, 238, 243, 244, 279, 295, 296, 298, 299, 316, 320, 328, 330, 331, 332, 334, 335, 340, 341

Reddit, 316
Reparations, 114, 172, 303, 305, 346
Restorative Justice, 300, 301, 302
Rhianna, 240
Rice, Tamir, 101, 380-381
"Rise Up October," 336, 337
Roof, Dylann, 42, 290-292, 293
Rose, Kwame, 110, 145, 332
Rough Ride, 187, 230, 343
Rush, Congressman Bobby (D-IL), 210

S
Sanders, Bernard "Bernie" (D-VT), 216, 217
Sandtown-Winchester, 118, 128, 179, 214, 239
"Say Her Name" Campaign, 246, 247, 339, 407
Schmoke, Kurt L., 42
Scott, Congressman Robert C. "Bobby" (D-VA), 50, 50f
Scott, Walter, 165, 185, 277, 288, 345, 383
September 11, 2001 (9/11), 255, 256, 299
Serra, Junipero, 322
Serra-gate, 323
Shabazz, Malik Zulu, 190-191
Sharpton, Rev. Al (see also the National Action Network), 42, 58, 332
Signs/Signage (Protest), 39, 164, 177, 246, 287, 320, 343-348
Social Network Conservation, 36, 81, 82, 83, 84, 113, 115, 230, 278
State of Emergency, 55, 58, 130, 151, 153, 164, 168, 215, 232, 329, 332, 385
Steiner, Marc, 47, 119
Stop-and-Frisk, 144
SWAT, 16, 246, 259-260, 267, 270, 271, 363, 370, 386, 389

T
Till, Emmett, 21, 106, 107, 108, 366
Timeline of the 2015 Baltimore Uprising, A, 327-342
Trumbull Park, 138
Toure, Kwame (FKA, Stokely Carmichael), 190, 311
Tulsa Race Riot, 135, 136, 394
Turner, Nat, 21, 36, 81, 84
Twitter, 110, 111, 145, 149, 189, 211, 232, 309, 319, 338

U
United Kingdom, The, 100, 114

United Nations (UN), The, 236, 304, 305

V
Vietnam War, 37, 46, 120, 140, 257

W
Waco Massacre, 41, 270, 271, 275, 276
War on Drugs, 129, 130, 131, 249, 305
Warren, Senator Elizabeth (D-MA), 217
Washington, Booker T., 77, 87
Watkins, D., 126, 321, 339
Watson, Henry, 71-72, 74
WEAA 88.9 (Baltimore), 118, 119
Wells, Faye, 227-228
Wells-Barnett, Ida B., 19, 51, 219, 311
West Baltimore, 38, 47, 56, 128, 129, 152, 154, 161, 164, 188, 194, 222, 239, 263, 269, 271, 272, 275, 330, 339
"While Black" Phenomena, 33, 35, 60, 62, 63, 64, 92
White Supremacy, 22, 90, 106, 107, 114, 136, 137, 150, 169, 178, 197, 198, 215, 277, 282, 283, 288, 289, 290, 291, 292, 293, 302, 303, 307, 308, 323, 343
Wilderness, 37, 38, 90, 121, 123, 124, 128, 129, 149, 150, 153, 243
Williams, Judge Barry, 297-298, 335
Wire, The, 40, 41, 96, 235, 248-253
World's Columbian Exposition (The Chicago World's Fair), 302

Y
Y2K, 16, 255, 322
Young, Bernard C. "Jack," 327, 329, 331
YouTube, 111, 189, 449

Z
Zero-Sum Game, 41, 172, 260
Zero-Tolerance, 54, 216, 217, 262
Zimmerman, George, 209-211, 373

†††

World To Come: Essays On The Baltimore Uprising, Militant Racism, And History

"…THIS MANUSCRIPT IS MY PROTEST SIGN."

www.ingramcontent.com/pod-product-compliance
Lightning Source LLC
Chambersburg PA
CBHW071434300426
44114CB00013B/1430